# Making Sense

# Making Sense

## Cognition, Computing, Art, and Embodiment

Simon Penny

The MIT Press
Cambridge, Massachusetts
London, England

This book was set in Stone Serif by Westchester Publishing Services. Printed and bound in the United States of America.

Library of Congress Cataloging-in-Publication Data

Names: Penny, Simon, author.
Title: Making sense : cognition, computing, art, and embodiment / Simon Penny.
Description: Cambridge, MA : The MIT Press, 2017. | Series: Leonardo book series | Includes bibliographical references and index.
Identifiers: LCCN 2017006487 | ISBN 9780262036757 (hardcover : alk. paper)
Subjects: LCSH: Art--Psychology. | Art--Philosophy. | Civilization, Western.
Classification: LCC N71 .P355 2017 | DDC 700.1--dc23
LC record available at https://lccn.loc.gov/2017006487

10   9   8   7   6   5   4   3   2   1

# Contents

# Series Foreword

## Leonardo/International Society for the Arts, Sciences, and Technology (ISAST)

Leonardo, the International Society for the Arts, Sciences, and Technology, and the affiliated French organization Association Leonardo, have some very simple goals:

1. To advocate, document, and make known the work of artists, researchers, and scholars developing new ways in which contemporary arts interact with science, technology, and society.
2. To create a forum and meeting places where artists, scientists, and engineers can meet, exchange ideas, and, when appropriate, collaborate.
3. To contribute, through the interaction of the arts and sciences, to the creation of the new culture that will be needed to transition to a sustainable planetary society.

When the journal *Leonardo* was started some fifty years ago, these creative disciplines usually existed in segregated institutional and social networks, a situation dramatized at that time by the "Two Cultures" debates initiated by C. P. Snow. Today we live in a different time of cross-disciplinary ferment, collaboration, and intellectual confrontation enabled by new hybrid organizations, new funding sponsors, and the shared tools of computers and the Internet. Sometimes captured in the "STEM to STEAM" movement, new forms of collaboration seem to integrate the arts, humanities, and design with science and engineering practices. Above all, new generations of artist-researchers and researcher-artists are now at work individually and collaboratively bridging the art, science, and technology disciplines. For some of the hard problems in our society, we have no choice but to find new ways to couple the arts and sciences. Perhaps in our lifetime we will see the emergence of "new Leonardos," hybrid creative individuals or teams that will not only develop a meaningful art for our times but also drive new agendas in science and stimulate technological innovation that addresses today's human needs.

For more information on the activities of the Leonardo organizations and networks, please visit our websites at http://www.leonardo.info/ and http://www.olats.org/. Leonardo books and journals are also available on our ARTECA art science technology aggregator: http://arteca.mit.edu/.

Roger F. Malina
Executive Editor, Leonardo Publications

# Preface

The philosopher John Haugeland used to say that he "certainly owned more nuts and bolts than most philosophers (and possibly more than any)."[1] In this wry poke at the scholarly establishment, he celebrates his interest in "lowly" materiality and, implicitly, the work of motor mechanics and plumbers. I suspect it is more than a witty aside. The author of *Having Thought: Essays in the Metaphysics of Mind* came to his position regarding materiality and mind results precisely from both engaging in and pondering material practices involving, among other things, nuts and bolts. I have taken pains to explain to generations of (generally bemused or baffled) students, that the lowly nut and bolt is nothing short of a technological miracle. Moreover, the intelligent use of nuts and bolts involves a sensitive understanding of the nature of materials and the deployment of complex sensorimotor skills that blur the false divisions between mind, body, and world in just the way Haugeland explains in "Mind Embodied and Embedded." And while Haugeland probably had more philosophy books than me, I have no doubt that I have more nuts and bolts. Indeed, I make them.

I want to emphasize that the theoretical issues articulated in this book *arise from material practice*, rather than via the critical consideration of other theorizing. This book addresses practice and seeks to be relevant to practitioners. Unlike many working in this field, I did not go to university. I went to art school, a context almost entirely devoid of academic intellectualism, theoretical speculation, or even books.[2] In their place, I learned to shape, harden, and temper tool steel over a coke forge. I learned to make molds, mill timber, and weld various metals. I taught myself to design, prototype, and build novel structures and machines from diverse materials. Learning iteratively in and through materially engaged practice informed my later work and this writing in a way that a conventional "academic" education could not possibly do. I remain indebted to my teacher Owen Broughton. I recall the finely wrought set of models of the Platonic and Archimedean polyhedra on the shelves in his tiny office, which adjoined the blacksmith's forge where I learned to make fine tools from old files.

Broughton had an encyclopedic knowledge of tools and making that spanned cultures and centuries. He could tell you how Vikings smelted iron, how Indians quarry granite with water and wood, how to accurately survey land on horseback, why the Rolls Royce factory uses straight fluted drills and how to drill a straight hole using mirrors. Broughton introduced me to the richness of traditions of making, a richness embedded in the artifacts themselves and in traditions of their use, passed on via artisanal apprenticeship, hardly touched by traditions of textual notation and learning. Broughton had been British sculptor Henry Moore's shop foreman, responsible for successfully casting Moore's gigantic bronzes. As a committed pacifist, Broughton volunteered as bomb defuser during World War II. He witnessed his workmate blown to pieces, which left him with a lifelong stutter, reducing his speech to barked vocal spasms. But in his lack of voice, he was eloquent. The understanding I gained of a kind of knowing almost incommensurable with the culture of the academy—a world of texts and speaking— informs at the deepest level the arguments I am making in this book.

In 1989, I became a faculty member at Carnegie Mellon, a position that matured into an interdisciplinary position as professor of art and robotics.[3] In this context, I negotiated the perspectives I had gained through my training and practice as an artist with the wildly different context of high-end (mostly military-funded) academic research. Carnegie Mellon, the campus of both Herbert Simon and Allen Newell, was one of three centers of artificial intelligence (AI) in the United States in the glory days of AI—the others being MIT and Stanford. In this privileged position, I had the immense good fortune to work with some of the leading figures of robotics and AI of the time.

At Carnegie Mellon, I attempted to deploy computational and robotic techniques in the making of cultural artifacts, and in the process I became profoundly aware of the starkness of the difference between my worldview (a worldview originating in art and material practices) and the worldview of many academically trained AI researchers and cognitive scientists. On one hand, this experience brought home to me the stark ontological differences between art making and academic scholarship and research. On the other hand, as a maker of machines, I understood the brutal pragmatism of robotics. Roboticists, they used to say, believe in the work ethic: "It has to work." The rigors of custom mechanical and computer engineering and design persuaded me of the deep wisdom captured in an aphorism: "The difference between theory and practice is greater in practice than in theory."

Over ensuing years, I have been preoccupied with the exploration of the depth and complexity of that divide. That inquiry has led to the writing of this book. Since then, I have become increasingly acclimatized to the culture of scholarship and the academy. I have become—to the surprise of many, no doubt—a professor. However, as an outsider to that culture, I remain stridently committed to the kinds of embodied, materially engaged knowing that are inherent in cultural practices—and I use the term *cultural* in the widest sense, to include the culture of clinical diagnosis or laboratory bench work, as well as the practices of Micronesian seafarers.

All adept practitioners (be they violinists or cabinetmakers), I suggest, understand their practices as intelligent, in a holistic way. Dualistic divisions between mind and body and between body and world are unpersuasive. The failure of conventional cognitive science to address embodied and situated dimensions of human cognition left a yawning chasm that contemporary research is beginning to address. My purpose here is to bring that new research into conversation with its richest exemplars in order to build a new discourse that usefully informs practitioners and theorist alike regarding the nature of intelligent embodied practice.

The concerns expressed in this book, and the subject areas explored, have arisen through practice. Over thirty years of interdisciplinary Art and Technology research and development practice, developing and deploying custom interactive technologies directed toward art and cultural goals, technical and theoretical issues in media arts have "shown up" for me and have demanded attention. I have remained generally skeptical of attempts by media theorists to apply critical theory to media art practice, because such attempts are seldom more than the laying of a theoretical veneer upon the products of technocultural practices, of which the authors often have a limited understanding. Worse, I have seen generations of students hamfistedly trying to implement or illustrate the ideas of such thinkers in their artwork.

In this book, I have attempted to avoid such styles of theorizing, and instead have worked toward theory from practice—cultural practices and scientific practices. I do not mean to imply that there is something wrong with the works of philosophers and theorists. The problem I address is the assumption that translation from theoretical abstraction to materiality (or vice versa) is straightforward. This may be a symptom of an enduring or resurgent Cartesianism, anachronistically reinforced in the minds of computer users through the reification of these ideas in the false dualism of hardware and software. One of the preoccupations of this book is the way that this mostly unquestioned endorsement of the doctrine of the separation of information and matter has been reinforced by the rhetoric around computing and AI rooted in a simplistic interpretation of the Cartesian separation of mind and body. This is found in the work of Newell and Simon, and in a common misreading of Shannon.

It may be possible to say something meaningful about the building of a drystone wall without taking part in the process. But such reflections will remain encapsulated as abstract symbolic representations that circulate in a universe of abstract symbolic representations. Contemplation alone cannot engage the deictic, enactive, sensorimotor, haptic realities of process: the heft of the boulders, the judgment of complex shapes and volumes, the grittiness and dusty dryness on the hands, the growth of calluses, the tiredness in the shoulders at the end of the day. Nor can such disembodied theorizing feed back into process; it is of no use to the stonemason.

Several years ago, in the PhD defense of an artist turned critical theorist, I (rather unwisely) made the observation that some critical theorists "see art in the way a cow sees grass." The idea that practical work and theoretical work can or should be separated I find entirely dubious. Cartesian thinking endures nowhere as strongly as in the academy, where theory and abstraction are valorized. Although I aspire to scholarly rigor, this book does not fit comfortably into the circuit of scholarly work. I hope to say something intelligent about (intelligent) practice that is relevant both to practitioners and to my academic colleagues. Contrary to the drive to abstraction that characterizes the academy, there *is* intelligent embodied practice, but its qualities are difficult if not impossible to enunciate in terms of internalist cognitivism. This is the heart of Polanyi's notion of "tacit knowledge," and it was the problem upon which first-generation AI foundered. "There are many activities which directly display qualities of mind, yet are neither themselves intellectual operations nor yet effects of intellectual operations," Gilbert Ryle (1949, 27) memorably enunciated. "Intelligent practice is not a step-child of theory. On the contrary, theorizing is one practice amongst others and is itself intelligently or stupidly conducted" (ibid.).

A 2015 review of *War and Peace* observed that Tolstoy "kept a scythe and saw leaning up against the wall next to his writing desk" ("The Secret to a Happy Life" 2015). Noting this juxtaposition of pen and plow in the novelist's lifestyle, the reviewer notes: "Tolstoy recognised that striking a balance between mind and body was an essential part of his creative process. He . . . regularly put down his pen to guide a horse-drawn plough across the fields." I suspect Tolstoy might not have endorsed the mind-body dualism the reviewer rather heavy-handedly imposes. As someone who is driven to punctuate his intellectual work with material practices—sculpture, gardening, building construction, sailing—I identify with Tolstoy's chosen lifestyle, if not this explication of it. The crosscut saw, the adze, the broadax, the level and plumb bob, and the other "primitive" tools I keep around me are not there as quaint pieces of rustic decoration, but for the way they imply complex skills and age-long accretion of human experience. They are objects to think with, in two senses: to contemplate, and with which to enact intelligent action.

The review continues: "In his last years, when writers and journalists came to pay homage to the bearded sage, they were always surprised to find one of the world's most famous authors huddled over his cobbling tools making a pair of boots." Cobbling, like so many other artisanal practices, is far from mindless labor, neither demeaning nor drudgery. As humble as it is, cobbling inheres the constant exercise of intelligence, judgment, and skill; having made shoes, I know. The image of the old man huddling over his tools, persevering in work he could easily have delegated and paid for, is emblematic of an acceptance of the temporal dimension of labor. As Gerard Manley Hopkins ([1918] 1985) celebrated: "Sheer plod makes plow down sillion shine."

I want to go beyond a sentimental appreciation of labor and skill. With many in the postcognitive community, I assert that that these kinds of practices involving bodies and environment and artifacts are constitutive of, not incidental to, intelligence. That intelligent action is in the world, not in the black box of the cranium. Intelligent action is, as Francisco Varela would put it, enactive and structurally coupled. Mark Johnson has argued, embodied experience is the source of abstract concepts. By these lights, the tool and the skilled practice associated with it *are* cognition and are generative of ideas, concepts, and theories, and shape the cognitive capacities of the user. Einstein was a small boat sailor and (it is said) credited his conception of relativity to his sailing activities. In the spirit of actor-network theory, we might venture that sailboats and sailing thought relativity theory with Einstein; scything, adzing, and horse-drawn plowing wrote *War and Peace* and whole new ways of thinking about Russian society. They didn't inspire, sharpen, or structure minds to do these things; they were integral parts of a whole system that did these things.

# Acknowledgments

As John Haugeland (1998) humbly stated in the beginning of his wonderful essay "Mind Embodied and Embedded," "little of this is new." In this spirit, I want to emphasize my deep gratitude for the work of a number of scholars who have had a lasting influence on my thinking on these matters. This list includes Jakob von Uexküll, Gordon Pask, Humberto Maturana, J. J. Gibson, Hubert Dreyfus, John Haugeland, Mark Johnson, Francisco Varela, Evan Thompson, Eleanor Rosch, Rodney Brooks, Philip Agre, Edwin Hutchins, Andy Pickering, Paul Edwards, Katherine Hayles, Peter Cariani, David Kirsh, Tim Ingold, Margaret Bowden, Michael Wheeler, John Sutton, Barbara Maria Stafford, Anthony Chemero, David Mindell, Lambros Malafouris, George Lakoff, Vittorio Gallese, Alan Costalls, Ezequiel Di Paolo, Alva Noë, Kevin O'Regan, and many others whose writing has given me substantial food for thought, and whose work is quoted and referenced in these pages.

Intellectual provocation and incisive critique are just part of the substantive relationships that make this kind of work personally worthwhile. I am grateful for the stimulating conversations and incisive critiques I have enjoyed with some of these people. I similarly thank Geoffrey Bowker, Georgina Born, Nell Tenhaaf, Maria Fernandez, Anne-Marie Duguet, Sally Jane Norman, Nick Gessler, Tom Jennings, Carrie Noland, Malcolm MacIver, Ian Horswill, Chris Salter, Michael Mateas, Noah Wardrip-Fruin, Phoebe Sengers, Emanuele Quinz, Samuel Bianchini, Narcis Pares, and Roc Pares for their encouragement, support, and convivial collegiality over many years.

I am especially grateful to Narcis Pares, who made possible my annual appointment as visiting professor in the Cognitive Systems and Interactive Media (CSIM) master's program at University Pompeu Fabra in Barcelona (2006–2013, until the economic crisis in Spain forced the curtailing of the program). These visits were a high point in otherwise difficult years.

This appointment gave me the opportunity to workshop many of the ideas and arguments in this book with the many wonderful students who went through that program. Last, I thank Charles Wheeler for his thoughtful reading and suggestions, Allison Dziuba for her meticulous editorial assistance, and Anita Ghazarian for her unwavering support.

Simon Penny
Los Angeles, California, 2016

# Introduction

The circling rivers the breath, and breathing it in and out,
The beauty of the waist, and thence of the hips, and thence downward toward the
   knees,
The thin red jellies within you or within me, the bones and the marrow in the bones,
The exquisite realization of health;
O I say these are not the parts and poems of the body only, but of the soul,
O I say now these are the soul!
—Walt Whitman, "I Sing the Body Electric" (1867)

This book is about different conceptions of intelligence and cognition and about how different cultural traditions and different technologies shape those conceptions. This book is about biological being and computationally simulated being. This book is about technologies that arise out of military research agendas and what happens when they become civilianized. This book is about two intersecting cultures—not the two cultures of C. P. Snow, but the culture of representation and the culture of performance. This book is about art practice and about media art practice. This book is about dualism and embodiment. How do all these things fit together?

## Art after Computing

This book is an attempt to reconsider the status of the arts practices in Western culture in the wake of the digital "revolution"—through the lenses of cognitive science, neuroscience, and philosophy of mind, as well as through art history, media arts, history of science and technology, anthropology, and other fields. If we are to make any progress in digital cultural practices, it is crucial to consider the extensive ramifications of the incorporation of a new kind of machine into human culture. Computers are cognitive machines. While it is commonplace to say that the "information revolution" is as resounding as the Industrial Revolution, I don't think we've fully grasped the psychoecological impact. We now share our cognitive ecology with machines. What is usually elided is that hardware and software, as designed artifacts, are products of human culture, and as such they reify culturally and historically contingent ideas: in this case, models of cognition. As the impact of these machines now extends into all aspects of human culture, we can't afford to reify outmoded, inappropriate models of cognition.

Another way to put this is that these machines *behave.* By this I mean that they vary their "output" due to reasoning based in an "awareness" of changes in their environments. This quasi-biological condition is now so commonplace that we do not notice it, but it is revolutionary in the history of human technology. I contend that we haven't come to terms with the ramifications of this novelty on philosophical, cultural, aesthetic, or technical levels. With respect to the arts, it is apparent that this new technology opens an entirely novel realm of aesthetics. Practice has preceded theory by thirty years or more. We have not yet formulated a coherent and embracing "aesthetics of behavior."

The motivation for writing this book lies in my own experience of several decades, developing interactive technologies for cultural practices and, more generally, negotiating the place of computing in culture during the period of radical development and popularization of computing that occurred in the 1990s. During this period, computing applications diversified, computer technologies morphed into digital appliances, and the culture of computing moved into diverse aspects of culture. It became clear to me at the time that within these technologies resided a particular set of values, a way of looking at the world that was seldom made explicit but was often at odds with the traditions of practice it intersected. For me, this was most directly experienced with respect to artificial intelligence and robotics. Computing offered tantalizing new possibilities for new kinds of cultural practices. Those possibilities, workshopped through the 1990s in the media arts community, are now fully instantiated in popular culture: social media, online gaming, "chatbots," and instant, global, multimedia information exchange. At the same time, the philosophical lineage of computing, deeply committed to a dualist internalism, was at odds with cultural practices, in which quantified information plays a minimal role. I became persuaded that this deep disjunction of basic values between the culture of computing and the cultures that became computerized was of critical importance, and my analysis has culminated in the book you are now reading.

There is a deep ontological rift between the culture of computing and the cultures of arts practices. This rift cuts deep into core ideas of mind and being. On one side of this rift, the reification of the mind-body dualism in computer technology is apparent in hardware and software. Attendant to this are other key concepts, such as the valorization of symbolic abstraction and a particular conception of *information*. Arts practices on other side of the rift endorse and implement, seldom explicitly, a holism that is both embodied and contextually embedded. It struck me that the kinds of difficulties encountered where computing interfaced with embodied practices—though often superficially technical—were rooted in a deep philosophical conflict, one which was seldom if ever enunciated.[1]

Traditional cognitive science views cognition as the logical manipulation of symbols by mathematical rules in an abstract reasoning space. This perspective renders the arts mysterious to cognitive science, and thus what I call "the intelligences of the arts"—which involve embodied and situated cognition—remained ineffable, at least in cognitive science circles. A corollary is that artists are seldom encouraged to reflect on the disjunction between the cognitive dimensions of their practices and their cultural naturalization to dualist explanations. Here, I develop a theoretical context that revalorizes the cognitive dimensions of artistic practices in terms of embodied and situated cognition. Recognizing the relegation, historically, of these intelligences to second-tier intellectual status, I call for a rethinking of the hegemony of representationalism in the academy. Such a rethinking could lead to a leveling of the academic playing field by providing new ways of explicating the intelligences of cultural practices and material engagement.

### Postcognitivism and the Arts

It is grandly ironic that during the late 1980s, as computing was emerging as a major cultural and economic force, the disciplines of artificial intelligence and cognitive science were experiencing a theoretical implosion. The *common sense problem* (see chapter 6) and the limitations of functionalism were becoming recognized, and new ways of thinking about cognition—reasserting the importance of embodiment, materiality, context, and temporal process—were proposed. These new approaches to cognition permit, for the first time in a century, a new kind of conversation about art and cognition, which holds the potential to not only recognize qualities of artistic intelligence but also, perhaps more importantly, relax the stranglehold that dualist internalist paradigms have had on ideas about intelligence and cognition.

The technical term *human factors* (as used in computer science) suggests that the qualities of human embodiment are peripheral "implementation details" in the development of computing systems. This speaks volumes about the worldview of the discipline of engineering. This is veiled cognitivism, in the sense that thinking is conceived of as abstract symbol manipulation and is taken to be an end in itself, rather than part of the process of ongoing lived being. A rather Victorian characterization of human perception and action as a serial process (input-output) informs computational thinking. The crisis of the cognitivist model has led to renewed attention to embodied, situated, and material aspects of cognition that the cognitivist worldview had elided. The new cognitive sciences are immediately relevant to the still-vexed human factors aspect of ubiquitous computing, precisely because they address aspects of human experience pertinent to the development of richer and more subtle—if not calmer—technologies of interaction.

Escape from the cognitivist cul-de-sac demands a wholesale paradigm shift and a new set of axiomatic assumptions: Mind and body are not separate or separable; self vs. world is likewise a questionable distinction; intelligence is making sense of (and in) the world; and thinking occurs at the fingertips and in the soles of the feet in the processes of interaction with the world. So-called context-aware technology implies a phenomenological understanding of "being-in-the-world" or, rather, of a performative doing-in-the-world, of situated sensorimotor action. Coming to understand the emergence of meaning through a temporal process of bodily interaction with things and people in the world is to engage what Andy Pickering has called "the mangle of practice" (1995). In his work of the same name, Pickering captures a key aspect of the paradigm shift I am arguing for in his distinction between what he called the "representational idiom" and the "performative idiom." In these terms, the cognitivist paradigm is firmly rooted in the representational idiom. The success of ubiquitous computing demands a postcognitivist approach attending to embodiment, to the performative relation to artifacts and the world, and to the relation of cognition to social and cultural formations.

I propose that *postcognitivist* cognitive science might offer a new way of speaking about and validating the embodied and situated intelligences of the arts. This might both correct the relegation of the (plastic and performing) arts to second-rank intellectual status and provide insights into the performative and embodied aspects of the arts of real-time computing, resulting in a more satisfactory aesthetic-theoretical discourse of technocultural practices. These new conceptions of mind and cognition offer new critical purchase upon and new modalities for the discussion and understanding of arts and cultural practices in general, and digital arts practices in particular. This would provide for

• a reevaluation and revaluing of arts practices, a way of discussing traditional practice that helps us understand embodied intelligence as intelligence per se and thus corrects some of the excesses of dualist academic epistemologies;
• a way to rehabilitate conceptions of intelligence from the excesses of cognitivism, which in turn suggests a reconsideration of the hegemony of the symbolic in the academy; and
• the development of a new aesthetic-theoretical context for interactive and digital practices.

This application of postcognitivist thinking to the arts is not a one-way street; the engagement of these practices within such discourses brings rich and complex examples and research opportunities to cognitive science.[2]

## Computing and Culture: A Millennial Cataclysm

A historically singular series of technological developments occurred in the second half of the twentieth century. The invention of the transistor and its subsequent utilization as a basic component in the construction of electronic components (logic gates) permitted the automation of Boolean logic. The ensuing miniaturization and mass production of microprocessors led to the rapid growth of a new industry, which in turn placed computational devices in diverse contexts outside of the technoscientific world.

Blindingly rapid technological development and diversification led to a culturally explosive moment in the 1990s during which we saw the birth and popularization of desktop multimedia, desktop publishing, interactivity, real-time graphics, 3-D graphics, 3-D animation, immersive interactive environments, the Internet, the World Wide Web, digital video, various classes of computer- and net-based gaming, online commercial and social networks, and virtual communities. Throughout the 1990s, for media artists—or anyone working closely with computer technologies—a kind of technological vertigo was a fact of life. The learning curve of tools and technologies was often longer than their lifespan in the market. A confusion of practices, rhetoric, and transdisciplinary ideas characterized the period as people tried to make sense of this new context.[3]

Over thirty years of explosive development, computing and digital cultures have coevolved. A technoutopian rhetoric of *convergence*, suggesting an image of the untroubled confluence of two streams, is as common as it is wrong; the image of a tsunami or a train wreck is more apropos. During this period, a new technology that inheres certain philosophical commitments collided with traditions of practice with very different commitments. Artists played an active role, grappled with issues theoretical and technical, and generated new cultural forms. Some of the most interesting work was produced by practitioners who possessed both a solid technical grounding and an interventionist critical intelligence that interrogated emerging technologies and social contexts. Such interdisciplinary expertise was generally hard won by autodidacts pursuing interests that often appeared contradictory or unrelated.

Art practices that engage computing as subject and as material are deeply interdisciplinary. Any good interdisciplinarian must engage fields vis-à-vis each other, comparing methodologies, principles, and cultural milieus. Some of the most thoughtful technological art engages the intellectual challenges at these interdisciplinary nexuses. The works of artists such as Paul De Marinas, David Rokeby, Jim Campbell, Natalie Jeremijenko, Nell Tenhaaf, Rafael Lozano Hemmer, Masaki Fujihata, Catherine Richards, and Perry Hoberman, among numerous others, functioned as meditations upon or interventions into technocultural discourses. Such works, one might say, assigned a rhetorical function to the aesthetic in service of the discursive. Practitioners usually eschew the intentionally didactic, as this would betray a basic commitment of contemporary art practice—a commitment to an enlightened pedagogy of active critical inquiry.

The question of why an artist would want to explore or deploy computational technology in the process of art making doubtless has as many answers as there are artists—likewise, the work of technologists who have been drawn to realize, in some technological context, something they regard as artistic or "aesthetic." As anyone who has considered the field for any time will be aware, many of these positions are influenced by vapid, popular rhetoric of convergence and technoutopianism, by dated notions of art preoccupied with self-expression, and by more or less sophisticated takes on the work of fashionable theorists.[4]

## Crystallization

In the last decade or so, the ground upon which "media arts" is practiced has changed substantially. The problem for practitioners in the 1990s was usually that the technology they wanted didn't exist or lacked required capabilities. The task of the artist was often to imagine and then develop the technologies themselves, from relatively raw components. While onerous, this task tended to ensure the synchronization of aesthetic goals with technical form. More recently (2000–2015), the technosocial and technocultural landscapes have stabilized as genres of digital products have emerged. We have witnessed a clear historical transition, which might be compared to the physical phases of water. According to this metaphor, the historical process of the development of digital technoculture has transitioned from a gaseous, undefined period (1980s), through a flowing and flexible period (1990s), to the current period of crystallization. The commercial dimension of this process is seen in the proliferation of highly specialized technological widgets predicated on assumptions regarding the desires of the user, which themselves are forced into increasingly narrow and commodified niches—game modding, for instance, or the preparation of brief videos for some social media app. The academic component of the process of crystallization is the progressive institutionalization of a recognized range of learning and practices (for instance, the proliferation of gaming programs in computer science schools), which soon cease to be identified as interdisciplinary and become an institutionalized discipline, albeit heterogeneous like any other.

This crystallization is evident in the technologies themselves and in their sociocultural placement. When such technologies find a sociocultural niche and functionality, this always puts the brakes on technological development, especially at the level of the interface, as marketing imperatives dictate that, regardless of changes "under the hood," the device and its interface must be historically consistent. For example: though automotive technology has changed radically—cars are now full of computers and even have electric motors—their basic interface topology (dials, levers, and pedals), seating positions, and general physical configuration have remained fossilized and resistant to change for almost a century.

Inevitably—as potential professional and cultural applications of these technologies are confirmed in provisional contexts such as the art world and youth subcultures—new markets emerge and new products fill their niches. Certain functions and combinations of technologies become commodified and socially instantiated. A winnowing occurs, and some forms go extinct. As capitalist economies of scale come into play, a technological "chunking up" occurs. Simple components are combined in increasingly complex and purpose-specific ways that inhere specific notions of function and design (such as the false enablement of plug'n'play). These assumptions float on a sea of usually unenunciated and often unrecognized ideological and philosophical commitments.

This scenario poses new problems for experimental arts practices in the field. In the current context, the market is flooded with chunked-up, purpose-built technologies. The task of the artist is no longer to imagine possible technologies but to decode the assumptions of the designers and to disentangle functionalities from these complex artifacts, or at least to proceed with an awareness of the sedimented imbrications of purposing. The notion of plug'n'play assumes the designer knows what you want to do and that he or she is right. Plugging and playing without critical perspective can create booby traps for artists.

This crystallization of new technosocial milieu and technocultural genres has a major impact on arts practices. Cultural instantiation opens the way for new industries, career paths, and college degrees. Entire fields of practice emerge (and die) within and upon new commodity devices: game modding, avatar building, smart mobs, flash animation for cell phones, geocaching applications for GPS-capable PDAs. The line between technoaesthetic inquiry and device-specific application development becomes blurred, as perhaps it should. The class of practice that in the "liquid phase" acquired the unfortunate moniker *new media* is now referred to by some as *old-school new media*. There is a generational aspect to this argument. Many "old-school'" video artists remained resistant to the digital, and a new old school of first-generation digital artists sense a historical shift that casts their goals and preoccupations in a yellowing light. As noted previously, in that period, fundamental technological research and development was complementary to aesthetic aspirations. This pursuit of technical R & D in the service of visionary art making is now almost incomprehensible, but that work contributed to the development of now commodified technologies.

Virtual communities such as Second Life and the diversity of multiplayer online games stand on the shoulders of the unacknowledged work of a generation of artists (including artists as diverse as Stelarc, Brenda Laurel, Jane Prophet, Sommerer/Mignonneau, and Char Davies), who, in different ways, labored to bridge the "embodiment gap" by articulating various forms of animated avatars in various forms of online, navigable, virtual worlds.[5] Similarly, there are (mostly unwritten) histories of artists' development of hypertextual and multimedia literature, vision-based interaction, social robotics, web-based systems, and various genres of human-computer interaction (HCI) and ubiquitous computing (ubicomp).[6] As these concerns moved out of the rarefied and often ghettoized worlds of the computer arts community and were transformed into industries, a great historical erasure has occurred. In a sense, the furious cultural maelstrom of the 1990s that asked of computational technologies "What is this stuff?" and "What should we do with it?" has been answered by capitalist historical process: It is for gossiping, for inducing sensational emotions, and for selling things, especially itself.

## Denaturalizing the Digital

We must resist our inclination to complacency in our increasing familiarity with our digital widgets.[7] This is not a naively luddite sentiment, but a call for deeper analysis of a complex and far-reaching technocultural sea change. Three great fictions have accompanied the rise of digital technology: The first is the utopian rhetoric that the technology is so new and different that history is not relevant; the second is that computational technology is neutral and applicable to all walks of life; the third is that digital technology makes difficult things easy (when in fact it deskills the user).

Regarding the first, we should recall George Santayana's famous aphorism, sometimes rendered as "those who cannot learn from history are condemned to repeat it," and simultaneously consider the work of social historians of technology such as David Mindell, who wisely noted that "our computers retain traces of earlier technologies, from telephones and mechanical analogs to directorscopes and tracking to radar" (2002, 16). The lessons to be drawn from these two observations, taken together, are rich. First, computing and ideas of computing culture have a long history.[8] Second, digital technologies are skeuomorphic and, like animals, carry traces of their evolutionary past. Nothing could mark this more clearly than the persistence of the QWERTY keyboard in handheld mobile devices. In the age of the mechanical typewriter, the QWERTY key layout was designed to *slow typists down*. Now we have no mechanical linkages to jam, not even mechanical keys, so why do we use QWERTY? The fact that the computer screen is skeuomorphically referred to as a *desktop* reminds us that until recently we sat at a desk to use a computer, and the kinds of tasks we performed with the computer were tasks conventionally undertaken at desks. Similarly, the MIDI convention in electronic music imposed the diatonic keyboard and the Western traditions of musical structure, and so impeded experimental practices, and even the implementation of already established avant-garde ways of thinking about sound, the production of sound, and the performance of music.

This observation affords purchase on the second fiction. Boolean logical operations instantiated in miniaturized electronics did not fall from the sky fully formed. They are the cumulative products of particular kinds of people with particular training and commitments, ensconced in particular kinds of institutions in specific historical contexts. Paul Edwards remarks, "The historical trajectory of computer development cannot be separated from the elaboration of American grand strategy in the Cold War. Computers made much of that strategy possible, but strategic issues also shaped computer technology—even at the level of design" (1997, 2) (see chapter 4). Edwards later elaborates: "For two decades, from the early 1940s to the early 1960s, the armed forces of the United States were the single most important driver of digital computer development. . . . Though most of the research took place at universities and in commercial firms, military research organisations such as the Office of Naval Research, the Communications Security Group . . . and the Air Comptroller Office paid for it" (1997, 43). The US military was a major force behind computer development, and the digital computer was integral to the rhetoric and practices of the Cold War. Edwards notes, "Practical military objectives guided technological development down particular channels, increased its speed, and helped shape the structure of the emerging computer industry" (1997, 44). Thus, the SAGE system and the related Whirlwind project (see chapter 4) inhered many of the characteristics of what was to become the personal computer (PC). At deep and structuring levels (both technical and rhetorical), those agendas have shaped the machines now deployed for cultural purposes. In my opinion, the impact of the militaristic logics embedded in the technology on cultural practices deserves far more incisive interrogation than it has received thus far. To highlight, by inversion, the questionable logic of *trickle-down*, imagine if we sent a SWAT team into battle with the best hairdryers and toaster ovens money could buy. The question of whether this military inheritance provides good technology for making anything other than military culture is seldom if ever asked. There are differences of opinion as to the implications of this military-industrial heritage. It is at least possible that the long-term entwinement of the development of computing with military agendas has left the technology with a particular cast that inflects everything we do with it. I have referred to this as the *Trojan horse syndrome*.[9] Such ideas are often shrugged off, but to me this shrugging itself reflects a naturalization to the mechanics of a militarized state. As Paul Edwards shows, the US military was responsible for 85 percent of the funding for AI research in the Cold War period. It is difficult to imagine that this has not left deep inscriptions.

However, this critique goes beyond identifying the skeletons in the closet—many of them in military uniforms. The development of computing technology has occurred within the intellectual context of the discipline of engineering, a discipline characterized by commitments to positivism, objectivism, reductivism, instrumentalism, symbolic abstraction, and Cartesian dualism. For example, the pervasive software-hardware dualism (an article of faith in computer science) is a reification of the mind-body dualism in Cartesianism. The rhetorical opposition of hardware and software is, on the material level, a fiction. The Cartesian dualism on which it is it based, and which has structured Western philosophy, is, we must emphasize, a metaphysical notion without a shred of scientific evidence to support it. Critical analysis of ideas reified in software and hardware has spawned new fields of software and platform studies, but the implications of this philosophical entanglement should be recognized more broadly.

## The Rise and Fall of Symbolic Abstraction

Since the mid-nineteenth century, scientific and scientized disciplines have steadily tuned systems—epistemological and technical—toward the elaboration of a worldview that valorizes abstract symbolic representation. This has occurred through the mathematization of science and the subsequent automation of mathematics in analog and digital computing.[10] The arts have been utterly "othered" in this process by their commitment to unmediated (or nonsemantically mediated) sensorial immediacy. A commitment to the specificities of materiality has obviated any possibility of making a case within the regime of generalized symbolic abstraction—hence the (modern) intellectual marginalization of art and artists. The arts have been discursively snookered.

An ironic historical twist now offers us the opportunity to reconsider the question of intelligence and thereby reposition arts practices within a broader notion of intelligence. Not accidentally contemporaneous with the rise of digital computing, a notion of intelligence emerged that came to be called *cognitivism* (or *computationalism*). This idea held that cognition consisted of the manipulation of symbolic tokens by logical rules—in this case, in the brain. This Platonic conception was supported by the *physical symbol system hypothesis* of Newell and Simon, which provided a theoretical basis for artificial intelligence. Thus arose a Janus-headed thing, a circular and self-reinforcing argument in which brains were held to be intelligent because they behaved like computers, and computers were intelligent because they purportedly manipulated symbols in a way analogous to brains. These approaches had the effect of implicitly asserting that the culmination and the goal state of intelligence was abstract symbol manipulation, as opposed to being part of the processes by which animals and people achieve things in the world. This statement captures the difference between the midcentury cybernetic conception and the later symbolic AI conception of intelligence.

A generation later, cracks were appearing in the edifice of AI, chiefly around the so-called common sense problem (see chapter 6). The common sense problem arose because it became evident that computers were not good at achieving things in the world. Hubert Dreyfus, applying a phenomenological critique, presciently signaled this crisis in his book titled *What Computers Can't Do* (1972).[11] During the 1980s, under pressure from the common sense crisis, cognitivist ideas about the nature of cognition and, in particular, the commitment to a thinly veiled Cartesianism came increasingly into question. Over the following two decades, new formulations of cognition arose, which in different ways have questioned the nature of cognition. According to these formulations, cognition is held not to occur (exclusively) in the head or necessarily in some immaterial space of logical manipulation of symbolic tokens. These approaches propose, in different ways, that cognition is embodied; integrated with non-neural bodily tissues; or extends into artifacts, the designed environment, social systems, and cultural networks. Such paradigms have arisen in neurosciences, cognitive science, and the philosophy of mind, and include the following:

- situated cognition (Suchman)
- enactive cognition (Varela, Thompson, and Rosch, and more recently Di Paolo, Noë, and O'Regan)
- distributed cognition (Hutchins)
- epistemic action (Kirsh)
- embodied cognition (Johnson)
- cognitive linguistics (Lakoff, Turner and Fauconnier, et al.)
- dynamical and emergent approaches (Beer, Kelso, Juarrero, et al.)
- post-Cartesianism (Damasio)
- extended cognition (Clark and Chalmers)
- cognitive archeology (Malafouris, following Ingold and Rowlands)
- neurocognitive studies (Rizzolatti, Gallese, et al.)
- neural Darwinism (Edelman)
- biology of noncranial and non-neural sensing and learning, such as work on cognition in the immune system, sometimes called *psychoneuroimmunology*

While these and related approaches vary and often disagree on details, they generally assert that we cannot meaningfully speak of intelligence as occurring exclusively inside the skull, connecting to the body and the world via mechanistic sensors and effectors. On the contrary, they assert that cognition is biologically material and embodied, and discussing it outside such contexts is of dubious value. Furthermore, cognition is dynamic; it occurs as a temporally ongoing relational engagement with architectures, artifacts, tools, language, human (and interspecies) relationships, and social systems.

We find ourselves at a curious moment: Computationalist theories of cognition have been *hoist with their own petard*, and new perspectives have come forth that offer the possibility of a significant reconfiguration of notions of cognition and intelligence. This is of substantial import for theorization of cultural practices. We now have an opportunity to reexamine, reconsider, and reevaluate cultural practices through the lens of these new approaches to cognition—and indeed, there is a groundswell building in this area, which in some quarters is referred to as the *cognitive turn*.

## The Reconfiguration of Arts Practices under the Influence of Digital Technologies

In the last half of the twentieth century, computationalism rose and reconfigured notions of cognition and intelligence. Previously I outlined the failure of its explanatory power and the emergence of postcomputationalist approaches. These approaches promise new ways of thinking about arts practices. Although the changes in computational technologies and paradigms are of huge popular interest and some attention has been paid to the question of cognition, some deep and fundamental issues remain undigested, and shifts (subtle and not so subtle) in practices and expectations often go unremarked.

The last quarter century has seen a remarkable about-face in the art world vis-à-vis digital technology. Twenty years ago, digital art was seen as a technological folk art inhabited by the nerdy equivalent of Sunday painters. Art theorists and art historians would not come near the field because it reeked of technophilia. As digital practices have developed, traditional practices are increasingly viewed—especially by those "born digital"—*in terms of* digital practices. New and necessarily interdisciplinary theoretical approaches have provided a vibrant discursive context, from the perspective of which traditional art historical approaches appear irrelevant and dowdy. At this moment in the development of digital cultural practices, it would be timely to reassess the condition of art and the practices of art making, both digital and nondigital.

The development of computer tools has brought forth a diversity of new practices, attitudes, techniques, processes, media, and devices, involving machine behavior based in real-time sensing and computation. The task of designing such behavior calls for aesthetic and theoretical support largely absent from traditions of theorization in the (plastic) arts—for an obvious reason: Until now, such practices have not had the capacity for ongoing dynamic change. At the same time, traditional practices have undergone significant change under the influence of computational technologies and discourses.

If practices have changed rapidly, then there is a clear call for ethnographic research to examine the impact of computing on practices in the arts—to ask what has been lost, what new has emerged, and in general how the ubiquity of computation has affected practices—while such practices survive, at least in memory. This is not just a call for a nostalgic oral history. In a way comparable to ethnobotanical research, cognitive ecologies that are on the verge of extinction may contain resources valuable for future developments. Such research can not only mark such changes but also contribute to the development of culturally enriched theories of cognition.

## Art after Computationalism

Critical discourses around computer culture have centered on networking, databases, interactivity, procedurality, and subthemes such as collaborative work. These approaches miss a fundamental point: The computer is a machine for manipulating symbols. The world is not symbols; *we* turn the world into symbols for the computer. Humans are the analog to digital interface between the world and the internet. The world remains outside the computer and outside the symbolic, but under the hegemony of the digital, the conflation of the products of computing with the world, bizarrely, goes unremarked.

In the spirit of cybernetics and autopoietic biology, we can think of the mind not as a quasi-mystical transcendental phenomenon but as biological, immanent in life, and see intelligence as suffused in the body and evidenced in successful action in the world. We can discuss intelligence in a way that reemphasizes relationality, contextualized by embodiment and situation. This move would redress the excesses of cognitivism and build conceptions of intelligence and cognition that more truly reflect the realities of intelligent human action in the world.

While other "information technologies" (writing, printing, etc.) have dealt in a currency of symbolic representation, information technology reduces the world to information, or at least positions information as primary and the world as secondary. But when I scramble up a scree slope or brace myself as the subway lurches or sniff melons for ripeness, symbolic representation is of marginal significance. The dynamical balance I must exercise, the subtle discernment of odors, cannot be reduced to symbols— or if they can, the experiences would be, in Philip Agre's felicitous wording, "hollowed through the false precision of formalism" (1997b, 148). This is a crux of my argument regarding computing and cultural practices: If we speak only in terms of information and of symbolic representation, we cannot effectively talk about art practice and the experience of artworks.

## How I Became Posthumanist[12]

The subject of this book might be interpreted as being roundly media art or computing and culture or ideas of cognition, but I am reaching further, beyond the foibles of the art world and perceived failures in the world of science and technology, toward fundamental assumptions of the modern Western worldview. Central in my sights are the mind-body dualism and the subject-object dualism. My general contention is that the dualistic conceptions that have characterized the modern worldview have rendered the qualities of our embodied selfhood obscure. This is a peculiar condition, regarding which Tim Ingold noted that "the division between design and implementation, or between the operations of intelligence and real bodily movement, is so deeply embedded in modern thought, and so heavily institutionalized, in diverse domains of contemporary Western society, that it is proving peculiarly hard to dislodge" (2001, 29). With regard to the separation of mind and body, John Haugeland memorably noted, "Only with this metaphysical conception in place, could the idea of solipsism—the idea of an intact ego existing with nothing else in the universe—so much as make sense. And behind that engine have trailed the sorry boxcars of hyperbolic doubt, the mind-body problem, the problem of the external world, the problem of other minds, and so on" (1998, 207). I propose that the mind-body dualism and the subject-object dualism (which are isomorphic and overlapping) have constructed our relation to the world, in art as much as in science. Paradoxically and ironically, it is the computer—that epitome of the objectivist worldview, that reification of dualism—that by its capability of producing quasi-biological behavior draws us ineluctably toward a rejection of those very dualisms.

## The Interdisciplinary Caveat

The scope of this book is broad and radically interdisciplinary. I recognize that few readers will share a background in the diversity of sources I am marshalling to make my argument. A reader who is a specialist in any of the many fields I visit might find this book engaging in its breadth and general argument but find my treatment of his or her field superficial, episodic, or inaccurate in some details. That is an inevitable side effect of the breadth of scope I am attempting here. I regret that many of my excursions into fields of research are unsatisfyingly brief. Sadly, it is impossible to simultaneously build a coherent and succinct general argument while engaging each individual field at the depth each deserves.

The various theories and methodologies discussed do not always sit comfortably with each other. I have done my best to get them to play nice. My intention is to connect ideas and events across disciplinary fields and discourses in ways specialist researchers may not have intended or perhaps not imagined. In a period of increasing specialization, I believe in the importance of this work, both for the argument I am making and as an intervention into conventional academic epistemology. If we allow the unexamined axiomatic assumptions of disciplines to create epistemological fiefdoms, we are the poorer for it. While specialists might chafe, I believe that in casting my net wide and juxtaposing ideas from divergent fields, the whole can be greater than the sum of its parts.

## Goals and Structure of This Book

To conceive of action in the world as constitutive of intelligence is an ontological shift with major repercussions for art theory, which affords the opportunity to evaluate and discuss practices in the arts (and related areas) in terms of embodied and situated cognition. Such attention may also put some pressure on the academic bias of the academy, which privileges knowledge encapsulated in abstract symbolic terms.

An "art of automated behavior" is a new aesthetic realm. Conventional art theory or art-historical approaches are of scant value here. To fill this gap, I draw together research in and critiques of artificial intelligence, robotics, cognitive science, HCI, and neurology, as well as relevant bits of art theory, cultural studies, science studies, and other disciplines, and meld them together as a way of laying the groundwork for a more usefully informed approach to methods and aesthetics of the field. I take it as given that culture and science are insinuated into each other with manifold mutually interpenetrating tendrils. Culture is scientized, and science is a cultural practice.

Much of this book focuses on a reevaluation of history, but my goal is to provide theory relevant to practice. Although theoretical work in digital cultures has become an established academic field, it tends to be rooted in traditions of literary criticism and critical theory. While practice steams ahead, there remains a need to build theories of cultural practice relevant to cultural applications of computing and resulting complex dynamical processes. Creative rationale and design methodologies related to new media modalities have received surprisingly little theoretical attention. Development of discourses around the evaluation of aesthetic richness in multimodal media design, sensor utilization, database coordination, interaction design, hypertextual strategies, or the deployment of autonomous agents is needed in order to provide a theoretical grounding for discussing emerging digital cultural practices—not simply to provide grist for the theoretical mill, but to provide support for the development of aesthetically rich and theoretically sound digital cultural practices.

Each of the three sections of this book builds on what comes before it. Part I provides an overview of a range of areas of research through the twentieth century that have bearing upon, or whose development culminates in, the topics discussed in part II. I expose the degree to which we are naturalized to dualism, internalism, representationalism, and computationalism, and the ramifications this naturalization has had on the way we understand what we are and how we operate in the world. This sets up part II, which focuses on the new postcognitivist theories of cognition, delving into some of the new paradigms—situated, distributed, extended, embodied, and enactive—reasserting embodied and material aspects of practices that, under the sway of cognitivism, have been elided. This discussion in turn provides a basis for part III, which relates these postcognitivist positions to discussions of art and cultural practices, including media art practices, to find ways of understanding and talking about art and cultural practices that provide an emancipation from dualist narratives and to deploy research in embodied, enactive, and embedded cognition in the formation of an approach to the design and understanding of behavioral and interactive systems. These foreground the dynamical and are key to the *aesthetics of behavior.*

# Intermezzo: Sugar and Slaves, Navigation and Cartography, Deixis and Representationalism

The following circular, looping story is a cameo, an analogy in miniature to the book. It involves medieval addiction to sugar; the evolution of Western cartography and nautical navigation; the early development of computing; the application of representationalism and particularly the concept of the *map* to AI and specifically to robotics; and the application of computational theory as an analytic tool for describing navigational practices and the simultaneous critique of those practices. All this is held together by the story of a non-Western, nonrepresentational navigational tradition.

Astronomy, mapping, and cartography were major sciences in Islamic culture, and Europeans on the periphery of the Islamic world were also interested. Notably, Norman king Roger II of Sicily (1130–1154) employed Islamic cartographer Muhammad al-Idrisi on his massive cartographic project begun in 1138, which produced the most accurate map of the world ever made. It remained so for the next three hundred years. John II, Christian king of the until recently Islamic territory of Portugal (1481–1495), had the idea to establish a system for gathering and processing observations and measurements made at sea and tabulate them in a standardized representational framework, combining the records and measurements of many sailors and explorers.

According to Sidney Mintz (1985), the period of European nautical exploration was prompted not by lofty ideas of discovery, but by the taste the European aristocracy had developed for sugar, which, as a result of the Reconquista, the Arabs refused to sell to Europe. Europeans tried to grow their own, first in the Balearic Islands, then, skirting Arab North Africa, in the Canaries and Azores, and finally (1493) on the islands of Sao Tome and Principe off the coast of modern Nigeria where slaves were brought from the mainland to work in the booming sugar plantations. Columbus stumbled across Hispaniola, and within a decade (by 1501) there were African slaves in the Caribbean. The already developed slave-based sugar production system was exported over the Atlantic. In 1526, the first Portuguese slave ship arrived, ushering in a 350-year period of large-scale transatlantic slave trade, in which 12.5 million were transported.

## Navigation as Computation

The problem of planetary cartography is fundamentally geometric: how to represent a spherical surface as a flat surface. Approximations to this geometrical impossibility are called *projections*. The Mercator projection (Gerardus Mercator, 1569) possesses a special quality that allows for the possibility of chart-based navigation. In the Mercator projection, a *rhumb line* (a path traveled according to a constant compass bearing) corresponds to a straight line on the map, a fact that simplifies navigation significantly.[1] This is not the case for maps in general, nor for other cartographical projections, which might preserve area (equal area) or distance (equidistant), instead of angle (equiangular).

The Mercator projection is a quintessential technical representation in which internal metrics of the representation correspond in some simple way to facts in the world, allowing for transfer of information in both directions. Calculations performed on the chart based on measurements taken in the world (speed, direction) are meaningfully transferrable back to the world and have predictive capability. The Mercator projection permits this at the cost of becoming wildly inaccurate toward the poles. In effect, the sphere is projected onto a cylinder. This creates paradoxes. The poles become not points but lines; areas falsely grow toward the poles. (This fault was not critical, as most of the zones of nautical adventurism [colonization] were in tropical or temperate zones where these inaccuracies were not significant.) The shortest path between two points on the surface of the planet—a great circle line—appears curved on the Mercator projection. Two ideas stand out: First, the Mercator projection is an analog computer. Second, metaphors and models make some realities seem implausible or counterfactual. The power of metaphors (both positive and negagive) is an idea that recurs in these pages.

The nautical chart is a repository of knowledge, an archive of data collected and corrected over decades, housed in a particularly useful data structure. It is a database in which information is organized by geographical position (as opposed to, say, size or color or alphabetical order). The complex of technologies that afforded the development of Western nautical navigation—the compass, nautical chart, and related chart tools such as protractors and parallel rules—when combined with certain tools and techniques of observation, reading, and drawing are an analog computational system. Edwin Hutchins notes,

It is essential to realise that a nautical chart is more akin to a coordinate space in analytic geometry than to the sort of simple map I may produce to guide a new acquaintance to my office. All maps are spatial analogies in the sense that they preserve some of the spatial relationships of the world they depict, but navigational charts depict spatial relationships in special ways that support certain specialised computations. . . . Plotting a position or a course on a nautical chart is just as much a computation as solving the set of equations that represent the same constructs as plotted points and lines. A chart contains an enormous amount of information, every location on it has a specifiable address, and the relationships of all the locations to all of the others are implicitly represented. (1995, 61–62)

Various sets of tables were important accessories in navigation, including tide tables—another pre-electronic database that offered predictive capability. For maritime powers, navigational expertise was a key aspect of imperial power. Ongoing technological research and development (such as the chronograph) was crucial. It is no surprise then that the proposed purpose of the original automatic computer—Charles Babbage's *difference engine*—was to prepare tide tables for the British navy. This was regarded as fundable due to a pressing need for such tables in order to support the naval superiority of a colonial and maritime Britain. Little has changed; the first task of ENIAC (Electronic Numerical Integrator and Computer) was to make calculations for the development of the hydrogen bomb. The GPS (global positioning system) in our phones is a satellite navigation system owned by the US government and run by the US Air Force.

## Navigation as Distributed Cognition

In his landmark work on distributed cognition, *Cognition in the Wild*, Edwin Hutchins described and analyzed the activity of a navigational team on a naval ship's bridge in rigorously computationalist terms: "The computation observed in the activity of the . . . system can be described in the way cognition has been traditionally described—that is, as computation realised through the creation, transformation, and propagation of representational states" (1995, 49). Hutchins identifies this group navigational activity as a case study in distributed cognition: "The functional system that realises this memory clearly transcends the bounds of the skull and the skin of the individual plotter. If we were to characterise this memory retrieval as a heuristic search, we would have to say that the search . . . is conducted in the space of the chart itself . . . The navigation system thus remembers which landmark goes with the current bearing and most of the structure and process of memory function is external to the human actor" (142).

*Distributed cognition* is one of several approaches that sought to liberate the idea of cognition from the individualist and internalist paradigm of traditional cognitive science. However, it should be noted that Hutchins's approach achieves this goal by extending the conception of representational computationalism beyond the skull. In this sense, his approach is a predecessor of the *extended mind* hypothesis of Clark and Chalmers (see chapter 13). This is in stark contrast to some of the more radical postcognitivist approaches to cognition, which reject, variously and to various degrees, internalism, computationalism, and representationalism, most notably enactive approaches (see chapter 11).

One can view Hutchins's exercise as one of disciplinary imperialism—validating nautical navigation in terms of computationalism. Maritime navigation is a long-established intellectual discipline with demonstrable achievements, involving refined instruments, measurements, and symbolic representations in a coherent logical system; this was Mercator's grand achievement. Techniques we now associate with symbol-processing artificial intelligence have been part of the Western tradition for five hundred years.

**The Skill of Map Reading**

We are thoroughly naturalized to maps and map reading. It is important to note that there is nothing "natural" in the practice, just as there is nothing natural in inferring "space" in a perspectival representation. Anthropological literature contains many examples of cultures in which one or both of these capabilities are unknown. Western cartography and perspective are expressions of similar motivations, involving representational abstraction rooted in geometry. It is important to recognize how culturally specific map reading is. It demands a specialized form of mental gymnastics involving the construction of a triple self. One self is in the world, struggling to correlate the (subjective) experience of the world with the representation on the map. A second self is at a location on the map. A third self is looking down from an impossibly high viewpoint, seeing the self with the map, as if looking at a map with the location of the self on it.[2] It is only by establishing these imaginary selves and negotiating the relationship among them that map reading is possible.

**Navigation, AI, and Robotics**

A representation implies a viewpoint; this is true with respect to visually based representations (perspective) and more conceptual constructions.

Implicit in the culture of the map is the idea of an all powerful, putatively "objective" viewpoint. In a more abstract sense, this "God trick" (Haraway 1988, 582) is isomorphic with the logic of scientific objectivity. Given the extended technical history of cartography and navigation; the Western naturalization to map reading as a technical representational practice; the association of both cartography and computer science with machinations of the military state; and the predilection of computer science to a scientistic notion of objectivity: It comes as no surprise that concepts of maps and planning on representations are fundamental to artificial intelligence.

The Western habit of projecting an imaginary and usually impossible viewpoint from which to extract authoritative knowledge is replicated in the top-down approach of Good Old-Fashioned Artificial Intelligence (GOFAI), as explicated in the Sense Map Plan Act (SMPA) paradigm. (*Sense* here means *measure*.) As such, Western chart-based navigation substantially informed concepts of robot navigation in the later twentieth century. Measuring, mapping, and planning are precisely what a navigator does. Ed Hutchins's choice of naval navigation as his field of study in distributed cognition inheres the same kind of historical circularity as the choice of the game of chess as the exemplar of AI.

## Micronesian Navigation and Deixis

In Western cartography, the world is fixed and the navigator moves across it. This may be an intuitive idea for terrestrial navigation. But the objectivizing representational convention of Western cartography is not the only possible mode of navigation. In Micronesian navigation, the navigator is the fixed point and the world flows past (more intuitive for a watery world). Historically, Micronesian techniques were found by Westerners to be paradoxical or irrational. The ability of the Micronesians to navigate over vast open water and make successful landfall on tiny islands over the horizon was regarded as mysterious.

In the middle of *Cognition in the Wild* is a remarkable essay concerning Micronesian navigation that combines computationalist reasoning with reflexive anthropology. Hutchins found anthropologists' explanations of the (then) almost lost art of Micronesian navigation incomplete. Insightfully, he proposes that this was because anthropologists naturalized to Western map-based navigational practices assumed, explicitly or implicitly (and contrary to any evidence), that there must be a map, even if it is a mental map. Hutchins then proceeded to demonstrate that Micronesian navigation techniques do not require maps. Hutchins established that it is possible to build an effective navigational system around a subject-centered (deictic) viewpoint that not only does not require maps, but precludes the possibility of a map. While incompatible with Western conceptualizations of navigational practices, Micronesian practices are fully functional and effective.

Hutchins showed that the Micronesian system is logically and computationally coherent. The source of the mystery was the inability of the original anthropologists to denaturalize their own acculturation to a particularly Western way of thinking about the world in terms of representation. The Micronesians do not indulge in the construction of multiple selves necessary for working with maps; their approach is inherently *deictic*. The observer is at the center of the system; the system is built around him, and there is no dissociation between the experiential and the schematic. "For the Micronesian navigator, all bearings originate at himself and radiate outward" (Hutchins 1995, 81). Hutchins makes claims about Micronesian navigation that seem simply incomprehensible in Western terms: "In this system there are no universal units of direction, position, distance, or rate, no analog to digital conversions and no digital computations [all key aspects of Western navigation]. Instead, there are many special-purpose units and an elegant way of 'seeing' the world in which internal structure is superimposed on external structure to compose a computational image device" (93).

**From Where I Stand**

Hutchins offers this thought experiment as validation of the Micronesian conception of navigation: "Go at dawn to a high place and point directly at the center of the sun. That defines a line in space. Return . . . at noon and point again to the center of the sun. That defines another line in space. I assert that the sun is located in the space where those two lines cross. Does that seem wrong? Do you feel that the two lines meet where you stand and nowhere else?" (1995, 81–82). The heliocentric Western view is only possible for an imaginary point of view outside the solar system! Indoctrinated in the heliocentric view, we Westerners habitually build this mental representation. Perhaps the origin of the "God trick" is the heliocentric model? (This would be ironic, since said model was originally seen as heretical.) In any case, its introduction highlights the privileging of the so-called objective viewpoint over the subjective and experiential, an idea that was to gain strength in succeeding centuries.

Ironically, even now, Western celestial navigation is conducted using a geocentric model of the universe. Hutchins notes that for the Micronesians, as for Western celestial navigation, the heliocentric point of view is irrelevant: "Modern celestial navigation is deliberately pre-Copernican precisely because a geocentric conception of the apparent movements of bodies on a rigid celestial sphere makes the requisite inferences about the positions of celestial bodies much easier to compute that they would be in a heliocentric representation" (1995, 82). As the Western and Micronesian navigational systems both work, so the geocentric and heliocentric conceptions both work. And each has conventions that make certain kinds of thinking easy and others more difficult.

For the Micronesian system to work, an assumption is made that seems unacceptably counterfactual to Westerners: It is assumed that the navigator and the stars remain fixed in position, while the world moves past the boat. Not only does this make sense when traveling at sea, but this is the experiential quality of optic flow or parallax. Watch the moon from a moving vehicle: The scenery glides past, and you and the moon are fixed. The Micronesian perspective is experientially accurate. Indeed, from the perspective of raw perception, we are always the center of the world. Neurologically, we have multiple systems of orientation, some of which are deictic and some of which refer to landmarks and world coordinates (see chapter 12). Micronesian navigation could not exist if it was not grounded in and supported by human cognitive capacity.

There is another aspect of the Micronesian context not immediately obvious to terrestrial cultures: Micronesia is almost entirely water. The familiar sorts of fixed points we navigate by—mountains, buildings, trees—simply aren't there. Indeed, there is no ground. Reference to the ground confirms to us we have changed direction (or haven't); we get it through our ankles and knees and hips as well as our vestibular system. On the water, the only fixed (terrestrial) point is the boat, and even that is unstable. Swells pass, currents flow, clouds drift; only the positions of the sun, moon, and stars provide a reliable basis for orientation.

Comparing the Micronesian and Western traditions, Hutchins insightfully notes that in the Western tradition there is "not just the development of the tools of measurement, but a passion for measuring and a penchant for taking the representation more seriously than the thing represented" (1995, 115). In comparison to the deicticism of the Micronesian approach, an imaginary overhead viewing position is part of the mental gymnastics needed to make the Western system work. To place oneself outside oneself is a radically disembodying cognitive act that Westerners are so utterly naturalized to that we don't realize we're doing it. Our view of the world, as neutral and natural and objective as we would like to think it is, is both culturally constructed and always inherently subjective.

# I  Minds, Brains, and Biology

# 1 How Did We Get Here?

A central goal of this book is to develop new ways to discuss the cognitive dimensions of cultural practices. A review of a range of background material is called for, to provide the foundations of arguments made later in the book. This book is interdisciplinary in scope and is directed at a diverse audience, so some of this may be familiar to some readers but not to others. The purpose of the following chapters is to review various conceptions of cognition and related concepts in differing fields through the twentieth century and also to document the history of computing through the same century, teasing out differences and schisms. This is important, because although we are acculturated to contemporary computing, an understanding of the way fundamental concepts were instantiated into computing as we know it is not well understood. The computer has become our "paradigmatic technology" (Bolter 1984; see below), especially for things mental, so it behooves us to understand the assumptions buried in the technology.

## Computing as a Twentieth-Century Meme

In March 1999, I received an email abstract for a guest lecture in the School of Computer Science lecture series at Carnegie Mellon. The first sentence of the abstract read as follows: "The brain is a computer." Specialists of all stripes talk of the brain as "the human information processor" and of the mind "applying algorithms" and "uploading programs." When I asked why the brain is thought of as a computer, a psychologist and cognitive scientist responded, "We don't even ask such questions anymore; we know that it is the case." This remark struck me as outrageous: the metaphor *brain is computer* declared a self-evident truth. The scientist's statement captures the circularity of what is referred to as cognitivism or computationalism and reveals the complementarity of cognitivist psychology and artificial intelligence: Cognitivist psychology purports to explain the brain in terms of computation, and AI pursues automation of mathematical logic as if it captured the essence of human intelligence.

Such metaphors have drifted quickly into popular language. When any such assertion is no longer explicitly understood as metaphor, we are already deep in an ontological mire. This linguistic sleight of hand has been part of the presentation of computing from the outset—for example, I have a book on my shelf from 1949 called *Giant Brains; or, Machines That Think* (Berkeley 1949).

Long ago, Jay Bolter (1984) developed the notion of *paradigmatic technology*, observing that in any historical period dominant technologies provide a major source for metaphors. For Descartes, the solar system and physiology were clockwork. Things still "run like clockwork." In the eighteenth century, blacksmithing and sailing offered new metaphors (e.g., we "lose our temper" or are "upset," we "forge" ahead, we "stay on an even keel" or are "taken aback"). In the nineteenth century, steam power and railway provided metaphors. When we are "all steamed up," things go "like they are on rails." In the early twentieth century, automobiles, electricity, photography, and radio provided metaphors. We "fire on all four cylinders," bring an idea "into focus," "have our antennas up," and "pick up signals." These paradigmatic technologies provide metaphors to describe human behavior among other things.

In the late twentieth century, our paradigmatic technology was computing. (It remains so, although computing itself has changed.) We casually deploy metaphors from hardware, software, and networking. A friend described someone as "having a very fast processor." Another remarked that a surprising experience had "crashed all her models" and apologized that she had "too many tabs open." We recognize these as lighthearted and inventive metaphors of our time, but they construct a particular sense of ourselves, different than if we identified with metaphors of gears and springs or steam pressure, or the growth and harvest cycles of agriculture, or the cycles of moon and tides.

Digital computing is not "neutral" or value-free, even if we are naturalized to it. There is nothing transcendental or God-given about bits or logic gates or Boolean algebra. Terms such as *artificial intelligence* and *knowledge engineering* make misleading and inflated claims for the techniques they describe. As Edsger W. Dijkstra poignantly noted, "The use of anthropomorphic terminology when dealing with computing systems is a symptom of professional immaturity" (1982, 130). The case of "memory" is particularly poignant. Borrowing a term from human activity (and subsequently dropping the quotation marks) caused a lot of confusion, especially when the computer paradigm was absorbed back into humanistic disciplines, as noted earlier. Computer *memory* is a digital filing cabinet. (In German, the term used is much more neutral, equivalent to *storage*.) Human memory is not data storage. The term *remembering* is instructive; human memory is creative, we put the arms and legs back on.

Sometime during the mid-twentieth century, several things happened that laid the groundwork for the "information revolution." A technical definition of information was established—and along with it a technical notion of communication as passage of information (Shannon 1948). A machine was designed that can process data via automated Boolean logical operations. The concepts of hardware and software were invented, and terms such as *memory* were anthropomorphically borrowed from human experience to describe the behavior of the machine. As the computer became our paradigmatic technology, these newly redefined descriptive terms were folded back on human experience, redefining human behaviors in terms of these mechanistic models. In the last fifty years, the expansion of applications of digital technologies has carried and reinforced these ideas. Basic theory of the digital computer now informs popular conceptions of the human mind. That theory of computing finds its axiomatic basis in the dualistic foundations of Enlightenment humanism.

Contrary to narratives of genius and originality (or proprietary interests), attitudes and technologies arise within historical and cultural processes. The information revolution was not a revolution, and the digital computer did not burst into existence in a blaze of glory in 1984 (or whenever). Both emerged in a long process of research and theorization peppered with serendipity, as numerous social and historical studies of science and technology have demonstrated. A full survey of these forces and trajectories would take us back to the Enlightenment and the "scientific revolution."[1] Here I will limit my discussion largely to the twentieth century and, in particular, to the history of the development of computational machines and the theories of life and cognition around them, attending as well to alternative views that were present concurrently in various sectors.

## Cartesianism and Embodiment

Zen commentator Alan Watts once said, "Most people think a body is something you have." Such an idea is often glibly referred to as Cartesianism, though to attribute it to Descartes is perhaps unfair, as his ideas on the subject were far subtler than the simplified notion that has become a structuring idea in Western thought of the last three centuries. The dualism that bears his name asserts that we are made of two parts, a physical body and an immaterial "thinking thing"—the *res extensa* and the *res cogitans*. There are historical reasons for this contorted idea—not least, Descartes's desire to reconcile his religious faith with his endorsement of emerging empirical and rationalist thought. Also he presumably wanted to avoid the fate of Giordano Bruno or Galileo.

The mind-body dualism is related to, but not identical to, the brain-body dualism (which is similarly problematic).[2] Some cognitive theory gives the impression that the body exists *for* the brain, solely as metabolic infrastructure for the brain. The opposite is the case. The operation of the brain can be properly understood only as part of a system of complex feedback loops that involve but extend beyond nonbrain neurology. We customarily refer to *my hand* and *my foot* as if the *me* who owns the foot is somewhere else. The fact that we locate the inner voices *in our heads* has much to do not with the location of our brains but with the locations of organs of voice and hearing.

The idea that people have separate thinking and doing parts is insidious and permeates our culture. The software-hardware binary in computer science reinforces the analogous dualism: information-matter and, ultimately, mind-body.[3] Over the second half of the twentieth century, with the rise of digital computation, the notion of the separation of matter and information has transitioned form being an abstruse philosophical idea to a technological fact. Digital computation reifies dualism. It reinforces the idea of the *res cogitans*, the thinking thing, and it adds implicitly that thinking is mechanistic reasoning upon abstract representations (symbols). A linear, serial (quasi-industrial) process of input–processing–output is fundamental to the architecture of the von Neumann machine (the architecture of the modern computer). These ideas—software-hardware, Boolean logical operations, and serial processing, along with the technical definitions of information and communication—characterize the digital computer and have been imposed on conceptions of mind and brain. Acts of perception and action are construed as translations from analog to digital and back again.

## The Circularity of Cognitivism and Artificial Intelligence

The discipline of artificial intelligence emerged in this context and, deploying the philosophical idea of functionalism (Putnam), made the astonishing claim that "thinking" could be implemented in machines that manipulate symbols. If this was the case, then, ipso facto, the brain is a computer. These arguments are circular and mutually reinforcing: Machines think and brains compute, and the currency in which these exchanges occur (in both cases) is symbols, manipulated by logical rules or algorithms. Implicit in this are two dangerous ideas: that sensing, thinking, and action are separate and separable operations; and that thinking happens in an enclosed, abstract, quasi-immaterial space of computation isolated from the world, where symbolic tokens are manipulated per mathematical rules. Artificial intelligence (of the first-generation, symbol manipulation variety) and cognitive science (or at least that variant sometimes referred to as *computationalism* or *cognitivism*) are thus mutually reinforcing inversions of the same idea, which permeates our culture. We find it reproduced everywhere, as numerous sci-fi scenarios from *2001: A Space Odyssey* to *The Lawnmower Man* attest.

As an intellectual pastime, the manipulation of symbolic tokens according to logical rules has preoccupied great minds for centuries. The system of logic implemented in digital computing was devised by George Boole, who died nearly a century before the first electronic computers. Contemporary digital computers implement and automate Boolean algebra. In order to *prove* the intelligence of computers, they were applied to tasks such as playing chess. When these machines beat humans at chess, they were deemed to be intelligent. Chess is a game for which the rules can be entirely stated in logical terms within a logically defined universe (as described by Kurt Gödel in his incompleteness theorem). Such a logically defined universe is isomorphic with the logical environments defined in computational systems themselves.[4] Here again is circularity: Systems of reasoning following logical rules are developed and—surprise, surprise!—they are successful in managing tasks isomorphic with those closed systems of rules. There is no dispute that this is a creditable testament to human intellectual achievement—but there is no evidence that human intelligence or biological cognition generally operate according to such systems of logical rules.

Most things in life are not so cleanly delineated as the rules of chess. From choosing what to have on a pizza to strategizing a route across town during rush hour to managing a relationship, attempting to solve such problems by implementing systems of logical rules is farcical (even though we sometimes persuade ourselves to do so). Tasking a computer to discern the better of two chocolate cakes is a far more challenging task than playing chess. Indeed, even identifying a chocolate cake among rubber replicas or discerning a carob cake from a photograph of a chocolate cake might be a challenge. Chess is playable by computer because it is entirely logically definable. New kinds of pieces with new behaviors do not occur. The board does not change shape. The big world is not definable by rules and, indeed, every time we attempt to define it by rules, exceptions crop up. This, in a nutshell, was the Achilles' heel of artificial intelligence. Over twenty years, from roughly 1970 to 1990, the AI/cognitivist paradigm was dominant, but problems of integration with the real lived world, previously seen as next steps in technical development, were increasingly acknowledged as problems *in principle* (see chapter 6).

## Calculation and Its Automation

The roots of computationalist and mechanist thinking can be traced back to the European Enlightenment. From there, we can trace a trajectory of the increasingly abstract and mathematized nature of (scientific) knowledge. In the late nineteenth century, devices like Karl von Vierordt's sphygmograph and Édouard-Léon Scott de Martinville's phonautograph rendered natural phenomena as graphical transcription. By mathematical description (analytic geometry, calculus, and Fourier transforms), those curves became numbers and equations. These two stages, the rendering of natural phenomena as graphical trace and the mathematical description of such traces, are major mileposts in the mathematization of the sciences in the late nineteenth century. They are also the prehistory of computing, for computing is nothing except the automation of this mathematics, and its conversion from a descriptive mode to a predictive and real-time mode. In this sense, computing can be seen as the Industrial Revolution coming belatedly to the territory of symbols—the automation of reasoning and calculation.

In the modern period, logico-mathematical thinking came to predominate across the sciences, originally in engineering. The effectiveness of such approaches in the context of modern capitalist industrial economy is indisputable, and that success lent the approach both rhetorical and pragmatic force. By the end of the nineteenth century, the idea that instruments could capture (graphical) records of environmental variables—which might then be analyzed mathematically—was accepted. With the rise of analog electronics, the graphical trace became an electrical waveform, and those signals could be manipulated and analyzed on the fly by electronic circuits. Like the curves inscribed on paper or smoked glass, the fluctuations of voltages (and other variables) had one-to-one correspondence with the dynamics of the physical phenomena that generated them. In this way, the electronic signals were truly *analogous*. This was the birth of *analog* computing.

Analog computation is fundamentally different from the kind we are naturalized to—that is, digital computation. In fact, it is not "computation" in that sense at all. So many terms of art have been (re)defined by the dominant discourse—in this case, digital computation—that explanation of the analog in terms of digital epistemology demands intellectual acrobatics. Yet analog conceptions are meaningful in their own right. Analog is temporally continuous; the so-called digital is discrete. Analog resolves to curves; calculus is its mathematical language. Digital computation requires that these analog processes be discretized into numerical values at a chosen resolution, and computation proceeds by arithmetic and logical operations upon these numerical values. Analog and digital computation are fundamentally different in the same way that geometry and algebra, verbs and nouns, and the performative and the representational are different.

## Cybernetics and AI

While AI still maintains something of the afterglow of a triumphal science, cybernetics is cast as old-fashioned, usually without explanation. Simplistic historical synopses tell us that AI supplanted cybernetics as digital computing supplanted analog computing. In fact, digital computing and AI emerged in the context of cybernetics and analog computing and only slowly differentiated through the 1960s. During that time, cybernetic and computationalist paradigms were in a process of formation and were not clearly distinguished. The preoccupation in AI with manipulating dematerialized information was explicit, whereas cybernetics focused on agent/environment feedback control functions. However, we cannot say that cybernetics was preoccupied with hardware, as the distinction was not clearly drawn at the time. "Software" *did not exist*. There was no "software," either in concept or in technological instantiation.

As technological discourses and systems of explanation, cybernetics and artificial intelligence are complementary. Cybernetics was generally externalist, whereas AI is inherently internalist. As digital computation developed, its rhetoric took an antithetical position to that of cybernetics: dualist software-hardware where cybernetics was holistic; internalist where cybernetics was externalist; abstract where cybernetics was materialized; and representational where cybernetics was, one might say, performative.

Cybernetics focused on the integration of an agent with its environment. AI focused on reasoning in the form of the manipulation of symbols. Cybernetics was heir to an engineering tradition of making things work in the world, as David Mindell has demonstrated. In cybernetics, intelligence existed at the interface with the world. This view is in stark opposition to the cognitivist view, which makes sensors and effectors secondary to the main event of information processing: symbol manipulation. The conception of the brain as a thinking organ, theoretically separable from the body, is a hallmark of computationalist cognitivism.

The influence of cybernetics waned through the 1970s, in part due to the ascendancy of digital computing technology and approaches related to it. Curiously, during the same time that cybernetics became unfashionable as a computational discourse, it was increasingly influential in engineering, biology, social sciences, and business management in the forms of systems theory, control theory, and operations research.

In computing circles, cybernetic ideas went underground but reappeared (cleverly disguised) as "artificial life" when the computationalist paradigm began to collapse. We can find the origins of the bottom-up thinking of the 1990s artificial life (ALife) movements in the cybernetic discourses around self-organizing systems, presaging "complexity theory" and emergent complex behavior.

AI descends from the tradition of mathematical and logical philosophy. AI constituted intelligence, in Cartesian spirit, as abstract and quasi-mathematical symbol manipulation occurring in a black box, separate from the world—manipulation of symbolic tokens occurring in an abstract immaterial space of logico-mathematical representations, whether that space was in a brain or in a machine. According to functionalism (see chapter 5), brain and computer were taken to be, in principle, interchangeable. For computers, the organs of translation were analog to digital peripherals. For brains, the world was accessible by organs of translation: the senses. According to the von Neumann paradigm, computing is a serial process of input, processing, and output.

That the senses are peripheral to thought is central to cognitivism. It speaks volumes that in computer science parlance sensors and effectors are referred to as *peripherals*. Under the influence of Weiner, von Neumann, and Shannon, the drive to mathematical formal abstraction was central. As Paul Edwards puts it, "Control and communication were computational processes susceptible to modeling in terms of devices and formal structures bearing no physical resemblance to the body or brain" (1997, 185). From this assertion of functionalist abstraction, the division of software from hardware evolved to the point that AI had no need for a model of mind as inherently embodied.

Functionalism was the philosophical device by which the AI community could argue that intelligence was "platform independent"—that brains and computer processors were interchangeable. Functionalism haunts later twentieth-century theories of cognition. Artificial life, at least in the hands of Chris Langton, was functionalist; the idea of life on a silicon substrate is incomprehensible otherwise. (There were others in the community, biological materialists, who rejected such analyses.) More recently, the extended mind hypothesis (Clark and Chalmers 1998) has been described by Michael Wheeler as a footnote to functionalism, and Andy Clark has himself admitted to "minimal Cartesianism" (1998). More radical thinkers in embodied cognition, such as the enactivists, reject some or all of the complex of Cartesian, representationalist, functionalist, cognitivist, computationalist approaches.

## Digital Computing and Dualism

Digital computing is, at root, simply the automation of mathematical logic. It perpetuates the Cartesian dualism in the fundamental division of hardware and software. This division is of course as false and unsubstantiable as the Cartesian dualism on which it is based. It remains one of the most extraordinary ironies of Western culture that although the mind-body dualism (and related dualisms) structures the Western worldview (and particularly scientific worldviews), it remains, as noted above, a fictive construction without a shred of scientific evidence to support it (see chapters 9, 17, and elsewhere).

At the heart of digital computing is an assumption regarding the separability—and inherent separateness—of matter and information. This commitment has ramifications in doctrines of the portability and platform independence of data and procedures. As Katherine Hayles rightly noted, "The point is not only that abstracting information from a material base is an imaginary act but also, and more fundamentally, that conceiving of information as a thing separate from the medium instantiating it is a prior imaginary act that constructs a holistic phenomenon as an information/ materiality duality" (1999, 13).

## Dualism and Holism in Biology

At the very inception of modern genetics, Watson and Crick took the idea of computer code—itself a somewhat ill-formed notion at the time—as the structuring metaphor in their interpretation of DNA, laying the groundwork for the Human Genome Project. It is commonplace to understand DNA as "code" analogous to computer code—an indication of the dominance of computationalist metaphors.

A very different tradition of thinking about cognition had developed in biology and in related disciplines, including psychology and ethology. The James/Lang theory of emotion proposed that information about emotion was relayed to the brain from the autonomic nervous system as feedback from muscle tone. This idea, anathema to internalists, was revived by Antonio Damasio in his book *Descartes' Error: Emotion, Reason, and the Human Brain* (1994). A tendency toward materialism, holism, and situated knowledge is a persistent thread in the biological sciences in the twentieth century. In the early years of that century, the discipline of ethology emerged, its stars being Konrad Lorenz, Nikolaas Tinbergen, and Karl von Frisch. Ethology is a holistic science, studying the animal in its environmental context. Another member of that founding generation of ethologists, Jakob von Uexküll, established biosemiotics. Ethology took a situated and material approach to animal cognition, a tradition perpetuated in the work of D'Arcy Wentworth Thompson, Karl Ludwig von Bertalanffy, Humberto Maturana, C. H. Waddington, J. J. Gibson, and others—physiologists, psychologists, neurologists, and ethologists whose disciplines did not subscribe to the mind-body dualism. Alvaro Moreno voiced early objections to the genetic determinism of the Human Genome Project. Twenty-five years later, the rise of epigenetics has destabilized genetic determinism, bringing histories of environmental context back into the picture in an almost Lamarckian way.[5] At the same time, revelations about the microbiome demonstrate that we are less individuals than symbiotic communities.

The autopoietic biology of Humberto Maturana and Francisco Varela asserts that cognition is not the province of *homo sapiens* but is present in all life-forms, being the process by which *autopoiesis*—self creation—is maintained. Maturana and Varela clarify the fallacy of what we might call *genetic informationism*:

It is the network of interactions in its entirety that constitutes and specifies the characteristics of a particular cell, and not one of its components. That modifications in the components called genes dramatically affect the structure is very certain. The error lies in confusing essential participation with unique responsibility. By the same token one could say that the political constitution of a country determines its history. This is obviously absurd. The political constitution is an essential component in any history but it does not contain the "information" that specifies that history. (1987, 69)

Here, Maturana and Varela contest the applicability of mechanism and reductivism to biology. They point to a case of fundamental attribution error and argue for a relational conception of life and the organism. It is important to note that mechanism and reductivism work perfectly well in man-made systems like threshing machines or autonomous agents built of separable components—that is, those that possess the quality of modularity. Reductivism works well for machines that can be reduced, but biology does not work that way.

## Conclusion

In order to create a discursive space for thinking about embodiment and intelligent action, it is necessary to review how we came, culturally, to possess a generally computationalist view of cognition.[6] This is the purpose of part I. Part I is a review of ideas about cognition, intelligence, reasoning, and related ideas as they arose in biology, psychology, computing, and related fields over the twentieth century. This chapter has introduced some of the key issues elaborated in the ensuing chapters of part I: the idea of the Cartesian humanist legacy reified in the computer and rehearsed in computationalist discourse, as compared with the more biologically based cybernetics discourse.

I frame this history in terms of an ongoing tension between materiality and abstraction, a tension that appears in Plato and Aristotle, and later between Descartes and Spinoza. In the twentieth century, this tension was expressed in a quest in certain aspects of science and philosophy toward the general, the symbolic, and the abstract, a trend generally lauded as the success of mathematized rationalism. Discussion of the relationship between Enlightenment philosophical ideas and the ethos of computing arises episodically throughout. This lays the groundwork for part II. According to the thesis of this book, art and cultural practices epitomize the sorts of intelligent action that have remained inadequately addressed by the reigning paradigm of cognition of the later twentieth century. There is scant reference to the arts as such in part I, but this section provides a discursive and historical context for later chapters.

## 2  The Biology of Cognition

Traditional theories have separated life from nature, mind from organic life, and thereby created mysteries.
—John Dewey, *The Later Works of John Dewey, 1925–1953*. Vol. 1, *1925: Experience and Nature* (2008, 212)

To see the organism in nature, the nervous system in the organism, the brain in the nervous system, the cortex in the brain is the answer to the problems which haunt philosophy. And when thus seen they will be seen to be in, not as marbles are in a box but as events are in history, in a moving, growing, never finished process.
—John Dewey, *The Later Works of John Dewey, 1925–1953*. Vol. 1, *1925: Experience and Nature* (2008, 224)

Living systems are cognitive systems, and living as a process is a process of cognition.
—Humberto R. Maturana, "Biology of Cognition," in *Autopoiesis and Cognition: The Realization of the Living* (Maturana and Varela 1980, 13)

Here we go, slithering and squelching on.
—Incredible String Band, "A Very Cellular Song"

Much of part I of this book deals with the history of computational technology and computational ideas. Yet the larger argument of this book is about human cognition. It is therefore appropriate to review biologically oriented theories of cognition through the twentieth century, in order to provide a backdrop for discussion of cognitive machines. This chapter reviews a diverse range of studies in biology, physiology, ethology, and psychology, which, in different ways, present noncognitivist ways of thinking about mind and body, intelligence, and selfhood. It is not my intention to provide a thorough or even balanced survey, but simply to present examples of research that, taken together, create a landscape of biologically based theories of cognition. The structure of this chapter is thus, necessarily, somewhat episodic.

The brain is complex and its relation with other parts remains somewhat mysterious, but it *is* a biological phenomenon. Here it is assumed that cognition and consciousness are, likewise, biological in origin. Implicit in this argument are biological materialism, a critique of human exceptionalism, a destabilization of conventional self-world dichotomies, and a questioning of notions of scientific objectivity. We are material biological beings, and our cognitive capabilities arise from our materiality and our evolutionary history. As such we are more like other animals, even insects, than we are different. We are primates before we are *homo sapiens*, and we are mammals before that. Nature does not separate mind and body. Our "mental" capabilities arise from our biology and are not so separate from other physiological capabilities, nor are they so different from those of our relatives. Rodney Brooks summarized the matter this way:

It is instructive to reflect on the way in which earth-based biological evolution spent its time. Single cell entities arose out of the primordial soup roughly 3.5 billion years ago. A billion years passed before photosynthetic plants appeared. After almost another billion and a half years, around 550 million years ago, the first fish and vertebrates arrived, and then insects 450 million years ago. Then things started moving fast. Reptiles arrived 370 million years ago, followed by dinosaurs at 330 and mammals at 250 million years ago. The first primates appeared 120 million years ago and the immediate predecessors to the great apes a mere 18 million years ago. Man arrived in roughly his present form 2.5 million years ago. He invented agriculture a mere 19,000 years ago, writing less than 5,000 years ago and "expert" knowledge only over the last few hundred years. (1990, 5)

Brooks's message is clear: Intelligence as we know it rests upon eons of biological evolution. The difference between one of us and, say, a lamprey, is far less than that between the lamprey and an amoeba. Once you nail multicellular organization, intelligence is a pushover.[1] In evolutionary developmental biology, to paraphrase William Gibson, evolution finds its own uses for things. The repurposing of parts of the body or brain for new activities is commonplace in evolutionary biology. As Elizabeth Bates and Brian MacWhinney observed, "Language could be a new machine constructed entirely out of old parts" (1988, 147). We were social omnivores before we had language, and our cognitive-cultural capabilities leverage existing neurological and physiological capacities, facilitating and facilitated by the invisible armature of language and culture. Like other humanistic dualisms, the nature-nurture dualism is outmoded. Nature and culture are inextricably bound together. It is not either-or; it is both-and. How could it be otherwise? The way infant learning occurs via the operation of mirror neurons is an illustrative example.

## Von Uexküll and the Life-World

Baron Jakob von Uexküll, scion of an aristocratic Estonian family, studied biology and physiology—including a period with the renowned physiologist Etiennes Jules Marey, better known to art history as the inventor of the chronophotograph.[2] By 1909, he had established his theory of sensory physiology in *Umwelt und Innenwelt der Tiere* (1909). After his *Theoretical Biology* of 1920, he published an unpretentious little volume in 1934, which in English was titled *A Stroll through the Worlds of Animals and Men* (not published in English until 1957). In this genteel text, redolent of the dying embers of Victorian gentlemanly research, von Uexküll ever so gently destabilized the objectivist basis of nineteenth-century science.

Von Uexküll argued that the experiential world of a creature is specific to that species, given to it by virtue of its particular suite of sensorimotor capabilities. He called this the creature's *umwelt*, which we might translate as *life-world* or *experience-world*. Put simply, in sensory experience, there is no objective world "out there." By this logic, mind and world are simultaneously cocreated. This sense of a developmental isomorphism of world and "mind" recurs in the psychology of Jean Piaget and of J. J. Gibson, in the autopoietic biology of Humberto Maturana, and in the enactive cognition of Francisco Varela, Evan Thompson, and Eleanor Rosch (see chapters 10 and 11).

Different species do not share umwelts, even if they happen to be physically colocated. Umwelts may intersect, like Venn diagrams, in which case different species can identify similar things. Creatures may cohabit the same "place" and be unaware of each other because their umwelts do not intersect, due to differences of scale, sensory capability, and so on. Some animals construct their umwelts via senses others do not have—such as the infrared sensing of some snakes, the echolocation of bats, the electro-sensing of platypus and some weakly electric fish, and the magneto-sensing of the hammerhead shark.

## Objectivity and "Experience-Worlds"

We believe in an objective world that includes such things as atoms and electricity, but our confidence in their existence is not given to us by our senses. Much of the "objective world" is experientially unknowable to us due to our limited suite of sensors. We experience this every day but seldom reflect on it. The cat has acute hearing in frequency ranges unknowable to us. Elephants and whales converse in frequencies lower than we can hear, rats and mice in frequencies higher. Taking the dog for a walk, we see that she has a vast and rich olfactory universe. We recognize that the olfactory worlds of dogs are far richer than our own, but we have no way to enter those worlds. Dogs and people can identify the smell of a barbecue, but the question of whether that odor "means" the same thing for dogs and people takes us into the territory of Gibsonian affordances (see below).

We are unable to sense the majority of the electromagnetic spectrum. It is no accident that the range of the electromagnetic spectrum we sense in vision corresponds to the most energetic wavelengths of the sun's emissions as measured on the Earth's surface. Yet the colorful world we inhabit is of our own making; there is no color in the world. Our awareness of space (beyond the peripersonal) is given to us by our sense of vision. An eyeless creature—say, a worm—might have no sense of space beyond the sense of physical contact on its skin, unless it possesses other "at a distance" senses, such as some kind of vibration sense, or "hearing."

The notion of an objective or observer-independent experiential world, even for humans, is not viable. "Objective," extra-specific evaluation of sensory experiences is untenable. We cannot know what it's like to be a bat (Nagel 1974). In proposing such ideas, von Uexküll put himself at odds with mainstream positivist and realist science, which aspires to the establishment of absolute scientific fact. By the same token, his position is sympathetic with his pragmatist contemporaries William James and John Dewey. These sentiments are precursors of the field of biosemiotics and were taken up in different ways by J. J. Gibson and Thomas Nagel half a century later (see below).

Von Uexküll also argued that various sensorimotor behaviors of creatures can be viewed as internally separate and latent until stimulated by environmental triggers. In this sense, integral selfhood is illusory, and the threads of selflets are integrated with the world, confusing the self/world boundary. The robotic architecture called subsumption, devised by Rodney Brooks in the 1980s, as a biologically based alternative to failed cognitivist approaches, implements this idea of behaviors as parallel threads. The idea that integrated identity or unitary selfhood is illusory or bestowed upon a creature by the observer presages ideas of both Maturana and von Forester as well as some contemporary neuroscience (such as David Eagleman).

## Pheromones and Jacobson's Organ

The emission and reception of pheromone signals is widespread among plants, vertebrates, and insects. Humans possess specialized pheromone receptors (the vomeronasal organ), but unlike olfaction, we are not consciously aware of the presence of pheromones nor their effect on our behavior; however, recent research demonstrates not only that pheremones play a role in mate selection but also that we *can* smell fear (Randerson 2008).

In 1959, Adolf Butenandt established that female silkworms signal potential mates by releasing the pheromone bombykol. In colonial insects, such as termites, ants, and bees, pheromones are a primary form of communication—active, for instance, when bees swarm. In many mammals, pheromones play a key role in mating behaviors. In reptiles and mammals, pheromone reception occurs in the Jacobson's organ located on the roof of the mouth. The strange open-mouth, teeth-exposing gesture sometimes seen in donkeys and horses signals exposure of the Jacobson's organ. Elephants touch the tip of their trunk to the organ. Snakes find their prey by using it. As with elephants, snakes touch the forked projection of their tongues on the two vomeronasal pits in the roof of their mouths after waving their tongues in the air; this is why snakes have forked tongues.

### "What the Frog's Eye Tells the Frog's Brain"

In 1959, "What the Frog's Eye Tells the Frog's Brain"[3] was published by Jerome Lettvin, Humberto Maturana (then on leave from the University of Chile in Santiago, Chile), Warren McCulloch, and Walter Pitts. This study established (at least for frog vision) that much of what we would assume to be higher-level "mental" pattern recognition in fact occurs in the eye itself, arising even beyond the neurology of the eye, as a consequence of the eye's physical topography.

In this groundbreaking paper, the researchers established that static aspects of the frog's world have no visual presence for the frog. The frog only sees moving things. Even a food object, such as a fly, is invisible if it is not moving. A frog will leap to capture an object that has the size and behavior of a normal food source, even if it is not, say, a worm, but a curved piece of wire. Here we see evidence of the isomorphism between creature and world that von Uexküll had identified. Indeed, von Uexküll described the hunting behavior of jackdaws in just these terms: For the jackdaw, when the grasshopper is not moving it ceases to exist. For the frog, there are not flies in the world, some of which are moving and some of which are not; there are just objects with the dynamical signature of food. This conception, that visual stimuli are already encoded with information without requiring interpretation, is what J. J. Gibson called an *affordance*.

In their experiment, Lettvin et al. determined that a network of connections *in the eye itself* would respond to moving objects down to three minutes of arc (i.e., one-twentieth of a degree) and that the response was stronger if the movement was jerky. In one case, they moved a color photograph of a normal frog environment seven inches in front of the frog, which garnered no response. If a black dot about one-degree wide (i.e., a fly-like dot) was moved with respect to the background, the frog responded actively. But if the dot was fixed to the picture, no response occurred. Here again we have evidence for the umwelt theory: The leaves and flowers in the picture that signify "frog environment" to us are invisible to the frog![4]

Contrary to the notion that the eye is a camera from which something like pictures pass to the brain to be interpreted, this experiment demonstrated that a substantial amount of the frog's visual perception is dynamical, and it occurs in the eye itself. That is,

the eye speaks to the brain in a language already highly organized and interpreted, instead of transmitting some more or less accurate copy of the distribution of light on the receptors. . . . The operations thus have much more the flavor of perception than of sensation, if that distinction has any meaning now. That is to say that the language in which they are best described is the language of complex abstractions from the visual image. We have been tempted, for example, to call the convexity detectors "bug perceivers." (Lettvin et al. 1968, 255–258)

The implications of this experiment are resounding, as they suggest among other things that some perception occurs extra-cranially, at least in frogs— that the sense organs are not dumb collectors of raw sensory data to be crunched in the brain-computer. Extrapolating to other senses, a person might easily conclude that perception is embodied and not exclusively "mental." The Cartesian theater, with the homunculus seated in the front row in a red velvet seat, is untenable, and not simply due to the infinite regress of homunculi. In the face of such research, it seems mysterious that cognitivism as a paradigm became so persuasive. Or, to put it differently, it explains why research like Lettvin et al.'s frog's eye, and similarly the work of J. J. Gibson, was incomprehensible to cognitivists.

The implications of the experiment are broad with respect to questions of what an organism "knows" about its environment, about the distinction between sensing and perception, and about where "thinking" occurs in the body. Contra cognitivism, the experiment suggests that perception, and what we are accustomed to calling "thinking," are distributed through the bodily tissues (at least). In their experiment, Lettvin et al. chose to use an approach that has become normal in *neuroethology*—that is, a combination of ethological and neurological approaches. The experimenters presented the frog with objects normal and unusual in its environment—normal food species as well as geometric shapes, and so on—while monitoring brain behavior. Although, per von Uexküll, we ought to assume that the frog was sensitive to the fact that it was not in a pond at the time, perhaps via sensory modalities the experimenters did not think to simulate. As we will see in the discussion of experiments by Hubel and Wiesel (see below), studying a creature outside its environment can result in wildly erroneous "knowledge."

Ross Ashby, the British neurologist and cybernetician, cited this study as the catalyst for his great work *Design for a Brain* (1952). Humberto Maturana, who had been part of the research team, went on to establish autopoietic biological theory, which undoubtedly influenced J. J. Gibson in the development of his ecological theory of vision. In the neurosciences, the frog's eye study is rightly regarded as pioneering work, around which the field of neuroethology is based. Contrarily, its implications appear to have been largely lost on mainstream philosophy and the AI community in the following decades. What this study established about the biology of vision should have had resounding consequences for the future of cognitive science; why it didn't remains something of a mystery. Perhaps computer science was still so thoroughly under the thrall of human exceptionalism that it was assumed that human vision just had to be fundamentally different?

### The Chance Meeting of a Cat and a Strobe Lamp on an Operating Table

To understand why Lettvin et al.'s 1959 paper was both unusual and consistent with cybernetic ideas, consider another famous experiment of the same period. The Hubel and Wiesel experiments of 1959 on the visual neurology of cats greatly expanded the scientific knowledge of sensory neuroscience. In one experiment, they inserted a microelectrode into the primary visual cortex of an anesthetized cat (with its eyes pinned open). They then projected patterns of light and dark on a screen in front of the cat. They found that some neurons fired rapidly when presented with lines at one angle, whereas others responded best to another angle, and yet other neurons responded best to lines of a certain angle moving in one direction.

The scenario of the experiment—which involved exposing the anaesthetized cat to visual stimuli unlike anything a cat would normally see—raises questions about what was learned. A cat's vision is attuned to hunting in the dark, to the perception of subtle movements of small animals betrayed by very subtle changes in light perceived by the cat's eye and brain. The bright bands of the experiments present a different kind of stimulus: large, simple, static geometrical shapes, in high contrast and high brightness. One would be hard-pressed to create a visual stimulus less like the ones the cat's vision system had evolved to be attuned to. To a cat hunting at night, the appropriate response to the sudden appearance of giant black and white bands—like the sudden appearance of car headlights—would be panic. Hubel and Wiesel observed visual experience far outside the cat's normal visual experience. Some knowledge was gained about feline brain structure, but whether anything useful could be inferred about how cats might behave in the real world remains an open question. What they recorded was likely the neural correlates of abject terror.

Here in the realm of neurology, we see two approaches that map onto the difference between the externalism of cybernetic and internalism of cognitivist styles. One context asks: How does the frog, as a system, work in coordination with its world? The other asks: How do parts of the brain of the cat work—as if they could be thought of in isolation from the rest of the cat?

## Autopoiesis

Anyone familiar with the ideas and historical moments of cybernetics and autopoietic biology senses kinship, and indeed, the connection between the two is direct. The frog's eye work of Lettvin et al. (1959) connects the neural network research of McCulloch and Pitts to the development of autopoietic biology by Humberto Maturana and Francisco Varela in Santiago, Chile, in the late 1960s and early 1970s. This research is captured in two foundational essays: Maturana's "Biology of Cognition" (1970) and Maturana and Varela's "Autopoiesis: The Organization of the Living" (1973). (These are published together in *Autopoiesis and Cognition: The Realization of the Living* [Maturana and Varela 1980]). An interesting detail confirming the historical connection between cybernetics and autopoiesis is that the preface to *Autopoiesis and Cognition* was written by none other than Stafford Beer, whose significance in cybernetics, in the history of Chile, and in the two together, is well known.[5]

Maturana forcefully asserts, "Cognition is a biological phenomenon and can only be understood as such; any epistemological insight in the domain of knowledge requires this understanding" (Maturana and Varela 1980, 7). Autopoietic theory constructs a framework of sensing and meaning that is fundamentally different from cognitivist/compuationalist conceptions. It intersects with and has been influential in biosemiotics and in the phenomenological theorizing of cognition. Consistent with von Uexküll's umwelt theory and with contemporary neuroscience, autopoietic biology sees the organism as a closed system, perturbed by outside influences. Key concepts of autopoietic biology include operational closure, structural coupling, the autopoietic notion of cognition, and the question of the observer. By *operational closure*, Maturana and Varela mean the mutually reinforcing interactions that constitute living: "It is the circularity of its organization that makes a living system a unit of interactions, and it is this circularity that it must maintain in order to remain a living system and to retain its identity through different interactions" (1980, 9).

## The Santiago Theory of Cognition

Maturana notes, "That which we . . . call cognition is the capacity that a living system exhibits of operating in dynamic structural congruence with the medium in which it exists" (2002, 26). Maturana's biologically derived description of cognition is incommensurable with the conventional cognitivist conception. In a cognitivist view, *cognition* is the correct identification of things objectively in the world. In autopoietic biology, *cognition* is the maintenance of a closed autopoietic system: "For every living system the process of cognition consists in the creation of a field of behavior through its actual conduct in its closed domain of interactions, *and not in the apprehension or the description of an independent universe. Our cognitive process (the cognitive process of the observer) differs from the cognitive processes of other organisms only in the kinds of interactions into which we can enter . . . and not in the nature of the cognitive process itself*" (Maturana and Varela 1980, 49; emphasis mine).

For autopoietic biology, as for cybernetics, successful cognition is successful structural coupling and the maintenance of autopoiesis. Maturana and Varela declare, "A cognitive system is a system whose organization defines a domain of interactions in which it can act with relevance to the maintenance of itself, and the process of cognition is the actual (inductive) acting or behaving in this domain" (1980, 13).

Yet relations among cybernetics, autopoiesis, and cognitivism are not entirely straightforward. N. Katherine Hayles notes:

In a sense, autopoiesis turns the cybernetic paradigm inside out. . . . In the autopoietic view, no information crosses the boundary separating the system from its environment. We do not see a world "out there" that exists apart from us. Rather, we see only what our systemic organization allows us to see. The environment merely *triggers* changes determined by the system's own structural properties. Thus the center of interest for autopoiesis shifts from the Cybernetics of the observed system to the Cybernetics of the observer. (1999, 10–11; emphasis in original)

Von Uexküll might have said that we see only what our systemic organization allows us to see. In the quotation above, Hayles indicates the line connecting von Uexküll with autopoiesis and second-order cybernetics—sometimes called *the cybernetics of the observer*.

## Adaptation, Development, and Creativity

Autopoiesis is a definition of the living, which, contrary to the reductive positivism of genetics, reproductive biology, and evolution, emphasizes self-organization and the holism of the organism. *Autopoiesis* means *self-making* and is essentially a systems-theoretic description of the phenomenon of life as defined by a network of processes that regenerate themselves. As cybernetics was the study of self-steering, "purposive," and self-organizing systems, so the preoccupation in autopoiesis is with the maintenance of organismic coherence, operational closure, and structural coupling. In autopoiesis, as in cybernetics, self-organizing systems are understood to be fundamentally conservative in the sense that they push toward prior equilibrium (i.e., homeostasis), correcting for perturbations and attempting to return to equilibrium. Autopoiesis moves beyond the inherently conservative cybernetic paradigm of self-stabilization to an active conception of ongoing self-creation.

Although Maturana and Varela asserted that an autopoietic system is a homeostat, it is a dynamical homeostat closer to C. H. Waddington's concept of homeorhesis. *Homeorhesis*, loosely put, is homeostasis with teleology, where *teleology* is used in cybernetic terms. For Waddington, homeorhesis described the way an organism maintained its coherence while adapting to its environment, a concept similar to autopoiesis. Yet, as noted by Di Paolo, Wheeler, and others, first-generation autopoiesis doesn't easily accommodate adaptation, development, and creativity (see chapter 11).

## Structural Coupling

In autopoietic biology, interaction with the environment is seen in terms of *structural coupling*, a concept closely related to what cyberneticians called *feedback loops* and to sensorimotor loops in contemporary cognitive science. Structural coupling is a central concept in autopoietic theory. The term describes the process by which structurally determined transformations in each of two or more systemic unities induce—in each other—a trajectory of reciprocally triggered change. Structural coupling triggers change in the organism but does not specify the nature of the change. The notion of structural coupling is taken to be cognitive; thus, in an autopoietic biological perspective, all living entities cognize. "If one does not see how it is that living systems do not have inputs and outputs," states Maturana, "it is not possible to understand cognition as a natural phenomenon, and one does not see that that which we call cognition is the effective operation of a living system in a domain of structural coupling" (Maturana, n.d.).

## Cognition without Information

Autopoietic biology contests the relevance of the concept of information, in its computational sense, as it contests other ideas of computaionalism, such as the linear flow if information from input to output. For Maturana, any attempt to explain the adequate behavior that in daily life we call cognition, as if it were the result of some computation made by the nervous system on the data or information that the sensors obtain of an external objective world, is doomed to fail because whatever occurs to or in a living system is determined by its structural dynamics. There is no information, and there is no computation. Varela asserted that "information, sensu stricto, does not exist" (1980, 45). He meant this in the spirit of second-order cybernetics—in that information is a quality attributed to a system by an observer. *Information* is a representational construction. If there is no representation within the organism, then there is no information as such: "The fact is that information does not exist independent of a context of organization that generates a cognitive domain, from which *an observer community* can describe certain elements as informational and symbolic" (Varela 1980, 45; emphasis in original).

Such epistemological clarity should have been a wake-up call to the AI community, but as Philip Agre observed, that community was itself epistemologically closed. Information does not exist inside the organism; inside the organism there are only complementary biological processes. And information does not exist outside the organism, because there is no "perception" (interpreted as the inflow of information from the environment). Hayles rightly observes, "Autopoiesis also changes the explanation of what circulates through the system to make it work as a system. . . . Indeed, one could say either that information does not exist in this paradigm or that it has sunk so deeply into the system as to become indistinguishable from the organizational properties defining the system as such" (1999, 11).

With respect to a study of color vision, Maturana states, "Perception should not be viewed as a grasping of an external reality, but rather as the specification of one, because no distinction was possible between perception and hallucination in the operation of the nervous system as a closed network" (Maturana and Varela 1980, xv). This is the sense in which Maturana and Varela describe the organism *bringing forth a world*, a sentiment that reminds us again of von Uexküll. As noted, such ideas are incomprehensible from a cognitivist perspective, which assumes that information is in the world and flows into the brain—as if world and organism were, per Shannon (see chapter 5), two computers on a network passing streams of bits.

### Reality and the Observer

As living creatures *bring forth* their worlds, so the question of objectivity and the observer emerges as a preoccupation in autopoietic theory. "Everything said is said by an observer" is perhaps the most quoted of Maturana's aphorisms. The idea of an objective world implies a realm that preexists construction by an observer. Maturana's locution is intended *not* to reinforce the notion of scientific objectivity—but rather to do the reverse. The implication, consistent with von Uexküll, is that any observer sees only what he or she has the ability to see (or senses what he or she has the ability to sense). There may be something "out there," but what comes to experience and the form it takes, for us and other animals, is determined by the organism's own organization: "No description of absolute reality is possible. Such a description would require an interaction with the absolute to be described, but the representation that would arise from such an interaction would necessarily be determined by the autopoietic organisation of the observer . . . hence the cognitive reality that it would generate would unavoidably be relative to the observer" (Maturana and Varela 1980, 212).

Heinz von Foerster famously said, "Objectivity is a subject's delusion that observing can be done without him"—a statement that captures the spirit of second-order cybernetics, preoccupied with the question of observation. Similarly, in terms that echo both von Uexküll and Maturana, von Foerster writes, "The environment as we perceive it is our own invention" (1980, 42). Time and causality are concepts imputed by the observer. An autopoietic system simply continues its autopoietic behavior at every moment. As Hayles notes, echoing Varela, genetic codes (and even the laws of nature) are abstractions invented by the observer to explain what is seen (1999, 139).

### Kittens in Baskets

In an experiment published in 1963, Richard Held and Alan Hein built a rotating balance beam device to accommodate two kittens—a kind of kitten carousel. The kittens sat in baskets; one basket had holes that permitted the kitten to walk. These kittens, designated "active kitten" and "passive kitten," were raised in darkness from birth to eight weeks and were exposed to the carousel for an hour a day (presumably after their eyes opened). Because of the design of the rig, as the active kitten propelled the rig around, each kitten had very similar dynamical visual experiences (one slightly delayed). After the experimental period of eight weeks, the active kitten was judged to be visually normal. The passive kitten was functionally blind.

The lesson from this experiment is that the visual world is not given, as if visual data simply lay around to be sucked up by an eye like some kind of optical vacuum cleaner. The eye is not a camera sending images to the little movie screen in the brain. As demonstrated by the research of Lettvin et al. (1959), vision isn't only, isn't always, and often simply isn't seeing pictures and naming objects. The phenomenon of blindsight reminds us of this. Vision, as spatial perception and in many other ways, is learned and calibrated through bodily experience. This has also been shown repeatedly in developmental psychology and in studies of previously blind people who have had their sight surgically restored.[6] This is the paradox of our sensory being-in-the-world. Our body is our means of having a world, says Dreyfus, following Merleau-Ponty (Dreyfus 1996). And the world we have is a consequence of the specifics of our embodiment, as von Uexküll asserts. The world we have is not "out there," nor is it a solipsistic neural construction. It is relational, as Anthony Chemero argues in his second-order affordance theory (2009).

## An Ecological Theory of Vision

James Jerome (J. J.) Gibson made several radical proposals in the psychology of visual perception during his long career. His early affiliation with Gestalt psychologists led him to reject behaviorist approaches. It was in two later books, *The Senses Considered as Perceptual Systems* (1966) and *The Ecological Approach to Visual Perception* (1979), that he formulated the theories and concepts for which he is best known. Gibson argued for a direct realist approach to vision, insisting that information was directly available in and from the environment. This contradicted the more conventional cognitivist approach that perception of the environment is constructed by inference and other mental processes. Gibson contested the notion of vision as "seeing pictures" predominant at the time. A key aspect of his theorization of vision was that visual information was not obtained through passive vision but was integrated with and dependent upon movement and temporality. "If object perception depends on invariant detection instead of form perception," he declared, "then form perception itself must entail some invariant detection" (Gibson 1978, 228).

Gibson's use of the term *invariant* in the context of the ambient optic array demands some elaboration. As we move toward an object, it appears to become larger; this is an aspect of what Gibson called *optic flow*. Optic flow is an invariant in the ambient optic array. This example shows that Gibson's ecological psychology has much in common with the *radical constructivism* of autopoietic biology: The organism responds to sensations on its retina, not to "objects in the world."[7]

Gibson's attention to the temporality of vision led to the notion that awareness of the speed and direction of movement is given by immediate experience of the ambient optic array. He proposed that animals guide their movement toward some goal by optic flow. The information needed to control movement is in the organization of the visual stimuli on the retina and does not require interpretation; it is already present in the ambient optic array. Gibson's notion of *perceptual systems* is a dynamical and embodied conception that emphasizes the role of the individual's self-directed movements in revealing environmental structure. This makes vision in Gibson's terms embodied and proprioceptively integrated. This idea is clearly in sympathy with Held and Hein (1963) and with contemporary conceptions of sensorimotor loops. Indeed, Gibson's work is celebrated as pioneering among postcognitivist researchers. Interestingly, Gibson admitted that his theorization of vision stumbled on the subject of actual pictures. His theory of direct perception works best in the nonsocial world (Gibson 1971, 1978): Only humans make pictures.

## Affordances, Umwelt, and Relationality

Gibson insisted that perception is *what we can do with* perceptual information. This pragmatism reminds us of the frog's eye experiments of Lettvin et al. (1959). According to Gibson, what are (directly) perceived in vision are functionally meaningful qualities for the perceiver located in the ambient optic array. Vision, for Gibson, is not the mental analysis of images. Gibson called these functionally meaningful properties *affordances*. Affordance is a relational concept. For Gibson, affordances are not mental constructions; they exist objectively as optical (or other sensory) information about the environment. An object might afford eating or danger or "sitting on" for one individual or species, but not for another. Affordances, we might say, are umwelt-specific.

Gibson's notion of direct perception is often taken to be radically external-ist. However, at least later in his career, Gibson himself was clear about what we would call the *relationality* of affordances, saying that the term *affordance* points both ways: "Affordances are both objective and persist-ing and, at the same time, subjective, because they relate to the species or individual for whom something is afforded" (1982a, 237). The relational quality of affordances is incommensurable with the structuring dualisms of computationalist, cognitivist, and representationalist approaches. As a conception of cognition, it is distributed, situated, and relational; it inheres a nondualist ontology: a difficult idea to grasp for those of us who are accus-tomed to thinking about our experience of the world in terms of object and subject.

In Chemero's more recent reconsideration of affordance theory (2009), the relational nature of affordance is foregrounded. Affordances are mutu-ally constituted by characteristics of the environment and the perceiver; echoes of the relativism and constructivism of autopoiesis and second-order cybernetics are clear. From the perspective of philosophy of mind, the direct realist notion of affordance offers an alternative to the solipsism that belea-guers dualist mentalism. If affordances are relational properties of perceiver and environment and are directly perceivable, then because conspecifics engage the environment similarly—having similar umwelts—qualities and aspects of the environment can have similar functional meanings among individuals.

The notion that information is present in the *ambient optic array*, as Chemero rightly states, is not *information* in the Shannon and Weaver for-mulation (see chapter 5)—not an atomist conception of information as composed of bits, tokens, or particles. In the current era of digital computa-tion, it is the Shannon-Weaver conception of information to which we are naturalized. When we read the word *information* in Gibson, it is confusing because we want to understand it in terms of Shannon-esque "bits," and that just doesn't work. The idea that affordance is neither in the world nor in the perceiver but in the relation between the two is made clear in the following example: Consider a simple, flat vista with a horizon and an object (say, a tree) of any size at any distance. For any perceiver, the height at which the horizon line intersects the trunk of the tree marks the height on the tree equal to the height of the perceiver's eyes. This *information* is located neither in the perceiver nor in the objects nor in the horizon, but in the interaction of all three.

## Sensory Integration and Neural Plasticity

We know from the inverting glasses experiment of George Stratton (1896) that if our visual field is inverted vertically, over a period of hours we can adapt and will regard the "inverted field" as absolutely normal, only to be immediately (but temporarily) disoriented when the glasses are removed. The nausea of motion sickness is explained as the result of a mismatch between vision and vestibular sense. In the 1990s, the US Navy had a problem with pilots crashing more planes than they should. It transpired that many of these crashes occurred shortly after a pilot had been in a flight simulator. In the simulator, the pilot sees the horizon move up and down and tilt left or right. But the pilot's bodily orientation does not change (unless a Stewart motion platform is used), so vestibular sensory experience is relatively passive. In this condition of contradictory sensory experience, visual information does not correspond with the sense information of the vestibular system (the semicircular canals). In the simulator, the brain avoids contradictory information by ignoring the signals from the vestibular system. This created a serious problem because the vestibular system doesn't "switch back on" without a period of deep sleep. Naval pilots were thus prohibited from flying for twenty-four hours, during which time they had a good nap. Motion sickness and seasickness are also a result of contradictory sensory signals, but in this case, the vestibular system registers movement but the visual system does not.

Like the kitten in the basket, these cases are not a matter of visual perception per se but of the correlation between multiple senses—not simply muscle action but proprioception: the rapid feedback, calibration, and correction procedure of the sense organs internal to the musculature and joints. This is the sense that allows you to clap with your eyes closed. Does the proprioceptive faculty maintain an internal map, a little proprioceptive homunculus represented in the brain? If not, then how are actions correlated and coordinated in real time? Is it the case that far less "control" is necessary than our Cartesian acculturation would have us suppose?

## "How Do You Catch a Fly Ball?"

A conventional cognitivist answer to the previous question involves the assumption that the mind is doing complex predictive ballistic calculations regarding trajectories in the mental computer. The truth of the matter is entirely different. McBeath, Shaffer, and Kaiser (1995) argue that the fielder effectively converts a temporal problem into a spatial problem in an embodied and sensorimotor fashion. That is, the fielder runs while watching the ball, and the object of the running is to keep the image of the ball moving in a *linear optical trajectory* (LOT). When the ball is high, the fielder is looking up, but as the ball falls, the visual angle of view becomes more horizontal. The upshot is that the recipe to catch a fly ball is as follows: You get the image of the ball in the center of your visual field and run to keep it there and—plop!—the ball is in the glove, more or less. No math, no reasoning. Note that there is no need to imagine Newtonian factors such as air resistance, wind, or spin, nor can the catcher predict where the ball will land. She does not need to. The process is a closed iterative loop, in enactive language, structurally coupled. This embodied deictic solution is similar to simple predator tracking behavior, and that is probably its evolutionary origin. Consistent with the lessons of evo-devo (evolutionary developmental biology), of morphological computing and of the bioenergetic equations of evolution, the organism solves problems in the most time- and energy-efficient way possible. The brain is an expensive organ to run, and if you can get your dinner without taxing it, then you live a little better. The brain did not invent the body; the body invented the brain.

In terms of skilled physical activities like playing sports, playing piano, and the like, it is well known that consciously thinking about what you are doing will ruin it. In fact, in most of the embodied activities we perform (e.g., driving or typing), the conscious mind only intervenes when something goes wrong. This is Heidegger's distinction between *ready-to-hand* and *present-at-hand*. As Hubert Dreyfus has elucidated (following Heidegger and Merleau-Ponty), the process of learning skills, even mental skills like chess, is a process of transition from laborious rule-following to the development of "muscular gestalts" (Dreyfus 1996). Achieving such muscular gestalts constitutes expertise and facilitates the sensation of "flow" celebrated by Csikszentmihalyi. Thus it is that great sports figures are usually unsatisfyingly vague when asked to explain how they, for example, scored an extraordinary goal. They literally have no idea, a fact underlined by John Sutton (2007) and famously by Michael Polanyi: "We can know more than we can tell" (1966, 4).

## TVSS: Seeing with the Tongue

From the late 1960s, Paul Bach-y-Rita built what became known as Tactile Visual Substitution Systems (TVSS), intended to provide a sense of sight to the blind. In the process, Bach-y-Rita (1967) conducted early and significant research in neuroplasticity. His TVSS machines substituted tactile stimuli for visual stimuli. His first machine (Bach-y-Rita et al. 1969) was built into the back of a chair. It had a panel of four hundred vibrating points upon which the experimental subject rested his back. The points translated a low-resolution pixelated monochromatic "image"—derived from a video camera mounted above the chair—as an array of pinpricks on the back.

As subjects became acclimatized to the chair, their experience transitioned from a sense of random points of excitation on the back to the sensing of the stimulation in terms of larger patterns, such as waves of movement from side to side or top to bottom. Ultimately the sense of excitations occurring on the back gave way to a sense of directly "seeing" (Bach-y-Rita et al. 1969, 1998). The rapidity with which tactile sensations could be interpreted as vision gave evidence of substantial neuroplasticity. Consistent with our discussion of the importance of proprioception, the pinpricks were only interpreted as "vision" if the camera was moved in concert with the subject's head movement. As the technology became increasingly compact, Bach-y-Rita made smaller and more portable devices. By 2000, research was underway using high-resolution electro-stimulation on the tongue.

## The Haptic Torch: TVSS in the Hand

Around 2004, Tom Froese and Adam Spiers, then graduate students, developed what they called the Haptic Torch, ostensibly a device for assisting the blind. It functioned like the laser measures commonly used in construction work. In form, it is a handheld flashlight (torch), with a motorized disc below the thumb (a simple servomotor used in radio control hobbies). A sonar sensor replaced the light bulb. The angular position of a bump on the disc corresponds to the distance measured by the sonar sensor—say, one o'clock for nearby and eleven o'clock for far away. As a user waves the torch around, the disc rotates and the bump is felt moving under the pad of the thumb. Very quickly, a user comes to interpret the rotary movement of the bump not as a sensation on the thumb, but *as distance*. More remarkably, with time a user comes to recognize patterns of movements of the bump as representing architectural features—such as a doorway or a corner or a room. Significantly, once again, this only occurs when the stimulus is associated with arm movement—the arm holding and moving the Haptic Torch. That is, the bump sensations only represent features in space when correlated with proprioceptive awareness of the rate and the direction of movement. Vestibular and proprioceptive senses give "sense" to the tactile stimulus: a thought-provoking example not only of neural plasticity, but also of the integration of sensorimotor functions.

### Eye of Fly and Ear of Bat: Morphological Computing

The line of thinking in the frog's eye research of Lettvin et al. (1959) has found a recent resurgence in the emerging field of neuroethology—and specifically what is referred to as *morphological computation* or *transneuronal and preneuronal signal processing*. The physical structure of a fly's eye or a bat's ear has been shown to perform computational work. The materiality of the physical structure does real data processing long before a neuron gets a look-in (MacIver 2009). Such realities, found all over the biological world, undermine conventional Cartesian/cognitivist assertions that *thinking* (as in reasoning on symbols) occurs exclusively bio-electrically in gray matter in the skull while the rest of the body is a mere meat marionette. The biomimetic and reactive turn in robotics in the late 1980s showed that embracing more holistic and situated models provided an alternative to the cognitivist paradigm that plagued robotics and AI.

The work of Egelhaaf et al. (2002) has established that in the case of a fly's compound eye, information regarding rolling (rotation around the axis of flight direction) is given directly and trivially by optic flow, because a row of ommatidia (the component subunits of the compound eye) that lie in a certain plane are connected to a single neuron. The signal of this neuron corresponds to the pattern of optic flow during rolling. Knowledge of rolling is given to the fly brain through exploitation of the ommatidia pattern and the spherical geometry of the eye itself; the reasoning occurs on the surface of the eye, as it were. As in the case of the frog's eye, no image is sent to the brain for "processing" (Lettvin et al. 1968). By extension, it is plausible that *all* vision in the fly occurs by such mechanisms; thinking, image processing, and reasoning on representations are minimal or nonexistent.

Another example concerns how bats locate their prey and other objects by sonar. Because bats are bilaterally symmetrical (with an ear on each side), locating the source of an echo on the horizontal plane is a trivial question of the timing and energy of echo in each ear. Vertical location is not so trivial. As Wooton, Haresign, and Simmons (1995) report, the intricate shapes and folds of the bat's ear (pinna and tragus) filter the echoes of the bat's sonar ping to give spectral cues that vary systematically with the angle of the elevation of the source of the sonar echo. "The conformation of skin and supporting tissue of the ear in the bat forms a computational device that solves a key problem in localization of prey in 3D space," MacIver observes (2009, 488).

Bat sonar is a case of *active sensing*, in which an animal generates a signal that it then senses; action precedes perception, and perception and action occur as continuously looped and inextricably linked processes. Active sensing is a specialized case of a sensorimotor loop, but in both the case of the fly's eye and the case of the bat's ear, a more complete picture of intelligent action in the world is revealed by consideration of perception and action as aspects of one process. Animals perceive in order to act, but they also act in order to perceive. The understanding of the integration of perception and action was present in the work of pioneer ethologists von Uexküll, Tinbergen, and Lorenz. It is also consistent with the ecological approach to perception of J. J. Gibson, the enactive cognition of Varela, Thompson, and Rosch, and much postcognitivist cognitive science.

## Thinking Muscles, Thinking Bones

Experiments in the robotics of legged and bipedal locomotion (Raibert 1986) show us that the substantial part of the real-time calculation inherent in a well-designed or evolved system, is evolved in hardware as it were—not even in calculatory hardware, in the digital or even electronic sense, but in mechanics, in the physics of joint movement, springs, and ratios of linkage lengths. A passive bipedal walking device can walk down a gentle incline with absolutely no computation. Computation is necessary only when there is unexpected change. Thus, the proprioceptive homunculus is unnecessary; it is provided by the body itself. Just as Rodney Brooks asserted that the "world is its own best model," the body turns out to be *its* own best model—its own homunculus (see chapter 8).

MacIver notes that human walking is highly economical in terms of energy consumption. He points out that the Honda Asimo (the well-known bipedal robot) consumes an order of magnitude more power to achieve bipedal locomotion than the human body. The efficiency of human movement is due to "having a skeletal structure and mass distribution that makes walking as energetically favorable to the body as swinging is to a pendulum" (MacIver 2009, 491). He argues that such structural dynamics are computational in the sense that they organize movement in the most efficient way they can; they "solve the problem." Such bodily functions have been implemented in hardware, so to speak. Events in the world that require rapid but varied responses are assigned to neurology, which consumes forty times more energy than an equivalent mass of bone. MacIver concludes, "At this level of description, there is no basis for an invidious distinction between bone and brain" (2009, 492).

Sten Grillner established, at least in the case of fish, that the muscle coordination that results in locomotion arises not in the brain proper but entirely in the spinal cord and the adjacent muscles. He notes, "Some mammals (such as the common laboratory rat) can have their entire forebrain excised and are still able to walk, run, and even maintain their balance to some extent" (Grillner 1996, 64). The case of Mike, the headless chicken of Fruita, Colorado (1945), is well known in folklore. Mike lived for eighteen months without a head (and posthumously ran for president in 2012).

Evidence suggests that such motor-control closed circuits exist in all animals, including humans. The speed of movement of the fingers of an expert violinist is faster than the time needed for a signal to travel from the finger to the brain and back. Here, "computation" is implemented in physiological design via evolutionary process. In these and similar examples, we are drawn to a conception of cognition as immanent in the whole creature—nerves, muscles, and bones—as opposed to a conception of a single intelligent part of the creature driving the rest of it.

## A Bag of Soup

We are encouraged, by the mechanistic explanations and metaphors from civil engineering that have framed physiology, to understand the human form in terms of industrial processes or metropolitan utility infrastructure. I recall drawings in school science textbooks of forty years ago in which the digestive system is depicted as a factory full of gantries, conveyor belts, hoppers, and chutes, populated by little balding, mustachioed, potbellied men in blue overalls brandishing shovels. The conception of the body as an assemblage of largely independent mechanical distribution systems hung on industrial structural armatures obscures the fact that as animals we grow from one cell and are made of the same stuff through and through.

Perhaps because I spent a lot of my youth wading about in semistagnant water and mud, entranced by the complexity of estuarine pond life (and I probably carry some souvenirs with me still), the image of the body as a pond full of nutrients, with tides and flows and concentration gradients and behaviors of its fauna and flora, makes more sense to me than metaphors of industrial hardware, with which I am also well acquainted. I am 70 percent water, the universal solvent. I am less a factory and more a bag of soup. The idea that neural activity consists primarily of electrical signals moving along biological "wires" and through "circuits" (as some neuroscientists like to call them) seems to ignore the fact that the whole system is bathed in solutions of neurotransmitters about which we know comparatively little.

Neurotransmitters, it transpires, are not exclusive to the brain but are general-purpose molecules that have different roles in various parts of the body. Bodily systems are thoroughly integrated. The molecules we call neurotransmitters do duty all over the body as triggers for specific metabolic processes in specific places—the endocrine and immune systems, for instance. Every white blood cell has receptors for twenty-eight (so-called) neurotransmitters. Serotonin, a molecule known as a neurotransmitter, is primarily produced and deployed in the gut and plays a crucial (negative) role in bone formation (Rosen 2009). While serotonin does not cross the blood-brain barrier, its precursor molecules do. Aromatase, which converts testosterone to estradiol (an estrogen), is produced in adipose (fat) tissue found on the bellies of overweight middle-aged men (among other places). Dopamine affects heart rate and blood pressure. And why not? The very fact that many so-called neurotransmitters are produced all over the body should give us cause to ponder. Brains are made of the same stuff as the rest of us. Nor should we forget that, embryologically, half of the neural matter of the fetus—the neural crest—splits off to become the central nervous system (the brain and spinal cord). The other half becomes the autonomic nervous system, comprising the sympathetic nervous system, the enteric nervous system, and the parasympathetic nervous system.

**One Hundred Million Neurons in the Gut**

Extracranial neural activity is far more extensive than previously thought. When someone had the silly idea of pointing an MRI at the stomach, he found three hundred times more neural structure than expected. The colon has its own "brain," complete with a blood-brain barrier. The enteric nervous system (ENS), sometimes referred to as a second brain, contains around one hundred million neurons—three orders of magnitude less than the brain, to be sure, but not an insubstantial number. Many quite clever animals survive with less; a frog, for example, has only sixteen million. The ENS constitutes a sheath that wraps around the entire gut. It utilizes more than thirty neurotransmitters identical to those in the brain and can function autonomously if the vagus nerve is cut. Surely, in some sense, it is producing thoughts or feelings—gut feelings, perhaps? The gut, the muscles, and the viscera are all busily doing something very like thinking. The endocrine and immune systems possess knowledge and cognition of their own. We do not understand the connections between these systems well (nor do we understand well the symbiotic relationship between the body and its teaming internal flora—the microbiota). We may ask: Is the autonomic nervous system part of what we might call the *cognitive unconscious*? (see chapter 16). Its connection to the central nervous system is tangential, and most of its operations are "unconscious." And what of the zones of crossover—such as breathing, which is amenable to both conscious and unconscious control? What of those adepts who are able to control by will processes regarded as "unconscious," such as heart rate and brain waves? If those processes are amenable to conscious control, then we must grant that they may have *thoughts* too, in Lakoff and Johnson's expanded sense, and that these thoughts might be involved in the formation of abstract concepts accessible to conscious reasoning.

In particular, we might muse over the thoughts of the gut. Giving credibility to such ideas opens up new, distributed ways of thinking about psychosomatic phenomena, addiction, and other disorders. Nor should we isolate our conception of cognition to neural tissues—that is, to a Victorian, mechanistic, "pipes-and-wires" conception of the body. As noted, the body is a big soup, with currents and tides and flows of hormones and neurotransmitters exciting or suppressing different aspects of different systems in different ways, being metabolized and metabolizing as they go. The brain is not the driver of a big meat bus. Parts of the brain participate in anarchic networks of generally self-regulating (but sometimes antagonistic) parts distributed throughout the body.

## The Microbiome Revolution

In the last decade of the twentieth century, the Human Genome Project encouraged us to believe that a mapping of the human genome would provide a master code, laying bare the computer program of human genetics. (As noted, the genome/computer code analogy has been part of genetics discourse since Watson and Crick). However, that dream has faded, and a new set of mysteries has presented itself: the biological self as ecosystem.

By cell count, I contain nine "foreign" cells for each cell that is genetically "me." For every human gene, I contain 150 nonhuman genes. The human microbiome accounts for around two kilograms of the average adult's body mass. Half the metabolites in the bloodstream are generated by internal microbiota. These foreign cells are found mostly in the gut, but sinus cavities, the vagina, mammary glands, and even eyes have local microbiomes. In each location, they operate symbiotically with cells that are "us" in the more normal sense. No wonder people often have adverse reactions to antibiotics! A course of antibiotics lays waste to complex ecologies of billions of organisms, many of which must be beneficial, or at least benign. Often dangerous bacterial monocultures grow in their wake.[8]

## Biologically, What Is "I"?

A particular molecule might have one effect on the ovaries, another effect on the digestive system, another effect on the amygdala, and another on the adrenal gland. In the gut, specific bacteria metabolize molecules the digestive system cannot, making products that are amenable to inclusion within human metabolic processes. What would happen to our sense of self, our study of physiology and medicine in general, if we took these phenomena seriously as an antireductive viewpoint from which to understand the body and metabolism?

Can we imagine ourselves according to a model in which organs large and small interact, not in a hierarchical feudalism with the brain on top, but—to continue the political metaphor—more like an anarcho-syndicalist commune? Imagine that there is no hierarchy, no central control. The illusion of an "I" (in the head) which is in control is just that—an illusion. The most plausible reason for the sense of individual selfhood (which objectivizes the body) is perhaps simply the physical location of several sense organs at the top end of the bag; in other words, it is from that stalk that I look down at the rest of me. I can imagine what I look like from the perspective of my left knee, but I can't actually see me from that perspective. (Mind you, if I deployed a device like Bach-y-Rita's TVSS and mounted the camera not on my head but on my knee, or simply hooked light fiber optics to my eyes from, say, each knee, who knows how my sense of physical selfhood might morph?)

## Constructivism, Relativism, and Biological Solipsism

This partial review of research over the last century reveals a "minor literature" in biology and psychology that challenges or at least problematizes the basic assumptions of positivistic cognitivist views of the last fifty years. Each of these examples problematizes the dualisms of mind-body and body-world, in their own way.

From von Uexküll, we get the idea of a mutual constitution of self and world, and this implicitly brings objectivism into question. Such ideas were developed in autopoiesis and in second-order cybernetics. These in turn inform trends in neuroscience, cognitive science, and philosophy of mind. Von Uexküll challenged the notion of a unitary self by arguing that individual sensorimotor behaviors are triggered and satisfied by environmental conditions. Such arguments challenge reductivism, dualism, and cognitivism.

Held and Hein demonstrate that functional vision is only possible when vision is integrated with and calibrated by embodied action. The lessons of morphological computing show us there is no simple way to isolate "thinking" or "intelligence" to cranial or even neural tissue. In a later chapter we review Benjamin Libet's work, which challenges the "neural Cartesianism," which holds that all the serious mental work is done by the conscious, while the unconscious is little more than motor reflexes (see chapter 16).

The researchers discussed here did not identify themselves as part of an organized movement, and indeed many would have their differences. But taken together, these ideas provide a grounding for alternative approaches as cognitivism crumbles.

# 3 What Was Cybernetics?

For many, the term *cybernetics* has a musty, "space age junk of the past" ring to it, its meaning muddied by images of the psychedelic 1960s and neologisms like *cyborg*, *cyberspace*, and *dianetics*.[1] These are little but distorted echoes. Cybernetics was a radically interdisciplinary movement that emerged immediately after World War II. It aspired to be a unified theory of systems, applicable across engineering and the natural sciences and beyond. In Norbert Wiener's formulation, it was positioned as an *ur*-science of "control," but we should not automatically assume the oppressive authoritarian connotation that today colors the word. Cybernetics certainly arose in the United States substantially out of military OR (operations research), but in the UK, leading researchers were neuroscientists. It may be understood more accurately as a science of systems and the role of feedback loops as a mode of organization. *System, feedback, homeostasis,* and other key terms of art gained their current meaning via cybernetic discourse. Cybernetics became a science of everything, in the sense that it concerned abstract notions of systems, organization, and control. As such, cybernetics was as applicable to thinking about the qualities of biological life as to machines, computational and otherwise. Central to cybernetic thinking were questions of self-organization and purposive behavior, the relationship of an entity to a (changing) environment, and adaptation.

A conventional history of cybernetics has it emerging in the 1940s out of American World War II military research. The torpedo and the antiaircraft gun are adduced as icons of feedback control, but, as David Mindell (2002) has shown, homeostatic machines had been under development for the previous fifty years. Operations research fed into the development of cybernetic system theory, and control theory grew out of it—but this is an engineering-centric account. Cybernetics was as much a discipline of the social and life sciences.

It was Walter Cannon, a distinguished physiologist, who coined the term *homeostasis* in 1926 (and elaborated upon the concept in 1929 and 1932). He described it thusly: "The coordinated physiological reactions which maintain most of the steady states in the body are so complex, and so peculiar to the living organism, that it has been suggested (Cannon 1926) that a specific designation for these states be employed—*homeostasis*" (1929, 400). As with many of the concepts brought together in cybernetics, Cannon's homeostasis was presaged by French physiologist Claude Bernard (1813–1878) in his concept of the *milieu intérieur*. Mexican cardiologist and founding cybernetician Arturo Rosenblueth worked with Walter Cannon at Harvard in the 1930s. The concept of *feedback* arose in analog electronics in the early twentieth century. The general systems theory of biologist Karl Ludwig von Bertalanffy (1937) became central to the emerging field of cybernetics. Via cybernetics, through the roles of Bateson, Mead, and others, systems theory came to have a major influence in the social sciences, as exemplified in the work of Luhmann and as described by Heims (1993).

Cybernetics was self-consciously propelled into the limelight as an interdisciplinary überdiscipline by Norbert Wiener. He achieved this in part by engaging the interest, cooperation, and collaboration of theorists and researchers not only from mathematics (von Neumann) and engineering (Pitts), but also those in physiology (Rosenblueth), neurophysiology (McCulloch), neurology (Lettvin, Ashby), biology (Maturana), psychology (Bateson), anthropology (Mead), philosophy (von Foerster), and other fields.

Wiener's 1948 cybernetic manifesto, *Cybernetics; or, Control and Communication in the Animal and the Machine*, put the project on firm footing. Cybernetics was predicated on the notion that machines and living beings are essentially similar in the way they relate to the world. In Wiener's spectacular diagnosis of ataxia, he demonstrated the power of cybernetic theoretical analysis by describing ataxia in terms of the disruption of neuromuscular feedback loops. In ataxia, the hand (for instance) overshoots the goal, is overcorrected, undershoots, and falls into a cycle of eventually damped oscillations. It was a watershed moment for the theory, and its generality was demonstrated by the fact that the same diagnosis was immediately applied in military research and resulted in a more accurate "predictive" antiaircraft gun.

## Military-Industrial Complex, Operations Research, and Cybernetic Socialism

Views into the house of cybernetics through different windows reveal very different scenes. The field saw rapid growth in the post–World War II years and by the early 1960s had attained the status of a scientific master discourse. The influence of cybernetics and systems theory was felt throughout the academic, business, and cultural world. It found application in anthropology, sociology, military strategics, business management, media theory, architecture, art, and even music—famously so with the use of feedback by Jimi Hendrix. Electric guitar amplifiers had much in common with the analog computers of the time. Indeed, analog audio electronic, radio electronics, and electronic calculation were aspects of one field and were largely made of the same stuff. The first generation of video artists was likewise taken with feedback effects. Hans Haacke's "real-time social system" and the ecological systems work of Newton Harrison and Helen Mayer Harrison are examples of deeper theoretical engagement in the arts. Jack Burnham's volume *Beyond Modern Sculpture* (1968a) was a major vector for cybernetic thought into the arts, as was his famous *Artforum* essay, "Systems Esthetics" (1968b).

World War II operations research (OR) created an abstract engineering discipline concerned with control, planning, and decision-making and contributed to early cybernetic ideas and techniques. At MIT and elsewhere, these ideas fed the growth of Cold War strategics and were applied in scientific management theory. Cybernetics was at the center of research in technological development, particularly of autonomous machines—machines that sense their environment, make decisions, and adjust their behavior accordingly. Wiener celebrated the self-guiding torpedo and the predictive antiaircraft gun as examples of cybernetic systems. Such autonomy was clearly deeply interesting to the military. Sci-fi images of the giant brain and the cyborg soldier emerged in this context. There is a direct line from the self-guiding torpedo to the contemporary unmanned aerial vehicle (UAV) or "drone."

Yet in the hands of Stafford Beer, Gordon Pask, Heinz von Foerster, Gregory Bateson, Margaret Mead, Buckminster Fuller, Marshall McLuhan, and others, cybernetics was variously playful, utopic, philosophical, and quasimystical. The writings of Bateson offer generous and deeply thought meditations on being human. At the end of his career as a world-renowned management theorist, Stafford worked at the invitation of Salvador Allende to establish a cybernetic socialist state in Chile. Their project, dubbed Project

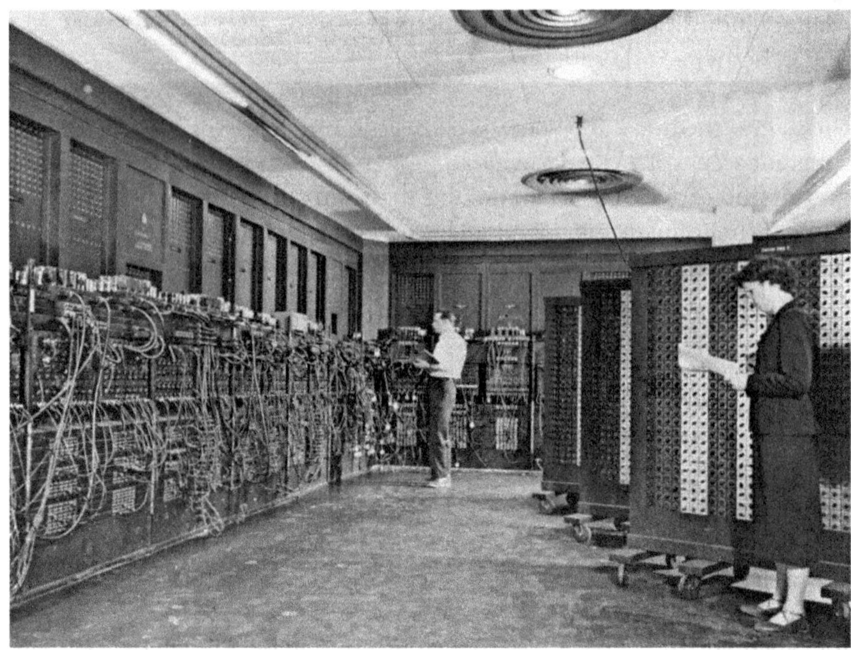

**Figure 3.1**
ENIAC. US Army photo.

Cybersyn, was cut short by Augusto Pinochet's coup and the assassination of Allende (Medina 2011). This was the Cold War, and Cybersyn (and Allende's socialism) was explicitly opposed by the US military and intelligence interests that supported the work of Jay Forrester and his colleagues in the SAGE/Whirlwind project at MIT.

### Icons of Feedback and Homeostasis

One of the technical icons of the cybernetics movement was the Boulton and Watts centrifugal governor, an early homeostatic mechanism that smoothed the power output of steam engines. The feed mechanism of the carbon arc lamp is another early homeostatic device. The thermostat and its role in the domestic furnace or automobile cooling system is a textbook example. Norbert Wiener used Heron of Alexandria's "automatic wine dispenser" as an example of a feedback mechanism. This makes the humble toilet cistern a cybernetic mechanism, too. Cyberneticians built more sophisticated devices, like Ross Ashby's Homeostat, William Grey Walter's

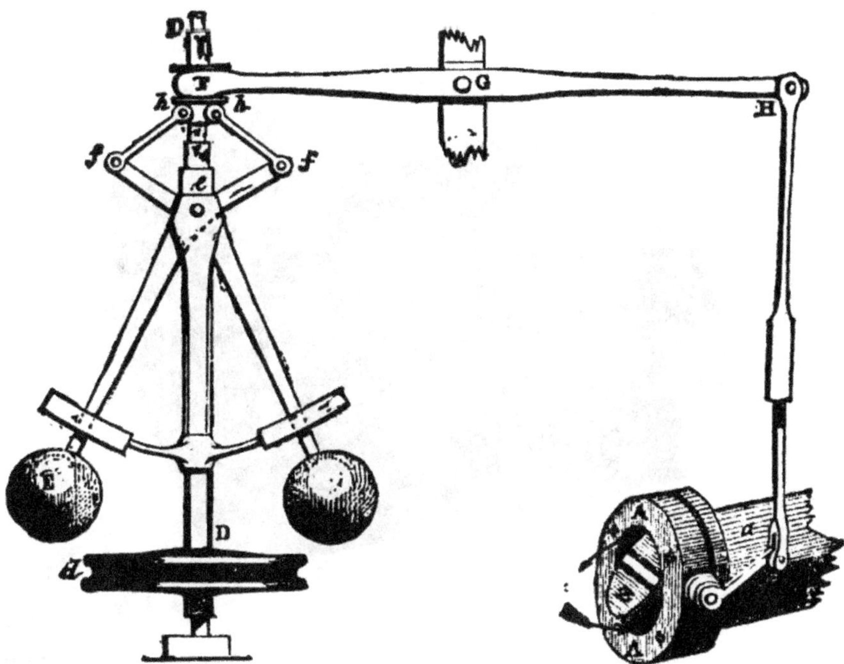

**Figure 3.2**
Boulton and Watts centrifugal governor, 1788.

"Turtles" (also referred to as "Tortoises"), Wiener's Moth/Bedbug, and Claude Shannon's Electronic Rat.

The self-steering vane designed by solo ocean navigator Herbert George "Blondie" Hasler in the early 1950s is a classic homeostat, in this case effective in a complex and changing environment. Hasler's pendulum servomechanism indicates that cybernetic ideas were in the air at the time. Lieutenant Colonel Hasler (DSO, OBE) had served in the Royal Marines in World War II and was doubtless familiar with maritime gyroscopic and servomechanisms, bearing out Mindell's argument regarding the prehistory of cybernetics in the servomechanisms of the nineteenth and earlier twentieth centuries.

Nonelectronic, or nondigital, servomechanisms of the mid-twentieth century inhere in a kind of "intelligence," which is largely incomprehensible to a generation reared to assume that machines can only be intelligent if they manipulate data microelectronically in "bits" via Boolean operations. The preelectronic automobile was full of subtle feedback and servo mechanisms, the tuning of which was rightly regarded as a black art, now largely lost. Consider the choke mechanism on the SU carburetor fitted to some

a.

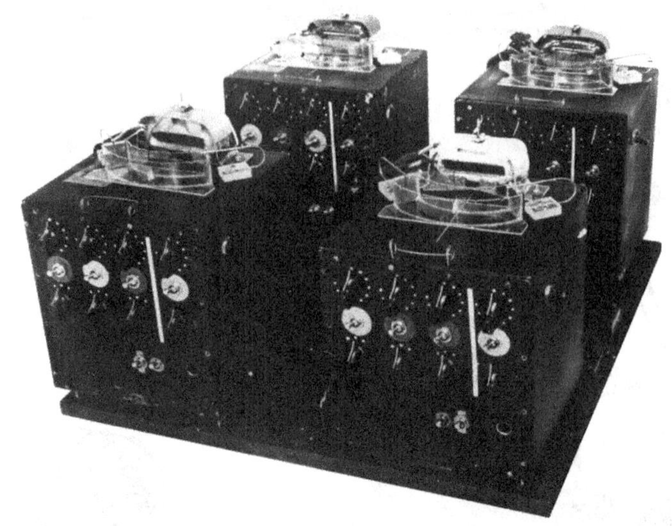

b.

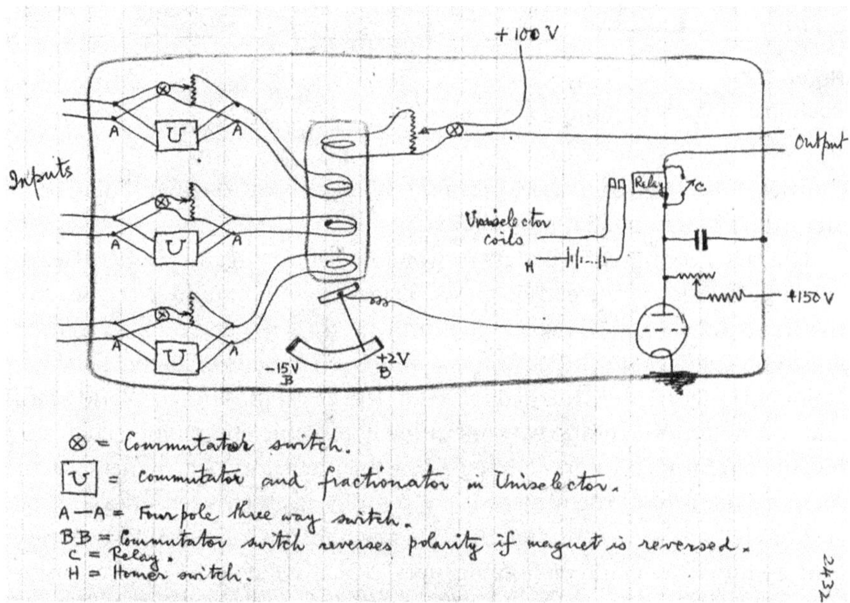


**Figure 3.3**

(a) Ross Ashby's Homeostat. (b) Ross Ashby's hand-drawn circuit diagram for his Homeostat. Reproduced with permission of the Estate of W. Ross Ashby.

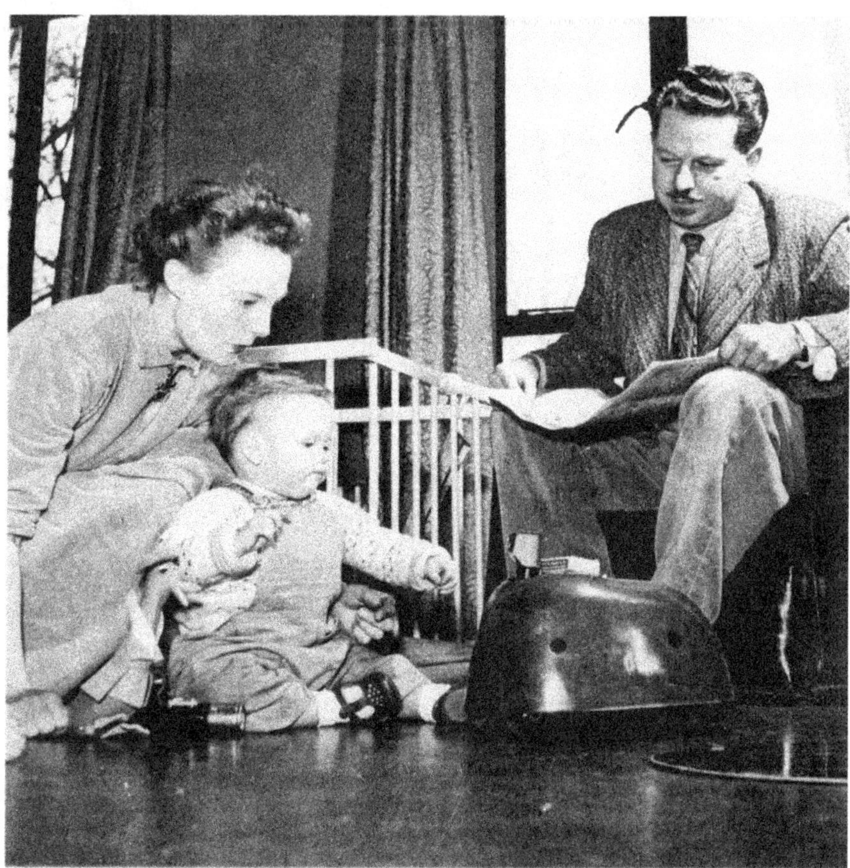

**Figure 3.4**

In this image, from Pierre de Latil's *Thinking by Machine* (1957), we see William Grey Walter and his wife Vivian Dovey with their baby Timothy and the robot Elsie. The original caption charmingly reads, "In their country home near Bristol, these parents have two children, one is electronic. Vivian Dovey and Grey Walter have two offspring: Timothy, a human baby, and Elsie, the tortoise of coils and electronic valves. Timothy is very friendly with his electronic sister."

Credit: Pierre de Latil, *Thinking by Machine: A Study of Cybernetics* (Boston: Houghton Mifflin, 1957).

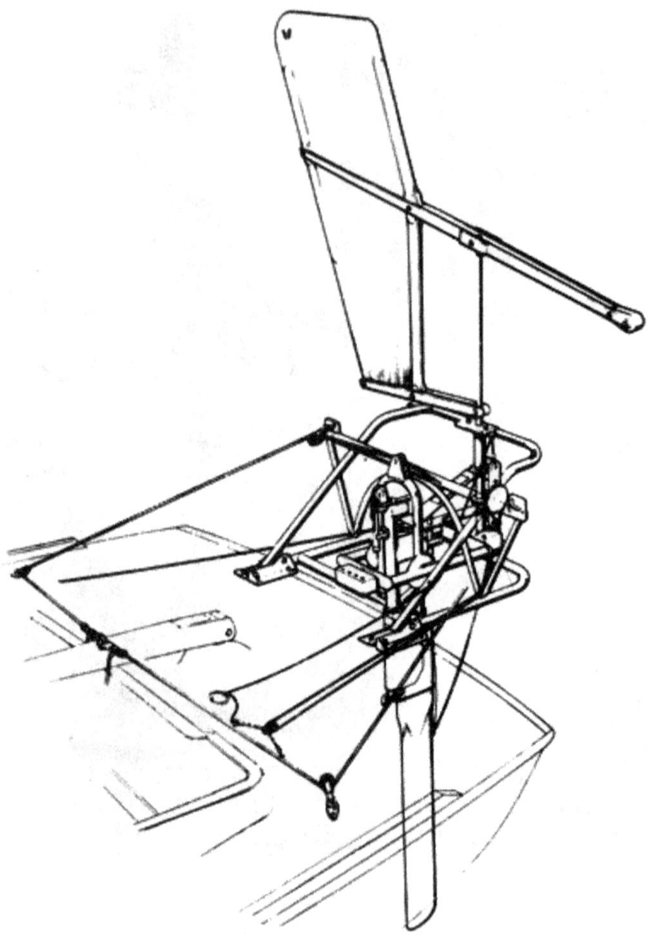

**Figure 3.5**
Small ship self-steering gear designed by "Blondie" Hasler. © Herbert George Hasler.
Image from V1SP sale material published by M. S. Gibb Limited, Warsash, Southampton, United Kingdom.

MGB sports cars—and considered a bear to tune. A cavity containing a bimetallic clock spring is fed by cooling fluid from the engine. As the engine warms up, the spring is heated and expands. This puts rotational pressure on a shaft at its middle. This shaft is the choke butterfly valve shaft. As the engine warms, the butterfly valve is slowly adjusted to an open position. This mechanism has other parts that respond to throttle and to throat vacuum. The forces of three different physical phenomena are merged by springs and cams.

Similarly, there is the vacuum advance mechanism for spark timing. The spark ignites the gasoline in the cylinder, but as the engine goes faster, the spark must ignite earlier so that the explosion is complete before the exhaust valve opens. But how can the distributor know how fast the engine is going? As the motor turns faster, it sucks more of the gas/air mixture through the inlet manifold. Thus vacuum on the manifold is proportional to revs. So take a vacuum line from the manifold and use that vacuum to suck a diaphragm, which pulls a lever in the distributor, advancing spark timing. Note that in the vacuum advance and choke mechanisms, as in the Hasler gear and all the other examples, *information, materiality, and motive power are inseparable*. Such examples exemplify the holistic nature of cybernetic thinking. They provide an insight into how to think intelligence in a nondualist and materially instantiated way. They expose the grand fiction of the separation of matter and information.

## System, Self-Organization, and Teleology

A key insight of cybernetics was that systems could be self-organizing and homeostatic (self-correcting) by way of feedback mechanisms between themselves and their environment. In 1947, neurologist Ross Ashby coined the term *self-organizing system*, and it was subsequently taken up by Norbert Wiener (1961), among others. The notion of self-organization in the early cybernetic literature involved adaptive, purposive, and even teleological systems. The concept has much in common with what today is called *complexity theory*, which refers to processes in which global patterns arise from multiple or iterated interactions in lower levels of a system. Canonical examples include the organization of social insects and the emergence of mind from neural processes. (Ashby's theories of self-organization and his law of requisite variety are discussed in detail in chapter 7.)

In 1941, Norbert Wiener joined Mexican cardiologist Arturo Rosenblueth and engineer Julian Bigelow at MIT's Radiation Lab, where Wiener developed his theory of feedback control, a theoretical analysis of servomechanisms.

In "Behavior, Purpose and Teleology" (1943), Rosenblueth, Wiener, and Bigelow proposed a special cybernetic sense of teleology, suggesting that its opposite is not determinism—in the fatalistic Laplacian sense of an utterly predictable future for anything, given adequate computing power—but nonteleology: probabilistic random behavior that is not goal directed. In other words, in a goal-seeking system, purpose is developed via negative feedback. In a sense, this paper updates the crisis Descartes felt between Newtonian causality and Christian (not cybernetic) teleology for twentieth-century physics of probability and entropy. In this way, cybernetics claimed philosophical high ground to bolster its experimental and technical successes and justified Weiner's celebration of it as a universal science. But this mixing of technical and philosophical ideas can be murky ontological territory, as Philip Agre has shown in the case of artificial intelligence (see chapter 5).

## The Genesis of Cybernetics

"Behavior, Purpose and Teleology" was a significant early position statement for cybernetics. The paper discussed iterative self-correction cycles that Rosenblueth, Wiener, and Bigelow (1943) called *negative feedback*. Inherent was the "redefinition of psychological and philosophical concepts in the terminology of communications engineering, [key analogies being] analyses of humans as components of weapons systems" (Edwards 1997, 181). The behaviorist language of stimulus/response was replaced with the mechanistic language of input/output. The input/output conception has its origins in early or even preindustrial hydraulic metaphors and was already applied metaphorically in communications. It is an oversimplified and vectorized model to apply to living organisms. *Behavior* was defined as "any modification of the subject, detectable externally" (183). At this point, the agenda of what Wiener was to call *cybernetics* in 1947 was essentially set.

The interdisciplinary field of cybernetics was formed during the 1946 conference on Teleological Mechanisms sponsored by the New York Academy of Sciences, the Hixon Symposium held at Caltech in 1948, and, most famously, the series of ten Macy Conferences (1946–1953). The Macy Conferences were a remarkable interdisciplinary phenomenon. Most of the attendees at the Macy Conferences were humanists, neuroscientists, and social scientists, rather than, as might be assumed, mathematicians and engineers. The series involved such luminaries as John von Neumann, Norbert Wiener, Warren McCulloch, Claude Shannon, Arturo Rosenblueth,

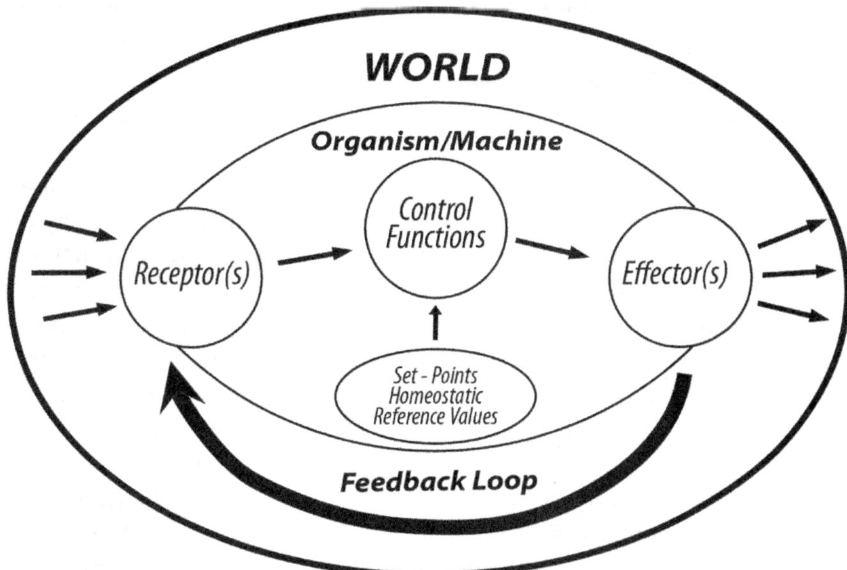


**Figure 3.6**

Homeostasis by negative feedback. This simplified diagram captures the essence of the process, applicable in both organisms and machines. Some homeostatic processes—like maintenance of body temperature in mammals—involve internal feedback as well as, or instead of, feedback through the "exterior world." This diagram captures the concept of sensorimotor loops and of enactive structural coupling. The diagram can be interpreted as having inputs and outputs, but, as Maturana and Varela emphasized, organisms do not have inputs and outputs. The notion of *input and output* applies to machines built to have such, but it is a falsely mechanistic explanation for organisms. Note that the operational amplifer (op-amp)—the quintessential device of electronic analog computing—is a perfect simple homeostat, comparing input value with a stored reference and adjusting output. Drawing by Evan Houston Stanfield after original by Penny.

Heinz von Foerster, Gordon Pask, Ross Ashby, Donald McKay, Lawrence Kubie, Gregory Bateson, and Margaret Mead.

The historic Macy Conferences were preceded by a gathering called the Cerebral Inhibition Meeting, held in New York in May 1942 and convened by Frank Fremont-Smith, the Josiah Macy Jr. Foundation's medical director. Among those in attendance were Mead, Bateson, neurophysiologist-turned-psychoanalyst Lawrence Kubie, Rosenblueth, and McCulloch (who, with Pitts, developed neural networks in the early 1940s). The subject of the meeting was twofold: hypnotherapy and the physiology of the conditioned reflex. It was at this meeting that Rosenblueth delivered the "Behavior, Purpose and Teleology" paper that motivated McCulloch, Bateson, and Mead to call for the Macy Organization to support what became the Macy Conferences.

Rosenblueth, clearly an intellectual titan as well as a pragmatic experimental scientist, was emphatic about models and metaphors in science and the dangers of mistaking the map for the territory. "The best material model for a cat is another [cat], or preferably the same cat," he remarked (Rosenblueth and Wiener 1945, 320). It is notable that among the founders of cybernetics, Rosenblueth, a Mexican, is least known and least celebrated.

The second Macy Conference, the Feedback Mechanisms and Causal Circular Systems in Biology and the Social Sciences Meeting, was held in New York in March 1946 and was more explicitly cybernetic. Among those attending this meeting were Warren McCulloch, the ecologist George Hutchinson, sociologists Kurt Lewin and Paul Lazarsfeld, Spanish neuroscientist Lorente de Nó, neuropsychiatrist Molly Harrower, psychologist Heinrich Klüver, and philosopher Filmer Northrop.

## Cybernetics in Ascendency

Wiener and others saw cybernetics as nothing less than a universal theory of knowledge, or at least a universal science. Bowker shows how cybernetics claimed simultaneously to be a metascience and a tool for other disciplines. Through it, probabilistic physics was extended into the realm of communication and thus into the social world of agents and actors. Thus, for instance, feedback theory led to discussions of purpose and teleology in the widest sense.

Cybernetics was in ascendency as a philosophy of the *intelligent* machine (among other things), though what the cyberneticians meant by *intelligence* was a rather different thing from what the artificial intelligence community came to understand by the term. In this respect, cybernetics was a philosophy of the situated machine and was preoccupied with ongoing sensorimotor engagement with the world, epitomized by the key cybernetic concept of feedback. The notion of autopoiesis proposes a definition of biological life in terms generally compatible with cybernetics. In a historically elegant way, it was Humberto Maturana's protégé Francisco Varela who applied autopoiesis to cognitive science and thereby played a major role in the development of a postcognitivist position in cognitive science.

## Ponds of Beer

Renowned British cybernetician Stafford Beer became a leading management theorist, basing his management theory on his viable system model (VSM). One of Beer's pet projects which he pursued outside his management consulting work was the notion that industrial and market systems might be governed by homeostatic organic systems. I use the term *governed* in its cybernetic-technical sense. Beer had the notion that one could run a large-scale industrial operation by feeding various production variables (material and labor costs, market demands, delivery times, etc.) into a fishpond, suitably encoded as nutrients and other chemicals. The idea was that the ecology of the fishpond would homeostatically balance itself with respect to the new conditions, and the necessary changes to the industrial system could be read off as chemical concentrations, microorganism populations, temperature changes, or other causes. This charming and wacky idea is antithetical to the obsession with reasoning in AI, but it is entirely in the spirit of artificial life. Note that Beer's pond might develop efficient solutions to problems, but, as with evolutionary programming and simulated neural networks, such solutions are often unlike any a human programmer would create, and sometimes they deploy obscure effects that are often impossible to reverse engineer.[2] Andrew Pickering has made the argument that at least some of the cybernetics research, like that of Beer, was "strange" because it purveyed a "performative" ontology very different from conventional representational science. In Pickering's terms, science in the *representational idiom* is a matter of notions and symbolic codifications, whereas science in the *performative idiom* is the "dance of agency" of science as a process (1995).

## Science in the Performative Mode

In a practice that harks back to late nineteenth-century scientific model making, cyberneticians, especially in the British group, liked to build machines. The most well-known are probably neurologist William Grey Walter's Turtles, Elmer and Elsie, the first autonomous robots. Around the same time, Ashby, also a neurologist, built his Homeostat, which Norbert Wiener called "a machine to think with." Ashby's project was a set of four more or less identical machines that mutually perturbed each other as they sought equilibrium. Gordon Pask was the most prolific machine maker of the group, his *electrochemical ear* being perhaps the most eccentric of the cybernetic machines (Cariani 1993). In the late 1940s, Pask built what has yet

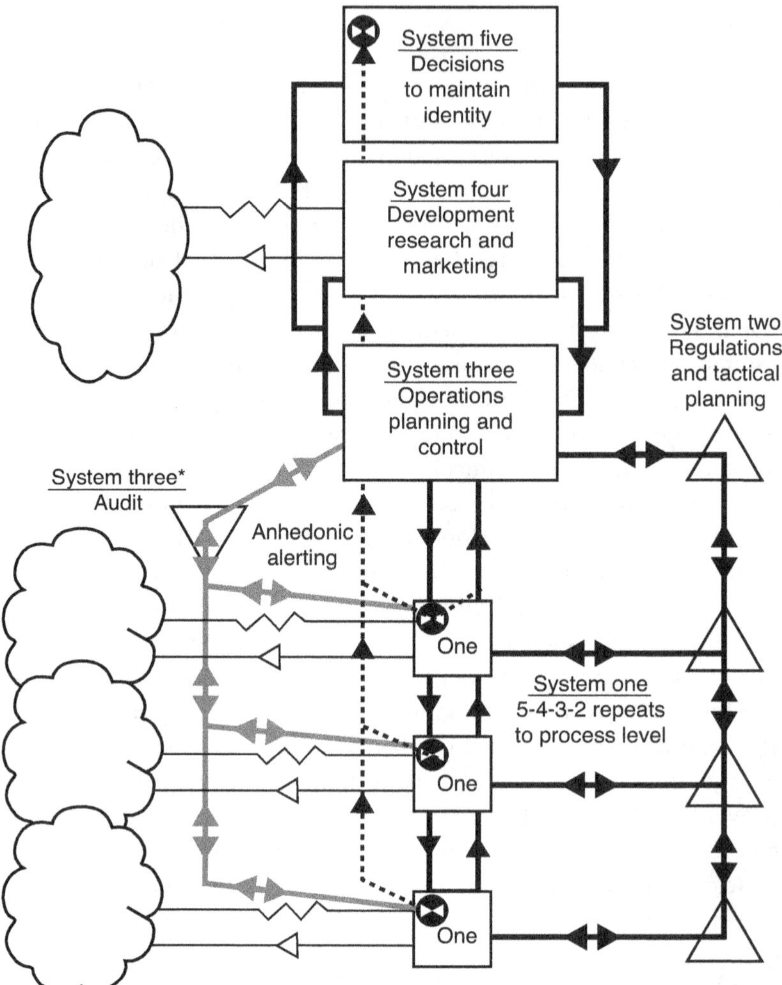


**Figure 3.7**
Stafford Beer's viable system model (VSM). Image by Nick Green, licensed under GNU Free Documentation License.

to be recognized as the first interactive art work. Musicolor, built largely of war surplus parts (like the homeostat), produced light patterns in response to the playing of a musician. But, much smarter than its latter-day disco namesake, Musicolor would become "bored" and provoke the musician to be more interesting. All this was achieved without software, without a Boolean operation, and, indeed, without a transistor. Pask, something of a dandy, said of Musicolor, "You need a mellow, elegant, South Kensington period in developing any cybernetic art form" (1971, 86). Sadly, Musicolor is lost and no images or moving footage of its behavior survive.

## Second-Order Cybernetics

In the early 1970s, roughly contemporary with the heyday of AI and the evacuation of research funds from cybernetics programs, cybernetics took a philosophical turn referred to as *second-order cybernetics*, which took up the implications of the observing subject as its key concern, memorably captured in a maxim of Heinz von Foerster: "Objectivity is a subject's delusion that observing can be done without him"—a postulation closely paralleled by Maturana's remark that "anything said is said by an observer" (Maturana and Varela 1980, 8).[3] In Ranulph Glanville's description, second-order cybernetics "is Cybernetics, when Cybernetics is subjected to the critique and the understandings of Cybernetics. It is the Cybernetics in which the role of the observer is appreciated and acknowledged rather than disguised, as had become traditional in western science: and is thus the Cybernetics that considers observing, rather than observed systems" (2003, 175).[4] The main organ for this movement was the journal *Cybernetics and Human Knowing: A Journal of Second-Order Cybernetics, Autopoiesis and Cyber-Semiotics*. Its title and subtitle demonstrate just how different the cybernetic notion of *knowing* was from the cognitivist one.

## Control and Communication in the Animal and the Machine

Taking a longer view of the history of ideas, this desire to understand animals as machines goes back to Julien Offray de La Mettrie, party boy of the Enlightenment and author of *L'homme machine* (La Mettrie 1996). (La Mettrie is said to have died as a result of eating a vast quantity of *pâté de faisan aux truffes*.) In *Leviathan*, a case study of Enlightenment mechanist thinking, Hobbes presages functionalism in suggesting that reasoning (along with imagining, sensing, and deliberating about action) might be performed by systems of various physical types. In the introduction to *Leviathan*, he asks,

"Why may we not say that all automata (engines that move themselves by springs and wheels . . .) have an artificial life? For what is the heart but a spring; and the nerves but so many strings, and the joints but so many wheels" (Hobbes 2016).

The analogies of cybernetics construct the human in terms of the machine: "Presuppositions embodied in the electronic rat include the idea that both humans and cybernetic machines are goal-seeking mechanisms that learn, through corrective feedback, to reach a stable state. Both are information processors that tend toward homeostasis when they are functioning correctly," says Katherine Hayles (1999, 65), regarding Claude Shannon's Electronic Rat. As Hayles correctly notes, "What tends to drop from sight is the fact that the equation between organism and machine works because it is seen from a position formulated precisely so it will work" (94).

## Matter and Information

Rosenblueth, Wiener, and Bigelow identified human practices that could be duplicated by machines (such as tracking and targeting), separating goal-oriented behavior from its "material substrate," and in the process implemented a functionalism and an abstraction characteristic of AI two decades later! In what is now called the Turing test, Alan Turing separated the content of messages from their embodiment. By 1948, Claude Shannon, himself part of the cybernetic circle, had established the technical concept of "information" as a phenomenon separable from physical instantiation. From these examples, we see that an easy opposition of cybernetics and AI is not possible. They are both mathematized, though in different ways, and mathematics *is* symbolic abstraction.

## Neural Nets

Warren McCulloch and Walter Pitts first proposed the idea of an electronic simulation of (a certain understanding of the behavior of) a network of biological neurons in 1943. McCulloch and Pitts pursued technical research and development on the topic in ensuing years. Such networks were found capable of learning and could be trained yet were resistant to reductive analysis. That is, while a network might display a behavior, half of the network would *not* display half of the behavior, and one neuron alone would not display one part of the total behavior. The idea of neural nets was a central theme in cybernetic research and rhetoric, characterized as it was by feedback, referred to as *reinforcement.* Consistent with cybernetic thought,

It was felt that the emulation of biological brain mechanisms could result in simulated intelligence.

Inspired by Turing's paper "On Computable Numbers, with an Application to the *Entscheidungsproblem*" (1936), Warren McCulloch and Walter Pitts applied Boolean logic in a (highly simplified) description of neural function. Their system was mathematically equivalent to a Turing machine. McCulloch showed that any proposition calculable by a Turing machine was also calculable by a neural net (McCulloch and Pitts 1943). The proof that a model (however simplified) of human neural process was equivalent to automata theory was, like Wiener's diagnosis of ataxia, a move of great rhetorical power for cybernetics, seemingly confirming the claim that a science of systems could apply equally to biology and technology. Wiener's diagnosis of ataxia as a feedback problem confirmed McCulloch's belief that the brain was less like other organs and more like a computer: "Brains do not secrete thought as the liver secretes bile but . . . they compute thoughts the way electronic computers calculate numbers" (quoted in Hayles 1999, 58). Here is, if not the origin of, an early statement of a computational theory of cognition that was to lead to computationalism. McCulloch and Pitts's theoretical work was largely ignored in the neurological community, but it was taken up in what would become the artificial intelligence community (Piccinini 2004).

As Hayles observes, "The McCulloch-Pitts neuron was made to stand simultaneously for a computer code and for human thought" (1999, 61). She repeatedly emphasizes that such mathematical generality is possible only by ignoring the specificities of particular embodiments. The symbolic abstraction characteristic of AI was inherent in cybernetic thought two decades earlier: "Transforming the body into a flow of binary code pulsing through neurons was an essential step in seeing human being as informational pattern. . . . Taken out of context, it is extrapolated to the unwarranted conclusion that there is no essential difference between thought and code" (61). Again we see the origins of what became AI in early cybernetics. In the big picture, this should not be surprising, as Enlightenment rationalism and Anglo-American analytic philosophy played a key role in the formation of all these thinkers. A reflexive awareness of the dangers of dualism and the importance of material instantiation is, by these lights, posthumanist.

In the early 1940s, Wiener introduced John von Neumann to McCulloch and Pitts's notation, which von Neumann then applied in his work on digital logics. Claude Shannon's communication theory, which was to become a major part of AI theory but was originally applied to telephone networks, also applied Boolean algebra (see chapter 5). In the first lecture of the first Macy Conference (held March 8–9, 1946), von Neumann discussed the characteristics and techniques of digital logic and its advantages over analog computation. Ideas of the brain as a computer, of thinking as mathematical reasoning, and of information as quantifiable in "bits"—which were to become the mainstay of artificial intelligence thinking—were present from the outset in the cybernetics community.

Bateson noted that the struggle between continuous (analog) and discontinuous (digital) approaches in the Macy Conferences echoed a similar debate in genetics decades before, in which the digital became the orthodoxy. Referring to McCulloch's theorizing, Hans-Lukas Teuber, a young psychologist who joined the Macy group midway through the conference, said, "Your robot may become capable of doing innumerable tricks the nervous system is able to do; it is still unlikely that the nervous system used the same methods as the robot in arriving at what might look like identical results" (quoted in Hayles 1999, 59). Sadly, critics continue to offer similar warnings to the robotics, cognitive science, and AI communities. Teuber continued, "Your models remain models—unless some platonic demon mediates between the investigators of organic structure and the diagram-making mathematicians" (quoted in Hayles 1999, 59). These remarks echo those of Rosenbleuth, Maturana, and others regarding the perils of mistaking maps for territories. Maturana queried the midcentury mathematical Platonism of the sort expressed by McCulloch: "A mathematical formalism is a conceptual and operational system that reveals the relational coherences of the space that it defines . . . But mathematical formalisms do not provide or create by themselves an understanding of the phenomena that an observer explains to him or herself through them" (Maturana 2002, 18).

Hayles cites McCulloch's telling response to Teuber: "I look to mathematics, including symbolic logic, for a statement of a theory in terms so general that the creations of god and man must exemplify the processes prescribed by the theory. Just because the theory is so general as to fit robot and man, it lacks the specificity required to indicate mechanism in man to be the same as mechanism in robot" (1999, 60).

## Cyborgs and Industrial Labor

Paul Edwards notes that semiautomatic weapons systems often cited paradigm examples of cybernetic control—the antiaircraft gun and the "torpedo with a target seeking mechanism" (1997, 184)—which were prototypical cyborg devices. They were key examples for cybernetic thinking, as machines with a level of autonomy closer to that of animals. Yet to the extent that they took the human out of the loop entirely, they were already postcybernetic. A key military application of cybernetics thinking was *human-machine integration*, the coordination of the human component performing the tasks yet beyond automation with the machine parts. Such integration was considered a stopgap until the technology advanced to the point that the human was unnecessary. This was exactly the model of human elements in the SAGE (Semi-Automatic Ground Environment) system. Humans were inserted into the machine complex via interactive interfaces (screens, pointers, and keyboards) to do the (pattern recognition) tasks that the machine was incapable of. In a sense the human operators were "plugged in." It is ironic that here, deep in the military industrial complex of Cold War paranoia, the origin of the purportedly liberating, and now ubiquitous, interface of personal computing is found (see chapter 4).

We should note that the cybernetic man-machine interaction is only different from previous forms in the more sophisticated calculatory power of the machine component. Warships, bombers, and submarines are quintessential "colonial cyborgs" (in the sense, commonly used in artificial life studies, of colonial organisms and insects). These techno-military systems reflect the disciplined man-machine complexes of Taylorist and Fordist industrial production—the model of the assembly line in particular. But this model of cyborgian industrial discipline has its origins in military imperatives. The first commodities with standardized interchangeable spare parts were guns (during the US Civil War). The disciplinary regime of US steam-powered "ironclad" warships is seen by some as a prototypical model of labor organization in the factory of the Industrial Revolution. Sidney Mintz (1985) offers a different and earlier origin, in the organization of slave labor on Caribbean colonial sugar plantations. Both systems are characterized by hierarchical authoritarian discipline. The cyborg discourse—which Edwards identifies and resoundingly demonstrates—seems to be consistent with the mentality of (an industrialized) military.

## Cybernetics and Behaviorism

Early cybernetic thinking perpetuated the assiduous externalism of behaviorism, embracing the notion of the black box, and extrapolated the analogy of the deterministic machine into the concept of homeostasis—the notion that the goal of a system is to reach an equilibrious rest state.[5] Machine behavior was discussed in terms of feedback and reflex arcs and stimulus/response translated as input/output. Consistent with the aspirations of cybernetics as a general science of systems, the machine is zoomorphized; simultaneously, analogies of cybernetic machines construct the human as machine. This circularity propagated into artificial intelligence with the comparison of the brain and the computer. As J. D. Bolter noted,

Wiener compared the new electron tubes to neurons and wanted to subsume the study of both under one discipline. Wiener's outlook was clearly as much influenced by pre-electronic control devices (feedback loops in various machines) as by the digital computers just being built . . . Those following Wiener's approach spoke of creating artificial brain cells and neural networks and allowing the machine to learn as a baby was presumed to do . . . But the theory of neural networks, which was developed mathematically, met with little or no practical success. (1984, 213)

This approach to artificial intelligence was also proposed by Alan Turing, but the biomimetic cybernetic approach was abandoned by the artificial intelligence community, which saw no need to emulate biology. Ironically, first-generation AI, which eschewed biological models, fell into crisis in the 1980s. This led to a return to biological models in artificial life, an approach that continues into the present in biomimetic robotics and the resurgence of neural networks (see chapters 6 and 8).

## Cognitive Psychology: In and Out of the Black Box

In an effort to remain "scientific" and to avoid the pitfalls of introspective philosophy of mind, behaviorism was committed to observation of measurable, external effects. The concept of the *black box*, common to behaviorism and systems theory, asserts that components of a system need only be understood in terms of their interfaces—their inputs and outputs. To say something psychologically useful, it was deemed unnecessary to know what went on inside the black box. From this perspective, internal processes were deemed irrelevant. Cognitive psychology, largely through the work of George Miller, emerged in opposition to behaviorist psychology, attempting to find a scientifically principled way back into the mind. Cognitive psychology dates back to the 1951 publication of *Language and Communication* by Miller. This cognitivist opposition to behaviorism was formative of early artificial intelligence. AI did not exist at the time, but already among cyberneticians, memory and language were seen in terms of formalizable transformations of information and feedback circuits, or control loops: "Cognition became, fundamentally, *symbolic information processing*, or computation on physically represented symbols" (Edwards 1997, 179; emphasis in original). This is what Newell and Simon came to call the physical symbol system hypothesis (see chapter 5).

## Cybernetics and AI

In some quarters, cybernetics is understood as relating to artificial intelligence in a way similar to the way alchemy is conventionally seen to relate to chemistry: as a misconceived and unprincipled precursor to "real information science." This notion has no validity. The theoretical reach of cybernetics was expansive. It was tied neither to a specific technology nor to a specific approach, so it could be applied as much to physiology as to economics. In this way, it differs from AI, which pursues the mechanization of "intelligence," defined in a specific logico-mathematical way. In contrast to the ideas that emerged later in AI, cybernetics saw intelligence in terms of environmentally situated agents engaged in feedback and homeostasic behavior with their environments. As Andy Pickering has shown, cybernetics—especially in the hands of the British cyberneticians—was situated and relational. Cognition was understood as operating at the interface between organism and environment. This again distinguishes it from AI, which is determinedly internalist. As I have emphasized, AI grew out of the cybernetics community, and although the two schools came to be opposed, until about the time of the Dartmouth Conference (1956), these ideas were intermingled and in development. A drive to symbolic abstraction was characteristic of both groups, as it was to all theoretical sciences.

The term *artificial intelligence* was introduced by John McCarthy and Marvin Minsky at the 1956 Dartmouth Conference on the simulation of intelligent behavior. That is not to say that all cognitive psychologists supported the AI project. Ulrich Neisser, echoing Rosenbleuth, observed, "It is true that a number of researchers, not content with noting that computer programs are like cognitive theories, have tried to write programs which are cognitive theories. . . . In a sense, the rest of this book can be construed as an extensive argument against models of this kind, and also against other simplistic theories of the cognitive processes" (1967, 9).

## Boolean Logic and Neural Nets

As digital computing became increasingly viable through the 1960s and 1970s (due in large part to the advent of the transistor and the integrated circuits that followed), neural network research was increasingly seen as a backwater. Seymour Papert and Marvin Minsky argued that a neural network could not learn an XOR (exclusive or) Boolean function. This argument was published in Minsky and Papert's book *Perceptrons* (1969) and led to the defunding of neural network research (Papert 1988). (Not long after, between 1972 and 1973, Grossberg demonstrated that neural networks *could* learn XOR.) The Minsky-Papert critique reveals, rather tellingly, the power structure of computational discourses at the time: It was incumbent upon neural networks to be able to emulate procedures of computationalist AI, but the presumed validity of physical symbol system techniques did not depend on successful emulation of the special behaviors of neural networks.

At root was a clash of paradigms: a biologically based paradigm of growth and adaptation, as opposed to a logico-mathematically based system of propositional reasoning on explicit representations. In later years, the question of representation became central to discussions at the nexus of AI and artificial life, with respect to genetic programming and with respect to Rodney Brooks's subsumption architecture, which some argued was representation-free. These qualities of neural networks—freedom from explicit representation and semiautonomous growth and adaptation—were sympathetic with, and informed by, the artificial life paradigm of the early 1990s.

## Computer Metaphors and the Rise of Biotech

In 1953, building on the work of Linus Pauling, Rosalind Franklin, and others, Watson and Crick announced the structure of DNA. Analogies from both cryptography and computer programming are everywhere in genetics language and seem to have been from the outset. Note the coincidence in timing: In 1952, a UNIVAC computer (the first "mass-produced computer" ever made) correctly predicted the outcome of the US presidential election between Dwight Eisenhower and Adlai Stevenson, based on early returns. This was also the first US presidential election to be coast-to-coast televised, so it was the first exposure to the general public of an "electronic brain."

Watson and Crick made explicit analogies between computer code and genetic "code," to the extent that DNA codons were conceived as words in DNA code script. They explicitly described DNA in computational terms as the genetic code, comparing the egg cell to a computer tape. The treatment of DNA as computer code laid the conceptual groundwork for mixing genetics and computing in genetic algorithms and biological computing, which take genetic and biological model programs composed of Boolean computational processes.

What is seldom noted is that the conception of computer code and computer programming in 1950 was radically different from what it became fifty years later. The analogy of DNA to machine code has some validity. The analogy of biogenetic operations to contemporary high-level programming environments is rather more tenuous and certainly demands critical interrogation. This historical drift of denotation has also permitted application of computing ideas in the emerging field of synthetic biology—such as the possibility of computer operations implemented in protein and amino acid interactions. Given the vastly complex cellular genetic processes, this kind of biocomputing seems ludicrous, like using a cell phone as a mirror.

## Artificial Life and Genomics

Cybernetics and digital computing deployed differing metaphors from biology, and, as we have seen, the conception of genetic information owed much to the conception of the computer program. The idea of the genetic program as deployed by Watson and Crick did not specifically dissociate the genetic information from its materiality, but by the late 1980s it was possible for artificial life adherents to speak in these terms. In the words of one of its major proponents, Christopher Langton, a basic premise of artificial life is the possibility of separation of the "informational content" of life from its "material substrate" (see chapter 8); the Cartesian dualism was written into artificial life at the outset. (When the Human Genome Project began in 1990, it was headed by none other than James Watson.)

Like any structuring metaphor, computer analogies doubtless had significant influence on the ways in which DNA and genetics are thought about, particularly by laying the fallacious software-hardware binary back onto biological matter—constructing DNA as "information" as opposed to the presumably information-free cellular matter. In recent years, this false binary has troubled genetics, as nongenetically controlled mechanisms are discovered. Embryological research indicates that the self-organizing behavior of large molecules provides (at least) a structural armature upon which the DNA can perform its work. That is, some of the "information" necessary for reproduction and evolution is not in the DNA but elsewhere, integrated into the "material substrate." Alvaro Moreno, Arantza Etxeberria, and Jon Umerez argue for a "deeply entangled" relationship between explicit genetic information and the implicit self-organizing capacity of organisms (Moreno, Etxeberria, and Umerez 1994). The contemporary rise of epigenetics is bearing these earlier warnings out. The reality of nongenetic inheritance is now well established and the authority of the genetic "program" is no longer regarded as absolute.

## Conclusion

The emergence of the discipline of cybernetics and its subsequent history is key to the formulation of technocultural ideas of the last half-century. The key precept, that animals and machines may be studies in an overarching discipline centered on ideas of feedback, homeostasis, and systems, leads directly to literature and theories on the cyborgian and the posthuman. The rapid spread of cybernetic notions into diverse fields all point to the significance of cybernetics as a social phenomenon worthy of study, from the civilianizing of systems theory as postwar corporate management theory by the RAND Corporation to applications of cybernetic ideas in psychology, sociology, anthropology, and other human sciences to the wholesale takeover of ecology by "systems ecology" (e.g., by Chunglin Kwa) to its application as art theory, most notably by Jack Burnham in the United States and Roy Ascott in the United Kingdom, and finally to the development of a distinctly "metaphysical" or mystical second-order cybernetics cult.

The demise of cybernetic discourses and simultaneous rise of symbol-manipulating AI is a complex and fascinating story with political, technological, and philosophical dimensions. Of equal interest is the way AI was bookended by biological paradigms. Cybernetic ideas resurfaced in artificial life discourse theory thirty years later, framed in terms of emergence, stigmergy, and bottom-up. Ideas of self-organization and emergent order percolated through the more systems-oriented parts of the ALife community. In artificial life, these ideas were clad in terms of autonomous agents, reactive insect-like robots, simulated evolution in fitness landscapes, emergence, and self-organizing criticality. Theorists like Peter Cariani explicitly bring systems theory and cybernetic theory to bear on artificial life.[6] Artificial life can be understood as a classic dialectical synthesis of previously opposed trends of cybernetics and artificial intelligence, as we will discuss in chapter 8.

# 4  Giant Brains of the Military-Industrial Complex

The computerization of society . . . has essentially been a side effect of the computerization of war.

—Frank Rose, quoted in *The Closed World: Computers and the Politics of Discourse in Cold War America* (Edwards 1997, 65)[1]

Cybernetic psychology began as an effort to theorize humans as component parts of weapons systems.

—Paul Edwards, *The Closed World* (1997, 180)

American weapons and American culture cannot be understood in isolation from each other. Just as the weapons have emerged from the culture so too have the weapons caused profound metamorphoses in the culture.

—H. Bruce Franklin, quoted in *The Closed World* (Edwards 1997, 7)

All the ideas that are going into the fifth-generation [advanced computing] project [of the mid-1980s] . . . ultimately started from DARPA-funded research.

—Robert Sproull, former ARPA director, quoted in *The Closed World* (Edwards 1997, 270–271)

This chapter describes the evolution of analog and digital computing in the mid-twentieth century from both sociopolitical and technical perspectives, aspects that are historically and culturally inseparable. It is not possible to understand the form "computing" took in the late twentieth century without understanding that the majority of fundamental computing research was pursued as (US) military research with military funding. From Colossus to the Manhattan Project to the SAGE system, computing systems were developed for and framed by military agendas. The development of both analog and digital computing bears the indelible stamp of the interests of the research sponsors. These sponsors were almost exclusively part of the *military-industrial complex*, a term coined by Dwight Eisenhower in his remarkable farewell to office speech. This chapter lays out milestones in that history to both describe key technological steps and elucidate the context(s) that motivated them.

Because histories of the computer focus on the emergence of the digital computer, one might be forgiven for assuming that it was the only game in town. A closer look at the history reveals that the success of digital computing was by no means a fait accompli. The history of computation, at least since Babbage, has swung between the poles of the abstract and the corporeal, the analog and the digital. Analog computing was successful, productive, and competitive into the 1960s. For the two decades that followed World War II (conventionally regarded as the period of the rise of the digital computer), analog and digital schools collaborated and differentiated. In the process, techniques and concepts once hazily conceived became clearly defined, including feedback, information, the software-hardware dualism, and the notion of symbolic manipulation. The universal engine Turing imagined in 1936 would not actually function until the Manchester Baby of 1948. Machines of this type would not be available even for research purposes until UNIVAC (UNIVersal Automatic Computer) in 1952.

## The Analog and the Digital: Cybernetics and AI

The distinction between analog and digital computing—like the distinction between cybernetics and artificial intelligence—is crystal clear from some perspectives and murky from others. What we mean by *analog* must first be explicated to avoid a fallacious and oversimplified analog/digital binary. It would be more accurate to name the sides of this binary *proportional* and *numerical*, so as not to confuse technological implementation with theoretical methods.

Cybernetics is native to the analog as AI is native to the digital. One way of understanding the bifurcation between cybernetics and AI is to recognize that the technological context of cybernetics was analog electronics. We should take this notion of analog seriously. Analog electronics *operationalizes analogy*; it is characterized by temporally immersed flows, curves, and gradual infinitesimal change: calculus is its math. If cybernetics is analogical and geometric, digital computation is both numerical and *representational*: arbitrary tokens are conferred discrete values upon which logical operations are performed. Oddly, this distinction between geometry and arithmetic corresponds to a similar transition between Gothic and Renaissance architecture.

## Proportion and Number: Medieval Masonry and Analog Computing

It may come as a surprise to many, naturalized to discretized and numerically based forms of measurement and mathematics, that the architecture of Europe's great cathedrals in the medieval period was done without numbers, as were the pyramids and Buddhist and Hindu temples. These practices employed "peg and cord" geometry, a set of procedures for geometrical constructions that derived *proportions* through simple geometric operations using a basic modulus, which in the case of some Gothic cathedrals was a stick the height of the master mason. An abrupt change in proportions can be seen in some cathedrals. As often as not, this was the effect of the death of the master mason and his replacement by another master mason of different stature.

Part of the abrupt change in the look of architecture between Gothic and Renaissance was not simply the adoption of Hellenistic models and forms but a shift to arithmetic procedures. The important lesson here is that computation can be done without numbers, can be continuous as well as discrete. This idea draws a connection between medieval geometry-based

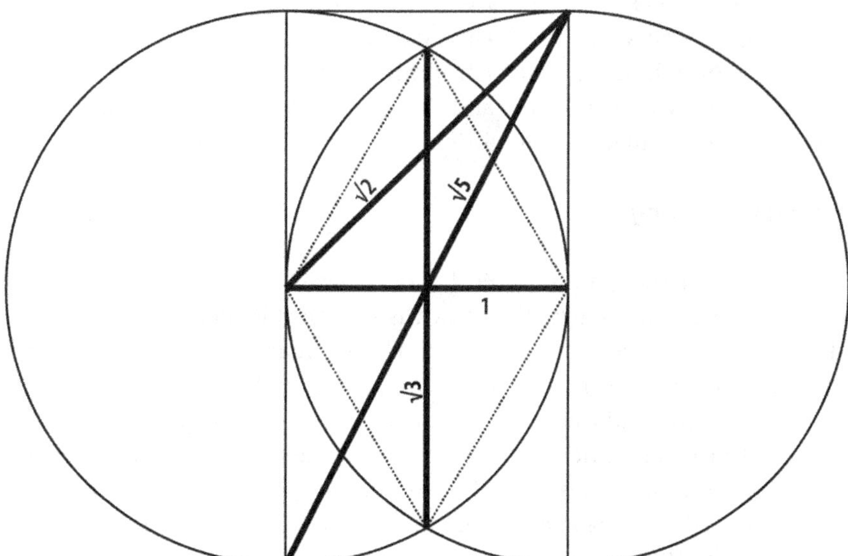


**Figure 4.1**

The *vesica piscis*—the shape of the intersection between two circles, in which the center of each is on the perimeter of the other. This construction gives rise to several important geometrical verities and ratios. Drawing by Evan Houston Stanfield.

masonry and the analog computing of the mid-twentieth century. The Gothic–Renaissance transition is paralleled by the analog–digital transition.

## As Simple as Clockwork

Astronomy and celestial navigation deal with calculation and prediction of continuous variables. Clockwork devices like the orrery accurately represent the movement of planets. Descartes and the mechanists made analogies for celestial movement, and much besides, from clockwork. Clocks and clockwork automata of the eighteenth century by Pierre Jaquet-Droz, Jacques de Vaucanson, and others were analog computers. There is a direct line between Jacquard's programmable loom and Babbage's difference engine. Clockwork performs math: A gear of twenty teeth driving a gear of ten teeth performs multiplication by two. Simple mechanical devices do computation.

This clockwork is much the same machinery as that of the mid-twentieth-century *mechanical* analog computers: the gears, racks, cams, integrators and differentials of the fire-control systems deployed on ships and planes. A cam follower, set in a specifically shaped spiral groove in a cam, computes the reciprocal of the input. The input is the rotational position of the input shaft. The curve is a representation of the equation, and the mechanism calculates (outputs) continuously and instantaneously. The operational amplifiers of analog *electronic* computing perform in an analogous way, deploying transistors, resistors and capacitors, and current flow instead of mechanisms and mechanical motion.

## Analog Computing

Analog computers of a mechanical variety have been known and used for centuries; the oldest currently known is the Antikythera device, found in the wreck of an ancient Greek ship. The Jacquard loom and clockwork automata of Vaucanson and Jaquet-Droz computed. The orrery, the astrolabe, the sextant, and the humble slide rule are all proportional calculatory devices. In the late nineteenth century and the first half of the twentieth century, numerous types of analog computers were developed, originally mechanical, then increasingly electromechanical and electronic.

In *Between Human and Machine: Feedback, Control, and Computing before Cybernetics* (2002), David Mindell has documented the development of control machinery from the late nineteenth century until World War II. From gyroscopic stabilization for naval ships to telephone switching machinery, specific business and military applications defined technological develop-

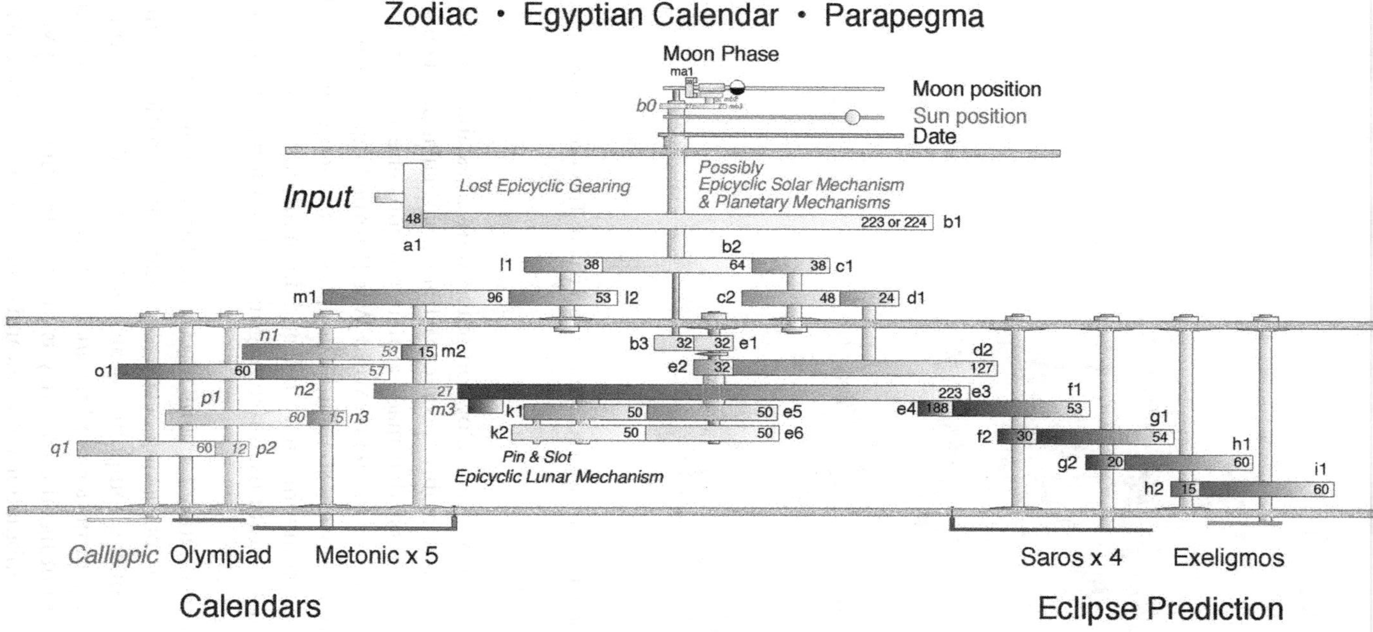


**Figure 4.2**

Diagram of the calculatory gears of the Antikythera device by Tony Freeth and Alexander Jones, 2012.

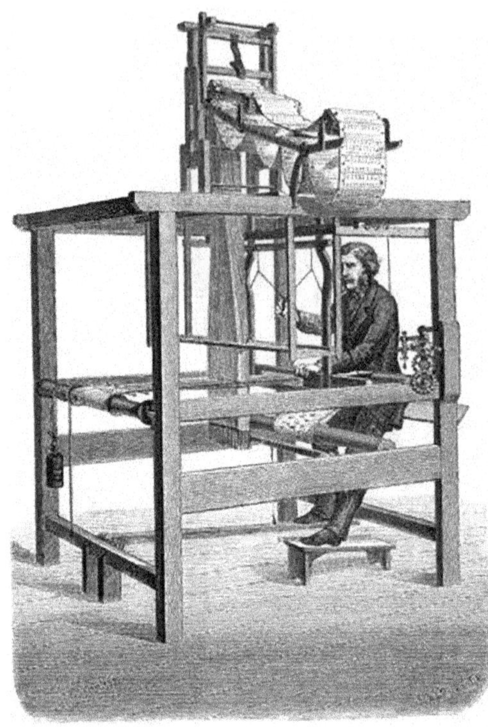

**Figure 4.3**
Jacquard loom showing punched cards linked in a chain. This was the first machine
with a variable "program."

ment. During World War II, analog computers were an established technology. These devices were highly specific, each for a particular problem—such
as analog "gun directors" that made antiaircraft guns effective against the
V-2 attacks on London in 1944. World War II torpedo guidance system
and antiaircraft guns were standard examples of homeostatic machines.
Mechanical analog computing (e.g., ball and drum integrators) continued to
be used for such applications as bombsights in US air force weaponry into
the Vietnam War era.

This kind of computing remains mysterious for many who are naturalized to the idea that computing occurs via logico-mathematical manipulation of symbols. Analog computing deals neither in symbols nor in logical
reasoning. The key to understanding analog computing is in its name. In
this form of computing, the currency is not bits but fluctuating voltages
and waveforms. Combinations of gears and cams or resistors and capacitors

a.  b.

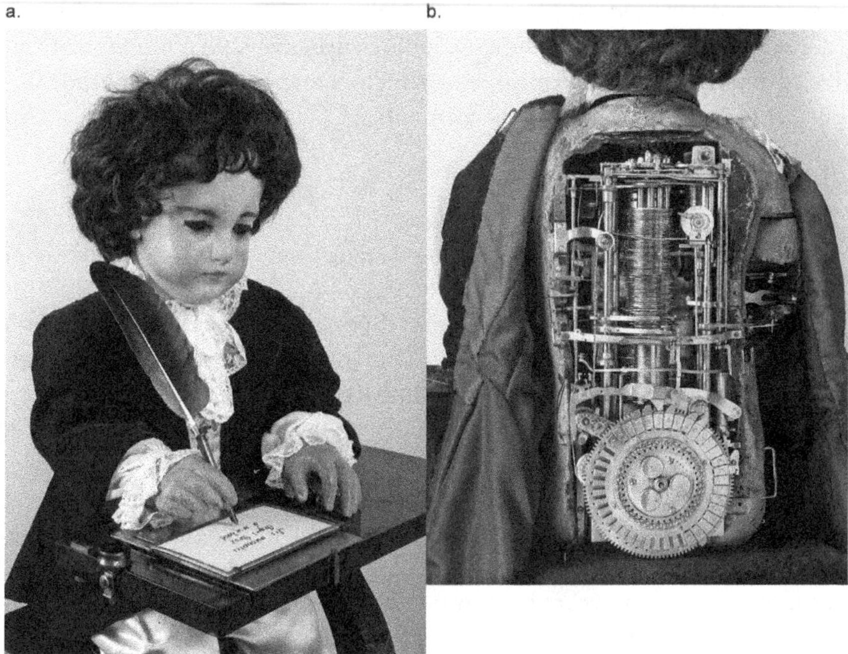

**Figure 4.4**
Pierre Jaquet-Droz's The Writer, the back showing the detail of the mechanism.
Courtesy of Musée d'Art et d'Histoire, Neuchâtel, Switzerland.

(or even the flow of water through pipes and valves) can be made to mimic other physical phenomena, such as acceleration curves.[2] The math native to analog computing is not binary arithmetic but calculus.

The histories of analog electronics and analog computing are intertwined. Radio and television broadcast and reception, audio electronics, and music recording all deployed analog electronics, as did radar and sonar. The first analog electronic synthesizer was the theremin, developed by Leon Theremin in the Soviet Union in 1920. The theremin is notable also for its gestural, nontactile interface and its continuous tonality. This marks it as radical with respect to much later (MIDI) devices, which slavishly emulate the piano keyboard interface and its diatonic tuning. The two musical instruments that characterized popular music in the mid-twentieth century—the electric guitar and electronic keyboards like the Hammond organ or the Fender Rhodes electric piano—were analog and depended on analog electronic amplification via vacuum tubes. In the popular mind, feedback became associated with psychedelic rock and roll. The BBC radiophonic workshop developed "space age" electronic sounds—such as the famous theme tune from Dr. Who. Analog audio synthesizers (like the Moog from 1964) deployed voltage-controlled oscillators and other circuitry indistinguishable from analog computing circuits.

## Analog and Digital Convivencia

From the 1920s through the 1960s, the clear distinction we now see between analog and digital did not exist. Indeed, the "digital" did not exist. This lack of differentiation mirrors the contemporaneous lack of differentiation between the cybernetics community and those who would become digital computing/AI stalwarts. From 1928 to 1931, Vannevar Bush and Harold Hazen built their *differential analyzer*, a mechanical analog computer that used ball and disc integrators to address an entire class of problems, those that could be specified in differential equations. The functions were computed by the geometrical relationships of the moving cylinder, sphere, and a flat plane [disc]. The significance of Turing's proposal for a universal computer, just a few years later, was not so much the concept of generality but its digitality. In 1938 Berlin, Konrad Zuse built the Z1, a floating-point binary calculator with some programmability. It had thirty thousand mechanical parts, mostly adapted from 35-mm camera, editing, and projection mechanics. In 1940, he built the Z2, replicating the functions of the Z1 with electromechanical relays.[3] The Z1 was a mechanical *digital* computer. The Z2 was a pioneering *electromechanical* digital computer.

The development and mass production of analog devices in World War II (gyroscopes, gun directors, etc.) had generated a substantial analog computing industry and a vigorous tradition of analog computation and control engineering. Work proceeded rapidly on (often huge) general-purpose electronic analog computers such as RCA's Typhoon. Aside from reliability and speed, analog machines had significant advantages. Analog computers interfaced smoothly with physical machines, whereas digital computers interfaced smoothly with the world of text and symbols. Analog computers integrated smoothly with control functions because their inputs and outputs were generally of the type needed to control other machines: analog voltages or precise mechanical movements. In comparison, digital machines had no interface with the world of physical phenomena; they could not control anything except for their own "printers"—in the early days, punch cards, an analog technology based on Herman Hollerith's punch card system developed in the late 1880s. (Hollerith's company was an integral part of what became IBM.) They likewise had no means of gathering data from the world, no sensors. The concept of analog to digital (A/D) conversion had yet to yield viable technology.

In the analog electronic boom after the war, George Philbrick, an engineer at the Foxboro Instrument Company, built the Automatic Control Analyzer (Holst 1982). Philbrick became a major name in electronic analog computing, introducing commercial modular vacuum-tube operational amplifiers, the famous K2-W, in 1953 (and transistor op amp units by 1961—the P2). A little later, at the Ballistics Research Laboratory (BRL) of the US Army Aberdeen proving grounds, Bush's differential analyzer was used to calculate firing tables. (At the same time, elsewhere on campus, rooms full of women—the original "computers"—with desktop calculators undertook the same task.) A second of Bush's differential analyzers was in use at the Moore School, where ENIAC was being built. Bush, who wielded substantial authority in the war research community, was skeptical of the digital approach, partly because vacuum tubes had limited reliability. Nonetheless, at MIT in 1942 he produced the Rockefeller differential analyzer, which could be

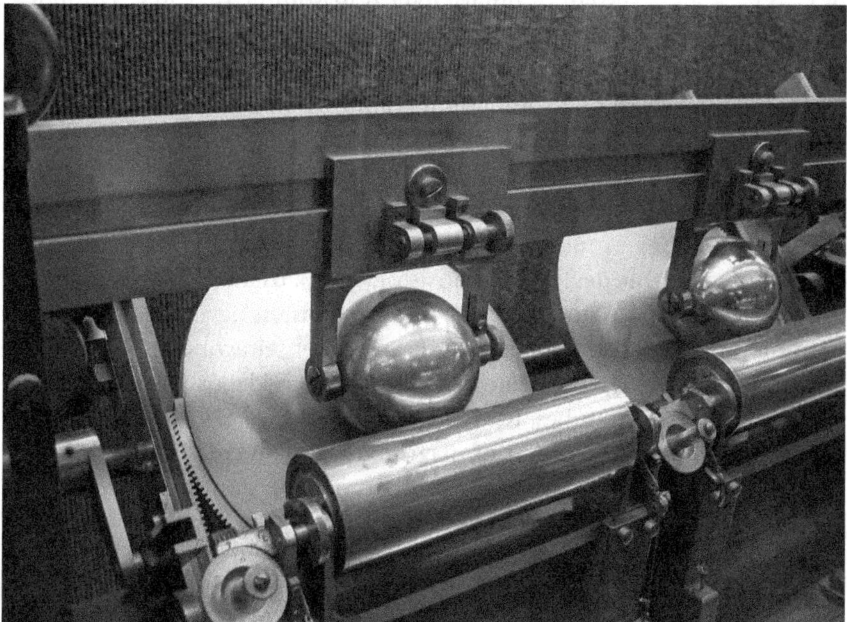

**Figure 4.5**
This image shows the ball and disc integrator, a mechanical computing device that performs integration by virtue of the movement and geometry of the forms. Photograph by Andy Dingley.

programmed with punched tape and had some electronic components. But digital computers were slow: "At Project Cyclone digital computers were . . . used to verify the accuracy of results from the analog computer. . . . In the simulation of a guided missile in three dimensions, the average runtime on the analog computer facility was approximately one minute. The check solution by numerical methods . . . took from 60 to 130 hours to solve the same problem" (Small 1993, 11). As Paul Edwards observes, in the decade after World War II, "the shape of computers, as tools, was still extremely malleable, and their capacities remained to be envisioned, proven and established in practice" (1997, 70). When, upon delivery in 1949, Eckert and Mauchly's Binary Automatic Computer (BINAC) failed to work, the Northrop Corporation switched immediately to available analog machines.

**The Transistor Transition**

The transition from analog to digital was undergirded by rapid changes in electronic engineering. Digital computing depends on the implementation of George Boole's system of binary logical reasoning as "gates" composed of switches or latches. These latches can be implemented mechanically, electromechanically, hydraulically, electronically, or in other media. Today, each *logic gate* in a digital computer is composed of transistors. The earliest digital computers used arrangements of relays (electromagnetic switches) for this purpose. They were replaced by electronic vacuum tubes, which operated at higher speeds but at high voltages, often around 350 volts.

The technology of modern digital computing is entirely dependent on the invention of one device: the transistor (1947), usually credited to Shockley, Bardeen, and Brattain.[4] In 1958, Kilby and others developed techniques to miniaturize and combine transistors and other semiconductors onto one integrated circuit (IC) chip, eliminating tedious and labor-intensive wiring. Compared to vacuum tubes, ICs reduced physical size as well as voltage and power consumption by orders of magnitude while increasing reliability by similar margins. Per Moore's Law, miniaturization continued steadily. In the 1970s, very large-scale integration (VLSI) put thousands, then tens of thousands, of transistors on a single chip.

Texas Instruments completed the first IC-based computer in 1961 for the US Air Force. The tight integration of technological development and military interests is reflected in the fact that "almost half of the cost of semiconductor R+D between the late 1950s and the early 1970s was paid by military sources" (Edwards 1997, 64). It was not until 1965 that the first commercial computer using ICs was marketed. While production was commercialized, funding and contracts remained largely military. This pattern persisted from the IBM 701 and the Texas Instruments IC computer in the 1960s into the late 1980s. Through the 1990s, 80 percent of the production of supercomputers by the Cray Corporation was said to have gone directly into black (classified) contexts.

## Science and Culture

Scientific ideas do not fall fully formed out of some value-free Platonic heaven; they develop iteratively in communities. Technologies arise in historical context and come to prominence through networks of influence and power. People commit effort and resources to achieve identified goals— even if once developed and immersed in culture, those technologies take on new and radically different roles. Computers are a case in point. In 1943, Thomas J. Watson, head of IBM, is reported to have said, "I think there is a world market for maybe five computers." That story appears to be apocryphal, but there is no reason why he shouldn't have said it, as it remained true for a decade. Similarly, Ken Olsen—founder of Digital Equipment Corporation (DEC)—said in 1977, "There is no reason anyone would want a computer in their home." In two generations, computers have morphed from machines that consumed the power of an entire town to desktop calculating machines to microcontrollers in cars, homes, and appliances.

The modern computer emerges as the confluence of three research streams:

1. The abstract and mathematical aspects of computation: the manipulation of logico-mathematical tokens (the tradition of Boole, Turing, von Neumann, and others)
2. The real-world, mostly military-industrial functions of sensing, measurement, and control
3. The increasing automation of calculation and record keeping in office work and business practices

Although the look and feel of contemporary computing devices is nothing like those walls of knobs and dials tended by men in lab coats, the underlying procedures and structures remain largely unchanged.

It is germane to ask whether the qualities of a device built for tracking rockets or financial accounting are optimal for the multifarious social and cultural purposes digital devices now serve. And by the same token, we must ask: Would these practices have developed, or how would these practices

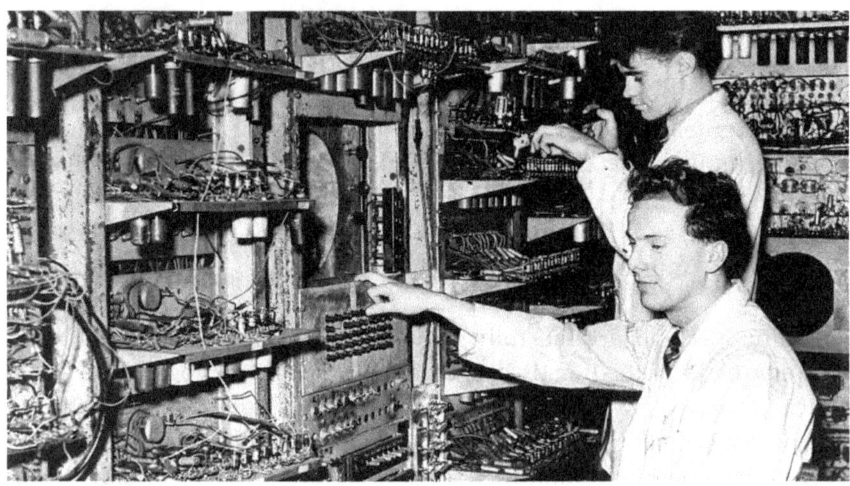

**Figure 4.6**
Early nerdy. Young men working on the Manchester Mark I. For an informative account of the development of the Manchester Baby and the Mark I, see https://www .youtube.com/watch?v=cozcXiSSkwE. Image courtesy of the University of Manchester.

be different, if they were not grounded in militaristic logic and were not formed out of military imperatives? This raises issues of cultural specificity and the skeuomorphic implications of "trickle-down." A common response to such questions relies on a fallacious truism: that the computer is a general-purpose machine. This assertion applies an idea arising from the history of mathematics to the sociocultural sphere in a way that demands interrogation. What we believe to be historical hindsight—often formed in large part by the rhetoric of vested interests—creates a sense of inevitability. But this sense of inevitability is often false, and the path of history veers wildly as a result of lucky, and unlucky, accidents. Consider the history of the steam engine–powered airplane—such as Clément Ader's exquisite Bat and Hiram Maxim's failed aerial behemoth of the 1890s (Maxim 1891, 1895). These seem absurd, yet early automobiles seem equally absurd. There were once steam cars, now they are "obsolete." There is a long history of electric cars, yet vested interests deemed them obsolete. We now foresee the resurgence of electric cars and the obsolescence of internal combustion engines.

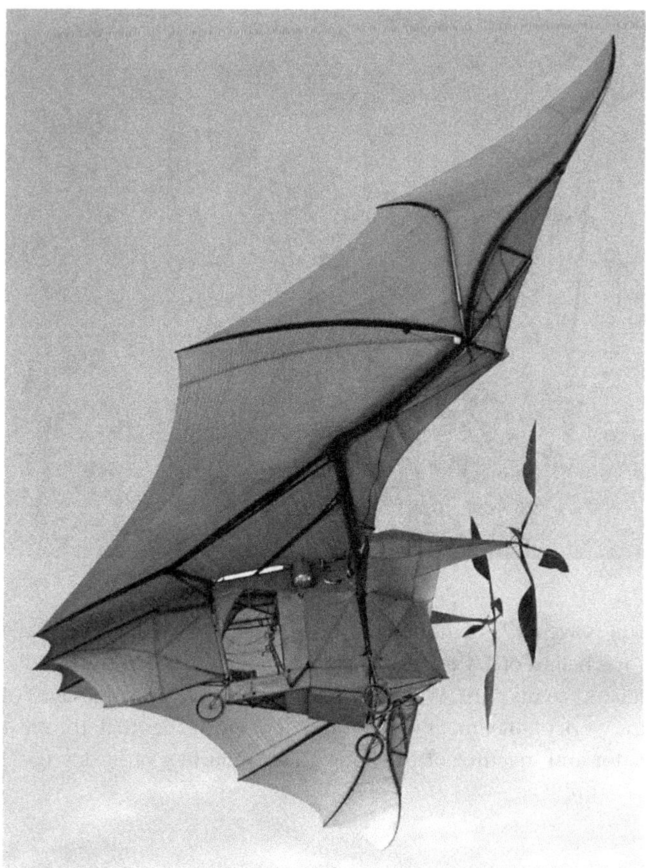

**Figure 4.7**
One of Clement Ader's exquisite machines, Avion 3, 1892–1897 (the epitome of steampunk). Courtesy of Musée des Arts et Métiers, Paris. Photomontage by Roby.

## The Military-Industrial Complex

As noted earlier, Dwight Eisenhower coined the term *military-industrial complex*. In his 1961 farewell to office speech, he said,

This conjunction of an immense military establishment and a large arms industry is new in the American experience. The total influence—economic, political, even spiritual—is felt in every city, every State house, every office of the Federal government. We recognize the imperative need for this development. Yet we must not fail to comprehend its grave implications. Our toil, resources and livelihood are all involved; so is the very structure of our society. In the councils of government, *we*

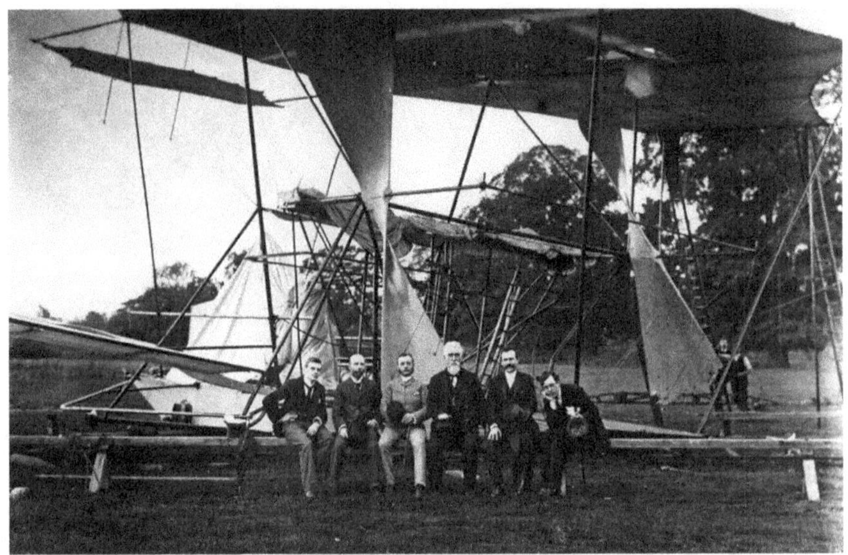

**Figure 4.8**
Hiram Maxim's steam-powered behemoth took off from railway tracks and flew, briefly—281 meters at a height of 1.4 meters. Maxim is the tall figure in the middle. H. G. Wells is immediately to his right. Wells based his short story "The Argonauts of the Air" in part on the work of Maxim, as well as on that of Otto Lilienthal, the great German pioneer aviator and inventor of the hang glider. Courtesy of Bexley Local Studies and Archive Centre.

*must guard against the acquisition of unwarranted influence, whether sought or unsought, by the military-industrial complex.* The potential for the disastrous rise of misplaced power exists and will persist. (Eisenhower 2005, 1038; emphasis mine)

These were astonishing, prescient, words for a Republican president (Richard Nixon was his vice president), retired general and the supreme commander of the Allied forces during World War II. Eisenhower was neither peacenik nor pinko, yet he warned the nation very clearly of the dangers he foresaw for his country. His words appear to have gone largely unheeded, then as now.

Edwards, in his remarkable work *The Closed World*, documents the close ties between the development of (digital) computing and Cold War military agendas. If we are to come to a deeper understanding of the nature of the computer by examining the context in which it was constructed, then the postwar decades in the United States must be examined in some detail. Campbell-Kelly and Aspray (1996), and others, have focused on the development of the computer as a business machine and a commercial phenomenon, but in light of the evidence Edwards presents, this history usually "tags along" with big business–gaining development contracts then "civilianizes" the results of research. The SABRE airline booking system, based in the SAGE Cold War defense system, is a typical example (see below).

Edwards argues that the image of an "iron triangle," comprising universities, industry, and the military, is more accurate than Eisenhower's conception of a military-industrial complex: "Though most of the research took place at universities and in commercial forms, military research organizations such as the Office of Naval Research, the communications Security Group . . . and the Air Comptroller Office paid for it" (1997, 43). Not only did the military fund it, but "practical military objectives guided technological development down particular channels, increased its speed, and helped shape the structure of the emerging computer industry" (44). Edwards observes, "MIT emerged from the war with a staff twice as large as it had before the war, a budget (in current dollars) four times as large, and a research budget ten times as large—85 percent from the military services and their nuclear weaponeer, the AEC [Atomic Energy Commission]" (47).

In *The Closed World*, Edwards persuasively demonstrates that the substantial force behind the development of digital computing was military in origin and that the digital computer was utterly integral to the rhetoric and practices of the Cold War: "The historical trajectory of computer development cannot be separated from the elaboration of American grand strategy in the Cold War" (1997, 2). The term *Cold War* was in common use by 1947, revealing a rapid transition in international relations from the alliance between the Soviet Union and the United States in World War II, which had ended only two years before.

Edwards continues, "For two decades, from the early 1940s to the early 1960s, the armed forces of the United States were the single most important driver of digital computer development" (Edwards 1997, 43). Elsewhere he says, "Computers made much of that strategy possible, but strategic issues also shaped computer technology—even at the level of design" (2). While military and intelligence interests drove technical research, the US taxpayer funded it. In 1950, he notes, "The federal government provided between $15 and $20 million (current) per year, while industry contributed less than $5 million—20 to 25 percent of the total. The vast bulk of federal research funds at that time came from military agencies." And the substantial part of the finding went directly to US corporations: "Between 1949 and 1959 the major corporations developing computer equipment—IBM,

General Electric, Bell Telephone, Sperry Rand, Raytheon, and RCA—still received an average of 59 percent of their funding from the government (again, primarily from military sources). At Sperry Rand and Raytheon, the government share during this period approached 90 percent" (61).

The pressing question that must be asked is: What mark has this intensely focused and highly funded period of research and development—at the formative stages of the technology—has left upon the digital appliances and infrastructure which now structures our lives? Computer scientists and engineers are, and always have been, notably shy on this subject. I have always attributed this to their fundamentally compromised ethical positions and to the lack of historical and humanistic perspective in their formation. However, social scientists, humanists, and artists have no such alibi. Does Edwards's conception of the iron triangle persist so strongly that universities and their faculty are silently complicit?

### Inscrutable Acronyms: IPTO, ONR, ARPA, DARPA, RAND

The RAND (Research and Development)—not to be confused with Sperry Rand or Remington Rand (or Ayn Rand, for that matter)—was formed by General Henry Arnold, commander of the United States Army Air Forces in 1946 to research future weapons.[5] Originally run by Douglas Aircraft, it was spun off as a nonprofit corporation in 1948. RAND was the quintessential military think tank. It developed systems analysis on the basis of the World War II technique of operations research (OR). Systems analysis, when eventually civilianized, became known as *cost-benefit analysis.* Another key tool at RAND was game theory, invented by John von Neumann and Oskar Morgenstern. Game theory was applied to the simulation of novel military situations, particularly nuclear situations. Key figures in artificial intelligence, including John von Neumann and Herbert Simon, were consultants to RAND. Allen Newell and Cliff Shaw were employed at RAND when, with Herbert Simon, they developed Logic Theorist, a "root document" of artificial intelligence. RAND spun off the Systems Research Laboratory (SRL) in 1950 to study human performance in complex man-machine interaction—the origin of the discipline of human-computer interaction (HCI). The idea of programming languages developed in this period. The Office of Naval Research (ONR) sponsored symposia on "automatic programming" in 1954 and 1956. Fortran subsequently emerged from IBM between 1956 and 1957, and in 1959 the Department of Defense (DOD) sponsored development of the so-called common business-oriented language, COBOL, though its early application was almost exclusively military.

The Advanced Research Projects Administration (ARPA), part of the DOD, was hastily founded early in 1958 by the Eisenhower administration in the wake of the 1957 Sputnik launch. Its responsibilities included several high-tech research areas, including the space program that became NASA in 1960. Late in 1962, ARPA's Information Processing Techniques Office (IPTO), headed by J. C. R. Licklider, founded the Systems Development Corp (SDC) to develop a time-sharing system. SDC, based in Santa Monica, California, grew out of the systems engineering group at the SAGE project (perhaps the engineers were tired of the gloomy Boston winters?). Completed by mid-1963, this system included the first graphical user interface. In 1972, ARPA became DARPA, the *D* standing for Defense. This rapid proliferation of information technology agencies evidences the role of the state in this process and exposes the networks through which funding traveled, as well as the nodal gatekeepers. SDC was privatized in 1969 and sold to Burroughs in 1980, which, after a merger with Sperry, became Unisys. By 1986, Unisys was the second-largest computer company, with a revenue of $10.5 billion. Such examples illustrate the mechanisms of trickle down—the corporatization of military research that drove the PC revolution.

The tight connection between computers, military interests, and the space race at the time was exposed by a report published in 2000. It revealed that in 1958 a team at the US Air Force special weapons center at Albuquerque, New Mexico, which included physicist Leonard Reiffel and a young Carl Sagan, was researching a plan to detonate a nuclear bomb on the moon as a show of military and technical strength (Broad 2000).[6] The space race, the bomb, the Cold War, the development of computing: these were deeply intertwined in the postwar period in the United States.

## SAGE: Icon of the Cold War

As much as any historical event, one choice tilted the scales of computer development in favor of digital machines—due in part to the vast sums committed to the project. The Semi-Automatic Ground Environment, or SAGE, was the high-tech keystone of the US ICBM early warning system during the Cold War. In December 1949, in the wake of the 1949 Soviet A-bomb test, the Valley Committee recommended that a comprehensive radar defense system be established to function as an early warning against Soviet ICBM attack. This system became SAGE; MIT spun off the Lincoln Lab for its development. The original plan was to utilize analog computing. Jay Forrester's Whirlwind became its computational centerpiece in 1950. The machine was found unsatisfactory for the task and, based on the success of the ENIAC, the decision was made to pursue vacuum-tube-based digital techniques.

Operational by 1961, Whirlwind was the largest, heaviest, and most expensive computer system ever built. It occupied two floors of the SAGE building, ran sixty thousand vacuum tubes, and consumed three megawatts of electricity. The total cost is estimated at $8 to 12 billion 1964 dollars (around $70 billion today), about triple the cost of the Manhattan Project. The SAGE system collected data from over one hundred radar stations in three lines: the Pinetree Line along the United States/Canada border; the Mid-Canada Line; and the Distant Early Warning (DEW) Line along the northern border of Canada. Twenty-seven direction centers carried data via phone lines and teletype machines to link these radar stations.

SAGE, built on the engineering achievements of Whirlwind, was the first computer capable of operating in real time. The Whirlwind (I and II) research generated or combined technologies and techniques definitive of the modern computer such as time-sharing, multiprocessing, A/D and D/A conversion, graphical displays, modems and networking, and many new

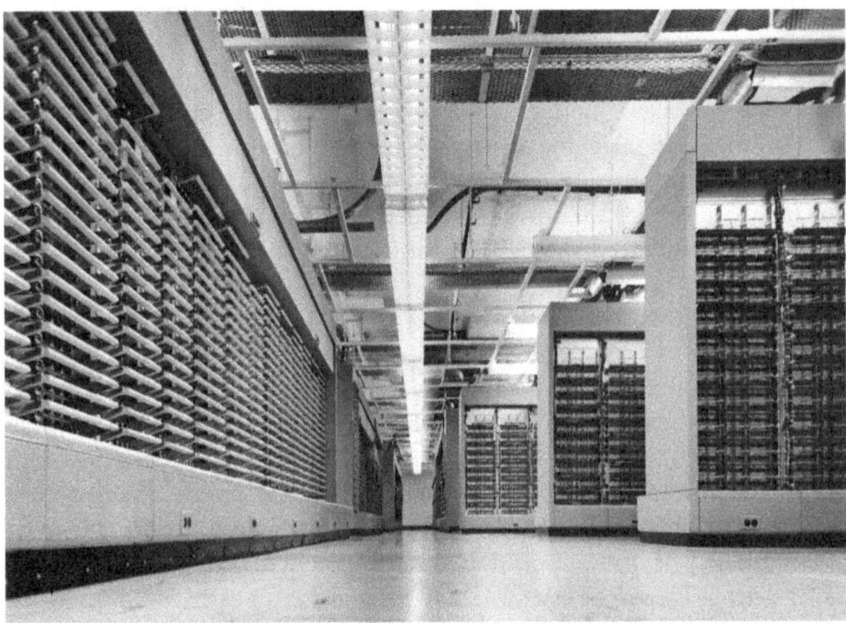

**Figure 4.9**

An A/N FSQ-7 Combat Direction Central computer—the SAGE computer. Courtesy of IBM.

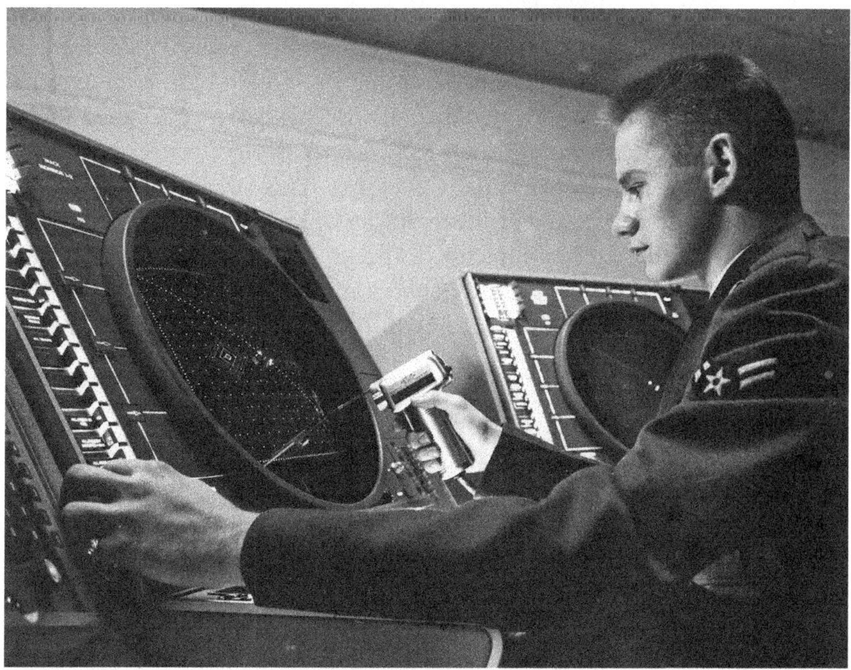

**Figure 4.10**
An operator with a light pen at a SAGE console. Courtesy of IBM.

technologies, including video displays, light pens, and Forrester's magnetic core memory. In the SAGE system, users interacted with keyboards and monitors using light pens, the prototype of the now-standard screen/keyboard/mouse computer interface. In addition, major developments were made in programming language and techniques.

IBM designed the production version of the Whirlwind II, called the AN/FSQ-7. IBM built fifty-six of these machines at about $30 million each. Edwards notes, "At the peak of the project, more than 7,000 IBM employees, almost 20 percent of its total workforce, worked on SAGE related projects; the company's total income from SAGE during the 1950s was about $500 million" (1997, 102).[7] IBM, however, balked at the job of programming the new machines. So RAND took on the project and spun off its SAGE programming operation as the System Development Corporation. It employed eight hundred programmers to produce the 250,000 lines of code for the SAGE system.

While many histories celebrate the establishment of the SAGE system, few document its deactivation in 1983. In twenty years of continuous operation, it did not detect one airborne enemy threat. It did not fail; there appear to have been no such threats. Whether the existence of the system contributed to this absence of threats would be very difficult to determine.

The only part of the SAGE software that "trickled down" was called SABRE (Semi-Automated Business Research Environment), adapted for civilian life by IBM for American Airlines flight bookings. This system still underpins many airline-booking systems, mostly in the United States. J. C. R. Licklider (who later became the first director of the IPTO) worked on the program, and its development of real-time networking influenced Licklider to support the development of ARPANET, itself the precursor to the Internet.

### Paranoid Rationality

In "Soldier, Cyborg, Citizen," Kevin Robins and Les Levidow explore the technological panopticon of the modern military from a psychoanalytic perspective, introducing the notion of "paranoid rationality":

Through a paranoid rationality, expressed in the machine-like self, we combine an omnipotent phantasy of self-control with fear and aggression directed against the emotional and bodily limitations of mere mortals. Through regression to a phantasy of infantile omnipotence, we deny our dependency upon nature, upon our own nature, upon the "bloody mess" of organic nature. We phantasize about controlling the world, freezing historical forces and, if necessary, even destroying them in rage; we thereby contain our anxiety in the name of maintaining rational control. (1995, 105–106)

Terms like *control* remind us of the military interest in both cybernetics and AI, which extend into our own period in programs such as the short-lived Total Information Awareness (TIA) program of 2003.[8] The idea—in cognitivist psychology—that problem solving is fundamental to human intelligence is a corollary. Contrarily, Philip Agre has proposed that the paranoid rationality of Cold War AI—full of spies and dangers and threats—is not relevant to daily life, which is mostly routine (see chapter 6).

### Giant Brains: A Brief Chronology of Early Digital Computers[9]

The following brief chronology lists various projects during the first decade of development of digital computing. Its brevity necessarily oversimplifies the complexities of the interplay among and within academic, industrial, and military contexts, but it makes clear the enormous influence of military funding and military agendas in US computer development. As with any debate about technological "firsts," there is ongoing debate regarding terminology and precedence in this history. Terms such as "programmable," "stored program," and "universally programmable" indicate the subtlety of these distinctions.

**1943.** At the end of World War II, Turing's Colossus, built at Bletchley Park intelligence headquarters in the United Kingdom, was the world's only functioning, fully electronic digital computer. In some ways more advanced than ENIAC, Colossus was a true electronic digital computer, but without the capacity for internally stored programs.

**1944.** Whirlwind was conceived at the MIT Servomechanisms Lab as the Airplane Stability and Control Analyzer (ASCA), an analog computer designed to function as a flight simulator. By mid-1946, it had metamorphosed into a general-purpose digital computer with a new emphasis on the cybernetic/military agenda of real-time functions, reliability, and interface to control functions.

**1945.** The Electronic Numerical Integrator and Calculator, or ENIAC, built by J. P. Eckert and John Mauchly at the University of Pennsylvania's Moore School of Engineering in Philadelphia, was not completed until after the war ended. ENIAC was not fully operational until 1946. Its first task was to create a mathematical model of the hydrogen bomb for the Los Alamos atomic weapons labs.[10]

**1948.** In June in the United Kingdom, the Manchester Mark 1 (or Manchester Baby) was the world's first functioning stored-program computer.

**1949.** The EDVAC, a project in which von Neumann was a key participant, was never completed, but it established the von Neumann architecture and was the first machine to incorporate an internal-stored program. Cambridge University's EDSAC, explicitly modeled on EDVAC in June 1949, preceded it into operation.

**1949.** BINAC, Eckert and Mauchly's successor to ENIAC, was commissioned by Northrop Aircraft to be used as a guidance computer for its Snark missile. Funding for the development of BINAC came from the US Air Force, channeled through Northrop. The first assembly language was the Short Code, devised in 1949 for BINAC, which didn't work well; Northrop quickly reverted to analog computers for the purpose.

**1950.** ATLAS, the second electronic stored-program computer in the United States, was produced by Engineering Research Associates (ERA) for the US Navy for cryptological work.

**1950.** MESM, the first universally programmable electronic computer in continental Europe, was built at Kiev Institute of Electrotechnology in the Soviet Union in 1948–1951; it ran its first program in 1950 (Fitzpatrick, Kazakova, and Berkovich 2006).

**1951.** Ferranti Limited (UK) built the first successful commercial computer, the Mark 1, and sold eight of them. The first Ferranti Mark 1 went into operation in February 1951, preceding UNIVAC by a few months.

**1951.** UNIVAC, produced by Remington Rand, was based on Eckert and Mauchly's military-funded work building ENIAC and BINAC. Much of the funding for it was channeled through the US Census Bureau (which purchased the first UNIVAC 1), but those funds were transferred to the department by the Army (Edwards 1997, 61).

**1952.** UNIVAC was loaned to CBS to predict the result of the Eisenhower presidential election, which it did to within 1 percent accuracy, using a 7 percent sample. To a large public, this was shocking "proof" of the arrival of the "intelligent" machine.

**1952.** John von Neumann's IAS machine, built at Princeton's Institute for Advanced Studies, was completed. Copies were quickly built at defense research installations, including the RAND Corporation and the Los Alamos, Oak Ridge, and Argonne national laboratories.

**1953.** The first true algebraic language was written for Whirlwind, but it was slow and specific to that machine.

**1953.** IBM's first production computer, the 701 (also known as the *defense calculator*) was developed at IBM's expense, but only after IBM had in hand letters of intent from eighteen Department of Defense customers (Edwards 1997, 61).

### Conclusion

We find the origins of digital computing, the Internet, and other characteristic technologies of contemporary computing during the Cold War in largely military contexts. It remains mysterious that so few media theorists and historians of technology have pursued basic questions of how and in what ways the computing technology we use today for a diversity of purposes is inflected by that history.

This chapter has focused on hardware and institutional developments. The development of artificial intelligence (the subject of the following chapters) ran parallel to the development of digital computing—and was recipient of substantial state largesse, as Edwards observes: "For over two decades almost exclusively a pure research area of no immediate commercial interest, [AI] received as much as 80 percent of its total funding from ARPA" (1997, 64). In 1962, John McCarthy left MIT to set up Stanford AI

Lab. Edwards notes, "Funding from ARPA was virtually automatic; Lick-lider simply asked McCarthy what he wanted and then gave it to him" (270). Between 1963 and 1970, ARPA funded MIT's Project MAC for about $25 million, supporting Minsky and his students (269–270). Some skeptics argue that the perceived progress of AI was not a result of better procedures but largely a matter of progress in computer engineering, with faster processors and increased storage capacity affording wider and deeper search functions. Today's *big data* processing—in which vast quantities of data are processed by relatively simple procedures—seems to bear this out.

Edwards has shown that the worldview of the US military in the Cold War and the worldview of computing research in the same period were inseparable and isomorphic. His research is invaluable in addressing three questions germane to the current enquiry: Why and when did the digital approach dominate the analog approach? To what extent is digital computation of military origin? What effect did these military origins have on later computer development? Several intertwined histories are pertinent here: the technical development of digital hardware; the interests driving its research agendas and funding; the theoretical drift and interplay of cybernetics and AI; the analog and the digital; and the embodied and the abstract. These issues are explored in further detail in forthcoming chapters.

# 5  The Rise of Artificial Intelligence

For me the notion of computation . . . is not a metaphor but part of a literal description of cognitive activity. This is not to say that there are not also metaphorical uses of computer concepts. But it seems to me that computation, and all that it entails regarding rule-governed transformations on intentionally interpreted symbolic expressions, applies just as literally to mental activity as it does to the activity of digital computers. Such a term is in no sense a literal description of the operation of electronic computers that has been metaphorically transported to the primary subject of mind.

—Zenon Pylyshyn, "Metaphorical Imprecision" (1979, 435)

## Cybernetics and AI: A Parting of the Ways

It would be inaccurate to portray cybernetics and AI as diametrically opposed, or to propose that AI supplanted cybernetics as a better solution to the same problems. Although there was some overlap, the stakes were different for the two fields. Cybernetics was interested in *systems*—often composed of heterogenous components—in an interdisciplinary and theoretical way that embraced, as we have seen, diverse fields from anthropology to neuroscience to mathematics. It was concerned with the interaction of an agent or artifact with its environment. Such agents were understood to sense and act in feedback loops, to adaptively stabilize their relation to the world, seeking homeostasis.

In the later 1960s, a new school of thought—which in key ways diverged from cybernetics—emerged. Symbolic AI rode on a different technological wave, that of transistor-based logic gates, and thus machines that dealt in representational tokens. The idea that in order to reason you must first construct an *abstract representation* of the object of interest is *fundamental* to digital computing. The very nature of computing is now assumed to necessarily involve symbols, models, and simulations. The software-hardware dualism (which reified the Cartesian dualism) emerged with, and is fundamental to, the digital but is absent from the analog. As a consequence, Zenon Pylyshyn or Herbert Simon could espouse a cognitivist-computationalist view of mind in a way that McCulloch or Ashby could never do.

AI was concerned specifically with the automation of intelligence, where *intelligence* was defined in terms of reasoning by mathematical logic. While cybernetics and computationalism are opposed on a number of axes, it would be historically inaccurate to suggest that they were always seen as such. Concepts we now find fundamental to digital computing (such as "software") evolved over the postwar decades, before the two paradigms diverged.

The first true stored-program computer, the Manchester Baby, was contemporaneous with the Macy Foundation meetings. By the time of the Dartmouth Conference of 1956 in which John McCarthy proposed the name *artificial intelligence* (see chapter 3), the fundamentals of digital computing technology were established. Brain modeling and symbolic processing continued to cohabit into the 1970s, as did analog and digital computing. Historical events are seldom as simple as schoolbook chronologies would have us believe. The Dartmouth attendees certainly had their differences, just as Macy and Dartmouth had commonalities. Many figures significant in the history of digital computing took part in the Macy Foundation meetings that established cybernetics.

The transition from analog to digital machinery had its parallels in cognitive theory. The orientation of cybernetics was consistent with the analog computer, with its direct interface with the world on the battlefield and elsewhere. Indeed, it might be said that they produced each other. If the digital computers were "giant brains," then the academic discipline that complemented them was artificial intelligence. If cybernetics modeled brains in bodies, AI modeled disembodied minds. The digital machines, whose relation to the world was symbolic, spoke of an autonomous power of mentation.

As the culture of digital computing grew, new qualities of emerging digital computing paradigms and discourse marginalized cybernetic approaches. There was an increasing commitment to the concept of intelligence as reasoning as opposed to intelligence as adaptation: "They managed . . . to wipe out interest in analog and neural models as far as engineering computing kinds of things and they essentially wiped out interest in similarities that cut across both biological and technical systems" (Whitaker 2011).[1] A clear distinction between information and matter was not axiomatic to the cybernetic paradigm. As digital dualism took hold, thinking by machine became a matter of the interaction of symbols, algorithms, and data storage. An increasing commitment to the software-hardware dualism made the idea of the integration of intelligence within (biological) matter itself problematic.

## Behaviorism and Functionalism

Cybernetics was informed by behaviorism, and this resulted in its externalist focus on the (measurable) interactions between entities, considered "black boxes." Behaviorism had declared that the operations of mind/brain were off-limits, as they were not accessible to experimental testing, so doctrinally behaviorism attended only to the inputs and outputs of black boxes—at their interfaces. The black box idea linked behaviorism with systems theory. This became a core analytic tool for cybernetics.

Hilary Putnam proposed that processes of mind (construed as reasoning) could be modeled as the manipulation of logical symbols by logical rules, or algorithms. He suggested that via this method, which he called functionalism (in 1967, and which he has since recanted), the mind might be studied as a cognitive system, without reference to (neuro)physiology. This became a central idea for AI, in the same way systems theory was for cybernetics.

Putnam's work provided AI with a philosophical basis for a scientific approach to simulating intelligence in computers. It claimed a principled way to bypass the radical externalism of behaviorism, and permitted looking into the (black) box, restoring scientific status to human mental life, and reestablishing introspection as an acceptable methodology (for better or worse). In cognitive psychology, functionalism provided a principled way to discuss internal mental states, an approach to studying the mind which permitted a principled bypassing of the constraints of behaviorism.

As a cultural imaginary, more so than in its technical development, AI was invested with a conception of intelligence as a closed and abstract capacity for logical symbol manipulation, and this conception influenced the parallel development of cognitive science, which purported to explain human intelligence in just such computational terms. Functionalism found application in various other disciplines. As mind and language are inseparable, these ideas were also adopted in an emerging school of linguistics, proposing that any grammar can be understood in terms of rules that manipulate otherwise meaningless formal symbols. As such, functionalism influenced the formation of generative linguistics. As AI developed, tasks of construction and interpretation of "natural language" became a central preoccupation, and generative linguistics was naturally compatible.

Like Descartes's dualism, functionalism was an a priori philosophical position not based on scientific evidence. Inherent in it are several problematic assumptions: that thinking is reasoning; that all reasoning can be described in terms of symbolic logic; that sensing, thinking, and action are separate and separable operations; that thinking happens in an enclosed space of computation isolated from the world; and that such symbolic operations in principle could be implemented on various substrates (i.e., organic or silicon).

The move to symbol manipulation retreated from engagement in the world. This resulted in a postponement of engagement with the real world, which sowed the seeds for the downfall of GOFAI (Good Old-Fashioned Artificial Intelligence) in the 1980s. As we shall see in the next chapter, by the late 1980s, the reactive robotics community and others said, "Enough postponing; interaction with the real world is the hard problem."

**Thinking as Reasoning on Symbols**

Thinking was understood as the manipulation of symbolic tokens in some abstract logical space—as opposed, for instance, to an ongoing engagement with the material world. The von Neumann architecture separates perception from cogitation and presumes that perception is a simple process of data gathering and translation, at which point the "difficult" task of reasoning takes over. (This is a dubious assumption.)

According to this approach, sensing is performed by "peripherals," which were conceived of as interchangeable (like attachments for a vacuum cleaner) and played no part in "cognition." Researchers expressed the opinion that limitations in sensing technologies were therefore not immediately crucial and that issues concerning sensing and perception could be pushed off into the future. This dovetailed neatly with the fact that many such problems, such as machine vision, presumed or depended upon technologies that were yet only partially developed. In this discursive context, it was reasonable to accept that shortcomings of these technologies were temporary. Certainly, sensing and interface technologies were poorly developed at the time. But this is circular. According a secondary role to sensing permitted research to be postponed. The combination of technical shortcomings and theoretical justifications obscured the possibility that the process of perception, in the sense of making salient qualities from the world available to cognition (in the sense of reasoning), may be intelligent activity in itself.

The development of capacity for logical symbol manipulation in computational contexts had the consequence of undervaluing the importance of processes of sensing and discerning meaning from the barrage of stimuli that press in upon the organism at every moment. Rather than residing in some darkened and isolated chamber in the brain, intelligence can be argued to reside precisely at the periphery of the organism, at the membrane, the interface to the world. Such an idea is literally unthinkable within the terms of cognitivist AI. As the discipline developed, a nagging suspicion arose that interface technologies were not as peripheral as their technical nomenclature suggested and inhered nontrivial problems beyond analog-digital conversion (see chapter 6).

Before delving more deeply into the methods and approaches that characterized the AI/cognitivist position of the time, it is necessary to recap some technophilosophical milestones that laid the groundwork for the formation of AI. These include Turing's universal machine, Shannon's communication theory, and Newell and Simon's physical symbol system hypothesis.

## The *Entscheidungsproblem* and the Universal Engine

Babbage, Lovelace, Leibniz, Boole, and Jacquard usually figure prominently in the history of digital computing, but it is generally accepted that theoretical origins of modern digital computing lie with the work of mathematician Alan Turing. When Turing began at Princeton in 1936, fundamental assumptions about the coherence of mathematics were at stake. It was five years since Kurt Gödel had, by his incompleteness theorem, resoundingly upset the grand unified theory of mathematics that Whitehead and Russell's *Principia Mathematica* (1910) aspired to.

The idea of mathematical coherence depends upon three qualities: completeness, consistency, and decidability. *Completeness* means that every mathematical statement is either provable or disprovable. *Consistency* means that it is impossible to arrive at two contradictory mathematical statements. *Decidability* implies that the truth of any mathematical assertion could be ascertained by a mechanical method—an algorithm or a "formal machine." Gödel addressed the first two qualities, demonstrating that all mathematical systems are incomplete and that they cannot be proven consistent. Turing's addressed the third quality, specifically taking on the challenge posed in 1928 by David Hilbert's *Entscheidungsproblem* (decision problem), now commonly referred to as the *halting problem*; it asks whether it is possible to determine in advance if any particular problem properly posed within a coherent mathematical system is solvable. In essence, the halting problem sets the task of determining if a particular calculation will "halt" or will continue indefinitely. In 1936, Alonzo Church (known for the lambda calculus) and Turing disproved the third point, showing that some mathematical problems are not susceptible to algorithmic solution. In "On Computable Numbers with an Application to the *Entscheidungsproblem*" (1936), Turing showed that a general solution to the Entscheidungsproblem is impossible. Church's approach formalized the idea of an algorithm. Turing's proof included a mathematical definition of a serial processing computer and program, which he called a *universal engine* (now commonly referred to as a *Turing machine*). Certain kinds of problems are incomputable (or *undecidable*) by a Turing machine.

Turing's universal engine was an imaginary machine with a paper tape of infinite length and a read/write head. The tape was divided into a row of squares in which a mark was present or absent (a binary code). The machine's operations were limited to moving the tape forward or backward one step, "reading" the tape, changing the value in a square, and stopping. With these limited functions, Turing showed the machine could be configured to enact any rule-based symbolic operation. Along with its binary logic and reading and writing functions, the universal engine utilized the concepts of a "program" (which Turing called *configurations*) and "memory" (the tape). Quite unintentionally, by contriving an imaginary machine for the purpose of making a mathematical proof, Turing invented the basic architecture of digital computing. The Turing machine provided the theoretical model upon which the von Neumann architecture was based. The von Neumann machine specifies a design of components and procedures for a serial processing machine and provides the basic plan for all commercial central processing units (CPUs).

The Turing machine is an abstract and theoretical machine, built upon analogies to technologies of the time. The logic of the machine may remind us of the magnetic tape recorder, with a read head and a write head and a tape upon which data and operating instructions (programs) are stored, read, and written. But at the time, magnetic tape recorders were a few years in the future (though wire recorders were in use). The general notion of keys marking a tape that could also be read was present in various automatic telegraph devices, particularly the stock ticker, and this is probably the analogy Turing was working with. The idea of a universal machine may also have its sources in the phonograph or gramophone. The late nineteenth century saw the flourishing of application-specific music machines—from the calliope and the pianola to Russolo's Intonarumori. These were all made redundant by the phonograph, a universal machine in the universe of music, musical sound, and musical instruments.

Turing's universal engine introduced the notion of generality to what would become, a generation later, computer science. As such, it sounded a death knell for all manner of differential analyzers, analog computers, and other parsimonious purpose-built mechanical calculating engines, just as surely as the jukebox sounded the death-knell for all the diversity of calliopes, nickelodeons, and other musical machines.[2] In the computer, as in the phonograph, generality is raised to a more encompassing register.

The origin of the modern digital computer in the Entscheidungsproblem reveals its origins in mathematical logic. To be amenable to decidability, problems must first be posed in, and posable in, mathematical language, with the desired result being yes or no (neither, maybe, and sometimes are not allowable). Clearly, beyond the idea of undecidability within mathematical terms, there exist situations that are inherently *incomputable*, in the sense that they cannot be put into a form amenable to computation according to Boolean logical procedures.

This might be because they cannot be posed in a mathematical language in the first place, they are not the kinds of questions for which a yes/no answer is meaningful, or they are complex arrays of multiple intersecting questions, or they are not questions at all. This relationship of computing to human culture more generally is reminiscent of the place of Newtonian physics with respect to nonlinear dynamics: Newtonian physics is explanatory for a small percentage of all physical situations in the universe and is useful only in highly controlled situations in which uncharacterizable or unpredictable variables are filtered out. Understanding the specificity of the Boolean logic of digital computing is important because the popular rhetoric of computing is that it is universal and applicable to all contexts. Problems arise when the mathematical notion of generality is applied in the sociocultural field. One result is that it is deemed acceptable to computationally operationalize those parts of a situation that *are* amenable to computation, and to omit those aspects that are not. The computational mindset thus obscures dimensions of, say, embodied activities, precisely because they are not amenable to algorithmic conceptualization. (This idea is developed below.) Regrettably—and this bears directly on the argument of this book—those aspects thereby rendered invisible are often central components of a practice (discussed in chapter 18). This is important in the contemporary cultural context, in which "computing" has metamorphosed from mathematical calculation of already quantified (i.e., engineering or financial) data to embrace all manner of cultural practices, aspects of which may be inherently incomputable.

### The Imitation Game

In his famous 1950 paper "Computing Machinery and Intelligence," Turing proposed a (very anthropomorphic) test for machine intelligence, based on a parlor game in which a man and a woman are separately secluded and a player exchanges written notes with them to determine which one is the woman. (It doesn't sound particularly exciting, especially for the audience.)[3] Turing proposed to replace one subject with a computer and ask the player to determine who was the human. If the player could not distinguish between human and machine, then the machine was intelligent. The test is played through the narrow bandwidth channel of teletype (raw text), so any and all qualities of embodied being—tone of voice, stature, odor, and so on—are absent. Here then is a defining moment in artificial intelligence: *intelligence* is defined in entirely disembodied terms of formal manipulation of symbols, and integration with the world is disregarded. It is precisely this rejection of embodiment and context that came to haunt, and ultimately defeat, AI fifty years later.

### A Mathematical Theory of Communication

The term *telecommunication,* invented by a French engineer at the beginning of the century, was institutionalized at the 1932 inaugural meeting of the International Telecommunications Union (ITU), formerly the International Telegraph Union. Telegraph was the first electric communication, and Morse's code of dots and dashes was binary, a precursor of Turing's notation. Consistent with the mathematization and electrification of the sciences occurring at the time, "information" began to take on a quantitative, technical meaning as "a unit of measure in a statistical theory of signals" (Mattelart 2000, 39).

In 1937, as a master's degree candidate at MIT, Claude Shannon proved that arrangements of electromechanical relays could perform Boolean algebraic operations, thus laying the technical basis for digital computing. (His PhD thesis of 1942 developed an algebra for genetics.) During World War II, he worked in cryptanalysis, and in that context he met Alan Turing. Out of this cryptographical experience came his major work of 1948, "A Mathematical Theory of Communication," in which he formalized his quantified information theory.[4] In this paper, the term *bit* is used in its modern sense as a contraction of "binary digit" (Shannon attributed the coinage to John W. Tukey). Shannon was explicit that the theory was concerned only with communication in the most mechanical sense of the relation between data sent and data received, and involved the statistical quantification of information, redundancy, and noise, deploying the notion of entropy from thermodynamics. "The fundamental problem of communication is that of reproducing at one point either exactly or approximately a message selected at another point," he explains. "Frequently the messages have meaning; that is they refer to or are correlated according to some system with certain physical or conceptual entities. *These semantic aspects of communication are irrelevant to the engineering problem.* The significant aspect is that they are selected from a set of possible messages" (Shannon 1949, 31–32; emphasis mine). This quotation indicates that Shannon quite clearly recognized that a theory of transmission of data does not constitute a theory of communication in a cultural sense of *transmission of meaning*, but sadly, numerous subsequent technocultural commentators seem to be unaware of this.

## Logic Theorist

The work of Alan Newell and Herbert Simon is fundamental to the history of AI. The program Logic Theorist, created at the RAND Corporation from 1955 to 1956 by Newell, Simon, and Charles Shaw, is regarded as the first artificial intelligence program, written before the field was named. Newell worked for RAND in logistics and organization, Simon was a political scientist, and Shaw was a RAND programmer. By 1956, Logic Theorist had found a more elegant proof of theorem 2.85 of the *Principia Mathematica* than any produced by human mathematicians, including Russell and Whitehead. Logic Theorist eventually proved thirty-eight of the fifty-two theorems in the *Principia*. This remarkable achievement, coming on the heels of UNIVAC's prediction of the outcome of the 1952 presidential election, propelled the dream of artificial intelligence. But more specifically, the successes of Logic Theorist gave credence to a notion that intelligence, generally, was a logical process of symbol manipulation.

The group followed up Logic Theorist with the General Problem Solver (1959), which was designed to solve any formalized problem in mathematical logic. The work of Newell, Simon, and Shaw rapidly raised to axiomatic status the idea that intelligence was indeed logical symbol manipulation, and could be successfully modeled or emulated by a computer. Newell and Simon were no doubt (justifiably) proud, but, giddy with success, they made some grandiose pronouncements. "There are now in the world machines that think, that learn and create," they declared. "Moreover, their ability to do these things is going to increase rapidly until—in the visible future—the range of problems that they can handle will be coextensive with the range to which the human mind has been applied" (quoted in Weizenbaum 1976, 138). Such assertions became typical in the field. In hindsight, they do seem to have been overreaching a tad.

Logic Theorist showed that automated logic systems could generate solutions previously only achieved by reasoning human minds. In an early refutation of cybernetic strategies of modeling biology, Newell, Shaw, and Simon asserted that such automated reasoning systems were not intended to model biological processes: "Our theory is a theory of information processes involved in problem solving, and not a theory of neural or electronic mechanisms for information processing" (1958, 163). This statement establishes that Newell, Shaw, and Simon subscribed to the philosophical ideas of functionalism (Putnam). Such pronouncements (like that of Pylyshyn at the start of this chapter) became standard fare in AI discourse. Functionalism allowed the divorcing of abstract cognitive processes from a specific physical substrate. If physical contexts didn't matter, then it could be claimed that brains do what computers do and vice versa. While Putnam later recanted functionalism, the idea persists in popular culture and underlies most claims for the viability or inevitability of artificial intelligence. As we shall see, this argument is inherently circular.

## Dartmouth: Intelligence Is Symbol Manipulation

In 1955, computer science as a discipline did not yet exist. Many members of the early AI community came to the field from psychology, others from mathematics and other fields. In 1955, McCarthy, Minsky, and others proposed that a "2 month, 10 man study of artificial intelligence be carried out during the summer of 1956 at Dartmouth College in Hanover, New Hampshire" (McCarthy et al. 2006, 12). They proposed the following:

The study is to proceed on the basis of the conjecture that *every aspect of learning or any other feature of intelligence can in principle be so precisely described that a machine can be made to simulate it.* An attempt will be made to find how to make machines use language, form abstractions and concepts, solve kinds of problems now reserved for humans, and improve themselves. We think that a significant advance can be made in one or more of these problems if a carefully selected group of scientists work on it together for a summer. (McCarthy et al. 2006, 12; emphasis mine)

This early and clear statement of the goals of the field is also an early example of what we might generously call its optimism. The assertion that "every aspect of learning or any other feature of intelligence can in principle be so precisely described that a machine can be made to simulate it," combined with the idea that a few scientists could knock out a goodly part of it over in a single summer, is indicative of the hubristic claims that would be characteristic of AI for the next thirty years.

The Dartmouth proposal included seven projects, including one project on "neuronal nets" (*sic*) revealing that no clear division existed between cybernetics and AI at the time. The seventh project was on Randomness and Creativity: "A fairly attractive and yet clearly incomplete conjecture is that the difference between creative thinking and unimaginative competent thinking lies in the injection of a [*sic*] some randomness. The randomness must be guided by intuition to be efficient. In other words, the educated guess or the hunch include [*sic*] controlled randomness in otherwise orderly thinking" (14). The notion that creativity amounts to randomness guided by intuition is so simplistic as to be laughable, as is the emphasis on efficiency. This trivialization of the nonrational, the commitment to a program of pragmatic technical innovation, and the absence of seriously reflexive critical analysis would characterize AI, to its detriment, for the next quarter of a century, as later explicated by insiders such as David Kirsh, Philip Agre, and Rodney Brooks. AI prided itself on formal coherence, but questions about what concepts like creativity, intuition, and efficiency entail are seldom deeply pursued. Indeed, key terms of art such as *representation, plan, symbol*, and *concept* remained uninterrogated.[5] Agre has argued that an emphasis on pragmatic technical innovation prevented the nascent discipline from interrogating its own structuring assumptions.

## Digital Computation Reifies Dualism

The preoccupation with abstraction and rejection of material considerations led to the formalization of the software-hardware dualism, reifying the *res cogitans–res extensa* (mind-body) dualism of Cartesianism. This is like saying that riding a bicycle is interesting, but the bike itself is irrelevant to the discussion. The rhetorical separation of hardware and software proposes that information can exist without physical instantiation. This is axiomatic in computer science. It should be noted that, at the time, all programs were custom, platform-specific, and handcrafted for particular machines. Software as a standalone information artifact was not reified as a commodity until well into the 1980s.[6] The first US patent for software was granted in 1981.[7] Even now, the notion of *platform independence* is rhetorical, a value that can only be approximated.

The development of *high-level programming languages* allowed the full extrapolation of symbol manipulation and in the process established paradigmatically the software-hardware dualism. John McCarthy wrote LISP (for *list processing*), a programming language that became the lingua franca of AI. In 1958, he and Marvin Minsky established the AI Group at MIT. At the same time (January 1959), McCarthy proposed the idea of *time-sharing*. His immediate motivation was to create a computational environment in which his programming language LISP could be more fully exploited.[8] By 1962 he'd developed a display-based time-sharing system.

The idea that people can or must have separate thinking and doing parts is part of the philosophical legacy of the Enlightenment.[9] The rise of digital computation and the software-hardware dualism over the second half of the twentieth century had the odd effect of reinforcing this notion, during a century in which its philosophical and psychological validity had been largely rejected. In digital discourse, the *res cogitans*, the "thinking thing," is digital, the world is analog, and acts of perception and action constitute a translation from analog to digital and back again. Artificial intelligence, leveraging functionalism, made the astonishing claim that thinking could be implemented in machines that manipulate symbols. If this was the case, then, ipso facto, the brain is a computer. This is a circular and mutually reinforcing argument: Machines think and brains compute, and the currency in which these exchanges occur is symbols, manipulated by logical rules. This generated the complementary double of artificial intelligence and cognitive science (or at least that variant sometimes referred to as *computationalism* or *cognitivism*).

## Logical Games

As an intellectual pastime, the manipulation of symbolic tokens according to logical rules has preoccupied great minds for centuries. The system of logical rules operationalized in modern computing was devised by George Boole, who died nearly a century before the first digital computers. Boole, the son of a shoemaker, with only primary school education, developed this logical system in the 1840s and 1850s.

In Western culture, a legacy of the Enlightenment and Rationalism is the idea that reasoning is the pinnacle of what it is to be human: *Cogito ergo sum*. As such, an appropriate test of intelligence in a machine would be an activity that has been considered a pinnacle of human intellectual achievement, such as playing chess. Thus, when machines beat human chess masters, they must be intelligent. There is a circularity in this "proof" that in retrospect is laughable. Build a machine that excels at performing logical operations in a closed logical domain, then assign it a task that has these characteristics. It's like asking why chocolate is chocolaty. There is no evidence that human intelligence or biological thought operates according to such systems of logical rules—even when playing chess, let alone when discerning degrees of chocolatiness.

## Generality and Culture

A fundamental commitment of computer science is the idea of the *general-purpose machine*. From the outset, generality was taken to be desirable, for reasons that are unassailable in formal terms. The principle of Turing universality is axiomatic to computer science. The computer is a technology designed to be capable of being something else, on its power of emulation. In a sense, every program passes the Turing test. "A universal machine can be *programmed* to compute any formally specified function," Pylyshyn noted. "This extreme plasticity in behavior is one of the reasons why computers have from the very beginning been viewed as artifacts that might be capable of exhibiting intelligence" (1989, 54; emphasis in original).

The virtue of generality—basic to the concept of the digital computer—was reinforced by the General Problem Solver of Newell, Simon, and Shaw. A problematic shift occurred in two parts, related to the economic principles of the computer industry and the rapid uptake of the computer in diverse sociocultural contexts far from the original applications of the machine. The first stage was the transfer of the notion of general purpose from the realm of mathematical theory to the beige-colored box and its big vacuum tube appendage. The idea of generality, entirely valid in formal mathematical terms, became identified with a physical commodity. This was convenient for the computer industry, as it seemed to justify the profitable mass production associated with consumer commodity economics.

The unquestioned axiomatic acceptance of the concept of generality as being a virtue in computational practice demands interrogation, especially when that axiomatic assumption is unquestioningly applied in realms in which it may not be relevant. Indeed, the fact that the question of its relevance is not asked indicates a problem that must be addressed. The notion of the general-purpose machine is, as I hope I have indicated, an ideological construct. As Agre reveals, all manner of finesse and compensation is undertaken in order to keep the illusion complete. While generality is taken as a virtue in computer theory, it also dovetails neatly with the idea of economies of scale. Contrarily, there are equally good arguments for specificity—a tool for every job and a job for every tool. Such tools are not required to carry the heavy weight of generality. They possess what we might call *machine parsimony*—a condition that doesn't aspire to universality and achieves specific goals with sustainable elegance.

## A Physical Symbol System: How the Brain Became a Computer

The physical symbol system hypothesis of Newell and Simon is the most general expression of the guiding principle of AI: "A physical symbol system has the necessary and sufficient means for general intelligent action" (1976, 116). It is this general assertion that intelligence consists of the manipulation of symbols that set AI on its quintessentially representationalist path (a path that began to be rather unclear by the mid-1980s). *Representationalism* (Jerry Fodor's "language of thought") is another key assumption of AI, integral to the separation of the mental from the physical. Representationalism assumes that thinking occurs on representations in the mind of aspects of the world in the form of symbolic tokens. Newell and Simon explained the idea of a physical symbol system in this way:

A physical symbol system consists of a set of entities, called symbols, which are physical patterns that can occur as components of another type of entity called an expression (or symbol structure). Thus, a symbol structure is composed of a number of instances (or tokens) of symbols related in some physical way (such as one token being next to another). At any instant of time the system will contain a collection of these symbol structures. Besides these structures, the system also contains a collection of processes that operate on expressions to produce other expressions: processes of creation, modification, reproduction, and destruction. A physical symbol system is a machine that produces through time an evolving collection of symbol structures. Such a system exists in a world of objects wider than just these symbolic expressions themselves. (1976, 116)

Artificial intelligence thus grew around the proposition that human intelligence could be modeled on computers as reasoning with symbolic logic. Cognitive science is premised on the idea that the functions of mind can be adequately described as algorithmic symbolic logical operations. Cognitivism or computationalism thus emerged as a variant of functionalism. AI and cognitive science are complementary interpretations of functionalism. So it was that the brain became a computer, and thinking became logical reasoning. Referring to the human cognitive architecture, Newell, Rosenbloom, and Laird noted, "The central function of the architecture is to support a system capable of universal computation" (1989, 103). The mechanism implicit in such statements may seem outlandish to us, and we might reasonably be surprised that such a paradigm garnered so much rhetorical and economic power.

## Maps, Plans, and Representations

First-generation AI assumed cognitivism: the idea that intelligence or thinking or reasoning can be adequately and more or less completely described as operations on symbolic tokens in some abstract, quasi-mathematical reasoning space. In turn, cognitivism assumes representationalism: the idea that (all) intelligent action consists of operations on mental representations and that the results of such cogitation are used to instruct mechanical bodily processes. Such a paradigm excludes the possibility of intelligent action directly upon or with respect to things in the world. As we will see, this shortcoming was to present insurmountable challenges to (good old-fashioned) AI, but in the early decades such issues did not seem so critical. Assuming representationalism, the next question should be: What forms do those representations take?

If intelligence is problem solving, if problems are posed as symbolic expressions and symbols are derived from the world, then implicit in the construction of those symbols is the problem of *representation*. Any synthetic system of knowledge representation, like a taxonomy, assumes not only identities but also relationships, including hierarchies and frames of reference and logics that operate on these structures. In AI, such systems of representation are called *ontologies*. This use of *ontology* and *representation*, like the term *artificial intelligence* itself, captures a characteristic of the culture of AI, in which complex and highly nuanced concepts are presumed amenable to reduction to simple serial procedures and are thus oversimplified: *knowledge engineering* is a more recent case.

*Plans and the Structure of Behavior* by Miller, Galanter, and Pribam (1960) quickly became one of the root documents of AI. That action in the world proceeds on the basis of a plan (a spatiotemporal representation) is a logical outcome of extrapolating the problem solving approach forward in time. The notion of planning became axiomatic and segued neatly with cognitivism on the one hand and the von Neumann architecture on the other. In robotics, this led to the Sense Map Plan Act (SMPA) paradigm (sometimes Sense Model Plan Act). According to this paradigm, a device or a creature would first *sense* its world, then combine data derived from that sensing to construct an internal map, then reason a plan or a path on that map, then output the result to end effectors, and only then re-sense to correlate world data with a presumed location on the internal map.

In practice, the SMPA strategy had several problematic aspects. The first was that to extract useful and accurate data about the world was a challenge in itself, so data from different sensors was often combined, but this "sensor fusion" had its own problems, adding layers of computation just to correlate the data from different sensors. All this culminated in the construction of a "map," but such a map was a representational problem in itself and was computationally expensive. Then came the problem of errors between an imagined position on this map and sensed position in the world. Every step required complex adjudication. The end result was that a robot like Shakey (see chapter 6), drawing on the power of a giant mainframe computer and the efforts of numerous programmers, managed to cross a room in seven hours.

## Conclusion

Classical AI was framed by the idea that thinking = reasoning = symbol processing. On the basis of this, key concepts such as *information* and *software* were formalized in AI and computer science in general. This process rendered qualitative and philosophical ideas amenable to automated calculation. In this sense, the mission of AI was to "engineer" concepts and practices that until that time had been native to humanistic disciplines. Such operationalization of increasingly diverse realms of human practice is a characteristic practice in AI and in computer science more generally. As such, Agre asserts that AI is an imperializing discipline that attempts to reformulate other practices in its own terms. (This idea is discussed in detail in the context of Edwin Hutchins's *Cognition in the Wild*; see part II.) Within AI, this permitted a complex and seldom-acknowledged epistemological two-step, in which claims were made that logical routines captured the essential mechanisms of intelligence, mind, and culture.

In our contemporary technocultural context, we often encounter confusion between the technical and cultural meanings of key terms in common parlance. Words like *intelligence, communication, information, knowledge, representation, memory,* and *sensing* now hover in an ontological limbo between quantity and quality. This is a result of the quantification and rationalization by which these ideas are, as Agre notes, "hollowed through the false precision of formalism" (1997b, 148).

As such, this "industrialization of intelligence"—to use Noah Kennedy's term (1990)—is part of the larger trend of mathematization and quantification of both human knowledge and human labor, of which the graphical

Instruments of the nineteenth century were a part, as were the industrial techniques of Taylorism and Fordism. But in AI, the process folds back reflexively upon itself, taking aim at the very mechanisms of the human intelligence that conducted the work in previous generations. And—in a way that is most germane to our current concerns—the most chimerical grail of the enterprise was, and remains, creativity.

At this point, the reader might pause to consider the deeper motivations for such an enterprise. An ostensible, if disingenuous, rationale for mechanization was the reduction of tedious manual labor—hence labor-saving devices. Labor was saved, ostensibly, to liberate people from their drudgery that they might pursue more fulfilling (intellectual and cultural) activities. However, when the mechanization is aimed at those activities themselves, one must begin to wonder. A side effect, or perhaps a cause, of labor saving is a general assumption that the less physical an activity is, the more its inherent value (however we now know that *embodied* intelligent activity is the best defense against Alzheimer's). To group skilled bodily practices such as playing a musical instrument with grunt labor such as breaking rocks in a prison yard is so simplistic as to suggest an ulterior motive.

It is no surprise that in the context of such work, notions of transhumanism and extropianism emerge. These sentiments, popular among the cyberpunk community of the 1990s, asserted that humans were destined to become increasingly cyborgian and the role of humans, in a kind of sci-fi, techno-Darwinist scenario, was to build the intelligent technologies that would be the evolutionary successors to biological humans. Kurzweil and others of that ilk refer to the moment this (theoretically) occurs somewhat melodramatically as *singularity*. A deep self-loathing seems inherent in such an idea, a loathing based on the false Cartesian dualism, which underpinned the entire enterprise from the outset.

This simplistic Cartesianism produces a desire to extract and valorize the symbolic aspects of practices (the aspects amenable to cognitivist theory). Such a process renders material instantiation and embodied enaction incomprehensible. A few decades into the information revolution, the academically accepted definition of *intelligence* is a cognitivist conception of the logical manipulation of abstract symbols. This encourages the denigration of bodily practices and the concomitant construction of a theory of intelligence that leaves no room for, and has no explanatory capability for, embodied practices. Ironically, practices that human culture has regarded as pinnacles of intellectual achievement for centuries remain inexplicable by cognitivist theory. (In the academy, as in virtual reality, we check our bodies at the door.) This scenario is of central importance in this book.

A new paradigm that encompasses the embodied, enactive, and spatially, socially, and culturally situated nature of human intelligence is called for, one that acknowledges that the entirety of human intellectual worth is not capturable within the terms of a theory where intelligence is a serial process of mathematical manipulation of symbolic tokens. Thankfully, such a paradigm is emerging.

# 6 Gravity Drowned: The Collapse of Computationalism

It is astonishing what havoc is wrought in psychology by admitting at the outset apparently innocent suppositions, that nevertheless contain a flaw. The bad consequences develop themselves later on, and are irremediable, being woven through the whole texture of the work.

—William James, *The Principles of Psychology* (1950, 224)

In this epigraph, William James sounds a warning regarding uninterrogated assumptions that has universal applicability. In the ensuing century of studies of mind, no field has been so guilty of such assumptions as artificial intelligence, which built an edifice of formalisms and justifications around the basic tenets of computationalism, fencing the discipline in. Such a framing prevented recognition of fundamental problems-in-principle. This, at least, was the assessment of Theodor Roszak, Hubert Dreyfus, John Haugeland, Philip Agre, and other well-informed critics.

This chapter addresses several of the philosophical debates that emerged as a result, largely of external critiques of AI, mostly in the 1980s. This resulted in the general recognition by the early 1990s that the AI paradigm, its rhetoric, and its methodologies had led the field into a cul-de-sac from which there was no exit without major reconfiguration. The previous chapter summarized the emergence of first-generation artificial intelligence; this chapter focuses on critiques of the program.

In *The Mangle of Practice: Time, Agency, and Science* (1995), Andrew Pickering notes that the practices of a field and the rhetoric around it could be quite different. AI is a case in point. On the one hand, AI aspired, at least officially, to the metascientific goal of creating artificial sentience. This dystopic theme runs through Western industrial culture from Mary Shelley and the golem through *Metropolis* (1927) and *Blade Runner* (1982), to name just a few. On the other hand, as a practice of technical toolmaking, its values were staunchly pragmatic.

The spectacular rhetoric of intelligent machines was often little more than promotional rhetoric for a technical agenda of developing automated mathematical reasoning. AI automated already existing mathematical and logical procedures and built upon them. The question of whether such procedures constituted intelligence was implicitly answered within an Enlightenment context of reason. For if mathematical logic was (self-evidently) the pinnacle of human intelligence, then a machine that could reason was intelligent. Further forays into philosophy were not required. If AI had restrained itself to claiming simply the automation of mathematical reasoning, it would have stayed out of philosophical hot water.

If the rhetorical claims were often little but PR, they certainly did their job.[1] The achievements of AI, such as the ability of Deep Blue to play grand master–level chess, reinforced rhetorical claims for human-like intelligence. Deep Blue beat chess grand master Gary Kasparov in a widely publicized event that had rhetorical power similar to that of the prediction of the Eisenhower presidential election by UNIVAC. The fact that Deep Blue achieved this by processes utterly unlike human intelligence should provoke some analysis of the deeper claims, as should the fact that the techniques used were the work of hundreds of human AI researchers.

Another critique of AI rhetoric (mostly argued by computer engineers) is that the only reason first-generation AI (roughly 1960–1990) "advanced" was because of advances in hardware engineering. Faster processors and more RAM permitted larger-scale brute-force searches. The absence of major breakthroughs in formal procedures or basic techniques of AI in the same period seems to support this argument. The computer upon which Deep Blue's chess program ran in 1997 was ten million times faster than the Ferranti Mark 1 upon which Dietrich Prinz's chess program ran in 1951, a statistic that adds force to this critique.

## Dissident Voices

A preoccupation with technical problem solving meant philosophical questions were seldom asked, and if they were, as often as not they were regarded as a distraction from the hard technical work that had to be done. The staunch pragmatism of the field worked against reflexive questioning. As a result, it generally had little capacity to distinguish between a technical problem (a bug) and a problem *in principle*. There is something endearingly American in this combination of plain-dealing puritanism and tough frontier pragmatism. The AI community was also overwhelmingly white and male—an aspect of this culture that has not gone unnoticed by feminist theorists (Adam 1998). Such questions might have included the following:

- Is thinking reasoning?
- Is reasoning dependent on symbolic representation?
- Is the kind of logic employed by Boole anything like the processes of the mind-brain?
- Is reason the pinnacle of intelligence?
- Are reason and emotion opposed?
- Is thinking (exclusively) in the head?
- Is perception simply a dumb front-end for symbol manipulation?

The AI paradigm was challenged politically and philosophically, ranging from questions regarding the connection of abstract facts to selfhood and the real world, to questions of human exceptionalism. Philosophers rankled, among them John Searle, Hubert Dreyfus, Stevan Harnad, and John Haugeland. Thoughtful insiders—such as Joseph Weizenbaum, Terry Winograd and Fernando Flores, Lucy Suchman, Rodney Brooks, and Philip Agre—offered critiques as well. Weizenbaum, who wrote the first software agent, Eliza, published *Computer Power and Human Reason: From Judgment to Calculation* in 1976. It is perhaps the first thoroughgoing philosophical reflection on computers and human culture by a computer science insider, and it contains chapters with provocative titles, such as "Against the Imperialism of Instrumental Reason." Arguments of this kind were usually reviled or more often simply ignored by the AI community, which, amid perceived rapid progress and massive funding was in no mood for critical reflection (the so-called AI winter notwithstanding). Another early dissenting voice was Theodore Roszak, who in 1986 pointedly stated, "Embodied in the machine there is an idea of what the mind is and how it works. *The idea is there because scientists who purport to understand cognition and intelligence put it there.* No other teaching tool has ever brought intellectual baggage of so consequential a kind to it" (217; emphasis mine). This theme of critique later was elaborated by Edwards, Agre, and others.

As we have seen in chapter 4, in *The Closed World: Computers and the Politics of Discourse in Cold War America*, Edwards revealed the tight integration of AI with Cold War military agendas and the related preoccupation with panoptical control and the informational omnipotence of what was known colloquially as the *God's-eye view* (Haraway). New approaches to HCI from Suchman (1987) and Winograd and Flores (1986) went beyond the technocentrism of the man-machine interaction of the SAGE era and engaged the social sciences and humanities.[2] Les Levidow more pointedly referred to the "paranoid rationality" of late twentieth-century military intelligence (see chapter 4).

There were questions in philosophy of mind regarding intentionality and from phenomenology on the matters of embodiment, learning, muscular gestalts, and common sense. Stevan Harnad identified the *symbol-grounding problem* (Harnad 1990). Critiques of this sort became generally grouped under the rubric *the common sense problem*—so named because any amount of abstract knowledge did not seem to protect AI systems from absurd errors (see Tale-Spin below). Attempts to include common sense in AI programs were dogged by the problem of *brittleness* and infinite regress as a result of the necessity to compute proliferating chains of contingencies (discussed later). Increasingly, it was recognized that this was a problem in principle and not simply a "bug," amenable to technical resolution.[3]

## What Computers Can't Do

Hubert Dreyfus, a Berkeley professor of philosophy and a close observer of AI since the late 1960s, proffered some salutary warnings about the AI project. He challenged fundamental assumptions of the field in *What Computers Can't Do* (first published in 1972, revised in 1979) and followed it up rather triumphantly in a third edition entitled *What Computers Still Can't Do* in 1992. In the 1979 edition, he stated, "Intelligence requires understanding, and understanding requires giving the computer the background of common sense that adult human beings have by virtue of having bodies" (3). Here, Dreyfus asserts an embodied notion of intelligence as something acquired in the mutual development of mind, body, and world. Such sentiments, rooted in the work of Heidegger and Merleau-Ponty, were largely incomprehensible to many in the AI community, in part because phenomenology (derisively referred to as "continental philosophy") was rarely taught in the United States and thus American scholars—including AI researchers—usually had no familiarity with its terms of reference. Philip Agre noted that in the culture of AI, philosophical critiques, whether coming from inside or outside the discipline, were found either arcane or irrelevant, or were taken as personal affronts.[4]

Some years later, in 1996, Dreyfus published a short paper that, in a position derived from Merleau-Ponty's phenomenology of embodiment, contested the computationalist theory of learning. In a spirit close to Csikszentmihalyi's notion of flow and sympathetic with the embodied cognition of Varela, Thompson, and Rosch (1991), Dreyfus argued that the attainment of expertise, be it in tennis or chess or driving, does not involve increasing competence and speed in mental computation following the classic cognitive approach of planning and prediction. On the contrary, Dreyfus asserts that only the beginner follows rules, which function as a recipe or as guidelines for establishing muscular gestalts. As he wittily says in a later paper, "After responding to an estimated million specific chess positions in the process of becoming a chess master, the master, confronted with a new position, spontaneously does something similar to what has previously worked and, lo and behold, it usually works" (Dreyfus 2005, 53).[5]

## The Chinese Room

An early philosophical challenge to AI came with John Searle's now famous Chinese room thought experiment (1980). His focus was on the claim that computers could think—or rather that they had knowledge. His thought experiment went as follows: Imagine a non-Chinese speaker in a room with appropriate instructions and resources for translating English to Chinese and vice versa—analogous to a program and a database. Questions in Chinese could be introduced to the room, and the room would output answers in Chinese. While the Chinese room *appeared* to know Chinese, it did not. It simply manipulated information by syntactical operations alone. The implication is that computers do not "understand" language and that the process of algorithmic operations on symbolic tokens does not inhere "meaning" and therefore does not constitute intelligence in the way humans understand the term. Searle's thought experiment asked philosophical questions that AI had elided about how mental states come to have meaning.

Rather cleverly, this scenario echoes the Turing test scenario, but implies that passing the Turing test does not constitute intelligence. The experiment therefore challenges not only the standard test but brings into question functionalist and computationalist assumptions. (Later, Edwin Hutchins argued, from a distributed cognition perspective, that the system *as a whole* did know Chinese, see chapter 11). The Chinese room argument elucidated questionable assumptions about algorithmic operations and complex notions like knowledge and understanding. It generated much debate and various counterarguments in the philosophical community and resulted in a separation between *strong AI* and *weak AI* communities, the former holding that such operations do constitute thinking and the latter that they only emulate it in a black-box fashion; that is, a certain output is produced from a certain input. (This distinction was mirrored a decade later in the hard ALife/soft ALife distinction.)

## Computationalism and Speech Acts

Winograd and Flores presented an early critical position on AI in their book, *Understanding Computers and Cognition* (1986). Their theorization of HCI was based on the premise that computer use is essentially an extension of language as a social practice, and that context clarifies the particular usage or nuance of a word and that it is those social structures, those *ways of life*, that ground meaning. As such, their approach took aim directly at the claims made by Allen Newell and Herbert Simon regarding formal systems: that a "physical symbol system" was "necessary and sufficient." Without sociocultural grounding, computational systems are vulnerable to infinite regress:

The rationalistic tradition takes language as a representation—a carrier of information—and conceals its central social role. *To be human is to be the kind of being that generates commitments, through speaking and listening.* Without our ability to create and accept (or decline) commitments we are acting in a less than fully human way, and we are not fully using language. . . . This key role [of speech act theory] develops from the recognition that computers are fundamentally tools for human action. Their power as tools for linguistic action derives from their ability to manipulate formal tokens of the kinds that constitute the structural elements of language. But *they are incapable of making commitments and cannot themselves enter into language.* (Winograd and Flores 1986, 76; emphasis mine)

This deployment of J. L. Austin's speech act theory is of historical interest, as it is the same theory that was key to the emergence of performance studies in the humanities around the same time (though there seems to have been no explicit communication between the fields). It is to the credit of these authors that amid the technophilic hype, they remind us that computer systems are ultimately designed by people and that they are, or ought to be, devices for facilitating communication between people. "In [computer systems literature] there is a pervasive misunderstanding," Winograd and Flores point out, "based on the failure to recognize the role of commitment in language" (1986, 77). The authors neutralized the possibility of putting the blame on an external object—the computer—as if it had intentions and instead placed the responsibility squarely on the shoulders of the designers (and users) of such systems.

## Symbol Grounding

A symbol has meaning in a symbol system by its coherent relations with other symbols in that system. Such a symbol, like a move in chess, has no meaning outside that symbol system. Searle argued that a computer system, like the Chinese room, is such a symbol system. Humans, on the other hand, know the meanings of words; they know their *referents*, to use semiological language. Identifying referents is what Stevan Harnad meant by *symbol grounding*. Harnad grounded his problem in an analogy derived from the Chinese room, which he called the dictionary-go-round: "Suppose you had to learn Chinese as a *first* language and the only source of information you had was a Chinese/Chinese dictionary! This is more like the actual task faced by a purely symbolic model of the mind: How can you ever get off the symbol/symbol merry-go-round? How is symbol meaning to be grounded in something other than just more meaningless symbols? This is the symbol grounding problem" (1990, 339–340; emphasis in original).[6] The problem Harnad raised in a theoretical way was already presenting itself in AI research, in key areas in which AI met the "real world," such as in natural language interpretation and robotics. Dreyfus, Searle, Harnad, and others, in various ways, focused on questions of meaning, intentionality, and the importance of real-world context—in the philosophical Achilles' heel of AI.

## Formal Domains and the Messy World

The success of AI systems in playing chess, far from being proof of the validity of the paradigm, can be seen as the exact opposite. Given that AI excels at logical problem solving in closed, known, and fully defined formal logical domains, few experimental objects could map onto the formal qualities of AI as well as chess.[7] Chess is a game for which the rules can be entirely stated in logical terms within a logically defined universe (as described by Kurt Gödel in his incompleteness theorem). Such a logically defined universe is isomorphic with the logical environments defined in computational systems themselves. As discussed in chapter 1, these claims of success in AI are circular: Systems of reasoning according to logical rules are developed, and they are successful in managing tasks compatible with those closed systems of rules. As Philip Agre insightfully observed:

The privileged status of mathematical entities in the study of cognition was already central to Descartes' theory, and for much the same reason: A theory of cognition based on formal reason works best with objects of cognition whose attributes and relations can be completely characterized in formal terms. Just as Descartes felt that he possessed clear and distinct knowledge of geometric shapes, Newell and Simon's programs suffered no epistemological gaps or crises in reasoning about the mathematical entities in their domains. (1997b, 143)

This circular technological story has contributed to the privileging of symbolic abstraction in the academy and throughout our society. The ivory tower is built around the valorization of abstraction and the power of generalization, be it in philosophy or physics. A consequence of the rhetorical power of cognitive psychology is that even our intelligence tests emphasize the extraction of abstract truths from the world, which are then manipulated in the immaterial realm of mental computation.

## Gravity Drowned: The Common Sense Problem

Hubert and Stuart Dreyfus quote Marvin Minsky's deliberations on the subject of common sense: "We still know far too little about the contents and structure of commonsense knowledge. A 'minimal' commonsense system must 'know' something about cause-and-effect, time, purpose, locality, process, and types of knowledge. We need serious epistemological research in this area" (Dreyfus and Dreyfus 1986, 140). Minsky recognized the common sense problem and seems to have assumed that it could be solved without undue trouble. He was wrong. Common sense turned out to be a fatal flaw for the grand aspirations of AI.

Hubert Dreyfus's response shows why he was not well liked in the AI community:

> Minsky's naïveté and faith are astonishing. Philosophers from Plato to Husserl, who uncovered all these problems and more, have carried on serious epistemological research in this area for two thousand years without notable success . . . Minsky seems oblivious to the hand-waving optimism of his proposal that programmers rush in where philosophers such as Heidegger fear to tread, and simply make explicit the totality of human practices which pervade our lives as water encompasses the life of a fish. (1992, 36)

It was in precisely these kinds of real-world problems (such as natural language processing) that the AI/cognitivist paradigm began to show some cracks. Language is contingent and dependent on context. Rules, at least in English, are inconsistent. Imagine a reading system confronted with the word *armchair*. If it knew the words *arm* and *chair*, it might deduce that an armchair is a chair shaped like an arm or that it is a chair for an arm, but it would be unlikely to arrive at what we commonly mean by *armchair*.[8] To take another example, *glass door bolts* might be bolts (i.e., nuts and bolts) for a glass door, door bolts made of glass, or door bolts (i.e., latches) made for glass doors. (*Bolts* could be interpreted as a verb, too, generating ludicrous scenarios.)

A case example is found in early AI work in autonomous story-generation systems. Tale-Spin (1976), a pioneering effort in the field by James

Meehan, generated passages such as the following: "Henry Ant was thirsty. He walked over to the river bank where his good friend Bill Bird was sitting. Henry slipped and fell in the river. Gravity drowned" (Meehan 1976, 129).[9] AI rule systems, operating in fully consistent logical spaces, are prone to such howling and nonsensical errors. The problem here is that the system knows that gravity is pulling Henry into the river, but it does not know that gravity is a force, not a character.

Gaffs like gravity drowning were common in AI systems for robotics, language, and other domains. It is all very well to propose that AI is intelligent because it can solve chess problems, but the chess world, as noted, is a closed and consistent world of logical rules. Contrary to the rationalist dream, this is exactly what the real world is not. Recognition that meaning depends on context-led AI ambitions of universal language understanding to be quickly scaled back to what became known as *expert systems*, which functioned in more or less closed and specifiable knowledge and vocabulary domains.

## Contingencies, Infinite Regress, and Brittleness

Connecting the world of symbols to the real world of experience became increasingly problematic. Symbolic AI is premised on the assumption that "higher"—that is, logical—aspects of human intelligence can be duplicated by decontextualized symbol manipulation. Implicit in such systems is the idea of explicit representation, affording a combinatorial style of reasoning: x with y, x with z, and so on. In a constrained domain (like a chess game), it is easy to list all the possible things that could matter, but in the real world it is often impossible. The following example, which occurred to me while on a train in Spain, elucidates the problem.

The problem for the railway thief is which bag to steal. The task is to assess which bag is most likely to contain valuables easily turned into cash. He must also consider the ease of the escape route: How close is the bag to an exterior door? Weighing these variables will help him decide which bag to steal. He sees the bags and sometimes knows which passengers they belong to. He can read the style and age of each bag, and he might be able to see if it is locked. He might watch to see the care or carelessness with which each passenger stows their bag in the baggage area. He can observe the passengers to see who is watchful of their bags. This might suggest that the bag contains valuables or simply that the owner is vigilant, but it would also make stealing the bag more difficult. How could he distinguish? It is always possible that the most jealously guarded bag contains goods of huge personal but zero cash value—a book manuscript or a mother's ashes. Or it's possible that the owner is obsessive. How could he decide? There is the possibility that really valuable contents might be camouflaged in a bag that looks old and beaten up. How could he tell? He might make some assumptions based on how a person is dressed: Is she wearing expensive jewelry? But is the jewelry fake or real? He might infer this or that by the appearance and demeanor of a passenger, but this involves subtle interpretation informed by a deep familiarity with fashion (local and international) and indicators of social class and of neurotic behavior. So it goes.

Every question opens out into a field of contingencies, and in each of these, new contingencies arise. The quality of the choice is determined by experience and acumen. People make such judgments every day, unconsciously. The proportion of decisions an average person makes by reasoning on an average day must be vanishingly small. But implementing such judgment on computers turned out to be difficult.[10] When programmers were confronted with such "common sense" scenarios, they often enumerated special cases in increasingly complex and proliferating conditional structures and rules about how and when to apply rules. Such chains of contingency and infinite regress resulted in a problem called *brittleness*, in which the system would crash under the weight of such webs of contingencies. In the pragmatic and technical culture of AI, problems like brittleness were usually presumed to be bugs amenable to technical fixes.

## Modularity and Schizophrenia

The challenge of brittleness was in part a result of an axiomatic endorsement of reductivism (and its design corollary, modularity). The doctrine of modularity comes into computer science from the engineering side. The notion of code components, which fit together like building blocks, works as well for code as it does for engine parts. This is because engine parts are contrived according to a logic of interchangeability that goes back to the small arms manufacture of Eli Whitney. Reductivism works well for systems designed according to that logic. Machine are designed according to that logic. Animals are not. In this sense, systems theory builds on the foundation of reductivism. Components in a system are so defined because their interfaces with other components are simple: two wires, a screw thread, an input and an output stream. However, biological and ecological systems are seldom defined by such narrow bandwidth connections. Every neuron in the human brain has thousands of synaptic connections with other neurons.

When complex systems are analyzed in reductive terms, transition sub units are invented to provide connections. But then transitions between transitions are required. This can lead to an infinite regress of the same kind that created brittleness in AI systems—contingency upon contingency upon contingency. A case study of this syndrome is found in the PhD thesis of Phoebe Sengers (1998), in which she diagnosed the behavior of autonomous agents as schizophrenic. She argued that modularity created abrupt transitions between behavior modules, which caused behavior we would, in humans, diagnose as schizophrenic. The "obvious" solution of creating transition modules led to the need for transition modules to join the transition modules and so on, leading to brittleness and infinite regress.

## The World Is Its Own Best Model

Like natural language understanding, robotics was a test case for AI's usefulness in the real world. AI autonomous robots such as Shakey and the Stanford Cart pursued a standard AI SMPA paradigm. As we saw in chapter 5, this paradigm had both pragmatic and theoretical problems. Shakey depended on a radio link with a vast mainframe computer; its machine vision involved bulky analog video cameras and entailed huge amounts of electronics and computation.

By the late 1980s, frustration had developed within the robotics community, as the application of conventional AI techniques to robotics had met with limited success. It was in this context that various researchers, notably Rodney Brooks and Luc Steels, pursued new approaches to robotics based on the idea that many creatures that demonstrably survive and thrive in the world have very small brains, are unlikely to reason, and are very unlikely to build internal representations of their worlds upon which to reason.

Several papers by Brooks, with provocative titles such as "Elephants Don't Play Chess" (1990), "Intelligence without Reason" (1991a), and "Intelligence without Representation" (1991b), documented and theorized his approach: situated, bottom-up, "reactive robotics." Brooks disturbed AI SMPA orthodoxy when he famously announced that "the world is its own best model." By this he implied that building and maintaining an accurate abstract representation of the world (a map) was both expensive and unnecessary. As a proper AI researcher, Brooks backed up his rhetoric with working examples, such as the robots Genghis and Herbert, that wildly outperformed other robots.

John Haugeland later paraphrased Brooks, saying that "it would be silly, for most purposes, to try to *keep track of* what shelf everything in the refrigerator is currently on; if and when you want something, just *look*" (1998, 219; emphasis in original). While such ideas were in the air, Brooks, clearly aware of the prejudices of the community, was careful to distance himself from *continental philosophy* (which was "code" for the phenomenological critique of Hubert Dreyfus). Brooks's *subsumption architecture,* which eschewed the centralized and hierarchical Cartesian top-down approaches of GOFAI, was inspired by von Uexküll's analysis of animal behavior. The general turn away from logic and planning and toward biological analogies, along with the terms *reactive robotics* and *bottom-up,* became central to the developing artificial life community, in which Brooks and Steels became major figures.

### Panopticism: The God Trick

While miniaturized digital computing technology is historically novel, the intellectual history of AI reaches back to the Enlightenment and before. In the West, we are as naturalized to the notion of the map as we are to the mind-body dualism (as discussed in the intermezzo). As such, and given the culture of AI, it is no surprise that the concept of the map was uncritically internalized into AI and taken as self-evident. The idea that AI systems would have total awareness of their contexts was consistent with the surveillance mania of the Cold War context (discussed in chapter 4). More recent government/military surveillance programs, such as the repugnantly panoptical Total Information Awareness program, are driven by the same instinct.

As feminist theory and later postcolonial theory have shown, such presumed universal, objective viewpoints are always surrogates for power and always support implicit power structures. Donna Haraway (1988) called it the *God trick*: making pronouncements about the world from an absolute nonposition without social or cultural context. Looking back at the emergence of feminist science studies, Sandra Harding said,

The women's movement needed knowledge that was *for* women. Women had long been the object of others' knowledge projects. Yet the research disciplines and public policy that depended upon them permitted no conceptual frameworks in which women as a group became the subjects or authors of knowledge; the implied "speakers" of scientific sentences were never women. Such subjects were supposed to be generic humans, which meant men, or even, as Donna Haraway famously put the point, God. (2004, 29; emphasis in original)

Patriarchy, objectivism, and other humanist philosophical baggage provided the uninterrogated philosophical ground on which AI was built. Agre has shown that the pragmatism of AI left no room in the discipline for the critical interrogation of the discipline.

## Deictic Programming

In AI, the assumption of the necessity for total awareness did two things. First, it placed a huge load on processing systems. In standard SMPA approaches, every object in the world had to be accounted for in every iteration—inducing brittleness. Second, it produced the multiple-viewpoints syndrome, which I discussed in the intermezzo in relation to the cognitive training that makes map reading seem natural to us. An agent in a simulated world (i.e., a VR environment or game world) has a subjective location and simultaneously has access to panoptical knowledge of its world.

It was in response to this theoretical and technical paradox that Philip Agre and David Chapman developed a style of programming they called deictic, based on the linguistic concept *deixis*. In their project Pengi (1987), they built an approach to programming in which an agent might behave successfully in its world without access to a God's-eye view. In linguistics, a deictic construction is one that requires or refers to contextual information. Its denotational meaning is conferred by context. If I say, "There are two hats, and one is mine. That is the dirty one" then the word *that* is performing a deictic function. In HCI, the term is used to refer to systems that are, in the debased HCI jargon, *context-aware*.

Pengi was a proof of concept for a deictic programming strategy, an autonomous agent designed by Agre and Chapman to play the game Pengo (a 1982 Sega arcade game), in which Pengo had to "kill" "bees." In Pengi, the player-agent did not have to keep track of the position of every bee in the "world" but contingently identified "the bee near me." This approach led to substantial efficiency in memory and computational load. A paper written a year later that discusses the project is called "What Are Plans For?" (Agre and Chapman 1990). This, like the title of Suchman's contemporaneous work, *Plans and Situated Actions: The Problem of Human-Machine Communication*, speaks to the general reassessment of key terms in the AI vocabulary at the time. Deictic theories have been found useful in various research projects (e.g., Ballard et al. 1997). On a philosophical level, they also reintroduce the possibility of subjectivity into the profoundly objectivized world of AI.

## Biology Comes Back

In the introduction to his 1988 book *Mind Children: The Future of Robot and Human Intelligence*, AI researcher Hans Moravec said, "Organisms that lack the ability to perceive and explore their environment do not seem to acquire anything that we would call intelligence" (16). This statement is indicative of the sea change that was in process in the AI and robotics communities in the late 1980s. Implicit in Moravec's statement is the recognition that organic intelligence exists in relation to and because of real-world interactions. It signals a return to biological models and a recognition of the environmentally situated and enactive nature of intelligent action; the two ideas were characteristic of an emerging postcomputationalist position in AI, robotics, and cognitive science.

This is significant, as Moravec was a leading roboticist with twenty years of conventional robotics and machine vision research behind him. He was part of the research teams that built both the SRI Shakey and the Stanford Cart, two of the earliest "autonomous" robots. (The term *autonomous* must be qualified, as their computation occurred in giant institutional mainframes connected to the robots by radio links.) Moravec's statement shows that some cognitive scientists, roboticists, and others at the time were casting about for alternative possibilities. These alternatives emerged largely in fields that became known as artificial life research and as embodied and situated cognition.

## Critical Technical Practice

In 1997, Philip Agre, math prodigy and PhD graduate of MIT's AI lab, published a most subtle, well-informed, insightful, and succinct critique of AI: "Toward a Critical Technical Practice: Lessons Learned in Trying to Reform AI" (1997b).[11] This essay is remarkable in its intelligence as well as its professional humility. It describes his gradual disaffection with his discipline and his attempts to denaturalize his training. In his book *Computation and Human Experience* (1997a), Agre identifies shortcomings in a humanities-starved computer science training and worldview: "The AI community has lacked the intellectual tools that it needs to comprehend its own difficulties. What is needed . . . is a critical technical practice—a technical practice for which critical reflection upon the practice is part of the practice itself. . . . critical research draws attention to structural and cultural levels of explanation—to the things that happen through our actions but that exist beneath our conscious awareness" (xii). This prescription for a reflexive critical practice, though alien to the technical disciplines, is familiar in the humanities and the arts. In art practice and pedagogy in the late modern and postmodern periods, such a critical technical practice has been central. Agre recognizes that AI is not *just* a technical practice, because it seeks to emulate and automate functions that are cultural and psychological.

The problem of the map and the territory is a recurring theme in these pages. Agre raised similar issues: "Metaphorical attributions of purpose were associated with the mathematics of servocontrol and realized in servo-mechanisms; metaphorical attributions of discrimination were associated with the mathematics of signal and noise and realized in communications equipment; and metaphorical attributions of communication were associated with the mathematics of information theory and realized in coding devices" (1997a, 1). Central to Agre's critique is his recognition of the slippage between rhetorical and technical domains. In computationalism, Agre argues, a potent stock of metaphors migrated from computer science to psychology, which made computer function appear naturally analogous to human thought: "a bit of metaphor attached to a bit of mathematics and realized in a machine whose operation could then be narrated using intentional vocabulary" (2).

## Panopticism, Problems, and Paranoia

Agre's work on deictic programming with Chapman was an example of a technical artifact motivated by critique. In this work, they showed that the panopticist God's-eye view was neither necessary nor optimal for AI systems. We know from Edwards that panoptical fantasies of total control were central to the worldview of the Cold War, and this worldview was formative for AI. AI conceives of life, at least mental life, as a series of novel problematic situations that demand thinking and planning. As Agre noted in that context, the world was construed to be a dangerous place full of unknowns. He questioned the assumption that cognition is *problem solving*.

In Agre's view, the day-to-day world is not (normally) a site of dangerous "problems" to be solved. The world is generally routine and benign. Agre asks, "If the world were not full of danger, but mostly routine, how could we then reconfigure our notion of intelligence?" He concludes that the bulk of our activities are routine, and when we encounter novel situations we tend to rely on already known routines. He called these novel situations *hassles*, to defuse the dire connotations of danger inherent in the diabolical combination of paranoid militarism and artificial intelligence so clearly outlined by Edwards. Echoing Dreyfus, Agre says, "The routine of everyday life is an emergent phenomenon of moment-to-moment interactions that work out in much the same way from day to day because of the relative stability of our relationships with our environments" (1997a, 7–8).

That is not to say that we or other creatures do not solve problems nor that problem solving is not an indication of intelligence. But in contrast to Cold War anxiety, our experience of the world is (blessedly) tedious, and novelty is rare. This is probably why we enjoy opportunities to gently surprise ourselves, in jokes and scary movies and roller coasters. Much of which we take to be pleasurable in play is structured around problem solving. But unpleasant surprises, like losing Internet service or being rear-ended in the car, are unwelcome. Situations that are constantly dangerous in novel ways demands constant vigilance that is stressful and fatiguing, resulting in post-traumatic stress disorder (PTSD).

The ability to flexibly adapt learned behaviors to novel situations is a key aspect of the exercise of human intelligence in the world. The groceries will always be bagged, but the packages are never quite the same in size, shape, and number. Likewise, a dancer makes a new combination of movements in relation to a novel context, but limbs do not suddenly change shape, and new limbs do not sprout. The component actions are already known in sensorimotor routines and seldom exceed the dancer's capability (when they do, injury can be expected). Humans easily navigate a continuum of variations. This demands judgment and nested contingencies. The human mind generalizes and extends such complex situations with ease—this is what we call common sense. The GOFAI balloon was popped by this recognition.

## The False Precision of Formalism

In "Toward a Critical Technical Practice," Philip Agre lucidly documented his own emancipation from the "false precision of formalism" via his reading of Foucault's *The Archeology of Knowledge* specifically and poststructural writing generally, noting that "they were utterly practical instruments by which I first was able to think clearly and to comprehend ideas that had not been hollowed through the false precision of formalism" (1997b, 148). It is precisely this false precision of formalism that hollows out embodied knowledge.

Agre elaborates elsewhere on the possibility of a reflexive computer science: "Instead of seeking foundations it would embrace the impossibility of foundations, guiding itself by a continually unfolding awareness of its own workings as a historically specific practice. . . . It would accept that this reflexive inquiry places all of its concepts and methods at risk" (1997a, 23). This quintessentially postmodern formulation is indebted directly to Foucault and Derrida that endorses radical interdisciplinarity. It restates the modus operandi of (avant-gardist) art practices, in which a primary generative activity entails upsetting received orthodoxies (even and especially within its own tradition). One can read modernist art movements as a kind of rhetorical calculus, reversing chosen terms in an aesthetic equation for the Socratic goal of testing the validity of the claim (which is almost always abandoned in the process). In this way, art has been as self-involved as any other discipline, and moments of engagement with the outside world have often been perceived by the establishment as eccentric, deviant, or simply irrelevant.

## Target Domain

"A computer, then," remarks Agre, "does not simply have an instrumental use in a given site of practice; the computer is frequently about that site in its very design. *In this sense and others, computing has been constituted as a kind of imperialism*; it aims to reinvent virtually every other site of practice in its own image" (1997b, 131; emphasis mine)—a sentiment presaged by Weizenbaum (above) and echoed by Theordore Roszak. Similarly, Paul Edwards observes that whereas "most tools produce effects on a wider world of which they are only a part, the computer contains its own worlds in miniature" (1990, 109). Agre refers to the location where the transformation of human sociotechnical process into computational representations occurs as *borderlands*: "Each of the borderlands is a complicated place; everyone who resides in them is, at different times, both an object and an agent of technical representation, both a novice and an expert. . . . every resident of these borderlands is a translator between languages and worldviews: the formalisms of computing and the craft culture of the 'application domain'" (1997b, 132). Agre notes, "The institutional relationships between the computer world and the rest of the world can be tremendously complicated—much more complicated than the relationships between the telephone world and telephone subscribers" (131–132).

Why are these relationships so much more complicated? A hammer, an electric motor, a speaker or a microphone, a capacitor or a resistor are not, in this sense, representational artifacts, because their natures reflect basic physical constraints and/or traditions of use. But, as Agre observes, "Computers are representational artifacts, and the people who design them often start by constructing representations of the activities found in the sites where they will be used" (1997b, 131). This mismatch between the world and code was observed by Roszak (quoted earlier), by Weizenbaum, by Edwards (discussed earlier), and by Agre. In chapter 9, we review the work of Edwin Hutchins from this perspective.

## Conclusion

Putnam's functionalism, the representationalism of Fodor and Pylyshyn, and its application by Newell and Simon in their physical symbol system hypothesis—these three ideas provided the philosophical grounding for artificial intelligence and for cognitivist cognitive science. Ed Hutchins observes, "Increasingly, the Physical Symbol System Hypothesis is a perspective into which things don't fit. It was a bet or a guess, grounded in a nearly religious belief in the Platonic status of mathematics and formal systems as eternal verities rather than as historical products of human activities" (1995, 370). The assumptions undergirding AI reflected a largely uninterrogated humanism and were configured according to precepts of Enlightenment rationality.[12] These precepts are the dualisms around which much of this book is also structured:

• The Cartesian mind-body dualism and its reification in the software-hardware dualism
• Nature-nurture, or biology-culture, often reflected in the science-humanities dualism
• The distinction between subject/object and the related distinction between self/world (as a result of the philosophical context of AI, the "thinking machine" is modeled on the construction of the autonomous Enlightenment individual)
• That other structuring dualism of Western culture: reason-emotion
• The human-animal dualism (human exceptionalism) so emphatic in Judeo-Christian traditions

The AI paradigm foundered on the frame problem, the symbol grounding problem, the common sense problem, and similar difficulties. The dream of universal AI systems evaporated (Cyc being the lone survivor). It seems that Hamlet was right: "There are more things in heaven and earth, Horatio, than are dreamt of in your philosophy" (Shakespeare 1.5.186–187). It transpired that turning the world into symbols and turning symbols back into the world was not as straightforward as had been expected and did not constitute intelligence. George Miller, one of the founders of cognitive science, like his former student Ulric Neisser, came to believe that "how computers work seems to have no real relevance to how the mind works, any more than a wheel shows how people walk" (quoted in Edwards 1997, 235).

It took a generation before almost anyone in the field recognized the folly of panopticism and the God's-eye view (not to mention the sympathy between such an omnipotent conception and the political agenda of the surveillance state). The increasing recognition of the common sense or symbol-grounding problem and the shortcomings of the SMPA paradigm led to the emergence of reactive robotics and a growing interest within the technical community in situated cognition (e.g., Suchman) and embodied perspectives. The aura of GOFAI was fading. In its place were arising approaches rooted in biology, ethology, phenomenology, and dynamical systems theory, which gave rise to new disciplines and fields—reactive robotics, artificial life, and new flavors of cognitive science—situated, distributed, enactive, and embodied.

In a way reminiscent of Pickering's thesis in *The Mangle of Practice*, Agre (citing Chapman) notes that the mentalist ideology of AI is contradicted by the very practice of the discipline itself. As Agre points out, the practice of AI is artisanal: "Building things, like fieldwork and meditation and design, is a way of knowing that cannot be reduced to the reading and writing of books . . . what truly founds computational work is the practitioner's evolving sense of what can be built and what cannot" (1997a, 10–11). The criterion of pragmatic proof-in-practice repressed innovation outside of a certain set of procedures and insulated AI from outside influence. Of criticisms from outside the field, such as those of Dreyfus et al., Agre notes, "The AI community has, by and large, found these arguments incomprehensible" (21), as AI lacked internal mechanisms for reflexivity. "The Cartesian lineage of AI ideas, for example, is held to be interesting but incidental, and critiques of Cartesianism are held to have no purchase on the technical ideas that descend from it." He captures the perils of this pragmatism and lack of capacity for reflexivity, ending this statement by saying, "This view, in my opinion, is mistaken and, moreover, forms part of the phenomenon needing explanation" (23).

## The Afterlife of AI

As the grandiose dream of AI faded, a more pragmatic generation applied AI techniques in realms such as computer gaming, data mining, online search engines, and the like. The popular name for autonomous agents in computer game worlds is *AIs*. It is an ironic footnote to the common sense problem that *it is only in entirely digital environments that AIs can succeed*, because online all data are already present in digital form (not always correctly, of course). The task of interpretation of sensor data is obviated as there is no "real world." The Internet is a post-GOFAI phenomenon. This afterlife of AI is only possible because almost everything that exists online has already been preprocessed into symbols and placed into data structures by humans. Humans, as the perceptual peripheral of the Internet, provide the functions AI could never achieve: discerning salience in a world of chaotic and multimodal stimuli, in just the same way that humans were harnessed in the first grand networked knowledge engineering project, SAGE—the Cold War semiautomatic ground environment in which humans were disambiguated blips on radar screens. (Ironically, not one ICBM was ever detected, and the efficacy of the system was never proven, because not one was ever fired at the United States.)

The applied fields of data mining and machine learning have demonstrated significant successes, and it's worth noting why this is. The tricky tasks of interpretation of sensor data derived from the electrophysical world and translation into bits have already been performed (largely by people): all that is left is symbols. This leaves the AI search and inference procedures to do the thing they do so well: sort data.

Human users serve as the perceptual front end of Internet-based machine learning, converting experience of the world into symbolic representations. They are the "peripherals" GOFAI felt justified in (temporarily) ignoring. Crowdsourcing is the perceptual prosthetic of data mining. From providing music metadata to identifying places and people in images, people prepare data that are then mined using the techniques of traditional AI. Humans provide the common sense to ground the symbols in the world.

Crowdsourcing and data mining (and all the human minds building the data-mining systems) are together cyborgian assemblages that, like Hutchins's interpretation of the Chinese room, may be said to exhibit intelligence. There is some irony in the fact that this situation provides a counterexample to conventional AI conceptions and at the same time is consistent with biological examples: sensing, or perception, not only requires intelligence, but also requires a kind of intelligence that AI systems still cannot provide.

# 7 Complexity, Nonlinear Dynamics, and Self-Organizing Systems

Big whirls have little whirls that feed on their velocity,
and little whirls have lesser whirls and so on to viscosity.

—L. F. Richardson, *Weather Prediction by Numerical Process* (1922, 66)

Because the development of computers arises within the discipline of engineering (notwithstanding the theoretical import of mathematics, physics, etc.), engineering as a discipline and as a discourse is central to the concerns of this book. While science and engineering are not a homogeneous entity, core ideas unite the scientific method, the logic of industrial production, and capitalism. The God's-eye view that characterized Bentham's panopticon also characterizes military Command, Control, Communications, and Intelligence (C3I), the Total Information Awareness of the surveillance state and the authoritative viewpoint of top-down AI. In a more general sense, core values of the discipline of engineering have been endorsed and reified in digital computing—such as reductivism, generality, and abstraction.

Over the second half of the twentieth century, experimental results in diverse areas led to a series of related theoretical inquiries, the results of which contested objectivism, determinism, reductivism, and other key tenets of the scientific method, in often surprising ways. These fields of inquiry included self-organizing systems, fractal mathematics, chaos theory, complexity theory, self-organizing criticality, dynamical systems theory, nonlinear dynamics, and emergent order. This research identified limits to conventional prediction techniques and motivated new methods. Ironically, and by historical happenstance, digital computing proved amenable to simulating and analyzing such systems as no technology had before. It was the iterative capability of digital computing that made the mathematical "monsters" of fractal geometry, nonlinear dynamics, and complexity theory tractable, leading to new insights into physics, the nature of biological growth, and the phenomenon of life itself.

## Reductivism

*Reductivism* asserts that phenomena can be usefully studied in isolation from their contexts. It allows that integrated systems can be broken down into component parts; the parts can then be assessed in isolation, and by combining the understanding of the parts, an understanding of the whole is attained. Implicitly, the whole is (nothing more than) the sum of its parts. The idea that phenomena can be reduced to components and that such components can be assembled additively to create larger structures, is axiomatic in conventional science and engineering.

This idea works well if the object at hand is a radio or a car—but not so well if it is a rabbit or a storm or an ecosystem. Reductivism is vulnerable to potential attack on the basis of *reductio ad absurdum*—is the quality of a ham sandwich determined by quantum effects? It is also susceptible to fallacious and untenable transitions between categories, such as the explication of *mind* in the physiology of *brain* or the explication of aesthetics in terms of (our current understanding of) neural processes. Systems theory provides a principled way of distinguishing where one component ends and another begins. Yet cybernetics emphasized the irreducibility of systems, especially self-organizing systems, whereas in computer science reductivism became key and motivated the doctrine of modularity in programming.

The idea that complex biological processes susceptible to analysis on the analogy of mechanisms dates back to *L'homme machine* (1747) (La Mettrie 1996). Reductivism affords the mechanistic analysis of organic and physical processes on the principle that the whole is only the sum of its parts. Applied to industrial capitalism, reductivism allows that a holistic socioeconomic system can be rationalized into chosen vectors that maximize productive output and hence profit with respect to input: materials, energy, money, and labor. The privileging of scientific discourses in our culture is in part due to the fact that this method has led to industrialization and the enormous accrual of wealth and power in the modern period. When these ideas are instrumentalized, they become the ideology of efficient production, what I call the *engineering worldview*, epitomized in Taylorism and Fordism. As Canguilhem argues, "The theory of the animal-machine is inseparable from 'I think therefore I am'" and is inseparable from the project of Enlightenment rationality (1992, 52).

## Mathematical Monsters and the Challenge to Reductivism

The scientific worldview of the nineteenth and early twentieth century recapitulated, or made corollaries to, a familiar set of Enlightenment values. They included the following: that mind is separable from body (Cartesian dualism); that it is possible to observe a system without that observation affecting the system (objectivism); that it is possible to understand a system by reducing it to its components and studying these components in isolation (reductivism, mechanism); and that the behavior of complex systems can be predicted (determinism).

The advent of machine-divided time (in the form of the clock and, later, global time coordination) is an emblematic precursor to the grand unified theory projects that typify the pinnacle of Enlightenment humanism in the late Victorian era, such as Whitehead and Russell's *Principia Mathematica*, unified field theories in physics, and the organization of biological taxonomic systems around Darwinian evolution. World War I demolished utopic dreams of social progress. Second-wave industrialization brought, internationally, further rationalization and disciplining of labor (Taylorism) and the social and economic order. In the Soviet Union and other Marxist states we see the implementation of an industrial socialism, which arose out of reflection upon the social changes brought by industrialization.

Meantime, in various sciences, anomalous results suggested standard Newtonian physics was not applicable, either because there were too many variables to compute or because systems developed behaviors that were not reducible to component subsystems. This idea is captured in the folk wisdom that the whole is greater than the sum of its parts. Such results destabilized the conventional scientific thinking at its mechanist root.

## Heteropathic Causation, Entelechy, and the Élan Vital

The question of what it is that distinguishes the living from the nonliving has been a constant theme in philosophy and science. Henri Bergson posited the idea of *élan vital*, or life force, an idea that received ridicule by mechanist scientists, who characterized élan vital as the phlogiston of the life sciences.[1] G. H. Lewes used the term *emergence* in its current sense as early as 1875, indicating the philosophical context for Bergson's élan vital. J. S. Mill embraced the concept of emergence. In *A System of Logic, Ratiocinative and Inductive* (2009; originally published in 1843), he applied the term *heteropathic causation* to situations in which an effect is the result of combined multiple causes. Heteropathic causation is anathema to reductivism—simple causation is fundamental to "normal science" and especially engineering. In his writings of the 1920s, Samuel Alexander proposed a general theory of emergence that purported to explain the transition from nonliving to living and from nonconscious to conscious. Such ideas were influential in fields as diverse as sociology and embryology. Hans Driesch, one of the founders of experimental embryology, subscribed to a notion of *entelechy*, a philosophical idea similar to élan vital that originated with Aristotle. The spirit of vitalism has recurred in various discourses around emergence and self-organization, ideas that have been central in cybernetics and artificial life. As we have seen, cyberneticians spoke of self-organizing systems, of purposive behavior and teleology (chapter 3). The mechanist/vitalist tension persisted throughout the twentieth century and is detectable in artificial life discourse (Hein 1972).

## Self-Organizing Systems

The notion of self-organizing systems was a key aspect of cybernetic theory. British cybernetician and neuroscientist Ross Ashby formalized the notion in 1947, and it was quickly taken up by von Foerster, Weiner, and Beer, among others. Ashby's work arose in part from his attempt to articulate the behavior of his homeostat. Ashby's 1962 paper, "Principles of the Self-Organizing System," summarizes the developments of the notion over the previous fifteen years. He interrogates the concepts of organization, self-organization, and machine, and uses terms that would be key in similar conversations in forthcoming decades, including *complex systems*, *dynamic process*, and *multiplicity of equilibrial states*—an idea that presages the "attractor basins" of chaos and complexity theories. According to Ashby, "The theory of organization is partly co-extensive with the theory of functions of more than one variable" (1962, 256). Ashby's Homeostat is an experimental environment for demonstrating the resolution of functions of more than one variable to multiple equilibrial states. Ashby emphasizes the nonreducibility of such phenomena and the relationality of the concept of *organization* as "partly in the eye of the beholder." He not only explicates the non-Newtonian nature of such systems but also articulates the agenda of second-order cybernetics and the relationality of observation: "The properties of any particular constraint will depend on both the real thing and on the observer. It follows that a substantial part of the theory of organization will be concerned with properties that are not intrinsic to the thing but are relational between observer and thing" (258). This idea recalls von Uexküll and presages the relational ontologies of Bateson, Maturana, Gibson, and later thinkers. Ashby asserts, "In any isolated system, life and intelligence inevitably develop," and he asks how we can generate intelligence synthetically (272)—a question to which the cybernetic answer was markedly different from the AI answer.

Ashby also developed a major weapon in the arsenal of cybernetic theory: his law of requisite variety (LRV) which states that a control system must permit a large enough range of variety to represent all parameters of the system in question. The LRV was fundamental to Stafford Beer's Viable System Model (Ashby 1962). With respect to the complex and intertwined histories of AI and cybernetics, it is important to note that the LRV is wholly representational. Moreover, Ashby cites Shannon's tenth theorem,[2] demonstrating again the undifferentiated nature of the cybernetics community before the "Dartmouth schism."

Like other aspects of cybernetic theory, the notion of self-organization was highly influential and applied diversely. These applications are not always fully compatible, but they generally include the idea that complex structures, organizations, or behaviors arise or emerge with no seeming causal antecedents and are thus irreducible. Such behaviors appear contrary to the second law of thermodynamics. Oft-cited examples include the behavior of slime molds; the social organization of colonial insects in, for example, termite building behavior (stigmergy); reaction-diffusion systems such as the Belousov Zhabotinsky; Conway's Game of Life; flocking and schooling in animal behavior; and the emergence of consciousness in the brain. In 1977, Ilya Prigogine, a pioneer of nonequilibrium thermodynamics, won a Nobel Prize for his theory of dissipative structures, which contested the time-agnostic notion of reversibility in physics. Twenty years later, in *The End of Certainty* (1997), Prigogine argued that determinism is no longer a viable scientific belief.

## Stigmergy

French biologist Pierre-Paul Grassé coined the term *stigmergy* in 1959 while studying the collaborative building behavior of termites. Derived from the Greek *stigma* (mark, sign) and *ergon* (work, action), he defined stigmergy as follows: "Stimulation of workers by the performance they have achieved" (Grassé 1959, 79). As von Frish and other first-generation ethologists had noted before, termites build enormously complex architectures that are highly efficient passive ventilation and air quality–control systems. Variables such as oxygen and carbon dioxide content, and temperature and humidity stay remarkably constant over time and across parts of the nest deep underground as well as above ground. In the absence of a master architect termite, the organized development and maintenance of such complex systems seems mysterious. It transpires that termites are stimulated to perform particular behaviors in the presence of certain pheromones and, in the process, produce more of those pheromones. In their building behavior, they will roll earth into mud balls, depositing a pheromone in the balls in the process. When that pheromone reaches a certain concentration in the air, they are then stimulated to use the mud balls to build walls, which then converge to form arches and tunnels. The robotic simulation of this seemingly organized but anarchic behavior by Beckers, Holland, and Deneubourg (1994) was one of the triumphs of artificial life reactive robotics research (see chapter 8).

The emergent nature of such behaviors and the absence of a master controller was also famously identified by Evelyn Fox Keller and Lee Segel in their paradigm-busting study of slime molds (1969). The idea that simple organisms, without memory or plan, can perform "intelligent," goal-based, complex, coordinated actions clearly challenges cognitivist assumptions in various ways. E. O. Wilson observed similar behaviors among ants. The general lessons we can draw from such examples is that top-down centralization is an artifact of human culture and that outside the rarified and particular realm of human abstract reasoning, nature tends toward rhizomatic mechanisms of self-organization, and intelligence or cognition tends to be decentralized and situated. Behaviors evolve in a context and are applicable to that context. In nature, generality is not a virtue; nature is pataphysical.[3]

## Mathematical Monsters and the Geometry of Nature

Lewis Fry Richardson (1881–1953), a meteorologist, polymath, and confirmed pacifist, pursued a lifelong project to mathematically analyze war. In the process, he came across a mathematical paradox. The question is beguilingly simple: How long is the coastline of, say, Sicily? Measuring with a one-kilometer ruler would produce a very different figure than that produced with a ruler of one meter. Scaling down further to rulers of, say, one centimeter, the numbers would continue to increase. If measured around the wetted surface of every grain of sand at a scale of 0.1 millimeter, the number would be astronomical. The length of the coastline is indeterminate, potentially infinite, and dependent on the unit or measurement. This so-called coastline paradox is now known as the Richardson effect, later celebrated by Benoit Mandelbrot as a ubiquitous example of fractal math in his 1967 paper, "How Long Is the Coast of Britain?" In a pattern that has become all too

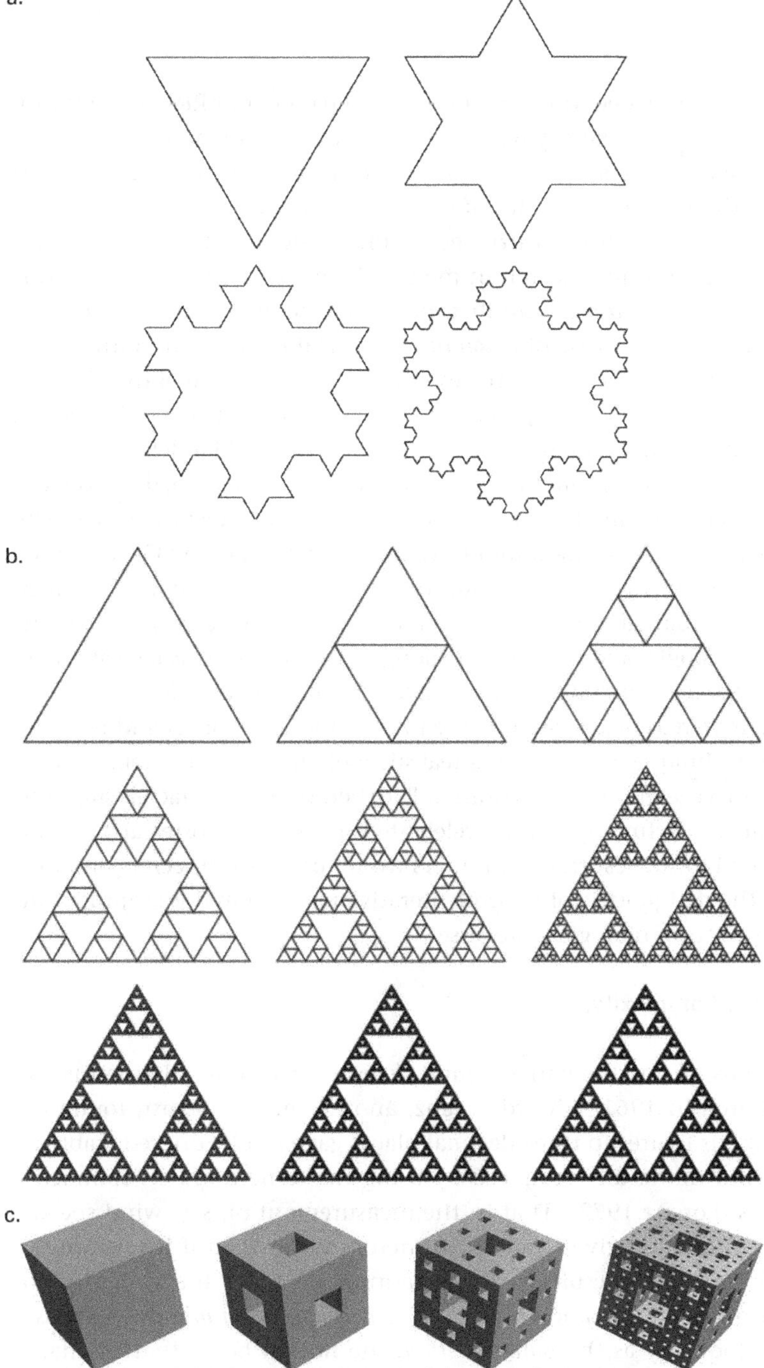

**Figure 7.1**
(a) Koch snowflake, (b) Sierpinski triangle, and (c) Menger sponge.

familiar regarding ideas that disrupt accepted paradigms, Richardson's work appears to have been largely ignored by mathematicians, at least until Mandelbrot used it to construct his notion of *fractional dimension*, a key concept in fractal theory and the source of the neologism *fractal*.

Richardson was clearly intrigued by phenomena at the edge of mathematics. Through his research in meteorology, he identified what is now known as the Richardson number, *Ri*, which quantifies turbulence. Turbulence is the classic case of a *nonlinear* physical phenomenon intractable in Newtonian physics. He saw the essentially fractal nature of the phenomenon, as indicated by the epigraph for this chapter, a witty riff on Swift.[4]

The extraordinary images of fractal patterns in Mandelbrot's highly acclaimed book *The Fractal Geometry of Nature* (1982) were made possible by advanced digital computing. The basic mathematics of fractals, of symmetry across scale, was over one hundred years old (developed by Georg Cantor, inventor of set theory), and the notion was well-known in the early twentieth century, exemplified by geometrical oddities such as the Koch snowflake, the Sierpinski triangle, and the Menger sponge. However, the visual elaboration of extended iteration only became viable with automated calculation.

Fractals were quickly implemented in computer graphics and became a standard technique for generating realistic-looking images of clouds, mountain ranges, vegetation, and coastlines. The rhetoric around fractals supported a generalized technomysticism (celebrated in popular poster art), as fractals seemed to suggest that computers would unlock the secrets of nature. Indeed, the design logic of multiply iterative procedures does capture some formal aspects of biological processes.

### Chaos and Complexity

Like fractals, the mathematics behind *chaos* was a century old (dating back to Poincaré). In 1961, Edward Lorenz, another meteorologist, found that rounding his figures to three decimal places gave results unpredictably different from the results produced by using the same numbers rounded to six places (Lorenz 1972). That is, the measurement of, say, wind speed as 17.584 km/h could give a radically different result than if it was rounded to 17.58 km/h. Such results were counterintuitive, to say the least. This phenomenon came to be known as *sensitive dependence on initial conditions* or more colloquially as the *butterfly effect*, the notion being that the flap of a butterfly's wing in the Amazon could instigate a chain of events that could result in a tornado in Oklahoma. Through the 1970s, the significance of nonlinear mathematics was recognized; the work of Robert May, for instance, had lasting influence in biology and ecology. "Chaos," an influential and widely cited paper by Crutchfield et al. (1986), contributed to increased popular understanding of these phenomena.

## Strange Attractors and Chaotic Regimes

The new sciences of nonlinear dynamics and complexity ushered in a new mathematical language of strange attractors and chaotic regimes—abstractions of the temporal behavior of dynamical systems. A simple image of the mathematical notion of an attractor or a basin of attraction is the rest point of a pendulum. As the pendulum loses energy (a dissipative system), it tends toward and eventually comes to rest at the point where its arm is vertical. A slightly more complex example—a marble released from the top of a hemisphere will roll to the bottom edge of the hemisphere. Note that the direction it rolls is sensitively dependent on initial conditions and its landing place could be anywhere on the circle of the bottom edge (recalling Ashby's multiple equilibrial states).

The mathematics of attractors is a key technique for description and study of chaotic and dynamical systems. *Strange attractors* have a fractal nature; they are nonperiodic (they do not repeat patterns), and the trajectories of these systems are not predictable—that is, they are "chaotic." It should be noted that the *chaotic regime*, contrary to its spectacular name, does not refer to sheer disorder but to the ragged edge of determinism, more accurately referred to as *deterministic chaos*, in which behaviors, though not predictable, remain susceptible to statistical analysis.

## Dynamical Systems Theory

Dynamical systems are nonlinear systems that develop over time. They are nonlinear in the sense that they are not amenable to analysis via standard Newtonian mechanics. Their evolution may be highly susceptible to initial conditions, and their behavior often involves proliferating perturbations due to those initial conditions. The paradigmatic example of a dynamical system is Lorenz's butterfly effect, discussed previously. The general phenomenon of turbulence in aerodynamics, hydrodynamics, and fluid mechanics generally is not amenable to deterministic analysis due to its fractal nature. Increasingly, problems, such as turbulence that in the past could only be empirically modeled using wind tunnels and test tanks, are now susceptible to computer emulation and analysis using nonlinear dynamics. Randall Beer explains the dynamical paradigm this way:

When one approaches some system from a computational perspective, one is concerned with what function the system is trying to compute, in what format the problem input is specified, in what output format the answer is required, how the relevant features of the problem are to be represented, by what algorithms these representations are to be transformed, and how the performance of these algorithms scales with problem size. In contrast, when one approaches some system from a dynamical perspective, one seeks to identify a minimal set of state variables whose evolution can account for the observed behavior, the dynamical laws by which the values of these variables evolve in time, the overall spatiotemporal structure of their possible evolution, and the sensitivity of this structure to variations in inputs, states and parameters. (2014, 135)

James Crutchfield, one of the authors of the now famous *Scientific American* paper on chaos (Crutchfield et al. 1986), summarizes the significance of science of complexity this way:

Defining structure and detecting the emergence of complexity in nature are inherently subjective, though essential, scientific activities. Despite the difficulties, these problems can be analyzed in terms of how model-building observers infer from measurements the computational capabilities embedded in nonlinear processes. An observer's notion of what is ordered, what is random, and what is complex in its environment depends directly on its computational resources: the amount of raw measurement data, of memory, and of time available for estimation and inference. The discovery of structure in an environment depends more critically and subtlely [*sic*] though on how those resources are organized. The descriptive power of the observer's chosen (or implicit) computational model class, for example, can be an overwhelming determinant in finding regularity in data. (Crutchfield 1994, 11)

Dynamical systems theory has been taken up as an alternative paradigm to functionalism/cognitivism in a range of postcognitivist discourses, from robotics to ethology, and has been applied in cognitive neurosciences and areas of psychological research, including early sensorimotor development (see, for instance, the work of Anthony Chemero, Alicia Juarrero, Tim van Gelder, Randall Beer, and J. Scott Kelso).

## Looking Back at Determinism

To say that the results of chaos theory were counterintuitive is simply to observe how thoroughly we are naturalized to Newtonian notions of simple causality and reductivism. Frank Durham and Richard Purrington have noted, "Perhaps the most remarkable thing about the universe is that it appears to be linear. Is this because we have been indoctrinated by three hundred years of [Newtonian] dynamics, or it is [*sic*] because human beings experience the universe in domains of time and frequency which admit of an approximately linear description? Is quasilinearity becoming a hypothesis we no longer need?" (1990, 221).

As any high school physics student knows, Newtonian physics fails when more than two variables are involved. This is known as the three-body problem and has been understood to be in general unsolvable since the late nineteenth century (established independently by Bruns and Poincaré)—hence the drive in engineering to simplified models and eliminating variables in order to produce tractable problems, and implicitly the aversion to heteropathic causation. The (strange) logic here is to get an answer at whatever cost, even if in the process crucial variables are ignored. The Achilles' heel of any model or simulation is that variables must be chosen (from the infinite complexity of the world) and others disregarded. "Noise" is eliminated on the assumption that it is irrelevant. The ghost of Lorenz's butterfly haunts this rationalization, and results, though consistent in controlled contexts, do not reflect real-world behavior (the map and the territory again). Oversimplification results in a "baby and bathwater" situation (not unknown in engineering), which can result in getting the right answer to the wrong question. An aphorism credited to Albert Einstein captures this: Everything should be made as simple as possible, but not simpler.

Symmetry across scale (in fractal mathematics), sensitive dependence on initial conditions (in complexity theory), and the development of nonlinear dynamics had a resounding effect on "normal science." These developments, on the one hand, provide purchase on previously intractable problems in fluid mechanics and, on the other hand, posed an in-principle challenge to reductivism and determinism on a philosophical level. This resulted in a growing realization that the clean lines of Newtonian physics and Euclidean geometry are part of a world of Platonic abstraction, and correspondence to the real world of phenomena is tenuous. The point, line, and plane of Euclidean geometry are abstractions with little relevance to the natural world. The iterative math of fractals captures an essence of biological growth. Newtonian physics provides minimal purchase on real-world problems such as calculating the drag on an airplane wing. Mathematical and computational modeling depends for tractability on reduction of data volume via approximation and generalization. The challenge posed by this new math is that such approximation and generalization—that is, any mathematical model of any phenomenon—is inherently a simplification and thus potentially unreliable. It is a testament to the intellects involved in these fields that such models work as well as they do.

## Monsters Are Everywhere

Clearly, we manage to get bridges and airplanes to stay up (most of the time), but one might argue that is largely because the materials and technologies have been engineered to conform to mathematical models. The very notion of a synthetic material is that it is constructed according to an idea of what the material should do and not do. We do not have that option with nature. The infinitesimal detail of biological systems is, in principle, resistant to the classical generalizations of Newton and Euclid. Nonlinear dynamical math is not, it transpires, an odd corner of the mathematical world inhabited by monsters. Contrarily, it is the general rule. The assumption that complex phenomena may be reduced to multiple simpler phenomena which can then be "summed"—and that this results in an adequate description of the original complex phenomenon—is rendered dubious. The fact that the whole is (almost always) greater than the sum of its parts brings the method of reductivism, axiomatic to scientific practice, into question.

## Conclusion: Sciences of Control

According to the argument followed in this book, the values that characterized nineteenth-century engineering ideology—quantification, abstraction, algebraic manipulation, and generalization—are reified in the digital computer. In an ironic historical turn, the computational capability of modern computers has in recent decades brought the values upon which that computation is based into question.

Although ideas of self-organization and emergent behavior were recognized in the heyday of cybernetics, it was complexity theory, nonlinear dynamics, and chaos theory in the 1980s that persuasively challenged the assumptions of reductivism and determinism. As we have seen, in the 1970s Mandelbrot discovered geometrical monsters, which he called *fractals*, by applying the iterative power of the computer to a nineteenth-century mathematical oddity. In a similar way, Crutchfield et al. shook the scientific establishment with the revelation that simple deterministic systems (a dripping faucet) can give rise to unpredictable and random behavior. They called this phenomenon *chaos* and noted that in principle it places limits on the power of determinism.

It is a baffling aspect of scientific history that in 1890 Henri Poincaré proved that a system composed of three (or more) bodies cannot be stable (i.e., not predictable), yet this proof was seemingly ignored for almost a century! (Not unlike the case of the frog's eye.) The scientific establishment retained its belief in principle in Laplacian causal determinism. Laplace had famously asserted in 1814 that if "an intellect" was to know the state of all forces and the position of all particles in the universe at a certain moment, then all past and future events could be predicted.

The assumption of the possibility of control of complex systems (in the face of Poincaré's proof) led to the flowering of what Chunglin Kwa (1994) called the *sciences of control*—that Paul Edwards has argued were key aspects of Cold War military strategy. Theoretically, the possibility of control is based on an assumption of predictability—that is, determinism, a key idea in Newtonian physics. It was assumed that with adequate computing power and adequate data, future developments could be predicted. It was only a matter of time before the edifice of large-scale control systems came tumbling down. Kwa has documented the failure of large-scale predictive models for urban and demographic planning, ecological and agricultural planning, and military planning and intelligence: "In the magazine *Science* it was suggested in 1976 that the International Biological Program was a failure, and that ecosystem models had not lived up to their professed ideal of total ecosystem management. . . . The air-defense system SAGE ceased to be the central component of the American air defense during the 1970s, apparently when its untrustworthiness was no longer conceived as something to be corrected with greater complexity and bigger computers" (1994, 377–378).

Kwa also noted, "Lee . . . correctly predicted the demise of what he saw as the futile efforts of the 1960s to develop large-scale, comprehensive, and integrated planning models (many of them specified with all the rigor that computerized mathematical modeling could then command) for metropolitan regions" (1994, 377; quoting Harvey 1989). It was chaos theory and nonlinear dynamics that provided the theoretical explanation for the failure of these and other grand projects of control.

# 8  Artificial Life: Emergence and Machine Creativity

Artificial Life [ALife] is the study of man-made systems that exhibit behaviors characteristic of natural living systems. It complements the traditional biological sciences concerned with the analysis of living organisms by attempting to synthesize lifelike behaviors within computers and other artificial media. By extending the empirical foundation upon which biology is based beyond the carbon-chain life that has evolved on Earth, *Artificial Life can contribute to theoretical biology by locating life-as-we-know-it within the larger picture of life-as-it-could-be.*

—Christopher G. Langton, *Artificial Life* (1989, 1; emphasis mine)

This is the way Christopher Langton defined the emerging field of artificial life. In part a response to the perceived failures of AI, artificial life claimed to create, simulate, or model *life*—as opposed to *intelligence*—and explored new ways to exploit digital computing as a way of emulating biological and social processes. Arising in the late 1980s from studies of emergence, self-organizing systems, nonlinear dynamics, and cognitive behavior among insects and nonhuman animals, ALife integrated the new computational techniques of complexity theory and nonlinear dynamics in order to model natural and lifelike systems in new ways. It preserved the drive to abstraction characteristic of AI while returning to many of the sensibilities of heretofore-taboo cybernetics.

Computationally simulated biological research laid the ground for and eventually became the main thread in the heterogeneous field of artificial life. The more extreme positions in this movement held that *in silico* systems that demonstrated lifelike properties were not just simulations but were in fact alive. Langton, an outspoken spokesman for artificial life, referred to it as a "biology of possible life" (1989) and was wont to make proclamations such as the following: "We would like to build models that are so life-like that they would cease to be *models* of life and become *examples* of life themselves" (Langton 1986, 147; emphasis in original).

Artificial life was a heterogeneous field that included such areas as evolutionary simulation, reactive robotics, social organisms, connectionism, and neural networks. The techniques of artificial life—such as cellular automata, genetic algorithms, evolutionary computing, and flocking simulations—provided a generative capability via a limited mimesis of biological processes. This was viewed as a viable alternative to AI-type computational approaches and applied to a wide variety of problems, from robot navigation to the design of coffee tables.[1]

Evolutionary dynamics is an engine for generation of variety, and the techniques of genetic algorithms and evolutionary computing were developed to simulate some aspects of biological evolution. Like any simulation, they were idealized, simplified, and abstracted. Such systems often implemented a process of mutation and selection over many generations, generating unpredictable novelty, which is a source of continuing fascination. However, evolution occurs in a teleological sense, toward a (predefined) goal state, defined by "fitness criteria." Each generation is culled to a few individuals that come closest to the fitness criteria. The question of the range and limits of possible variety available within the "computational" vis-à-vis the biological was reflected upon by more philosophical members of the community, such as Peter Cariani.

The artificial life community purported to divide itself into "hard" and "soft" factions, reminiscent of the "weak" and "strong" AI factions. The hard ALifers maintained that silicon-based "life" was indeed alive by any reasonable definition. They argued that biology must include the study of digital life, deriving universal laws embracing "wet life" and digital life. Soft ALifers retreated from claims of living digital systems and preferred to speak of models and emulations. A third grouping, the wet ALifers, were concerned with doing things to/with actual living organisms, work that laid the groundwork for contemporary synthetic biology. The notion that artificial life *is* life created a philosophical firestorm concerning intelligence, creativity, and generativity in evolving and adaptive non-carbon-based life forms. Unfortunately but inescapably, such debate was often muddied by Extropian rhetoric asserting that in computers and robotics humans were building the machine successors to biological (human) life.

## Artificial Life as a Dialectical Synthesis of Cybernetics and AI

Artificial life arose in part in response to the common sense crisis in AI (discussed in chapter 6). This crisis concerned the incompatibility of Platonic abstractions as implemented in Euclidean geometry, Newtonian physics, and Enlightenment abstraction generally with the real world. This tension recurs in the philosophy of science. One sees, in Weiner, Waddington, and Langton, a drive to find universals as opposed to identifying specificities of the embodied particular. This desire for a privileged position from which to generalize, for an "objective" viewpoint from which to look down with authority, is like the God's-eye view of cartography or the authoritative viewpoint of Renaissance perspective: a desire for abstraction and disembodiment, for transcendence.

Undergirding artificial life was a return to materiality and the material instantiation of information. It looked to biology for inspiration, particularly evolution and social organization. It valorized, explored, and replicated the mysterious phenomenon of "emergence." The rise of artificial life in the 1990s was then both a reaction to the perceived failures of the *physical symbol system* conception of AI and a renewed interest in biological models, which hearkened back to cybernetic ideas. Some ALife work can be viewed as cybernetics research implemented in digital systems. Artificial life could not have emerged as a persuasive paradigm without the easy availability of computation. This is not simply to proclaim, as did Christopher Langton, that artificial life was an exploration of life on a noncarbon substrate, but to assert that artificial life is "native" to computing in the sense that large-scale iterative processes are crucial to the procedures which generate (most) artificial life phenomena.

The second generation of thinking about biology, cognition, and computation—artificial intelligence—focused on the implementation of mechanized logico-mathematical reasoning systems, the assumption being that if such reasoning were the epitome of human intelligence, then duplications of such behavior in a machine would constitute synthetic intelligence. The fallacy in this reasoning was threefold (at least): First, human intelligence is not exclusively or even largely a matter of reasoning. Second, such reasoning is part of a historically and culturally specific intellectual tradition. Third, such reasoning depends upon a substrate of nonreasoned sensorimotor behaviors, which are mostly nonconscious and as embodied as they are cerebral.

In artificial life, to the extent that intelligence or cognition was considered, it was generally not seen as something *mental* in the cognitivist mode, but, per autopoietic biology, it was a quality of living creatures engaging with their environments, a product of biology and evolution. Along with the return to biological models (so unfashionable in the AI world), artificial life was critical of representationalism. The antirepresentationalist theory of embodied and situated robotics captured in Rodney Brooks's adage that "the world is its own best model" became a key theme in the bottom-up approaches of ALife, often explicitly opposed to AI's top-down, God's-eye view approaches. Concepts of distributed, self-organizing systems and bottom-up cognition opposed the hierarchical centralization of AI and SMPA notions of behavior. Artificial life was generally anticognitivist and anti-internalist. It emphasized the specificity of an environmental situation over aspirations to abstraction and generality.

The logic of ALife was evolutionary and rejected human exceptionalism. Many creatures metabolize, but only some are mobile. Only a small percentage of creatures are multicellular, and few have nervous systems and organs. Of those, only a few have a proper brain and sensory organs. And of those, only a few can plan, and so forth. From this perspective, human intelligence is a late byproduct of a long evolutionary history. In a similar non-exceptionalist spirit, cognition was taken—at least by those who accepted the principles of autopoietic biology—as a universal characteristic of the living, as opposed to being a capacity of (human) minds. In these notions, we see a resurgence of a sensibility suppressed for a generation. Artificial life was, dialectically, a third generation of thinking about the qualities of biological life with respect to computational machines. It was a moment of novelty and expansive thinking: a somewhat joyous celebration of emancipation from an increasingly gloomy cul-de-sac of cognitivist AI thinking, which nonetheless perpetuated key ideas of AI, including, in some quarters, functionalism. Langton's notion of life on a silicon substrate is textbook functionalism. Artificial life thus represents an awkward dialectical synthesis of cybernetics and digital computing ideas.

### Cellular Automata, Evolved Graphics, and Procedural Modeling

The paradigmatic example of artificial life dynamics is an iterative mathematical game called the Game of Life developed by John Conway in 1970. The game was prototyped on paper and only later computerized. Conway's Game of Life is an example of a class of mathematical processes called *cellular automata*, originally devised by John von Neumann as a part of his discussion of the possibility of self-replicating machines. The dynamics of Conway's Game of Life echo themes of self-organizing systems in the cybernetic period. Played out on a (potentially infinite) square grid, Conway's game generated surprisingly complex emergent dynamical behaviors from simple, local rules operating on individual pixels. This stunningly elegant game provides an immediate analogy to the idea of emergent complexity in the living world: the emergence of complex molecules from atoms, the

**Figure 8.1**
One time step in a sequence in Conway's Game of Life. Running the program, or watching a video recording of the running program, is far more informative.

emergence of metabolism and reproduction from such molecules, cellular interactions and the emergence of consciousness from neural processes. As such, it quickly became an emblem of ALife.

In the 1980s, digital 3-D animation was a young field; attempts were being made to automate the movement of entities through virtual, animated spaces. It was in this context that Craig Reynolds developed a set of "steering behaviors" that resulted in remarkably persuasive simulations of the flocking and schooling behaviors of virtual entities he punningly called "boids" (2007). As with Conway's Game of Life, and analogous to social insect behaviors, each boid knew very little—a general direction of travel and the distance to its nearest neighbors. The "steering behaviors" kept each agent at an optimal distance from its neighbors. Note that this system is distributed and, like Agre and Chapman's Pengi, deictic. The larger theoretical implication of such work was that simple autonomous behaviors by numerous simple agents could produce (the appearance of) large-scale organized behavior (organization, as Ashby, von Foerster, Varela, and others observed, being in the eye of the beholder). Reynolds's boids thus were taken as an exemplar of emergence, and they provide an early model for multiagent systems. Reynolds was invited to present this research at the first artificial life workshop in 1987, and the boids became an icon in ALife.

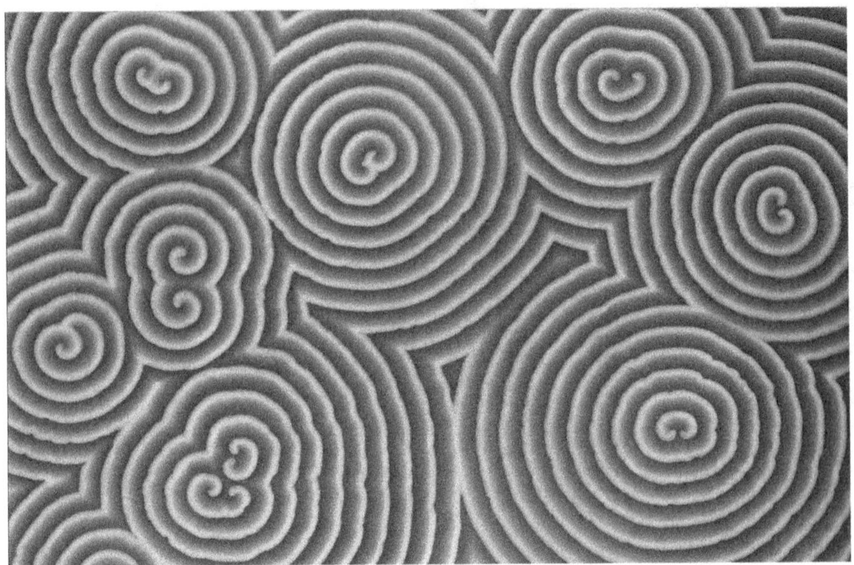

**Figure 8.2**
A moment in an ongoing Belousov-Zhabotinsky reaction.

In 1992, Andrew Witkin and Michael Kass won the Ars Electronica Golden Nica for computer graphics for *RD Texture Buttons*, a system that generated plausibly "natural" patterns and textures based on *reaction diffusion*, nonlinear partial differential equations (Prix Ars Electronica 1992). This work was a simulation of the canonical example of self-organization in chemistry, the Belousov-Zhabotinsky reaction. It deployed the mathematics of nonlinear dynamics and represented significant progress in computer graphic research at the time.

The desire to describe "nature" mathematically has a long history, one of its landmarks being D'Arcy Wentworth Thompson's magnum opus *On Growth and Form* (1917). Combining the biomathematical research of Thompson with aspects of fractal math and deploying simulated evolution and 3-D modeling, British sculptor William Latham evolved an array of biomorphic forms, mostly existing as virtual sculptural objects. As computational capabilities—particularly graphical capabilities—advanced, so the modalities of the work developed: through still graphics and animation to interactive (and sometimes immersive) real-time systems.

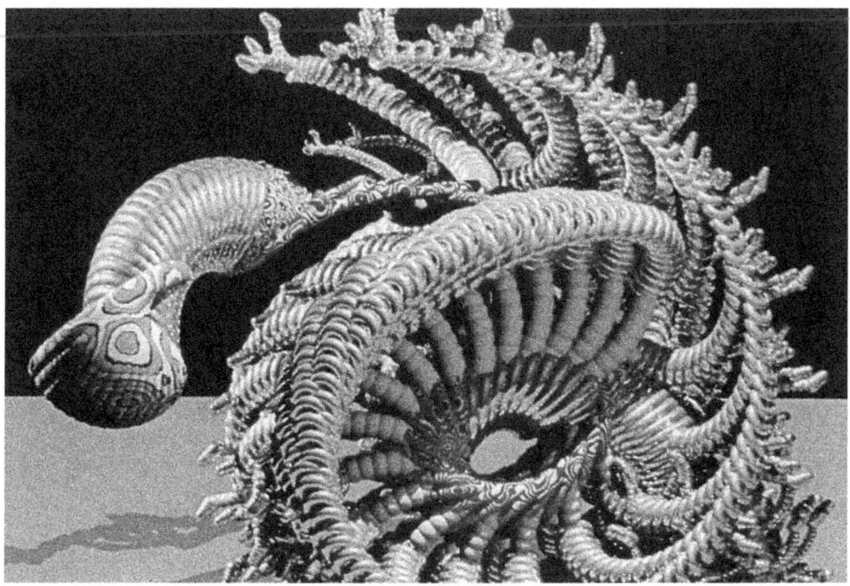

**Figure 8.3**
William Latham, *Mutation Raytraced on the Plane of Infinity*. Prix Ars Electronica 1992,
Honorary Mention (Computergraphics). Courtesy of William Latham.

## Genetic Algorithms and Synthetic Evolution

In 1975, John Holland published *Adaptation in Natural and Artificial Systems*, in which he outlined the notion of a genetic algorithm as a method of problem analysis based on Darwinian natural selection. This publication brought previous work in computational modeling of genetics and evolution to a larger ALife audience.[2] In such systems, an initial population with randomly generated characteristics is evaluated by some method (called *fitness criteria*) to establish the most successful members, which are mutated and crossbred to produce a new population, which is then tested against the same criteria. This process is repeated numerous times, and increasingly fit products are generated. This technique often arrives at novel and mysterious solutions, creating code structures that are not like human-written algorithms and are resistant to reverse engineering. They work, but we don't know why.

Genetic algorithms have been deployed in a host of application domains to design or evolve machine-vision systems, diesel engines, stock market prediction systems, coffee tables, artworks, and robots. Karl Sims's spectacular

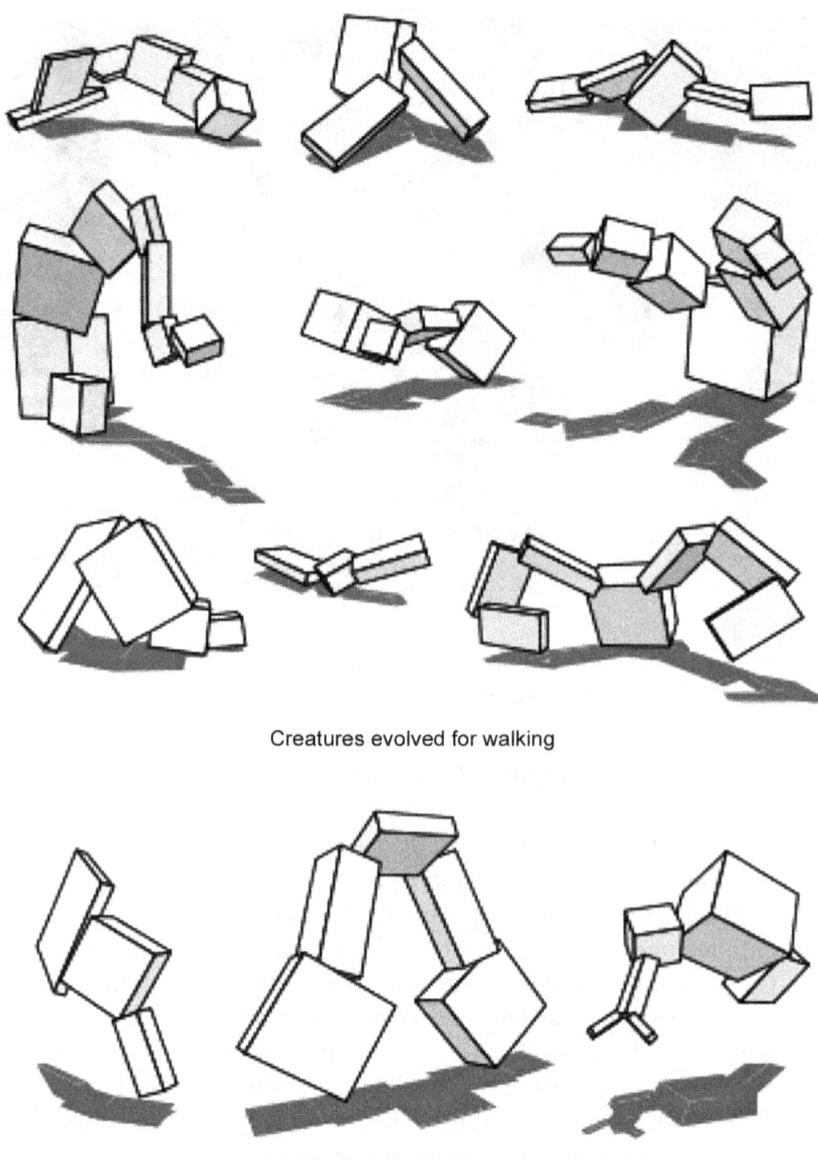



**Figure 8.4**
Images from Karl Sims's *Evolving Virtual Creatures*. Courtesy of Karl Sims.

evolved virtual creatures were poster children for this technique (1994a, 1994b). Over the next decade, Sims played a leading role in developing technologies and works—an early example being the animation "Panspermia" (Sims 1991). A year or two later, his project Evolved Virtual Creatures (developed when he was in residence at Thinking Machines, a developer of innovative massively parallel computers) had a resounding influence, as it demonstrated highly persuasive animations of computationally evolving ALife creatures.

## Parallel Distributed Processing and Connectionism: The Resurgence of Neural Networks

Much ALife inquiry focused on mechanisms for generating novelty, including phenomena such as consciousness and aspects of intelligence that might be understood as more associationist than deductive. Connectionism (aka *neural nets*) received renewed interest, offering the prospect of ways of addressing the common sense problem.

Parallel distributed processing (PDP) deviated from a representationalist approach based on explicit symbols, framing knowledge and learning in terms of networks of connections: "There is, on this view, no such thing as 'hardwiring.' Neither is there any such thing as 'software.' There are only connections. All connections are in some sense hardwired (in as much as they are physical entities) and all are software (in as much as they can be changed)" (Rumelhart, McClelland, and PDP Research Group 1986, 141).[3] This kind of approach, disparaged in the AI period, was a continuation—at least in spirit—of work begun by McCulloch and Pitts. "Knowledge is implicit and distributed across the entire pattern of interconnections," Rumelhart, Hinton, and McClelland argue. "It is 'in' the connections rather than in a change of state of any isolated unit in the system" (75–76). Implicit in this work is a relational sensibility that bears some similarity to the rhizomatic thinking of Deleuze and Guattari, popular in critical theory circles in the same period. Inherent also is a critique of representationalism, in the sense that these systems can perform intelligent work but do not contain representations that input data are compared with. This brings not only the idea of mental representation but the entire SMPA paradigm into question, for computers and robots as well as for human minds: "Schemata are not explicit entities, but rather are implicit in our knowledge and are created by the very environment that they are trying to interpret . . . in the conventional story, schemata are stored in memory. . . . In our case, *nothing stored corresponds very closely to* a schema. What is stored is a set of connection strengths which, when activated, have implicitly in them the ability to generate states that correspond to instantiated schemata" (1986, 20–21; emphasis in original).

Today, research in Artificial Intelligence is almost exclusively connectionist, a radical turnaround from the dismissal of neural nets by Minsky and Papert in the heyday of GOFAI (see chapter 5). Google has taken up and deployed this research, especially in its pattern recognition technology. Inceptionism (2015) is a Google feature recognition tool designed to identify features (dog's heads, trees, pagodas, and so on) in images. When provided with random "noise" files, the software "hallucinates," generating alarming, psychadelic imagery. Google's Go-playing system, AlphaGo (released in 2016), is making inroads into automating that game, for which GOFAI methods made little headway. This is a testament to the capabilities of neural net systems.

**The Failures of Top-Down Thinking**

Typically, when AI techniques were applied to problems of robot navigation, data was gathered by sensors and an internal map of the environment of the robot was generated, over which a path was planned. Instructions were then sent to output devices. As the robot proceeded down this path, the environment was remeasured, position plotted on the map, and map and path corrected if necessary. This method is classically top-down, rooted in Enlightenment-Platonic dualistic abstraction: The map is a pure, true, abstract representation, from which decisions about the world are made without recourse to the world. In practice, these systems were very slow (but we must allow for the fact that the computers of the period of first-generation AI were, by modern standards, very slow). It was noted with chagrin that a cockroach, with only a handful of neurons, was better at crossing a road than the most powerful computer—and could do more complex things besides! Rodney Brooks observed that cockroaches don't map and iconoclastically proposed that AI should stand for *artificial insects*. According to Brooks, it was bald-faced hubris to imagine we could build a human-like machine intelligence if we could not build a machine with the capabilities of a cockroach.

The top-down paradigm, with its centralization of control perpetuates panoptical models; its dualism replicates and reinforces the traditional dualisms of master and slave, general and soldiers, boss and workers, and, more abstractly, nature/culture, body/mind, form/content, and hardware/software. Bottom-up theories, by contrast, dispute hierarchical authoritarian power structures and are sympathetic with horizontal and rhizomatic power structures. (That is not to say that research in the bottom-up school has avoided philosophical pitfalls.)

### Reactive Robotics: Fast, Cheap, and Out of Control

A concern with embodied and autonomous agents was characteristic of the artificial life movement of the 1990s—hence the focus on reactive and bottom-up robotics, a robotics that found fault with the computationalist worldview and turned for inspiration to biology (an approach which had been unfashionable for a generation).[4] For an artifact to behave in the world implies autonomy and thus quasi-biology—for what has autonomy except organisms? To the extent that they are sensing and acting systems, robots constitute a kind of quasi-organism.

Expatriate Australian roboticist Rodney Brooks was a major figure in this movement. The most resounding early proof of principle of reactive robotics were Brooks's two robots, Allen and Herbert (named for Allen Newell and Herbert Simon), described in "Elephants Don't Play Chess" (1990).[5] They had the task of tooling around the hallways of the MIT AI Lab collecting empty soda cans. These robots had no powerful central processor that took in symbolic representations of sensor data and planned routes or executed can-collecting maneuvers. Rather, the robots had a hardware architecture of independent parallel sensorimotor systems that Brooks called "subsumption," entailing little or no manipulation of representations. These simple, independent systems interacted closely with the world itself rather than with representations of it. Robots structured this way executed their tasks in more robust ways than did robots using more traditional methods.

The reactive/subsumption paradigm is important, not only because of its pragmatic success but also because it inhered several radical ideas. First, the robots were phenomenologically grounded in the world: they did not deploy or require a process of abstraction of the world into symbolic representations to be effective. Second, they were nonhierarchical: They did not depend for their success on the amalgamation of all input data into an authoritative model from which all output was computed. Third, they did not plan. The notion of parallel behaviors was no doubt influenced by Marvin Minsky's *The Society of Mind* (1986). Subsumption provides a model of a functioning creature in which there is no unitary self, except as imputed by an external observer, a current idea in neuroscience.

Brooks made explicit reference to von Uexküll, and one can trace his subsumption logic to von Uexküll's analysis of sensorimotor behaviors. He is less explicit about his debt to cybernetics, though later in life he recalled being inspired as a child by seeing William Grey Walter's Turtles. The connection is clear: like Allen and Herbert, Walter's Elmer and Elsie were entirely reactive and grounded in their environment. For them, as for von Uexküll's tick, the world was the only model.

## Stigmergic Robotics

As discussed in chapter 7, colonial organisms and insects—from slime molds to sponges to bees, ants, and termites—were a subject of great interest in the artificial life community. One of the more remarkable early proofs-of-concept of synthetic emergent systems based on biological models was the work of Beckers, Holland, and Deneubourg (1994), which emulated termite building behavior in small robots.[6] Following the work of Wilhelm Bosch, Eugene Marias, and Pierre Paul Grassé, Beckers, Holland, and Deneubourg emulated pheromone-driven behavior changes among termites. In this experiment, a small group of independent robots, each with very simple behavior and no large goal or plan, generated large-scale organized behavior. Each robot had a little scoop at the front. Their behavior was simple: It consisted of moving forward and turning a random number of degrees when it encountered a degree of resistance. The robots wandered in a field strewn with styrofoam blocks that the experimenters called pucks. When they had scooped up three pucks, the robots would dump, reverse, and turn. This behavior eventually put all eighty-one pucks in their pen into a single pile—without any centralized coordination or master plan.

Such results fed the idea in artificial life that biological analogies held promise for solving some problems than had been intractable for AI. In combination with ideas such as flocking and emergence, conceptions of multiagent and swarm robotics were developed to link robotics with the study of social insects. Biological and nonbiological systems that demonstrate emergent complex behavior came to have special importance in ALife circles.

## Dynamical Systems

Distributed emergent systems are everywhere in nature. Think of the growth patterns of a tree: A leaf grows if and only if there is available sunlight. There is no master plan of growth. There are only local circumstances that encourage or discourage growth. The leaves form a canopy, a surface at the extremities of the branches. Beneath this surface, leaves do not grow. The result of this process, in combination with competition from adjacent trees, gives rise to an optimal design for gathering maximal sunlight with minimal structure, adaptive to the specific and changing context, responsive to environmental factors.

Such ongoing dynamical processes reveal the limitation of the notion of homeostasis. To return to the stable local minimum of an attractor basin offers no explanatory value for questions of ecological, evolutionary, or cultural development. However, an overly "teleological" explanation has its own implicit problems. That natural systems can appear to have trajectories in the absence of an evident master plan or centralized control is one of the mysteries of biology. Such phenomena are both general and beyond the explanatory capability of reductivism but are clearly intelligent in a way incompatible with cognitivism. It was in response to such dilemmas that C. H. Waddington developed the concept of homeorhesis (see chapter 2), which connotes the return of a system to a trajectory rather than a state. He also coined the associated term *chreod*, meaning *necessary path*, which is the trajectory to which the system tends to return.

## Artificial Life, Emergence, and Surprise

In recognition of the stymied hopes for generating computer-based creativity via artificial intelligence methods, a central concern in the new field of artificial life was the development of mechanisms for generating novelty by simulating biological processes. The notion of creativity has affinity with emergent order and emergent novelty and more generally with ideas of self-organizing systems that immediately links back to cybernetic and systems-theoretic thinking. Loosely speaking, a *self-organizing system* is one that manifests new organization de novo.

Artificial life confronted the question of "creativity" in synthetic systems in quite a different way from AI approaches. The question of whether a computer could be creative was not in this case reduced to inference procedures but was connected to the emulation of emergence—and specifically, emergent complex behavior and self-organization in digital environments. Improvisation, surprise, generativity, creativity, and novelty are all explicit or implicit in artificial life literature. In the discourse of complex, self-organizing, and dynamical systems, "surprise" is conceived of as *emergent*—as arising (meta)properties that were not previously present in a system. The key quality of emergence is that it is fundamentally nonreductive and thus creates tension with basic principles of scientific experiment of the divide-and-conquer kind. Emergent phenomena arise out of and are constituted by underlying processes, but the behaviors and categories of phenomena manifested therein are independent from the underlying processes and irreducible to them. Oft-cited examples include the complex collaborative behaviors of colonial organisms such as corals, sponges, and slime molds; the architecture of ants, bees, and termites; and the arising of consciousness from neural structure.

## Emergence Defined: Cariani

The term *emergence* is often applied loosely, and one man's emergence is another man's predictable (if complex) system.[7] If artificial life is about surprise, then the question of what constitutes surprise must be asked. Over several decades, Peter Cariani has provided some analytic precision on questions of what constitutes novelty or emergence by deploying systems-theoretic approaches to analyze various categories of emergence in the context of robotics and artificial life.

Cariani makes a primary distinction between what he terms *combinatoric* and *creative* emergence: operating within a framework of set constraints versus creating new frameworks (2012). Combinatoric emergence consists of the recombination of existing symbol primitives (reminding us of Gödel's notion of closed logical systems). This is the kind of emergence that can be pursued in software systems. Although this space can be large, it is countable and not infinite. Creative emergence is akin to "thinking out of the box." According to Cariani, creative emergence requires the generation of new primitives; in the computer world, this would correspond to the development of new procedures, if not new hardware.

The limits proposed by Cariani are consistent with phenomenological critiques of AI, Searle's Chinese room, and the symbol-grounding problem (Harnad 1990). Such limits concerned the givenness in ALife of the silicon hardware substrate and the flexibility (via evolution) of the hardware substrate in biology.[8] Cariani argues that the ability to evolve new sensors generally exceeds AI and ALife techniques.[9] The idea of evolvable hardware comes close to von Neumann's grail of the self-reproducing automaton. The conception of combinatoric emergence suggests an isomorphic fit between improvisational practices and computational procedures. An example of Cariani's *creative* category is the community of musical instrument inventors (acoustic, electronic, and digital) who have followed in the path of Harry Partch by creating new hardware substrates for new behaviors. In general, then, any kind of prosthetic technology is creative—if we adopt an extended and cyborgian conception of identity.

## Emergence In Digital Systems

In genetic or evolving computational projects, the inherent dualism of computer systems persists. Algorithm is separate from data. In the physics of the virtual, the force of the algorithm works upon the mass of the data. In the genetic paradigm, the evolved code establishes an intermediary step, but it is the design of the environment (the fitness landscape) that generates the code that becomes the designed or (meta)creative act. Even if an individual was to propose the breeding of these environments themselves, or to propose that the "fitness landscapes" were configured so as to evolve responsively to the pressures of the populations evolving within them, the design function simply moves one step into the background—or to put it another way, the system is jacked up another level off the ground. This infinite regress is like Sengers's diagnosis of schizophrenia in autonomous agents.

At root, such systems always ground out in Boolean logical operations, fixed in hardware. Where does this leave beguiling arguments for emergence—in particular, arguments of the emergence of consciousness? Cariani has argued that computational emergence always devolves to exclusive logical operations and is thus not emergent at all.[10]

## Sensors and Perception

Consistent with the second-order cybernetics of von Foerster, Cariani (1992) argues that such systems are only emergent relative to the observational frame of an observer. Put simply, if it is a surprise, then it is emergent; if it's not, then it's not. Cariani identifies true emergence with *adaptation* (a key cybernetic term) and reserves it for systems integrated into and open to the physical world that can evolve their own sensors. In his terms, *syntactically adaptive* systems can evolve their response to sensor data, and *semantically adaptive* devices alter the relation between environmental state and internal representation by evolving new sensors. Such ideas are cogent in the world of physical, biological phenomena but become murky in the digital world, and here we see disingenuousness in the rhetoric of the hard ALifers.

The fact is that in the digital realm, everything is potentially definitive and knowable; there is no need for interpretation or determination of salience (of sensor data) as there is in the physical world. This is the sense in which Michael Mateas asserts that "software is a perfect material" (pers. comm.). The notion of virtual sensors that collect particular data from a stream of digital data (e.g., Internet traffic) is as common as it is false. The conception of a *virtual sensor*—code that watches for other significant code events, be they in a digitized video data stream or a mail agent sorting email—is metaphoric at best. Sensors convert electrophysical phenomena in the world into digital representations. Data streams are already representations. Virtual sensors are not sensors; they are, at best, filters or sorting criteria.

Perception is not simply sensing; it is *sense-making*. Inherent in the notion of a virtual sensor is the idea that sensing is data collection and that data is simply present, waiting to be mechanically collected. Perception implies determination of salience, at least, and determination of salience is intelligent behavior. So perception is a kind of intelligence, but the serial SMPA paradigm precludes intelligence at the sensor and effector extremities.

The separation of sensor and processor may work for the von Neumann architecture but it is invalid for biological systems. In digital systems, conversion from an analog sensor signal to digital data is axiomatic, but in biological systems it is nonexistent or occurs in multiple, finely graduated steps. In the fly's eye, some computation occurs "in hardware," in the physical layout of the light-receptive cells (see chapter 2). The imposition of an analog-to-digital discontinuity on biological systems is obfuscating computationalist dogma.

### Gödel Again: "Emergence Relative to a Model"

Clearly, conventional software-based generative and interactive systems depend on combinatoric emergence. Software systems, as logically coherent domains, are constrained by Gödel's incompleteness theorem. In the context of our larger concerns, we might ask: Do human improvisatory practices broach the combinatoric/creative barrier, or do they fit into the category of combinatorial emergence within a general taxonomy of emergence? That is, does improvisation generate ontological novelty? In general, improvisatory practices remain genre-bound and thus in the realm of the combinatoric. In certain cases, improvisatory practices have generated entirely new genres—the case of the Living Theater comes to mind, as well as some live video–based improvisatory practices of the 1970s (e.g., the early work of William Wegman, Vito Acconci, and Peter Campus). However, such genre-busting events are rare and sporadic, like successful mutations. In this way, these cultural revolutions are consistent with Kuhn's paradigm shifts and with Gould's punctuated equilibrium. When these breakthroughs occur, they tend to be disturbing and disorienting, at least until new worldviews grow around them.

The growth of new worldviews—like the stabilization of an ecology around an introduced species—is roughly comparable to *emergence relative to a model,* a major idea in Cariani's analysis (Cariani 1992). This idea is rooted in the second-order cybernetics of von Foerster et al. and in the radical constructivism of von Glasersfeld. The notion is that the occurrence of creative emergence is only palpable when the behavior of the system becomes inexplicable according to the descriptive or explanatory model deployed by the observer. This model is an externally imposed reference and must be known and shared for the behavior to be perceived as improvisatory. The point relevant to the current context is the necessity of a preexisting (and shared) model, representation, or frame of reference for improvisation to "make sense." Responses such as "It doesn't make sense" and "It's just noise" imply the lack of a shared model between musician and audience.

The problem with a machine that possesses "creative emergence," then, would be that it would constantly exceed our capability to conceptualize its frame of reference. It would be confusing; as such, it would likely exceed the psychological comfort zone of any viewers/users, and the experience would be perceived as unpleasant,[11] not unlike the experience (for many) of the works of Survival Research Laboratories (SRL) or the Catalan performance group La Fura Dels Baus.[12]

## The Generative

What is a generative system? A novel with two possible endings can hardly be regarded as generative, nor can a choose-your-own-adventure book. The range of possibilities is firmly encoded in ink on paper, and any surprise quotient is minimal and predefined and occurs only once for any reader. The surprise is written on the page, just waiting for you to read it. Card games (e.g., poker, bridge, or 500) are generative, but only within the combinatoric range of the existing cards and the established rules: You'll never get an eleven of diamonds. A computer poker game is generative only in the most trivial sense: If a computing device happened to have stored all possible outcomes, how could we tell? A random number generator (or a pseudorandom number generator; who can tell the difference?) is generative, but it is hardly interesting—at least to creatures like us.[13]

What then constitutes interest? Some kind of pattern and some kind of development? That is, establishing a pattern, then breaking it, only to develop a larger pattern of which the prior smaller pattern and its breakage can be seen to be a part (metapatterning)? This sounds like a compositional strategy: A language is established; its rules are broken, producing a phase of incomprehensibility; then a new rule set is established that includes the rules of the first pattern and the "rules" of the breakage.

## Tierra and Artificial Life Art

Within the (small) community of interdisciplinary and technically literate computer artists, many were highly attentive to the emergence and activities of the artificial life community, because these practices promised a kind of supercharged interactivity: autonomously behaving art that could make its own decisions based on its own interpretations of the/its world. The methods of artificial life suggested the possibility of the holy grail of machine creativity and autonomous agency. Not simply reproducing the one-to-one man-machine model, but expanding the notion of computer interactivity to synthetic and hybrid ecologies.

One of the early celebrated artificial life experiments was named *Tierra*, built by biologist Thomas Ray. In Tierra, (digital) forms evolved to compete better, and various kinds of biological survival strategies emerged, such as host/parasite relations and predator/prey relations, involving cycles of development of aggressive and defensive behaviors (Cho and Ray 1995).[14] In the ALife art world, response to Tierra was double. As an idea, Tierra was exciting, but like much scientific research, one knew it by interpreting data and numbers. The challenge to the art community was how to open such phenomena to direct sensory experience.

Given such a world of creatures, one might reasonably want to watch them, follow them, construct them, and constrain them. The artist would become a gardener, a metadesigner, imposing constraints upon the environments of her creatures, which would then respond in potentially surprising ways. This entailed visualization and interaction/interface design. A community of "art breeders" arose in the early 1990s and explored the generation of aesthetic artifacts via various ALife and genetic procedures; the community included the aforementioned Karl Sims, Andy Witkin, and Willian Latham, as well as Jon McCormack, Scott Draves, Jeffrey Ventrella, Bernd Lintermann,[15] and others. Digital creatures and communities of behaving and often interactive digital life forms became common. Researchers developed underlying evolutionary and ecological architectures and interaction schemes based on biological and ecological analogies. In *Turbulence* (1994–1995), Australian computer graphic artist and computer scientist Jon McCormack presented a digital animation of an array of evolved and synthetic life forms in an installation context. User interaction was restricted to navigation of the database of clips. In this context, we must also mention the hallucinogenic biomorphic computer animations of Yoichiro Kawaguchi of the 1980s and 1990s, which, while not "evolved," were an inspiration to many.

*Interactive Plant Growing* by Christa Sommerer and Laurent Mignonneau (1993) was an early foray into the performative visualization of artificial life. Five potted plants were monitored for changes in their galvanic condition. As visitors approached and fondled the plants, these galvanic changes were utilized as variables in the program, which grew virtual plants on the screen in response to the visitors' fondling. *TechnoSphere* by Jane Prophet and Gordon Selley (1995) involved a web-accessible, computer-generated landscape/environment in which users could release creatures they had built from components available in the application. Creatures would then interact and compete by fighting, attempting to mate, and so on. Along with the modeling of an artificial ecology, *TechnoSphere* engaged other contemporary challenges in digital media arts, such as the creation of navigable virtual landscapes, strategies for real-time interaction, and utilizing the web as a presentation environment.

Much of the media art research which occurred through the 1990s was commercialized in the following decade, including much generative computer art. In some cases it might be charitable to suggest that the techniques were reinvented and that the media art world was just a decade ahead of the commercial world. *Spore*, a 2008 video game developed by Maxis and designed by Will Wright, and other games like it represent the commercialization of the cumulative research of the artificial life art community.

## Conclusion

By the late 1980s, it was clear that highly iterated computational processes held the paradoxical potential to simulate processes that seemed to defy the ordered predictability of Boolean logic and Newtonian physics. The artificial life community pursued research based in nonlinear systems, which challenged conventional reductive and mechanistic science and engineering. Research into fractals, nonlinear dynamics, cellular automata, genetic programming, and related practices provided a context in which artificial life might develop. Stuart Kauffman's expansive *The Origins of Order* (1993) quickly became one of the primary texts of the movement, and Stephen Wolfram's *A New Kind of Science* (2002) became its epilogue. Artificial life can be seen as a dialectical synthesis of cybernetics and AI. While artificial life, as a field, dwindled in the following decade, the research that originated in that community was rapidly adopted in diverse fields, from computer graphics for games and movies to the modeling of social and demographic processes to the development of military swarm robots. The artificial life movement was contemporaneous with the rise of postcognitivist theories of cognition. The two communities had strong sympathies and much source literature in common.

# 9   Rethinking Cognitivism

Why must we seek explanation in either Body or Mind? It seems a false dichotomy.

—J. J. Gibson, *The Ecological Approach to Visual Perception* (1979, xii)

Idealism and Materialism are answers to an improper question. The "reduction" of the material world to mental states and processes, as well as the "reduction" of mental states and processes to physical states and processes, presuppose the legitimacy of the disjunction "Either there exist minds or there exist bodies (but not both)." It would be like saying, "Either she bought a left-hand and a right-hand glove or she bought a pair of gloves (but not both)."

—Gilbert Ryle, *The Concept of Mind* (1949, 22–23)

To the extent that the engineering field is prescriptive by design, this kind of epistemological blunder is still workable. However, it becomes unbearable and useless when exported from the domain of prescription to that of description of natural systems. To assume in these fields that information is some *thing* that is transmitted, that symbols are *things* that can be taken at face value, or that purposes and goals are made clear by the systems themselves is all, it seems to me, nonsense . . . Information, sensu stricto, does not exist.

—Francisco Varela, "Describing the Logic of the Living: The Adequacy and Limitations of the Idea of Autopoiesis" (1980, 45; emphasis in original)

The three quotations above dispute mind-body dualism and other aspects of a mechanistic approach to biology and cognition. As such, they draw out tensions between the Enlightenment humanist values reified in computing, AI, and cognitivism, and contrary arguments arising in biology, ethology, nonlinear dynamics, and artificial life (as elucidated in part I). This prepares the reader for part II, in which postcognitivist paradigms are introduced. Postcognitivism is the term I use to describe new approaches in cognitive science that emerged during and since the "common sense crisis": The recognition that the common sense problem and symbol-grounding problem in AI were not bugs amenable to technical tweaking but were in fact fundamental problems in principle.

Suppose a person were to ask, "What was the fundamental commitment of computationalism, around which all of its capabilities and limitations were arrayed?" I think that "a Platonic/Cartesian commitment to the notion of the immateriality of cogitation" would be a fair answer. One of the enduring problems engendered by this neo-Cartesianism is the reification of the key tenets of this philosophy in a major technology. The separation of software and hardware and the presumed immateriality of information are articles of faith in the cult of computing and are direct analogs of the Cartesian dualism. Such separation is fundamental to the formulation of artificial intelligence. From this axiomatic assumption fall a variety of methods and approaches that characterize the AI/cognitivist attitude, many of which transpired to be problematic (not surprisingly) with respect to the application of these ideas to an understanding of mind and cognition, and as AI moved toward real-world situated problems, such as robotics and natural-language processing.

Identifying reasoning as the pinnacle of human intelligence, the AI community aimed straight for it. As a result, interaction with the world was seen as peripheral to intelligence proper. This choice belied the philosophical commitments of AI, and it had its consequences. It was also pragmatic. The symbol-manipulation approach would require, eventually, automatic devices that would extract symbols to be manipulated from the world, but the necessary technology did not yet exist. It was assumed (wrongly) that the "translation" required to perform this symbol manipulation would transpire to be relatively straightforward. This was a reasonable hedge at the time. For instance, while the idea of interfacing a camera with a computer was conceivable in 1965, the task of interfacing a television camera (the only electronic camera at the time) with a computer would have demanded all the processing power of a room-sized computer. While computer vision as a research project was proposed in 1960 (Roberts), it was not until 1978 that David Marr outlined a potentially viable way forward. Half a century later, even though cameras are now part of every phone, the task of extracting the content of pictures still preoccupies major players such as Google.

In the meantime, research proceeded by providing reasoning systems with human-built streams of symbols, which were taken to be similar to those that might be produced by an appropriate sensor/interpreter system when it came along. In the event, this turned out to be overly optimistic, as the common sense problem demonstrated. Without the experience of making these vision systems work, conjectures regarding the mechanisms of biological vision or workable synthetic vision remained conjectures. The hypothesis that visual experience could be reduced to streams of symbolic tokens was untested, and was already dubious, given the research of Gibson and others. But the culture of AI was a closed culture, and the dictates of functionalism rendered such inquiries irrelevant. Part of the radicality of Rodney Brooks's research program was that he insisted that every layer or module be tested in the world as a stand-alone system, before building it into more complex systems. He was insistent on this, due no doubt, to his awareness of problems encountered attempting to adapt AI "castles in the sky" or "toy problems" such as "block world" to real-world situations.

## Cognition as Reasoning

From a history-of-ideas standpoint it is important to note that cognitive science emerged in the context of Anglo-American analytic philosophy and was thereby invested in notions of representation and disembodied logical reasoning from the outset. Cognitive science and artificial intelligence were born joined at the hip and shared a commitment to the idea of thought or intelligence as symbol manipulation. As heirs to the Anglo-American philosophical tradition, functionalism and its offshoot computationalism are inherently committed to mentalist or internalist explanation—to the idea that such phenomena as intelligence and cognition occur in the mind (a nonphysical thing) or at least in the brain (a special organ for reasoning) as algorithmic manipulations of representations. Regarding this philosophical heritage, Jerry Fodor rightly said, "Insofar as the Representational Theory of Mind is the content of the computer metaphor, the computer metaphor predates the computer by about three hundred years" (1981, 140).

## Validation and Automation of Symbolic Representation

Through the modern period, scientific and scientized disciplines have become increasingly mathematized. Scientific epistemology has drifted from emphasis on empirical data and physical models and demonstrations toward a valorization of abstract symbolic representation. Computers and computing are isomorphic with this worldview in the sense that they deal in symbolic representations. The culture of computing has validated this epistemology. However, this valorization of abstract symbolic representation has serious implications. Noting that "the privileged status of mathematical entities in the study of cognition was already central to Descartes' theory," Philip Agre cogently observed, "a theory of cognition based on formal reason works best with objects of cognition whose attributes and relationships can be completely characterized in formal terms" (1997b, 143). Humberto Maturana made similar remarks, emphasizing again, the role of the observer and the map/territory problem: "A mathematical formalism is a conceptual and operational system that reveals the relational coherences of the space that it defines. . . . But mathematical formalisms do not provide or create by themselves an understanding of the phenomena that an observer explains to him or herself through them" (2002, 18).

Without a doubt, Newell, Shaw, and Simon's *Logic Theorist* was a tour de force of intellectual achievement. But its chosen object, a proof in formal logic, was hardly a big reach, given that the language of the program and the procedures of the machine are nothing but an operationalization of precisely that tradition. As discussed in chapter 6, the kinds of contingent, situated judgments that people make every day, often unconsciously, are often not amenable to this kind of reasoning—are not *computable* (at least by conventional symbolic AI techniques). However, such tasks would have been seen as trivial precisely because the kind of thinking most valorized in the Western tradition as the epitome of intellect is precisely logico-mathematical reasoning; the *Principia Mathematica* (Whitehead and Russell 1910) was seen as the high point of that tradition.

The public demonstration of AI's success in the development of grand master–level chess playing programs is (as discussed in chapter 6) similarly tautological, in the sense that chess is a closed logical world amenable to complete formal description—precisely the kind of (abstract and artificial) environment that computers do best in. While this achievement was by no means trivial, prosaic real-world tasks, like route planning for deliveries, turn out to be more challenging to compute due to the rapid proliferation of alternatives, each with its own contingencies. The resulting breakdowns in AI systems are referred to as *brittleness*. Beer, Chiel, and Sterling put it this way: "When even the most mundane contingency arises in our everyday interactions with the real world, we may draw upon an incredibly diverse collection of cognitive skills and a lifetime's worth of accumulated knowledge to cope with it" (1990, 170).

The concept of the physical symbol system, and Alan Newell and Herbert Simon's assertion that "a physical symbol system has the necessary and sufficient means for general intelligent action" (1976, 116), was central to AI and cognitivism. Digital computing operationalizes propositional logic and is thus the epitome of the Enlightenment rationalist ideal—a machine that reasons without body, without affect. Computational explanations have limited explanatory power regarding experiential lived-being. As Philip

Agre wisely observed, "Just as Descartes felt that he possessed clear and distinct knowledge of geometric shapes, Newell and Simon's programs suffered no epistemological gaps or crises in reasoning about the mathematical entities in their domains" (1997b, 143). The much-touted successes of digital computing in tasks of abstract reasoning (such as playing chess) have a hollow circularity about them, and they reveal the way the AI/cognitivist community has controlled discourse around matters of intelligence and cognition.

This confusion between intelligence as reasoning and intelligence as successful operation in the world continues to the present day. It is precisely this confusion that has rendered cognitivism a liability in explanations of intelligent action in the world, of which the arts provide epitome examples. This is why the new postcognitivist paradigms seem, to this author, to provide such an important breakthrough in discussions of the intelligences of the arts.

According to functionalism and to the physical symbol system hypothesis, algorithmic procedures of intelligent reasoning were taken to be transferable in principle to some other substrate, from brains to computers or vice versa. Like modularity and seriality, this quality, which in its technical realization in computer science is called *platform independence*, is an axiomatic restatement and reification of the functionalist doctrine of multiple realizability. This conception serves to reinforce the reigning cognitivism of popular psychology, even if these ideas might be found dubious in parts of the academy.

This hegemonic epistemology of the purported possibility of *hardware independence* in AI and artificial life discourses denies the possibility of materially specific modalities of cognition and thus preempts a nontrivial conception of embodied intelligence. It marginalizes or renders meaningless claims to certain kinds of knowledge—notably, sensibilities of the arts. This matter is of resounding import for the arts and specifically for arts practices that involve computation.

## Denaturalizing Dualism

Computer culture has been highly effective in reinstating certain dubious dualisms. The center of this is the reification of the Cartesian mind-body dualism in the software-hardware dualism, often cast in terms of immaterial information as opposed to intelligence-free matter. Such distinctions often arise in a casual way but become axiomatic. Due to the shortage of critical reflection in technical disciplines which Philip Agre outlined, computer scientists are seldom given rein to critique such assumptions—even though, like the mind-body dualism, the software-hardware dualism is a belief rather than a scientifically demonstrable fact.

The mind-body dualism is a fundamental concept in Western philosophy. Could it be possible that a substantial part of Western philosophy is based on a false premise? Is it plausible that the mind-body split simply doesn't exist? Have philosophers for generations been barking up not just the wrong tree but a nonexistent tree? Is the Cartesian *res cogitans–res extensa* a false construction? Is the mind-body problem akin to the problem of angels and pins? If this sounds heretical to some, then perhaps it is: a contravention of some faith-based premise that exists outside the realms of both science and reason. After all, in two thousand years of active inquiry, Western philosophy has not made any progress at all in isolating the transcendent repository of Platonic ideals, the location of immaterial mind or the mysterious thread that connects the *res cogitans* to the *res extensa*. We would be better off forgetting about the whole thing. The mind-body problem is an idea that has had its day. It not only is without scientific merit, but also stands in the way of a better understanding of ourselves and of the design of better technologies.

The Cartesian impasse has bedeviled Western philosophy since La Mettrie and Spinoza, but for all that it is an illusory can of worms. It is not my intention here to rehearse that history in all its rich and circuitous detail. But—hindsight being what it is—one has to marvel at the reign of the singularly powerful but also completely unfounded notion of the mind-body split and the tenacious grip it has held on the minds of (many) philosophers. Perhaps this says as much about philosophers and the tradition of Western philosophy (and religion) as it does about the nature of human being and experience. If one is taught to seek authoritative knowledge through introspection (listening to internal voices) and abstract reasoning on symbols held in the mind, then one will naturally gravitate toward kinds of explanations that involve noncorporeal reasoning on mental representations, whether those operations are rhetorical, textual, or implemented as machine code.

What monsters this chimerical mind-body notion has brought forth: explanations involving homunculi, the idea that thought is propositional reasoning on mental representations, and, more pragmatically, the dualistic notion of hardware and software, an abstraction that structures discourse in computer science even as it has no reality in fact. Recall Friedrich Kittler's admonition that *there is no software*—there is no such thing as immaterial information. It's time we got off John Haugeland's train with its "sorry boxcars" and pushed it over the cliff.

## Serial Processing and the Sense Map Plan Act Paradigm

The internal processes of computing (in its serial von Neumann form) involve the assumption of passive sensors and the notion of sensing as data gathering. Sensors, by this logic, are analog to digital preprocessing front ends that prepare *data* for *processing*. According to this paradigm, the processing happens (only) in the central processing unit, by retrieving and manipulating stored representations derived either from *sensing peripherals* or from previously constructed representations (derived from sensing peripherals). These are then *output* to analog conversion and performed by *end effectors*, which are taken to be as dumb as a bag of hammers. The SMPA paradigm reiterates this seriality and assumes a centralized model of reasoning. This industrial seriality and centralized processing requires that sensor data be made compatible and combined (via sensor fusion) before a plan can be constructed. Not only is this computationally expensive, but it is not how evolved organisms make their way in the world.

## The Fallacy of Information

In our contemporary technoculture, the word *information* is ubiquitous. Phrases such as *information economy* and new disciplines such as *informatics* attest to this. The range of common contemporary uses of the term suggests that it is almost meaningless in a rigorous sense. Over the past half century, under the influence of Shannon's communication theory and the development of digital computing utilizing Boolean operations in a von Neumann architecture, information has undergone ontological drift: It has become quantified in terms of bits, permanently separated from materiality.

*Information* is an idea, a theoretical construct, that has become fundamental to computer science and fundamental to cultures that engage with computing. The discipline of computer science is structured by a working definition that conflates *information* with *computability*. The idea of the separability of information from matter—and the further assumption that information is inherently quantifiable—implies objectivity and absolute external reality. We have become naturalized to quantifying information. As a result, only that which can be *represented* as number and symbol is validated, and anything that is not amenable to digitization ceases to contain information. When all these axiomatic assumptions are internalized, certain ways of thinking about intelligence, awareness, being, and selfhood become impossible.

It may be argued that this is a perfectly acceptable and pragmatic assumption, on the basis of which technical practice is simplified and smoothed.

But as we have seen in examining the common sense crisis, the result of sweeping such concerns under the rug is that they come back later to bite. As N. Katherine Hayles notes, "The point is not only that abstracting information from a material base is an imaginary act but also, and more fundamentally, that conceiving of information as a thing separate from the medium instantiating it is a prior imaginary act that constructs a holistic phenomenon as an information/materiality duality" (1999, 13).

Like Humberto Maturana, Francisco Varela is lucid on the limits of mechanistic explanation. He acknowledges both the physical concreteness of actual processes and the symbolic or systems theoretic explanation, but he emphasizes that this artifice of explanation should remain in full view at all times as an antidote to those in computer science and systems engineering who mistake a symbolic description for an operating one, assuming that "information and information processing are in the same category as matter and energy." In the passage by Varela quoted at the beginning of this chapter, he makes it clear—as the second-order cyberneticians did before him—that information is in the eye of the beholder, as it were: "To assume in these fields that information is some *thing* that is transmitted, that symbols are *things* that can be taken at face value, or that purposes and goals are made clear by the systems themselves is all, it seems to me, nonsense" (1980, 45; emphasis in original). Underlying this statement is what Varela rightly refers as an "epistemological blunder"—the application of reductive mechanistic explanation to complex biological and ecological systems—that fails to recognize a clear distinction between proscriptive and descriptive theory. Machines, and engineering in general, are constructed according to theory. The concept of information as objectively quantifiable fails in the real world—or at least it becomes irrelevant in terms of human activity. How much information is in a page of writing? How much information is in a page of my (rather illegible) handwriting? How much information is in a page of German to a person who does not speak German? How much information is in a page of Wittgenstein? To a four-year-old? Such questions prompt the common sense answer that it depends on who is reading, what kinds of criteria they impose, and what kinds of questions they are asking. To people, *information* is relativistic and relational.

To paraphrase Maturana, everything known is known by a knower. Previous learning and experience grants us the ability to have experiences from which we derive meaning. I look at the sea and I see glittering patterns of reflected light, a fisherman sees a school of fish under the surface, and a sailor reads the direction of the wind. When a geologist looks at a cliff, she sees geological history. To the civil engineer, the same cliff is a public danger to be stabilized. How do you assess the information content of a tree, of a dance, of the skill of a masseur or that of a machinist, or, better, of the cyborgian complex of him, his machine and their practices together? Environmental cues detected by an aboriginal tracker, a Micronesian navigator, or an Inuit hunter may not be information for me. I am simply not aware of them; they do not exist for me.

The computational conception of information implies objectivism. A simplistic interpretation of Shannon's theory proposes that information is objectively "out there" and is constant (we know Shannon was cognizant of the danger of this extrapolation). Other approaches see information in terms of systems of meaning that are necessarily subjective, consensual, or negotiated. As with other discontinuities between the technical and humanistic mindset, here science is premised on the assumption of the possibility of objective truth, and the humanities are premised on the understanding that this is an impossible quest.

## Digital and Analog and Everything Else

An underlying assumption of computationalism is that evolved biological "mechanisms" are interchangeable with computational emulation. There are equally good arguments to suppose they are incommensurably different. Such questions are often presented in terms of the analog/digital binary, but this simplistic opposition is framed within digital discourse, as if *the digital* were a natural phenomenon. Thinking with the analog/digital binary bends reality around the digital pole. It is like opposing drinks and tea, or fruit and raspberry.

While *digital* describes a specific set of symbolic procedures, *analog* can refer to a number of things: mid-twentieth-century analog electronic processes computing, which automated calculus; any other method of calculation (quipu, for instance); or alternately everything else in the world that is not digital computing. The automation of Boolean logic is a variety of automated digital reasoning, which is a subset of automated calculation (analog and digital), which is a subset of calculation as performed by animals and machines, which is itself a subset of things done by animals and machines. Neural "computation" (and even using the term is dangerous) does not follow the logic of analog or digital electronics. What we currently choose to identify as computation is determined by our naturalization to digital and cognitivist conceptions of information and computation.

## Is the Human Body a General-Purpose Machine?

In its implementation of functionalism, the physical symbol system hypothesis assumes *platform independence*, the notion that symbolic processes can be implemented in a variety of physical substrates. The AI/cognitivist community embraced this conception of the operation of the mind. However, the human body is nothing like a general-purpose machine. It has highly specific qualities that are necessarily biologically instantiated. Paradigms of embedded, enactive, and extended cognition inherently dispute the multiple realizability of functionalism.

The extensive theoretical work on universal Turing machines and the idea of a general-purpose computer create a reassuring impression that software running on hardware has some relevance in explaining biological cognition. Alan Costall notes, "Yet how could anyone seriously have supposed that the human *body*, with its specific skills and limitations, could be likened to a general-purpose machine whose functioning is solely constrained by instructions?" (1991, 158; emphasis in original). In the same paper, Costall quotes James Russell (1984) to amplify his point:

The analogy between the program and the mind does not stand up to even the most cursory examination because accepting it means accepting a model of the mind as an instruction-giving entity *distinct from any realisation (not just from a particular one)* and as influencing the brain, if not through the pineal gland, then through the interface between the brain or "brain-code" and some kind of mental compiler. It is partly to avoid this kind of embarrassment that proponents of [the computation theory of mind] maintain a degree of ambivalence in their overall aims: an ambivalence between modelling the "mind" and modelling the brain. (1991, 158; emphasis in original)

Russell rightly argues here that functionalism is invalid as a theory of human cognition due to the embodiment of the mind and the tight integration of the body and mind. Haugeland (1998) argued in a similar vein. In part II, we explore a range of newer conceptions of mind and cognition, which find a way out of the cognitivist impasse via the embracing of embodiment and context.

By virtue of evolutionary selection, direct cognitive correlation exists between the world and the bodily experience of it. This performative, embodied, situated knowledge provides a basis for cogitation irreconcilable with the cognitivist physical symbol system hypothesis. Because *the world is its own best model*, and because there is a direct (non)cognitive correlation between the world and the bodily experience of it, postcognitivist positions have a biological validity that cognitivism could never attain. This is the lived solution to the symbol-grounding problem. It is a true paradigm shift, and its ramifications are only now beginning to be felt.

## Disciplinary Imperialism and Computational Explanation

In 1995, Edwin Hutchins published *Cognition in the Wild*, his remarkable work of interdisciplinary scholarship that combined anthropological field work with cognitive science and computational theory. (I discuss this work in more detail in part II.) Hutchins analyzed the group activity of navigation on a ship's bridge as a case of *distributed cognition*, in which a group of people perform specific roles and communicate with each other in specific ways using a highly developed set of tools to perform computational tasks. Hutchins speaks of these distributed processes in computational terms. *Cognition in the Wild* explains a functioning and historically coherent system as computational procedure—implemented in an array of men, machine, and activities. In this sense, it is a case study for Agre's argument about the imperialism of AI. When Hutchins translates one activity into the terms of another—explaining collaborative navigation in terms of computation— the authority of this translation is given by the (presumed) authority of computational discourse. The effectiveness of the practice—the ability of the crew, their training and process, tools, and artifacts—was established long before computational explanation. Recall that the expressed purpose of Babbage's difference engine was to calculate tide tables for the British Navy—an aid to precisely the kind of navigation Hutchins observed.

In what way and for whom did *Cognition in the Wild* "explain" the procedures of coastal navigation? To put it another way, what is the power of the computational explanation? An unreconstructed computational explanation would necessarily explain observed phenomena in functionalist terms. Hutchins's cognitivism is more nuanced. For him, cognition is embedded in the network of artifacts and practices and actors—but it is still understood as, or explained in terms of, computation.

As cognitive science reaches out into cultural realms in which computation is an alien concept, distinctions between technical and popular usages become increasingly hazy: the imperializing project of computing insinuates itself into the wider culture. This is not a conspiracy theory; it is simply a way of speaking about the mechanisms by which paradigms proliferate. It is a specific example of a problematic identified in this book: Is the logic of computation relevant to noncomputaional aspects of human culture, and how has the proliferation of computing into those practices perturbed them?

## Subsumption, Externalism, and Antirepresentationalism

The bottom-up, reactive robotics and subsumption architecture of Brooks were major technical and theoretical breakthroughs in robotics in the late 1980s. Brooks's robots were better, faster, and cheaper. Central to the success of this paradigm was a theoretical refutation of cognitivist representationalism, which Brooks captured pithily in his remark repeatedly referenced in this book, because it concisely captures a key tenet of postcognitivism. Brooks's robotics research and his writings found relevance in both the artificial life movement and in the emerging paradigms of embodied, situated, and distributed cognition.

The subsumption paradigm has gained currency in diverse fields—from neuroscience to cognitive archeology—not so much because it solved some technical problems of the time and resulted in better robots, but because subsumption proposes an ontology that is radical with respect to AI internalism and cognitivist metaphors built around the von Neumann architecture. Subsumption eschews the serial logic of the SMPA paradigm and the centralized hierarchy of top-down in favor of a model of cognition grounded in and temporally integrated with the world (*structurally coupled*, as the enactivist would say). Subsumption also allows for the destabilization of the notion of an integrated selfhood, allowing that (per von Uexküll) separate behaviors can be directly triggered by and performed in the environment, largely in isolation from each other.

## Computation, Cognition, and Biology

Does a bacterium compute? Does an ecology of freshwater organisms compute? Maturana would argue that bacteria cognize, but such a conception of cognition is at odds with cognitivism/computationalism, which is human-exceptionalist. Stafford Beer proposed that the homeostatic behaviors of ecologies, such as a fish pond, could be deployed to control technological systems. Artificial life sought to expand the kinds of computational processes that could be emulated or implemented in computers—such as evolutionary genetics, neural networks, and multi-agent interactions. However, much of the artificial life community remained committed to functionalism, as indicated by Chris Langton's characterization of "life on a silicon substrate." Contra this version of artificial life, we must distinguish between biological and silicon-based computation—that is, between computation achieved as neurochemical process and computation achieved via manipulation of symbolic tokens, with appropriate analog-digital and digital-analog translation processes on either side of the computational process. In the latter mode, the computation is locked in a box away from the world, whereas in the case of the fly's eye the computation occurs at the interface to the world. We must avoid being trapped by the rhetoric of the enemy: Cognition *is not* computation. Cognition is not satisfactorily explained as manipulation of symbols in an input–processing–output translation chain.

One of the rhetorical battles that established the superiority of the computationalist paradigm was Minsky and Papert's critique of neural networks (1969), in which they argued that a Boolean symbol-processing approach was superior to connectionist or neural-network approaches to the automation of cognition. Such a rhetorical battle established—temporarily—the superiority of symbol processing in terms defined by computationalist discourse. The fact that neural networks possessed capabilities beyond those defined by computationalist discourse—such as learning, which was also of importance to AI—demonstrates only that the battle won was rhetorical, further establishing AI as a master discourse. To frame intelligent biological behavior in terms of computation is, in Agre's terms, an imperializing move, which recasts its object in its own terms.

The cognitivist position privileges algorithmic explanation—that intelligent behavior is necessarily and sufficiently explained as the logico-symbolic manipulations of representations, as defined in the physical symbol system hypothesis of Newell and Simon. This hypothesis proposes a physical grounding of symbols, but the assertion that thinking is algorithmic does not appear to be widely supported by neurophysiological research.

The idea that computation is necessarily native to digital microelectronics is an unfortunate misconception, common particularly in the born-digital generation. Computational events, in the sense of logical operations, can occur in various media—from mechanical latches to hydraulics to children in a classroom passing bits of paper. That said, the project of resolving material, mechanical, analog-electronic, chemical, genetic, or physiological processes to algorithmic/digital equivalence is an exercise that is inherently intractable in the sense that different approaches will generate values and categories that are irreconcilable. To put it simply, the map is not the territory. Such elision of representation and reality, as we have seen in various contexts, generates a confused epistemological context, making it difficult to distinguish raw fact from paradigm-inflected interpretations.[1]

## Biological Systems Do Not Have Inputs and Outputs

Biological processes are not binary, not serial, not Boolean, nor defined by exclusive logic. They are not separable from their material substrate and do not proceed from input to output. It should go without saying that although gross processes such as digestion have obvious inputs and outputs, such linear constructs are of marginal value in understanding physiology. Nutrition may be understood as the *output* of digestion, and all manner of other biological processes are involved, so the whole process is more compatible with cybernetic metaphors of systems, feedback loops, and homeostasis.

Note that such models are dynamical and processual, performative, and relational; the meaning in the system is not located in informational objects located in specific places but in the system as a whole. Like an analog electronic circuit, there is no input or output; the entire system resonates with changing vibrations, and "information" can be picked off at any point. In computational jargon, *peripheral* implies an ancillary and secondary status with respect to the central processing unit within which the important stuff happens. Such a reductive, serial model assumes that the system can be broken up into relatively separable subsystems, implying relative autonomy and mostly one-way communication. This is the ethos of reductive modularity at work. Again, it is an idea from engineering that does not map well onto biological structures.

## Neuroethology and Human Exceptionalism

Except for those of a fundamentalist persuasion, the notion that humans are unique and separate from the rest of biology and that the mind is bestowed by God solely upon humans is regarded as anachronistic. We know that animals, mammals, and primates behave in intelligent ways, and some have a theory of mind. Genetically, we are almost indistinguishable from chimpanzees, share 96 percent of our genetic material with mice, and have a substantial amount in common with the housefly (yuck!). This implies that the way we perform cognition is like how apes do it. There is something extra, no doubt, in the human mind, but to recognize this is far easier than to explain how it got there. Increasingly, comparative neuroscience shows us the evolutionary utilization of old capabilities for new functions. Our brains, like our digestive system, evolved to cope with the exigencies of a tribal hunter-gatherer lifestyle, not to cope with literacy, mathematics, elevators, or cars.

The idea that perception is the unproblematic conversion of phenomena in the world into symbolic tokens for cognition and that cognition is where the real mindwork is done contradicts biological evidence. This evidence is found in studies of flies' eyes and bats' ears, going all the way back to the foundational paper "What the Frog's Eye Tells the Frog's Brain" (Lettvin et al. 1959; as discussed in chapter 5). The analogy of the eye as a camera seems to originate with Johannes Kepler in 1604 (long before photography), and that long history testifies to the ubiquity of optical technologies and the paradigmatic power they came to have in the West since early modern times. Lettvin et al. (1968) demonstrated that the frog's eye is far from a camera for the brain. The topological organization of rods and cones, neurons, and synapses perform image analysis—that is, perception. Thus, processes that occur in the eye and at other neural/nonneural nexuses are properly cognition, not noncognitive preprocessing for cognition.

The intelligence of discernment, of determining salience, begins at the interface between body and world, often in nonneural tissues. By this reasoning, ears and eyes and arguably kinesthetic and proprioceptive sensing partake in intelligence. The picture that arises from all this is that intelligence permeates the physical body, and nonneural tissues of all sorts partake in its circuits. Further, intelligence is enacted in ongoing temporal engagement with the world—a world that, in the human case especially, is "always already" pre-structured with the armatures of culture. It is these armatures, from tools to town layouts to language itself, that bootstrap an infant mind into culture and provide a scaffold to be leveraged by the acculturated adult mind.

## Cartesianism and Language

One way to peek around the obstacle of our dualist and craniocentric conditioning is to "gray out" the term *mind* in this conversation. Immersed as we are in the Cartesian sea, any talk of mind might inadvertently reintroduce the very dualisms we are seeking to move beyond. Such linguistic patterns are insidious and widespread; for instance, the Wikipedia entry on "Embodied Embedded Cognition" notes that "the state of your body is a direct factor of importance on the kinds of cognitive processes that may arise in the higher parts of your brain" (Wikipedia contributors, n.d.). Even though this entry purports to explain "Embodied Embedded Cognition," we find in this short passage all the hallmarks of the deep naturalization of hierarchical dualism: Bodies have states, and brains have cognitive processes; the brain has "higher" parts, and clearly, by the same metaphor, the brain is higher than the body.[2]

Perhaps if we were to cease to think in terms of mind somehow separate from body, and instead decided that *mind is immanent in and coextensive with body*, we might make some headway in explaining to ourselves the story of being. Not that this is easily done, for language thwarts us at every turn. We seem to be constrained to know parts of (our own) body as separate from the subvocalizing part. Take the simple statement "I touch my nose." What is the "I" that is separate from and owns "my" nose? Is that separation culturally constructed and culturally specific, a linguistic implementation of Cartesian dualism? "I hand touch I nose" makes no sense in English. Does a linguistic construction such as "The hand part of I touch the nose part of I" more accurately mirror the topology of the self?[3] Yet we cannot deny the indisputable "I," the voice in the head, speaking endless soliloquies in mentalese. It is there, subvocalizing these words as I type them.

## Humpty Dumpty Took a Great Fall

A recurring theme in these chapters has been the compatibility—nay, the isomorphism—of reductivist analysis with machines and systems, and the incompatibility of reductivism with biological and environmental systems, so clearly articulated (as noted earlier) by Varela (1980): "Information, sensu stricto, does not exist" (see chapter 2).

The linear, serial nature of digital computing belies its intellectual antecedents in the industrial production automation—the *production line* — and the sequentialization of sensing, computing, and output. But *we* perceive actively, in engaged iterative feedback loops, with the environment. We often act in order to cognize and calibrate further action, based on the perception of our actions in the world. The schisms between the logic of the natural world and the logic of the engineered world reveal the Cartesianism inherent the separation of materiality and abstraction—assumptions that, though commonplace, are fundamentally false. They have (and have had) broad and problematic ramifications when applied to human practices, particularly in the discussion of arts and cultural practices.

As a result of the critiques discussed in chapter 6, by the late 1980s the cognitivist/computationalist paradigm was beginning to look distinctly unstable. The authority of the various neo-Cartesian discourses of the second half of the twentieth century[4] succumbed to attacks on multiple flanks: from phenomenology (Dreyfus), from biology (Varela), from psychology (Thompson et al.), from sociology (Pickering; Latour; Callon; Law), from neuroscience (Edelman; Damasio; Gallese), and more recently from postcognitivists of many stripes, who emphasize variously the situated, enactive, and embodied nature of cognition. The idea that mind, intelligence, consciousness, cognition (call it what you like), might be thought of in other terms than *mentalese* (Fodor and others) began to be explored on a variety of fronts.

As outlined in previous chapters, although neo-Cartesianism has held sway, there is no shortage of intellectual patrimony for notions of embodied and situated cognition in the modern Western tradition. Such ideas have often been regarded as eccentric voices in their own disciplines, marginalized by a dualist intellectual establishment and derided as mystical, unscientific, or unprovable. This trend in holistic embodied thought has included biologists, psychologists, cyberneticians, philosophers, and interdisciplinarians of pragmatist and radical constructivist persuasions, including William James, Jakob von Uexküll, John Dewey, Alfred North Whitehead, Gilbert Ryle, Arthur Schopenhauer, Ross Ashby, Maurice Merleau-Ponty, J. J. Gibson (among others), whose work has more recently been attracting renewed interest and reassessment.

In recent decades, the various dimensions of neo-Cartesian explanations have been interrogated. Among philosophers of mind, AI researchers, cognitive scientists, and others, previously axiomatic Cartesianisms have been questioned, and some have recanted or modified their positions (Hilary Putnam being a case in point). Embodied (Dreyfus), and enactive (Varela, Thompson, and Rosch) critiques suggest that mind is not locked in the cranium but extends throughout the body. Situated (Suchman; Lave) and distributed (Hutchins; Kirsh) approaches to cognition emphasize the extension of cognition beyond the body, into tools, structured spaces and social networks. Discourses around dynamical systems and emergence (Kelso) and neuroethology have provided non-Cartesian models, some of them implemented in biologically inspired robotics (Brooks; Steels; Beer et al.). Taken together, this represents a true paradigm shift.

The extended mind hypothesis of Clark and Chalmers (1998) (see chapter 14) was a philosophical challenge suggesting that mind extends into artifacts. This proposal covered ideas formulated in the situated cognition of Suchman and Lave or the distributed cognition of Hutchins and Kirsh, and it provided a lively platform on which such ideas were debated (Menary 2012). But, as Chemero has cogently argued, these approaches sometimes project the cognitivist paradigm out into the world, seeing marks on paper as ersatz mental representations and social procedures as algorithms. Other approaches, which go by labels like *enactive* (Varela, Thompson, and Rosch) or *dynamical* (Beer; Kelso), contest the necessity of mental representation either entirely or in much of cognition and propose that intelligent action in the world does not proceed via reasoning on representations, internal or external. J. J. Gibson provided nonrepresentationalist models of cognition, which is why his work is experiencing something of a revival.

There appears to be, from a variety of disciplines and persuasions, no shortage of well-reasoned arguments in support of an embodied, enactive, and situated notion of being that is incommensurable with mind-body dualism. Such incommensurability defines a change of ontological ground, constituting a Kuhnian paradigm shift that continues to have major repercussions. The destabilization and denaturalization of these structuring dualisms—a large task in itself—portends a rethinking of what we understand by consciousness, selfhood, and the Enlightenment conception of the individual—all key tenets of humanism.

With the softening of the borders between mind and body, self and world, and a new awareness of the processual in the form of enactive cognition, comes the possibility of a momentous ontological shift toward the performative and relational.

# II  A Body of Knowledge

# 10  Mindful Bodies

The skill of a lute player is . . . partly in the muscles of his hands.
—René Descartes, *The Correspondence* (1991, 144)

Living systems are cognitive systems, and living as a process is a process of cognition. This statement is valid for all organisms, with or without a nervous system.
—Humberto Maturana and Francisco Varela, *Autopoiesis and Cognition: The Realization of the Living* (1980, 13)

In a world where education is predominantly verbal, highly educated people find it all but impossible to pay serious attention to anything but words and notions
—Aldous Huxley, *The Doors of Perception* (1954, 62)

Preceding chapters have probed twentieth-century ideas regarding mind, brain, body, and world. The accretion of scientific evidence in a diversity of fields has challenged cherished tenets of humanistic science and philosophy in various ways. The idea that *mind* exists in some mode or realm separate from *body* is one of the most powerful structuring dualisms in Western thought. It has held on tenaciously in our so-called scientific culture, even in the face of the fact that there is no scientific evidence to support it. It is a *belief*. This belief has become enmeshed in everyday language and the assumptions of science, law, and religion and has influenced the formulation of social and technological systems, not least among them computing. Along with the big Cartesian bogeyman come related ideas concerning the nature of thought as *reasoning* on *representations*. We are naturalized to such ideas, even if on some occasions we adopt postures contrary to them.

## Before and after Cognitivism

In the early years of the twentieth century, among the first generation of ethologists (von Uexküll), among philosophers who came to be known as pragmatists, and in early phenomenology (Husserl), the development of the study of cognition seemed to be headed in an embodied and embedded direction. Thinkers like John Dewey sensed the inherent flaws in the mind-body dualism. In 1928, Dewey observed, "We have no word by which to name mind-body in a unified wholeness of operaton [*sic*]. . . . What the facts testify to is not an influence exercised across and between two separate things, but to behavior so integrated that it is artificial to split it up into two things" (6–7). He continued, "From all sides the artificiality of isolation from one another of mind and body are commencing to be seen" (18). In this passage, Dewey confirms that Cartesianism was dominant at the beginning of the twentieth century; however, he seems to sense a sea change. Sadly, either Dewey was overly optimistic or something happened to suppress that trend. As I have shown in part I, the rise of a technology (digital computing) unreflexively predicated on Enlightenment humanist notions of dualism and representationalism certainly did not help. Non-Cartesianism persisted throughout the twentieth century, usually in localized pockets of resistance against master discourses: the philosophy of the American pragmatists (e.g., James and Dewey); the phenomenology of Husserl, Heidegger, and Merleau-Ponty; the philosophy of Gilbert Ryle and Michael Polanyi; the biology of Humberto Maturana; the psychology of J. J. Gibson; the anthropology of Marcel Mauss; and the sociology of Bourdieu.

As the rise of computationalism reinforced an otherwise retrograde Cartesianist trend, phenomenologically informed critiques of AI by Hubert Dreyfus and the work of philosophers of mind such as Mark Johnson, Francisco Varela, Evan Thompson, Michael Wheeler, and John Haugeland offered interpretations of mind and cognition that were, in one way or another, anticognitivist. Work in neurology and neuroscience by Edelman, Ramachandran, Sacks, Gallese, and others revealed new dimensions of the mind-body relation.

## Cognition in the Brain and in the World

Today, most people, without much critical reflection, adhere to the orthodox idea that cognition occurs largely or exclusively in the brain. I argue that the renewed currency of dualist, functionalist ideas is in large part due to the infiltration of digital computing into diverse aspects of human culture. Computing, as our paradigmatic technology, became the main source of metaphors for human cognition. Yet in day-to-day life we are presented with very different experiences of cognition as it is lived. Strangely, we seem to be content with a philosophical explanation that is at odds with our lived experience.

The Google definition of *cognition* includes the following: "The mental action or process of acquiring knowledge and understanding through thought, experience, and the senses. Synonyms: perception, discernment, apprehension, learning, understanding, comprehension, insight; reasoning, thinking, thought" (2016).[1] Such a definition reflects the conventional view and at the same time is replete with inconsistencies and debatable generalizations. Is cognition (exclusively) mental action? What is mental action? Most of the terms cited reflect an internalist or mentalist conception of cognition: Cognition occurs (exclusively) in the brain. Yet the very notion of "experience, and the senses . . . perception" already implies a contextualized and relational condition. The terms *learning*, *understanding*, and *comprehension* all imply consciousness; *reasoning* implies mental representation. Fundamental attribution error is implicitly at play here; there is no doubt that the brain plays a role in cognition, perhaps even a primary role. But likewise, cognition necessarily implies cognition *of* and *via*.

A fundamental problem in these discussions is the deep ambiguity that arises out of the tacit adherence to the Cartesian dualism, which suggests that the mind is somehow immaterial, despite the fact that it is assumed to be in the head. Nuwan D. Leitan and Greg Murray state, "As a discipline, psychology is defined by its location in the ambiguous space between mind and body, but theories underpinning *the application of psychology in psychotherapy* are largely silent on this fundamental metaphysical issue" (2014, 1; emphasis in original). The very assertion of the existence of this ambiguous space is a product of a self-contradictory axiomatic position. If there is no mind-body dualism, then there is no ambiguous space between the mind and body. Premising psychology on ambiguous spaces between mind and body is no more scientific than believing that some wine in a church is Christ's blood. A theory of cognition based on imaginary ideas, or at least entirely unprovable ideas, doesn't seem particularly useful.

While the blood-brain barrier is taken to be paradigmatically indicative of a difference in kind between brain and body, the brain is a biological part like the appendix or the foot. In order to avoid the philosophical quicksand of fallacious solipsisms of the "brain in a vat" kind, it is necessary to accept that the mind arises within biology. (To say *human biology* would be to assert a human exceptionalism, which would similarly demand justification.) Cognitive events are embodied events. To propose that the part of the cognition that occurs on the membranes of the body or in non-neural tissue is not really part of cognition raises questions. It calls to mind Herbert Simon's rhetorical sleight-of-hand deployed in his famous hedge: "Now I should like to hedge my bets a little. Instead of trying to consider the 'whole person,' fully equipped with glands and viscera, I should like to limit the discussion to Homo sapiens, 'thinking person.' I myself believe that the hypothesis holds even for the whole person, but it may be more prudent to divide the difficulties at the outset, and analyze only cognition rather than behavior in general" (1996, 53). Contra Simon, there is no principled way in which the thinking person can be separated from the whole person. Simon avoids reference to aspects of the body involved in obvious ways with sensorimotor engagement with the world. Recognition of sensorimotor engagement would have jeopardized his argument.

The notion of higher-level function is itself dubious. Why do we say that the processes of imagination, for instance, are qualitatively different, more refined, or otherwise better than pulling your hand out of a flame? The notion of higher-level functions presumes a value-laden hierarchy of neural processes occurring in separate departments within the brain. This hierarchy is reminiscent of industrial employment, in which remuneration is usually inversely proportional to the thickness of calluses on the hands.

Contemporary neuroscience continues to show us that a model of the brain with "faculties" located in specific places—a bureaucratic analogy with departments for different cognitive functions—is anachronistic. The brain is wildly cross-connected, and faculties seem to be distributed. Various areas are in constant contact with others, and mental operations are neurologically dispersed. To think that vision is *here* and language is *there* reflects outmoded notions of mental capacities reminiscent of phrenology. For example, Gallese and Lakoff (2005) argue that so-called higher-level mental properties like *concepts* arise in the territories of paradigmatically lower-level areas like motor circuits. This conjoining of "primitive" motor functions with "higher" reasoning contradicts the hierarchical faculty model.

In terms of intelligent action, is there a principled division between brain and not-brain? In chapter 2, we reviewed ideas of morphological computing in neuroethology, which argues against making any "invidious distinction between bone and brain" (MacIver 2009, 492). Cosmelli and Thompson (2010) examine brain-in-a-vat arguments to argue that cognition cannot happen without embodiment. Haugeland (1998) argues that there is no justification for a separation of brain and body from a systems-theoretic point of view. The connections between brain and body are all wide-bandwidth, neurologically as well as physiologically. It makes more sense to divide cognition "horizontally" and by function: this bit of brain plus this bit of body plus this bit of world achieves this task. For instance, we cannot meaningfully speak of the act of handwriting without referring to hands, eyes, pencils, paper, chairs, tables, and light, natural or artificial. Together, they constitute the realm of the cognitive act of handwriting. This way of thinking, which sees cognition as embedded within procedures that involve learned procedures with artifacts in contexts, hearkens back to von Uexküll and has been technologically validated in Brooksian subsumption architecture.

Cognition includes experience; it is being *in the world*. There is no cognition except for current experiences in the world or reference to past experiences in the world. You can't reason about Plato's cave without having had situated, embodied experiences that make the metaphor meaningful. As David Kirsh (1991) established, many behaviors we call *cognitive* in the narrow and conventional sense are facilitated by or cannot occur without physical action in association with artifacts and tools. In this sense, cognition is not only embodied but embedded.

## Implementation Details

*Implementation details* is a phrase that stands in for an entire corpus of disciplinary rationalizations to justify the disembodiment of AI, as articulated by Herbert Simon in *The Sciences of the Artificial* (1996). This arbitrary and convenient limit permitted the excision of embodied, situated materiality from AI and cognitive science for a generation. The devil is not so much in the (implementation) details as in the belief that it is acceptable or possible to ignore them. Explanation of a group human activity in terms of computation will inevitably render invisible the significance of embodied practice, because the irrelevance of embodiment is axiomatic to the rationale of the discipline. Hutchins insightfully observes, "From the perspective of a formal representation of the task, the means by which the tools are manipulated by the body appear as mere implementation details" (2010a, 445). The phrase *implementation details* tells the score before the game begins. It belies a commitment to dualism that will automatically render invisible or irrelevant aspects of embodiment. However, implementation details cannot be swept under the rug. Like the anachronistic and double-edged phrase *human factors*, the term has allowed the technical community to sidestep serious engagement with human contexts. Such engagement would demand an interdisciplinary approach, which always has the awkward potential of destabilizing axiomatic assumptions.

## Embodied Cognition

The framing of group performance on a ship's navigation bridge as distributed computation in a computational-cognitivist worldview was a tour de force by Edwin Hutchins. Yet, as he himself recognized later, his style of analysis rendered the bodily dimensions of thinking obscure:

The processes that underlie the "Aha!" insight remain invisible to a computational perspective in part because that perspective represents everything in a single monomodal (or even amodal) system. A careful examination of the way a navigator used his body to engage the tools in the setting, however, helps to demystify the discovery process, and to explain why and how it happened when it did. The insight was achieved in, and emerged out of, the navigator's bodily engagement with the setting through enacted representations. (Hutchins 2010a, 436–437)

In such statements, Hutchins comes close to the work of Johnson (1987) and Lakoff and Johnson (1999) regarding the origins of abstract concepts in embodied experience. Such (embodied) thinking is not reasoning in the cognitivist sense. Attempts to interpret embodied thinking in terms of computation necessarily force it through awkward transmogrifications to fit such immaterial, noncontextualized models of representation.

The cognitivist paradigm has had a negative influence on interface and interaction design in the sense that it encourages designers to discount the performative dimension of bodily engagement with material artifacts and tools developed over years or generations, which, taken together, facilitate embodied cognition. The navigator's chart protractor—which Hutchins (but evidently no one else) calls a *hoey*[2]—like the engineer's slide rule, the machinist's caliper, and the carpenter's square, in combination with the techniques of their use, are amenable to computational explanation. Loosely, they enact a relatively simple translation of geometry to algebra, of material proportions to numerical values. Here we are reminded of Andrew Pickering's insistence on the difference between performative ontologies and representational ontologies (see chapter 24). Stuck as we are in a world of things, of *nounishness*, it is difficult to verbalize the way meaning arises in processes. The two modalities are incommensurable, and any attempt to explain one in terms of the other is folly. This situation is reminiscent of similar clashes of paradigms, such as Minsky and Papert's refutation of neural networks or, indeed, the entire general schism between cybernetics and computationalism.

As Hutchins recognizes, "Interactions between the body and cultural objects constitute an important form of thinking. These interactions are not taken as 'indications' of invisible mental processes; rather they are taken as the thinking processes themselves" (2010b, 95). Suggesting that bodily motion may constitute a medium of thinking is a radical assertion for a cognitivist. However, it is a commonplace to the dancer or practitioner of martial arts or to any thoughtful person while rock climbing or hanging out the laundry. We must not underestimate the profundity of this sea change in cognitive science. It indicates a hard-won emancipation from our naturalization to the dualist tenets of AI. And, indeed, Hutchins is making much the same point that Hubert Dreyfus made many years earlier in his phenomenological critique of AI: "My personal plans and my memories are inscribed in the things around me just as are the public goals of men in general" (1992, 266). John Sutton similarly noted, "Thought is not an inner realm behind practical skill, but itself an intrinsic and worldly aspect of real-time engagement with the tricky material and social world" (2008, 50).

In the epigraph included for this chapter Aldous Huxley observed, long ago, that "highly educated people find it all but impossible to pay serious attention to anything but words and notions" (1954, 62). Huxley proposes that there are valuable qualities of human cognition/intelligence that are non-linguistic. Numerous students of embodied cognition, from Michael Polanyi to Evan Thompson to John Sutton, have stated what practitioners and teachers of embodied cultures have always known: The skills of bodily know-how are notoriously hard to document, because such thinking is inherently non-textual and does not intersect with textual representation and text-based reasoning. Dreyfus, after Merleau-Ponty, refers to such knowledge as "muscular gestalts" (1996). Sutton notes it in regard to the skill of a potter: "Because this kind of expertise relies on an immense reservoir of practical skill memory, embodied somehow in the fibres and in the sedimented ability to sequence technical gestures appropriately, verbal descriptions of it (by either actors or observers) will be inadequate. . . . What the expert remembers is in large part consciously inaccessible as well as linguistically inarticulable" (2008, 49).[3] Philip Agre makes a complementary point when he observes that computational fields "concentrate on the aspects of representation that writing normally captures. As a result, theories will naturally tend to lean on distinctions that writing captures and not on the many distinctions that it doesn't" (2003, 290). We could not survive in the world without tacit knowledge. The arts are built around the refinement of tacit knowledge. Yet it is notoriously difficult to translate from the performative idiom to the representational idiom.

### Fleshy, Wet, Pulsing

In Western culture, the dualistic construction of *body* has been woven into particular kinds of philosophical ideas and beliefs.[4] At a raw cognitive level, we have the sense that the "I" is different from "me," but this is contradicted by the reality that I am nothing but my fleshy, wet, pulsing self.[5] This fleshy, wet pulsing is my connection to my world, and without it I do not have a world—or an "I." Indeed, theorists from von Uexküll to von Foerster to Dreyfus to Varela have argued that the world I have is defined by the embodiment I have. I am involved in a temporally and spatially immersed and autopoietic dance of negotiation in relation to the world I am given by my embodiment. Indeed, my existence is nothing but that dance. Cognition is the process by which the cognizer builds and maintains a world.

To conceive of cognition as the processing in the brain of data gathered about the world involves a strange inversion, as if somehow processing in the brain were an end in itself. When reading some cognitive scientists, one has the sense that they believe the body exists for the pleasure of the brain. Such brain-first definitions that imply that the body is a marionette driven by the brain, instantiate a mind-body dualism that, as we have seen, has no basis in biology.

## Recasting Cognition

We are culturally accustomed to thinking about being in a dualistic way: We believe generally that we perceive, cogitate, and act, with those distinctions and in that order, with cogitation being different in kind. Increasingly, neuroscientific research is showing us what is obvious from an evolutionary perspective: The brain is—before culture, before consciousness, before language—the organ that enables us to move in and interact with the world. Contemporary roboticist Vytas SunSpiral puts it this way:

The primary purpose of the brain is to control motion. At first this might seem odd—the motor cortex is only a small part of the brain, and there are so many other functional aspects that don't seem related. But . . . perception and thought are prerequisites for intentional motion. When we build autonomous robotic systems we find that simple motor controllers are not enough. To move in the real dynamic world (not just a lab or factory) we need to sense and understand the environment we are moving through. . . . But just sticking a camera on a robot is not enough either—that just gives you a bunch of colored dots. Interpreting that data might start by reconstructing a 3D scene from those dots—but even that is not enough. What is the scene? What dangers lie around you? What opportunities? Where should you move? What might be tasty and good for you if you ate it? What might eat you? Every act we do, from eating to talking and emailing requires an intentionally coordinated set of motions. In every moment, even when laying on the bed thinking, we have to choose from the infinite set of possible actions which of those actions we will manifest. That is what our brain does. All the complex decisions, desires, motivations, social norms, emotions, habits, and other "higher level function" boil down to the simple question of deciding how our physical body will interact with the physical world. It all ends up being about motion. (2010)

I believe it is justifiable to assert that knowledge is embodied, not in a dualistic sense that knowledgable action is performed by a body, but that knowledge and skill arise in and abide in the body. Intelligent action shapes joints and muscles into a holistic cooperation of (motor) neurons, muscles, bones, and fascia: sensory organs for proprioception. No matter how much knowledge I acquire, I cannot play piano if I do not have fingers, nor can I play well unless I have my proprioceptive and sensorimotor systems attuned to the task—attunement achieved only by practice—playing scales at speed, hearing harmonies, and so on. Nor could I play piano if it were not built to human scale: Imagine a double scale piano! The keys would not fit my fingers, nor the keyboard my armspan. To the extent that such knowledge is *knowledge in practice*, it is effectively nonexistent except in the context of its actual performance.

This is not simply a matter of motor skills. With Mark Johnson, I argue that abstract concepts arise in bodily experience; with Lakoff and Gallese, I find the hypothesis of neural exploitation persuasive as an explanation of the evolution of cognitive capabilities. We know that neurons first evolved for motor control. We also know it is foolish to attempt to build a robot without consideration of factors of physical embodiment: physical masses, the compliance of structures and the power of motors, as well as the nature of the environment. Modern robotics confirms the validity of the holistic real-time structural coupling of enactive cognition.

## Conclusion: Rethinking Being and Consciousness

We are not minds that happen to have bodies to do their physical work. Rather, we are bodies that seem to have minds. We are bodies in motion that happen to produce a subjective sensation we call *consciousness*, which gives us the impression that we are something more than, or something other than, bodies. This is the remarkable illusion we call *mind*. When that illusion is granted not only identity but an identity of a higher order, embodiment is devalorized and the inherent value of embodied practices is denigrated.

The dualisms of mind-body and self-world are untenable. The idea that exercises of intelligence are computational must be reconsidered. We must recast cognition as dynamical, relational, and performative doing in the world. I'm not saying that there is no room for symbolic representation.[6] I *am* saying that a filter that extracts analysis and symbolic representation from bodily practices and privileges the abstract over the embodied may have jettisoned the larger and richer part of the intelligent behavior in question.

Research questions arise within research paradigms. Many of the questions that can be asked in postcognitivist inquiry are unaskable under the internalist paradigm. In this new postcognitive context, one can ask questions like, "If intelligence does not occur (entirely) locked within the cranium, and if it does not occur (exclusively or at all) in algorithmic manipulation of immaterial symbols, then what and where is it?" Aspects of this new paradigm are captured in the new approaches to cognition: embodied, embedded, enactive, extended, situated, distributed, which are explored in the following chapters of part II.

The purpose of this part of the book is to build up an integrated, embodied account of being and consciousness that exposes the fetters of false dualism and is washed clean of transcendentalist mumbo jumbo. Such an account involves conceptualization around ideas such as the following:

• We cognize as integrated biological creatures, and any attempt to mechanistically separate faculties into organs and systems can only be understood in the context of an overarching multimodal integration.
• Intelligence, thinking, cognition is situated and embodied. We think in engagement with the world; in other words, active engagement with the world constitutes thinking.
• Skill is intelligence. Skill is the traditional, nonscientific descriptor for the capabilities that permit epistemic action and distributed cognition.
• Abstract cerebration, the mental manipulation of symbols, is a special case, and even then such thinking leverages (and would be impossible without) a history or embodiment.
• Mind and consciousness are epiphenomena of embodied being and have no existence outside embodied being.

From this base, one could lay out a new account of cultural action, based in new approaches to consciousness and cognition:

• Reconceptualization of conscious/nonconscious thought/action
• Reconceptualization of nature and nurture through the idea of cultural bootstrapping of latent capacity and neural exploitation
• Reconceptualization of cognition as embodied, enactive, and integrated with the material and cultural world

This is what is so exciting: The current revolution in cognitive science provides new ways of speaking about embodied, materially engaged intelligent action. It has the potential to provide an entirely new register in which to speak about what we might call *cultural cognition*. This promises the possibility of a new paradigm for embodied art and cultural practices, to be viewed in a new way that gives full recognition to the materially, socially, and spatially situated intelligences involved in activities of both high and low culture. Framing this new paradigm for the intelligences of the arts is the purpose of part III. Such an approach also holds the potential to level the (academic) playing field that has for so long been tilted in terms of the abstract and the symbolic.

Postcognitivism—and its inherent critique of cognitivism—is directly relevant to computer-automated cultural practices, simply because interactivity is necessarily distributed and relational. At a deeper theoretical level, cognitivist ideas structure computing at all levels of hardware, software, and theory. These Trojan horses have the potential to—and I would say regularly do—subvert well-justified and well-intentioned projects in human-computer interaction. In digital arts pedagogy as in computer science, this level of theoretical interrogation is rarely if ever engaged.

Now more than ever, such historical and philosophical contextualization is crucial to denaturalize assumptions about computing among current and future born-digital generations.

# 11 The New Cognitive Science—Embodied, Embedded, Enactive

Interesting philosophy is rarely an examination of the pros and cons of a thesis. Usually it is, implicitly or explicitly, a contest between an entrenched vocabulary which has become a nuisance and a half-formed new vocabulary which vaguely promises great things.

—Richard Rorty, *Contingency, Irony, and Solidarity* (1989, 9)

Embodiment is not an aspect of cognition; cognition is an aspect of embodiment.

—Paul Cisek, "The Affordance Competition Hypothesis" (2008, 204)

The meaningful is the world itself.

—John Haugeland, "Mind Embodied and Embedded" (1998, 231)

What a thing is and what it means are not separate, the former being physical and the latter mental, as we are accustomed to believe.

—J. J. Gibson, "Notes on Affordances" (1982c, 408)

In the late 1980s and early 1990s, AI and cognitive science fell into a crisis. Increasingly through the 1980s, the caving in of the functionalist-internalist-representationalist paradigm provided opportunities for open interdisciplinary inquiry. New approaches to cognition—embedded, embodied, and enactive (and others)—emerged, many informed by phenomenology, anathema to the Anglo-American analytic tradition that had informed the theorization of computing.

Theoretical critiques began with the work of Weizenbaum, Roszak, Winograd and Flores, Searle, Harnad, Dreyfus, and Haugeland (and others), creating "a half-formed new vocabulary which vaguely promises great things" (Rorty 1989, 9). These critiques fed new research and new ideas in the work of Lucy Suchman, Jean Lave, Rodney Brooks, Pattie Maes, Luc Steels, Francisco Varela, Evan Thompson, Philip Agre, David Kirsh, Edwin Hutchins,

George Lakoff, Mark Johnson, Michael Wheeler, Scott Kelso, Randall Beer, and others. Each addressed shortcomings of internalist and representational theories of cognition from differing perspectives, generating an increasingly substantial postcognitive position.

## Disciplines and Emerging Paradigms

During the middle of the twentieth century in the United States, the Anglo-American analytic school of philosophy held sway. In the United States, European phenomenological and existential philosophy and psychology—the work of Heidegger, Husserl, Merleau-Ponty, Sartre—derisively referred to as "continental philosophy" were either unknown or ridiculed. Through the 1970s and 1980s, as feminism, poststructuralism, and postcolonialism emerged, new European philosophy became influential in the humanities. Due largely to the conservatism of institutionalized philosophy, new programs and departments had to be established often with the moniker "critical theory" so as not to encroach on the territory of dusty old philosophy. Foucault was particularly influential in his social and historical contextualization of the intertwining of knowledge and power. However, poststructuralism was double-edged, as the "textual turn" remained invested in representationalism, a tendency countered to some extent by feminist embodiment theory, performance theory, and social studies of science and technology (in its various acronymic forms: STS, SSSS, and SSK). These have become major theoretical forces in the humanities and social sciences but have remained mostly unknown in cognitive science, even in emerging situated and distributed variants. This lack of a potentially productive flow of ideas between disciplines reveals a danger of disciplinary conservatism. Such conservatism is less powerful in disciplines in formation. In some quarters, human-computer interaction (HCI) became increasingly interdisciplinary, embracing actor-network theory (ANT), ethnomethodology, and activity theory. In Europe, especially in Scandinavia, "humanistic informatics" was taken seriously, and in the United States more progressive informatics programs have engaged psychologists, anthropologists, and sociologists.

As acceptance of the shortcomings of the cognitivist paradigm became more widespread, new kinds of inquiry emerged in and around cognitive science. The critiques of the computationalist paradigm (representationalism, planning, intelligence as symbol manipulation, etc.) defined a wide range of new research programs, among them reactive robotics, deictic programming, genetic and evolutionary computing, and a resurgence of interest in connectionism and neural network research. Human interaction with technology in work and social contexts was addressed more intensively, as evidenced by the rapid growth of computer-supported collaborative work (CSCW), and related areas of research.

Emerging fields go through a period of interdisciplinary epistemological "hunting and gathering" until paradigms gel and drift inexorably toward ossification. Postcognitivist research continues to engage anthropology, sociology, psychology, biology, neuroscience, and philosophy of mind, as well as computer science and robotics. This signals an important and healthy reconnection of cognitive science with other disciplines.

Various emerging research fields are also part of the postcognitivist zeitgeist, even if they are not directly connected, such as neuroethology and morphological computation. Beyond cognitive science, the reappraisal of cognitivism has had a strong influence on HCI, reactive robotics (Brooks, Mataric, Steels, Maes), cognitive neuroscience, and psychology more generally (Costall et al.). As the neuroscientific turn permeates the social sciences and humanities, new research areas have opened, including material anthropology and cognitive archeology (Ingold, Renfrew, Malafouris, Rowlands).[1] The application of these ideas from anthropology is particularly significant to the project of this book, as they provide different perspectives on concepts of skill and material engagement.

## What Do We Mean by Cognition?

Confusion arises when discussing cognition, because several schools of thought have quite different interpretations. As noted in part I, the autopoietic conception of cognition is incompatible with the cognitivist conception (which is derived from Anglo-American analytic philosophy, though analytic philosophers have accused cognitivists of being a bit sloppy). Continental philosophers (phenomenologists) draw distinctions differently. When Lakoff and Johnson talk about the cognitive unconscious, their conceptions of the conscious and unconscious diverge from Freudian ideas.

One reason for this confusion of terminology is precisely the condition of the paradigm shift itself. Neologisms (some of them clunky) and borrowings from other languages abound because existing language is built around dualist concepts. New language is needed. Maturana and Varela coined *autopoiesis*. Gibson invented *affordance*. Likewise *umwelt* and *enactivism* and other terms are now part of a new vocabulary.

One way out of this spiraling vortex is to come back to action in the world. There is something to the metaphor of having your feet firmly on the ground. Damasio, Lakoff, and others challenged the primacy of logic and reason, reintroducing metaphor, emotion, and affect into the conversation. Johnson developed schemes for a biologically materialist explanation of higher mental capabilities. Maturana and Varela proposed a biological, nonhuman exceptionalist notion of cognition. Advances in neuroscience research revealed new dimensions of the mind-body relation. In *Philosophy in the Flesh: The Embodied Mind and Its Challenge to Western Thought* (1999), Lakoff and Johnson challenge conventional philosophy of mind on the basis of new experimental results.

## Situation, Enaction, and Structural Coupling

In cognitive science, the self-world binary is as bedeviling as the mind-body dualism. In technology as in biology, systems are tightly coupled to other systems, embedded in other machines, such as airplanes or automobiles. It is a question of philosophical debate whether such tight coupling constitutes situatedness or integration. For now, let's propose that tight coupling is constituted by ongoing and actively reciprocal sensory, electronic, or mechanical connection. Whether we speak in terms of Suchman's situated cognition (1987); Hutchins's related distributed cognition (1995); Varela, Thompson, and Rosch's enactive cognition (1991); or, for that matter, current work in material anthropology and cognitive archeology, the notion that mind ends where the brain ends is now dubious. Nor is the idea that mind stops where body stops easily defended. Intelligence can be contextual and social. The notion that we own our intelligence and our selfhoods, portably in our skulls, is a cultural construct of Victorian individualist humanism, and as we know, is not as strongly held in many other cultures. In the following passages, I draw out some discontinuities with cognitivist thought. That is not to say that postcognitivism is monolithic. Subsequent chapters explore incompatibilities between postcognitivist paradigms.

## Disambiguating "Embodiment"

*Embodiment* has become increasingly important in philosophy of mind, cognitive science, sociology, and anthropology, as well as HCI and art and media theory. Like any such term, as it has been deployed in various contexts, and it has come to have a range of usages, some of which attach specialized meanings to the term and some of which trivialize the idea. The following guide aims to clarify various usages of the term.

*Material "embodiment."* To say that something is embodied *simpliciter* is to say little but that it materially exists. The term can be applied to both the living and the nonliving. With respect to humans and cognition, it connotes the simple fact of bodily materiality, but usually implies a recognition of physical instantiation as being a necessary aspect of and for human cognition, a position that refutes brain-in-a-vat arguments (Cosmelli and Thompson 2010) and accepts the reality of morphological computation (per MacIver, discussed in chapter 2). *Embodiment* is sometimes deployed in distinctions between hardware and software (as though software were immaterial) as per the mind-body dualism. When applied to robotics, the term has an analogous meaning of *physical instantiation*. It implies that a machine situated in a physical environment must manage the qualities of that environment and can exploit aspects of its own embodiment and materiality.

*Physiological embodiment* pertains to the specificities of a creature's physical makeup: senses, physical size and shape, characteristics, and number of limbs. It thus defines the kinds of sensorimotor functions a creature might have and what Jakob von Uexküll calls the creature's *umwelt*. In Gibsonian terms, a chair *affords* sitting for humans of a certain height, because we bend at knees and hips in appropriate ways. A chair does not afford sitting for a snake or a flamingo.

*Biochemical embodiment* indicates the holism of immunological, endocrine, metabolic, genetic, and epigenetic aspects of an organism's existence, including molecular aspects of biochemical cognition such as neurotransmitters, pheromone emission and response, endocrine and immune response, and interaction between the autonomic nervous system and the *microbiome*—ecologies of internal flora.

*Neurological embodiment* implies the brain is in (and of) the body and that the body is "in" the brain, in the sense of the title of Johnson's pioneering work, *The Body in the Mind: The Bodily Basis of Meaning, Imagination, and Reason* (1987). It implies a nondualist holism—or at a least a complementary one. The nondualist and biologically materialist rejection of dualism holds that the brain is not a general-purpose and platform-independent machine but that it is thoroughly integrated with the "body proper": the not-brain or not-mind. As Johnson, Dreyfus, and, before them, Merleau-Ponty put it, we have the kind of minds we have because of the kind of bodies we have. The old fatalism that the brain cannot grow or change has been refuted by neuroplasticity research, from Paul Bach-y-Rita onward. Especially in childhood development, neural structures are built through bodily and cultural experience (Edelman 1987). The theoretical question of whether a brain in a vat could cognize is by these lights nonsensical. Brains are not transferrable. A brain without the sensorimotor experience of being—not simply embodied but codeveloped with a particular body—*may* be able to reason (though Johnson, Lakoff, Gallese, and others would refute this assertion). But a reasoning brain in a vat would have the same common sense problem that brought first-generation AI to its (metaphorical) knees.

*Conceptual embodiment.* Elizabeth Bates, Mark Johnson, George Lakoff, Vittorio Gallese, Susan Hurley, and others argue that abstract ideas emerge out of embodied experience, and according to the logic of biological evolution, higher functions (such as reasoning or language) exploit and adapt existing (i.e., sensorimotor) systems. Conceptual structures are built through interaction with the world in infancy. Accident, amputation, or paralysis does not necessarily impair the use of the developed cognitive facility.

*Extended or prosthetic embodiment* involves motor and cognitive extensions and the development of skills and cultures around them. Neurological embracing of the blind man's cane is paradigmatic. Use of the bicycle, automobile, microscope, and Internet all demonstrate the temporary or permanent adaptation of sensory and motor homunculi. Such incorporation is fundamental to cultural embodiment. Cultures develop specific ways of weaving, riding horses, or playing flutes.

*Cultural embodiment.* As a result of acculturation to chairs, Europeans tend not to squat, and even find it uncomfortable. But in many cultures, squatting or sitting cross-legged is normal and chairs are unusual. People in different cultures dance in different ways. In general, bodily behavior and interaction are culturally formed, and different cultures have different sensibilities associated with proprioception and peripersonal space. As Hutchins argues, culture "is a human cognitive process that takes place both inside and outside the minds of people" (1995, 354). He proposes "an integrated view of human cognition in which a major component of culture is a cognitive process . . . and [a major component of] cognition is a cultural process" (354).

While the term *brain* is amenable to a fairly simple physiological definition, the implicit nesting of *mind* within brain is questioned here and in various postcognitivist approaches. Variously, mind may extend into body, into artifacts and tools, into structure spaces, and into procedures, rituals, and social interactions.

## Schools of Postcognitivism: A Primer

The notion that intelligent action necessarily and centrally involves the logical manipulation of symbolic representations is held far less surely than it once was. The new generation of postcognitivist cognitive science is based in a general conception that cognition occurs in a living body (which may or may not contain a brain) and is (at least) markedly enhanced when that body is active in a pre-structured physical and social context. Genres of postcognitivism—including embodied, enactive, extended, distributed, and situated—contest generic cognitivist positions in different ways, though they all tend to endorse biological materialism and dispute the centrality of internalism, representation, reasoning, and human exceptionalism. Some approaches—which Anthony Chemero calls *radical embodied cognitive science*—reject representationalism entirely and endorse dynamical systems theory as an alternative theoretical formation.[2] On the other hand, some approaches maintain aspects of computationalism or representationalism. As noted in chapter 9, Hutchins's distributed cognition is explicitly computationalist. The extended mind hypothesis of Clark and Chalmers, as Clark would put it, is "minimally Cartesian." What follows is a synopsis of the entailments of these new genres:

*Embodied cognition*, informed by phenomenology, focuses on contesting the mind-body dualism. It asserts the origins of higher cognition in bodily and "unconscious" processes (Lakoff and Johnson 1999). Rather than conceiving of perception as a relatively trivial preprocessing stage of cognition, it allows generally that perception *is* cognition, that perception itself is an exercise of intelligence. It emphasizes the embodied dimensions of cognition, variously extending cognition beyond the cranium and beyond neural tissue. The vexed question of the location of perception is thus sidestepped. If sensing is not "dumb" (as noted in the cases of the frog's eye, the fly's eye, and the bat's ear), then cognition extends throughout the body.

*Enactive cognition* emphasizes the iterative, temporally extended, and dynamical quality of embodied and situated cognition. Developed by Varela, Thompson, and Rosch (1991) and founded on the process ontology implicit in autopoietic biology, it emphasizes the fundamentally biological nature of cognition as a defining aspect of the living. Elaborated on by, among others, Alva Noë, Kevin O'Regan, and Ezequiel Di Paolo, *enactivism* contests the linear input–processing–output model and the cognitive reality of the subject-object binary, emphasizing the tight integration of an agent with its environment and the inseparability of perception and action in sensorimotor loops. This ongoing sensorimotor feedback, called *structural coupling*, is sympathetic with *temporal coupling*, harking back to the iterative cycles of cybernetic feedback loops. The reconfiguring of cognition as structurally coupled allows that we often act in order to sense, and that our understanding of the world is not separate from our exploration of the world. Varela borrowed the phrase "laying down a path in walking" from Buddhist philosophy to capture this quality of the enactive approach. The enactive approach focuses on holistically embodied cognition. Other paradigms pursue the idea that cognition is not bounded by the body membrane but spreads out into the world of designed spaces, artifacts, and social organization.

*Extended cognition* has its roots in the now famous paper by Andy Clark and David Chalmers entitled "The Extended Mind" (1998). This hypothesis proposed that if a *cognitive prosthetic* plays a role equivalent to an aspect of biological cognition, it should be regarded as an extension of mind outside the body. This became known as the *parity principle*. In the extended mind hypothesis, the mind is deemed to be "extended" on the basis of the parity principle—the example used was memory, and its replacement with a notebook, a passive cognitive prosthetic. For Clark and Chalmers, such storage is deemed to be part of the mind because it is both specific to the individual and tightly coupled.

The strictures of the parity principle were quickly relaxed to permit the idea of *complementarity*—that cognitive prosthetics can complement internal processes. This more general formulation has become known as *extended cognition*. Ezequiel Di Paolo and Michael Wheeler have argued that enactive and extended cognition paradigms are mutually exclusive (see chapter 13). This raises the question of other kinds of mental extension, such as those discussed by McLuhan, Donald, and Kirsh. Marshall McLuhan famously saw media technologies as "the extensions of man."[3] These sensory extensions are cognitively prosthetic. Merlin Donald identified the storage media of cultural memory—such as cuneiform tablets, hieroglyphs on friezes, and books—as generationally persistent cognitive extensions, which he dubbed *exograms*.

*Situated cognition* (Lucy Suchman, Jean Lave) proposes that memory and problem solving can be distributed in interpersonal and spatial contexts, and thus cognition must be understood as a cultural and social phenomenon occurring in structured environments. Suchman's *Plans and Situated Actions: The Problem of Human-Machine Communication* (1987) was an early foray into such studies. Various interpretations allow that cognition extends out into the world, in symbiotic coordination of structured environments (information systems, offices, architectures, street layouts), artifacts (tools and instruments), documents (maps, diagrams, plans, tables), and social systems (rituals, procedures, collaborative work and play). When documents and traditions are considered, such studies embrace a notion of temporally displaced cognition and cultural memory. If the structuring of environments and cultural practices makes us intelligent, is intelligence an individual possession, or is it culturally constructed? Can we make a principled boundary of intelligence at the biological boundary of the creature? In posing such questions, situated cognition thus preempts many of the issues raised in extended cognition.

*Distributed cognition.* Under the banner of distributed cognition, Hutchins, Kirsh, and others have explored how certain kinds of cognitive functions are supported by, or only occur with the use of, specially structured artifacts. Kirsh and Paul Maglio are responsible for the useful concept of *epistemic action.* In their article "On Distinguishing Epistemic from Pragmatic Action" (1994), Kirsh and Maglio make a distinction between actions that change the world (pragmatic) and actions that change the nature of our mental tasks (epistemic). They assert that thinking is enhanced or made possible by the manipulation of things in the world and identified with artifacts (and associated sensorimotor procedures) as *epistemic action.* Thus, the use of pencil and paper enhances our ability to do arithmetic. Their experimental context was the computer game Tetris. Success at Tetris requires effective real-time response and so served as a vehicle by which Kirsh and Maglio could explore how the offloading of cognition onto the external world could simplify or speed the task at hand. It was established that players who rotated the *zoids* on a screen via keyboard as they fell did measurably better than those who performed the computation in their heads. Such actions were dubbed *epistemic* because they had cognitive benefits. These results make claims for pure internalism dubious and encourage consideration of the roles of tools, artifacts, procedures, and structured environments in cognition. This line of argument connects to Lakoff and Johnson in the sense that bodily experiences build abstract concepts. For instance, embodied experience of a container provides sensorimotor resources for metaphors of *inside* and *outside,* processes of filling and emptying, and being full, empty, or overfilled—not to mention that the concept of *level* is given by water level.

In his masterwork, *Cognition in the Wild* (1995), Hutchins takes coastal navigation on a naval ship's bridge as a case study of distributed cognition, and shows that cognitive activities often occur as group activity in the context of richly developed social organization. Hutchins addresses formalized social interactions as part of a cognitive assemblage in ways that are reminiscent of both situated cognition and ANT. Hutchins notes, "If we ascribe to individual minds in isolation the properties of systems that are actually composed of individuals manipulating systems of cultural artifacts, then we have attributed to individual minds a process that they do not necessarily have, and we have failed to ask about the processes they actually must have in order to manipulate the artifacts. This sort of attribution is a serious but frequently committed error" (1995, 173). By this line of reasoning, Hutchins extends a computationalist theory beyond brain and body to embrace artifacts and social behaviors. (On the basis of which he has offered a novel response to John Searle's Chinese room; see chapter 6.)

## Turning Cognitivism Inside Out

The distributed cognition paradigm identifies heterogeneous *cognitive systems* made up of people, instruments, procedures, documents, and other agents and disputes the traditional notion that cognition is *internalist*—that is, occurring exclusively inside the brain. Distributed cognition remains computationalist while rejecting internalism, preserving representationalist ideas of traditional cognitive science but allowing that such processes may include extracranial events. Hutchins reframes Newell and Simon's physical symbol system hypothesis by saying that it does *not* model the operation of a mind but precisely *does* model the operation of a distributed cognitive system. "It is no accident that the language of the physical-symbol-system hypothesis captures so much of what is happening in domains like ship navigation," he writes. "The physical-symbol-system hypothesis is based on the operation of systems of this type" (Hutchins 1995, 363).[4] He cleverly argues that the failure of the internalist/cognitivist program has its roots in the fact that Turing's model was a materially instantiated model of a person in a sociocultural context, but that later cognitivists (Newell and Simon) took the computer to be a model of the brain. In the process, the symbols were moved from the outside world into the brain. He writes, "When the symbols were put inside, there was no need for eyes, ears, or hands" (Hutchins 1995, 365).[5] The irony here, if we take Hutchins's reading, is that Newell and Simon based their argument for an abstract and internalist view of cognition on a thoroughly embodied and social process.

In *Cognition in the Wild*, Hutchins inverts the internalism of the physical symbol system hypothesis, saying, "The physical-symbol-system architecture is not a model of individual cognition. It is a model of the operation of a sociocultural system from which the human actor has been removed" (1995, 363). Hutchins completes this theoretical tour de force by attacking the cognitivist division between perception and cognition: "The existence of perceptual and motor processes that are distinct and separate from so-called cognitive processes is not an empirical fact: it is simply a hypothesis that was made necessary by having constructed cognition out of a mechanized formal symbol processing system" (365).

Distributed cognition is sociological and anthropological in the sense that it moves cognition away from the individual cranium and out into the social and cultural world. By leveraging the possibility that cognitive events in such contexts can be observed and measured by standard anthropological methods (intracranial cognitive events are not amenable to such observation and measurement), such studies reveal complex interactions between people, processes, and artifacts, which usually do not figure in conventional cognitive science research.

## Autopoiesis and Structural Coupling

Enactive cognition arose out of Francisco Varela's project to extend autopoietic biology into what he referred to as the *neurobiology* and *neurophenomenology* of cognition, informed by phenomenological philosophy. According to the enactive approach, cognition is the ongoing lived process of an organism embedded in its environment. It is dynamical, iterative, structurally coupled, and dependent on sensorimotor feedback loops.

In *The Embodied Mind: Cognitive Science and Human Experience*, the pioneering work on enactive cognition by Varela, Thompson, and Rosch (1991), the authors argue that cognitive science reached an impasse due to the inability of cognitive scientists to reconcile the results of their research with their own lived experience. The authors propose a radical alternative approach to the study of cognition, which they call *enaction*; it conceives of cognition as an ongoing, self-organizing, and groundless lived process based on the idea that "cognition has no ultimate foundation or ground beyond its history of embodiment" (1991, xx). The authors of *The Embodied Mind* alert us to the absence of the body as an object of concern or consideration in this paradigm. The organism and its environment coevolve, they argue. Any organism—particularly the human organism—actively shapes its environment, so the clear distinction between self and objective world becomes untenable. They also problematize the valorization of problem solving in conventional cognitive science: "The usual tendency (of conventional cognitive science) is to treat cognition as problem solving in some pre-given task domain. The greatest ability of living cognition, however, consists in being able to pose, within broad constraints, the relevant issues that need to be addressed at each moment" (145).

Varela, Thompson, and Rosch recount examples of cognitive science research that make untenable the notion of a unified self, and they pair this with quotations revealing the inability or unwillingness of these same researchers to accept the implications of their research. They argue that clinging to a notion of the self-inviolable is an impediment to the development of cognitive science. They assert that the idea of the inviolable self and of *objective external reality* are implicit in each other and that this entails further assumptions: that the qualities of the outside world are fixed and objective; that we recover these properties by internally representing them; and that there is a separate subjective "I" that does these things. "These three assumptions amount to a strong, often tacit and unquestioned, commitment to realism or objectivism/subjectivism about . . . how we come to know the world" (1991, 9). In this way, the authors of *The Embodied Mind* sought to reorient cognitive science from cognition as reasoning on representations to cognition as embodied action. Varela, Thompson, and Rosch propose that nothing less than a thoroughgoing rebuilding of the philosophical foundations of the discipline is required.

The authors refer to this history of embodiment as an *emergent phenomenon* and thus link their enterprise with complexity theory, emergent order, and self-organizing systems. The rejection of the possibility of objectivity and simultaneous rejection of the stability of the cognizing subject resonates with the writings of many feminist and poststructuralist theorists and with von Uexküll, Gibson, Bergson, Dewey, and James. By associating themselves with these various schools of thought and with the phenomenologically informed critiques of AI, the authors make it plain that they are positioning their discussion not within the confines of the discipline of cognitive science but in a broader critique of the scientific method and the traditions of the Enlightenment. The authors cite Merleau-Ponty's notion of *double embodiment* as fundamental: "For Merleau-Ponty, as for us, *embodiment* has this double sense: it encompasses both the body as a lived, experiential structure and the body as the context or milieu of cognitive mechanisms" (Varela, Thompson, and Rosch 1991, xvi; emphasis in original). The authors call for a "radically new approach to the implementation of Merleau-Ponty's vision" (xvii).

The authors of *The Embodied Mind* assert—the work of Merleau-Ponty, Heidegger, Husserl, and Nietzche notwithstanding—that the Western philosophical tradition is largely bereft of the tools necessary to deal with the issue of the insubstantial nature of the self. Here, they make an admirable counter-Eurocentric move, drawing upon a long tradition of experientially based philosophy of cognition in certain aspects of Buddhist thought—the Madhyamika tradition and specifically the philosophy of Nagarjuna—which has been developed and refined for many centuries. It is in the Madhyamika tradition that the authors find both an experiential dimension of study, which complements and redeems cognitive science from being lost in abstraction, and a system of thought that finds no need of objective ground, that indeed counsels against the clinging to or grasping of such ground as fallacious. There ensues an introduction to the notions of ground-lessness and of the nonunified or decentered self in the Buddhist tradition, along with explication of a system for enlightened living based on this notion of groundlessness and egolessness in the same tradition. In this system, the authors find support for their program of enactive cognitive science.

Varela, Thompson, and Rosch make arguments similar to those made in previous chapters. They point out the ubiquitous presence of the computer metaphor in cognitive science:

The central tool and guiding metaphor of cognitivism is the digital computer. . . . A computation is an operation performed or carried out on symbols, that is, on elements that *represent* what they stand for. . . . Cognitivism consists in the hypothesis that cognition—human cognition included—is the manipulation of symbols after the fashion of digital computers. In other words, cognition is *mental representation*: the mind is thought to operate by manipulating symbols that represent features of the world or represent the world as being a certain way. (1991, 7–8; emphasis in original)

They contest the assumption that cognition is fundamentally representational: "We explicitly call into question the assumption prevalent throughout cognitive science—that cognition consists of the representation of a world that is independent of our cognitive and perceptual capacities by a cognitive system that exists independent of the world" (xx).

*Structural coupling* is a key concept in enactive cognition: "These issues and concerns are enacted from a background of action, where what counts as relevant is contextually determined by our common sense" (Varela, Thompson, and Rosch 1991, 145). The emphasis on histories of structural coupling as the ground of ontology is drawn from the autopoietic theory of Humberto Maturana and Francisco Varela. *Autopoietic cognition* is inherently biological and noncognitivist. The notion of enaction emphasizes *ongoing becoming* arising from iterative sensorimotor coupling, epitomized by the notion of *laying down a path in walking*. Such a focus on the precedence of process and ongoing self-creation is as consistent with Waddington's conception of homeorhesis as it is philosophically orthogonal to the preoccupation with objects and states typical of conventional cognitive science.

The idea of structural coupling as grounding cognition is in sympathy with Brooks's notion that *the world is its own best model*, with Malafouris's assertion that "there is no mind apart from the world" (2004, 60), and with John Haugeland when he says, "The meaningful is not in our mind or brain, but is instead essentially worldly. The meaningful is not a model—that is, it's not representational—but is instead objects embedded in their context of references. And we do not store the meaningful inside of ourselves, but rather live and are at home in it. These are all summed up in the slogan that the meaningful *is the world itself*" (1998, 231; emphasis in original).

As cognition in the enactive sense is constituted by structural coupling and is not representationalist, the common sense problem or symbol-grounding problem (the Achilles' heel of AI) is rendered meaningless.[6] As such, it sidesteps the hoary mind/world dilemma, the related realist/idealist dilemma, and the desire for an absolute ground or foundation, which Richard Bernstein called *Cartesian anxiety*. The notion of enaction as a dynamical embodied sensorimotor phenomenon has given rise to a range of variants employing the term and the approach, the *enactive approach* of Alva Noë being one of them. Kevin O'Regan refers to this approach as the *sensorimotor approach*. Anthony Chemero has distinguished between enactive approaches, which he refers to as *radically embodied* cognitive science, and approaches that preserve the idea of cognition as symbol manipulation and extend it out into the world. The distributed cognition of Hutchins and the extended mind hypothesis of Clark and Chalmers are examples of the latter.

### Enaction, Evolution, and Artificial Life

The use of the terminology of emergence would seem to affiliate enactive cognition with artificial life. However, there is an interesting and clear difference between the two positions on the subjects of evolution and emergence. The ALife community generally seems to embrace an unproblematized emulation of Darwinian selection and thus presents the possibility for the reification of all sorts of nineteenth-century social Darwinist notions. In addition, certain parts of the community seem all too willing to adopt the analogy of genetics as algorithm, and DNA as code, uncritically embracing the original analogy of Watson and Crick and perpetuating the computationalism of cognitivism. Such thinking is open to critiques similar to those that the authors of *The Embodied Mind* level at cognitivism; the analogy with digital computing is counterproductive: "Baldly stated, representationism [*sic*] in cognitive science is the precise homologue of adaptationism in evolutionary theory, for optimality plays the same central role in each domain" (Varela, Thompson, and Rosch 1991, 194). In contrast, the authors of *The Embodied Mind* offer the idea of evolution as natural drift, which contests the idea that evolution forbids anything that is not survivable (survival of the fittest) and offers a liberatory idea that evolution admits anything that can survive. This opens the evolutionary field to mutations that do not impair survivability and permits seeing evolution as *bricolage*—that species exist not because they fulfill some ideal design but simply because they are possible: "There are therefore reasons to ask whether the very program of studying evolution as trait fitness optimization is not fundamentally flawed" (189). In the same way, an enactivist conception of emergence cannot be realized in digital technologies by virtue of Cariani's distinction between syntactic and semantic emergence.

## Cognitive Anthropology

First-generation cognitive anthropology and cognitive archeology shared the cognitivist, internalist, rationalist, and representationalist assumptions of cognitive psychology. As in AI, the implicitly reflexive nature of this inquiry was seldom acknowledged. The assumption is that "we" occupy a pinnacle of development, and thus the mental characteristics "we" (loosely speaking, highly educated, middle-age, middle-class, white Western males) take to be of supreme value are indeed fundamental to a superior being. Conventionally, those qualities have included abstract symbolic thought and a denial of "irrational" emotional behavior. Postcognitivist cognitive archeology interrogates such assumptions.

A central question of cognitive archeology is, "How and when did the predecessors of modern man come to possess the mental capacities we now identify as especially 'human'?" Inferring mental capability from skeletal remains and scant artifacts is a tenuous, even dubious pursuit. Many conditions have been proposed as generative of such changes, including the opposable thumb, language, cooking food, and Jayne's notion of the bicameral mind. However, it is well established that the human brain and body have not significantly changed (evolved) since long before the period in which these cognitive breakthroughs are assumed to have occurred. So human cognitive development appears to be a cultural, as opposed to a biological, phenomenon.

It is satisfying to see, then, that as distributed cognition bridged cognitive science and anthropology, recent cognitive anthropology is embracing postcognitivist notions of cognition. The notion of cognition as intelligent engagement with the world has introduced new perspectives to the cognitive anthropology and cognitive archeology community (including Ingold, Malafouris, Renfrew, Rowlands, and others). For instance, in the work of Lambros Malafouris, we clearly hear echoes of Kirsh and Hutchins in statements such as this: "The efficacy of material culture in the cognitive system lies primarily in the fact that it makes it possible for the mind to operate without having to do so: i.e., *to think through things, in action, without the need of mental representation*" (2004, 58; emphasis in original).

Malafouris makes strong arguments for the necessity of considering cognition and material culture together in ways that are reminiscent of justifications for neuroethology: "Cognition and materiality intersect, mutually catalyzing and constituting each other" (2004, 53). He laments, "I am afraid that, as long as cognition and material culture remain separated by this ontological gulf, our efforts to understand the nature of either is doomed to failure" (53–54). Malafouris draws on a wide range of postcognitivist research—including autopoiesis and Brooksian robotics—a commendably interdisciplinary reading list for an archeologist. He quotes Daniel Dennet: "Tool use is a two-way sign of intelligence: not only does it *require* intelligence to recognize and maintain a tool . . . but a tool *confers* intelligence on those lucky enough to be given one" (Dennett 1996, 99–100; emphasis in original). Malafouris, Ingold, and Rowlands mount a concerted argument against cognitivism. Malafouris argues, "If we are to succeed where cognitivism has failed we need to develop our own means to grasp the engagement of the mind in culture . . . the objective should be to develop a more detailed classification of the types of mnemonic operations involved, keeping in mind that object traditions allow a [to quote Rowlands] 'direct re-engagement with past experience in ways that are prevented in language'" (2004, 57). Such sentiments hearken back to Polanyi and recall John Sutton's work on memory in (the game of) cricket (Sutton 2007).

A postcognitivist rejection of representationalism is not a denial that mental representation ever happens. Except in the most radical positions, it is only a rejection of that idea that all cognition is operation on mental representations. (A similar distinction is made regarding internalism. A noninternalist position does not necessarily declare that cognition is exclusively external but simply that it is not exclusively internal.) Language, and certainly written language, is symbolic representation. The relation between material experience and symbolic abstraction remains one of the mysteries of cognition, and transition from materiality to abstraction demands attention. Malafouris notes, "The point is not to deny altogether the existence of mental models, schemata and internal planning procedures as active in the course of any creative process, but rather to recognize them as the temporally emergent and dynamic products of situated activity" (2004, 60). Such ideas recollect the work of Agre and Horswill (1997).

Malafouris contests the traditional cognitivist distinction between skill and cognition: "This is precisely the assumption that should be questioned by collapsing the dividing lines between perception, cognition and action, and rejecting the methodological separation between reason and embodiment" (2004, 59). He goes beyond distributed cognition, far beyond the parity principle and even beyond Sutton's complementarity principle when he says, "Mind is immanent . . . in the sequence of technical gestures required for the production of the tool and the various media that are brought to bear on that sequence, and . . . in the skillful actuality that transforms the tool into an agent imbued with cognitive and social life" (60). This reading of past human culture captures precisely the project of this book. Cultural practice is cognitive—not in the functionalist sense, but in an enactive, temporally grounded sense. Following Malafouris, we should think cultural practice and embodied cognition through the thematic of *cultural cognition*: a study of embodied cultural practices drawing upon contemporary cognitive science, and focusing on creative practices, especially those aspects that fall through the cognitivist net.[7] Such an emphasis on the doing, on process, was a key part of the theorization of art practices of the late 1960s and 1970s. Process ontology was a part of art theory long before it became a topic in cognitive science.[8]

## Feminism and Embodiment

The critical and political analysis of the mind-body split and its relation to patriarchy were central to feminist discourses from the outset. The range of publications, from 1970s activist self-help texts like *Our Bodies, Ourselves* (Boston Women's Health Book Collective 1971; the title says it all) to Adrienne Rich's *Of Woman Born* (1976) to Iris Young's "Throwing like a Girl: A Phenomenology of Feminine Body Comportment Motility and Spatiality" (1980), and Jane Gallop's *Thinking through the Body* (1988) testifies to the extended intensity of this work.[9] However, scour the bibliographies of orthodox cognitive science; you'll find nary a whisper.

How is it possible that two fields ostensibly concerned with the same issue (albeit from very different perspectives) seem not to have crossed? It would be a caricature to suggest that the (mostly white male) cognitive science community looked down upon *women's work*, left it at home in the dormitory suburbs with the mothering of children and the domestic chores, so far from the heady concerns of the ivory tower. However, a full thirty years of feminist theory seems to have been ignored or, worse, unacknowledged. How could this have happened? It is not as though universities are devoid of women; indeed, many progressive campuses nurtured feminist activism and institutionalized departments of Women's Studies during the decades when cognitivism reigned. Gallop insightfully notes,

Men have their masculine identity to gain by being estranged from their bodies and dominating the bodies of others. . . . men are more able to venture into the realm of the body without being trapped there. Men who do find themselves in some way thinking through the body are more likely to be recognized as serious thinkers and heard. Women have first to prove that we are thinkers, which is easier when we conform to the protocol that deems serious thought separate from an embodied subject in history. (1988, 7)

Indeed, it is the gendering of the mind-body split and the essentializing of woman as "natural" and driven by biology that privileges men in the academy.[10] In the last two decades in the humanities and the arts, gender balance has been significantly addressed, but on the technical side of campuses even now, at least in the United States, female students are rare and female faculty rarer, especially in engineering.[11]

With respect to Nietzche, Foucault, and Deleuze and Guattari, Elizabeth Grosz notes, "None of the male theorists discussed here is very enlightened about or illuminating on the question of sexual specificity. None seems prepared to admit that his researches, if they make sense of the body, do so with reference to the male body. None seems aware that the specificities of the female body remain unexplained" (1994, xiii). These sentiments are of a piece with Donna Haraway's *God trick*. If this can be said of these philosophers, then so much more is it characteristic of the AI/cognitive science community. Even given the presence of a few influential women such as Lucy Suchman, cognitive science remains almost untainted by the politics of gender. N. Katherine Hayles relates that she recommended Mark Johnson's *The Body in the Mind* to a female graduate student, who threw the book down when she encountered his gender-blind use of a passage from *Men on Rape*, treating it without comment, as if the story were as benign an instance of human life as walking the dog. As Hayles remarks, "Johnson launches perhaps the most severe attack on objectivism. Thus it is ironic that he reinscribes objectivist presuppositions in positing a universal body unmarked by gender, ethnicity, physical disability or culture" (1999, 206). She continues, "With stunning reticence, [Johnson] never remarks on the gender politics so obviously foregrounded by this series of propositions, treating the example as if it were sexually and culturally neutral" (206). Even today, studies in situated and embodied cognition are unwilling to grant the reality of cultural, economic, and physical difference—not just in gender, but in race, ethnicity, and class.

The title of one of George Lakoff's books implies misogyny: *Women, Fire and Dangerous Things: What Categories Reveal about the Mind* (1987). While these authors explore the cognitive ramifications of metaphor, they avoid questions of cultural bias in metaphor and the power of outdated ideas. This shortcoming demonstrates the value of the kind of reflexive criticality advocated by Agre, that has arisen in postcolonial and feminist studies, in which humanism is critiqued for the universalization of Western white male and the marginalization of the experiences and histories of women and the racially or ethnically other. If Hutchins can reflect that his notion of distributed cognition in *Cognition in the Wild* was "strangely disembodied," then we must also recognize the *Vitruvian Man* implicit in much embodied cognition. The old ghosts of Enlightenment patriarchy still rattle their chains. One only hopes that the ascent of man does not imply the descent of woman.

## Conclusion

The foregoing discussion has attempted to capture the spirit of postcognitivism by discussing the work of several representative theorists and schools. If the body behaves intelligently in direct sensorimotor engagement with the world, then the notion that intelligence dwells in the logico-mathematical manipulation of symbols in some immaterial Platonic idea-space comes under some pressure. This should lead us to reflect on the valorization of modalities of symbolic representation in our intellectual culture, modalities such as textual and numerical expressions.

If concepts arise from bodily experience in the world, then the symbol-grounding problem, that bane of AI, never arises, because symbols or concepts were always grounded in lived sensorimotor experience. Physiologist Paul Cisek's crucial insight is that the central question that dogged cognitivism in the common sense crisis—how to attach meaning to symbols—puts the boot firmly on the wrong foot. Cisek (1999) argues that meanings are primary and the world is full of meaning. As Haugeland said, *we abide in the meaningful*. The problem cognitivism failed to recognize was how to attach symbols to (already present) meanings! This idea resonates with Hutchins's inversion of the symbol-grounding problem discussed previously, and it is consistent with the work of Lakoff et al.

In the cognitivist conception, perception is regarded as a relatively trivial process of the production of logical tokens through perception. However, perception is by no means a simple process; it is not a matter of referencing a look-up table. Discernment of salience from the overwhelming cacophony presented to our senses *is intelligence*. Contra the cognitivist value system, one might well argue that once the construction of symbols is done, the operation of the algorithm is relatively trivial.

I believe that taking such ideas together offers a new purchase and new perspective on creative practice. Embracing and applying them to a theorization of arts practices promises a new way to understand arts practices and their position in the larger culture. If cultural practices—be they dancing or throwing a pot—depend on techniques learned in a Dreyfusian sense, then intelligent judgments made below the level of consciousness are central to arts practices. Indeed, this is what Csikszentmihalyi identifies as the flow state. Out of this comes a new way of thinking about art practices, engaging conceptions of the cognitive unconscious as the sensorimotor unconscious. Sutton (2007) has argued for a subtle interplay of the conscious and unconscious, of automaticity, awareness, memory, and introspection in playing sports. If this is the case in sports, it is more so in arts practices, in which conscious intentions regarding historical and cultural context and predictions of audience reception are interwoven with muscular gestalts and intuitive decision-making.

---

**Summation**

The new postcognitivist paradigms offer useful and explanatory perspectives including the following:

1. A (variously qualified) rejection of the notion that cognition, reasoning, thinking, intelligence, mind, or self is located exclusively inside the cranium.
2. An understanding that the human being is not divisible into the *res cogitans* and the *res extensa* but is suffused throughout the biological body (at least) and does not trade in what neuroethologist Malcolm MacIver calls "an invidious distinction between bone and brain" (2009, 492).
3. A commitment to the materialist idea that cognition is biological and does not require magical explanations.

Take-home points about noncognitivist conceptions of cognition include the following:

• Knowledge comes from interaction with the world and is directed toward interaction with the world.
• Knowledge of the world derives from active exploration.
• Fluency in the world is developed through increasingly fluent sensorimotor action.
• The directional and serial notion of perception-thought-action is false.
• Rarely is there a clear separation of perception and action. Action often precedes perception, and perception is concurrent with action.

• The idea that (all) intelligent action presupposes reasoning on internal representations is dubious at best.
• Abstract thought and language arise from interaction with the world.
• Much cognition or intelligent action in the world occurs without conscious awareness.
• Capacities for abstract thought arise in a distributed way throughout the brain/body, piggybacking on existing systems for sensory and motor functions.

One might summarize the tenets of cognitivism in the following way:

1. Human thinking occurs via algorithmic manipulation of symbolic tokens.
2. Human thinking, or acting in the world, consists of a serial process of perception, cogitation, and action.
3. Human thinking occurs in a closed physical or logical space.

An alternate view of human intelligence might be summarized in the following way:

1. Human intelligence resides at the intersection of the body and the world—in our fingertips and our bellies and the muscles around our knees.
2. Sensing and action are inseparable; sensorimotor loops hold our umwelts—our experience-worlds—together.
3. Action in the world is characterized by iterative feedback loops and close integration of body and world. (In the autopoietic tradition, this is called *structural coupling*.)

The body is our general medium for having a world.
—Maurice Merleau-Ponty, *Phenomenology of Perception* (2002, 169)

Mind is a leaky organ, forever escaping its "natural" confines and mingling shamelessly with body and with world.
—Andy Clark, *Being There: Putting Brain, Body, and World Together* (1996, 53)

The brain is an organ whose role is to control the interaction between the body and its environment.
—Paul Cisek, "The Affordance Competition Hypothesis: A Framework for Embodied Behavior" (2008, 230)

There is no mind apart from the world.
—Lambros Malafouris, "The Cognitive Basis of Material Engagement: Where Brain, Body and Culture Conflate" (2004, 60)

The structuring dualisms of humanism produce a paradoxical way of thinking about being, selfhood, mind, body, and world. Broadly, according to this conception, mind is immaterial and abstract but is housed (exclusively) in the brain, though the details of that colocation are unclear. The brain is a biological organ of the body, but the body does not partake in mind. The self is subjective, but the world is objective and "out there." In perception, we take in *information* (which is lying about in the world) and turn it into symbols (representations). Thinking involves reasoning on representations, or "symbol processing." Each pillar of this theory is dubious, and the logic of their separation and separability is likewise dubious.

The disciplines of psychology and, later, cognitive science adhered in general to this formulation.[1] Enough has been said in previous pages about cognitivism that it needs no further elaboration. Our problem is that these dualisms are wrong: The location of mind may not be entirely in brain, but mind, like brain, is surely in and of body. While autopoiesis demands a dividing membrane, the body is embedded in and integrated with the world. The relation between body and world is given by evolutionary processes, which provide a generally good match between body and world—even though change in human culture has outstripped the speed of evolutionary change, demanding technologies of compensation, such as wisdom tooth extraction, and technologies of enhancement, from contact lenses to the Internet. The old explanations have ceased to hold explanatory power, and fundamental assumptions about the nature of mind and body and their relationship are in question. We are confronting a wholesale paradigm shift.

## Systems and Subsystems

In *Having Thought: Essays in the Metaphysics of the Mind*, John Haugeland deploys systems theory in a *reductio ad absurdum* argument against an internalist notion of intelligence (1998, 211–214). A key procedure in systems theory is to break systems into networks of subsystems. This approach has its roots in the cybernetic idea of *black boxes*. To understand how a subsystem functions as a component of a system, it is not necessary to know how the subsystem works internally but only what happens at its interfaces—that is, at its inputs and outputs. But how do we divide an integrated system into subsystems in a principled way? What is an interface to another subsystem? In systems theory, an *interface* is by definition a low-bandwidth connection between subsystems; whatever passes between subsystems at the interface is simple with respect to what is going on inside the subsystems. This works well for machine parts, but for more complex "systems," isolating "inputs" and "outputs" is dubious. When everything is connected to everything else in a multiplicity of ways, assigning inputs and outputs is arbitrary. Per Francisco Varela's assessment of information in a biological system, *sensu stricto*, systems, subsystems, interfaces, inputs, and outputs do not exist. They are externally imposed a posteriori theoretical abstractions.

Haugeland proposes that if an internalist position is correct, we ought to be able, according to systems theory, to find low-bandwidth interfaces between mind, or brain, and body, and likewise between body and world. He proceeds to look for such interfaces but finds none, and, on the contrary, finds only broad-bandwidth connections. In terms of systems theory, it is not possible, he argues, to break the mind-body-world into subsystems. On the basis of this, he argues that internalist ideas about mind are wrong, and mind is indeed "embodied and embedded." One might question whether his choice of systems theory is an appropriate speculum with which to examine mind, but there is some rhetorical merit in using the tools of one's opponents to demolish their axiomatic assumptions. Echoing Haugeland, Michael Silberstein and Anthony Chemero explain, "When the constituents of a system are highly coherent, integrated, and correlated such that their behavior is a nonlinear function of one another, the system cannot be treated as truly a collection of uncoupled individual parts. Thus, if brain, body and environment are non-linearly coupled, their activity cannot be ultimately best explained by decomposing them into sub-systems or into system and background" (2011, 4).

## Mind in Body

It seems as though some collusion between philosophy of mind and neuroscience has encouraged us to believe that the mind is in the brain, even if *mind* retains its peculiar immateriality. This situation is at best not entirely straightforward, and, as we have seen in preceding chapters, it is open to dispute from a number of directions. George Lakoff and Mark Johnson take an admirable biologically materialist position in arguing that "an adequate theory of concepts and reason must provide an account of mind that is cognitively and neurally realistic" (1999, 79). We must be careful not to assume Lakoff and Johnson seek an account of mind *in brain*. That may seem absurd—of course the mind is in the brain! Nonetheless, I would like to hold that door open slightly—though not in the sense that mind is wholly elsewhere; certainly, it is not beamed in from some supernatural elsewhere via the pineal telegraph! On the contrary, from a biologically materialist and culturally contextualized position, *mindedness* is an aspect of the whole organism; arrangements of receptors in the retina, neural behavior in the gut, and proprioception in the knee joints all contribute to mindedness. Further, dynamical and enactive loops with the world, with cultural artifacts, and with other people together constitute mindedness. This discussion *is* confusing, hopefully not because of my clumsy writing, but because in breaking down conventional distinctions between mind, brain, body, and world (not to mention sensing, perception, cognition, and intelligence), the implicit definitions we rely upon become contradictory. This is the nature of a paradigm shift.

*In Steps to an Ecology of Mind*, Gregory Bateson asks, "Is the mind in the brain?" (1972, 16). His answer is no: "The mental characteristics of the system are immanent not in some part, but in the system as a whole" (316). He continues: "We may say that 'mind' is immanent in those circuits of the brain which are complete within the brain. Or that mind is immanent in circuits which are complete within the system brain plus body. Or, finally, that mind is immanent in the larger system—man plus environment" (317). Bateson's words, as they reflect a cybernetic holism, presage the postcognitivist movement. Lettvin et al. (1959) demonstrated that the frog's eye is not a camera for the brain (see chapter 2). The topological organization of rods and cones, neurons, and synapses perform image analysis—that is, perception. Neuroethology is replete with similar evidence of cognition integrating neural and nonneural tissue.[2] Recent work on central pattern generators (CPGs) shows us that the very materiality of neural structure provides organization for neural processes (Ijspeert 2008).

Intelligence permeates the physical body and nonneural tissues of all sorts partake in its circuits. (Some readers may balk at this dogmatic assertion. Yet what is the conventional position except a similarly dogmatic assertion?) Intelligence is *enacted* in ongoing temporal engagement with the world, a world that is prestructured with the armatures of culture. These armatures, from tools to town layouts to language itself, bootstrap an infant mind into culture and provide a scaffold to be leveraged by the acculturated adult mind. If the body behaves intelligently in direct sensorimotor engagement with the world, leveraging the artifacts of culture in acts of epistemic action, then the notion that intelligence dwells in the logico-mathematical manipulation of symbols in some immaterial Platonic idea-space becomes nonsensical.

## Umwelts, Affordances, and Autopoiesis

In the early years of the twentieth century, Jakob von Uexküll developed a thoroughly relational perspective on organism and environment. According to von Uexküll, the world a creature has is given to it by virtue of its particular sensory and motor physiology, which he called its *umwelt*, or experience-world (see chapter 2). The corollary being that different species can be physically colocated but be unaware of each other's presence because their umwelts do not intersect. As we have seen, the fly has no spatial world with objects in it; it has only optic flow on the surface of its compound eye. We may perceive many animals occupying "our" space, but each one has its own umwelt and its own space, and other creatures show up in the way that the sensory capabilities of the perceiving animal render them. These species-specific sensorimotor suites are what prevent us from knowing what it is like to be a bat (as Nagel showed); we cannot say how a blind mole-rat perceives a snake.[3] We cannot know the world known by species around us. Our human perception is not absolute or objective; these animals appear to us as they do by virtue of the capacities of our senses. We do not, for instance, share the olfactory or auditory richness of a dog's umwelt. To a dog, we are each probably a cloud of subtle and complex odors before we are a visual phenomenon. The autopoietic biology of Maturana and Varela confirms the isomorphism of entity and environment implicit in the notion of the umwelt. According to autopoietic biology, cognition is a quality inherent to life and the living. This biological-materialist, anticognitivist, and anti-human-exceptionalist position has been influential in subsequent noncognitivist theorizing, as well as in artificial life.

In his ecological approach to visual perception, J. J. Gibson affirms that an organism and its environment are mutually constituted, a notion generally compatible with von Uexküll's umwelt. Gibson argues that this mutual constitution results in the possibility of direct perception of *affordance*. The concept of affordance has two parts. A flight of stairs *affords* climbing for an adult human (but not for a stork or for a crawling baby) due to the length of legs and the way knees bend. Gibson argues that the corollary is that objects in the environment, via visual perception, directly indicate the functions an animal can make of them. This second idea is the core of Gibson's radical externalism. In "What the Frog's Eye Tells the Frog's Brain" (1959), Lettvin et al. provide an example. For the frog, a fly is perceived not as a dark object of x angular dimension moving at y speed in z direction (and why, on God's green earth, should it be?) but directly as *edible*. Gibson calls such characteristics *high-order invariants*. In the frog, this provokes an immediate response to fire the tongue in that direction. As in the case of the fly's eye, the behavior is a rapid and unified sensorimotor event with little or no reasoning involved.

From a cognitivist position, the challenging part of Gibson's notion is that he asserts that affordances are *directly perceived*. This robs a cognitivist of a crucial axiomatic construction: the Cartesian theater. If the eye is not sending raw data to the brain—which interprets light changes as images—then cognition has already happened, in the eye. Some may object to this loose language, but surely it is preferable to presuming imaginary faculties.

The reason that Gibson's theory is so roundly misunderstood is that affordance is neither wholly internalist nor wholly externalist. Affordance is located neither in the brain of the subject nor in the objects of the environment. Rather, it is located in the specific relationality of a subject of a particular physiognomy and a set of characteristics in the environment. The realism, relationality, and externalism at the heart of Gibson's work made it incomprehensible to the (internalist) cognitivist community.

If comprehensively and rigorously pursued, it destabilizes the ground of the subject-object dualism upon which cognitivism rests. Nor should we attempt to understand relationality as an abstract object. The phenomenon is processual and performative.

Such *process philosophy* has been a minor literature in the West since Heraclitus, and it was pursued in the twentieth century by Whitehead, following Bergson, James, and Dewey. Karen Barad's *Agentieller Realismus (Agential Realism)*, and the work of Andrew Pickering are contemporary expressions. In non-Western traditions, "process" perspective is characteristic of much Daoist and Buddhist thought, and has been found relevant to postcognitivists, Varela, Thompson, and Rosch in particular. An important caution must be issued, identifying a "trap for young players": The term *process ontology* has been appropriated in representionalist AI, as has the more general term *ontology*. This kind of technical application of a highly nuanced philosophical idea is paradigmatic of the kind of dumbing down that occurs when such ideas are, as Agre puts it, "hollowed through the false precision of formalism" (1997b, 148).

## Merleau-Ponty and Dreyfus

Hubert Dreyfus, after Merleau-Ponty, said, "Our bodies determine what shows up in our world" (1996). Phenomenology has become a philosophical bulwark for embodied cognition and has contributed to the development of postcognitivist approaches, particularly in the work of Dreyfus, Philip Agre, Francisco Varela, and Evan Thompson.[4] This quotation from Maurice Merleau-Ponty captures the relevance of phenomenology to embodied cognition:

The body is our general medium for having a world. Sometimes it is restricted to the actions necessary for the conservation of life, and accordingly it posits around us a biological world; at other times, elaborating upon these primary actions and moving from their literal to a figurative meaning, it manifests through them a core of new significance: this is true of motor habits such as dancing. Sometimes, finally, the meaning aimed at cannot be achieved by the body's natural means; it must then build itself an instrument, and it projects thereby around itself a cultural world. (2002, 169)

When Merleau-Ponty emphasizes that the world we have is given to us as a result of our specific sensorimotor makeup, we are reminded of von Uexküll. In this, both thinkers reject objectivism—in the sense of a fixed world *out there*—and thus implicitly refute basic tenets of cognitivism.

Dreyfus, drawing upon Merleau-Ponty, critiqued the cognitivist notion of learning. Along the way, he clarified the matter of *affordances* as they pertain to human embodiment and the human cultural context. Dreyfus identifies three modalities of affordance, which he calls *innate structures*, *basic general skills*, and *cultural skills*. The first pertains to our raw human physical conformation. He quotes Merleau-Ponty: "In so far as I have hands, feet, a body, I sustain around me intentions which are not dependent upon my decisions and which affect my surroundings in a way which I do not choose. These intentions are general . . . they originate from other than myself, and I am not surprised to find them in all psycho-physical subjects organized as I am" (Dreyfus 1996).

The second sense of affordance for Dreyfus (again based in Merleau-Ponty), is that as we develop skills, things show up as offering affordances; as we refine our skills, affordances proliferate. Affordances may be negative. As toddlers, we come to understand that a descending staircase affords tumbling down. Thus, "what affords walking on, squeezing through, reaching, etc. are correlative with our bodily capacities and acquired skills" (Dreyfus 1996). His third sense of affordance, drawn from Gibson, is that a mailbox affords mailing letters—a historically and culturally specific affordance. To Descartes or Shakespeare, a mailbox would not afford mailing letters and a phone would not afford making calls. Paraphernalia of their time—for handling hot coals or tightening corsets—would not be affordances to us, so we would not develop the attendant sensibilities and practices. Dreyfus notes, "The cultural world is thus also correlative with our body; this time with our acquired cultural skills" (1996).

## Biology and Psychology

Functionalism provided cognitivism a principled way out of the constraints of behaviorism by arguing that material substrates were in principle irrelevant for information processing. (Tolman destabilized the orthodoxy of behaviorism with his cognitive maps research in 1948.) By imposing a dualist metaphor of hardware and software, it was asserted that biology and psychology were different sciences. Establishing that logical (computational) processes of an abstract kind provided a principled way to sidestep behaviorist constraints and permit discussion of mental states. A dubious by-product of this move was to permit introspection as a methodology.

The recent emergence of cognitive neuroscience is an attempt to reconnect psychology with biology, but it is hampered by the fact that it inherits theoretical positions from cognitive psychology. As a result, much cognitive-neuroscientific research is framed in terms of cognitivist paradigms. As emphasized in chapter 10, questions askable in postcognitivist inquiry are unaskable under the internalist paradigm. Thus, cognitive neuroscience researchers might seek faculties or centers in which activities of perception, cognition, and action control can be isolated, and the brain confounds them by not functioning in this manner. Evidence increasingly points to the idea that perception and action cannot be separated, even in the brain, and the purportedly separate cognitive function is merged with, and emerges from, sensorimotor networks.

The first paragraph of Haugeland's essay "Mind Embodied and Embedded" reads:

Among Descartes's most lasting and consequential achievements has been his constitution of the mental as an independent ontological domain. By taking the mind as a substance, with cognitions as its modes, he accorded them a status as self-standing and determinate on their own, without essential regard to other entities. Only with this metaphysical conception in place, could the idea of solipsism—the idea of an intact ego existing with nothing else in the universe—so much as make sense. And behind that engine have trailed the sorry boxcars of hyperbolic doubt, the mind-body problem, the problem of the external world, the problem of other minds, and so on. (Haugeland 1998, 207)

Haugeland's charmingly hokey "sorry boxcars"—bringing Thomas the Tank Engine imagery to mind—aptly ridicules Cartesian solipsism. Cognitivism and cognitive neuroscience perpetuate the mind-body dualism. In biologically based traditions we find approaches that bypass the cognitivist dilemma. Maturana's definition of cognition is thoroughly biological, and more contemporary work in neurophysiology continues in this spirit. Physiologist Paul Cisek provides a good example of noncognitivist approaches, maintaining a pragmatic evolutionary biological logic: "The nervous system did not evolve for the kinds of abstract tasks to which formal computations and descriptive representations are best suited. It evolved for controlling interaction with the environment, and was constrained by the pragmatic concerns of that control" (2008, 233). Cisek combines this biological pragmatism with a pointed critique of cognitivism: "The bottom line of survival is how we deal with the challenges posed by the environment, and not how deeply we may contemplate them" (230–231). It is from this perspective that Cisek asks, rhetorically, "Should we expect that a conceptual framework which developed for many years in deliberate isolation of [*sic*] biology would provide the most promising foundation for the interpretation of neural data?" (208). He continues, "Perhaps the concepts of separate perceptual, cognitive and motor systems, which theoretical neuroscience inherits from cognitive psychology, are not appropriate for bridging neural data with behavior" (209).

Cisek destabilizes two central ideas of cognitivism: centralized control and unified representation. The linear perception-cognition-action model centralizes decision-making in a "'central executive' which issues orders to the rest of the brain" (2008, 224). However, "cognitive psychology's assumption of a unified and stable representation does not appear to be well-supported by the divergence of the visual system and the widespread influence of attentional modulation" (217). Indeed, neural data often "does not strongly support the distinction between decision-making and movement planning or between planning and execution" (221). That is, it does not support the cognitivist paradigm. Importantly, "decision-making . . . appears to be distributed throughout the brain" (224). Behavior of the posterior parietal cortex "does not appear to neatly fit into any of the categories of perception, cognition or action. Indeed it is difficult to see how neural activity in this region could be interpreted using concepts of cognitive psychology" (219).[5] This challenge to a standard paradigm is reminiscent of the situation of AI in the late 1980s, when it was increasingly perceived that stumbling blocks in research were not technical glitches but problems in principle.

More generally, the concept of localized brain faculties is not supported by contemporary neuroscience. On the contrary, when each neuron is connected to ten thousand others, even in a brain of one billion neurons, each is connected to every other with only a few degrees of separation. This scale of connectivity exceeds the capabilities of human technology by several orders of magnitude.

Long ago, Rodney Brooks observed that while *representation* was axiomatic to AI, no one agreed on what the term meant. Extrapolating from the physiological reality of the separation of dorsal and ventral streams in vision, Cisek builds a perceptual model, distinguishing between what he calls *descriptive* and *pragmatic* representations: "'Pragmatic representations' are not primarily concerned with descriptive accuracy at all. Instead, they are most concerned with the efficiency of the behavior to which they contribute" (2008, 211). A "representation" without descriptive quality looks like an *affordance*. Cisek's pragmatic representations are akin to the *contingent action plans* discussed by Gallese and others. In a key passage, Cisek argues that "the existence of a unified internal representation is not necessary. . . . pragmatic representations specifying potential actions and pragmatic representations collecting selection criteria need not be explicitly bound together, because the operation of the specification and selection system can be integrated simply by focusing each on the same spatial region of interest through overt gaze orientation . . . or covert shifts in spatial attention" (233). This passage reinforces the principle of situated cognition from a biological point of view (the world is its own best model), and it reminds us of the multithreaded selfhoods of von Uexküll and Brooksian subsumption.[6]

Elsewhere Cisek notes, "Numerous theorists have proposed that grounding must come from situated interaction with the environment . . . which is performed as an extension of physiological control through the environment by exploiting the consistent properties of that environment" (2008, 233). Cisek here asserts that, biologically, *the existence of a unified internal representation is not necessary for cognition.* In so saying, he makes a radical claim that the processes of cognition are not required to be coherently logically organized or even rational! This upends cognitivism. The sensor fusion of the SMPA paradigm is not a biological reality: "As long as the mixture of features leads to adaptive behavior, the confounding of variables within a single neural population is perfectly acceptable and will be supported by natural selection" (211). Cisek thus justifies the formulation of a different paradigm, suggesting that the activities of the posterior parietal cortex are evidence of a process of negotiation or competitive winnowing of possible action scenarios in the form of pragmatic representations, informed by perceptual updates. In a nod to Gibson, he calls this the *affordance competition hypothesis.*

## Neuroethology

Like Gibson's higher-order invariants, the complex cognitive scenarios Cisek explores are not amenable to reductivist experimental methods in controlled laboratory contexts. To deploy such a method would likely erase or obscure precisely what is of interest. To illustrate, consider the 1959 Hubel and Wiesel experiment discussed in chapter 2. Typically, in experimental contexts of this sort, variables are controlled in order to capture "knowledge." The cat is chemically paralyzed and strapped to the table, its eyelids pinned open, and electrodes put in its brain. A bright light like a strobe or flashgun is set off at close range, and neural responses are timed and measured. While the technical achievement of measuring anything happening in the brain of a live cat in 1959 is remarkable, the usefulness of the resultant findings for explaining how cat vision works—for the cat, in the world—seems dubious for at least three reasons.

First, because the stimulus is orders of magnitude greater than a normal visual stimulus, especially for night vision, any reaction in the cat's brain is to a cataclysmic event. There is no assurance that resulting neural activity bears any similarity to normal visual activity; in fact, the contrary is more likely. Presumably, the cat's vision is attuned to subtle variation—say, that created by a scared mouse quivering in leaf litter at night—stimuli as different from a strobing projected stripe of light as night is from day.

Second, the experiment seems to assume *cognition* in the sense of reasoning on representations. If the frog's eye is any indicator, salient visual effects are likely to be of a different order.

Third, as the cat is deprived of the opportunity to respond, the controlled experiment offers little insight or predictive value for normal behavior of a normal cat in a normal environment. Not only that, but the cat's paralysis and awareness of being disabled and constrained presumably create panic responses, which may disrupt more subtle responses that the experiment purported to measure. Clearly, a less invasive technique would likely result in more useful data. Technologies have advanced: many subtle, miniaturized, and wireless monitoring systems now permit measurement while the animal is conscious and mobile, and in a more "normal" environment.

Consideration of the full sensorimotor engagement between animals and their worlds calls for an interdisciplinary approach—hence, neuroethology. Ethology looks at behavior in the world, neurology at neural activity. Neuroethologists argue that it is necessary to look at behavior in the world and neural activity together to gain an understanding of how behavior happens in the world and to avoid fundamental attribution error (see below). In the same way that sensing peripherals were put temporarily by AI researchers in the too-hard basket, the technological challenges of real-time monitoring of animal brain activity in the wild were seen (rightly at the time) as prohibitive by neuroscientists. Notwithstanding this technological dodge, tensions bedevil the merging of ethology and neurology, which mirror the internalist/externalist tensions in human cognition. As in neuroethology, in studies of human behavior, cognitive science, and cultural anthropology must likewise necessarily converge, and this, happily, is beginning to happen.[7]

In such interdisciplinary initiatives, we must be vigilant not to impose a disciplinary imperialism of the sort that Philip Agre has alerted us to and that Edwin Hutchins, in an exemplary way, has acknowledged in his own practice (see chapter 9). Disciplinary hubris and methodological misunderstandings rooted in uninterrogated and mismatched axiomatic assumptions create booby traps for interdisciplinary enterprises. For any such enterprise to be successful, these misunderstandings must be preemptively addressed. Sadly, this fundamental problem is rarely acknowledged, let alone addressed.

## Neurocentrism and Fundamental Attribution Error

In neurocentric research, having found brain activity in a certain location, the assertion that "this is where this behavior/skill/ability resides" seems to follow. Attribution error runs wild in this territory, as in genomics rhetoric. It would not be unreasonable to assert that the entire program of conventional cognitive science is guilty of fundamental attribution error (also known as *correspondence bias* or *attribution effect*). Gerd Gigerenzer spells it out: "The tendency to explain behavior internally without analyzing the environment is known as the 'fundamental attribution error'" (2007, 50). Lambros Malafouris elaborates: "It is one thing to say that the brain, or more specifically the right hemisphere, plays a special role in the creation of the self. It is indeed another, quite different thing to say that the self 'resides' in the right hemisphere" (2008, 1995). Ecological psychology, neuroethology, and many embodied cognition paradigms embrace relationality, proposing that cognition extends beyond the skull, beyond neural matter, and beyond the outer membrane of the body.

I propose a way of thinking about embodied and diffused cognition that aims at decentering the brain and providing a way of thinking of the mind as distributed. This scheme is sympathetic with many of the ideas discussed previously and is structurally reminiscent of subsumption architecture. In essence, it is as simple as it is anticognitivist, and its key justifications are necessity and sufficiency.

## The Subsumption Self: Heterogeneous Functional Networks

While the "voice in the head" is taken to imply residence of the self and mind in the brain, it has an obvious embodied explanation—that the voice *is* in the head, in the resonant cavities of the mouth, throat, and nasal cavity. Therefore, it stands to reason (as they say) that we would imagine the mind as being in the head, as much as we associate breathing with the lungs and kicking with the feet.

The brain/body binary not only emphasizes the differentness and separateness of brain and body but also conjures a sense of the brain as undifferentiated. When speaking of mind, intelligence, and consciousness, we tend to regard the brain as an undifferentiated whole, though in some abstract way there is a separation of consciousness and the unconscious. The brain, more correctly, is an assemblage of organs with various functions, all interconnected. In neurophysiology and physiology generally, we are encouraged to believe top-down centralized hierarchical metaphors that have obviously sociopolitical origins. However, we are presented with distributed, horizontal, decentralized, nonhierarchical, and rhizomatic models of parts in cooperation (or competition) with each other, from slime mold behavior (Keller) to stigmergy among colonial insects (Grassé) to Minsky's society of mind and other models of multiple selves and negotiated selfhoods.

I propose a different logic of mind-brain-body, analogous to ideas of von Uexküll and Brooks. First, let us assume not a monolithic brain but numerous brainlets or specialized brain organs, massively interconnected. Specific brain organs might be better connected with specific noncranial parts than they are with other parts of the brain, even given the truly awesome number of synaptic connections in the brain. These heterogeneous functional networks include sense organs and nonneural tissues. They do things in the world: eating, running, or typing. I stress "they do," not "the brain tells the muscles to do." There is substantial literature on neural activity that never gets to the brain, in locomotion (Grillner 1996) and the activities of the autonomic nervous system, not to mention endocrine and immunological circuits in the "bag of soup" (see chapter 2).

Any human behavior (broadly construed) involves a bit of the world (with qualities like gravity, temperature, language, sociality), some aspect of one or more senses, some neural sensorimotor function, some muscular behavior, and so on. Any number of these processes are constantly happening in parallel and influencing each other. In this conception, it is meaningless to say that a behavior is in the brain. It can only occur *when all aspects of the heterogeneous network are involved*. There is no input and output; there is sensorimotor process. Various parts resonate together in mutually excitatory (or inhibitory) ways. The analogy of analog electronic circuitry with its allover resonances is more useful than the hierarchical linearity of the von Neumann paradigm.

If we pay attention to any prosaic bodily experience, the input-output paradigm is immediately dubious. I rub my right shoulder; my left hand finds the swelling of the offending bug bite; the right shoulder feels the pressure of the left hand, exciting the irritation and causing me to scratch with the left. Somewhere in the middle, the greasiness of my skin on this hot summer afternoon and some grit left over from gardening also register. In the scratching, tension on the hair follicles is felt (differently) in the shoulder and under the fingers. All these sensations drive one another in subtle ways; they draw my vision to my shoulder, where I now see what was previously only felt: a welt. Simultaneously, I feel sensations in my neck caused by three things combined: the left hand grasping, sensitivity due to a recent strain, and the turning of my head.[8] As Kurt Vonnegut would say, "So it goes." If we take the time to sensitively examine any activity—whether cutting a loaf of bread or pushing a heavy wheelbarrow—while attempting to avoid craniocentrism and the fallacious linear processing analogy, then we find such endless ramifications and echoes. The roughness of the handles of the wheelbarrow (thoughtlessly left out in the weather) is felt in the hands; the heaviness of the load is felt in the shoulders, in the lower back, in the thighs, in the soles of the feet; pressure is felt in the temples if the load is too heavy.

When we consider highly skilled embodied and interactional cultural activities such as dancing the tango, the scenario becomes increasingly complex. All kinds of sensibilities are at play: feeling the smell and texture of our partner's clothes, and through that a sense of the ease or tension in the muscles. A faltering or lilt of our partner's movement informs us about the desires and abilities of our partner—not to mention the music, the crowdedness of the dance floor, and so on. It is absurd to propose that the dancing is happening in the mind. It is a process that integrates immediate kinesthetic, proprioceptive, and peripersonal understandings with bodily memory and skills, varying degrees of understanding of the subtleties of a cultural tradition, and complex interpersonal dynamics expressed as bodily gesture.

Why do we objectify the body, describing sensations from the position of a self who is elsewhere, as it were? This is, in a sense, the question Descartes asked. His answer got us into this mess. This objectification of the body by a viewpoint previously ascribed nonbody status is a deep theoretical issue for postcognitivist theorists. In theories of embodied cognition, we often encounter a new dualism: the experiencing self and the experienced self (Legrand, Hurley, Thompson, Gallagher). Hanna and Thompson (2003), following Husserl, called this the *body/body problem*: They distinguish the lived, embodied self from the body as object, thus displacing the mind-body problem and reframing the consciousness question in embodied terms, but the reframing perpetuates dualism. Are we as a species doomed to dualize? Is the resolution of this conundrum a kind of cosmic joke? Is dualizing fundamental to our biology as bilaterally symmetrical creatures, implicit in the fact that we say, and think: On the one hand, x, and on the other hand, y?

### I Am, Therefore I Think

As our body is our general medium for having a world (Merleau-Ponty), so our thinking is facilitated and constrained by our embodiment. It is ironic to reflect that our tendency to construct binary oppositions might be the upshot of our bilateral symmetry. Von Uexküll's division of perceptual space seems a projection of Cartesian space. Yet it can be argued that it arises out of embodied experience. As vertical creatures, we stand perpendicular to the ground, the original gnomon, our vertical axis parallel with the direction of gravity. We are frontal: Experientially, there is always "the direction I am facing" and its opposite—my "backside." We are bilateral: two eyes, two arms, two legs, a left and a right. Our primary vertical axis, our frontality, and our bilaterality construct the axes of Cartesian space. Right angles and perpendiculars are natural to us. Cartesian space is vertebrate bodily space. Would starfish philosophy have pentisms instead of dualisms? Or a binary characterized not by front and back, nor past and future, but rather

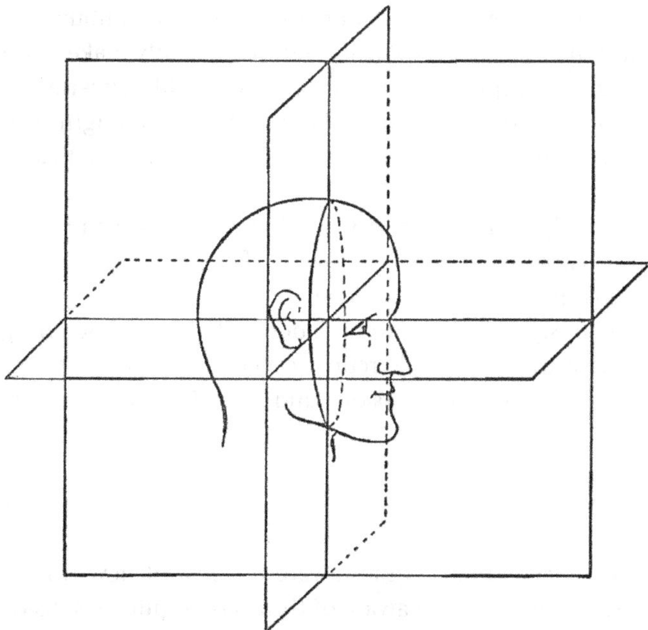

**Figure 12.1**

Head with Cartesian planes, from von Uexküll, *A Stroll through the Worlds of Animals and Men* (1957).

another conception arising from their form—their armored and exposed side and a protected, vulnerable, and blind underside?[9]

**Space and Place**

We interact with the physical space in three or four main ways. These ways are reflected in different neurological systems:

We move parts of ourselves with respect to other parts—deploying proprio-ceptive and kinesthetic awareness, along with stereoscopy and hand-eye coordination. In neuroscience, this is called *personal space*.

We occupy space and move about locally. This is referred to as *peripersonal space*. We extend our embodiment prosthetically. We interact with tools, artifacts, and objects. We expand and adapt our sensory and motor homunculi. Heidegger's *present at hand* refers to when our adaptation to a prosthetical homuncular extension fails.

We move bodily through space, deploying place and grid cells, exploiting the structuring of spaces. This is *extrapersonal space*. Vision and hearing informs us of things and events beyond peripersonal and ambulatory space and beyond the range of stereoscopy, but we can only make sense of visual and auditory impressions based on prior bodily experience. If we had never approached and climbed a mountain, we might well assume that the jagged triangular forms on the skyline were flat card-board cutouts.

We interact interpersonally and socially in ways that, via culture and tech-nology, are not constrained by physical space. We use language, face to face and in various space- and time-extended modes.

We respond unconsciously to pheromones and to hardwired learning functions such as mirror neuron circuits, especially in infancy. We read and deploy subtle facial expressions and body language, usually unconsciously.

**Finding My Way**

When one is in a new place, one becomes aware not just of new things, but reflexively, of the quality of being aware of things that quickly subside into muscular gestalts. When I moved into an apartment in a new city, I became aware of the miniscule details of navigation that had to be con-sciously managed: the way to turn and push the front door, how much I had to lean against it to counteract its heft, the height of the step up before the elevator, the wrinkle in the carpet, the behavior of the ancient elevator call button, the distance down the hall, the orientation of the key and the direction it turned to let me into the apartment. The subtle but typical musty-dusty smell of the hallway stays with me. Slowly and steadily, procedures became unconscious, routine, and automatic. This quotidian poetry of experience is commonly attended to in the arts. These kinds of everyday experiences demonstrate a fluid interchange between situatedness and representationalism, and the development of *intelligent action*, which is not reasoned nor entirely representational.

How could one make a robot that could internalize such environmental learning, effectively leveraging the environment as an armature for more effective or intelligent behavior? What would it take to build a device capable of such learning? The tools of AI have largely developed around paradigms of reasoning and planning and the construction of internal abstract representational schemes. In this paradigm, *thinking* occurs upon these representations and then is transferred to the world.

As an alternative to the cognitivist paradigm, we might say that intelligence exists, in an autopoietic sense, on the membrane, at the interface between organism and world and between self and other. Evidence in many cases from neuroscience, ethology, and psychology supports this idea. Under such a paradigm, many of the tools of AI and cognitivism would have no relevance, and attempts to apply them would only result in confusion—like trying to apply a torque wrench to a cow.

## Location, Location, Location: Proprioception, Deixis, and Place

When we navigate large spaces of landscape and architecture, our networks of grid and place cells provide us with orientation with respect to landmarks. The space around the body within reach of the hands or reachable in one step, more or less, is managed, neurologically, in quite a different way from more remote visual and acoustic space. Tasks in peripersonal space involve fine proprioception in coordination with vision, hearing, and other senses. Reaching for an apricot on a tree, swatting a mosquito, embroidering, playing an instrument, hand-to-hand combat, and lovemaking all involve a subtle intermingling of finely tuned sensorimotor behavior. Peripersonal space is deictic space.

Our physiology and neurology are formed around the fact that seeing is integrated with other sensorimotor activities. Note that the field of human vision almost exactly covers the extent of space reachable by the hands. Try it for yourself: stand facing forward. With arms outstretched, and without moving the head, trace the largest arcs of your hands, from by the thighs to above the head. Notice that, looking forward, your hands are always just in your peripheral vision. Your visual field closely matches the space you can reach with your hands.[10]

Our stereoscopy, our 3-D vision, is only useful in peripersonal space—the space we can reach or jump to. The interoptic distance determines the useful range of our stereoscopy. Stereoscopic acuity is best within arms' reach directly in front—exactly where you need it when you're assembling a motorcycle engine on the bench. It is especially useful at close range, such as when we manipulate small objects (say, a knife and a carrot), which are necessarily in arms' reach. Useful stereoscopy drops off quite quickly, and beyond the space we can leap to in a stride or two, it is of marginal value. If our eyes were farther apart, then we would have deeper stereoscopic vision, but we don't need long-distance stereoscopy. Other depth cues such as occlusion are demonstrably sufficient for other activities; we drive cars at speed, for instance.[11] The mountain might be a cardboard cutout, but it really doesn't matter until we get there. Indeed, the space within our stereoscopic range is the only space in which we can be fully 3-D in our actions. At a larger scale, we are little more than two-dimensional: We navigate on a two-dimensional plane; our mobility in the third dimension is severely restricted due to gravity and our inability to fly. In the big world, our dimensionality is fractal, we're about 2.2-dimensional.

No wonder, then, that current neurological research shows evidence of visuotactile multimodality: It's (neuro)logical! The biological holism of the body and pressures of evolution demand the integration of all kinds of systems that reductivism has falsely cleaved apart. If we embrace current understandings of spatial perception—in which we have not just one spatial context but at least two—as models for selfhood, then we can think selfhood in two ways simultaneously, as nested and overlapping: in a binarizing subject-object sense within the world coordinate system and in a deictic and intersubjective mode that enfolds artifacts, local contexts, and other people.

### Where Am I? Place and Grid Cells

How do we know where we are? In 1971, O'Keefe and Dostrovsky identified so-called place cells in the hippocampus—so named because each fired when the test animal was in a specific place. The finding was taken to confirm what, in 1948, Edward Tolman had called *cognitive maps*. There are hundreds if not thousands of place cells in the hippocampus. In any given environment, every position a rat occupies will stimulate the firing of a specific place cell. When moved to a new environment, a previously active place cell may or may not be activated in the new environment, tagged to a new place.

Are place cells a *map* in the top down AI sense? A 2013 blog entry called "Place Cells, Remapping and Memory" (recalling the work its author, John Kubie, had done with Bob Muller in the 1980s) sheds some light on this question. "An important concept is that the map is entirely in the brain. In this description, a map is defined by the relation among hippocampal neurons, not by the relationships between neurons and the environment. The linkage to the environment is critical, but does not define the map" (Kubie 2013). Kubie emphasizes, "The temporal relations are important for two reasons. First, neurons in the brain do not know about space directly, but they know about time. Neurons can code the timing relations of the neurons that project to it, but not the spatial relations. In other words, within the brain, the map is a timing map that encodes the temporal overlap between cell pairs" (2013). What Kubie does not draw out here is that this place cell mapping is deictic; the temporality says, "I was there, now I am here." This subjective, self-centered map is not the "objective" map of SMPA, but is consistent with Agre and Chapman's deictic programming, which proved to be a parsimonious alternative to the God's-eye view approaches of conventional AI (see chapters 5 and 6).

The work of Muller and Kubie informed the work of May-Britt Moser and Edvard Moser at the Kavli Institute for Systems Neuroscience in Trondheim, Norway, in the early 2000s—for which they won a Nobel Prize. They discovered correlates to place cells, so-called grid cells in the medial entorhinal cortex of rats. These brain cells fire as a rat moves around and complement the functioning of place cells. The behavior of grid cells is remarkable. As the animal moves about, each individual grid cell will fire when the animal passes over a node on a regular grid, which is laid out over the world, as it were, by the cell. Grids are not permanent or universal; rather, like place cells, they are contingent and environment-specific (i.e., situated). They arise when a rat enters a novel environment and usually persist while the creature is in that environment. Anchored perhaps to places and calibrated by the animal's gait, grid cell activity does not require visual input; they are regulated proprioceptively. The grid has axes at 120 degrees and nodes that are equidistant, forming equilateral triangles. (Some researchers refer to this as a hexagonal grid). As the animal moves, say, northwest-ish, the cell will fire every time the animal is at a point a fixed distance away from the start point. Several adjacent grid cells will lay out grids in the same orientation, with the same axes of symmetry, but offset (and at different scales); each cell will fire when the animal crosses a point in that cell's grid. Grid cells code for direction of movement—not position with respect to some objective or allocentric map.

There are layers of grids of differing scales in the entorhinal cortex. Cells in a particular zone have the same scale, but as you move down the entorhinal cortex the scale grows bigger, from around 5–10 cm up to around 3–4 m. Each grid cell is encoding for movement on a series of aligned but offset grids of varying scales. The combination of this information gives the rat a capability for distance measurement or *odometry*. This seems to be how an animal is constantly aware, while fossicking about, of how far and in which direction it has moved. Whether the grid cells provide this information or are provided with it is unclear.

In 2013, researchers found evidence of human grid cells. (Interestingly, the tests on human subjects by Jacobs et al. [2013] were performed with bedridden subjects, and a navigable VR environment was used.) These findings imply that our internal navigation system is active even in the absence of bodily movement in physical space. This result seems in tension with the idea that grid cells do not require visual input, as the bedridden subject navigating a 3-D computer game has only visual input. One way to read this potential contradiction is as evidence for Lakoff and Gallese–style metaphorization and sensorimotor multimodality. Assuming the subjects have at some time been ambulatory, their proprioception would have calibrated their vision—unlike Held and Hein's kitten in the basket (see chapter 2). The visual experience of the 3-D world may assist in mapping and orientation based on grid cells. What about navigation in dreams or when forming a mental map of directions given in verbal form or when playing Dungeons and Dragons? The evidence from VR-using test subjects suggests that grid and place cells function for imaginary environments. Such translation to more abstract contexts seems to support a metaphorization of sensorimotor routines, of the kind proposed by Lakoff and Gallese. Consistent with the arguments of the book, one assumes that imaginary navigation occurs only because real-world navigational skills integrating vision, proprioception, and the operation of grid and place cells has been developed and is thus available to be metaphorized or deployed in other abstract or dematerialized ways.

In addition to grid and place cells, there are also head direction cells. A fourth kind of cell, the conjunctive grid/head direction cells fire when grid and head direction cells fire. Head direction information is combined with distance information to generate dead reckoning with respect to place cells. *Dead reckoning* is a traditional nautical navigation technique that interpolates direction and distance traveled (by compass and log) in the absence of *pilotage* (navigating with respect to landmarks) or celestial navigation, both of which tend to be more accurate.[12] In animal neurology, navigation of known, roughly horizontal spaces appears to be achieved by coordination of place cells and grid cells. *Place cells* identify known places, and *grid cells* provide a sense of relation between places. Together, this system of landmarks and spatial relations permits us to navigate our worlds. These neural behaviors are disrupted when animals navigate vertical spaces. Our neurology is adapted to the fact that we tend to, or mostly, navigate on the horizontal plane (see below).

Yet another class of cell codes for borders or boundaries and is subjective or deictic. A particular cell will fire for borders or gaps, say, on the left side, and it will fire for all borders on the left side, say, in the case of a maze. The behavior of place cells is different depending on whether the animal is in an open space or in a narrow, confined space, perhaps because of the influence of border cells. Local borders seem to anchor the grid cells to the local environment. This combination of grid, head orientation, place, and border cells negotiates subjective deictic coordinates with world coordinates and seems to be the neural basis for orientation in extrapersonal space, providing the ability to move about in the world without becoming disoriented.

### What Is a Place? What Is a Map? What Is a (Mental) Representation?

The hippocampus is understood to be important for memory, and though memories have many components, they usually involve location and orientation. The behavior and integration of these cells brings up a number of interesting questions, not least about the nature of representation, memory, and maps. The question "Where am I?" does not have to mean "Where am I in relation to an internal world representation?" or "Where am I in relation to a set of absolute coordinates?" Representations could be fundamentally temporal rather than spatial/pictorial: "Where am I with respect to that mountain, tree, or wall that I passed a while ago?" Does the combination of signals arising from the grid, place, head, and border cells constitute a representation? Are these signals stored and coordinated in a centralized representation?

Does all this conform to an internalist SMPA model, or does it support an enactivist interpretation? Is it dynamical, pragmatic, constructed on the fly, laid down in walking? The behavior of grid cells is temporal and structurally coupled. It is in a relational or deictic mode (referred to more commonly in neuroscience as *egocentric*), and at the same time it is allocentric: "I moved from there to here, in roughly that direction with respect to that doorway, tree, or sandwich." It identifies physical locations, and, once established, it is preserved in memory. Successfully finding our way in the world is a basic cognitive behavior, an act of intelligence in the situated and embodied sense. The management of mobility in extrapersonal space can be a test case for the negotiation of the enactive/dynamical and representational/computationalist interpretations of cognition.

Aside from these central questions, there are others. Why does the grid have this triangular geometry? Is there a kind of neural parsimony that makes a triangular grid more viable? Is 120 degrees more biologically basic than 90 degrees? The answer to this riddle is found in the basic geometry of space filling or close packing. The grids are triangular for the same reason that a bee honeycomb is hexagonal or that marbles on a vibrating tray will pack in that pattern. What determines the orientation of the grid? What line or axis is the grid aligned to? Given that it is triangular, one axis can be straight ahead, but then there cannot be an axis at right angles to that, across the body to the left and right, which would seem intuitive. The brain, at this level, thinks in triangles, not according to the rectilinear grid we are acculturated to.

### Almost Flatland: Living in Fractal Dimension

Almost all grid cell experiments have been conducted on flat, horizontal, and usually rectilinear surfaces, so the data are entirely two-dimensional. But rats, as we know, climb up and down on ropes and trees and inside walls. Does the triangular grid lend itself to 3-D manifolds like burrows and trees? Hayman et al., the authors of one of the few studies in this area, state the following: "It seems that grid cell odometry (and by implication path integration) is impaired or absent in the vertical domain, at least when the rat itself remains horizontal" (2011, 1182). They continue, "Grid cells, which show periodic firing in the horizontal plane, showed no vertical periodicity" (1186). Therefore, "neural representation of allocentric space has intrinsically different properties in the vertical dimension from those in the horizontal" (1186). The authors make a general hypothesis: "Path integration does not function effectively for movement in a dimension that is perpendicular to the long axis of the animal (such as, for surface-dwelling animals, the vertical dimension). An analogous finding has been reported in head direction cells, which encode directions only in the plane of locomotion; this apparently produces a planar compass signal, but one that can be oriented vertically if the animal . . . orients its body plane vertically" (1187).

They propose that "the mammalian cognitive map may be a contextually modulated two-dimensional map (or set of maps) rather than a true volumetric representation" (Hayman et al. 2011, 1182). This would tally with the fractal idea that animals are not 3-D in their large-scale mobility but are fractionally "2.x"-dimensional. This applies to birds and fish too, though the "x" would be larger in those cases. The only fully three-dimensional creatures would be those for which vertical movement is no different from horizontal, which would seem to restrict this designation to very small and unicellular aquatic organisms.

## An Excursion into Geometrical Mysticism

On a triangular grid, there can be six directions of movement—six directions along which there will be increased cell firing. By the same token, there will be six in-between directions in which cell firing is low. Putting these together, we get a clock face of twelve points. In human counting systems from the Egyptians and the Babylonians, duodecimal (base twelve) counting has been predominant, even though we don't have twelve of anything. We have two eyes, knees, and sides of the body; four limbs, ten fingers, ten toes. Therefore, counting in base two, four, five, ten, or twenty would make sense. So why twelve inches? Why a dozen? Why twelve hours on the clock and twelve houses of the zodiac? Notice also that the clock face resolves the triangular grid with the quadrants of the compass and the rectilinear grid, which, as we found previously, has bodily correlates. Are we looking down the barrel of a neural anthropic principle?[13]

The presence of a triangular or hexagonal radial geometry in deep neural functions is suggestive of an *internal* embodied source of concepts, different from Johnson's external sensorimotor experience sources. On the other hand, as navigation and mobility are quintessentially embodied and spatialized practices, we might ask the questions, "Do we *feel* duodecagonal directions or radii as we rotate in the world? And is such a feeling an expression of this neural duodecagonal geometry?" This would doubtless be a difficult conjecture to test. At least until the digital clock generation, our culture was naturalized to the clock face, although one might argue the naturalization to the right angular grid and cardinal points would be stronger.

## Conclusion

The idea that mind is an abstract and disembodied phenomenon clearly fails in its explanatory power when confronted with the phenomenal realities of being in the world. No doubt, we engage in abstract thought and in mental representations, but these are the tip of the iceberg of cognition, and the vast majority of mental activity is integrated with body and world. Forthcoming chapters explore different aspects of this integration.

# 13  Mind beyond Brain: Extending Cognition beyond the Individual

In 1998, Andy Clark and David Chalmers proposed the *extended mind* (EM) *hypothesis*, in which external cognitive aids that do work equivalent to that usually done by the mind were granted the status of being part of the mind. This paper has provoked an ongoing debate, some of which is captured in Richard Menary's anthology on the subject (2012). Here, I will discuss the extended mind hypothesis in terms of types of epistemic actions undertaken in cultural practices.

In their extended mind thought experiment, Clark and Chalmers probed questions of internalism and externalism and proposed an interrelationist and *minimally Cartesian* argument for extended mind. The paper poses a thought experiment involving an Alzheimer's sufferer who consults his notebook as if it were his memory. The question was whether the mind can be said to extend beyond the brain or beyond the body. Clark and Chalmers propose a special variant of generic externalism they call *active externalism*, which implies a temporally ongoing interaction with artifacts, thereby associating their thesis with paradigms of distributed cognition and with the structural coupling of enactivism.

The extended mind paradigm problematizes the location of mind not simply within the body but with respect to the "world." Clark and Chalmers ask whether artifacts in distributed cognitive processes simply support cognitive behavior or partake in it. They assert that mind extends beyond body and that external artifacts can function as part of an (individual) mind. The matter turns on questions of portability and tight coupling, as they demonstrate in their now famous story about Inga and Otto.

Both Inga and Otto want to go to the Museum of Modern Art (MOMA) in New York, and both know it is on Fifty-Third Street. Inga knows this in the normal way, but Otto—who has Alzheimer's—"knows where it is" because it is written in his notebook, which is always with him. Clark and Chalmers assert that "the notebook plays for Otto the same role that memory plays for Inga" (1998, 13). They called this idea the *parity principle*. The extended mind hypothesis asserts that if an artifact serves an equivalent function to some native cognitive process in the brain, then it should properly be considered as a part of the mind: "If, as we confront some task, a part of the world functions as a process which, *were it done in the head*, we would have no hesitation in recognizing as part of the cognitive process, then that part of the world *is* (so we claim) part of the cognitive process" (8; emphasis in original). Artifacts are thus incorporated into the process of cognition but remain physically outside the organism.

The root of the extended mind debate is the question of whether the mind is delimited by the cranium, the neural tissue, or the perimeter of the living individual organism, or whether it can extend into nonorganic matter. Per our discussion of postcognitive approaches, such extension may have many dimensions, including texts (exograms), tools, active and calculatory machines, physical spaces that act as cognitive supports (such as the layout of a library or a city), or telematic extensions (such as the Internet). Cultural practices, such as line dancing or playing football, might count as cognitive if the group activity informs individual activity or if the behavior of the group as a whole seems goal directed (pun intended). This group cognition tends toward Borg-like communal cognition, such as that found among colonial organisms, when it is referred to as *stigmergic cognition* (discussed in chapters 7 and 8).[1]

The parity principle is a narrow constraint, as it limits what can be counted as mind on the basis that it duplicates normal mind functions. In their original paper, Clark and Chalmers focus on one example that—they claim—duplicates memory: a passive resource to be polled, as opposed to an active device like a calculator. Note that the assumption that a notebook has parity with human memory is based on a further assumption that human memory is storage—a computationalist idea. Thus the supposition that remembering and consulting external data storage are comparable or have parity is questionable. The extended mind hypothesis is analogous to John Searle's Chinese room argument (see chapter 6), in the sense that we can see the extended mind hypothesis as a question of which entity knows or does not know Chinese.

Regarding Searle's Chinese room, Edwin Hutchins observed that though the man in the room does not understand Chinese, the entire extended system (or actor network) does: "Notice that when the symbols are in the environment of the human and the human is manipulating the symbols, the cognitive properties of the human are not the same as the properties of the system that is made up of the human in interaction with these symbols.

The properties of the human in interaction with the symbols produce some sort of computation. But that does not mean that the computation is inside the person's head" (1995, 361). Hutchins continues, "The Chinese room is a socio-cultural cognitive system. . . . Together he [Searle] and the characters and the rulebook in interaction seem to speak Chinese. But Searle himself speaks not a word of Chinese" (362). Hutchins articulates a conception of cognition that, while remaining symbolic, rejects the idea that such symbol manipulation resides entirely inside the skull. By this logic, Otto without his notebook is not cognitive; the notebook without Otto is also not cognitive; but the system of Otto plus notebook *is*. This shifts the argument from whether the human mind extends into external artifacts to whether *human plus artifact* systems are enhanced cognitive systems, which Kirsh and Maglio and others already experimentally established (see chapter 14). Internalists argue these systems are not cognitive but are material supports for cognition.

While this is an intriguing philosophical debate, my goal is to probe the extended mind hypothesis for its usefulness as a way of thinking about material cultural practices that does not erase or diminish the richness of their material qualities. For me, the question is not so much, "Is Otto's notebook a truly cognitive component in Otto's cognition, or is it (just) an exogram?" The challenge instead is to elucidate how extended human/artifact systems function cognitively in cultural contexts without reducing such processes to dematerialized internal computation. I take it as given that computational tasks can be achieved in a distributed and materialized fashion—or, to put it another way, that heterogeneous networks of agents and artifacts, utterances, and procedures can achieve computational tasks that would be more challenging or impossible for an unaided individual. The challenge is to make the same claim for activities that may be construed as cognitive outside computationalist terms of reference.

As Hutchins puts it in a later synopsis: "The 'Classical' vision of cognition . . . was built from the inside out starting with the idea that the mind was a central logic engine. . . . Attempts to reintegrate culture, context, and history into this model of cognition have proved very frustrating. The distributed cognition perspective aspires to rebuild cognitive science from the outside in, beginning with the social and material setting of cognitive activity, so that culture, context, and history can be linked with the core concepts of cognition" (2000, 10).[2] Here, differences between non-internalist paradigms of cognition become more clear. Hutchins's expansive and anthropologically informed conception of distributed cognition is incompatible with (first-generation) extended mind theory, because of the individualism of extended mind, which insists the artifacts involved must be *personal*. Clark and Chalmers assert that Otto's notebook must not be useful to anyone else, nor would anyone else's notebook be useful to Otto. It could be written in code, or Otto's handwriting might be illegible to anyone else. What if Otto's notebook were a commercial street directory? This would constitute a shared social memory, even if Otto were closely coupled with it. Otto's notebook is therefore specifically not cultural memory in the sense of Merlin Donald's exograms. Contra distributed and situated cognition, the extended mind hypothesis and its parity principle endorse a humanistic notion of individuality.

The artifacts addressed by Clark and Chalmers are, like exograms, largely static. The artifacts and procedures discussed by Hutchins are dynamic—calculators or compasses or clocks—devices or procedures that are mind-like in other ways, such as in actively computing or assisting pattern recognition.[3] Clark and Chalmers explicitly reject extending the extended mind paradigm to include pocket calculators, for instance, on the basis that they are not permanent fixtures and are not personalized. According to Clark and Chalmers, they are too easily decoupled to count as cognitive. The possibility of decoupling doesn't seem to matter to Hutchins and Kirsh. The distinction drawn by Clark and Chalmers is between artifacts that can truly be considered part of an individual's mind and artifacts and external systems that function as cognitive prosthetics. This distinction hinges on the assumption of a humanistic individual mind. If we were to soften the individualism inherent in their argument, the all-important personally specific aspects of the devices Clark and Chalmers allow as mind extenders might cease to be so relevant.

While the extended mind paradigm extends mind beyond body, the parity principle declares that an external component can only be regarded as mind if it duplicates a function of mind. Otto is a cyborg, but not an enhanced one. His notebook is a prosthetic in the surrogate sense only. Otto's notebook stands in for his impaired memory, doing something his memory would normally do. This doesn't help us much in thinking about doing new and different things. Most cognitive prosthetics enable us to achieve more than we could otherwise, not to do the same by other means. Even Rumelhart's paradigmatic example of paper and pencil for performing sums can move quickly from duplication to augmentation. Arguably, adding a column of one thousand numbers is not something I can easily do unaided, yet it is straightforward, if tedious, with pencil and paper. If this was not true, the methods of accountancy would not exist.

McLuhan's arguments for media technologies as cognitive *extensions* can in this sense be seen to presage extended and distributed cognition. Far earlier, Baron von Uexküll concluded "A Stroll through the Worlds of Animals and Men: A Picture Book of Invisible Worlds" (1957) with a discussion of the astronomer, whose umwelt is extended into space via his telescope. Another way of thinking through the limitations of extended mind is to propose, as an alternative, *extended body*. The work of performance artist Stelarc, whose career has focused on the development of bodily extensions, real and virtual, local and distributed, provides examples via which the Cartesianism of extended mind is thus thrown into relief. It would be absurd to propose that, for instance, a diamond saw blade is a tool because, in cutting concrete, it does what I can do with my teeth. A theory of extended body provides a different way to think about tool use and the blind man's cane. The navigators on Hutchins's ship's bridge do what they do together, leveraging collaborative procedures and the capabilities of artifacts (compass and chart) enriched with the accretion of the intelligence, experience, and skills of generations. We need to find ways out of the dualist snares laced so tightly into language—to think of cognitive engagement with the world beyond the dualisms of mind-body and self-world.

## Structured Environments, Situated Cognition

Is Otto's notebook the only cognitive aid he needs to get to the museum? Is Inga's memory the only cognitive aid she needs to get to the museum? Both these aids only function because they are integrated into a web of already existing environmental structures, key among them our acculturation to the Cartesian grid and the adoption of it in urban design and street layout. Otto's notes can only exist in such a condensed form due to the designed nature of the city itself. We know where the MOMA is because the city is arranged in a way that supports our knowing where it is, in a geometrical, numerically predictable (and classically Cartesian) way that is easy to mentally reason about ("I'm at Forty-Seventh Street, going uptown, so Fifty-Third Street is ahead") even if we've never been there before. The scheme of the grid city leverages cultural knowledge of the cognitive schemes of parallel lines and checkerboards and coordinate geometry and schemes of sequential counting, which we project onto a landscape—paradigmatic representational reasoning. The fact that Clark and Chalmers's extended mind story takes place in Manhattan, a canonical grid city with sequentially numbered streets, calls for some discussion. Otto's notation that MOMA is on Fifty-Third Street wouldn't be very useful if he were not already culturally naturalized to rectilinear grids and their numerical ordering—a technique whose ubiquity masks its cultural and historical specificity—nor if the numbered names of streets happened not to be sequential.

The New York City grid is a highly rationalized layout designed to perform computation or offload computational tasks. Since ancient Greek times at least, the grid layout has provided a cognitive scaffold for anyone who knows the system, which in turn assumes literacy and numeracy. Otto's notes are only complementary to the numbered grid, which allows Otto's notes to work for Otto in New York. This brings into question the assertion that what Otto is leveraging to assist in his cognition is *individual*. What he does is on the order of an annotation on a memory structure that is cultural and shared.

The grid layout affords computational efficiencies to a numerate person naturalized to the Cartesian grid. In addition, knowing the blocks are the same size, I can calculate distances. Knowing how long it takes me to walk one block, I can estimate time to destination. By virtue of the fact that the city is laid out in such a way, Otto is able to build a mental model and, by simple counting, find his way. It is no doubt possible to devise an ordered city layout (or geometry of any sort) based on triangular grids, concentric circles, or other ordered geometrical patterns that would be predictable if we were naturalized to such patterns. If Otto were a bee, the rectilinear grid might be confounding, but a hexagonal grid might be "intuitive."

Any designed road system is a cognitive system and an exogram. If Otto were in Los Angeles and looking for the Getty, his notes might say, "210W to 110S to 10W to 405N"—admirable shorthand for a fifty-mile journey. Without the freeway system and its nomenclature and signage, his notes would have to be more extensive. We organize our environments in order to behave more intelligently and efficiently in them.

Otto's technique is not applicable in, say, the Centro Gotico of Barcelona, where straight or parallel streets are rare. The grid city is a classic case of the organization of an environment to offload computational load. A substantial effort at the outset provides citizens and visitors, for hundreds of years, with a way to economize on individual cognitive work, obviating the need to do such things as produce and carry maps, triangulate landmarks, or use celestial navigation techniques. Navigating such a city enacts a culturally and historically extended intelligence or form of mind. If Otto were looking for the Tate, his notes would be more copious due to London's irrational layout. In fact, they might not work at all in a nongrid city. There *are* roads, but there are no right angles, and there is no simple mnemonic to help Otto predict the name of the next street, because there is not predictably sequential structure.

Needless to say, without named streets, numbered routes, and signage, the task would be even more difficult, to say nothing of the task in the absence of roads or paths. In a medieval town, or in a forest, we use a different kind of memory, one more kinesthetic and complexly multimodal (see the discussion on grid and place cells in chapter 12). We navigate by narratives and cues: There is a bar with a yellow sign, then (before or after?) a bent lamppost . . . just near the place where Johnny had a bicycle accident . . . the road becomes narrower and turns upward to the left, and the cobblestones become uneven (I must take care not to twist my ankle). Otto could not write this down so easily.

When I am looking this direction, it (whatever it is) is on my right. When I sit at my desk, the book I want is up there, at arm's reach on the left, in a trajectory between my left ear and my left eye. It's not at x23, y45, z10; it's "up over there." Such location is defined by proprioceptive and peripersonal awareness. This is the kind of embodied cognition Edwin Hutchins means when he refers to a navigator "thinking like a compass." We know where we are in the book by the thickness of the pile of pages on the left and on the right. We might recall a particular passage is "about a third of the way through the book, on the lower left." Such useful material cues are often lost in software emulations.

Pilgrimage and trading routes are marked by cairns, temples, and mythologically significant geographic formations and narrated in a temporally extended and deictic way, utterly different from the God's-eye view of the grid city. European colonial history is full of stories of aboriginal trackers and native guides reading cues invisible to European explorers. Terrestrial navigation in such situations is achieved via narratives referencing features of the landscape: "Follow the riverbed, keeping the mountain on your right until you come to the cliffs," or, more colorfully, "Go to where the sky serpent did battle with the great bear, then follow the route of the wounded eagle back to its eyrie."

Nautical navigation beyond sight of land must be achieved without reference to "landmarks," which explains why the maritime navigational techniques of the people of the Pacific are incommensurable with terrestrial navigational techniques. The lack of fixed reference points in the open ocean is no doubt why navigational expertise was traditionally held in such esteem and why so much effort was expended improving devices—astrolabes, compasses, and chronometers—that function as cognitive prosthetics. With GPS, all this complexity is hidden behind veils of user-friendly graphical interfaces. Who reflects, as they bicker with Siri, that she is correlating your position with the positions of multiple orbiting satellites?

## Culture as Cognitive Parsimony

It is a commonplace of situated cognition that humans structure their environments in order to offload computation. This is simply to restate in cognitive terms a characteristic of human cultures. We may view human cultures as systems by which knowledge and ideas and activities are shared and promulgated, not simply in the form of static records—as per Donald's exograms—but in appliances and tools and artifacts, which, when combined with skills and procedures, result in enhanced capability and a reduction of effort on the part of those who share in that culture. Killing a bison with a bullet is far easier and less dangerous than killing it with a rock, but the bullet implies a vast network of technologies and practices.

I heard a construction worker instruct another, "twenty-six and a half by twenty-eight"; in this brief utterance, he defined a shape and size. Such economy is only possible in a world of defined units, and in which mass-produced materials and structures rigorously conform to a rectilinear *xyz* spatial-grid system. Making things square and level was once the mark of the skilled artisan. Now it is subsumed into systems of standardized, industrially produced components that produce the flatness of floors and verticality of walls at lowest cost, with the least-skilled workers. "Twenty-six and a half by twenty-eight" is a useless utterance when building a wattle and daub hut out of mud and branches or a boat or an igloo—situations in which flat planes and right angles are rare.

## Extended Mind Extended

While extended mind engages the internalism-externalism debate, it preserves the distinction. Like Hutchins's distributed cognition, extended mind is computationalist; it preserves the idea of cognition in terms of operations upon representations. The extended mind hypothesis has generated extensive debates, and proponents of differing theories of situated, embedded, distributed, and extended cognition, including Michael Wheeler, John Sutton, and Ezequiel Di Paolo, have scrutinized the hypothesis from their various perspectives. Basic questions that concern internalists and externalists alike include "What constitutes cognition?" and "Is cognition computational?" Part of this conversation reflects the tensions previously discussed between cognitivist and more dynamical conceptions of cognition. Adams and Aizawa (2008) contest extended mind from a conventional internalist cognitivist position, asserting that cognition is a computational event in a neural substrate, a position that excludes any nonneural event from being cognitive.

This position excludes some kinds of processes in the brain that are taken to be cognitive by connectionists. On the other hand, postcognitivists of various stripes see the extended mind hypothesis itself as being restrictive of notions of cognition.

A second wave of extended mind theory extends the theory itself by superseding the parity requirement. John Sutton argued for what he called the *complementarity principle*, which embraces some of the problematics of reliance vis-à-vis the concept of parity. "In putting complementarity at the heart of distributed cognition, then," he argues, "we acknowledge that relations between agents and artefacts may be asymmetric and tangled in different ways and thus that such relations are often dynamically reconfigured or renegotiated over time" (2008, 43). By replacing parity with complementarity, Sutton radically reconfigures the extended mind hypothesis, defusing the instrumental/individualist cast and bringing it closer to distributed cognition and ANT, in which cognition is situated and social.

**Enactive or Extended?**

In "Minds, Things and Materiality" (2010; originally published in 2008), Michael Wheeler outlines a debate that extended mind catalyzed in the postcognitivist community, to which Ezequiel Di Paolo responded in 2009. Both papers probe the relations between extended mind and enactive cognition. Wheeler argues that extended mind and enactivism are incompatible. His analysis turns on two matters: one inherent in extended mind and the other inherent in enactivism. He exposes the debt of extended mind to Putnam's doctrine of multiple realizability. He asserts that Putnam's functionalism, and not extended mind, was the radical gesture and goes so far as to say that extended mind is a footnote to functionalism. On this basis, Wheeler proposes that extended mind is simply extended functionalism. Computationalism is predicated on functionalism and multiple realizability, fundamental components in the rhetoric of AI. Like the Cartesian dualism, functionalism has no in-principle proof (we might take the collapse of first-generation AI as a demonstration of its inherent fallacy).

Wheeler's second line of argument concerns enactivism and its roots in autopoietic theory. We have already surveyed the central ideas of enactive cognition originated by Varela, Thompson, and Rosch on the premises of Maturana and Varela's autopoietic biology (see chapters 2 and 11). We can summarize Wheeler's argument as follows: Autopoiesis as a definition of living is premised on the idea of autonomous self-organizing systems that maintain a boundary, or membrane, between the organism and the world via a network of recursively dependent processes, maintaining structural coupling with the world. In autopoietic terms, the maintenance of that membrane is the result of, and the primary goal of, cognition. Organisms "constitute the system as a unity," as they say (i.e., they *live*): "Living systems are cognitive systems, and living as a process is a process of cognition" (Maturana and Varela 1980, 13). Enactivism emerged from this theoretical context.

This is a curious twist. Extended mind, rooted in functionalism, provides a principled justification for externalism in terms of multiple realizability. Enactivism, on the other hand, is revealed to be, in this sense, internalist. "If the living system is identical with the cognitive system, then the boundary of the living system will coincide with the boundary of the cognitive system," Wheeler notes. "Since autopoietic theory and (therefore) enactivism are committed to identifying the cognitive system with the living system, the enactivist simply cannot endorse EM. In other words, enacted minds are not extended minds" (2010, 35). If cognition is taken to be materially specific and biologically grounded, then extended mind is untenable. In an autopoietic or enactive approach, the premises of functionalism are themselves fallacious. Thus, enactivism and extended mind are incompatible, according to Wheeler.

Di Paolo refutes Wheeler, but does so by proposing a broadening of autopoiesis. Di Paolo's rejoinder in "Extended Life" (2009) disputes the assignation of internalism to enactivism and argues that, for enactivism, cognition is relational—a move not unlike Anthony Chemero's recasting of Gibsonian affordances as relational (see chapter 2). This claim does require some revisionism regarding the links of enactivism with autopoiesis. It also requires some theoretical "development" of enactivism to embrace what Di Paolo calls *adaptivism*. Di Paolo's revision turns on a subtlety of binary differences and matters of degree. Wheeler notes that "raw autopoiesis" (2008, 819) is, per Di Paolo, an "all-or-nothing norm: organisms live as long as they don't die" (Di Paolo 2005, 436). Adaptivity implies gradations and choices: it is "better" over here; it's "worse" over there. Such a sensitivity to gradients is what Evan Thompson calls *sense-making*.

## Extended Life

Ezequiel Di Paolo argues that the original paradigm of autopoiesis, as incorporated into enactive cognition, presents certain stumbling blocks that have not been fully explored. These limitations are revealed in his attempts to reconcile enactivism with the paradigm of extended mind; they boil down to the differences in apparent position on the relation between life and cognition in extended mind and enactivist conceptions. Di Paolo recognizes there is paradoxical and residual Cartesianism in autopoiesis and in extended mind. The inside/outside division fundamental to autopoietic theory mirrors a circularity found in extended mind—the circular definition of cognition as that which "goes on in our heads." Extended mind is a symptom of the blind spots of traditional cognitive science (understood as cognitivist accounts of the mind that are largely representational and functionalist). Di Paolo asserts (with respect to the assumptions that underlie the parity principle), "The intuitions about cognition that EM relies on are inevitably tied to the boundaries between inner and outer that it wishes to undermine" (2009, 10). Thus, it is at root both circular and dualist.

Along the way, Di Paolo takes extended mind and conventional cognitive science to task, alerting us that "the disappearance of any scientific, phenomenologically informed and useful notion of a cognitive system as an autonomous agent" (2009, 11) from cognitive science is nothing less than pathological in its avoidance of basic questions "about individuation, autonomy, agency, normativity, and the nature of cognition" (10). He adds, "This avoidance is pathological in the strict sense that it leads to ill-posed problems and creates a 'moth-around-the-candle' effect." He concludes, "The EM hypothesis has the form of an unfinished *reductio ad absurdum*" (10). Di Paolo asserts that such matters are not only central to, but also explained by, enactivism: "For the enactivist, mind was never in-the-head in the first place" (10). He elaborates: "Cognition is a relational phenomenon and thereby has no location" (9). He argues that in EM two different kinds of boundaries are conflated: "The boundary of the organism (or its brain) as the 'intuitive' locus of what we refer to as a cognitive system, and the more abstract boundary between processes, engagements, relations, mechanisms and systems that deserve the name cognitive and those that do not" (10). He calls these the *relational* and *operational* domains.

Di Paolo articulates the problem of reconciliation of the operational and relational domains as follows: "The first pertains to the functioning of the autopoietic network so that it constitutes a unity (a composite system), the second to the relations that such a unity enters into in its structural coupling with the environment" (Di Paolo 2009, 17). He finds further fault with extended mind for not making the second boundary explicit. Obviously aware that the distinction between relational and operational domains has a distinctly Cartesian ring to it, he is quick to qualify: "The enactive approach does provide a workable and non-species-specific definition of cognition, it does not fall into paradoxical situations of breaking boundaries while re-introducing them through the back door as regulatory principles" (19).

## Di Paolo's Revisionism: Autopoiesis+

Di Paolo then confronts a quality of autopoietic theory that recalls its cybernetic roots. Autopoietic systems are homeostatic, and homeostatic systems revert to a prior equilibrium. Di Paolo's proposal hearkens back to the cybernetic debates about teleology and purposive systems and reminds us of Waddington's homeorhesis, which addressed similar concerns. "We . . . cannot derive from the definition of autopoieis that an autopoietic system will attempt to ameliorate a situation that leads otherwise to future loss of autopoiesis . . . a *bare* autopoietic system cannot be a cognitive system and so it cannot be an extended cognitive system either" (Di Paolo 2009, 13; emphasis in original). For Di Paolo to assert that autopoietic systems are no longer cognitive is a rather audacious move. Di Paolo then proposes *autopoiesis+*, or adaptive autopoiesis, which would, under certain circumstances, regulate its states in a predictive way to avoid situations that would otherwise lead to a loss of autopoiesis (otherwise known as death). "This property," he states, "is perfectly operational but not implied in the definition of autopoiesis" (14).

Di Paolo builds his extension of first-generation autopoiesis around adaptivity, thus climbing out of the homeostatic trap: "An adaptive autopoietic system is able to operate differentially in (at least some) situations that, were they left to develop without change, would lead to loss of autopoiesis" (14). He elaborates, endorsing a dynamical and relationist middle way reminiscent of Evan Thompson's: "The proposed grounding of cognition in life is quite different from the simple statement of co-extensiveness of the living and the cognitive. Nor is it at any point possible to infer an internalist view of cognition in the enactive story. Indeed, neither an externalist one! Cognition is sense-making in interaction: the regulation of coupling with respect to norms established by the self-constituted identity that gives rise to such regulation in order to conserve itself" (19).

Such an extension of autopoiesis links the theory of enactive cognition with the theorization of emergence elegantly articulated by Peter Cariani in his "Emergence and Artificial Life" (1992) and with conceptions of the integration of agent in environment via feedback loops that originated in cybernetics. This circular story of autopoiesis, artificial life, and cybernetics reminds us that Maturana, as a young man, worked with McCulloch, Lettvin, and Rosenblueth.

## Extended or Distributed?

In the parity principle, extended mind asserted the role of artifacts as equivalent to native biological cognition. The artifacts are incorporated into the process of cognition according to the multiple realizability thesis of functionalism, but remain outside the organism as a biological entity. Ezequiel Di Paolo decouples cognition from biological coherence. Autopoiesis asserts that the coherence and integrity of the bounding membrane of the biological organism is fundamental, but, as Malafouris argues, if we simply give up the Cartesian obsession of distinguishing what is mind and what is not and, as Di Paolo proposes, see cognition as relational, then it is possible to accept the autopoietic biological origin of cognition without demanding that the one maps onto the physical boundary of the other.

It is patently evident that social procedures and structured environments make us smart. The notion of extending mind beyond body is tantalizing, but in doing so under the banner of functionalism, it confirms Chemero's accusations of covert Cartesianism. As with AI and ALife, perhaps it is time to distinguish strong and weak versions of the extended mind hypothesis. What would a "strong EM" position be? If it means to hold the ground for representationalist functionalism, then this would be taking sides in an old philosophical battle. To accept a "weak" extended mind preserves the autopoietic basis of enactivism and allows that social procedures and structured environments make us smart—without being mind. The autopoietic position holds a self-world boundary as fundamental. Autopoiesis—that is, life—ends when the boundary between organic and nonorganic is ruptured. By decoupling cognition from the precinct of metabolism, Di Paolo's relational approach is consistent with that of Chemero and Beer.

## Conclusion: Post- and Neo-Cartesianisms

There are more and less radical approaches to embodied cognition. As Anthony Chemero rightly argues, there are two general positions in post-cognitivist cognitive science. A group we might call *extended cognitivists* allow that cognition might be embodied and/or distributed in various ways—shifting the edge of mind to the edge of body, for instance—but the fundamental assumption that cognition is computational remains in place. Extended cognitivists preserve all or many of the trappings of functionalism-representationalism-computationalism, including an implicit or explicit *res cogitans–res extensa* binary. Such tinkering is, in my opinion, a kind of false consciousness: an attempt to preserve familiar assumptions and constructions even in the face of contrary evidence. These closet Cartesians are outed by theorists who reject all or most of the central tenets of cognitivism and embrace some form of externalism—asserting that cognition is not (or not exclusively) a matter of mental representation and does not occur (or does not occur exclusively) inside the skull.

First-wave autopoiesis preserves a biologically based internalism and also endorses biological materialism, assuming that biological life is both necessary and sufficient for intelligence and that therefore intelligence might be suffused throughout the flesh—or at least that mechanistic separations of mind from body and intelligence from action are untenable or unnecessary. Many in this camp endorse relational and dynamical systems approaches, and some endorse posthumanist and process ontologies of various sorts. Recalling Rorty's observation about the asymmetry of paradigm shifts, tenets of the dynamical-processual-enactive alternative remain unresolved but hold titillating potential. Reasons for the rejection of cognitivism should by now be clear. However, as this chapter has shown, embracing embodied, distributed, and dynamical conceptions does not lead into a field of new certainties but instead into a lively field of exciting questions, which, per Rorty, offer great promise.

# 14  Tools, Cognition, and Skill

There are many activities which directly display qualities of mind, yet are neither themselves intellectual operations nor yet effects of intellectual operations. Intelligent practice is not a stepchild of theory. On the contrary theorizing is one practice amongst others and is itself intelligently or stupidly conducted.

—Gilbert Ryle, *The Concept of Mind* (1949, 26)

In modern Western culture, rational and conscious reasoning—expressed in the abstractions of symbol, number, text, and spoken language—have been privileged over human practices that are social, embodied, and materially instantiated. This hierarchy has been reinforced institutionally, not least by the academy itself, in which modalities of symbolic representation are valorized. Yet the quotation that opens this chapter gives ample evidence of ongoing unease with this cognitive chauvinism. The material in this chapter provides further arguments supporting this critique.

The use of tools, machines, instruments, prosthetics, and appliances designed and made to extend capabilities, enhance performance, achieve technical goals, or offload cognitive load is a special aspect of embodied cognition. Here, I explore the cognitive dimensions of instruments, artifacts, and tools from the perspective of embodiment, enaction, and materiality.

Tool use, generally speaking, involves an artifact attuned over time to a specific task domain, combined with equally attuned skill. Skill and tool are complementary and isomorphic. In order to effectively use a specialized artifact, specific skills must be developed. The skill with no tool is dormant, while the tool with no skilled user is worthless.

No cognitive extension performs its task without a tradition of complementary bodily practice. Cognitive economy is gained in part by the encapsulation of prior experience in the tool or instrument and its corpus of practice. This preservation persists over generations and centuries, but only if the complementary bodily cultures of tool making and tool use persist. The cognitive economy is achieved by *muscular gestalts*—learned bodily procedures that, though cognitive, are implicit and automatic.

## Tools and Tool Use

Skilled tool use always involves a three-way isomorphism and structural coupling between user, tool, and context. The act of chiseling cannot exist without the chisel—and a chisel is not fully a chisel unless it is wielded with appropriate chiseling skills and is situated in a chiseling context of mallets, vises, benches, and wood appropriate to the task.

A tool has no value without the presence of complementary skill. A tool, in the hands of a novice, is ineffective or dangerous. The tool does not change; the capability of user-with-tool is enhanced by enhanced skill. Skill is developed through bodily practice. Learning from a book, a lecture, or a video does not impart skill. How is skill acquired? In an appropriately structured environment, in a culture of training and practice. If I want to use a block plane to smooth a piece of wood, the work piece must be secured in such a way that it will allow access for the gestures required. Grain will catch if I plane in one direction. Such characteristics of the task I know from prior experience or will learn by practice. Different kinds of wood take the plane differently, demanding adjustment to tool and stance, extension of reach, and force applied. The setting of the blade is quickly understood, as proportional to the hardness of the wood and the strength of the user. The correct setting and the sharpness will come to be sensed by passing a finger lightly along the bed. A parsimonious working rhythm will emerge from practice, producing a quality result with a minimum of effort.

Cultures of tool use and tool making are dynamic; they adapt to design and material developments (steel replaces wood in the body of the plane), and such developments incrementally change practices. Radical technological changes, such as the addition of electric motors, produce radical changes in practices and the culture of tool use generally.

Relationships with tools, instruments, and other prosthetic enhancements are key aspects of arts and cultural practices. Artisanal and cultural practices have occupied a marginal place in cognitive science, because the tight and ongoing intercourse with materiality confounds notions of cognition understood as abstract reasoning. In tool use, conscious reasoning takes a backseat to muscular gestalts. Such studies have thus been the province of anthropology and sociology, as opposed to cognitive science. The application of postcognitivist approaches can make substantial contributions to a new theorization of tool and instrument use.

## Incorporation

Micronesian canoeists gather knowledge about undersea geography and the presence of islands over the horizon "by the seat of their pants" (if they're wearing any): Through a subtle integration of proprioceptive and vestibular cues related to the movement of their craft (vaka) as a prosthetic extension of their embodiment. To ask if this cognition is occurring in the brain or not in the brain is to fall into the false dichotomy of cognitivism. If we accept that the way our brains are is a result of evolution, then it is clear that they exist as parts of a more complex system, a system of which the general goal and purpose is survival in the world. A useful theory of cognition should address questions of how it is that we do the things we do in the world—as opposed to treating the brain as something with its own goals that the body is deployed to achieve. Viewed from this perspective, divisions between brain, body, and world become if not irrelevant, then at least less significant for structuring analysis.

When I learn to use a simple hand tool or implement, like a hammer or a knife, I quickly and unconsciously incorporate the dimensions of the tool into my activities. My arm muscles apply more effort in rising up and driving down when the hammer is in my hand. I accommodate its mass and the shock that, on impact, passes up its handle and into my arm. I learn to interpret the nature of that shock as the indication of a clean or glancing blow. When I put down the hammer, my arm resumes its normal dynamics, but when I pick the hammer up again, I know how to use it, and its mass and length are immediately incorporated into my extended self. In this context, *incorporated* must be understood in its richest sense: The hammer becomes part of me. However, neither "part of me" nor "of my body" are accurate. The hammer is part of a larger cognitive cyborg that "I" become.

As we become adept in the use of a tool, incorporating its use into increasingly precise and modulated muscular gestalts, it becomes neurologically incorporated into a physical sense of self. The blind man's cane becomes an extension of the blind man's index finger, though the cane has neither nerves nor muscles. This kind of cognitive extension is as marvelously mysterious as it is prosaic. When we wield a baseball bat or an axe, we likewise *incorporate* the mass and physics of these entities—arm muscles compensate for load and leverage in a way that confounds simple distinctions between the mental and the physical.

## What Is a Muscular Gestalt?

In *What Computers Can't Do* (1972), Hubert Dreyfus refers to the concept of a *muscular gestalt*, which he drew from Merleau-Ponty. Max Wertheimer (1924) encapsulated the notion this way: "There are wholes, the behavior of which is not determined by that of their individual elements, but where the part-processes are themselves determined by the intrinsic nature of the whole. It is the hope of Gestalt theory to determine the nature of such wholes." While gestalt psychology has been a major influence on psychology generally, the concept is confounding, because its antireductivism and implicit emergentism make it incompatible with cognitivism. In recent years, the new dynamical neuroscience gives us evidence of the neurological basis for gestalts.

The gestalt concept became clear to me as I reflected on a simple task. I was flummoxed by my Bluetooth headset; somehow, it just wouldn't fit. I fiddled this way and that, matching/mismatching the shape of the device to my ear. Upon examination, I saw that the clip was flipped to the "right-ear" position. I flipped it over and clipped it on in a smooth operation. In the process, I noticed the "thinking" was all in my fingers; my "knowledge" did not involve mental representation or cogitation. Instead, it involved a sequence of actions, each one made possible or provoked by the result of the last. "One thing leads to another" is more than a trivial observation. The aphorism captures the reality of a temporal unfolding in which plans are superfluous. Or more accurately, to quote Dwight Eisenhower, "Plans are useless, but planning is indispensable."

The "thinking," it seems, could not occur without the physical presence of the ear, the Bluetooth, and the hand, their conformation and scale with respect to each other, and with the temporal kinesthetic logic of process they define and constrain. To describe this process in internalist terms would involve a circuitous explanation that William of Ockham would discourage. This is a highly *situated* cognition, and it shares the temporally contingent logic of subsumption architecture. By these lights, there is sympathy between gestalt theory and enactive cognition (a series of codependent, contingent, temporally coupled actions, not a plan) and with Gilbert Ryle's (1949) *knowledge-how*. Like Andrew Pickering's performative idiom, Ryle's *knowledge-how* is irreducible to book knowledge, *knowledge-that*.

## Tools as Cognitive Extensions

Offloading computation onto prestructured environments, tools, and artifacts was a key theme in first-generation situated cognition. In early distributed cognition, emphasis was placed on human interaction in group procedures, as well as interaction with devices and instruments. As the discourses of embodiment and situation have matured, the role of bodily practices and procedures in which computation—that is, "thinking"—is achieved *by doing* have received increased attention. Kirsh's epistemic action laid the groundwork for this, but the richness of the isomorphism between procedures and instruments has yet to be explored in the depth it deserves. A cognitive study of artisanal practices of tool use is an interdisciplinary project with rich potential.

Edwin Hutchins noted that, in using navigational tools, cognitive functions are enacted with minimal user effort. Prior to the advent of digital tools, the world was full of analog calculators—such as slide rules and the legendary Curta—parsimonious and elegant arrangements of mechanisms, matched to the hand, that performed sophisticated mathematical functions by simply arranging settings and reading off values. Such tools are more than exograms; these cultural artifacts not only store information in a passive way but also store and facilitate the implementation of procedures. For millennia, simple instruments—the abacus, the carpenter's square, the humble ruler—have provided such cognitive offloading functions. With each of these cognitive prosthetics came a bodily culture, a way of organizing

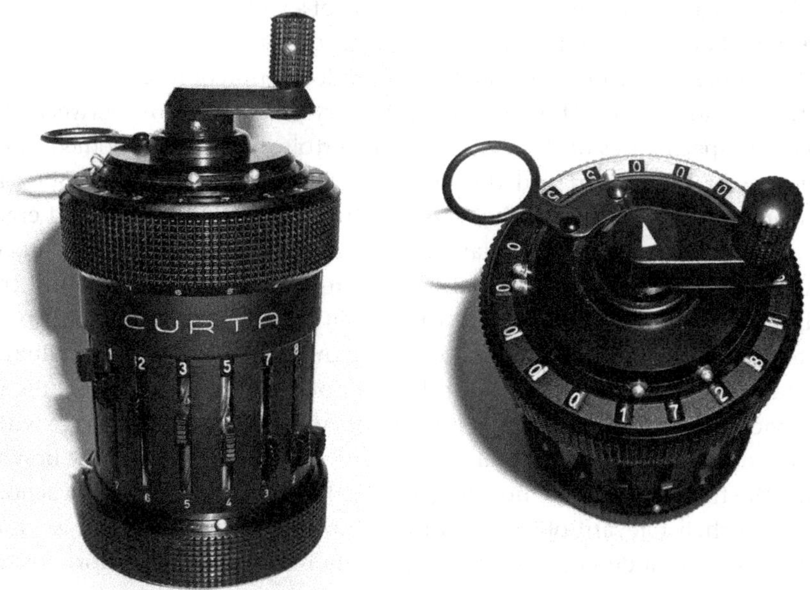

**Figure 14.1**
The Curta mechanical calculator. Photograph by Clive Maxfield.

sensorimotor functions in order to generate the desired results as well as more abstract conceptions. From a Platonic perspective, a ruler is little but an emblem of an abstract *metric*—a system of stable references—and likewise the clock. The standardization of timekeeping was an infrastructural and managerial innovation that undergirded the effectiveness of national railway systems.

## The Stradivarius and the Kitchen Sink

Bodily cultures and artifacts coevolve. Knowledge-how (Ryle) is invisible and worthless without the artifact/object it is associated with. The artifact makes it possible to demonstrate the knowledge related to it. As a practice becomes more refined, the artifact becomes more specific and vice versa; a more sophisticated artifact permits more refined practice, whether we are talking about an adze or a skateboard.

The refinement of an instrument, tool, or artifact is the result of intelligent observation, design, and craft. This process defines the range of practices the instrument facilitates, and new subtleties of form permit further extension and refinement of practices, which in turn become embedded in the tool itself.

What makes a Stradivarius so much more of a violin than a cigar box with a rubber band stretched over it? The special quality of such an instrument is that it has been formed through an extended period of interplay between artisans and players. This produces a history of coevolution between the material specificities of the artifact, the repertoire, and the embodied intelligences of the artisan and the musician. Similarly, a kitchen evolves as a workplace through use—chains of intuitive technique, design and ergonomic tweaks, a subtle interplay between ingredients, artifacts and procedures of specific cuisines, spatial layouts, technological changes, and the physical capabilities of its users. An array of utensils and ingredients on a kitchen bench might suggest action, while the shape of the knife facilitates certain kinds of actions and not others. Knowledge resides in the knife or the violin. However, it is not possible to demonstrate that knowledge without complementary practices and contexts. Assertions like "I know how to play the flute" or "I know how to get to Little India from here" are vacuous without their relevant objects. Transcription into a symbolic form, such as text, results in a description that necessarily remains a description. Recipe books and books to teach yourself harmonica do exist, but that knowledge cannot be implemented without the support of both the relevant artifacts and a background of situated bodily culture. If you've never lit a stove, if you've never melted (but not burned) the butter, if you've never separated eggs or sifted flour, then you won't be able to make a soufflé from a recipe.

Sailing is similar. Each boat has its own qualities that a person becomes familiar with through hours of attentive practice (and the occasional improvisation under pressure), and a sort of generalized awareness develops, such that a sailor will often respond to a situation without knowing what triggered the response: Was it a pull on the tiller, an odd roll of the boat, the cessation of the grinding of the prop-shaft, the sound of the flutter of the upper leach of the jib hidden behind the mainsail, or any of a thousand other internalized subliminal cues?

## The Tool-Using Homunculus

*Skill* is a way of describing a kind of prosthetic selfhood that envelops a tool, realizing extended cognition-in-action. This general statement applies to hammers, bicycles, cars, and the canonical blind man's cane. It applies to virtual prosthetics (software) and telematically extended prosthetics, such as scanning tunneling electron microscopes and the tools of robotic surgery, in which kinesthetic and proprioceptive sense are relayed across space and scale. Instruments are perceptual or sensorimotor prosthetics. We *incorporate* instruments. What happens in the brain as skilled tool use is attained? Do the sensory and motor homunculi grow and distort with each prosthetic? When I put down the hammer and pick up the pen, do I switch from one extended homunculus to another? Or is this a fallacious construction comparable to the Cartesian theater? As we become fluent with a tool or instrument, what changes? Once you know how to ride a bicycle, it becomes a difficult thing not to know. Destin Sandlin (2015) made an elegant demonstration of this with his reversed-steering bicycle. It took him months to learn to ride the new device, at which point he could no longer ride a normal bike. How does such knowledge contribute to the building of new metaphors and new categories? Lakoff and Johnson have shown how the topology of objects can generate metaphors, but bodily procedures are also a rich source of metaphors, such as when we make an imaginative leap or step up to a responsibility.

## Measurement and Epistemic Action

Kirsh and Maglio (1994) made the distinction between epistemic and pragmatic action, yet in practice the distinction is not so clear. The kinds of tools arrayed around any craftsman's workshop can be loosely organized into two general categories: tools for pragmatic action and epistemic tools. A mason has a plumb, square, and level; these define the mason's art, which is as much about geometry and geodetics as it is about banging rocks with hammers. A carpenter has saws and chisels, but also a bevel gauge and calipers. The cook has scales and measuring cups. But on closer analysis, the pragmatic/epistemic distinction is seldom clear. The humble block plane has both pragmatic and epistemic aspects, and the depth of the blade below the bed is subject to fine adjustment. In some planes, the angle of the blade is also precisely adjustable, from 15 to 7.5 degrees. A car mechanic has wrenches and hammers, and he has feeler gauges. He also has a torque wrench—a pragmatic tool with an epistemic dimension. But if I can tighten a head bolt to a certain torque with a regular wrench, my action still has an epistemic dimension. In fact, an adept knows that one can shear a bolt or trip a thread with an ordinary wrench. So every tightening of a nut is epistemic.

A machinist has dial indicators and micrometers and all manner of precision measuring and marking tools, the center finder being an elegant example. The lathe and the mill are instruments as much as tools, finely engineered and calibrated to provide variations of distance and angle to high precision. The interpolating scales on such tools, like those on oscil-

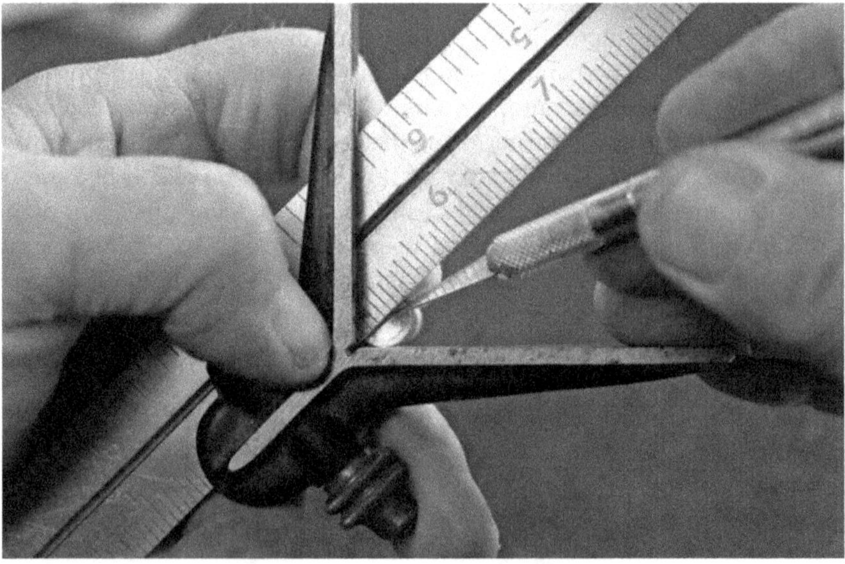

**Figure 14.2**
The center of the small disc is found accurately and simply by nesting it in the V and scribing along the rule, then rotating the object some arbitrary angle and scribing again.

loscopes and other twentieth-century technical instruments, are little analog computers. Likewise, navigators' tools—the astrolabe, the sextant, the
compass, and the chart rule—are all epistemic. Hutchins notes, "These tools
thus implement computation as simple manipulation of physical objects
and implement conceptual judgments as perceptual inferences" (1995, 171).
He elaborates, "The computational constraints of the problem have been
built into the physical structure of the tools" (171). The parsimonious
elegance of such solutions is often staggering.

## The Slick and the Scythe: Embodied Cognition and Making

Some tools have cognitive aids built in. The block plane has a blade adjustment screw with reference marks; the circular saw, in fixed or portable form,
allows blade-height adjustment. Some tools have no such cognitive crutches
and depend on the user's fine sensorimotor control as well as brute strength.
Consider the shipwright's *slick*. This large chisel tool for fine-contouring
wooden boat hulls—a massive billet of tool steel with a long straight

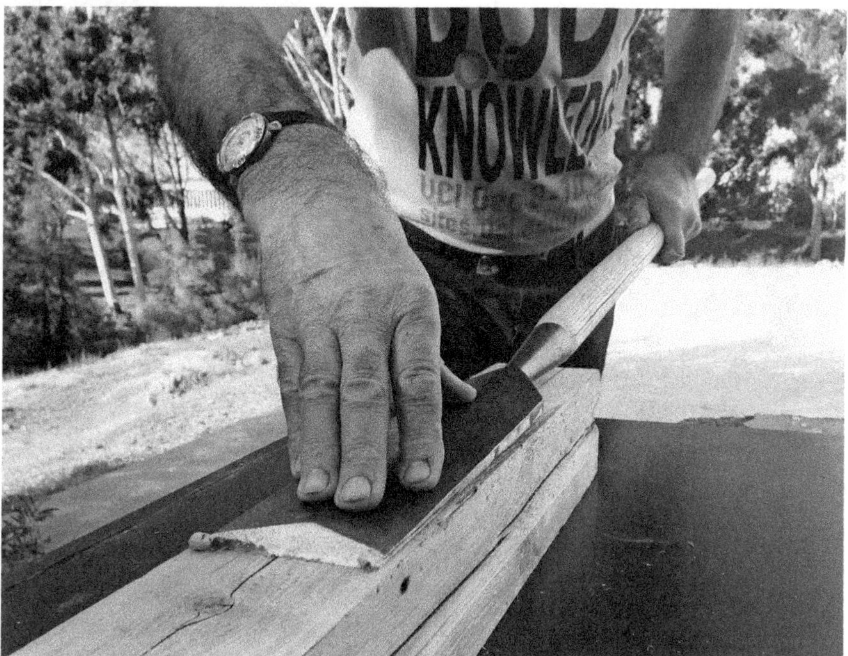

**Figure 14.3**
Author with slick.

handle—is wielded with both hands and the entire body. The shipwright pushes the blade against the wood surface via the handle, precisely gauging the depth of cut by managing the location of a sliding fulcrum—the point on the underside of the blade that slides on the hull surface behind the cutting edge—thus deftly monitoring cut depth at every instant by miniscule variations of angle made possible by the length of the the handle. A slick is a plane with all parts removed except the blade. With respect to the slick, the plane offloads computation.

The harvester's scythe is, even more so than the slick, a whole-body tool, with its sinuously curved shaft and ergonomically adjustable handholds.[1] Deceptively simple, the shape of the tool conforms exquisitely not only to the shape but also to the motion of the body. The scythe user makes graceful swings—pendulum-like. Skilled scythe use is, bioenergetically, highly efficient and places minimal stress on bones or wear on joints, allowing maximum weight of cut hay for minimum caloric output and minimum bodily wear.

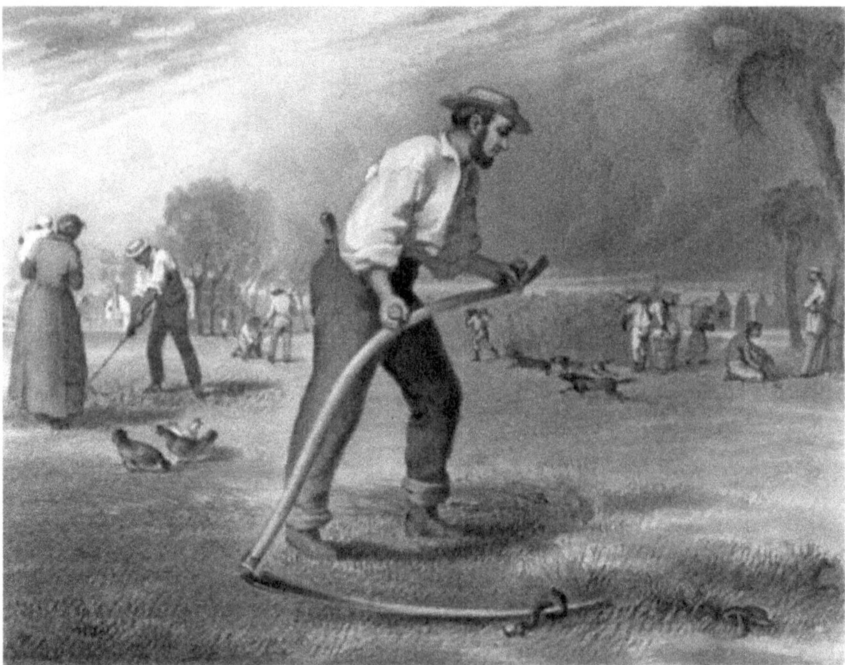

**Figure 14.4**
Man swinging a scythe. Courtesy of Library of Congress.

## Skill and Tacit Knowledge

There is a lot more in the technology of paints and brushes than a novice comprehends, and there is a lot to the sensibilities developed in doing the work. Painting is one of those practices that has been dumbed down by the do-it-yourself rhetoric of big box hardware stores. I was reminded of this recently while painting my boat with a less skilled helper. I watched her dip the brush in the paint up to the handle, and wipe the brush against the surface with the middle of the bristles, as opposed to the tips. I saw areas with too little paint and areas with too much. I saw her work a dry brush; I saw that my painting was faster than hers. I considered my own brushing technique, I noted the way I dipped the brush in the paint and wiggled it a bit, collecting the most paint the bristles could carry, but then I wiped the brush on the side of the can just enough to stop drips en route to the painting area. I noticed I used quick strokes to distribute the brushload, then came back with longer strokes to spread it evenly, using the bristles almost like a broom. Occasionally I used a quick scumbling movement, holding the brush not by the handle but at the shank between thumb and fingers. I was wary not to scrub a too-dry brush on the surface; doing so gives the impression of extending coverage, but it produces too thin a coat. The goal is to get the right amount of paint on the surface, not too thin but not too thick, avoiding pools or drips to reduce the need for cleaning or sanding, thereby maximizing speed of coverage and minimizing effort. At edges, I used the brush leading with the narrow edge, at an angle inclined forward, with enough pressure to flex the bristles. This produced a bead of paint flowing just ahead of the bristles, producing a clean, straight edge. I kept a *wet edge* so that the next brushful would blend without a roughness that I would have to sand later.

Paint flows, and its viscosity must be managed with additives. Latex paint flows differently from alkyd and different surface textures require adjustment to technique. Because paint is as a liquid, consideration of gravity is key. Gravity is an asset or a liability in different ways when painting vertical and horizontal surfaces. A different repertoire of actions is required to paint a vertical surface than a horizontal one—not to mention overhead! The stiffness of the bristles produces different effects with different kinds of paint. Longer, softer bristles give a smoother coat. These are the sorts of understandings a person comes to through aware practice. The longer one does it, the better one gets, honing skills and developing more subtle distinctions about paint viscosity and other variables. In any artisanal practice, techniques develop exploiting peculiarities of the physics of tools and materials and this in turn generates concepts—hence the *wet edge*.

## Saving Labor

Technophilic rhetoric about tools often emphasizes enabling, while actually deskilling. The advent of consumer power hand tools has a deskilling aspect. The marketing rhetoric of "saving labor" and "no experience necessary" has encouraged the idea that the addition of external power negates the need for skill. For instance, the crucial importance of blade sharpness can be ignored if power is (perceived to be) free. With brute force, a blunt drill can usually be forced through. A power screw gun can strip the hole or mash the head. External power and precision are not synonymous—indeed, often the opposite is true. It comes as quite a surprise to some students that precision is not exclusively the province of automatic industrial machinery. One can achieve precision of one thousandth of an inch with hand tools.

Hutchins notes, "By interacting with particular kinds of cultural things, we can produce complex cognitive accomplishments while employing simple cognitive processes" (2010b). We might invert Hutchins's statement to say that large effects can be achieved by attaching relatively simple cognitive processes to sophisticated cultural artifacts. This is the recipe for user-friendliness, plug'n'play, and all kinds of simplified home improvement products.

Tools make an activity more efficient, more precise, or less fatiguing. In the mid-twentieth century, the notion of the labor-saving device was an effective marketing angle; since the 1990s, we have come to accept the notion of cognitive labor-saving in the form of software tools. We are accustomed to the understanding that a tool relieves us of drudgery. We also have an expectation that tools are easy to use and make tasks easier. The term *tool* has come to have the connotation of easing burdens in both physical effort and learning. Tools, in the contemporary context, are often deskilling. Software tools extend and diminish the concept of the tool further. The development of software tools, like all mass-produced commodities, is motivated by the desire for financial profit, and these tools trade upon desires for productivity and efficiency and, often, simple laziness. Any product that alleviates cognitive effort is potentially deskilling. We happily embrace calculators and lose the capacity to do mental arithmetic. It's a Faustian bargain.

## "Sheer Plod Makes Plough down Sillion Shine"[2]

I admit to feelings of visceral antipathy when people express sentiments regarding the drudgery of repetitive labor. I think such expressions are not only pathetic and lazy, but ignorant. In addition to an almost religious commitment to physical labor, I also find it an interesting object of study.

However humble a task, there is beauty in the negotiation of a relationship between design or desire, tools and materials, and the development of skilled practices and procedures. Leo Tolstoy was clearly of the same mind. From a wealthy family, he ploughed his fields with a horse-drawn plough and made his own shoes. Repin's painting of Tolstoy in his study, often seen cropped, shows a bow saw and a scythe in the background and a shovel in the foreground. (The painting may be somewhat romanticized; photographs show a desk piled with books.)

We are persuaded that repetitive physical labor should be avoided, that it is boring, that it is to be done by a computer or a machine or by workers in a sweat shop in El Salvador or Malaysia, but not by us, because our time is too valuable to be squandered in such tedium (yet oddly, we pay money to perform narcissistic repetitive labor at the gym). Why, amid my labor, do I find the tedium of my tasks fascinating? I think because the work is precisely *not* mindless, but demands abiding attention in a way antithetical to modern conceptions of labor. Skilled repetition is not stupid; it evinces intelligence and expertise, and it produces value. Fordism and the production line increased output by deskilling work. Intelligence is evidenced not only by problem solving—the management of constant novelty being a benign consumer version of Cold War paranoia—but by the application, attention, and constant improvisation implicit in skilled embodied work.

As part of a project, I had to scrape many pounds of stiff clay out of a plaster casting, taking care to remove the clay but not scratch the cast. I made hundred of cuts with chisel and scraper—not one cut could be allowed to hit the cast. In such practices, there is physical effort, and there is superficial repetition. But in detail, there is constant exercise of awareness, constant adjustment of actions to subtle changes of context. With awareness, any activity becomes iteratively richer, subtler, and more complex. Tim Ingold (2006) has made similar observations about sawing wood. Probably every embodied action is like this. Even the most menial procedures are replete with this kind of embodied cognition—not just sawing and painting but also vacuuming and washing the dishes.[3]

Such activity is not simply performance in the narrow sense of an enacted set of behaviors. It is more than critical technical practice. It is enactive, not just in a simplistic sensorimotor mode, but in a reflexive way with a back-and-forth between the *cognitive nonconscious* (in N. Katherine Hayles's terminology) and consciousness. That, in itself, is a subject for awareness and contemplation. How did I become consciously aware that the paint has become too viscous on this hot day? At what point does the added drag of the brush alert me that it is time to thin the paint? What are we to say

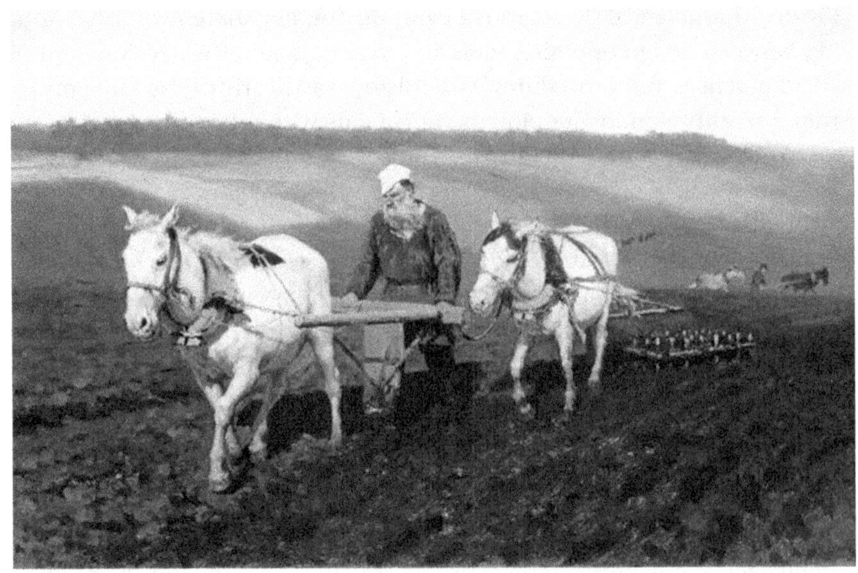

**Figure 14.5**
*Tolstoy Ploughing* (Ilya Repin, ca. 1889).

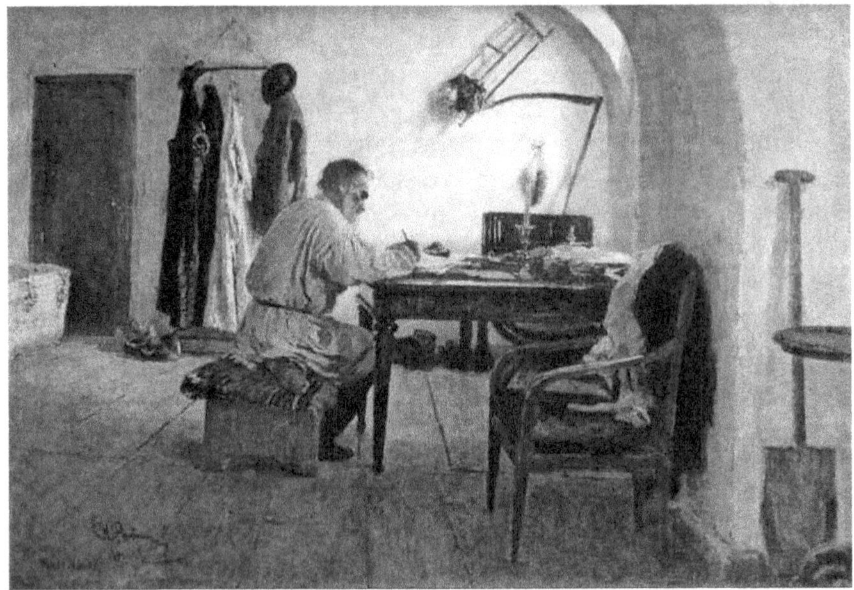

**Figure 14.6**
*Tolstoy in His Study* (Ilya Repin, 1891).

about these sorts of activities in terms of cognition? These are by no means dumb mechanical actions. Yet *reasoning on symbols* seems an irrelevant way of explaining the intelligences involved. Nor is it simply a matter of *tacit knowledge* (Polanyi 1966), because what we are aware of here is a constant honing and tuning and adaption. Awareness of the subtlety of embodied practice is not new, as the following passage from *Inner Chapters* by Chuang Tzŭ (or Zhuangzi), dating from about the fourth century BCE, demonstrates:

Duke Huan was reading a document at the upper end of his hall, and the wheelwright Bian was making a wheel at the lower end. Laying aside his hammer and chisel, Bian went up and said, "Dare I ask my lord what words you are reading?"

The duke said, "The words of a sage."

"Is the sage with us?"

"He already is dead."

"Then, isn't what my lord is reading just the dregs of a man of ancient times?"

The duke said, "When I read a document, how do you get to discuss it? If you can explain, OK; if you cannot, you die!"

The wheelwright said, "I, your servant, observe from my own work. In making a wheel, if I go slowly, it is easy but not a solid [fit]; if I go quickly, it is toilsome and [the parts] do not go together.[4] Neither too slow nor too fast, I get it with my hands and respond with my mind, but my mouth cannot speak [of it]; there is a skill I maintain in this: I cannot teach it to my son, and my son cannot receive it from me. In this way, I am now seventy and have grown old making wheels. The ancients—and what they could not pass down—are dead. Thus what my lord is reading is just the dregs of the ancients. (Translated by Michael Fuller, pers. comm., 2011)

"I cannot teach it to my son, and my son cannot receive it from me": This is knowledge that can only be acquired by *doing*. It is, in Pickering's terminology, *performative* —a mode of learning diametrically opposed to that of Duke Huan at the other end of the hall. The document Duke Huan is reading is, to use Merlin Donald's terminology, an *exogram*: externalized and temporally extended cultural memory or, more accurately, storage. This ontological circuit is at the core of human culture—the transference of the dregs of life-as-lived into fossilized records. It is not a translation, as Bian rightly asserts; it is *dregs*, the sediment left when the life is drained away.

The tension between embodied and performative ways of knowing and symbolic and textual ways of knowing was brought to our attention by philosopher Michael Polanyi when he famously said, "We can know more than we can tell" (1966, 4), a sentiment also at the heart of much Zen Buddhist teaching. The notion of *tacit knowledge* asserts that there are aspects of certain kinds of knowledge, such as that required to play a violin or ride a bicycle, that are not capturable or transmissible via spoken language or text. In the wise words of, as far as I know, an anonymous sage: "The difference between theory and practice is greater in practice than in theory."[5]

## Mind and Culture: Culturally Specific Learning

Compared to the chimpanzee brain, the human brain has no novel structures. Yet humans enjoy a complex linguistic and cultural life unavailable to chimpanzees. This implies that the human brain is replete with latent capability and/or a remarkable flexibility to shape its own processes and that this is achieved through the cultural process. An infant human brain is bootstrapped by engagement with culture into capabilities it would not in isolation attain, as we know from the various wolf boy/Caspar Hauser kinds of stories. In the process of that bootstrapping, the child becomes part of a specific culture and then plays a role in the communal perpetuation of that culture. Research into mirror neurons (Rizzolatti, Fogassi, and Gallese 2009) gives us some inkling of how such bootstrapping occurs.

A young person develops in response to their world, in terms of language, social structures, physical activities, and interaction with artifacts and spaces. Every component of a culture teaches. Climbing Western stairs is different from climbing the stairs of a Mayan Temple, and climbing ladders and rope ladders are different again. A coffee mug trains the hand in a certain way different from that of a teacup or a Chinese tea bowl. Manipulating a mug full of hot liquid is different in significant sensorimotor ways from manipulating a fine porcelain teacup. Neither technique is good for drinking from a martini glass, a half coconut, or an animal horn. Perceptual distinction and articulation of spoken sounds and words in Hmong is different from in English.

## Epistemic Prosthetics

The painter's brush, the violinist's bow, the harvester's scythe, and so many other artifacts are complex and sophisticated devices because they have evolved in a deep structural coupling with the rhythms of bodies and sensorimotor loops, and are integrated into complex cultural practices. According to extended cognition, aspects of the environment are deployed as off-board memory. In Hutchins's notion of distributed cognition, computation is offloaded too. While we accept externalization in these cases, we continue to deploy computationalist metaphors. Must we justify action in the world as computation in order for it to count as cognition? To say that the scythe is an epistemic prosthetic is to suggest that such tools are devices for thinking, but this would be to endorse the *cart-before-the-horse* nature of *cognitive chauvinism.* When Hutchins (recalling his colleague David Kirsh's notion of epistemic action), says that "motion in space acquires conceptual meaning, and reasoning can be performed by moving the body" (Hutchins 2010b), is he proposing that successful doing in the world is a matter of reasoning? This would be to reduce action in the world to computationalist terms that, however subtly, reinstate a Cartesian separation between action and thought. No! The violin, the scythe, the brush: these are cognitive prosthetics that integrate user, tool, and world at a deep and more organic level, precisely because they *do not involve* a translation into and out of logico-mathematical computation.

## Navigation and Embodiment

As Hutchins explains, "A good deal of the computation performed by a navigation team is accomplished by processes such as hand-eye coordination. The task of navigation requires internal representation of much less of the environment than traditional cognitive science would have led us to expect" (1995, 132). This critique of representationalist cognitive science is consistent with Brooks's "the world is its own best model" and Haugeland's idea that "we abide in the meaningful." In the following passage, Hutchins considers the question of how to describe the distributed and extended cognition on the ship's bridge and, by extrapolation, cognitive action involving artifacts more generally: "Clearly, a good deal of the expertise in the system is in the artifacts (both external implements and the internal strategies)—not in the sense that the artifacts are themselves intelligent or expert agents, or because the act of getting into coordination with the artifacts constitutes an expert performance by the person; rather, the system of person-in-interaction-with-technology exhibits expertise" (155). These kinds of inquiries are strongly reminiscent of the concerns of actor-network theory (Latour, Callon, Law), which was emerging in sociology while Hutchins was engaged in his cognitive anthropology. It is interesting but sad to note that the two fields did not actively connect. Latour *was* aware of and impressed by Hutchins's work, as indicated in his review of *Cognition in the Wild* in the journal *Mind, Culture, and Activity* (Latour 1995).

The "cognitive" capabilities of humans are difficult to characterize in computational terms because they are not primarily pointed toward deductive reasoning. Consistent with arguments made here, Hutchins notes,

These tools permit people using them to do the tasks that need to be done while doing the kinds of things that people are good at: recognizing patterns, modeling simple dynamics of the world, and manipulating objects in the environment (Rumelhart, Smolensky, McClelland, and Hinton 1986). At this end of the technological spectrum, at least, the computational power of the system composed of person and technology is not determined primarily by the information-processing capacity that is internal to the technological device, but by the role the technology plays in the composition of a cognitive functional system. (1995, 155)

The successful cognitive cyborg is not successful because of the capacity of the tool to perform Boolean operations, but because of the capacity of the person/tool union to achieve human goals in the world, by exploiting *complementarity* (see previous discussion of extended mind in chapter 13). This complementarity, we must recall, was also paradigmatic of first generation HCI systems: the humans in the loop in the SAGE system (see chapter 3). Hutchins went on to sound a warning to the discipline of HCI and to computer scientists generally, a warning that seems to remain largely unheeded:

The computational constraints of the problem have been built into the physical structure of the tools. . . . These tools thus implement computation as simple manipulation of physical objects and implement conceptual judgments as perceptual inferences. But perhaps this refinement will be lacking from the next generation of tools. By failing to understand the source of computational power in our interactions with simple "unintelligent" physical devices, we position ourselves well to squander opportunities with so called intelligent computers. The synergy of psychology and artificial intelligence may lead us to attempt to create more and more intelligent artificial agents rather than more powerful task-transforming representations. (171)

Hutchins's admonition is a prescription for an entire design enterprise: the utilization of computing technology that is in synchrony with human capability, understood as embodied cognition, rather than the pursuit of developing computational tools as extrapolations of a dualistic philosophical position.

In a more recent paper, entitled "Imagining the Cognitive Life of Things," Hutchins reflected upon his own previous research in the great work *Cognition in the Wild*, observing that the model of distributed cognition he presented was lacking in explanatory power because it was *oddly disembodied*. His revelation demands quotation at length:

In the last chapter of *Cognition in the Wild* . . . I argue that cognitive science made a fundamental category error when it mistook the properties of a person in interaction with a social and material world for the cognitive properties of whatever is inside the person. One enduring problem with this claim is that it demands a description of how cognitive properties arise from the interaction of person with social and material world. *Cognition in the Wild* provides an answer to this question, but I now believe a change of focus is required. . . . For the most part, the cognitive processes described in *Cognition in the Wild*, and in other treatments of distributed cognition, are presented without reference to the role of the body in thinking. That is, in spite of the fact that distributed cognition claims that the interaction of people with things is a central phenomenon of cognition, the approach has remained oddly disembodied. (2010b, 91)

Such a reconfiguration of a worldview is rare, and Hutchins deserves only credit for this laudable act of self-criticism. Axiomatic assumptions and the lacunae they generate are so often *the* great obstacles to clear apprehension. One wonders about the circumstances under which this reconfiguration happened. Such wholesale inversions of premises rarely occur in the echo-chambers of academic disciplines.

## Knowing How, Culture, and Affordances

In 1945, Ryle proposed that knowing-how is incommensurable with knowing-that. According to Ryle, knowing-how is logically prior to knowing-that, and knowledge-how is not reducible to knowledge-that. *Knowledge-how* is an ability. We might say that knowledge-how is knowledge of affordance. To say a chair affords sitting is to say we have the knowledge of how to sit on it (see chapter 2).[6] This is elementary knowledge-how but has an aspect of culture about it (see chapter 12). *Knowledge-that* is expressed in regulative propositions. The dorsal and ventral streams of human vision provide a neurological analogy. The dorsal stream, sometimes called the *where* stream, heads to the parietal lobe, whereas the ventral *what* stream heads toward the temporal lobe.

A scanning tunneling electron microscope affords examination of matter at the molecular level to someone who has been trained to use it. There are handles that afford grasping and knobs that afford turning, meters that afford reading, and so on. Knowing-how itself rests on a tacit knowledge of affordances, and such "knowledge" of affordances is as inaccessible to conscious awareness as the rest of Gallese and Lakoff's *cognitive unconscious* (see chapter 16).

Gallese and Lakoff provide a neurologically based hypothesis for the elaboration of abstract meanings from sensorimotor circuits, which in turn provides a plausible neurological explanation of the distinction between know-how and know-that. Know-how cannot be verbalized, or not verbalized with veracity, because it is sensorimotor knowledge located in the cognitive unconscious. *Know-how* is relational and context specific. *Knowing-that* is the culture of the exogram (Donald) and the representational idiom (Pickering)—symbolic knowledge amenable to alphanumerical expression.

While linguistic or textual knowledge might be said to accumulate over historical time, (tacit) knowledge ("skill") associated with artifacts comes and goes with those artifacts and the cultures of their use. Knobs and dials, once the interface to all technical instruments, are now viewed with steampunk nostalgia. The clock face itself, that icon of the Enlightenment, is becoming unfamiliar. No one today knows how to build a Gothic cathedral with donkeys and chisels, without the use of hardened steel drills or wire rope or diesel engines or concrete. Doubtless, professors of gothic architectural history could *tell you* how it was done, but *no one can do it*. The boilermakers' art—the knowledge of how to make, with iron sheets shaped at a blacksmiths forge, joined with hammered red hot rivets, a vessel resistant to the intense pressure of superheated steam—is likewise almost lost. The skill of surveying and mapping land from horseback, as employed by the great surveyors of the British Empire, is a dead art. Most of the celestial navigation traditions of Pacific peoples, which permitted exploration, colonization, and travel across the great expanses of the pacific for hundreds of years before Westerners arrived, are lost. (Desperate attempts have been made in recent decades to rescue surviving remnants). The ability to send and receive messages in Morse code, the code that created a global communication system far more revolutionary than the Internet, is now rare. So it goes.

## Instrumental Incorporation

When we incorporate a tool into our bodies, we change our relationship to the world at large as if we had evolved a new body part. That is, we create a new semantic relation with the world. We notice this process most when we are in the transition phase of establishing the automatic linkages needed to incorporate the tool into our bodies. This is Dreyfusian learning, culminating in muscular gestalts that in turn inform our cognitive unconscious (Lakoff and Johnson 1999). Phenomenologists from Heidegger to Merleau-Ponty, Polanyi, and Bateson have pondered these kinds of temporary sensory and motor extensions. Polanyi observes:

Our subsidiary awareness of tools and probes can be regarded now as the act of making them form a part of our own body. The way we use a hammer or a blind man uses his stick, shows in fact that in both cases we shift outwards the point at which we make contact with the things that we observe as objects outside ourselves. While we rely on a tool or a probe, these are not handled as external objects. We may test the tool for its effectiveness or the probe for its suitability, e.g. in discovering the hidden details of a cavity, but the tool and the probe can never lie outside the field of these operations; they remain necessarily on our side of it, forming part of ourselves, the operating persons. We pour ourselves out to them and assimilate them as parts of our existence. We accept them existentially by dwelling in them. (1962, 61)

Merleau-Ponty argued that the tip of a blind man's cane extends his hand to the ground—but the extension is unimodal: The tip of the cane does not feel heat or pain. The physicality of the cane, like any tool or prosthetic, extends only a part of the capability of the finger. Yet we do "feel" through prosthetics. We "feel" the road when we drive. Musicians play by "feel." You certainly feel it when your spade hits a rock hidden below the surface. Heidegger's *present-at-hand* captures the moment when that smooth incorporation fails. Is it part of me or part of the world? Something I manipulate or something I manipulate with? Such questions may not lead to useful answers, as Gregory Bateson elucidates in his cybernetically inflected observation: "These questions are nonsense because the stick is a pathway along which differences are transmitted under transformation, so that to draw a delimiting line across this pathway is to cut off a part of the systemic circuit which determines the blind man's locomotion" (1972, 318). That is to say, the cane and the person achieve a cyborgian unity. The cane has been made ready-to-hand by the learned practice of incorporation.

## Temporary Cyborgian Unions

It is easy for us to comprehend the incorporation of tools when they are handheld, small relative to ourselves, and extend a simple physical function—hitting, poking, or cutting. But we incorporate in other ways as well. Every car driver knows the somatic sensations of reverse parking. This sense of extension is not just a passive sense of dimension and mass; it is active and specific. Our skill conforms to the car we know, its size and its steering capabilities. When I drive my car (but not always when I drive another car), I feel comfortably acquainted with its dimensions and behavior. I identify with the physical extent of my car. When I am reverse parking in a tight spot, I feel a twinge in my right buttock. The body of the car maps onto my flesh, my lower rear right extremity corresponding to the lower rear right of the car. Yet the identification of body part to car part does not follow a simple logic, and my bodily actions in driving are not analogous to running or walking. I do not use my arms to turn when walking. The speed of the car is not determined by the rate of my alternating leg movements.

I stand in the shower, adjusting the water temperature. My left hand is on the faucet, my right under the water flow. I twist the faucet and, some-time later, my right hand senses a temperature change, hotter or colder. My perception of temperature is not linearly proportional to my kinesthetic sense of rotational movement. My faucet hand is integrated with the fau-cet artifact; my muscular action turns about the axis of the faucet. I feel the subtle changes of the friction of the washer against its seat, through the handle of the faucet. I know, from past experience with plumbing, the structure of the interior of the faucet, but I do not need to know this in order to incorporate the behavior of the faucet into my behavior. I automatically calibrate my effort to the friction of the faucet, to the changes in the rate of flow according to the position of the faucet and to the relative temperatures of the hot and cold water as felt by my right hand. The body-shower system is one cyborgian unit. When the temperature is okay, I detach myself from the apparatus. The temporary extension of me into the plumbing/water system retracts, and the apparatus becomes an object.

The giant crane in a modern container harbor dwarfs the crane operator as he rides inside it in a moving cabin, conducting the machine like it is a gargantuan exoskeleton, lifting shipping containers like LEGO bricks. Oper-ating a scanning tunneling electron microscope or a giant crane demands the extension of a sense of embodiment that embraces radical variations of physical scale. When we incorporate and abandon these prosthetics, we mys-teriously don and jettison these extended bodies at will. As we extend our embodiment into telematics or virtual realms, this *incorporation* becomes still more mysterious. It would be quite wrong to cast the skills involved in robotic surgery as *mental* skills; these systems work or don't work accord-ing to the precision with which their interfaces and dynamics map onto our bodily conformation and capacities—conformations and capacities that are both mental and physical, to the extent that such a distinction is meaningless. As the kind of world we have is a result of the kind of embodiment we have, so the kind of mind we have is given by the kind of body we have.

## Virtual Prosthetics

Kirsh alerted us to the reality of epistemic action and, in doing so, disrupted assumptions of the easy separation of thought and action. The *epistemic action* could not have occurred by manual actions alone; no amount of complex finger gestures could have achieved the result. Skill with the computer afforded epistemic, cognitive action.

Physical tools often function as cognitive scaffolds. The virtual tools we work with are graphical and, to greater or lesser degrees, immersive and interactive. The cognitive complexities of such tools demand deeper analysis in terms of embodied cognition. When tools are primarily graphical, they are representations, but they, like code itself, are also machines. This makes virtual tools and virtual prosthetics ontologically complex. At the coming out of virtual reality (VR), at SIGGRAPH in 1989, Jaron Lanier waxed poetic about his experiments in virtual embodiment—inhabiting the body of a virtual lobster and learning to drive its many limbs via VR eyephones. Lanier's lobster raises provocative questions regarding neural plasticity. From a biologically holistic and evolutionarily pragmatic position, my brain is seamlessly integrated in the body it is a part of. As such, it has the capacity to coordinate the movements of four limbs and no more. Changes in shape and scale can be accommodated, in the same way that physical tools and prosthetics are incorporated. What are the limits to the brain's topological flexibility? We know that although humans can adapt to up-down inversion of the visual field (Stratton), our visual system does not adapt to inversion of dark for light (like a photographic negative). Can I swing twelve virtual hammers at twelve different targets (without twelve independent eyes or pairs of eyes)?

With another generation of technological development, virtual reality is again big business, but the basic paradigm has not changed since the 1980s. The rhetoric of VR was an *embodying* technology. This was, and remains, hollow. Today's VR is an improved means to an unimproved end, as Henry David Thoreau memorably remarked about the telegraph in 1854: "Our inventions are wont to be pretty toys, which distract our attention from serious things. They are but improved means to an unimproved end, . . . We are in great haste to construct a magnetic telegraph from Maine to Texas; but Maine and Texas, it may be, have nothing important to communicate" (1966, 67).

In simulating only visually stereoscopic spatial experience, VR dissected the body into hand-eye coordination and everything else. Yet regular users of what we now call *immersive environments* will attest that they can achieve a fluency or flow in which every space and turn of the virtual environment are known. This fact is implicit in flight simulators and military simulators, as it is in immersive games including first-person shooter games. It is also well established that skills learned in the virtual environment can transfer into the real world; otherwise, simulators would be useless.[7] Proprioception is largely absent in simulators and computer gaming, so this knowing is a curiously synesthetic condition where vision stands in for proprioception.

But this should not be surprising, given all we know about how vision is calibrated and made useful through proprioception in infant development, not just in kittens (Held and Hein 1963) but in human infants as well.

In gaming and in VR, the avatar of the user is an extension of the user's self. Pointer, cursors, and point of view (POV) are cognitive extensions that extend Merleau-Ponty's blind man's cane into what we used to call *the virtual*. However, in the game/gamer situation, it is not simply the avatar that functions as an abstract extension of the user's body; the world is also prosthetic. Agency is extended into a virtual world via a virtual body, which is observed *unisensorially* (visually) but experienced in a way that conjures proprioceptive response—not simply rapid keyboard action, but ducking to avoid (virtual) projectiles.

## Skill as Anti-Cartesian

As studies of cognition escape the cranium and ooze out over culture, the territories of cognitive science and anthropology intersect. Speaking in an anthropological context, Ingold repositions intelligence as situated skill in a way that has relevance to the present conversation on behaving artifacts and the notion of a performative or processual ontology. He warns, "Attempts to render such practices in a propositional form misconstrue the very nature of skill, which . . . consists not in acquired mental representations but in developmentally embodied capacities of attention and response" (2001, 30)—that is, muscular gestalts. By this logic, we are embodied creatures who engage, via the specifics of our umwelts, in a socially and physically situated and temporally unfolding way. Cultural practices are part of this, and this is human culture, widely construed. On the other hand, modernity has constructed us as reasoning internalists—isolated masterful individuals in a world of objects upon which we act.

For Ingold, the terms *art* and *technology* occupy positions in the discipline of anthropology that recapitulate a Cartesian dualism, with technology occupying the position of body and art the position of mind. (He is not referring to the Art+Technology art movement of the 1960s and 1970s.) Thus, technology refers to brute production and art to intentionality. Ingold problematizes this dualism around the concept of skill. *Skill*, for Ingold, is anticognitivist; it is performative and situated. He proposes to "recover the essence of skill, as 'both practical knowledge and knowledgeable practice'" (2001, 20). It is this notion of knowledgeable practice, or know-how, that characterizes much of human practice that has been denigrated in cognitivism.

For Ingold, skill is relational, in a similar way that affordance is for Chemero: "Skill, in short, is a property not of the individual human body as a biophysical entity, a thing-in-itself, but of the total field of relations constituted by the presence of the organism-person, indissolubly body and mind, in a richly structured environment" (2001, 21). From here, Ingold inverts a cognitivist conception of learning:

I do not deny that the learning of skills involves both observation and imitation. But the former is no more a matter of forming internal, mental representations of observed behavior than is the latter a matter of converting these representations into manifest practice. For the novice's observation of accomplished practitioners is not detached from, but grounded in, his own active, perceptual engagement with his surroundings. And the key to imitation lies in the intimate coordination of the movement of the novice's attention to others with his own bodily movement in the world. (21)

He continues, "The clumsy practitioner is precisely one who implements mechanically a fixed sequence of instructions, while remaining insensitive to the evolving conditions of the task as it unfolds" (24). This reiterates the phenomenological interpretation of learning as the establishment of muscular gestalts by Hubert Dreyfus (1996). Contra cognitivism, rule following typifies only the practice of the learner and not that of the adept.

## Conclusion

In previous chapters, I observed that, paradoxically, it was the iterative arithmetic of the computer that opened to doors to exploration and understanding of nonlinear and dynamical systems. Similarly, by ironic historical happenstance, the machine that is the very reification of representationalism has provided us with the possibility of reasserting the embodied and performative. Art, design, and cultural practices have always been embodied/performative. It is the immiscibility of such conceptions with cognitivism that has rendered the intelligences of the arts opaque or obscure. Ingold puts it well when he says, "If one were to ask where culture lies, the answer would not be in some shadowy domain of symbolic meaning, hovering aloof from the 'hands on business' of practical life, but in the very texture and pattern of the weave itself" (2001, 28). Recognizing the reality of human cognition as embodied and performative provides a new purchase on the problems of design in HCI, and it also has the potential to provide us with a new language and a new set of perspectives by which to speak of the practices of the arts.

# 15　Representation

The mainstream thinking of cognitive science in the past thirty years leads us to expect to have to represent the world internally in order to interact with it. This theory of "disembodied cognition" (Norman, 1990) has created systematic distortions in our understandings of the nature of cognition.
—Edwin Hutchins, *Cognition in the Wild* (1995, 132)

Culture, thus conceived, cannot be understood to comprise a system of intrinsic rules or schemata by means of which the mind constructs representations of the external world from the data of bodily sensation.
—Tim Ingold, "Beyond Art and Technology: The Anthropology of Skill" (2001, 28)

The specter of *representation* haunts these pages. Inherent in the conventional idea of cognition is the idea that the mind, intellect, or reason operates on mental representations. Representationalism is a part of the Western philosophical legacy and is fundamental to an internalist view of cognition. Like the Cartesian dualism itself, it is an axiomatic assumption without good evidence to support the idea as a general claim. It creates a false impression of what we are and how we work. As such, it leads to improper research, in the sense of getting the right answer to the wrong question.

Many, if not all, disciplinary discourses are undergirded by axiomatic assumptions that, in Gödelian spirit, are intractable within the terms of the disciplinary discourse itself. Key terms remain undefined until put under pressure, at which point discontinuities, fractures, and imponderables often arise. Terms such as *concept, symbol, representation,* and *information* occupy such a position in cognitivist discourses.

The idea of the Cartesian theater—full of little homunculi munching homunculus popcorn—is ludicrous. However, it does raise questions: What *are* mental representations (if or when such things occur), and how are they deployed? Committed representationalists argue the impossibility of thought without internal representation. Some reject the notion of mental representation altogether; some occupy a middle ground, permitting its existence in some cases. It is difficult to refute that "in my mind's eye" I can see the face of, say, my mother. But *thinking* and *representation* are tautologically linked. If thinking requires representation, then nonrepresentational mental events are not thinking. This gets us nowhere.

Internalist and representationalist accounts of cognition require that cognition is constituted by logical operations on representations. But, as Rodney Brooks observed twenty-five years ago, though representation was a key theme around which AI research was organized, there was no clear or shared definition of what constituted representation. Brooks made this point clear in the opening lines of "Intelligence without Representation" (1991b, 139): "Representation is the wrong unit of abstraction in building the bulkiest parts of intelligent systems. Representation has been the central issue in artificial intelligence work over the last 15 years only because it has provided an interface between otherwise isolated modules and conference papers." Internalist theories of cognition are in a similar situation: They all depend on representation, yet there is little clarity or unanimity on what a representation is, on any level of analysis, from the symbolic to the neurological.

Many things occur in my neurology that do not seem to require representation. Are sensorimotor loops *representations*? Such debates quickly move toward sophistry—angels on pins—a direction we should avoid, because our question should be, "Do we interact with the world or with mental representations of it?" That is, as biological creatures, do we interact in and with our world in an unmediated way, or does cognition occur inside a cranial black box, as operations on symbolic tokens? As discussed (in chapters 6 and 9, and elsewhere), the idea that cognition is constituted in manipulation of abstract representations is an aspect of cognitivism reflecting its philosophical base in functionalism.

That said, thinking about thinking is a circular trap. Our ability to imagine possible mental structures and processes is limited by what we are mentally capable of. This idea is related to the positions of the New Mysterians (among them Owen Flanagan, Colin McGinn, and Steven Pinker), who say essentially that we're just not smart enough to understand consciousness. This idea might also be seen as an introspective variant on umwelt theory or a neural variant of the anthropic principle. Nonetheless, one of the miracles of the brain is that, so far, it seems capable of accommodating any and every explanation!

## Does the Mind Operate on Mental Representations?

While contemporary neuroscience is making rapid inroads into various mysteries of the brain and various preconceptions have been overturned, fundamental questions of mind, cognition, and selfhood remain mysterious. To assert that all mental events depend on internal representations seems dubious. Not only have we had great difficulty locating mental representations and repositories for such in the brain, but there is little agreement even on what to look for. The idea that such representations are pictorial in the conventional Western sense—mental movies showing in the Cartesian theater—is clearly culturally specific, related to our long acculturation to image technologies and metaphors drawn from them. What form does representation take in the case of nonvisual or multimodal phenomena or temporally extended and contingent sensorimotor routines? Grid and place cells (discussed in chapter 12) build a contingent and analogous spatiotemporal representation, but they are very different kinds of representation from the abstract, universal, logical entities of symbolic AI.

Our way of thinking about the world and about what we do is constrained by representationalist models. Cognitive capacities such as knowledge-how and the cognitive unconscious do not easily conform to this orthodoxy of logical operations on representations, whatever we mean by *representation*. When I speak to you across a table over coffee, I am really engaging with an image in my brain—this cognitivist explanation feels like a contorted fiction. Casting a fly while trout fishing is not easily explained using the physical symbol system hypothesis. It seems evident that perception and cognition are of a piece. The question is, where is the "I" doing the perception (see chapter 16)?

Lakoff and Johnson (1980) have shown us that metaphor, far from being an ornament of language, is key to the way meaning is constituted for humans—and that basic metaphors arise from embodied experience. Are metaphors representations? At an appropriate level of abstraction, metaphors can be blended (Turner and Fauconnier 1995) and new meanings created without the requirement of Boolean logical operations. Reasoning, metaphor, and representation seem to imply one another.

Reasoning in the Western sense seems not an innate biological capacity but rather a cultural one. That we seem—to ourselves—to be representational might be culturally specific and historically contingent, or it may be an epiphenomenon of the (epi)phenomenon of consciousness, if consciousness is taken to be our capability for telling ourselves stories about our experiences. In one account, what we understand as our recollection of dreams is the rapid narrativizing of a jumbled cacophony of mental imagery in the transitional stage before fully awakening. Humans seem to have a penchant for telling stories. Perhaps this proclivity is (all) the evidence we need to understand the nature of mental representation. The *Iliad* and the *Odyssey*, the Icelandic sagas, the *Bhagavad Gita*, the Koran, and the Bible—storytelling is how humans propagate culture. The capacity to relate an extended autobiographical narrative is a key aspect of selfhood. But the bedrock of selfhood seems to be prereflective, pre-representational, proprioceptive selfhood: the capacity to know, for instance, that my hand is "mine" (Legrand, Hurley, Metzinger, Zahavi).

We believe we have mental representations, although we have no (conscious) access to the mechanisms whereby those representations, or the illusions of such, are conjured. Until the neutral correlates of mental representations are identified, we cannot know how much of our nonconscious mental life is based on representations, if any. If nonconscious operations provide the basis for conscious operations, is mental representation only a characteristic of the 10 percent of brain activity that is conscious? Maybe using the word *representation* is a way of persuading ourselves that we know what we're talking about, when we don't have a clue!

Such questions are perplexing and fold in on themselves, drawing in concepts of intelligence, consciousness, cognition, selfhood, and being, which seem often to be defined in terms of each other. Going that way leads us into an inward spiraling philosophical vortex. As Hubert Dreyfus noted in response to Marvin Minsky's perceived optimism about the common sense problem, philosophers from Plato to Husserl have been working on that problem for two thousand years without notable success.[1] If introspection only provides access to the 10 percent of the brain's operations of which we are conscious, then, beguiling as it is, it is not a useful tool (see chapter 16).

## Computation and Representation

Counting sheep in a field is tricky, unless they're dead or asleep. Counting them as they pass through a gate reduces the problem substantially. Once that number is known, a person may want to perform operations on that number. Using pebbles to represent sheep in a one-to-one correspondence permits arithmetic operations to be performed on the pebbles rather than on the sheep. Making variously sized piles is easier with pebbles than with sheep. We might divide the number of pebbles among a number of people—this many sheep per person. Pebbles, the abacus, the Incan quipu, and the five-barred gate (or tally mark) are counting notation systems of increasing abstraction. They are external and perform work that the brain finds difficult unaided. We need not presume that mental representation precedes externalized representation. The reality may be the reverse; as discussed later in this chapter, Lambros Malafouris argues: Embodied action on material artifacts bootstrapped human culture into representation.[2] If simple pebbles provide such a resource for representation, then how much richer a source might the procedures of making a bow and arrow be? Recalling our discussion of tools (chapter 14), proportional measurement can occur without a generalized metric. With a balance—an ancient instrument with numerous variants—the calculation of equivalence does not depend on a standardized metric, a pound or gram weight. You can put pebbles on either side. This much (cow dung) *equals* this much (gold). If you move the fulcrum, you make it computational. The *klepsydra* (water clock) and the hourglass deploy quantities of water or sand to metaphorically quantify time. A metaphor is a *representation*; a grain of sand here is a *symbol*. (It is, at the same the time, a grain of sand; that's what makes it a symbol.)

In the klepsydra or the hourglass, we can introduce calibrations, a scale like a ruler (of course, the hourglass is not cylindrical, so the scale must indicate equal volumes, not equal distances). The volume of sand or water stands as a representation of a more abstract idea: a period of time. In these examples, we map the world onto symbols, operate on the symbols via a materialized algebra, then output back to the "matter" at hand. We might say that representation is fundamental to computation, at least in the sense we have come to understand computation in the context of digital computers. A computation, in this sense, involves the following stages: a system of correspondence is established between the phenomenon of interest and a symbolic token (a pebble or a graphical mark); algebraic operations are performed upon the tokens; then the value of that computation is transferred back to the object of interest.

The preceding examples involve physical tokens, and the computation occurs, if not outside the head, then in some relational way that embraces brain, manual actions, and objects. This way of thinking puts the cognitive boot on the other foot, so to speak. Rather than the mind—with its mysterious capacity for abstract representation—*implementing* physical representations, the process seems to work in reverse: Action in the world generates the capacity for mental representation. In this light, embodied cognition is the source of abstract or *disembodied* thought. Those forms of thought that we traditionally deem to be higher are themselves dependent upon this nonrepresentational, nonsymbolic, and nonlinguistic substrate, both evolutionarily and phenomenologically.

The nature of analog and digital representation was discussed in chapter 4, and some qualities of tools were discussed in chapter 14. A bevel gauge or a caliper captures data—an angle or a length—and allows that data to be transferred, but it requires no standardized metric. A protractor or a vernier caliper converts such data into measurements with respect to a metric: inches, millimeters, degrees. To take a measurement is to quantify according to some metric. In each case, you build a device in order to subject matter to measurement, whether it's the thickness of a steel plate or the weight of a sack of flour. At root, what is involved is a translation of geometry to algebra—of materialized relations of proportion to numbers (symbolic tokens) with reference to an abstract reference system.

When Rodney Brooks developed his subsumption architecture for robot control, there was some debate as to whether the system had (some form of) internal representation—a debate he sidestepped. This debate was rooted in particular ideas of representation within the AI community. Clearly, computer code is a representational system. However, it is possible to implement subsumption in analog electronics.[3] Where, then, are the representations? The idea that representation and translation into representation are necessary components of computation is validated by the physical symbol system hypothesis, which contentiously asserted that it was *necessary and sufficient* for intelligent action—that is, that reasoning on symbols accommodates all those capabilities we consider intelligent, and capacities that

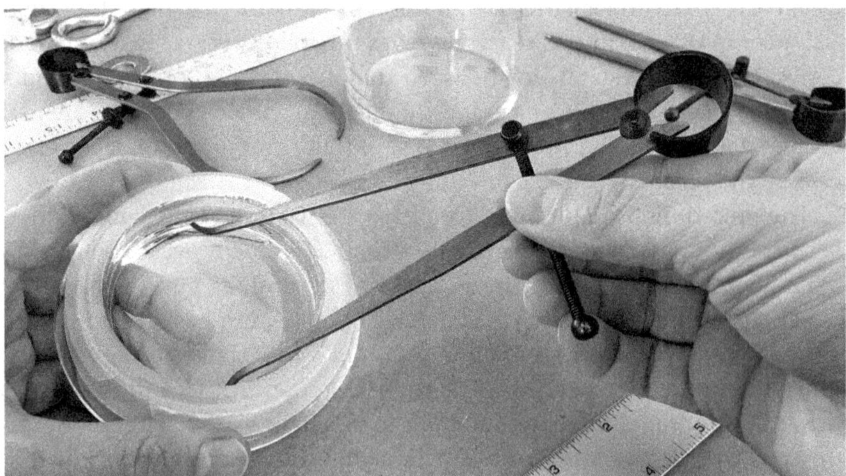

**Figure 15.1**
How to use an outside caliper. Photo courtesy of Steven Hoefer.

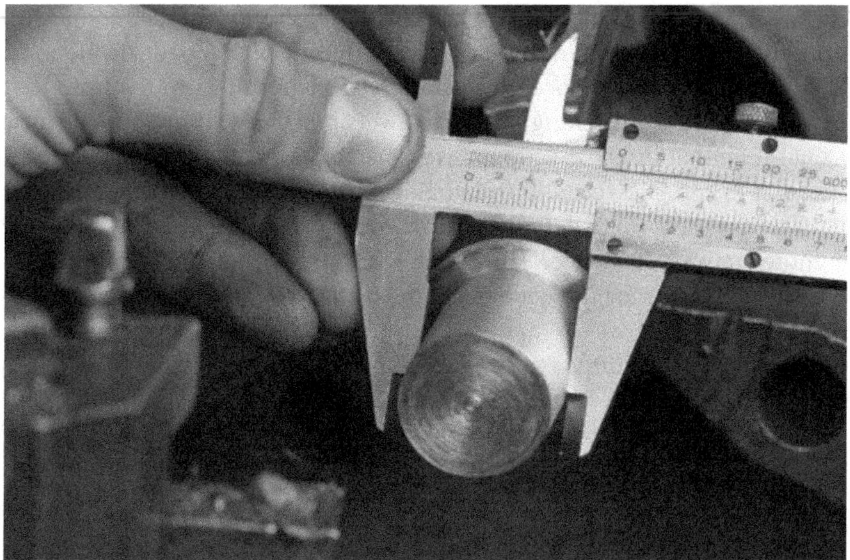

**Figure 15.2**
Using a vernier caliper.

do not require reasoning on symbols are thereby not intelligent. Again, an unsatisfying circularity.

## Do Muscular Gestalts Compute?

Do the pheromonal reactions of von Uexküll's tick compute (see chapter 2)? The tick's perceptual metabolism is a biological equivalent of Brooksian subsumption architecture. Do muscular gestalts compute? When a cat plays with a soft toy, the toy represents a prey animal. This is representation—but is it computation? Computation in this sense is a manipulation of abstract quantities. Is reasoning on symbols the only valid and relevant sense of computation?

About halfway through my walk to work, I was considering two possible routes. I could go left, up the stairs and across the bridge, or right, through the tunnel and up the hill. I found myself gesturing, enacting this or that possible route with my outstretched hand. Unconsciously, my hand enacted my path in miniature in front of me. The movement of my hand forward, wending left and right, up and down, enacted my path in miniature out from my torso. My hand mapped two paths sequentially, and the "time of flight" of my hand determined which path is shorter. This clearly entailed some kind of proprioceptive representational process, upon which I made deductions. A kinesthetic and proprioceptive act derived the result I wanted from that representation. I was telling myself two versions of a spatiotemporal story. Could it be that by these actions I was enacting a small-scale deictic modeling in grid and place cells? Is this analogous to "marking," in the sense that dancers use the term to describe spatiotemporally condensed shorthand for a choreographic sequence? This would correlate with Lakoff and Gallese's general argument for the generation of abstract concepts from sensorimotor routines.

Here, we have a curious case of epistemic action—not on material objects but on a mental representation. I call it a mental representation, but naming it so emphasizes the way in which the term serves as an indication of an incomplete or hazy concept. There is no imagery involved; I do not see a map in my "mind's eye," nor do I see a mental movie of my path. My mind's eye does not "see" anything. My hand enacts a motor representation of my path in miniature. We might say that my hand knows a scale model of the local topography.

Recall the story of how to catch a fly ball (see chapter 2): Fix the ball in the center of the visual field and run toward it, keeping the ball in the center of the visual field. The ball should hit you between the eyes. Is this intelligence? Joking aside, this mechanism resembles analog fire-control computing and involves much the same kinds of phenomena, trajectories, moving targets, and servo-mechanisms, only here the target is the active party trying to catch the projectile. Can we shoehorn this kind of sensorimotor "thinking" into paradigms of mental representation? Not without doing it some violence, or at least significant distortion. Discussing representation and dynamical systems Randall Beer asks:

How are we to understand the nature and role of this internal state within a dynamical agent? The traditional computational interpretation of such states would be as internal representations. But possessing an internal state is a property of physical systems in general, and these states can covary with states outside the system in quite complicated ways. Unless we wish to grant representational status to all physical states (does a thunderstorm represent the topography of the terrain over which it passes?), there must be additional conditions that license the modifier "representational." Unfortunately, despite the fundamental role that the notion of representation plays in computational approaches, there is very little agreement about what those additional conditions might be. These considerations have led me to adopt a position of representational skepticism (not, as some have suggested, anti-representationalism). (2014, 139)

Many postcognitivist theorists have elaborated upon kinds of cognition that precede—or seem to proceed without—mental representation. Maxine Sheets-Johnstone (2010) has argued in detail for the kinesthetic cognition of infants. Ed Hutchins (2010a) has articulated in detail the embodied and kinesthetic representational process involved in chart-based navigation. Examples such as those discussed here propose a notion of intelligent action in the world as consisting largely of nonconscious proprioceptive knowledge and kinesthetic procedures tightly coupled with skilled use of artifacts and prosthetics. If mental representation is present at all, it does not seem to take a form compatible with the "Cartesian theatre."

## Doing and Representation

*Doing in the world* (a) obviates mental representation or (b) permits the doing of things that might be impossible solely by mental representation and/or (c) contributes to the development of better mental representations. Whatever combination of a, b, and/or c applies, it's clear that as we plumb the realities of acting in the world, the Cartesian meat robot becomes untenable. We "do in the world" in order to obviate the need for (working with) mental representation or because doing in the world permits kinds of thinking internal representation alone cannot support. Malafouris reiterates Hutchins in arguing that it makes little sense to speak of one system representing the other: "Although we may be well able to construct a mental representation of anything in the world, the efficacy of material culture in the cognitive system lies primarily in the fact that it makes it possible for the mind to operate without having to do so, i.e., to think through things, in action, without the need of mental representation" (2004, 58).

Most postcognitive positions, from those of Suchman and Kirsh and Hutchins to that of Malafouris, share the idea that we operate intelligently in interaction with tools and contexts. Intelligent action is not so much guided by mental representations as it *arises* in relation to tools and contexts. Such contexts are often especially felicitous because they make mental representations redundant—offloading computation, as they say. In many cases, manipulating artifacts and tools permits achievements that mental representation cannot. This is the principle of complementarity in second-generation extended mind theory. Across the landscape of postcognitivist thought, there seems to be general concurrence that cognition extends beyond the body and incorporates all kinds of worldly structures and processes.

## Plans, Models, and Representations

David Marr began his influential book on vision by saying, "Vision is the *process* of discovering from images what is present in the world, and where it is" (1982, 3; emphasis in original). This passive view of perception is embedded in our language and our technologies, yet research from von Uexküll through Lettvin et al. to Gibson seems to suggest otherwise. The school of thought called *computational neuroscience* (originated by Michael Gazzaniga at Cornell in the late 1970s and continued at MIT by David Marr) proposed that perception (especially and paradigmatically, visual perception) consists of the inflow of visual information into the brain, where representations or models of the world are constructed and upon which reasoning is performed. The sensory front end to perception takes in the world passively, somehow turning sensation into information in the form of symbols, which funnel into our brains to form rich internal representations of the world for guiding our behavior. The idea that perception precedes action and that the two are mediated by cogitation is part of the Western philosophical legacy discussed in the beginning of this chapter. As Ed Hutchins notes, "The existence of perceptual and motor processes that are distinct and separate from so-called cognitive processes is not an empirical fact: it is simply a hypothesis that was made necessary by having constructed cognition out of a mechanized formal symbol processing system" (1995, 365). As we have seen, in many cases action guides perception.

The idea that sensing or perception are simple processes of transduction and that all of the cognitive heavy lifting is done by the "reasoning department" is an aspect of the computationalist prejudice that is axiomatic in the popular mind.[4] An alternative approach argues against the idea that information flows unproblematically into the brain via the senses. Contrarily, the notion that perception is a temporally extended process of active, embodied engagement with the world is at the center of contemporary neuroscience. Rather than developing rich internal models, animals—which include people—allow the world to be their own best model through close sensorimotor contact between it and our nervous system. The integration of skillful action and perception is central to enactive cognition. Sensing must be combined with active behavior for the world to make sense, as was demonstrated so conclusively by Held and Hein (1963) so long ago.

## We Reason and We Represent

I can see the image of my son in my mind. I can hear, in my mind's ear, the beginning chords of Bach's Toccata and Fugue in D Minor. I can "visualize" the qualities of a boat I will build. A person cannot deny the phenomenological reality of these experiences. It is difficult to deny the obvious presence of some kind of mental representation as being central to conscious thought. But the nature of those representations is unclear. The importance of mental representation is downplayed by externalists; in extreme cases, any necessity for any mental representation is denied.

That said, we do seem to infer, deduce, remember, correlate, abstract, and build structuring metaphors and analogies. We seem to act on the basis of reasoning on such representation, but this must be said with caveats. The degree to which such activities are available to conscious introspection is unclear. There is often a difference between what we do and what we believe we do. In many cases, conscious representation has been shown to be a false representation of things that occur nonconsciously. We are (obviously) unaware of nonconscious dimensions of things we believe we are conscious of (see chapter 16).

The further we probe the question of mental representation, the less we seem to know. Representations, paradigmatically, are pictures. The term *representation* is itself a metaphor. We consciously represent and reason, but it is far from clear that all mental activity deploys such techniques. We have no evidence to assume such "reasoning" occurs via some equivalent of computational process involving algorithms, symbolic tokens, and Boolean operators. We cannot assert that all thought or human knowing occurs in the brain or even in exclusively neurological processes in the body. How do we mentally represent dynamic action? Research into the behavior of grid and place cells is suggestive. Exploring the location and role of symbolic reasoning in the cognitive activities of the cricket batsman or the chicken sexer would demand a new kind of research methodology that acknowledges the possibility that such activities are embodied, dynamical, embedded, and enactive.

## Perception and Problem Solving

As quoted earlier, Varela, Thompson, and Rosch note, "The greatest ability of living cognition, however, consists in being able to pose, within broad constraints, the relevant issues that need to be addressed at each moment" (1991, 145; see chapter 11). Problem solving is valorized in traditional cognitive science, but little attention has been given to the precursor to problem solving. The process of extracting salience from the world—problem *framing*—involves holistic synthetic thinking about heterogeneous qualities, the very opposite of the analytic mode of problem solving. You can only solve a problem once you have determined that there *is* a problem and you think you know what that problem is. That is, you have formalized a problem in a way that makes it amenable to solving. Even then, you can't be sure you have the right problem, even if you do successfully solve it.

William James observed, "Consciousness, from our natal day, is of a teeming multiplicity of objects and relations, and what we call simple sensations are a result of discriminative attention, pushed often to a very high degree" (1950, 224). The task of determining salience from the heterogeneous and incommensurable diversity of life and mind lies outside the gamut of the physical symbol system for the simple reason that this determining of salience is the process by which symbols are constructed. The world does not come equipped with symbols like labels or barcodes that can just be picked off. Symbols must be made in order to have symbols we can reason upon; for that reasoning to be of (practical) value, the symbols must represent their referents. This "creative" dimension of cognition is not a matter of deduction but of determining salience from a heterogeneous cacophony of sensory experiences. We know from studies of active sensing and sensorimotor circuits that sensing is embodied and temporally extended.

Cognitivism relegates the process of asking the right question to sensory peripherals, as if constructing symbolic representations from worldly experience were a simple transduction. Perception is the creation of meaning(s). In essence, it is the common sense problem, upon which the AI colossus stumbled and fell. As Varela, Thompson, and Rosch put it: "These issues and concerns are enacted from a background of action, where what counts as relevant is contextually determined by our common sense" (Varela, Thompson, and Rosch 1991, 145).[5]

Except in the case of the couch potato, the capacity of vision, of seeing, is a temporal, enactive, and structurally coupled process, as anyone who has ever hit or caught a ball will attest. The enactive approach of O'Regan and Noë (2001) provides contemporary research and validation in this area. Such work is a continuation of the spirit of autopoietic cognitive theory, Gibsonian ecological psychology, and von Uexküll's ethology. All of these confirm a tight integration of self and world. The objectivist view of perception is refuted in diverse aspects of human culture and, paradigmatically, in various art forms, for both their makers and their audience.

### Between Frogs' Eyes and Mental Movies

Central to Enlightenment thinking is the privileging of (a certain conception of) vision and of optical technologies, from the magic lantern and the camera obscura to stereoscopic virtual reality. Indeed, the entire pictorial tradition in Western art encourages the idea that vision is the creation of mental representations. We can take this in two ways: that vision itself is a process of creating mental representations or that our *experience* of vision is a result of our process of creating mental representations. Either way, we take it for granted that vision *is* mental pictures, displayed in the Cartesian theater of the mind.

Yet studies of the neurology of vision in lower animals—from the fly (MacIver 2009) to the frog (Lettvin et al. 1959) to the raven (von Uexküll 1957) to studies of blindsight in humans—demonstrate that vision is and always has been dynamical, temporal, and unconscious, before it is seeing and identifying objects. Phenomena like blindsight show us that much human vision and other sensing have precognitive aspects and need entail no conscious or even preconscious process of pattern recognition or name giving. Vision itself does not require that an object of vision be identified, named, and its representation stored and compared to other similar images. Separation of figure from ground is more fundamental and is achieved through a variety of capabilities, including stereoscopy, motion parallax, optic flow, and other temporal dynamics. Can we imagine a mode of seeing without differentiation? The most basic form of vision, the most primitive eye, would be a generic ambient light sensor, as in the light sensing of simple animals such as nematodes, analogous to a single phototransistor or a cadmium sulphide photoresistor. This is the extent of vision in many lower animals, and, indeed, it was the nature of vision in the pioneering cybernetic robots built in the late 1940s by William Grey Walter (discussed in chapter 3): active, enactive vision linked directly to motor functions, resulting in phototactic behavior.

Once the viewed field is broken into sectors, as in the insect's compound eye, increasing resolution permits differentiation between cells and the tracking of changes across a field. In the case of the fly, a major function of its "sight" is the stabilization of flight via something like optic flow—a function that does not require object recognition and has no meaning outside of a sensorimotor loop. Importantly, this ability is conferred by the partially nonneural topology of the elements of the eye itself. This intelligence is not in the brain. Even if we consider the eye as a part of the organism's neural structure uniquely close to the external membrane of the organism, the information conferred is a product of the physical configuration that confers the data structure, not of mental reasoning on an internal movie. The fly is not looking at the world, nor identifying things in the world, nor is it viewing mental movies. Neural signals from the ambient optic array are locked into a sensorimotor feedback loop with motor routines that govern flight stability.

In an important sense, there is no world for the fly; there's just a pattern of light on the elements of the eye, an ambient optic array, which is exploited to stabilize flight. While we might call it *vision*, in some sense there is no *sight* in the sense of localizing and identifying objects. This is an example of von Uexküll's notion of the umwelt in the sense that the sensorimotor capabilities of a species confer upon it a "world" specified by those sensorimotor capabilities. There is no conscious executive decision-making on the part of the fly—no "oops, I'm leaning to the left, I must do something about that." Nor do we feel the need to assign selfhood to a fly. When we avoid the teenage skateboarder or catch the falling glass, we must allow that there might likewise be no object identification or conscious executive decision-making; we might also propose there is no "self" involved.

Humans possess a sophisticated capability of image vision, visual memory, and word/image association. Yet the preceding examples caution us not to project our sense of what is constituted by vision onto other species. We are taught to believe in—and we are taught to develop—capabilities of internal imaging, so we are naturalized to the phenomenon of the mental movie upon which we introspect. Much philosophy of mind is predicated on introspection, but aspects of vision such as blindsight cannot be introspected, exposing a blind spot in such philosophizing.

Neurologically, the optic nerve splits into a dorsal and ventral part. The ventral heads off to the well-known vision centers, such as V1–4. The dorsal goes north to the parietal lobe, where rapid nonconscious actions are taken. That is, the optic nerve heads straight into sensorimotor circuits. These two modes of vision correspond to what Paul Cisek calls *descriptive* and *pragmatic representation* (see chapter 12), though to refer to the second in terms of representation seems to stretch our conventional notion of a representation. Optic flow is useful in camera-based robot navigation and related pursuits precisely because it is not premised upon, and does not require, analysis of images as composed of (identifiable and nameable) objects positioned at various angles and distances in the visual field. Optic flow is a dynamical and nonrepresentational conception in the largely image-centric, frame-based, machine-vision culture. It should come as no surprise that J. J. Gibson, whose ecological conception of vision was at odds with conventional notions of vision, identified optic flow as a mode of visual knowledge.

## Paleolithic Representation

How and when did humans come into representation? Conventionally, the occurrence of Paleolithic cave painting is taken as a historical marker of the onset of representational capability. The conventional explanation is that human brains came to have the capability of mental imagery, and Paleolithic imagery provides a temporal marker for when this happened. But as Malafouris rightly points out, this says very little. In his paper "Before and Beyond Representation: Towards an Enactive Conception of the Paleolithic Image" (2007), Malafouris makes a particularly thought-provoking intervention into the conventional story of acquisition of representational capability, observing that the conventional story explains only *when* representation occurred, not *how*. In a charming inversion, he proposes that the act of mark-making bootstrapped the Paleolithic mind into representation. This makes mental representation a cultural phenomenon, further blurring nature-nurture dualisms. This way of thinking about mental representation as arising from embodied practice resonates with the work of Gallese and Lakoff (2005).

Mark-making here was not so much epistemic action as *generative action*. More than enhancing an existing ability, it catalyzed a new mode of thinking: mental representation. Malafouris's insight that situated sensorimotoric engagement with environment and artifacts may have bootstrapped human culture into representation is a lodestone in the context of a reconfiguration of conceptions of intelligence with respect to cultural practices: "The boundary between the 'internal' concept seen in 'the mind's eye' and its external representation on the wall of the cave should be questioned. The cave wall was not simply a 'context' for the 'mind inside the head,' it was the outward membrane of the 'mind inside the cave'" (Malafouris 2007, 299). If it was the act of marking the cave wall at Lascaux—or elsewhere—that catalyzed the cognitive ability to represent, then by extension, *cultural practices with artifacts and tools are processes by which new ways of thinking are generated.*

Almost heretically, Malafouris suggests that representation may not hold the key to understanding the human mind. More subtly, he issues a caution against simplistically assuming that we can extrapolate from our own experience of these images what the perceptual experience of the makers might have been: "Whilst it probably makes perfect sense to see the Paleolithic image as a representation *of* something—from our contemporary habits of seeing and perceiving—to assume uncritically that this was also the way the image was experienced in its original context is to take as our starting point what should have been the end of our analysis" (2007, 292; emphasis in original). Like any good anthropologist, he is wary of unintentional cultural back-projection: "It is one thing to say that the people of the Upper Paleolithic were creating representations—they certainly appear as representations to the modern observer—it is another to say that the Paleolithic people were aware or knew they were making representations in some arbitrary symbolic sense" (292). That is, though the Paleolithic images are clearly depictions, we should not assume they are representations in the way we understand the idea. This proposition is both reasonable and tantalizing; we must accept it while also accepting our inability to share or even conceive of the Paleolithic experience of an image. We can't know what it is like to be a Paleolithic person any more than we can know what it is like to be a bat (Nagel).

Most of us have not seen Paleolithic cave paintings, except in photographic reproductions in which they are arrayed in the conventional rectangular formats of Western pictures. We forget that a cave wall is seldom a flat, smooth, vertical, evenly lit surface like an art gallery wall or a movie screen. Caves are dark, and surfaces are curved, inclined, pocked, jagged, and occluded.[6] For the original makers and viewers, light sources were flickering flames, whether from a fire on the floor of the cave or a torch carried by hand and possibly moved in particular ways. This might shed some light (as it were) on the phenomenon of multiple profiles often encountered in such paintings. They might have been "movies"—or at least Paleolithic zoetropes! A moving, flickering light source combined with shadows caused by protuberances in the rock surface produce a zoetrope-like experience. Without being too fanciful, one might suggest that such images might have been performative in a way similar to Erkki Huhtamo's explication of precinematic *magic lantern* shows. Huhtamo cautions us not to imagine them as slide shows of still images (2012). Many of the slides were mechanized to make moving images, fades were used, and the images were integrated into extended spoken narratives. Magic lantern shows were more like movies than we might assume, and the "telling" of cave paintings may have been similarly performative.

Malafouris does not work through the process of this bootstrapping in detail, but the idea has undeniable appeal and a certain intuitive insight. We know we are neurologically primed to find recognizable patterns in our visual field. We see faces in clouds and animals in Rorschach inkblots. We are equally sensitive to temporal patterning—and a temporal pattern may suggest a form without that form being depicted, as Shakespeare knew, indicated by Cassius's remark: "'Tis Cinna. I do know him by his gait" (*Julius Caesar*, 1.3). It seems not unreasonable to imagine that a formation on a cave wall, illuminated by a flickering flame, might suggest something in the larger world for which there might have been a name, and thus the act of enhancing that resemblance with a piece of charcoal seems like the kind of thing a person might do. If this hypothesis is correct, representationalism, both on the wall and in the brain, does not have, or need, a neuroessentialist explanation. Like language, it is learned. There is no bison neuron, as there is no grandmother neuron. In the spirit of Elizabeth Bates's remark that language is a new machine made of old parts, preexisting visual capabilities are repurposed to support a *culture* of representational mark making.

Such proposals have a corrective effect upon the kind of biological or neural determinism that characterizes recently fashionable neuroaesthetics. A radically cultural-relativist position is just as problematic; a person could not have representation without eyes or a sophisticated visual cortex—but having complex eyes and a visual cortex is itself not sufficient. Again, we see that the *science wars* were a symptom of an artificial dualism—in this case, that of biology-culture or nature-nurture.

An aspect of the Paleolithic paintings not discussed by Malafouris is that they were generated and used in a social context, and those interactions were temporally extended over seasons and thousands of years. While we can only conjecture about the sort of activities that occurred in relation to these sites, it is probably safe to assert that they indicate the existence of a shared notational system or pictorial language used not only inside the cave but as part of distributed cognitive practices in the lives of Paleolithic people. At the conclusion of "Before and Beyond Representation," Malafouris (2007) draws his argument together to reorient the entire notion of mental imaging and argues that the external sensorimotor scaffold of the cave may have not only generated the capability of mental representation but also created the context for the emergence of *metaconsciousness*— thinking about thinking.

We are taught to "see" images on paper and on screens before we can talk. As a result, we are so naturalized to seeing depictions in perspectival images (photographic or handmade) that it is difficult not to see them. But some surviving cultures do not—and many of the past did not—have pictorial representation or do not share our particular Western style of representation. Into the 1970s, there were some New Guinea highland groups who could not see their images in a Polaroid photograph. In African cultures and in Chinese painting traditions, the convention that diminished size connotes the object is in the far distance is unknown. Like vision, representationalism emerged gradually and, like language, has many variants.

## Conclusion

The question of whether cognition is achieved via operations on mental representations seems at this point passé. Evidence appears overwhelming that a substantial amount of what we used to call *cognition* is achieved in nonconscious ways, with no call for those processes to be universally representational. Across the postcognitivist spectrum, representationalism is disputed entirely or qualified in various ways. The fault lines are various, as are the proposed solutions to perceived binaries such as the internalism/externalism dualism. That said, few would insist that we do not represent in complex ways. The interesting questions now are about the extent of the capabilities of nonrepresentational cognition, about the nature of mental representations—whether representations are exclusively of the conscious mind or how they *become* conscious—and about how these representations are dynamically coupled to the flow of living in the world.

# 16 Consciousness, Selfhood, and the Cognitive Unconscious

If there is no other, there will be no I. If there is no I, there will be none to make distinctions.

—Zhuangzi (Chuang-Tzŭ), fourth century BCE

The life of consciousness—cognitive life, the life of desire or perceptual life—is subtended by an "intentional arc" which projects round about us our past, our future, our human setting, our physical, ideological and moral situation.

—Maurice Merleau-Ponty, *Phenomenology of Perception* (2002, 157)

It is all to the good when "consciousness" is thrown overboard as a substance or separate process designated by a noun: for "ness" indicates that the noun is abstract and results from erecting a quality of action into a thing in itself. But the quality of being conscious remains; the difference between behavior that is aware of what it is about and routine or impulse behavior is as marked a factual difference as we can anywhere discover.

—John Dewey (1928, 16)

This chapter poses the question of consciousness. Not in the sense of "what is this wondrous phenomenon?" but in the sense of "who cares?" Consciousness, however marvelous a thing it is to wonder about, is a surface effect of deeper processes, themselves not available to introspection; this is why we call them *unconscious*. Consciousness is just the glittering reflection on the surface of the deep lake of the nonconscious. What purchase can be gained by speaking of those aspects of cognition, mentation, awareness— choose your term—that happen to rise to consciousness as a *separate realm*, an ontological a priori? The notion of consciousness as an object of study seems to me to be predicated (again!) on a fallacious structuring dualism. It's like talking about your face as if it exists independent of your head.

Consciousness has long been a key theme in popular philosophy of mind. It became faddish with the rise of interest in psychedelic drugs and

Eastern spiritual thought in the 1960s and 1970s, when these new influences widened the popular conception of consciousness (astral travel, anyone?). Through the last century, philosophy of mind in the Anglo-American analytic tradition—almost entirely based in introspection—shared the stage with Freudian psychoanalytic conceptions. Freud was a neuroscientist before he was a psychoanalyst. Today, contemporary neuroscience is providing evidence of brain and neural processes that challenges many long-held philosophical ideas. Andy Clark is one of several philosophers who have engaged this new knowledge. George Lakoff and Mark Johnson (1999) were outspoken in their rejection of a preoccupation with consciousness and speak of the cognitive unconscious making an "end run" around philosophy itself in their book *Philosophy in the Flesh: The Embodied Mind and Its Challenge to Western Thought* (1999), discussed later. Recently, N. Katherine Hayles has introduced a similar notion she refers to as the *cognitive nonconscious* (2017). Contemporary neuroscience increasingly shows us that consciousness is the tip of the iceberg. Consciousness-chauvinism is increasingly anachronistic.

## Qualia and the Hard Problem

According to Western philosophy of mind and conventional cognitive science, reason is the pinnacle of intellect, and reason is, paradigmatically, conscious; *cogito ergo sum*. It is possible that the reason that consciousness seems so vexing is precisely the way it is framed, within a context that privileges conscious thought and denigrates "lower" or unconscious thought or neural activity. A key concept in philosophy of mind is *qualia*. Qualia are the subjective qualities of experiences, and their nature (and existence) has been debated from various positions—physicalist, functionalist, representationalist, panpsychist, mysterian, and so on. The paradigmatic example is the experience of seeing red (the experience of nodding off while reading this passage might be another). As with any philosophical debate, various philosophers have their own interpretations, which makes answering the question of what qualia are tricky.[1]

Are qualia a philosophical invention? John Haugeland constructed an amusing image of the Cartesian train, with the locomotive of the *res cogitans* leading, and "behind that engine have trailed the sorry boxcars of hyperbolic doubt, the mind-body problem, the problem of the external world, the problem of other minds, and so on" (1998, 207). Qualia are thus one of Haugeland's "sorry boxcars."

According to David Chalmers (1995), the hard problem of consciousness is how we come to have the feeling of what it is like to experience (anything)—that is, what it is like to have awareness of oneself as a conscious-perceiving self. He took qualia as being central to his *hard problem*. This problem has been a center of debate for some time during the emergence of postcognitivist positions. By some lights, the hard problem does not exist. Various philosophers, including Lycan, Dretske, Block, Dennett, and others, have offered differing explanations. Fred Dretske, as a representationalist, contends that all mental facts are representational facts; however, his interpretation of qualia is not internalist: "I know of no plausible psychosemantics, no plausible theory of what makes one thing *about* another, that isn't externalist in character" (1996, 143; emphasis in original).

In this chapter, I will sidestep such debates, as it seems that in debating the subtleties of sensory experience in terms of conflicting paradigms it is easy to go a long way and not get anywhere. My interest is in exploring aspects of consciousness, mind, and selfhood that are largely avoided or ignored in conventional debate (but, as Francisco Varela and Evan Thompson emphasized, are dwelt upon in Buddhist philosophy). Mind you, magical, supernatural, or esoteric explanations—spirits, the little psychic telegraph station in the pineal gland, quantum phenomena, or other such ideas—are, by Ockham's razor, unnecessary. There is more than enough complexity in the biology of being to preoccupy us without positing mysterious mechanisms or forces.

## Consciousness and Everything Else

The privileging of conscious over the nonconscious duplicates the Cartesian dualism. The privileging of consciousness is both humanist and human exceptionalist and closely tied to Western conceptions of individual identity. If we are to make any headway in understanding cognition as intelligent action in the world, we need to denaturalize—and break away from—dualist patterns of thought. Consciousness, Descartes's *cogito*, is scaffolded by a teeming multitude of nonconscious structures and processes involving grid cells, pheromone reception, proprioception, language formation, language understanding, image processing, remembering, forgetting, and so on. These processes, as discussed in previous chapters, extend beyond brain, beyond neural tissue, and beyond body in sensorimotor chains. A commitment to a self-world dichotomy, in the form of a subject-object dichotomy, is axiomatic to much modern Western thought. It undergirds and structures modes of culture and kinds of technology and science. It has the sense of being *natural* to us because of this consistency across Western culture, not because of its "truth" or explanatory value.

Only a small proportion of the activities of the brain are accessible to consciousness. When you speak, you hear words come out of your mouth without any awareness of the coordination of breath, larynx, and vocal tract movement that produces the stream of sounds. Yet you intend to speak, and speaking occurs. We usually have no awareness of, and do not consciously control, the functions of our larynx and vocal cavity to give voice to those intended words. As physiologists like Paul Cisek emphasize, much of the brain's activity is integrated with bodily processes and with movement. When I decide to dive into the pool, the coordination of muscles in processes of priming and springing and leaping and pointing downward and preparing for impact and holding my breath and righting myself and surfacing is utterly opaque to me. Long ago, Benjamin Libet showed that the mental activity that gives rise to consciousness is itself unconscious (see below).

Consciousness is partial, fallible, and in some cases false. Some things the unconscious is doing may be too important or too urgent to tell consciousness about. Conscious mental life, and selfhood itself, might be epiphenomenal. So let's begin by deprivileging consciousness, and go on to query the notion that the conscious and the unconscious are monolithic or permanent in their boundaries.

The separation of the conscious and the unconscious is far from obvious, and things move into and out of consciousness in different ways. There are many modalities of the unconscious (as of the conscious). As with the discussion of representation in the previous chapter, key terms are used in a variety of ways, not always consistently. The image of consciousness as *arising*—just cropping up, in patches, epiphenomenally—counteracts the more conventional image of a faculty housed in a particular area.

As a result of cognitivist paradigms and the employment of introspection as a traditional philosophical technique, we have come to privilege consciousness and ignore the obvious fact that we survive and prosper through acts of unconscious intelligence. William James observed, "Consciousness, from our natal day, is of a teeming multiplicity of objects and relations, and what we call simple sensations are results of *discriminative attention*, pushed often to a very high degree" (1950, 224; emphasis mine). This chapter reviews perspectives on the conscious, the nonconscious, and the self, with respect to the umwelt and to embodied action in the world.

## Consciousness and Introspection

Most of us seem to have a fairly keen sense of being conscious when we are conscious. This seems to be a defining characteristic of the condition. Yet defining consciousness has proven troublesome, to say nothing of finding its neurological origin and location, a project that remains at the level of conjecture. "Consciousness, then, does not appear to itself chopped up in bits. . . . It is nothing jointed; it flows" (James 1950, 239). In so saying, James seems to assume that we can know mind through introspection and that what we introspect upon (consciousness) is mind.

In *Philosophy in the Flesh* (1999), Lakoff and Johnson argue that only 10 percent of cognitive activity is conscious; the rest they call the *cognitive unconscious*. If major aspects of mind and intelligence are not conscious, then, with Lakoff and Johnson, we must conclude that introspection is not a useful technique for knowing the nature of mind, let alone the behavior of brain. If for every conscious event there are nine or ten nonconscious neural events involved, then you can't understand cognition by thinking about consciousness.

As Lakoff and Johnson (1999) point out—somewhat gleefully—this implies that the larger part of Western philosophy (which relies on introspection to determine the operations of the human mind) has dubious value in the scientific study of cognition because it relies on introspection to reveal the operations of the human mind (this relates to the circularity problem noted in chapter 15). Not only does that include a substantial part of the Western philosophical corpus, but it also includes most of AI, as the procedures created by AI professionals were almost always autobiographical, and the validity of introspection as a method was seldom if ever interrogated.

## Benjamin Libet and the Readiness Potential

Over his career, and largely in the 1970s, Libet conducted a series of experiments that challenged the notion of the autonomy of conscious decision-making, the perception of the passage of time, and the notion of free will. In one experiment, he had subjects hold out their arms and, at any chosen moment, flex their wrists. The moment of their decision, the moment of brain activity related to the physical action, and the onset of the action itself were all monitored with electrodes and timed. The surprising result was that the decision to act came significantly after the brain registered preparation to act—the signature of which is called the *readiness potential*. The readiness potential preceded the action by 550 ms, but the decision to act preceded the action by only 200 ms.[2] The implication is that we become consciously aware of the decision to do something only after our brain is in the process of already beginning to do it.

In related experiments, where he had access to the brains of patients who were conscious while undergoing brain surgery, Libet directly stimulated the sensory cortex with an electrode. He found that even with such direct stimulation, it took consciousness at least half a second to register a sensation. These results raised questions regarding our perception of time. What is the nature of the conscious perception of "now" if sensory stimuli take half a second to become conscious? What, then, is the mechanism whereby we, demonstrably, take more or less instantaneous action—as in the case, for instance, of slamming on the brakes in a freeway driving emergency?

In essence, Libet hypothesized that in order for various sensory stimuli to be correlated and not to generate a confused or contradictory conscious experience—a state he called *cerebral neuronal adequacy*—a time delay occurs, followed by a kind of neurological back-dating that antedates the perception of the experience (Libet 1993). Sensational reports suggested that such results brought the concept of free will into question. It would be more accurate to infer that his experiments demonstrate only that the true decision-making faculty is not accessible to introspection; that is, it is not part of the conscious mind. This is itself a challenge to traditional philosophy with its emphasis on introspection, the limitations of introspection being that it can only access consciousness.

Libet's work sowed seeds of doubt regarding the presumed primacy of consciousness. While consciousness is normally assumed to be the seat of intelligence, it increasingly becomes clear that much of the activity that results in intelligent judgment, languaging, and the like occur nonconsciously. The experiments of Libet seem to show that our cherished consciousness is an epiphenomenon of the real work of the brain. As the experience of selfhood is so tied to consciousness, selfhood itself starts to feel somewhat illusory.

## The Unconscious

What we call *consciousness* is thoroughly underpinned and structured by nonconscious processes. While consciousness is indeed mysterious, it is an accessible mystery. Surely, it's just as interesting to ask what is *not* conscious? In my opinion, the larger mystery is in the iceberg proper, of which consciousness is only the exposed tip. The image of an iceberg seems apropos because of the volume below the surface and for the very image of the water surface, a surface that is permeable and fluctuating. Of all the neural events going on at any moment, we are conscious of just a few. How do things become conscious? What are the processes by which, from the plethora of sensations and neural processes, a small number of things become conscious? How, finally, do things recede from consciousness? The back-and-forth of signals and sensations across the conscious/nonconscious divide must be constant and multifarious. There is not just one doorway into consciousness. The way a memory of school days becomes conscious might be quite different from the way in which we become aware of a painful blister, and these are both different from coming to understand a phrase in a foreign language or detecting the smell of jasmine in the night air. Likewise, there is no one mechanism or sensation or exit door where things exit from consciousness.

There are many kinds of unconscious phenomena: the unconsciousness of low-level motor routines, the unconsciousness of memories not present to consciousness, the unconsciousness of displaced anger, the unconsciousness of the gut. In each case, there is a process by which we become conscious of something, a way in which a thought or sensation makes itself known. Becoming aware of a scent is different from the dawning awareness that you're in big trouble.

## The Human Brain Is like an Enormous Fish

Throughout this book, I have drawn attention to how metaphors can structure inquiry in a way that leads people down a false path. "The human brain is like an enormous fish: It is flat and slimy and has gills through which it can see," says Graham Chapman in one of many absurd but insightful Monty Python skits.[3] Analogies of water surfaces and the like create an image of stratification, the imagistic succinctness of which can be dangerously seductive. Perhaps to speak of doorways or icebergs and water surfaces is to conceptualize the problem wrongly. How do we combat—or at least maintain vigilance against—this danger? We must model to build a hypothesis, and a model is a metaphor—yet we must be vigilantly aware that a metaphor can overwhelm or wrongly frame the phenomenon itself. Like the mind-body binary, construction of the conscious-unconscious as a binary may be just that kind of dangerous metaphor that prevents our better understanding.

## The Cognitive Unconscious

The work of Lakoff and Johnson, Gallese, Dreyfus, Libet, and others presents an idea of the relation between conscious and unconscious that problematizes the conventional view. According to Gallese and Lakoff, concepts arise from the unconscious parts of sensorimotor circuits (see below). According to Dreyfus, conscious learning becomes unconscious—muscular gestalts. Not only do we take actions motivated by perceptions we are unaware of (blindsight, pheromone reception) but, according to Libet, even in the case of consciously chosen actions we are taking them before we are aware of choosing to do so. As Lakoff and Ingold have argued from different perspectives, there is no simple and clear separation between conscious ratiocination and bodily skill. Indeed, the distinction simply reproduces the axiomatic Enlightenment privileging of the abstract.

According to the Cartesian hierarchy, the (cognitive) unconscious—that aspect of mental functioning previously relegated to lower status—is linked to and identified with the body. Much of the presumedly lower mental work is involved with enacting sensorimotor routines in feedback loops with the environment, to say nothing of the activities of the vast and complex autonomic nervous system—the "brain in the gut" that is by definition unconscious. The degree to which the autonomic nervous system takes part in the activities of the cognitive unconscious is increasingly an open question, especially as the influence of the microbiome on neural processes becomes better understood. Out on the peripheries of holistic neuroscience, the fascia, heretofore more or less ignored in physiology, is attracting increased attention. Stilwell points out, "There are 10 times as many sensory receptors in your fascial tissues as there are in your muscles" (quoted in Myers 2011). Fascia plays a role in transference of vibrations mechanically, at a rate far exceeding the rate of nerve impulses.[4]

Gallese and Lakoff assert that "rational thought is . . . largely unconscious" (2005, 473). If rational thought is largely unconscious, then by what definition is it rational? Moreover, how do we know it happens in the brain and not, for instance, in neural and nonneural loops through viscera, muscles, or fascia? Or in epistemic action feedback loops through body and world?

Expertise in sports, dancing, or arts practices is holistic embodied intelligence, a kind of heightened being in the world, in which bodily systems take part in creative cognition—even the structure of bones and the shape of joints. The quick and skillful finger movements of the pianist or violinist occur in less time than it takes for a nerve signal to go from brain to hand and back, and neurophysiological evidence exists that certain motor behaviors are coordinated via remotely self-contained subroutines. Certainly some kinds of motor behaviors involve neural circuits that never make it to the "headquarters" (Grillner 1996). Some may object to the fish examples by claiming that fish are evolutionarily remote and thus not relevant, but this would be human exceptionalism showing its ugly face again. We should remember the lessons of evo-devo (evolutionary-developmental biology): We are genetically 96 percent the same as a mouse and have more in common with the housefly than we would probably like to think.

Muscular gestalts are precisely what a dancer or a footballer depends on to act intelligently in the moment. Is the operation of a muscular gestalt a kind of thinking? Or is it skill? To answer the latter would simply confirm the power of the Cartesian hierarchy, which we already acknowledge is baseless. And where do muscular gestalts live? In the lowly reptile brain? What of the spinal cord and the afferent and efferent nerves that extend to the extremities? Are they not "brainstuff"? What constitutes "thought" and where such thought is located is unclear. According to the mythical *res cogitans–res extensa* binary—a seemingly biologically principled distinction between brain and body—cogitation purportedly occurs within the confines of the cranium and perhaps only in certain privileged neighborhoods. That distinction has been contested by Haugeland in a systems theoretic argument, and by Robert Hanna and Evan Thompson from an enactive standpoint (2003).

## Where Do Concepts Come From?

One of the questions conventional Western philosophy has had some difficulty answering is how we come to have the capacity to think in abstract terms. That is, how—barring some kind of quasi-spiritualist mumbo jumbo concerning Platonic ideals or the pineal telegraph—do we come to possess the components of abstract thinking? This is an area in which embodied cognitive science and philosophy of mind have viable and testable proposals.

In *The Body in the Mind: The Bodily Basis of Meaning, Imagination, and Reason* (1987), Mark Johnson argued for the origin of abstract concepts in bodily experiences. After generations of denial of the significance of embodiment in mainstream Western philosophy, Johnson identified that the crisis of rationality could be resolved by acknowledgment of the physically instantiated nature of mind in body.[5]

Johnson elaborates his argument with numerous examples. He argues, for instance, that the abstract notion of equivalence is rooted in the sense of balance. This is easy to understand. If I come home with a bag of oranges in one hand and a bag of books in the other, and I am not pulled off balance by my loads, then in some sense the oranges "equal" the books. Johnson argues that, in this way, abstract concepts are generated metaphorically, noting that metaphor has been denigrated in traditional Western philosophy. Johnson, on the contrary, makes metaphor fundamental to reason. In this spirit, Johnson and Lakoff coauthored the better-known *Metaphors We Live By* (Lakoff and Johnson 1980). Johnson and Lakoff argue that, contrary to Enlightenment convention, reason—and by extension much of higher cognition—is metaphorical "all the way down."

In *Philosophy in the Flesh* (1999), Lakoff and Johnson bring this argument to bear as a critique of Western philosophy itself: "Whenever a philosophical theory seems intuitive to us, it is primarily because it is based on metaphors that are deeply embedded in our cognitive unconscious and are widely shared within a culture. . . . Nobody would understand Kant's moral theory at all if it didn't make use, albeit creatively, of the same metaphors that underlie our cultural models of morality" (541). Central to their argument is the idea that thinking is rooted primarily in metaphor, as opposed to reason. They base this argument in neuroscientific research, arguing that cognitive metaphors arise through *cross-domain mappings* in which sensory-motor concepts provide the foundations for abstract reasoning. They explicitly dispute a linguistic-cognitivist explication of metaphor: "Contrary to long-standing opinion about metaphor, primary metaphor is *not* the result of a conscious multistage process of interpretation. Rather it is a matter of immediate conceptual mapping via neural connections" (57; emphasis in original). Cognitive metaphors are acquired in child development through embodied activity in the world.

In "The Brain's Concepts: The Role of the Sensory-Motor System in Conceptual Knowledge" (2005), Vittorio Gallese and George Lakoff propose neural mechanisms for the embodied origins of metaphor and abstract concepts. "The sensory-motor system not only provides structure to conceptual content, but also characterizes the semantic content of concepts in terms of the way that we function with our bodies in the world" (456). In so saying, the authors present a model for neurological and cognitive details of how abstract concepts might come to exist out of bodily experience. That is, they provide plausible neuroscientific explanations for the process outlined by Johnson two decades earlier, arguing that neuroscientific evidence accumulated over the last two decades enables us to say quite new things about the way the brain works.

Contemporary dynamic brain-imaging technologies (such as fMRI), are providing an unprecedented view of neural processes and structures. Much of that work is marshaled to support established paradigms and research agendas, while some is informed by postcognitivist ideas of sensorimotor integration. According to Gallese and Lakoff:

The very same neurons that control purposeful actions also respond to visual, auditory, and somato-sensory information about the objects the actions are directed to. They do so because they are part of a parietal-premotor circuit . . . in charge of overall control of purposeful bodily actions in peri-personal space. This contrasts with the old notion that sensory-motor integration is achieved at a "higher" level at which separate neural systems for motor control and sensory processing are brought together in a putative "association area." (2005, 459)

This passage disputes conventional conceptions of brain functions. The idea of the separation of motor and abstract neural activity or the idea that different kinds of processes (e.g., reasoning, memory, or language) occur in specific specialized departments in the brain has a musty, Victorian smell to it.

Driven by a theoretical program that acknowledges embodiment and dynamical sensorimotor process, Gallese and Lakoff can say that parietal and premotor areas are deeply integrated and neurons are inherently multimodal. That is, a single neuron might respond to both performing an action and seeing that action performed. This integration permits that these areas "serve the function of constructing an integrated representation of (1) actions together with (2) objects acted on and (3) locations toward which actions are directed" (Gallese and Lakoff 2005, 460). Drawing on the prior work of researchers in Parma, Italy, on mirror neurons (see, e.g., Di Pellegrino, Fadiga, Fogassi, Gallese, Rizzolatti 1992),[6] they argue that doing a thing, imagining it, and reasoning with it use the same neural circuitry.

Hubert and Stuart Dreyfus (Dreyfus and Dreyfus 1980) elucidated a process of learning in which tasks begin as explicit, conscious, and reasoned and become increasingly automatic and embodied as muscular gestalts (see chapter 15). If we accept (per Dreyfus) that learning is a transition from explicit conscious representation to muscular gestalt, this is an example of mental traffic *going the other way* from conscious to (cognitive) unconscious. If, per Lakoff and Johnson, sensorimotor functions are far closer to abstract thought than we have allowed, then Enlightenment humanist conceptions of reason, intellect, cognition, and mind fail. A wholesale reconfiguration of basic ideas about conscious and nonconscious, brain and body, abstract thought and embodied practices is required. If all this is the case, then traditional artisanal and artistic methodologies take on new relevance as exemplary of these complex processes and should themselves become a subject for study.

Gallese and Lakoff (2005) illustrate their argument for the origin of abstract concepts in motor routines, taking *grasping* as an example. The physical act of grasping is coordinated by motor circuits. When we *imagine* grasping, they say, we use the same circuitry: the same neural events occur in same neurons, the "output" is just suppressed. They go on to argue that the same circuitry generates the *idea* of grasping, which can then be deployed in metaphorical ways as abstract concepts: We *grasp* an argument. They argue, by an Ockham's razor, that there is no need for the concept (and the word) to reside elsewhere in the brain. The abstract concept and the motor action are the same thing, and the concept is generated by firing the motor circuitry for grasping.

They elaborate, based on neuroscientific evidence: Once a sensory motor process is learned, the neural process itself can be activated while physical action is suppressed. This process is employed as a simulation for feed-forward control. Imagining the action uses the same activation of the same neural circuits, with conscious access. According to Gallese and Lakoff, "These data all together show that typical human cognitive activities such as visual and motor imagery, far from being of a disembodied, modality-free, and symbolic nature, make use of the activation of sensory-motor brain regions" (2005, 464). They argue that inference and understanding regarding a sensorimotor function draw upon the activation of those brain regions. That is, that reasoning is not context-free manipulation of symbols but is thoroughly grounded in embodied experience.

Gallese and Lakoff then move to the relation of concepts to language. According to their sensorimotor hypothesis, they assert that language makes direct use of the same brain structures used in perception and action. Consistent with their denial that reasoning is disembodied, they also assert that there is no "language module" in the brain: "Neither semantics nor grammar is symbolic, in the sense of the theory of formal systems, which consists of rules for manipulating disembodied meaningless symbols" (2005, 473). They conclude, "According to our hypothesis, rational thought is an exploitation of the normal operations of our bodies. As such, it is also largely unconscious" (473).

Supported by neuroscientific research, the authors thus assemble a hypothesis and a set of related claims that, taken together, propose an embodied explanation for higher mental functions and challenge not only computationalist cognitive science but much in the Western philosophical tradition.

## Abandoning the Humanist Self

In the Cartesian construction, the "I" is immaterial and mental, and a clear separation is maintained between the mental and the bodily. Such a separation undergirds internalist and some embodied theories of mind—Andy

Clark's minimal Cartesianism being a contemporary example. Such quasi-embodied theories maintain a principled separation between mind and body, even if they move the boundary or make it permeable in various ways. Many of the thorny problems of modern Western philosophy have centered on reconciling lived experience with Cartesianism. The challenge therefore is to develop conceptions of selfhood, intelligence, and awareness that are not predicated on false mind-body and self-world dichotomies. It is obfuscating, and simply unnecessary, to say "this is mind and that is body," "mind ends here and body starts there." Maturana and others might assert that, biologically, Descartes had it backward: *I am, therefore I think.*

Questions about the relation of mind, brain, body, and world in studies of cognition necessarily lead to questions of selfhood, self-awareness, and consciousness, about embodiment and the sense of self. Examples of such inquiry include Susan Hurley's (1998) ideas of preconscious awareness in her shared circuits hypothesis. Dorothée Legrand (2006) worked in similar territory, plumbing the subtleties of self-awareness in her work on prereflective self-consciousness, where she argues that a prereflective bodily awareness (given by proprioception) must necessarily precede a sense of selfhood itself (see chapter 21 for further discussion). Could such prereflective awareness be given by the operation of sensorimotor routines identified by Gallese and Lakoff (2005) as the source of abstract concepts? This in turn links with the work of Maxine Sheets Johnstone. Johnstone is adamant regarding the primacy of movement, and this brings us back to the biological and evolutionary fact that the brain originated as the organ that coordinates movement.

In an important paper of 2003, Hanna and Thompson reconfigure the mind-body problem as the *body-body problem* and discuss the matter in Husserlian terms of subjective consciousness. They address questions of subjectivity from an enactivist perspective, usefully reframing the mind-body problem as the mind-body-body problem, deploying terms from the German: *leib* and *korper*, the body as subject and the body as object.[7] Their deployment of the German terms *leib* and *korper* is reminiscent of Gallagher's body schema and body image (2005).

Hanna and Thompson's discussion cleverly destabilizes the mind-body problem; subjectivity is understood in bodily terms, so questions normally associated with mind become questions associated with the body. Thus, Nagel's "something it is like" is explained in terms of the living body or *korper*. Subjectivity is an aspect of the living and lived body. From an enactivist point of view, having subjectivity, having what seems to be a mental state, is really the product of being a living, lived body. This approach seems to sidestep Chalmers's hard problem.

In "Between Brains, Bodies and Things: *Tectonoetic* Awareness and the Extended Self," Lambros Malafouris considers the evolution of self in cognitive archeology and pointedly rejects projection of the humanist self onto past eras. He asks, "When and how did humans develop the experience that they own their bodies (sense of ownership) and started to feel as the authors of their actions?" (Malafouris 2008, 1993). He emphasizes, "The constant danger is that our modernist epistemic predisposition towards questions of the 'what is this 'I' that I know?' type may blind us to any alternative possibilities" (1994). Malafouris is here sounding warnings about the dangers of metaphors and uninterrogated axiomatic assumptions, similar to my own remarks in these pages. In a similar spirit to his argument about representation, Malafouris's reflexive proposal is that the notion of self is a historical assemblage or incremental accretion: "Even the footprints from the muddy floor of the Niaux cave in France or the impressive handprints and hand stencils from the Chauvet cave do not suffice, *in themselves*, to give us access to the presence of selfhood or the absence of it—they can certainly be seen as indexes of an acting human body but provide no direct evidence of a self-aware acting body" (1993; emphasis in original).

Citing Snell (1960) and Bernard (1993), Malafouris notes that even as late as Homer, it can be argued that selfhood *as we know it* did not exist (an idea first proposed by Julian Jaynes): "The Homeric epics show an absence of awareness of a unitary self and thus that no Homeric person can be seen to act as a fully integrated and autonomous agent" (Malafouris 2008, 1994). While this discussion is based on a literary form and not on evidence of daily life of the period, it allows Malafouris to make a radically relativist objection of the kind he makes in "Before and Beyond Representation: Towards an Enactive Conception of the Paleolithic Image" (2007; see chapter 15): If we cannot confirm the presence of a humanist self in Homer, it is presumptuous to assume it for the Paleolithic.[8]

### Humanist Selfhood and Language

The construction of the individual is fundamental to Enlightenment humanism; a sharply defined self/other distinction is implicit. Like any such fundamental assumption, this frames and defines what can be said and thought and what cannot. As such assumptions broadly take hold, cultures become naturalized to them, inculcating these ideas in young minds as unquestionable, incorporating them into conceptual schemas, linguistic structures, and religious and cosmological systems.

The construction of the Western modern "individual" has been a focal concern in political and social theory (most obviously in the work of Foucault and in the work of Foucauldian, feminist, and postcolonialist thinkers). Likewise, the related binary constructions of subject-object and self-world have been queried in posthumanist thought. In cognitive science, neuroscience, and philosophy of mind, Enlightenment assumptions regarding mind, self, and consciousness are increasingly seen as pseudo-problems, no more substantial than the emperor's new clothes.

## Art Practice and Consciousness

How sensory experiences—or more correctly, enacted sensorimotor experiences—*become conscious* is a question at the forefront of neuroscience and philosophy of mind. As most human neurological process is nonconscious, much of the process of experience of art must be nonconscious in this sense. Much of the decision-making involved in music, arts, and design practices is nonconscious in the hands (as it were) of the adept practitioner (Dreyfus 1996).

Aesthetic decision-making involves exquisitely subtle and complex flows of association and affect, visceral response and imagery, back and forth across the conscious/nonconscious rubicon. In the same way that it is difficult if not impossible to reverse-engineer a process evolved by genetic programming or grown in a neural network, so it may not be possible to consciously reverse-engineer aesthetic decisions. If cognition is embodied and most of cognition is nonconscious, then art-theoretic attempts to discuss art in terms of the conscious processes are invalid for the same reason introspection is invalid—which brings us back to Polanyi.

## Conclusion

In this chapter, I have tried to bring together various examples that highlight features in the landscape of a posthumanist, postcognitivist notion of selfhood. Combining these trends leads to the possibility of conceiving of a notion of self that surpasses the mind-body dualism, softens the self-world binary, and accommodates dynamical, processual, performative, and relational conceptions. Orienting ourselves to such a shift is an intellectual challenge, because it destabilizes ideas deeply inculcated in culture and embedded in language. Our late modern Western conception of individuality and selfhood is historically and culturally specific. Self and mind are cultural constructs.

Infancy and childhood are neurologically explosive periods when the brain grows around and into culture and language as a vine grows around a tree; so too do culture and language constrain and shape that growth, in the way that a vine trapped by an overhanging eave grows along under it. The cultural specificity of particular notions of self and mind form and exist as adapted biology. We are all relieved about neural plasticity, but unmaking and remaking—or a second parallel making—is still real work, as any adult student of a foreign language knows. Nothing is more difficult than denaturalization.

If we accept that the Cartesian independence of the mental realm is fallacious and assume that mind is dependent upon situated and distributed mechanisms—language, culture, artifacts—then only an enactive and extended mind makes any sense. However, if, in the pursuit of a more distributed, enactive self, we create a separation between self and mind, then this only generates another binary where we seek to diffuse them. If we are to embrace a diffuse mind, then the self must go with it. We must find modes of diffusion that diffuse both self and mind.

# III Toward an Aesthetics of Behavior

# 17 Postcognitivism and the Aesthetics of Behavior

Thought is not an inner realm behind practical skill, but itself an intrinsic and worldly aspect of real-time engagement with the tricky material and social world.
—John Sutton, "Material Agency, Skills and History" (2008, 50)

Cognition and materiality intersect, mutually catalyzing and constituting each other.
—Lambros Malafouris, "The Cognitive Basis of Material Engagement" (2004, 53)

## Our Story So Far

In the first section of this book, I reviewed significant episodes in scientific and technical history pertinent to questions of cognition. I provided a general introduction to conventional cognitive science and computational discourses and surveyed nondualist positions in a variety of disciplines. In the process, I drew attention to Enlightenment dualisms—chief among them the mind-body dualism—that have structured our discourse about being, became deeply rooted in diverse disciplines, and shaped our paradigmatic technology. In part II, I provided an overview of postcognitivist views of mind and cognition, discussing several of the new paradigms, discussing the work of several leading thinkers, and identifying parallel work in differing fields. This inquiry teased out commonalities and tensions between these paradigms as well as clarifying differences between postcognitive positions and conventional cognitive science.

Having reviewed the historical and philosophical formation of ideas around cognitivism and AI, the limitations of that paradigm, and the emergence (and reemergence) of alternate approaches, I will now position these notions within a larger historical and cultural field, particularly with respect to our central project: the application of such notions to traditions of cultural practice. The purpose of part III is to draw together the diverse threads of previous chapters toward a focus on arts and cultural practices.

My goal is to provide a basis for a new kind of theoretical discourse for arts and cultural practices, one grounded in postcognitivist ideas—countering the denigration of embodiment, materiality, and process inherent in cognitivist theories of intelligence and cognition that valorize abstraction. I do this not in order to create yet another fashion in theorizing, but to provide a discursive armature that is found to be helpfully explanatory for the inquiring practitioner and teacher, as well as philosophers and theorists. I do it also to map important new ground for interdisciplinary research between the cognitive sciences and the arts.

I hope it will be evident by now that I attempt not to pursue this goal with disciplinary hubris or in a way that effects a kind of disciplinary imperialism: The last thing I want to do is explain art (away) via science. On the contrary, I deploy this theory to denaturalize cognitivist preconceptions in order to consider these practices in their fullness, embracing embodied and material aspects of cultural intelligence. This theorizing arises out of practice and has as its most important application a resource for practitioners to enhance practice.

The relationship with computing explored in this book is complex. I pay special attention to problematics of cultural practices with computational tools, because (biographically) the concerns of this book arose out of practice—specifically, three decades of developing interactive cultural artifacts utilizing computing and robotic techniques. It was precisely in the attempt to develop a new modality of art practice—in which real-time computing facilitated the design of behaving cultural artifacts—that philosophical and theoretical schisms between computing and cultural practices became increasingly obvious. The fact that postcognitivist discourses were arising as a result of the failure of GOFAI— at the same time that computing was becoming a commodity—makes that period a "perfect storm." Part III discusses cultural practices generally, and makes regular reference to cultural practices with computational tools. This is done with constant recognition of the ways that values reified in the tools have the potential to undermine the integrity of the practices themselves.

## The Big Picture

An odd historical confluence has led us to this place. Enlightenment humanism and its structuring dualisms promulgated a false separation between the arts and the sciences, as between the passions and reason. As Antonio Damasio argued in *Descartes' Error* (1994), the same dualism stained cognitivism. For at least a century, dualist discourses held sway in the arts as much as in the sciences. However, arts practices differ from Enlightenment conceptions of intelligence and knowledge in the following way: They do not (usually, primarily) *mine the world for symbols*. The historical emergence of the academy itself is a product of these Enlightenment values in the sense that it valorizes the distillation of abstract symbolic representations from the world. Art operates directly upon embodied, sensorial materiality, making physical, material, and temporal permutations that are invested with intelligence *unintelligible* from a cognitivist perspective. These intelligences have been relegated to the realm of skill, the *merely artisanal* because they engage materiality directly and do not traffic primarily in the symbolic notations that have become the lingua franca of our age.

Enlightenment humanism instigated (in the West) a drive to automate reason, which led to the development of the digital computer. In one of the grand ironies of modern history, the cognitivist worldview began collapsing—like the Roman Empire, from the center—at the same time that commercial and popular digital computing rooted in that worldview surged ahead on the frontiers. Dualist and reductivist ideas that underpin and are reified in the structural organization of the computer—and its functionalities— have been carried out across culture like Trojan horses, promulgating cognitivist notions like "thinking is reasoning" and "the brain is a computer." As computation continues to insinuate itself into all corners of our lives, we must remind ourselves that there is nothing *natural* about computation facilitated by logic gates made of transistors, which automate the logical calculus conceived by George Boole. Automated reasoning and embodied and materially-engaged human cultural practices are *not* inherently compatible.

Maxine Sheets-Johnstone, in the introduction to her pioneering anthology, *Giving the Body Its Due*, says: "Cartesianism itself is a cultural disease" (1992, 15). As discussed in chapter 9, postcognitivism arose to address perceived failures in the cognitivist worldview. The field promises to redress the excesses of cognitivism and, in the process, permit a reassessment of art and cultural practices in a way that *gives the body its due*. This is precisely what was absent from cognitivism, but arts and cultural practices are inherently embodied and temporally extended.

The focus of this part of the book is to explore arts practices as cognitive processes involving intelligences of real-time structural coupling, sensorimotor feedback loops, and engagement with materiality, artifacts, embodied procedures, and know-how. The new paradigms of cognition—which I call postcognitivist—offer new ways to understand cultural practices, which involve the construction of artifacts, organized spaces, and systems of gestures and movements as *cognitive* in a rich and sophisticated way. Within the corpus of postcognitivist literature and research, there are several directions of research immediately relevant to these goals. In part II, I dwelt on several aspects I believe have immediate relevance and usefulness: the phenomenological theorization of learning by Hubert Dreyfus, which leverages Maurice Merleau-Ponty's muscular gestalts; David Kirsh's notion of epistemic action; and Edwin Hutchins's meticulous teasing out of thinking with things. George Lakoff—with Mark Johnson and with Vittorio Gallese—has argued that symbolic thinking can arise from embodied experience, and in the process it destabilizes the presumed autonomy of conscious thought. These authors do not, however, elaborate on the possibility that embodied metaphors can play a role in a circuit of material-meaning generation in which language plays a minimal part. The integration and extension of such ideas is part of the foundation of a new theory of (embodied) practice.

Andrew Pickering's distinction between the performative idiom and the representational idiom has, in my opinion, resounding relevance to the formation of a theory of materially engaged practice and a study of performing artifacts. To argue that cognition is supported, enhanced, or enabled by artifacts and procedures developed by people over years, generations, or centuries is to argue that cognition is cultural and that human culture functions to propagate postevolutionary cognitive capabilities.

The cognitive anthropology of Tim Ingold (2011) and the cognitive archeology of Lambros Malafouris (2007) are particularly relevant here. The link to archeology, which might appear tenuous, is particularly rich, as the business of archeology is the interpretation of material residues of cultures. Thus, archeology has a particularly refined way of understanding what artifacts say about cultures. Merlin Donald's concept of the exogram (1991)—the notion that cultural artifacts are transgenerational information storage systems—and the developmental psychology of Michael Tomasello (1999)—who proposes that an evolved capacity of imitation is the biological armature that supports complex human culture—provide further background for a new interdisciplinary approach to art making as distributed cognition. Such work can inform the way we think about art making and the utilization of sophisticated tools and systems.[1] It also modulates the tired old nature/nurture debates in ways that can bring us to new and productive positions regarding the relation of culture and biology, positions that challenge dogmatic biological and genetic determinism and social constructivism.

By leveraging these new perspectives, several complementary goals may be achieved. First (and in my mind most importantly), cultural practices can be examined in a new frame that revalorizes intelligent human bodily activity. Second, such reconsideration of embodied intelligences might encourage a timely broadening of the notion of intelligence in our culture. Third, such a consideration can bring to cognitive science rich contexts for further research.[2] Postcognitivist discourses are thus of particular relevance to the theorizing of the production and consumption of cultural practices.

## Computationally Articulated Cultural Artifacts

Postcognitivist discourses provide a new kind of leverage and resource for an aesthetic theory pertinent to cultural practices involving behaving artifacts—practices I call *real-time computational art* (RTCA) or *computationally articulated cultural artifacts* (CACA)—in which artifact and experiencer are dynamically engaged in ongoing feedback loops. These terms are designed to draw the crucial distinction between digital tools that create static or temporally linear output—pictures and movies, for instance—and forms in which *behavior* is a central part of the artwork in its presented form and in which the designing of behavior is a central part of the practice. This extends aesthetics into unknown territory that I refer to as the *aesthetics of behavior.* This territory presents a challenge to aesthetics because ongoing chains of interaction utterly destabilize the subject-object dual of conventional aesthetics (see chapter 21).

The perspectives of the new neuroscience, cognitive science, and philosophies of mind—which focus on situatedness, embodiment, and ongoing sensorimotoric action—inform analyses of cultural or aesthetic experience and, in particular, cultural or aesthetic experience of computationally articulated cultural artifacts (CACA), in new and rich ways. We have, in computational technologies, tools with which it is possible to simulate quasi-biological behavior or even cognition itself. Making work in this mode constitutes nothing less than *a radical ontological shift* in the nature of arts practices. No longer confined to engaging in frozen representations of visual experiences or gestures or emotions, artists can build systems that inhere the capacity to enact an intention while remaining sensitive to varying environmental changes.

Art is no longer a recording, a recollection, or a representation of something doing something: It *is* something doing something. This is Pickering's representational/performative dualism in its clearest form. Such a reconfiguration of the artwork into something that takes action and the artist into someone who designs behavior is an ontological shift far greater than that inherent in the emergence of the celebrated technocultural forms of the late nineteenth and early twentieth centuries: photography and cinema.

As cinema became *the* art form of the twentieth century, so computation-ally based interactive practices will (have already) become *the* art medium of the twenty-first. Computer games—so recently poo-pooed as trivial and adolescent—are increasingly rich in theoretical, literary, and political dimen-sions.[3] Yet the aesthetic, design, and philosophical questions arising from this unprecedented historical event have hardly begun to be addressed.

## Cognition and Practice

The idea of intelligence—construed as action in the world, as bodily prac-tice, as *skill*—is incompatible with an internalist cognitivism. The cognitiv-ist conception of cognition has little explanatory power regarding cultural intelligences, which engage embodiment, materiality, artifacts, and the spatial and sensorial world directly. They remain largely irreducible to text or numbers and are thus inexplicable in those terms. The effect of this is to exclude those intelligences from accounts of intelligence as conventionally understood. This leaves us in the anomalous position of recognizing cul-tural practices as pinnacles of human achievement while at the same time excluding them from the criteria by which we evaluate intellectual worth.

Doubtless, some will rankle at my calling embodied engagement with materiality, artifacts, and the spatial and sensorial world *intelligence*. I do this intentionally, because it focuses my discursive intervention on the material/immaterial dualism—the false hierarchy of intelligence and skill—lurking beneath our conventional notions of intelligence. Consider the common example of the potter at a wheel: The clay is pushed and pulled and stretched in tight, dynamic muscular play; there is a feel, and when the feel is right the material can be encouraged to do remarkable, unnatural things, like stand up on a thin wall. As Michael Mateas put it, "You push against the materials and the materials push back" (pers. comm.). Sometimes, if you don't have the feel or the *flow*, it all collapses in a soggy pile. Few would argue that such practice is without intelligence, even though some may want to reinstate a skill/intelligence dualism. Once we accept the intelligence in practice, then the task of drawing the line at which mind ends and body begins, or body ends and world begins, is, as John Haugeland (1998) argued, impossible and unnecessary.

The collapse of the cognitivist worldview has ushered in a range of new approaches to cognition: the embodied and dynamical approach of enac-tivism, as well as architecturally, artifactually, and socially contextualized approaches of situated and distributed cognition. These variously attend to embodied, material, and social dimensions of cognition, and they should be specifically applied to embodied, material, and social dimensions of arts and cultural practices.

Reconsideration of practice in this way both counteracts the lacunae of cognitivism, which have hog-tied theories of practice, and provides much-needed leverage for the task of designing behavior in computational media practices by permitting the cognitive significance of proprioception, gesture, and movement.

## The Intelligences of the Arts

To the extent that a cognitivist conception of intelligence is explicitly involved with internal manipulation and external representation of symbolic tokens, some art and cultural practices appear to contain little intelligence. Attempts to discuss art practices in cognitivist terms engage in discursive contortionism or they are simply incapable of recognizing the aspects of intelligent action in art practices not packaged as arrangements of symbolic tokens.

Art, design, and cultural practices involve direct engagement with the world, with materiality. The production of and reasoning upon symbolic representations may be marginal to some practices, though most cultural phenomena are simultaneously symbolic *and* material. From distributed and enactive cognition theory, as from art practice, we know thinking and working are iterative, holistic, and structurally coupled. The idea that things in the world are executed on the basis of fully formed internal representations—as if the brain pressed Print—is nonsense.

By engaging postcognitive discourses, we can speak about the intelligences of arts practices in ways that do not throw the baby out with the bathwater by reducing embodied, embedded cultural practices to disembodied symbolic tokens. These new paradigms allow us to build a dynamical, situated, and relational language to talk about the intelligences of the arts, which is not so simplistically dualist and thus can articulate the somewhat inchoate rhetoric in the arts of "process."

Art practices are intelligent engagement with materials and artifacts, with tools, with bodies, with spaces. To describe the intelligences of the arts in terms of representationalist conceptions of cognition, as was done for much of the twentieth century, is to willfully ignore the cognitive holism of such practices. It is to suggest that manual activities, perceptual activities, and sensorimotor activities in general are stupid and that around the neck somewhere is some line at which intelligence stops and dumb physical action takes over. This, as Haugeland has argued, is implausible. By Ockham's razor, it is simpler to imagine that intelligence suffuses the body, in the way autopoietic biology asserts that cognition is immanent in the organism. The subtle, ongoing interaction with the world evidenced in many kinds of artistic practice is done better justice by deploying postcognitivist explanations.

The reliance upon the idea of internal symbol manipulation in a cognitivist rendering of cognition makes an explicit separation between reason and embodiment and constrains the notion of intelligence to symbolic reasoning. It excludes the "irrational" intelligences of the arts—that is, the generation and judgment of affect. It ignores the cognitive unconscious, presuming that intelligence is action of the conscious mind in which unconscious events play no part. It separates perception, cognition, and action per the input-processing-output paradigm. As noted, such arbitrary and indefensible (reductive) divisions render the intelligences of arts practices obscure. Arts practices are, we may say, intelligent in ways orthogonal to, or incommensurable with, cognitivism.

## Cognitivism and Art History

The assumption that knowledge inheres in (and only in) symbols has led twentieth-century art theory on a wild goose chase of rhetorical contortions that seek to justify material practice in symbolic terms. While we are surrounded by examples of high (artisanal) intelligence, we have minimal discursive tools to validate this intelligence. In the arts, activities in which symbolic processes were difficult to identify were relegated to the condition of *craft*, creating a hierarchy within the arts between artisanal art and "smart" art. Conceptual art, by rejecting materiality and craft, abandoned the traditional footing of arts practices in materiality. The downside of this move was that in claiming the nonmateriality of art "information," conceptual art was forced, by its own rhetoric, to deny the validity of material and embodied dimensions of practices in order to maintain or pretend to status among the disciplines of the intellect in the academic world—a project similar to the notion of *passing* in racialized cultures. The notion that there is no intelligence in material engagement is as stark a Cartesianism as one could imagine and, as such, prevents us from speaking intelligently about the intelligences of material engagement.

## Cognition and the Arts: New Research Agendas

I see five separate and equally important research agendas arising from the foregoing:

1. *Arts and cognitive science research.* Art practices involve manipulation of "raw" materials, physical artifacts, and bodily gestures within constructed spaces and constructed times in order to build persuasive multimodal sensorial and sensorimotoric interactions and experiences. The arts provide the postcognitivist community with domains of study that move beyond the instrumental and "toy" contexts conventionally studied, and draw cognitive science into a deeper consideration of cognitive dimensions of cultural practices involving richly developed embodied traditions often hundreds of years old. To date, cognitive scientists interested in embodied practices have chosen to deal with tractable and quantifiable examples—games like Scrabble and Tetris—for good scientific reasons of experimental control and quantifiable results. An intrepid few (including Hutchins, Kirsh, and Sutton) have pursued more anthropological approaches, even venturing into the territories of the arts. Evelyn Tribble has made pioneering efforts by applying distributed cognition to Shakespeare studies. Such "in the wild" contexts are far more complex and inherently less controllable than the lab experiment, and demand an interdisciplinary approach—similar to that of neuroethology—that brings anthropology and cognitive science together around the role of artifacts and materiality in cognition.[4]

2. *New ways to understand the intelligences of arts practices.* Such interaction between arts and cognitive science communities will have the complementary effect of catalyzing new discourses within the arts while affording them new credibility—as cognitive practices—in the academy.

3. *Correcting the skewing influence of cognitivism on the theorization of arts practices.* There is a historical irony in the fact that postcognitivist studies, which emerged as a reaction to the functionalist internalism of the AI/cognitive science complex, might now be deployed to interrogate the infiltration of the cognitivist paradigm into the arts. Such a reevaluation and revaluing of traditional practices will elucidate the largely unstudied effect of computational discourses on traditional arts practices.[5] The emphasis on disembodied information, the packaging of skills as menu options, and the general separation of thinking from making, has undermined traditional practices and traditional styles of pedagogy that emphasized learning through artisanal practice—the Bauhaus being a paradigmatic example.

4. *Deployment of postcognitivist understandings to advance computational art and design practices involving behavior and human interaction.* As noted, the corpus of conventional aesthetic theory is nigh bankrupt in elucidating temporally contingent action, especially in hybrid behaving systems of machines and people. Such a study is crucial to the ontologically new condition of the arts that has emerged as part of the digital revolution, in which the artist is reconfigured as a designer of behavior.

5. *Correcting the excesses of the humanist academy.* Finally, in the broadest way, postcognitivist thought provides means to rethink the relationship between intelligence and embodiment. That is, to critique sedimented assumptions in the philosophical legacy of Enlightenment humanism.

---

**The Revalorization of Experiential Knowledge (an Autobiographical Aside)**

The deep motivation for this work arises from an abiding awareness that something is missing from (academic/literary) accounts of artistic process, that academic descriptions do not capture something inherent in the creative process, something ineffable that seems to sidestep locution. I say this with some trepidation, knowing that adherents of (over-)intellectualized poststructuralist approaches may scoff at sentiments that appear to echo mid-twentieth-century anti-intellectualism or the romanticism of which it was a late incarnation. Suffice it to say that I do not subscribe to such ideas, at least not in an unreconstructed way.

The intelligences involved in the making of and in the reception of arts and cultural practices are not primarily or centrally a matter of manipulation of symbols in an abstract reasoning space but a matter of direct engagement with the world, with things in the world, with spaces, procedures, and social orders, with direct sensorial engagement. I *know* this as a result of reflection upon forty years of active practice, and observation and critique of the practices of others. The practice of art is (to me), first and foremost, the complex and subtle modeling of multimodal sensorial experience in order to optimally stimulate a rich (and not necessarily differentiated) visceral, emotional, and intellectual experience. Art does not seek to bypass the senses as scholarly textual communication does. In this sense, the "direct neural jack" is anathema to art.

Because the motivation for this work arises out of practice, I am in no need of persuasion about the validity of paradigms of material agency and situated action. My professional experience and formation are rather different from that of many of my academic/scholarly peers. As an art student, I had the enormous luxury of having free rein to imagine, design, and build eccentric structures and machines. While most of my present colleagues were poring over books and taking exams, I was gathering skills in diverse traditions of making, from blacksmithing to precision machining, honing my sensitivities to the changing ductilities of red-hot iron, feeling in my arm and back the consequences of a glancing blow, attuning my ear to the ringing of the anvil. I have a lifetime of experience manipulating matter with tools in both gross and subtle ways and in developing strategies to do so. I know the stubbornness of material agency in a way that is etched into my flesh. Like anyone, my muscles and sensorimotor routines have formed in a subtle negotiation between desire and matter that Andy Pickering would call a "dance of agency" (1995). I have a foot in both worlds. I speak from (and for) embodied experience, and I seek to translate those realities into the representational idiom and the academic milieu—a realm in which they are, to a greater or lesser degree, incomprehensible.

Interdisciplinarity is thoroughly native to the arts in our era. In arts practices, unlike most other pursuits, a practitioner has the unquestioned right to meld wildly heterogeneous elements: political and social content, philosophical and theoretical approaches, stylistic borrowings, and often bizarre material choices—plumbing fittings (Marcel Duchamp), sawn animal carcasses (Damian Hirst), vaseline (Matthew Barney).[6] Every aspect of an artwork "speaks." The artist must negotiate every shape and material choice and surface texture and the cultural meanings associated with all of these and the way they interact. One negotiates the corrosion resistance of an aluminum tube with the need to defuse readings of high tech so as not to imply an extropian agenda while emulating animal behavior. The process of realization—from hazy ideas through incremental materialization in drawings, models, and prototypes—demands constant attentiveness to the lessons to be drawn from these material instantiations.

In our culture, artworks are expected to be accessible to everyone—all ages and ethnicities and educational backgrounds. This is a rigorous expectation not made of physicists or philosophers. With such a diverse audience, an artist cannot be assured that every individual will hear the same thing. A Socratic, as opposed to didactic, method is implied.

These are some of the ways in which arts practices are *strange* in the context of the academy. By the same token, it is why this book may seem a little strange to some academics. I am a practitioner, and the questions in this book have arisen out of practice. I'm interested in providing a body of theory that helps practitioners understand better the cognitive dimensions of what they do and how their work is understood.

## Conclusion

We are not minds that happen to possess bodies to perform their material work. Rather, *we are bodies that happen to have minds*. We are bodies in motion that happen to be able to abstract certain aspects of their experience in a sensation we call consciousness, which gives us the impression that we are something more than, something other than, bodies. This is the remarkable illusion we call mind. When that illusion is given not only identity but a superior identity, embodiment is devalorized and the inherent value of embodied practices is denigrated. In the following chapters, I marshal ideas from recent cognitive science and evidence from contemporary neuroscience motivated by the following general proposition: *Embodied experience affirms the wholeness of our embodied being and challenges the internalized, internalist rhetoric of Cartesian dualism.*

The attempt to explain art practices in a dualist or internalist way necessarily must elide the performative dimensions of practice and material engagement. Our paradoxical challenge, then, is to find a way to speak about practice that does not reduce practice to theory. My goal is to attempt to build a framework for an aesthetic theory that takes as its starting point a nondualist and enactivist conception of being, in which meaning is immanent in gesture—that is, in which a gesture and its meaning are seen not in terms of the latter driving the former nor of the latter arising from the former. Beyond a call for the recognition of the fundamentally embodied and distributed nature of cognition, the upwelling of arguments (in fields as diverse as performance studies, science studies, cognitive science, and neurosciences) that contest axiomatic binaries of subject-object or world-representation suggests a fundamental and large-scale change in ontology, a paradigm shift: a shift of great relevance to the arts.

In the following chapters, I argue why this area of research is of particular relevance to the production and consumption of cultural practices with behaving artifacts. I lay out the rudiments of an aesthetic theory based in this work, which offers explanatory power regarding such work and offers practitioners real purchase on the problems confronted in performing such work.

The following chapters plumb issues arising around the status of the arts in Western culture in the wake of the digital revolution. (That is not to say they exclusively concern emerging digital practices.) Making culture with behaving technologies implies the development of an *aesthetics of behavior*. While the field of HCI has focused on pragmatics, the need for a general aesthetic project is seldom acknowledged.

More generally, the incursion of computing into culture has thrown into relief the retrograde cognitivism inherent in computing culture, and this in turn has revealed the hegemony of cognitivism over the last century—a discursive hegemony that has rendered embodied, materially engaged practices inexplicable or inarticulable *as cognitive action*. Application of postcognitivist perspectives promises the rehabilitation and explication of the *intelligences of the arts*.

Embodied in the machine there is an idea of what the mind is and how it works. The idea is there because scientists who purport to understand cognition and intelligence put it there. No other teaching tool has ever brought intellectual baggage of so consequential a kind to it.
—Theodore Roszak, *The Cult of Information* (1986, 217)

A computer . . . does not simply have an instrumental use in a given site of practice; the computer is frequently about that site in its very design. In this sense and others, computing has been constituted as a kind of imperialism; it aims to reinvent virtually every other site of practice in its own image.
—Philip Agre, "Toward a Critical Technical Practice" (1997b, 131)

In the flow of ideas in this book, the digital computer has been a constant presence—as the product of a certain kind of thinking and as a technological commodity that has supported and promulgated attitudes about intelligence, thinking, and things cognitive generally. In the 1970s and 1980s, the digital computer migrated beyond the research labs and military installations into wider society—into corporate offices, schools, and homes—and is now into the pocket and the purse. This incursion of digital computing into society brought with it the influence of computational procedures and rhetorics. Outside their original context, values inherent, historically, in computer culture are anathema to various kinds of cultural practices, just as those practices are alien to traditional computer culture. This chapter draws together ideas raised in previous chapters relevant to questions of computing and cultural practices.

Over the past twenty-five years, computer use in arts and cultural practices has introduced new techniques and terms of reference into these fields. In the process, methods and metaphors from computationalist discourses have become incorporated into art practices. This has usually happened under a sense of pressure to be contemporary. Consistent with the argument of this book, the implicit reinforcement of mind-body dualism and a linear, sequential, and mechanistic conception of sensing and action merit deeper critical consideration. Such ideas destabilize contexts shaped by native (and naïve) cognitive holism.

Long ago, J. D. Bolter coined the term "paradigmatic technology" to describe the role computing plays in the formation of metaphors that structure our way of thinking about the world (Bolter 1984). This remains a useful concept as it reminds us that the influence of the technology is not just in what it does or allows us to do, but in how it influences the way we think. The insinuation of computationalist values into arts cultures and their effect on traditions of practice are matters overdue for interrogation. Digital technologies have catalyzed a flurry of new creative practices, and simultaneously, the underlying philosophical commitments reified in the technology have destabilized and undermined values central to traditional practices in the arts. To put a different spin on it, the influx of the underlying value system of computer science into the arts has, as a side effect, drawn attention to a lack of theoretical elucidation regarding core values and methods in the arts. The tension I wish to dwell upon here lies between the valorization of logico-mathematical abstraction in the mathematized and academicized technical sciences and the relatively poorly ennunciated commitment to embodied and performative practices in the arts. As digital technologies become ubiquitous across the arts, and mathematized and academicized practices frame discourses in the digital or media arts, a devalorization of embodied practice has inevitably resulted.

## Computing and Cultural Practices

There is nothing *natural* about computing. Its highly specific procedures have a particular intellectual provenance. At root, it is the automation of a particular kind of Victorian logic undergirded by a Victorian conception of the desirability of the dominion of rationality over all aspects of life.

As any new technology moves into any part of culture, accommodations are made in both directions. We develop new cultural practices that incorporate technologies, and the technologies change due to cultural applications. I doubt that in their wildest dreams Turing or von Neumann could have imagined that dating and gossip (social media) would become major functions of the computer and digital communications network.

To use an old-fashioned term, *computerization* has changed everything—in as broad-sweeping a way as electrification did a century before (Marvin 1990). As with industrialization, electrification, the telegraph, the railway, and other world-changing technologies of the nineteenth century, computerization has caused old practices to quietly disappear (or become nostalgically celebrated—viz steampunk). New practices, or ways of proceeding in the world, emerge and fit into a new life-fabric. We adapt to and exploit messaging technologies from the postal service to the telegraph and the telegram to email, SMS, Twitter, and Instagram. The term *search engine* has a steampunk ring to it, though we never notice. Neologisms like *blogosphere* testify to the new ways we do things. The development of a vast (vastly profitable and vastly resource-hungry) data-industrial complex has utterly changed the way we communicate and acquire knowledge, from the most trivial tasks—like finding somewhere to have lunch—to the most portentous events—such as wars, revolutions, plagues, and disasters.

In a technological revolution, everything changes in some way.[1] As part of this process, computers—and with/through them, a computational mindset—have infiltrated the world of the arts. This is a historical fact, irreversible, with many positive qualities. As computing has impacted cultural practices, traditional arts practices have been altered and a plethora of new practices have emerged, practices that will mature into fully fledged cultural forms. Gaming, for example, is in the process of doing just that. For two decades, it has been obvious (to some) that networked computer gaming will be to the twenty-first century what cinema was to the twentieth. It will have its Eisensteins, its Fellinis, its Fassbinders, its new kinds of cultural practices and venues.

As we consider the retrospective questions discussed above, we must also ask: In what ways does adopting or incorporating these machines into previously established practices change or disrupt them? This is, of course, a huge question with a huge answer: *in every way, wherever they appear.* So much so that we must accept that painting today is not painting of fifty years ago—even if done with precomputational technologies—and we cannot see a painting painted fifty years ago as it was seen then. Even if computer use does not occur in the actual process of making the work, the presence of digitally treated and computer-mediated imagery has become ubiquitous, and this has changed our frames of reference for all images. Our relationship with images occurs substantially via digital media, and that context—from its pixilation to its sophisticated pattern-recognition algorithms—shapes the way we see and think about images. The same is true, of course, for sound and music and for text and the written word. Until a decade or so ago, we could maintain a vaguely principled distinction between a photograph and a digital image (or between a book and digital file)—but no more, because there is nothing else.

The availability of real-time computational tools over the last twenty-five years has led to the growth of new modes of design and aesthetic production. Most digital media tools and work environments were modeled on predigital modalities, and as a result the new tools skeuomorphically preserve procedures and metaphors of predigital technologies, ossifying or fossilizing aspects of these practices in new contexts. Examples are everywhere: in computer-aided design (CAD), digital painting, digital photography, digital animation, digital audio, and digital video. This is a somewhat trivial historical observation, but Philip Agre has elucidated a key aspect of these transformations. Per the quotation at the beginning of this chapter, he points out that software environments are *representations*: not just digital emulations of predigital tools, but reifications of procedures and cultural contexts. Paul Edwards concurs: "Most tools produce effects on a wider world of which they are only a part, *the computer contains its own worlds in miniature*" (1990, 108–109; emphasis in original). Software tools prescribe the way work will be performed, the sequentiality or workflow, the criteria by which products will be sorted and arranged. They are, after all, usually the work of people who are primarily technicians responsible for building a machine rather than anthropologists, and their understanding of such systems is often incomplete or superficial.

## Interrogating Ubicomp

The much-acclaimed vision of Weiser and Brown of a "calm technology" (1995)—now referred to as *ubiquitous computing* or *ubicomp*—was conceived as a reaction to cumbersome and clunky first-generation technologies, and proposes that computing should "disappear into the woodwork." Twenty-five years later, embedded microcontrollers, high-speed networks, wireless communication, and the "Internet of Things" are well in place. Sophisticated, miniaturized, and inexpensive sensors/input devices and output devices are embedded everywhere. Yet to disappear computing into the woodwork is not the same as making it go away; indeed, a covert presence may be more problematic than an overt one.

The ubicomp program assumes the ubiquitous presence of computing is an incontrovertible good. The assumption seems to be that the way computing technologies and procedures reconfigure our lives is unquestionably good. Querying this would seem incorrigibly Luddite. I think we should ask this question, on all levels, from the way Boolean algebra prescribes a particular reasoning to the way our smartphones reconfigure our sociality.

In what more or less subtle or insidious ways does the bending of human activities to the conditions of ubicomp stain or perturb the richness of those practices? I am thinking of skilled embodied practices in particular, practices that have developed organically over generations, subtly adapted to the complex richness of human formation, in which artifacts have coevolved in ways that adapt and optimize subtleties of human sensorimotoric capabilities, which may never have been nor have had to be made explicit. It is this implicit, or *tacit*, embodied knowledge that confounds software designers most of all, due to the omnipresence of a cognitivist mindset.

N. Katherine Hayles observes, "The point is not only that abstracting information from a material base is an imaginary act but also, and more fundamentally, that conceiving of information as a thing separate from the medium instantiating it is a prior imaginary act that constructs a holistic phenomenon as an information/matter duality" (1999, 13). How does the imposition of dualist assumptions and other philosophical baggage of the engineering worldview impact user experience? Is the rationalization of social relations on Facebook a result of underlying computational structures or assumptions within the discipline of computer science, or is it a digital implementation of bookkeeping methods that themselves influenced the structure of software? Every aspect and layer of the technology—from VLSI circuit design to the development of programming languages, operating systems, and interfaces to the topology of the Internet—originated in highly specific historical and cultural contexts (as discussed in chapter 4). Computing *is* ubiquitous and underpins everything from healthcare to advertising to military action. Should we then accept it as a neutral foundation? No. We should review the aspirations of ubicomp and its current implementations, and the "always online, everywhere" catchphrases of pervasive computing, and consider the desirability of the technological trajectory they imply—especially for the arts.

## Digital Commodities and Software Appliances

Rapid advances in technology permit interfacial cosmetic niceties undreamable twenty years ago. The technofetishism of higher resolutions and faster bit rates serves the needs of an industry that depends on obsolescence (as perceived or by planned material breakdown) to remain profitable, often deploying superficial novelty to obscure a void of significant technological advancement. Higher resolution and bigger screens do not improve the same old junk TV content.

So-called new media art practices have, of course, naturalized to lower latency, higher bandwidth, higher resolution, and the development of mobile and handheld devices to the extent that content of a decade ago *looks* primitive even if it is conceptually sophisticated. Improved means to an unimproved end, as Henry David Thoreau might say. While the technologies have advanced, the design and aesthetics of interaction have not advanced so much. The same old paradigms that involve pointing, icons and keypads, and an individualistic deskwork modality—developed during the Cold War for military man-machine interaction—still dominate contemporary applications. Artists and others harness themselves to such interface paradigms with minimal reflection, and allow the technology and its underlying ideology to shape what they do, perpetuating these ideas in the works they make. The Trojan horses not only flourish but reproduce!

## Computing in General

To attempt to speak of "computing in general" is almost preposterous today. So many aspects of culture integrate computing technology. To the contemporary user of the iPhone, of Facebook, and so on, the fundamental mechanics of digital computing are invisible and irrelevant. It was easier, in a way, to have this conversation twenty years ago, when the tools were less cosmetically enhanced and the logic of the digital was more obvious. Now, it is buried under layers of user-friendly interfaces and integrated into systems of communication, wireless and wired networks, and all the complex organization of the so-called cloud (which is in fact a vast and very material system of energy-consuming and globe-warming data factories). Only specialists "close to the machine" have a sense of the computational mechanics subsumed under these layers.

Over the last thirty years of hardware and software development, long-term users and practitioners have been constantly destabilized by a conceptual shifting of scale or frames of reference, in which fundamental verities around which practices were structured have sunk into the mud of invisibility and inaccessibility and systems have increased in complexity. There is a fractal logic to this: Machine code undergirds assembly language, which undergirds C, which undergirds Java, which undergirds custom scripting languages and authoring environments. The verities of assembly are still valid, but engagement with them is pointlessly micrographic, subsumed as they are by layers of higher-level automated procedures. The layering of user interfaces and protocols follows a similar trend. The scenario is not unlike the increase in complexity from single-celled to multicellular animals to vertebrates or from quantum to atomic to macromolecular phenomena.

This situation raises curious theoretical problems. To what extent does the deep logic of the machine—the logic gates and shuffling of bits in and out of registers—have any relevance to the surface effects? Or, to cast the question in a historical light, to what extent does the fact that the computer's basic operational procedures—developed in the context of the "paranoid rationality" (Levidow 1994) of Cold War military intelligence—influence the form and behavior of seemingly benign applications such as Facebook? Simply put, is our machine-mediated sociality disciplined by a military-industrial logic? If the answer is yes, what can we do about it? Or is that history subsumed and rendered irrelevant in a process of technological accretion like the rain of diatom skeletons laying down calciferous sediments on the sea floor? How could we tell?

## A Cognitive Turn

As we exploit computers as tools and resources for artistic/creative/cultural ends or purposes, it behooves us to pursue an exploration of these deeper ramifications of values that underlie computational technologies and that insinuate themselves into daily life. This excursion begins with the recognition—with Agre—that the machine is more than a tool; it is a carrier of ideas that have been reified in the course of its development. That information is immaterial and that hardware and software are complementary—each of them possessing what the other lacks—is such an idea. The general Cartesianism of computer culture separates information from matter and mind from body. The heritage of digital computing as the continuation of a specific tradition of mathematical logic has generated the unusual idea that intelligence consists of logical operations on symbols embedded in a linear process of perception-reasoning-action. We must not lose sight of how ludicrous it is that these ideas inform the generally accepted model for human cognition, the result of a spurious discourse linking brain and computer.

This scenario is of particular import for the arts, as arts practices present a very different conception of cognition, one that is externalist—dynamically engaged with matter, with tools, with spaces, and with other people—and seldom conforms to production line process. This is why new approaches to embodiment and context are so important for an understanding of arts practices and for reinstating cultural practices as intelligent (and by the same token, for leveling the cognitive playing field and the intellectual hierarchy of the academy). The intelligences of the arts *are* intelligences.

This has been obscured by the dominance of a mechanistic conception of intelligence. Recognition of this necessitates a reconceptualization of what we mean by *intelligence*.

## Embodied Practices

As species face extinction at an alarming rate, we commonly hear a principled (if instrumental) argument for protecting biodiversity. A similar argument can be made for cognitive diversity. There is some awareness, internationally, of what might be lost as indigenous knowledges disappear. A similar question should be asked regarding art practices that predate computing before such practices are lost entirely.

It sounds distinctly old-fashioned to claim that "traditional" cultural practices have certain qualities and that many of these are incompatible with computing technologies and antithetical to the values of computer culture. Cultural practices are usually highly embodied and engage materiality in a direct and ongoing way. Cultural practices are often social: group activities that occur at a specific place and time, for good cultural reasons. The qualities of cultural practices seldom involve values such as productivity or efficiency. Cultural practices seldom endorse a mind-body dualism or a linear conception of cognition as proceeding via perception, reasoning, and action, in that order.

Twenty-five years ago, the pressure to adopt computing was palpable among artists and art educators, as among other groups. Given the substantial mismatch between a technology for numerical operations and a practice of (say) image manipulation, it should come as no surprise that early software tools were woefully misbegotten and misconceived, having been designed by software engineers with a naïve or anachronistic conception of art practice. In particular, the embodied, materially engaged dimension was lost, due precisely to the denigration of the value of such factors in computing culture. As computationalist perspectives have become normative, the arts community has been incapable of coherently elaborating the importance of the embodied dimension of practices, at least in terms that make sense to those who shape the technology. Postcognitivist discourses can belatedly facilitate this enunciation.

## Generality

One of the most unfortunate slippages in computer science discourse is around the concept of *generality* (likewise modularity and reductivism). Tur-

ing's mathematical formulation of the *general-purpose machine* has undeniable value in its context. The story of how this highly specialized and
technical concept was leveraged to suggest that a logic machine with a
small screen and a typewriter keyboard had optimal application to diverse
human practices has yet to be adequately told. This transition bears similarity to the habit in the AI community, noted by Agre, of attaching a highly
specific technical procedure to a loose cultural metaphor. Certainly, the idea
of a general-purpose computational commodity would have been be very
attractive to those interested in mass production and economies of scale.

The word *bureau*, as in *bureaucrat*, has a mixed etymology. In British parlance, it can refer to a slant-top writing desk, but more generally, it refers
to an office of regulation and policy. In any case, it conjures an image of
an environment of rules and procedures, with people sitting at desks doing
deskish things—writing, calculating, and making and checking records. This
is the environment that the desktop computer and its original software were
designed to fit into. Whenever we pull out our tablets or phones, we are reaching down into a mire of skeuomorphs. Of all the things I do in my life, only
some of them suit sitting at a desk in front of a glowing surface, poking at buttons. The transition to miniaturized portable versions—with buttons smaller
than my fingers and text so small I have to put my reading glasses on—may be
less of a radical change than it seems. That is not to say that all kinds of wonderful capabilities have not ensued from the integration of Internet, Wi-Fi, and
GPS, but these are not the qualities we would expect to be celebrated.

Robotics often offers counterexamples to the general trend of computing, precisely because robots are situated machines and therefore occupy
particular and specific real-world contexts. There is no such thing as a
general-purpose robot, and no roboticist would pretend there was. Contrary
to computer science dogma, *there is a tool for every job and a job for every tool.*
Artists and artisans understand this. The extent to which a tool is general-
purpose is precisely the extent to which it is horrible. A good tool makes an
artisan more effective, but in the hands of a dolt, a good tool is ruined. A
good tool isn't a good tool unless it's wrapped in a complementary context
of skilled practice. Such tight linking of artifact and practice is as consistent
with postcognitive ideas as it is incompatible with cognitivism.

The corollary with computer use is clear. Computers are now digital appliances, mass-marketed consumer commodities. As such, much of the rhetoric
of computer marketing emphasizes the "no experience necessary" rhetoric
of plug 'n' play. Menu options, commodified templates, and formats create
a false sense of achievement and contribute to the deskilling of the user. In
such contexts, the application of digital technologies almost always has the

effect of thinning out the experience in question, due to an emphasis on generality and with problem solving on the symbolic plane—and the ensuing elision of situated, embodied action.

This syndrome maps onto imperatives of computer engineering such as modularity, reductivism, standardization, generality, optimality, efficiency—that is, instrumentality generally. These criteria are valid in their home territory: I want my laptop battery to have maximum life; I want my file to be compatible; I do not want anyone taking aesthetic liberties with the shape of an airplane wing. But the validity of these criteria wanes as they are applied in territories further from home. Optimization of *King Lear*, Beethoven's Fifth, Dylan's "Sad-Eyed Lady of the Lowlands," or a Buddhist chant by elimination of redundancy is an inherently ludicrous proposition.

It is not meaningful to inquire about the informational content of a painting. It would be of no value to estimate the number of assessments, decisions, and negotiations per hour or square centimeter. If there is knowledge, it is somehow in the active, dynamical relation between the painter and the work or the viewer and the work. The concept of knowledge as an abstractable, extractable thing is part of the representational idiom. Computing, which deals exclusively in symbols (representations), is the technology of the *representational idiom* par excellence. It may thus be fundamentally incompatible with cultural practices that engage the *performative idiom* (Pickering).

## Instrumentality and Interaction

The forgoing conversation leads us to the recognition that the way we think about the aesthetics of (digital) interaction has been formed, in large part, by conceptions of instrumental interaction imported from HCI and the design of (commercial and business) hardware and software interfaces for *instrumental interaction*. However, the utilization of computers for interactive cultural practices does not necessarily imply a simplistic logic of instrumental interaction. In an interactive artwork, I do not take an action to achieve a preconceived goal; rather, I act to create possibilities, to expose myself to possibilities. An emerging aesthetics of interaction has been done no favors by the rhetorical steamroller of commercial digital tools. Indeed, one can make a sound historical argument that the predigital interactive art of the Art and Technology movement was more diverse and creative than computer-based interactive art (see chapter 19).

The idea that instrumental modes of interaction found in commercial software are a priori adequate for interactive art seems, ironically, stronger today than it was twenty years ago. A shift to deictic, dynamical, and enactive theorization will permit the development of new approaches. As any thinking practitioner discovers, much of the work in digital art practice involves kludgy workarounds for the structures and expectations built into commercial products—or building tools de novo.

## Gaps in Scholarship

Many of the details discussed in this chapter are well known to scholars and researchers in media studies, software studies, humanistic informatics, and related fields of sociology and anthropology. They turn up in the popular press often enough. But it is surprisingly difficult, even now, to find a paper that discusses ethical and philosophical implications of deep computational processes or assesses the impact of computing on cultural practices. This is a broad field with major repercussions, but these issues have tended to fall through the gaps between institutionalized disciplines. The reason, I think, is twofold. First, such concerns, like the technology, are new, and as the academy came to embrace them, it did so in a haphazard way, established disciplines attaching themselves to aspects that seemed familiar or tractable. Second, the economic boom of the "information sector" encouraged technophilia, on university campuses as elsewhere. As a result, activities celebrating the technology attracted and attract funding, while others fend for themselves.

Media theory, institutionally speaking, often emerged as an outgrowth of film theory and cinema studies, disciplines that had previously adapted to and embraced television. Cinema studies–inflected media theory's view of the digital focused on the aspects of digital culture that corresponded with the phenomena of film and television—narrative, characters, plots, camera angles, editing techniques, soundtracks. Thus, it largely missed the critical ways in which digital, and especially interactive forms were different.

Art history simply chose to ignore the whole phenomenon. A generation later it has finally begun to engage the digital, probably because the new generation of art historians were "born-digital." Sadly, the discipline thus missed the field's formative and perhaps most important historical period. Media theory and art history, as parts of the humanities, traditionally take a dim view of technics, both as subject matter and as a practice for scholars. The standard formation of humanists robs scholars of the necessary background to take anything but a superficial view of the digital phenomenon. Some art history programs expose their students to studio classes in painting, even sculpture. Some media studies programs offer filmmaking. Students in literary criticism are expected to be able to write. Even today, it is a rarity to find a media studies or media art history program that requires courses in programming, computer engineering, or even web design. This chasm between theory and practice, I think, has only negative consequences for theory. As a consequence of this situation, fanciful, poorly researched, third-hand, and plainly false information is not uncommon on paper—and more so online.

Computer science, as a technical discipline, has staunchly avoided tangling with messy cultural aspects, sidestepping them, even in such blatantly cultural areas as gaming! HCI programs often struggle with the interdisciplinarity implicit in the pursuit and tend toward the instrumentality of the larger discipline.

Scholars in education and art education who showed any interest in the new technology seemed to follow the received wisdom that computerization of the classroom is a general good and rarely grappled with deeper questions of pedagogy and practice. As such they concerned themselves with short-term pragmatic questions of getting computers into the classroom and integrating curricula around the new order. The current fashion is the 3-D printing craze. The idea that teaching students to output plastic tchotchkes teaches them anything about 3-D visualization or design practice generally is, I believe, sadly misguided.

Cultural anthropologists and sociologists necessarily take a somewhat more grounded approach, but have tended to look at mass practices, such as gaming and social media or "work and home" types of interaction (characterized by acronyms like CSCW, or computer-supported collaborative work). HCI scholars focus on commercial applications (for reasons of funding as well as social impact). Cognitive scientists traditionally avoid art like the plague, since it falls outside the Enlightenment conception of the rational. AI practitioners have recognized that creativity is a hallmark of human intelligence but have been hampered by the same theoretical strictures as cognitive scientists.

Neuroaesthetics, a field that has experienced a recent boost due to the revolution in neuroimaging technologies, is hobbled by a scientistic internalism. As the reader might expect, in this author's view seeking the aesthetics neuron or the creativity neuron perpetuates a Cartesianism that has been made obsolete by its lack of explanatory power. More generally, we must observe great caution regarding the *cognitive turn* in the humanities, as it is susceptible to a timid philosophical backsliding in the face of triumphal science.

Artists and other interdisciplinary practitioners themselves commonly had the best grasp on the nature of the new media, emerging practices, and theoretical implications. Contemporary students of the computer culture revolution are advised to seek out such writings, which remain the most authoritative reports of the period.

The academy moves like a speeding glacier, and a generation or two into the "information revolution," contexts that successfully integrate the many dimensions of the phenomenon and provide students with an adequate curriculum remain scarce. The broad interdisciplinarity demanded of the new technocultural formation is impeded by the disciplinary divisions of the academy. (These matters are discussed in greater depth in the epilogue.)

Internationally, some new institutions, schools, and programs have recognized the complexity of the field and have forged radically interdisciplinary formations that more adequately provide the necessary theoretical, historical, technical, and creative resources. But sadly, in recent economic downturns many of these programs have felt the bean counter's knife.

### Conclusion—or Rather, a Commencement

Looking beyond digital arts practices, the demise of cognitivism and the emergence of postcognitive conceptions offer the possibility of the development of a rhetoric of (art and cultural) practices that revalorizes materially engaged practice. Such rhetoric corrects the excesses of internalist discourses—which, as discussed, generally made a large detour around embodied experiential, performative practices because that discourse found them incomprehensible as cognition. The following chapter discusses in more detail the ramifications of ideas discussed here on the period of the emergence of the media arts.

This chapter traces some striking parallelisms in the development of the arts and of computational discourses through the second half of the twentieth century, beginning with the explosions of new forms in the 1960s, and culminating in the emergence of digital arts practices in the 1990s. The 1960s were a veritable cultural pre-Cambrian explosion that generated a diversity of forms and approaches. The conventional notion of the plastic arts as defined by material genres—painting, printmaking, and sculpture—was dismantled, giving rise to a primeval soup of new forms that burst the boundaries of the normal institutions: happenings, mail art, body art, performance, installation, site-specific environmental art, and conceptual art. Neologisms were coined to describe new methods, including the term "intermedia" created by Fluxus artist Dick Higgins. This concept may be seen as a precursor of interdisciplinarity generally, which is formalized in academic settings a decade or two later (in the United States, the Association for Interdisciplinary Studies was founded in 1979). These new practices were often referred to collectively as *post-object art*, a term redolent of Burnham's *unobject* and identified as a trend in Lucy Lippard's *Six Years: Dematerialization of the Art Object from 1966 to 1972* (1973). The term *post-object* was applied because a key quality of the new practices seemed to be a rejection of conventional genres that celebrated traditions of artisanship in art objects, or objets d'art. This was seen as retrogressive. In the new practices, temporal and artisanal process was celebrated, as opposed to the resulting material product: the entire period is permeated with a nascent process ontology. Artworks could be transient, impermanent; indeed, the artwork would never need to physically exist or be made.

To speak of a general class of post-object art obscures a deeper and profound binary arising in the 1960s and early 1970s. The period was characterized by new practices that were embodied, lived, materially instantiated, and socially and environmentally situated. Body art, site-specific art, and related practices were materially and geopolitically situated as political and activist practices engaged with community issues. Conceptual art, which often eschewed materiality entirely, also flourished. Much conceptual art sought a dematerialized and neo-Platonic condition of pure immaterial information—artwork finally rid of the inconveniences of its *res extensa*. The notion that the "essence" of the artwork was an immaterial idea and that the artwork could exist as written specification and need never be materialized was proclaimed with varying inflection by numerous "conceptual" artists, such as Sol LeWitt, Lawrence Weiner, Douglas Huebler, and Robert Barry. For example, Barry's *Inert Gas Series* (1969) consisted of photographic "evidence" of the release of a quantity of an invisible gas—that is, no evidence of an invisible event that may or may not have happened.

## Art and Cybernetics

Cybernetics was influential in art circles, as indicated by Nam June Paik's "Cybernated Art" manifesto (1966)—as garbled as it is brief. (No matter, it was not just artists who made garbled statements about cybernetics and computing in the 1960s.) Internationally, a slew of exhibitions in the late 1960s celebrated cybernetics, including *Cybernetic Serendipity* (1968), *Software* (1970), and *Information* (1970) and the Experiments in Art and Technology (EAT) events. In the EAT projects, Bell Labs engineer Billy Kluver paired leading artists such as Robert Rauschenberg, Jasper Johns, and David Tudor with Bell Labs engineers to make collaborative works. Kluver was a colleague of Claude Shannon and part of the larger East Coast cybernetics circle. In Europe, in the 1950s and 1960s, Gordon Pask, Nicholas Schoffer, Jean Tinguely, and others made cybernetically informed, behaving, electronic and electromechanical artworks.

Art historian and theorist Jack Burnham was a major vector by which cybernetic and systems-theoretic ideas influenced the art world. He dedicated a full third of his 1968 tome *Beyond Modern Sculpture: The Effects of Science and Technology on the Sculpture of this Century* (1968a) to cybernetics. Later that year, his influential essay in *Artforum*, "Systems Esthetics" (1968b), began by claiming, "A polarity is presently developing between the finite, unique work of high art, i.e., painting or sculpture, and conceptions that can loosely be termed 'unobjects,' these being either environments or artifacts which resist prevailing critical analysis" (31). He went on to assert, "The specific function of modern didactic art has been to show that art does not reside in material entities, but *in relations between people and between people and the components of their environment*" (31; emphasis mine). Here is a clear enunciation of an art concerned with process and system, as well as a prescient relational sensibility. Passages in this essay, such as the following, sound like they would be more at home in a journal of cybernetically informed ethology or sociology: "Art, as an adaptive mechanism, is reinforcement of the ability to be aware of the disparity between behavioral pattern and the demands consequent upon the interaction with the environment. Art is rehearsal for those real situations in which it is vital for our survival to endure cognitive tension, to refuse the comforts of validation by affective congruence when such validation is inappropriate because too vital interests are at stake" (Morse Peckham, quoted in Burnham 1968b, 31–32).

There are resonances of Ashby's law of requisite variety in this passage, but the idea that art plays a role of challenging preconceptions—and by way of this, prepares humans for survival in challenging circumstances—leads Burnham beyond cybernetic homeostatic orthodoxy to a more social, complex model in which artists play a socially relevant, disruptive role. This sentiment is reminiscent of McLuhan's famous remark, "I think of art, at its most significant, as a DEW line, a Distant Early Warning system that can always be relied on to tell the old culture what is beginning to happen to it" (1964); McLuhan's explicit use of this terminology is redolent of the Cold War zeitgeist. He was metaphorizing the line of radars across Canada's arctic that was the first line of sensors in the SAGE system (see chapter 4).

## System and Process

A concern with processes occurring in systems was a fundamental concept in systems theory, operations research, and cybernetics. This focus on systems was part of an ontological shift that, as mentioned earlier, rendered some cybernetics research quite "strange" according to the conventional scientific subject-object binary (see chapter 3). The destabilization of this subject /object duality is philosophically developed in Heinz von Forester's second-order cybernetics and finds echoes in the autopoietic biology of Humberto Maturana.

Similar concerns with process arise in the art world, in the explicitly named *process art*, in systems aesthetics, and in various forms across the breadth of 1960s avant-garde practices, from the happenings of Alan Kaprow to the event scores of George Brecht. Such concerns have resonances in the music, literature, and dance of the time, in the generative chance operations of artists like Brion Gysin, John Cage, and Merce Cunningham. While *Condensation Cube* (1965) and *Real-Time Social System* (1971)—two works by Hans Haacke—are wildly different from a media/genre point of view, they share a concern with *systems* as opposed to static appearances. As noted, the notion of *system* was central to cybernetics discourse (see chapter 3). This preoccupation was evident across diverse kinds of practices, from Robert Morris's *Box with the Sound of Its Own Making* (1961) to the walks of Richard Long to the early video installations of Bruce Nauman, such as *Video Surveillance Piece: Public Room, Private Room* (1969–1970). While philosophical grounding for these works may be found in the works of Alfred North Whitehead and Henri Bergson, no doubt the culturally ubiquitous discourse of cybernetics was immediately influential.

This focus on process cohabited with a neo-Platonic drive in some aspects of conceptualism and the linguistic turn in theory, both of which reaffirmed a representationalist drive to abstraction. A concern with process is strongly felt in the arts, because the material, temporal, and artisanal dimensions of practice can never be denied. Whether we talk of painting or dance, art practices are quintessentially embodied and performative, in Pickering's terms, and incompatible with the representational idiom.

## AI and Conceptual Art

As noted above, there is a dialectical tension between Cartesian Platonism and a drive to situated, materialized, and embodied holism within the diversity of 1960s art. Sometimes, confusingly, these contradictory drives are found in individual works, and often in the oeuvre of particular artists. Materiality and abstraction are not always in opposition, as was the case with minimal sculpture; Carl Andre's well-known tile works are a case in point. In 1967, Donald Judd proclaimed, "Everything sculpture has, my work doesn't." (On the contrary, Judd's work *is* sculpture, at least as we have come to understand it, in that his work and sculpture share the basic quality of materiality.) There is much more to say about the tensions between materiality and concept in art of the 1960s and 1970s.[1]

This materiality/abstraction dialectic of the 1960s in the arts was contemporary with a similar dialectic in the sciences of information. Indeed, we might see in the former a reflection of the latter. It was the moment of differentiation between cybernetics and the emerging digital computationalist ethos. The historical and theoretical association between, on the one hand, situated, materialized, and embodied works and cybernetics and, on the other, more dematerialized conceptual work and artificial intelligence is highly suggestive. Put plainly, the historical transition from the situatedness of cybernetic theory to the Platonism of digital computing and artificial intelligence is contemporaneous with and directly paralleled in the emergence of conceptual art.

According to some modernist narratives, conceptualism can be understood as a final gesture in the reductivism of twentieth-century avant-gardism, stripping away affect, technique, and materiality. However, conceptualism arose simultaneously with with the rise of the AI/cognitivist paradigm as the metaphysical epitome and theoretical grail of digital computing and the emerging discipline of computer science. It thus arose precisely when the notion of software as dematerialized information was formalized and the Cartesian dualism was reified in the software-hardware dualism. As we have seen, stories of giant brains and artificial intelligence titillated the general public. The obsession in conceptual art with dematerialized information makes sense in the context of the ubiquitous presence of digital computational rhetoric at the time.

While these parallels between the art world and the world of technology are clear, we must be vigilant to avoid readings that are historically inaccurate. It is instructive to review what the artists in Jack Burnham's exhibition *Software* meant by "software." We find that the notion of software is very hazy compared to our contemporary understanding of the commodified information object. Indeed, it is *in formation*, just as computers themselves were in formation.

## The Neo-Cartesian Zeitgeist

The rise of quantitative mathematical methods in the late nineteenth century and the demonstrable power of these techniques led to a widespread shift in scientific ontology, away from analogic and materially instantiated model building and toward mathematical "proof" based on data supplied by recording instruments. The first signs of this shift were seen in the mathematization of engineering in the late nineteenth century as electronics developed. These techniques were automated in analog computing and the trend accelerated in the 1960s with the rise of digital computation and automated algorithmic reasoning. Concurrently, we see the rise of semiotics and cognitivism in psychology, with similar trends in other areas of the social sciences and in the arts, all of which are preoccupied with abstract symbolic systems. Across sciences, humanities, and the arts, the second half of the twentieth century seems to have been under the sway of a neo-Cartesian zeitgeist. What can account for this resurrection (as it were) of neo-Cartesianism? One explanation is that it was driven by the infiltration of computing into increasingly diverse fields, the commodification of software and the acceptance of the notion of the dematerialized information commodity that went along with it. The emergence of consumer-grade computers carried the dualistic axioms of computer science into diverse aspects of culture previously insulated from direct contact with such conceptions.

Conceptual art is *cultural software*. It pursues a rhetorical commitment to the idea of disembodied information in parallel with the emergence of the information commodity. Conceptual artwork often consists of notations made in some abstract symbolic system that specify an output if and when a machine is set in motion. Sol LeWitt's famous statement that *"the idea* becomes the *machine* that makes the art"* (1967; emphasis mine) sounds very like the specification of a computational machine. Similarly, Lawrence Weiner asserted, "The piece need not be built" (1969),[2] which implies that the artwork is complete in its symbolic specification, *sans materiality*. Conceptual artworks are thus "art algorithms." This trend toward ephemeralization began in the visual arts before computers were readily available. Ezra Pound asserted, "Artists are the antennae of the race" (Pound and Fenollosa 1967). We can see conceptual art (or *information art*, as it was sometimes called) as a working out of the cultural, theoretical, and aesthetic implications of "pure information" and "information technology" without tangling with the hardware.

## The Digital Art Revolution: A Perfect Storm

In the late 1980s and early 1990s, the technologies of digital computing were developing and diversifying at a blinding rate. Groundbreaking new tools became obsolete while you were learning them. Life in the digital arts world of the 1990s was an addled scrambling through fog and dust over the wreckage and rubble of an ongoing collision, occasionally stumbling across a fortuitous mutation, some weird hybrid fused together by the force of the explosion. In the midst of this, some managed to make significant artworks. Some of these works are now recognized as historical markers in the development of digital arts. Sadly, most of these are lost because the hardware and operating systems they were built on are irredeemable.

Arts practitioners found themselves deterritorialized. The discursive impact of computing was as resounding as the technological impact. The computationalist incursion was inherently explicit, instrumental, pragmatic, and representational. In the face of this, the arts community could only mutely articulate its value system, inherently performative and tacit as it was. Indeed, the apprenticeship traditions of artisanal disciplines rendered their explication in an explicit textual mode unnecessary.

In the 1990s, computing technology advanced rapidly, became cheaper and easier to use, and reached out into new sociocultural realms, creating uses and requiring solutions undreamed of in earlier decades. To call the digital consumer appliance that emerged in the 1990s a computer is like calling a Prius a horseless carriage. Likewise, the digital appliance in your pocket is unrecognizable as a computer in the sense in which the word was understood in the 1990s. The kinds of functionalities that were central to computer research in the 1960s and 1970s are now so deeply buried under interfaces and applications and operating systems that any elaboration of them leaves users as flummoxed as an explanation of internal combustion does most automobile drivers.

## A Nod to History

Although marketing rhetoric encourages us to imagine that all things digital are without precedent, digital art is predicated on the revolution in practices of the 1960s. Movements like Fluxus and Art and Technology provided the theoretical and methodological basis. The tradition of technical experimentation typified by Pask, Schoffder, and Ihnatowicz was carried into video and multimedia by the Vasulkas, Dan Sandin, Nam Jun Paik, Myron Kreuger, and others, who created the identity and context for the *artist-technologist*. Higgins's Fluxus conception of *intermedia* describes the interdisciplinarity demanded of digital media artists (Higgins [1981] 1995). The explosion of electronic and digital media experimentation of the 1980s and 1990s, and the emergence of the *artist-programmer* simply could not have existed without this history.

As with so many aspects of what we now call digital culture, fundamental concepts of today's social media were prototyped in the art world. Kit Galloway and Sherrie Rabinowitz's extraordinary *Hole in Space* (1980) predates video call apps such as Skype by nearly half a century. Indeed, *interactivity* itself was an art world invention. Pioneers were at work in the early 1950s and even 1940s; consider Nicolas Schöffer's *CYSP 1* (1956) and the progenitor of all interactive art, Gordon Pask's *Musicolour* (1953). During the art and technology years of the 1960s, artists were making interactive and robotic artworks, such as Juan Downey's *Against Shadows* (1968), Pask's *The Colloquy of Mobiles* (1968), and Edward Ihnatowicz's interactive robotic sculpture *Senster* (1970).

Conceptualism, idea art, and information art laid the groundwork for software art, but the situated and embodied aspects of the 1960s revolution continue to challenge the underlying commitment in computing to the dissociability of matter and information, and this is evidenced in the disruptive quality of artist's interventions in virtual reality in the 1990s. The conflict between the commitment to the specificities of material instantiation in the arts and the yearning for abstract Platonic truths in computing underlies the turmoil of the first decades of digital art, when the materiality and sensorial immediacy of art was challenged by the valorization of dematerialization in computing. The concept of *virtuality* framed much first-generation digital art. In retrospect, much of this concern with dematerialization was in fact a concern with *rematerialization*—making computational phenomena experiential through innovative interface and system design.[3]

## Art and Artificial Life

As the computer, in the guise of the PC, began to make its presence felt beyond sci-fi and military-academic research contexts, the philosophical commitments of computationalism were falling apart. AI, informed by Putnam's functionalism and Newell and Simon's physical symbol system hypothesis, was brought to its knees in the later 1980s by the common sense problem, the frame problem, and the symbol-grounding problem; by Searle's Chinese room; by Dreyfus's phenomenological critique; and more generally by the giant holes shot in reductivism by chaos theory, complexity theory, dynamical systems theory, emergence, and self-organization (see chapters 7 and 8).

Artificial life (discussed in depth in chapter 8) was an attempt to reconfigure the landscape of computational thinking in light of the failures of computationalism and the implications of complexity and dynamical systems theory. This process included a reconsideration of cybernetic thinking, taking biological systems as models—evidenced in genetic algorithms, synthetic stigmergy, and biomimicry generally. The common sense problem was circumvented by building systems that were grounded in the real world and thus did not fall into computationalist solipsisms of mapping and planning. As noted by Rodney Brooks, "Elephants don't play chess."[4] Artificial life can be seen as paradigmatically dialectic—a resolution of cybernetics and AI in computational models of biological phenomena—or, as Chris Langton might put it, as *life* on a silicon, as opposed to a carbon, substrate.

Throughout the 1980s, the rise of real-time computing capabilities permitted the exploration of iterative processes that came to resemble or simulate biological and environmental phenomena. Paradigmatically, fractal geometry deployed iterative computational capabilities. Complexity theory, chaos theory, and dynamical systems theory applied iterative computation to previously intractable problems of turbulence in aerodynamics and other diverse areas (e.g., in J. A. Scott Kelso's work). These computational capabilities flowed over into computer graphics. Craig Reynolds was a pioneer in "procedural modeling," simulating the behaviors of flocks and schools by modeling ongoing temporal dynamics (2007). The utilization of iterative computing to model biology was not limited to the movement of individuals or particles, deployed to simulate the evolutionary process in genetic algorithms (Holland 1975).

The process ontology inherent in autopoietic biology resurfaces in the enactive cognition theory of Francisco Varela, Evan Thompson, and Eleanor Rosch (1991), which affirms not only the tight integration of an agent with its environment but also the ongoing sensorimotor feedback called *structural coupling*, which might also be thought of as *temporal* coupling. Around the same time, Rodney Brooks developed an antirepresentationalist theory of embodied and situated robotics, famously saying that "the world is its own best model." John Horton Conway's Game of Life (1970) was a mathematical game that became an icon of artificial life. It generated surprisingly complex emergent behaviors from simple iterative mathematical rules. The game was prototyped on paper and only later computerized. The dynamics of the game echo themes of self-organizing systems in the cybernetic period.

By the end of the 1980s, the groundwork had been laid for computationally simulated biological research, which became a main thread in the heterogeneous field of artificial life. The more extreme positions in this movement held that *in silico* systems that demonstrated lifelike properties were not just simulations but were in fact alive. Artificial life was defined by a spokesman for the field, Christopher Langton, as follows:

The study of man-made systems that exhibit behaviors characteristic of natural living systems. It complements the traditional biological sciences concerned with the analysis of living organisms by attempting to synthesize lifelike behaviors within computers and other artificial media. By extending the empirical foundation upon which biology is based beyond the carbon-chain life that has evolved on Earth, *Artificial Life can contribute to theoretical biology by locating life-as-we-know-it within the larger picture of life-as-it-could-be.* (1989, 1; emphasis mine)

In Langton's terms, artificial life, while rejecting key aspects of the AI paradigm, preserved functionalism. This position was not universally endorsed in the field.

In the early 1990s, amid the furor created by the explosion of consumer and prosumer digital computing tools, digital multimedia, the digitization of sound and imagery, and the turbocharged rhetoric of the computer revolution, digital media artists were scrambling (both technically and theoretically) to understand the rapidly changing landscape of computers and computing. Meanwhile, in artificial life, a new approach to deploying computing technologies as generative process was emerging. The approach was concerned with processes, systems, dynamics, and generative procedures rather than with databases (glorified filing systems), "multimedia," and an instrumental notion of interactivity. As such, the spirit of artificial life was sympathetic to ontologies of art practices, even though the technological medium, in its dematerialized abstraction, presented challenges to conventional modalities of practice.

It is no wonder, then, that a small community of technologically inclined artists viewed artificial life with intense interest (see examples in chapter 8). The ideas of artificial life offered an intriguing alternate set of approaches for computational novelty and creativity. Such approaches, not nearly as insistent on a Cartesian hierarchy of mind over matter, were more sympathetic to the kinds of embodied intelligences native to art practices. The possibility of crafting a behaving aesthetic artifact—which manifested behavior and process—as a simulated organism in a virtual world or as a physical artifact (robot) in the physical world was very attractive. Artificial life art explored the aesthetic potential of computational simulations of the living and of lifelike computational behaviors in generative, performative, and processual ways. It was, and it remains, an art genre that extends Cezanne's dictum that art is "harmony parallel to nature," from visual mimesis or static depiction to realms of behavioral mimesis.

## After the Storm

Ironically, at the same time that the computer industry was becoming a major global economic engine, paradigms on which the industry was (intellectually) based were imploding. Cognitivism (also called computationalism), the theoretical underpinning of AI, was in crisis (see chapter 6). Cognitivism assumes that intelligence consists (exclusively) of the logical, mathematical manipulation of symbols in an abstract reasoning space, without easily accommodating the possibility of intelligence occurring in the process of ongoing embodied and environmentally engaged doing. That is, cognitivism tacitly or explicitly assumes that all intelligence is performed upon mental representations (see chapter 5). Although the functionalist, representationalist, cognitivist, computationalist approaches seemed to deliver intelligence-as-reasoning, they failed in situated and embodied contexts.

For many, the cognitivist paradigm lingers on in a kind of uninterrogated afterglow, but its authority as a useful general theory of cognition is finished. Now that the dust has settled, we are in a position to reflect on the intelligences of the arts in the aftermath of the computationalist paradigm. Consider the intelligences of the chef, the welder, the sailboat skipper, the equestrian, the surfer, the potter, the musician, the painter, the dancer—activities that we take to be, in various ways, pinnacles of human achievement: These are inexplicable in cognitivist terms. The assumption of mental representationalism reinforces the authority of extrapolated, symbolically encoded physical documents (equations, texts, scores, and programs) but provides minimal explanatory power regarding action in the world. Michael Polanyi's dictum that "we can know more than we can tell" (1966, 4) points in the direction of other sorts of knowledge, and we might extend this dictum to assert that we can tell more than we can encapsulate in alphanumeric codifications. Many kinds of arts and cultural practices, and especially improvisatory practices, inhabit these realms of tacit knowledge. This difference is key to the ontological gap between such practices and academic cultures of (instrumental) text and number. The new postcognitivist paradigms provide not only a way for media art (and HCI) to be liberated from the strictures of a view of human cognition imposed by the ideology associated with the technology, and to apply ideas about cognition that are more explanatory, but also directions for better design.

Part III of this book is a reevaluation and revalidation of arts practices through the lens of postcognitivist conceptions of cognition and intelligence. In this chapter, I focus on the construction of a new aesthetico-theoretical corpus applicable to and explanatory of cultural practices in the computational milieu. It seeks to reorient the terms in which the making of and experiencing of art—and more specifically, behaving art—is understood. By "behaving art" I mean the creation of artifacts involving sensors and real-time computing, which respond to changes in their environments.

The emergence of the desktop computer and the Internet had momentous impact on cultural practices and on the social fabric in general. While there has been much celebration of the enabling aspects of these technologies, less attention has been paid to the deeper theoretical questions concerning the ontological drift of practices under the influence of these technologies and the rhetoric surrounding them. Through the 1990s, as computing came to have a presence in diverse contexts in the arts, an intense but seldom enunciated theoretical crisis emerged—most clearly experienced at the interface between computing (in the box) and the world of sensing bodies, the realm of *interaction.* In designing interaction, traditions of crafting sensorial experience (the arts) collided with traditions of symbolic abstraction (mathematics and computing) like an unstoppable force hitting an immovable object. The quiet violence of this collision is easy to understand if we see it as the coming together of the opposing poles that structured the modern Enlightenment worldview: reason and "passion." Seen from this perspective, *the need for new and relevant aesthetic theory is glaringly obvious.*

### New Aesthetic Territory

While *interactive multimedia* (to use almost forgotten terminology) is now at least a quarter-century old, an aesthetics of behaving technologies seems remarkably ill-developed. Conventionalized actions, complete with templates, style guides, and tutorials, have become customary. Specific modalities became reified in authoring systems of now well-established genres, such as web design, video editing, interactive animation, screen-based games, and the ubiquitous PowerPoint. A point Philip Agre made with respect to AI has parallels here—such practices are preemptively commodified into technical niches, in which reflexive *critical technical practice* seems a distraction from the exigencies of production. Yet as a formal inquiry, aesthetically fundamental questions about design criteria for behaving media are seldom explored. Indeed, the very neologism *behaving media* is paradoxical. Traditionally, *media* are passive substrates upon which action is taken. Electronic media (radio, TV, video) were active and ephemeral, but they did not have agency.

As a result of a confluence of technological and cultural trends, we are presented with a new cultural scenario: a behaving cultural artifact. This novel conformation requires of its audience ongoing quasi-social behavior. This condition of cultural interaction is as unfamiliar in the fine arts as it is in computer science. Practitioners, theorists, and students need ways to understand what's going on. Fortuitously, the advent of these automated, temporalized, and spatialized cultural forms is roughly contemporaneous with a rethinking of perception, cognition, and action based in new paradigms of situated, embodied, and enactive cognition. These approaches owe a great deal to continental philosophy—specifically, phenomenology and hermeneutics. Such work provides insights around which to build a new aesthetics relevant to these new forms.[1]

**Toward an Aesthetics of Behavior**

The recognition that interaction is both embodied and performative provides a perspective from which to build relevant aesthetic theory. While interaction design and interface design are well established fields, we rarely see articulated the general notion of an *aesthetics of behavior*. Below, I outline a way of proceeding upon which research can occur and that can inform and support practitioners and contribute to the enhancement of practice and product.

1. Offer an introduction to an enactive/sensorimotor approach to cognition, including some relevant and persuasive examples (for those who might be unfamiliar with this area of research).
2. Argue why this area of research is particularly relevant to the production and consumption of cultural practices with behaving artifacts.

3. Lay out the rudiments of an aesthetic theory which offers both explanatory power and real purchase on the problems confronted by practitioners.[2]

## Performative Technologies, Behavior, and Interaction

Scholarship on interaction and interactivity occurs, generally, in two modes, which reflect the two cultures they arise from. A technocentric view focuses on interaction as the capacity of a machine system: *Users* exist peripherally as *human factors*, pressing buttons and getting rewards at designed-in appropriate moments. Humanists, on the other hand, have tended to focus on the experience of the user, less concerned with and less familiar with the mechanics of the technological system. As Matthew Kirshenbaum observed many years ago, "If the devil is in the details, media studies has been positively angelic."[3] Both perspectives yield valuable insights, yet the user-machine binary characterizes conversations on both sides. The subject-object dichotomy imposes an impediment to understanding the phenomena in question. As Karen Barad has argued, "Phenomena do not merely mark the epistemological inseparability of 'observer' and 'observed'; rather, *phenomena are the ontological inseparability of agentially intra-acting 'components.'* That is, phenomena are ontologically primitive relations—relations without preexisting relata" (2003, 815; emphasis in original).

The experiencing of art is, first and foremost, a multimodal sensory experience of an artifact or situation that has been crafted in order to conjure affect and associations in the mind of the experiencer. This reality has been confused by the rhetoric of computing and the *information revolution*. As discussed in chapter 5, Claude Shannon's formulation of quantified, immaterial information became axiomatic to computer science. Shannon's theory concerned the passing of unambiguous and error-free data between machines. Shannon himself was emphatic that semantic content was irrelevant to his theory. Yet in a prime example of the cultural slippage of technical ideas into cultural contexts, Shannon's theory has been taken to be relevant to contexts in which communication is never between identical machines and can never be error-free because human communication is a matter of interpretation.

In cultural theory, in aesthetics, the questions of what it is we experience and how we know we experience it—of *phenomenal consciousness*—are fundamental. While the term *experience* adequately defines a holistic, embodied perceptual event, it does nothing to erode the sensing/acting dualism. The way forward is a theoretical approach that addresses experience in terms of sensorimotor loops, integrating sensing and action, self and world in a dynamical, performative, and structurally coupled way. Unlike approaches invested in representational explanations, enactive approaches to the question of phenomenal consciousness emphasize an ongoing and contingent process of linked sensation and action immersed in a world—which Varela, Thompson, and Rosch (1991) called *structural coupling*.

## Real-Time Computation, Agency and Performativity

Scholars and pundits have opined about what they regard as the fundamental qualities or significant aspects of the digital revolution. Lev Manovich (2002) at one time championed the database; for Pierre Levy (1997), as for Roy Ascott and others (1999), it was telematics and the emergence of a global "consciousness" via the Internet. Janet Murray, Sherry Turkle, Brenda Laurel, and, more recently, Tom Boellstorff have focused on virtual theaters for identity play. Much has been made, in the literature of multiuser gaming and digital sociality, about the implications of fictitious identities and fictitious social spaces. The sensorimotoric orders that undergird such interaction are seldom addressed. They are the ground on which innovation in design and invention occur. The call and response of hypertext is a basic and well-established kind of ongoing temporal aesthetic process. More sophisticated kinds of interaction involve quasi-social or quasi-ecological engagement with a scenario of multiple agents, in virtual or real space. Spatiality, whether real, virtual, or augmented, is a quality of such experiences. This spatialization and temporalization demand ongoing and embodied (inter) action. To put it another way, interaction is inherently extended in both time and space.

In my opinion, the definitive characteristic that marks this technology as novel is the ability to construct artifacts that possess *behavior*. Rampant commercialism has created a weird situation in which we have somehow become blasé to the existence of synthetic entities with agency, before we even comprehend the social and cultural implications of the phenomenon and its aesthetic dimensions. Procedurality, genetic programming, emergence, and artificial life have been celebrated as effects of this new environment, but these are conditions of the more general condition of behavior modeling that has developed in the new technosocial environment. An *enactive aesthetics*—an aesthetics of performative, structurally coupled action—provides a nexus between the new cognitive science and studies of performativity. This kind of approach will bring back to center stage the elided dimensions of cultural cognition.

## Doing, Not Viewing: From Contemplation to Enaction

In the emergence of computationally facilitated cultural forms, designers, makers, and users are confronted with novel aesthetic conditions in the interaction between users and artifacts/systems that respond to changes in their environment. Such activities provide a radically different cognitive scenario from that of the passive viewer of a picture, a cinema or television screen, or a theatrical stage. This aesthetic scenario is novel with respect to conventional theory, and the reason is obvious: *conventional art objects do not talk back*. The term *object* is symptomatic. We now have cultural artifacts that are in some sense "subjects."

To be alive is to live in flow, immersed in temporally extended, structurally coupled, and dynamical experience. The psychology of visual perception and the aesthetics of the plastic arts have been preoccupied with static entities. An aesthetic approach to behaving technologies in these terms misses the bus. It wantonly ignores dynamical, enactive, and deictic aspects of cultural experience. It is hard to imagine how we can gain traction on dynamical art forms without considering the temporal process of active engagement. Engagement with real-time computational cultural artifacts and systems of artifacts involves—but goes beyond—the gamut of conventional aesthetic theory and presents conditions not encountered in such contexts. Self-evidently, if artworks of the past have not inhered in the capacity of behavior, there is very little in conventional aesthetics that has relevance to questions of agency, behavior, performativity, and relationality of an artifact.

If conventional aesthetic theory, arising in the context of the traditional plastic arts, has minimal purchase on the inherently dynamic, subjectivized temporalization and spatio-temporalization of real-time computational art and design practices, then we must necessarily look elsewhere for ideas to borrow and adapt. Happily, this dynamic, subjectivized temporalization is the stock-in-trade of (some aspects of) postcognitive cognitive science. The qualities identified and distinctions made in studies in cultural anthropology of dance or martial arts, for example, may also be useful to augment conventional aesthetic theory. We can deploy such perspectives to develop new ways of talking about arts practices—and real-time computational art in particular.

## Aesthetic Contemplation and Victorian Objectivism

The conception of passive contemplation is isomorphic with Western perspectival representation, with conventional theories of visual perception, and with the notion of scientific objectivity. All three ideas posit an authoritatively positioned observer who is external to events—anathema to an enactive sensibility. With respect to this complex of ideas, Heinz von Foerster's admonition that "objectivity is a subject's delusion . . . that observing can be done without him" (quoted in Poerksen 2004, 3) is apropos. Any theorization of enaction, aesthetic or not, must be wary of philosophical boobytraps entailed in a *partial* escape from Cartesian cognitivism, as explicated by Anthony Chemero (2009).

Conventional aesthetics deals with conventional art *objects*, and these objects, according to tradition, lie passively at a distance and are contrived to give up their meaning in the correct way (only) when viewed—passively—from such a distance. The theory, like the objects, is from another era. Such aesthetics is simply not adequate for a context in which a cultural artifact responds in real time to its environment, interpreting sensor and other input data and producing behaviors to which human users respond. (I am here discussing conventional aesthetics of the plastic arts. Since the 1960s, performative practices have been a key aspect of the arts, and theorization thereof, as discussed in chapter 19).

The concept of the distanced, contemplative "observer" is as fundamental to art (theory) as it is to science. In the same way that second-order cybernetics interrogated that assumption for science, interactivity forces the abandonment of such values in art. The distanced and passive contemplation of Victorian objectivism is built on dubious Enlightenment axioms. A conception of perception based on such ideas has long been under scrutiny, because the experimental procedures on which it was based made invisible the qualities of temporally and spatially immersed perception. Any aesthetic theory built on this foundation is thus also rendered dubious.

To craft a performative aesthetics adequate to real-time computational art practices, we should look to phenomenological perspectives on embodied experience and ongoing sensorimotoric flow and revisit the feedback loops of cybernetics. This seems necessary even to reassess the creation and reception of conventional static or passive cultural forms, but it is crucial for forms for which distanced passive contemplation is irrelevant. A new aesthetics appropriate to behaving systems must engage enactive cognition and embrace embodied and action-guided perception.

When a person interacts—a contingent, temporally, and structurally coupled process—that person engages in an iterative, enactive circuit of signification. It is impossible to adopt an objective view in such a situation, just as it is impossible when one is engaged in a game of tennis or football. It is logically incoherent to posit an observing self that exists outside the engagement with an interactive system. When a person is immersed—mentally if not physically—experience is subjective and deictic. An objectivist explanation is incoherent because part of the aesthetic phenomenon a person is observing is one's self in the process of interacting. As a consequence, any implicit or explicit appeal to an objectivist posture in theorizing interactivity is a mistake. There is no object external to me, observing the observer. Instead, there is an evolving scenario including me and the phenomena I am interacting with. In explicating this lacuna in aesthetic theory, I move between discussion of the artifact, the experience of the interactor, and the space of interaction (the interface)—conscious of the fact that none of these is itself an adequate perspective. What is needed is a relational process ontology that addresses the entire system. I use the term *system* here in the fullness of its cybernetic elaboration. Indeed, it was second-order cybernetics that articulated the duplicity of the objectivist stance.

We might propose that a person can *observe* behavior, but this would be to endorse a conventional notion of passive perception—the seeing couch potato. To adopt such a stance would be to willfully ignore enactive conceptions of perception from cybernetics to enactivism. If an observer maintains a "looking in from the outside" stance with respect to the object of interest, many conventional notions of aesthetics remain intact. However, as soon as the observer takes action in the scenario, she becomes a part of a system, and the possibility of (or pretense to) an objective stance is curtailed.

Conventional aesthetics provides minimal purchase on the spatially engaged and temporally extended dimensions of cultural experience. The shortcomings of conventional aesthetics in the context of computational arts are akin to the limitations of the SMPA paradigm in GOFAI as an explication of the ongoing dynamics of action in the world.

The fact that technical computing traditions and traditions of Western aesthetics share philosophical commitments contributes to the presumed intuitiveness of the idea that computation and the arts are unproblematically compatible. The *experience* of computational art often argues the opposite: Neither the philosophy of artificial intelligence nor that of conventional aesthetics is particularly useful in working on problems posed in the design, making, and experiencing of CACA. The mode of ongoing interactive aesthetic engagement contrasts radically with the conventional aesthetics of the contemplation of static artifacts, which (as discussed) inheres a rather Victorian conception of perception as an inflow of pictures from the world—a conception loaded with ideas of objectivity and mental representation. The cognitivist version of this idea adds that perception is a *peripheral* analog to digital transformation—turning the world into symbols.

Interactive cultural practices destabilize the self-world dualism. Any practice that involves the design and deployment of computationally based artifacts prescribes a mode of engagement that is spatially and temporally immersive and interactive. An adequate aesthetic theory must exceed discussion of forms that are passive and static, or temporal but narratively linear, to embrace contingent change. This demands a new aesthetics rooted in postcognitivist perspectives that refute the separation of sensing and action and the separation of self and world, acknowledge the centrality of sensorimotor feedback loops, and refute the *peripheral* nature of perception.

## The Spectactor

Indicative of the novelty of this realm of inquiry is the scarcity of adequate terminology for modalities, fields, artworks, and participants. New media (itself an unsatisfyingly empty neologism) artists have struggled with a name for their audience, often submitting to the inadequate but academically and commercially condoned term *user*. I like the term Augusto Boal (1985) devised to describe participants in his activist theatrical work: *spectactor*. While slightly awkward, it captures the condition of an interactor in an interactive artwork far better than the more commonly applied *user*, which suggests an instrumental relationship.

A spectactor is simultaneously an actor and a spectator; this person not only attends to whatever events are unfolding as a result of their actions but also simultaneously and reflexively attends to their own kinesthetic, proprioceptive, and perceptual experience. Interaction immerses the spectactor in a temporally extended, structurally coupled process. From the perspective of the spectactor, the aesthetic experience cannot be fully objectified— that is, conceived as external to the interactor. The aesthetic experience is neither internal, as in a drug experience, nor external, as in looking at the Sistine Chapel. The experience of embodied interaction is in part *kinesthetically introspective* and involves a sense of "I am doing this now." It is precisely such (performative) aspects of the aesthetics of embodied interaction that demand theoretical elaboration.

CACA is not mostly, not always, or sometimes not at all about depiction. It is not so much concerned with representation as it is with experience—and not the experience of the artist as related through the artifact. It is about providing a context in which a spectactor can reflect on the nature of their own experience.[4] The *subject matter* (if such a term is even applicable) is constituted by the spectactor's experience; the job of the artist is to create a catalytic context. This is art in the performative mode, as Andy Pickering would say.

Yet to speak simply of the artifact/organism system is to ignore the equally substantial shift in the conditions of making and of reception. Inasmuch as the work is immersed in and responsive to an environment, so the spectator is reconfigured as spectactor and the experience of the work is inseparable from the spectactor's situated and embodied experience of her own proprioceptive and peripersonal trajectory. In this process, the opposition of (observing) subject and (fixed) passive object that defines the conventional aesthetic calculus is demolished and replaced by a relational and performative mode.

The spectactor of real-time computational art is immersed in an ongoing spatiotemporal experience. Conventional aesthetics of the passively perceived, static, and distanced object (and attempts to automate this view of the relation between self and world) are of marginal value. The experience of real-time computational art demands a cognitive-aesthetic theory that explains situated and enactive experience.

## Embodied Interaction

Edwin Hutchins reflected that his original explications of distributed cognition were "strangely disembodied" (see chapter 14). Explications of screen-based and immersive modalities of interaction often make the same error. All interaction is to some extent embodied. Some interactive artwork has dwelt, reflexively, upon embodied interaction as its subject matter as well. Embodied interaction challenges fundamental assumptions about cognition that are integral to a humanist worldview, such as the Cartesian mind-body dualism, the self-world dualism, and the objectivism implicit in the notion of an external individual who observes from a viewpoint that is both detached and privileged. One cannot occupy an "objective" external viewpoint because one is, in Agre and Chapman's terms, in a *deictic* position at the center of a dynamic, contingent, and subjectively formulated spatiotemporal situation. In many cases, the physical shape and extent of the system or installation prevents an authoritative viewpoint; it may be temporally extended or involve multiple spaces (virtual or physical).

Through the 1990s, much media artwork was enmeshed in rhetoric of the virtual. In that period, Jeffrey Shaw (1993) explicitly described his work as a formal exploration of the "modalities of the virtual." With hindsight, much of this work was less an exploration of the virtual than a grappling with the task of making the virtual *tangible*. Early interactive artwork arose in a theoretical vacuum due to the absence of adequate theory of interactive, virtual, and behaving media. Whatever the theoretical tools available to address matters of form, color, expression, and embodied sensorial engagement in the canon of the aesthetics of plastic arts, those traditions had little to say about ongoing, dynamic, temporal engagement, because *traditional art objects do not behave.*

## Interaction and Biology

Scientific and humanistic narratives collide in interactive art, being, as it is, a radically interdisciplinary realm. The *science wars* have been a constant backdrop to work and theorization in the field. Yet to the extent that interaction is an embodied process, neat separations of biology and culture are collapsed. Interaction with technologies of any kind *makes sense* to the extent that it is consistent with or analogous to the learned effects of action in the real world, from the calibration of vision by motor action in infancy. Our ability to predict—and find predictable—behaviors of digital systems is rooted in our evolutionary adaptation to embodied experience in the world. We are embodied beings whose sensorimotor acuities have formed around interactions with humans, other living and nonliving entities, materiality, and natural phenomena. We understand digital environments on the basis of extrapolations upon such bodily experience–based prediction. This is easy to understand in mimetic environments such as Second Life, but it is equally present on a more basic mouse-to-screen level of interaction. If children become acclimatized to digital interfaces with arbitrary physics earlier and earlier in development, permanent sensorimotor maladaption may result. This possibility is yet another justification for developing a deeper understanding of the sensorimotor dimensions of digital interaction.

## Designing Behavior

The capacity for interactivity and behavior facilitated by real-time computation is the most thoroughly novel quality of the "new" media. The corollary is also true: Experience of real-time computational art demands a subjective, situated, and enactive mode of engagement. The design of interaction is the implementation of technological systems that enact or perform responsive procedures through time. While this might be seen as a kind of automation, it is also a new genre of design, compositional, or literary practice that combines the envisioning of multiply unfolding responsive and contingent scenarios with the specific technical capabilities of computer programming and computer and electronic engineering.

Almost all digital systems involve the designing of behavior through coding. Coding is writing a script for a process, similar to dramaturgy or choreography, except that it is enacted by machines. The script of a play or a musical score involves symbolic representations of temporal processes, recipes to be followed—but they almost never involve contingency. Structures of coding, such as if-then statements, plan for contingency. Interactive systems—a theme park ride, an interactive installation, a piece of hypertextual literature, or a multiuser game—are multisensorial, spatialized, and time-extended, and require ongoing physical movement and decision-making. Undergirding all these examples is a capacity for real-time computation based on data from sensors.

In most interactive media, modalities of interaction are taken as transparent and given. They are *ready-to-hand*. In HTML, for example, the dynamics of interaction were conceived of as nonlinear linking mechanisms. Meaning was found in the content of the work. When interface and interaction modalities are deployed as mechanisms for exploring content, this results in a conservative notion of interaction that I refer to as *instrumental interaction*. The exploitation of differences and nuances in modalities of interaction as meaningful in themselves is rare. In more experimental cases, the performative dynamics of interaction play a key role in the accumulated meaning or experience of the work.[5] However, even when relational and processual approaches are pursued, interaction dynamics complement other aspects. The subtleties of negotiation between *content* and *dynamics* are part of the new aesthetics.

To the extent that an aversion to didacticism and an acceptance of interpretation is central to any art practice, you can't design the interaction a person will have—but you can design *for* interaction. (In contrast, you *can*—and *must*—design interaction if you're designing an ATM, because the goal is to limit actions to a simplified set [*instrumental interaction*].) The task of interaction design for cultural application is more open: to create a context in which interaction can facilitate (or thwart) certain kinds of responses.

## Agency, Behavior, and Performative Technologies

Theoretical purchase on interaction design can be enriched by understanding interactivity as a subset of a larger category of *performative technologies*. Of all behaving systems, only some are interactive in the conventional man-machine sense.

*Agency* is a key word in any conversation about behaving systems and performative technologies. The term is widely used in a range of disciplines from sociology to artificial intelligence. As theories in different fields emerge, the term has accrued various shades of meaning. Actor-network theory, instruments, and bacterial cultures are granted agency. Different approaches to agency in inanimate phenomena lead us toward panpsychism or toward Manuel DeLanda's (1992) ideas of nonorganic life.

In our context, sentience is not a necessary condition for agency. Whether an agent is biological or technological, its capacity to decide and take action is the defining quality. In this sense, a computer system that makes choices based on varying (sensor) inputs is an agent.

Interaction involves two (or more) agents engaged in ongoing, dynamical exchanges. A computer and a person may be agents in interaction, as may a frog and a fly. The dynamics of agents in interaction are relational. In this sense, *interaction confers agency*. Such a perspective reaffirms the relevance of much of the theory discussed in previous chapters, from von Uexküll's umwelt to Gibson's affordance theory to Barad's agential realism.

It is sometimes proposed that any experience of any artwork is *interactive*. To propose that an artwork is interactive because the viewer experiences subjective change in the process of engaging it is, in the terms of this discussion, fatuous. This sort of argument makes the term *interactive* useless for any theoretically useful purpose. We must impose some terminological discipline to avoid such annoyances. The video game Tetris is interactive (though in a formulaic and instrumental way); a photograph simply is not. Mobiles and kinetic sculptures—which in the arts are seen as historical precursors of interactive systems—do move but do not exhibit agency. The capacity for interactivity depends on the capacity for (agent-like) behavior on both sides. The design of sophisticated behavior necessarily precedes the design of the interaction.

Noncomputational cultural forms (in the performing arts) can be interactive between performers: this is called *improvisation* (see chapter 23). Interaction between performers and audience is less common; the audience is usually passive. Popular cultural practices, such as tango dancing, martial arts, and team sports, are both improvisatory and interactive. Unlike theatrical arts, they are played for the pleasure of the players and are not, primarily, performed for an audience.

## Agentic Ecologies: A Systems Approach to the Quasi-biological

*Interactivity* has been defined by the HCI community almost exclusively as an interaction between one person and one machine. However, any theoretically well-informed approach to that relationship—informed by cybernetics, artificial life, dynamical systems theory, ANT, enactive and distributed cognition, and other relevant theoretical perspectives—must see man-machine interaction (to use the cold war era term) as a subset of a general scenario involving the interaction of human and nonhuman agents. In analysis of an analog electronic circuit or the ecology of a fishpond, a reductivist separation of *effectors* and *effecteds* often does violence to integrated systems, obscuring precisely the phenomena of interest: mutually enmeshed structural coupling via feedback loops. The tyranny of reductivism must be countered by a systems holism. This is true for an analysis of the synthetic ecologies of interactive systems, as it is for analog electronics or ecology proper.

A technology, or a technological complex, that has the capacity to *behave* in a quasi-biological way has a quasi-biological status. It possesses, or seems to possess, agency. It can "assess" its relation to its "world" at any moment in order to "decide" and take action. (The scare quotes denote metaphor—the last thing I want to do is to imply that computers possess human awareness.) It may exhibit behavior with respect to direct human action. It may display behavior that resembles other systems, such as traffic flow or the flocking of birds. It may do so with respect to distributed sensor systems, such as those along the San Andreas Fault, or with respect to abstract global or non-geographical data systems, such as automated stock trading (high-frequency trading [HFT]).

A behaving artwork is an agentic system that changes its nature and/or its expression in real time due to changes in its environment. The novelty of this condition cannot be understated. It is simultaneously artifact and pseudo-organism. With hindsight, we can identify precedents, such as the automata of the eighteenth century by Jaquet-Droz and Vaucanson and, more recently, the cybernetically inspired artworks of the mid-twentieth century (discussed in chapter 19), such as Gordon Pask's *Musicolour*, Nicolas Schöffer's *CYSP* series, and Edward Ihnatowicz's extraordinary *Senster*.

The real-time processing capability of the computer, when suitably interfaced with the world via sensors, has permitted advancement in agentic capability by orders of magnitude. Programmable devices and the flexibility of coding—in a variety of special-purpose languages—permits rapid testing, and this has qualitatively advanced the practice of the design of behavior. This qualitative leap, a phase change in the designing of agents, highlights the paradoxical nature of code: Code is text that performs: It straddles the representational and performative idioms.

### Agents, Emergence, and Interaction

An agent, then, has a quasi-biological capacity for behavior. The notion of an agent, consistent with both artificial life and cybernetic theory, is agnostic regarding whether it is carbon or silicon based. As such, the extensive literature of the artificial life community (laid down in the 1990s) is a rich resource for further thinking about the design of behavior and *culturally intelligent agents* (I coined this term in the late 1990s when the analogous idea of *socially intelligent agents* was emerging in the AI community). As discussed in chapter 8, one of the foci of artificial life was the exploration of *emergent* phenomena that confounded reductivist analysis—the behaviors of social insects being paradigmatic. In the reaction to the shortcomings of symbolic AI, the recognition of emergent phenomena hearkens back to cybernetic ideas of self-organizing systems.

Emergence *is* mysterious, largely because it resists reductive analysis, like the related fields of complexity theory and dynamical systems theory. Among artificial life thinkers, Peter Cariani explicated the theoretical dimensions of emergence in ways that are directly relevant to agentic art practices (see chapter 7). From a scientific perspective, emergent phenomena are fascinating, be they the behavior of slime molds, the dynamic shapes of a flock of starlings, or the emergence of consciousness. They all have the common quality of metapatterning, which is *of the whole system* but not reducible to parts owned by entities of the group. This phenomenon is perfectly valid as subject matter for cultural practices. The utilization of the mechanics of emergence as a component of an artwork is a little more arcane. In paragraph 7 of Cornelius Cardew's *The Great Learning*, composed in 1968, the score *emerges* as the result of a procedure observed by each singer, with some freedom of interpretation (Cardew 1971). This results in a field of flowing sound, one of the best examples I know of the use of emergent mechanisms in performance. Recalling Pound's assertion that "artists are the antennae of the race," as with so many other examples, Cardew explored the potential of ideas that came to the notice of scientific researchers a generation later.

Emergence elicits the sensation of surprise. The value of surprise in art and cultural practices, especially dynamic practices, should not be trivialized. It is relatively easy to do the unexpected, in the sense of unpredictably random effects. It is a subtle task to design that effect to draw the user into consideration or exploration. Because there is no compulsion in art, the artist bears the burden of enticing engagement.[6]

## Circuits of Agency

An interactive system can be analyzed from several perspectives: from the perspective of the designer/author engaged in creative practice; in terms of the experience of the human interactor; and from the perspective of the technological system's behavior. As in linear temporal forms such as film, theater, or music, the external expression of the system/artifact changes through time, but its behavior also varies in a responsive and often unpredictable way. The system undergoes internal reconfiguration as a result of changing environmental conditions. Per von Uexküll, Merleau-Ponty, and Dreyfus, the world of an automonous agent is given to it by its sensors. In more sophisticated cases, the generation of variety utilizes procedures such as genetic algorithms, machine learning, neural nets, and multiagent systems. Such a technological assemblage is a hybrid *agent-artifact*: It has "agency" of a quasi-biological kind and possesses its own umwelt.

Yet to regard the technological assemblage as a standalone artifact is to run afoul of the fallacy of the subject-object construction itself. The spectactor is engaged in an unfolding that is a relational product of his behavior and the (behavior of the) technological assemblage. The complex of spectactor and agent-artifact defines a system in which the aesthetic effect on the spectactor is a combination of perceptions of the behavior of the system and awareness of the spectactor's own activity and agency in the system. The whole process can only be properly understood from a viewpoint that subsumes subject and object in a performative and ecological view of processes among a network of actors in circuits of agency. An adequately complex approach to the aesthetics of embodied interaction must involve perspectives that address the technological assemblage, the spectactor, and the emergent, relational condition of the system as a whole.

## Paradigm Shift

The upwelling of arguments that contest presumed axiomatic binaries of subject-object or world-representation—in fields as diverse as feminisms, performance studies, science studies, and cognitive and neurosciences—along with calls for the recognition of the fundamentally embodied and distributed nature of cognition, suggests a fundamental and large-scale ontological change. I believe we are in the midst of a Kuhnian-style paradigm shift toward embracing embodied and situated notions of intelligence (part of a larger critique of humanist ideas—in this case, individualism). This shift provides a new perspective on conventional narratives in both the sciences and the arts, and it allows us to formulate an aesthetic theory that embraces embodiment, dynamical systems, and other aspects of postcognitivist theory. In combination with ideas of (inter)subjectivity, performativity, and relationality, this new perspective provides a theoretical basis for the development of and discussion of new modes of creative practice facilitated by real-time computation. I point not only to interactivity and interaction design but also to creative and design practices in all manner of dynamical, generative, and reactive systems, which we might call *heterogeneous performative assemblages*.

## Conclusion

Artistic practice with computational technologies ushers in nothing less than an ontological shift in practice. This shift was catalyzed in realms of digital practice, but it has ramifications throughout the arts. I have discussed the ways in which traditional canons of aesthetic theory are not adequate to the task, and I have outlined a set of issues that I believe lays the groundwork for an aesthetic theory of practice in which real-time computational technologies are utilized for cultural purposes. Such a theory recognizes that the technology itself is historically contingent. In order to establish a useful sociocultural theory, computer-based art practices must be seen in historical context as the deployment (but usually not the détournement) of a technology the history of which resides in realms of scientific calculation, business management, and military application: realms of calculation and control far outside the normal realms of artistic practice. A viable theory of computer art must incorporate this perspective, because the axiomatic commitment to quantitative and objective knowing that structures the history of computing is largely at odds with the ontology of the arts that emphasizes affect and the immediacy of sensorial experience.

There is a beautiful irony in the fact that out of this reductive rationalist agenda can emerge a generative cultural technology. An entirely new aesthetic dimension is introduced in using these new tools: the designing of automated behavior and the construction of ongoing, intersubjective, embodied, temporal interaction—in other words, a quasi-social, quasi-biological, dynamical engagement. All aspects of media art partake of this capability, from the lowliest graphical user interface to the most sophisticated artificial life ecosystem or AI-based poetry generator.

In order to pursue the development of cultural practices of integrity and rigor under such conditions, it is incumbent on practitioners, theorists, and teachers to actively interrogate the intellectual and social history of such technologies, as well as their technical conformation and behavior. While historico-theoretical background—such as an understanding of techniques of Boolean algebra and the intellectual milieu of its technological implementation and reification— is crucial, we must also come to understand the aesthetico-theoretical implications of what it affords and what it precludes.

This in turn demands the integration of contemporary theories of cognition into a theory of computational media practice. It is only by denaturalizing the dualist and internalist axiomatic assumptions that inform the structuring of the technology—and thus the modes of interaction implicit in them—that practitioners can develop a more relevant grasp on the cognitive dimensions of such practices, which include embodied, materially and spatially engaged, and social aspects.

Most importantly, such theoretical inquiry can lead to better purchase on problems that practitioners have continued to face, which in many cases compromise the works themselves. A reflexive critical practice is long overdue—a practice that, in a sophisticated way, sees technology not as neutral tools but as culturally loaded artifacts.

# 21  Applying Postcognitivist Approaches to Arts and Cultural Practices

The goal of this book is to bring postcognitivist thought to bear on considerations of art and cultural practices in order to provide much-needed balance to the internalist rhetoric of cognition, which has held sway for most of the last century and has provided minimal purchase on the embodied, enactive, situated, and materially engaged nature of cognition as it happens in the arts. To bring postcognitive thought into connection with arts practices, we must contradict some conventionally accepted notions of cognition and also counter some conventional discourses of arts practices. To work against the grain of conventionally accepted ideas demands constant vigilance reminiscent of Philip Agre's prescription for critical technical practice (discussed in chapter 6).

As previously demonstrated, the new cognitive science, informed in part by the phenomenology of Heidegger, Husserl, and Merleau-Ponty, has brought into question not only cognitivist representationalism but also the Cartesian binaries of mind-body, self-world, subject-object, and nature-culture. New work in the cognitive science and philosophy of mind communities has generated a groundswell of research in which mind and cognition are taken to be biologically and materially grounded, embodied, and situated. This destabilizes the humanist and Cartesian ground upon which conventional cognitive science was founded. Our "modern" aesthetics is premised on similar philosophical foundations and is ripe for destabilization by the same arguments.

Epistemic action, structural coupling, the parity principle, and other key concepts constitute signposts in a new landscape of postcognitivist thought, an interdisciplinary landscape where cultural anthropology meets cognitive neuroscience. Taken together, key ideas in postcognitive discourse, such as sensorimotor loops, enactive cognition, deixis, material engagement, and a consideration of cognitive prostheses, lend new ways of thinking about the development of interactive art, interface design, and HCI in general.

If the conventional binary of subject-object is a false construction in science and in art and if self and world are mutually co-constituting (*umwelt*), then we must approach the relation of person(s) with artworks as mutually influencing systems to be interpreted not in terms of active viewer and passive object, nor in terms of perception (of an object world) followed by action (upon an object world), but rather as relational, structurally coupled, and agentic cognitive ecologies. Moreover, if we come to know the world through acts of sensorimotoric probing, then those very movements, actions, choices, and responses construct and constitute meaning in a proprioceptive way.

These sensorimotoric probings are not simply actions through which information is vacuumed up and dropped into the collecting basket of the cranium. Rather, they are themselves complex sentient actions by which we build our sense of place in the world. If such performance involves not only pragmatic, instrumental action but also *epistemic* action, then action generates meaning.

Our experience with art and cultural practices—dancing, doing yoga, exploring a classical ruin or a Richard Serra sculpture—often involves embodied sensorimotor action. Postcognitivist thought provides purchase on this aspect of the arts, which has been sidelined under the cognitivist paradigm. Ahead, I offer a summary of some key ideas in postcognitivist thought, which provide new insight into arts practices. By bringing these ideas into intersection with each other, I hope to create a discursive framework within which to flesh out an embodied approach to thinking about art and cultural practices.

Note: In this chapter, arguments which have been built throughout previous chapters are brought to a culmination of theoretical focus. In order to do this, many topics are revisited and references re-cited. Owing to the length of this book, it seems advisable to restate rather than rely on recall. For those who find this repetitious, I plead indulgence.

## Umwelt

It is appropriate to begin with a pioneer, a voice that predates cognitivism, reminding us that cognitivism has a short history. Jakob von Uexküll's concept of the *umwelt* affirms the inexorable isomorphism of an organism and its world. The experiential world I have, the world I believe to exist *out there*, is given to me through the ways I know the world: through my senses. In my world, imminent collision is not given to me through hearing, as it is to a bat. I cannot sense the body heat of a (scared) rodent, as can a snake. I cannot navigate the world by the magnetic qualities of rocks, like a hammerhead shark can. And I can't know who has been in the neighborhood by sniffing a fire hydrant.

The concept of the umwelt supports the phenomenological arguments of Merleau-Ponty and Hubert Dreyfus that the kind of world I have is given to me by (the specifics of) my particular embodiment. As Dreyfus (1996) puts it, "The body is our general medium for having a world." By the same token, this fundamental idea destabilizes the easy subject-object binary on which so many of our assumptions—scientific, philosophical, and legal—are based. There is no objective world out there. The relativism of the umwelt concept is the precursor to similar ideas in autopoietic biology, in second-order cybernetics, and in radical constructivism.

## Epistemic Action

David Kirsh and Paul Maglio (1994) coined the term *epistemic action* to describe the gathering of knowledge through action in the world. They observed that certain kinds of things can only be thought, or can be thought more quickly, efficiently, or richly, by concurrent manipulation of objects in the material world. Kirsh gives the example of moving Scrabble letters about to suggest words. Kirsh and Maglio's Tetris experiments address time-constrained problem solving: Players who were allowed to manipulate the tokens as they fell performed better than those who were not (see chapter 11). The general lesson of epistemic action is that we leverage the world to help us think. The Tetris experiment focuses on the home territory of cognitive science: reasoning and problem solving.

The challenge of applying the concept of epistemic action to interactive art practice is that only the most tedious kinds of interactive art, and only the most tedious approaches to interactive art, can be treated as puzzle-solving tasks. Cognitive science, with its quantitative scientific affiliations, has shied away from more open-ended inquiry. Insomuch as creation in the plastic arts consists in part of intelligently moving matter about, observing and reflecting on the results of combinations and placements, it is epistemic action par excellence. However, creative exploration extends the concept of epistemic action. In its original sense, epistemic action was applied to preexisting problem domains. In the Tetris case, the task is clearly defined and logically circumscribed—the very epitome of cognitivist problem *solving*. In our discussion of tools (chapter 14) it became clear that the distinction between epistemic and pragmatic action was not straightforward. In art practice, the problem itself is seldom so constrained. Indeed, the practice is often a matter of discovering or articulating the "problem" through what we might call *embodied epistemic speculation*. Epistemic action in arts practices expands on the concept to facilitate generative action—the creation of new possibilities or problem *creation*.

Action can be, in Johan Huizinga's (1950) terms, *ludic*—not only analytic or instrumental but also playful. (There is no line between the end of epistemic and the beginning of ludic.) Play can be exploratory, experimental, generative—and art is often celebrated as having such qualities. Studies in cognitive science often hew closely to reductive analytic tasks. Art practices tend to be synthetic and interdisciplinary, mixing heterogeneous elements. This distinction between reductive analytics and generative combinatorial play is the difference between getting the (right) answer and asking the (right) question.

Consistent with the ludic, experimental spirit of art, the conditions in most interactive works are contrived for an inquiry for which the outcome, while framed, is open-ended, allowing the possibility of hypothesis formulation rather than simply resolution. Indeed, we might say that an exemplary work of interactive art might entice a user to "hang" in an unresolved situation far longer than they would tolerate otherwise, in order to explore that sense of anxiety and expectation as an experience in itself.

In the same way that the extended mind hypothesis was extended beyond the parity principle to embrace complementarity, arts and cultural practices leverage tools and traditions of practice with those tools. In this sense, *cultural* cognition is always extended. In the realm of cultural cognition the notion of epistemic action expands to embrace speculative action, generative action, and creative action. This reminds us of Fluxus artist George Brecht's *irrelevant process* and of John Cage's notion of *experimental action*, a term he used as early as 1955: "An experimental action is one the outcome of which is not foreseen" (1961, 39). Cage advocated aleatory procedures to "bypass taste and memory." This kind of exercise moves beyond the limitations of conventional cognitive science research of the problem-solving kind by recognizing the constraint of problem solving with respect to a model or hypothesis. Cage's method is *metacognitive* in the sense that it critiques the tendency to make predictive models itself.

## Distributed Cognition

Distributed cognition—in Edwin Hutchins's formulation—provides ways of thinking about cognition and cognitive action that arise through the coordination of multiple (skilled) human actors, procedures, and instruments and devices, such as the nautical chart and the compass (see chapter 11). This conception of cognition as collaborative and situated applies to theatrical rehearsal as it does to navigation on a ship's deck, as Evelyn Tribble (2005) has shown in her distributed cognition–inspired approach to longstanding puzzles related to Shakespeare's Globe. Hutchins's conception of the role of artifacts and procedures is sympathetic with Merlin Donald's concept of the *exogram*—a cognitive cultural artifact that inheres in previously acquired knowledge and capabilities (see chapter 17). However, whereas the exogram is a passive document, the artifacts in Hutchins' scenario take a more active role in cognition. That said, Hutchins's approach does not embrace the agency of nonhuman actors as thoroughly as ANT does (see chapter 20). In Hutchins's later work, he articulates his own recognition that thinking can occur in and through bodily action. As with epistemic action, sometimes bodily action does not enact or represent prior existing thought; it generates thought—or rather, it *is* thought.[1]

In front of her canvas, the painter moves back and forth—close in for detail, at arm's reach for a brushstroke, then back out to gain the big picture, from side to side to check surface reflection effects and to accommodate (or exploit) anomalies of vision such a parallax. The welder deftly judges the gap between the electrode and the work piece as the bead of molten iron flows into the partially molten cavity. We have been long accustomed to providing mentalist explanations of the exercise of intelligence in such cases. Ockham's razor proposes a simpler explanation. Accepting that we think with our whole selves in movement dispenses with circuitous explanations in the same way that the heliocentric model of the solar system dispensed with circuitous calculations.

## Bootstrapping the Mind into Representation

In his paper "Before and Beyond Representation: Towards an Enactive Conception of the Paleolithic Image," Lambros Malafouris (2007) offers a cunning inversion of the standard story of Paleolithic cave painting. He not only offers an embodied and enactive account of how the representational threshold was crossed, but also allows that representationalism is not so much a neurological capability as a cultural capability—implying that the transmission of representational capability is passed on culturally. He proposes that enactive mark-making bootstrapped the Paleolithic mind into representation, both internal and external, and that representation may not be an innate (neurological) capability but rather a property of human culture propagated via bodily practices and cultural training. Such an idea links the work of Donald with that of situated and distributed cognition and the sociology of Marcel Mauss (1934) and Pierre Bourdieu (1972). It permits the general idea that human cultural practices are cognitive and reminds us that any line drawn between cultural and cognitive practices is false.

Cognitive archeology may seem a stretch from discussion of the arts, but we must bear in mind that archeology is making inferences about otherwise unknown cultures through the study of material artifacts. The deep question Malafouris asks is how we, as humans, came to be representational. His answer exposes that conventional explanations weren't really explanations; they assume the priority of mental representation but do not explain how it came to be. Malafouris provides a hypothesis that turns conventional wisdom on its head, and in the process it provides support for narratives of thinking-through-doing that are common in art folklore: Barbara Hepworth's thinking hand holding the chisel or Paul Klee's taking a line for a walk. Ludic action and enactive mark-making converge.

## Abstract Concepts Arise from Bodily Experience

In his foundational work *The Body in the Mind: The Bodily Basis of Meaning, Imagination, and Reason*, Mark Johnson (1987) asks, "Where do concepts come from?" Disallowing esoteric explanations, he argues for the origin of abstract concepts in and from bodily experience. His hypothesis—later provided neurological explanation by Gallese and Lakoff and others—is simple: We learn by bodily experience, and concrete experience gives rise to abstract concepts. A typical example is the origin of the abstract concept of equivalence in the bodily experience of balance—not simply on the teeter-totter or seesaw, but in daily life. I have two shopping bags, one in each hand. One has beers in it; the other, groceries. The pull on my left arm is like the pull on my right. I do not have to struggle to stay upright as I walk. In a sense, the beers equal the groceries. This *is a sense*, or a sensing in the proprioceptive sensors in my joints and fascia.

This bodily sense becomes an abstract concept through metaphor. As Damasio, Lakoff, and others have been at pains to point out, metaphor is not a pretty decoration on reason; it is the way we build meaning. This provides a way of thinking about abstract thought that liberates one from the solipsistic fallacies of Cartesianism and Platonism. When combined with Kirsh's epistemic action and Hutchins's embodied cognition, we can begin to see a vision of human action in the world as embedded, dynamic, contingent, and relational—a way of thinking about self and world that does not give automatic priority to a mental realm of abstract ideas but rather sees mind arising out of interaction with the world.

In their *Pengi* work, Agre and Chapman (1987) developed a charming workaround for the computational challenges encountered in top-heavy, God's-eye-view, top-down AI programming (see chapter 6). In essence, they said that it is not necessary for me to know the location of all of the ants in the world in order to act intelligently with respect to the ant biting my toe right now. Such a subjective spatial and temporal frame of reference is *deictic*. People and animals proceed in the world in a deictic way; it is parsimonious. When people engage in interactive installations and virtual environments, their perspectives are likewise deictic.

## Enaction and Structural Coupling

The general framework of enactive cognition of Varela, Thompson, and Rosch (1991) provides that not only is cognition *situated* (they would say *structurally coupled*), but this structural coupling also is temporally extended and enacted in iterated sensorimotor feedback loops. Enactivists emphasize that basic sensorimotor realities anchor interaction in a way that dissociated contemplative vision never could. As embodied beings, we conduct our paths through the world in the form of sensorimotor circuits that have neither beginning nor end, a sentiment captured in the phrase the authors borrowed from Buddhist philosophy: *laying down a path in walking*.

Contrary to received wisdom, humans rarely perceive then act, but instead understand the world in a synesthetic and proprioceptive fusion of sensing and action, often acting to perceive. For instance, when I take a photograph, I incline my head left and right and move back and forth to frame my shot. An aesthetic theory of interaction, then, must include a choreographic understanding of perception and action. In their enactive approach, Alva Noë and Kevin O'Regan (2001) emphasize the integration of sensing and action. The idea that we act to perceive rather than perceive then act provides cognitive grounding for processual, performative, and relational approaches.

## Ecological Psychology and Affordances

James Jerome Gibson's (1979) emphasis that perception is a bodily practice—or, as he put it, that perceptual systems integrate proprioception—fits with enactivist conceptions of sensorimotor loops. As discussed in chapter 2, Gibson believed that functionally meaningful qualities of the world are directly perceived in the ambient optic array. Gibson called these functionally meaningful properties *affordances*. For Gibson, affordances are not mental constructions; they exist objectively as optical (or other sensory) information about the environment. The optical experience of a chair, to me (but not to an elephant), is the perception of "sit-ability" (it can be sat upon). The concept of affordance has been taken up in design and HCI circles, but the idea of *direct perception* and of the *ambient optic array* that underlies affordance theory has encountered more resistance, because it negates internalist positions. The idea that information is not a product of internal analysis, deduction, and inference, but is directly available to perception, is alien to a cognitivist mindset. The notion of direct perception and the notion of affordance continue to be debated in the Gibsonian community and beyond.

The extreme externalism of Gibson's original formulation is tempered by the idea of culturally specific affordances. Dreyfus notes that a mailbox affords mailing letters—but only if one understands the role of the mailbox in a larger process. The concept of affordance is rich in its potential application to the design of interactive and virtual environments. The existence of such cultural affordances provokes the possibility of utilizing a theory of *affordance architectures* as a technique for design. Can an interactive installation or an online game be usefully analyzed in terms of architectures of affordances?

## Cognition and Dynamical System Theory

Randall Beer disputes the notion of passive perception and neatly sutures dynamical systems theory, Gibsonian psychology, and autopoietic biology to develop a *behavior-oriented view of perception*:

Perception is generally viewed as a means by which an agent extracts information about its surroundings from the raw sensory signals and internally represents the structure of its environment. But a dynamical system follows a trajectory specified by its own internal state and dynamical laws [reminiscent of autopoietic theory]. Sensory inputs cannot in general place a nonautonomous dynamical system into some state uniquely characteristic of a given external object. Rather, the most that they can do is bias the intrinsic tendencies of the agent dynamics by selecting some particular trajectory from the set of possible trajectories that the agent's dynamical laws allow from its current state. This suggests a more behavior-oriented view of perception that is reminiscent of Gibson. (2014, 138)

An interactive artwork is an environment like any other, in which we deploy sensorimotor behaviors. Beer's formulation allows us to understand the trajectory of a spectactor through a work in a way that respects the conventional distaste for didacticism in art and allows us to think of the design of interaction in terms of *aesthetic affordances*—how the artist makes cultural references or facilitates associations.

## The Meaningful Is the World Itself

In his subsumption architecture, Rodney Brooks demonstrated that it was possible to realize an effective robotics without the representationalism inherent in early AI. This both destabilized the edifice of representationalism and reinforced the idea that a nonrepresentationalist theory of cognition was viable (turning the pragmatic work ethic of AI against itself). As John Haugeland recognized, Brooks's achievement was notable from a philosophical as well as a pragmatic perspective. Haugeland paraphrased Brooks's anti-internalist notion that the world is its own best model, saying, "We abide in the meaningful, the meaningful is the world itself" (1998). Physiologist Paul Cisek covers similar ground when he cleverly inverts the cognitivist symbol-grounding problem. He points out that from the perspective of cognitivism the problem was how to attach meanings to a prior system of abstract, immaterial symbols. Cisek shows that cognitivists had the boot on the wrong foot. The problem, he explains, is not in the attachment of meaning to a preexisting network of abstract symbols. He argues that as sentient beings, self-evident meaning is all around us. As such, the challenge for cognitivists was to make their network of symbols meaningful by attaching it to the meaning already present in the world. This characterization elegantly captures the fallacy of internalism.

The common sense problem was exactly this: An internally coherent abstract symbol system, though true and provable in a mathematical sense, does not necessarily have useful effect in the world. It would be like negotiating a parking lot according to the rules of chess. The rules of chess are consistent within their frame of reference, but cars have limitations; they can't jump over other cars, for instance. On the other hand, we can be fairly sure that a cockroach does not reason about its path across the alley by plotting possible trajectories on an imaginary map and calculating their probabilities. The take-home lesson for the arts, and for designing behavior here, is that human experience grounds-out in the sensorimotoric experience of phenomena of the world. Meaning is given by sensory experience.

## The Cognitive Unconscious

Lakoff and Johnson challenge the cognitive primacy of consciousness with their notion of the *cognitive unconscious,* and Gallese and Lakoff provide a persuasive neurological hypothesis for a process by which abstract concepts emerge out of sensorimotor circuits. This idea loops back to Hutchins's declaration that bodily actions can be cognitive, can be thoughts; aspects of human behavior that evade consciousness or linguistic elaboration can be cognitive. This reminds us of Michael Polanyi's idea that embodied knowledge is tacit. We often "feel our way" through tasks, relying on intuition—and what is intuition except a reinforcement of particular neural pathways by repeated experience? These are important ideas because they free us from a mentalist conception of art experience.

The discovery of mirror neurons by Gallese, Rizzolatti, et al., shows (at the very least) that vision links directly to motor circuits. Claims have been made for mirror neurons as a source for more complex social behaviors such as empathy—and many of these claims have been contested. However, the raw fact of mirror neurons appears indisputable—learning occurs via multimodal nonlinguistic, nonsymbolic channels. "Monkey see, monkey do" has more profundity that we thought. Gallese and Lakoff, Elizabeth Bates, and others in the field argue for *evolutionary exploitation*, the idea that higher cognitive faculties leverage existing neural architectures. Gallese and Lakoff's hypothesis that concepts (and language) arise in motor circuits is an example of such thinking and provides neurological justification for Johnson's theory.

John Sutton (2007), in his work on memory in cricket, explores and updates ideas of tacit knowledge and *flow* (à la Csikszentmihalyi) in skilled bodily performance. In this paper, he elucidates just how complex the intersection between representational and kinesthetic/proprioceptive memory can be. He makes the case for a middle way between extremes of internalism and externalism and for combining representationalism and performativity.

A useful understanding of the intelligences of the arts must involve consideration of the bodily dimensions of cognition. This is necessary to right the skewed view we have been working with, but adopting a fully externalist position (see chapter 15) seems to contradict introspective evidence. Humans clearly have the capacity for mental representation, even if there is no consensus on what a mental representation is. Resolution of this question depends on a definition of representation, which was absent from the cognitivist establishment and continues to be elusive. Questions of whether and to what degree any neural correlate is a representation are fundamental to any coherent neurocognitive theory.

Artworks are representational, in the sense that they refer to images and ideas not directly present in the physical work itself. The myth of hardware and software encourages us to imagine that things are either material or informational. This is nonsense. Symbols are not exclusively immaterial; a physical object can also represent an idea. Work such as Sutton's helps to elucidate the complex nature of meaning in embodied practices and artworks.

## The Dance of Agency: Process Ontology and the Performative Idiom

Andrew Pickering's formulation of performative and representational idioms (1995)—originally applied to questions of scientific knowledge and practice—is rich in potential for application to a critical analysis of art practices. Artifacts of conventional plastic arts (paintings and sculptures) are representational artifacts par excellence, even though they do not usually partake in a regime of formalized abstract symbolic tokens (like number systems or written language). Orchestral scores and scripts for plays partake in the *representational idiom*, but are then the basis for performance. In this sense, music does Pickering's process backward. While performative scientific lab practice generates representational artifacts (scholarly papers), music goes the other way. Computer code, too, is written, then performed, in this case, by machine. Interactive cultural practices, though deploying representational components, prescribe a performative ontology (true of some more than others). The performative, as Pickering defines it, resonates with notions of process that are central to arts practices. The ontological orthogonality of representational and performative idioms provides a framework for developing an enactive theory for art practices.

Pickering's image of a *dance of agency*, arising as it does from observations of scientific research, maps onto art practices—if anything, more smoothly than it does onto scientific practices. *Making* in the arts does not conform to an industrial conception of punching out exact replicas according to a blueprint. Making implies a cognitively active process of being open to possibilities. In this sense, Kirsh and Maglio's epistemic action is a subset of what we may term ludic or generative action. In Japanese aesthetics, notions of *shibui* and *wabi-sabi* describe an attitude of receptiveness to accident and imperfection in process—not in the sense of accepting failure, but as a mechanism of generation of variety, reminiscent of Brecht's generative schemes. No wonder Brecht, like many of his peers (including Cage), had a lifelong interest in Zen.

## Actor Networks

In actor network theory, Latour, Callon, and Law explored circuits of non-human agency in a way similar to Pickering's approach.[2] The spirit of ANT is captured in the following quotation from Latour:

Pasteur acts so that the yeast acts alone . . . he creates a scene in which he does not have to create anything. He develops gestures, glassware, protocols, so that the entity, once shifted out, becomes automatic and autonomous . . . Who is doing the acting in the new medium of culture? Pasteur, since he sprinkles, and boils, and filters, and sees. The lactic acid yeast, since it grows fast, uses up its food, gains in power . . . If I ignore Pasteur's work I fall into the pitfalls of realism . . . if we ignore the lactic acid, we fall into the other pit . . . of social constructivism, forced to ignore the role of nonhumans. (quoted in Pickering 1995, 22)

Latour's description aptly captures the work of the artist engaged in writing code and designing behavior: "He creates a scene . . . so that the entity . . . becomes automatic and autonomous." He chooses a middle way between realism and social constructivism. This scenario resonates with Varela, Thompson, and Rosch's integration of internalism and externalism in their proposal for an alternative, enactive form of cognition. Is an artwork better seen in terms of a representationalist cognitive *extension* (as described by Clark and Chalmers) or an *enactive* structural coupling? Is aesthetic cognition constituted not in the subject but rather in a cultural/cognitive assemblage of distributed cognition (as theorized by Hutchins)? Is it better conceived in terms of actors and agents (as conceived by Latour, Callon, and Law)? Critical analysis of the shades of difference among these theorizations, along with assessment of their relevance to art practices, defines a rich new realm of aesthetic inquiry. Against this backdrop, Nicholas Bourriaud's briefly famous *Relational Aesthetics* (1998) is old news. His essay cites among sociologists only Guattari and Bourdieu, but it clearly owes much to ANT and related social theory.

The field of neuroethology, especially in its dynamicist modes, provides persuasive evidence for the reality of the integration of mind, body, and world, especially in terms of nonneural control functions (Rieffel, Valero-Cuevas, and Lipson 2010). Neuroethology reminds us that the brain is not an alien organ squatting in the body—the brain's original function is to coordinate motion. Neuroethology reinforces anti-human-exceptionalist sentiments. ANT is anti-human-exceptionalist in a different way. The theory describes networks of actants in a way that provides purchase both on the agency of software and on the role played by physical structures and scenarios. As such, ANT has direct relevance to the understanding of arts practices as *heterogeneous performative assemblages*.

## Selfhood and Consciousness

At the core of inquiries into cognition lie questions about selfhood, self-awareness, consciousness, and the relation of mind, brain, body, and world. This complex subject was explored in chapter 16. Any ideas about what art is and how it works must eventually be grounded in ideas of who and what we are. I argue that the cognitivist story is not simply wrong or radically incomplete; it also positions arts practices as incommensurable with cognition. The traditional valorization of cultural dimensions of human society shows us this latter is also wrong. The work of Evan Thompson, Lakoff and Johnson, Susan Hurley, Dorothée Legrand, and others already cited provides us with ample material for the construction of an aesthetic theory that "gives the body its due" (Sheets-Johnstone 2010).

Lakoff and Johnson complicated the conscious-nonconscious dualism in a useful way by identifying the cognitive unconscious as the location of most cognition. Thompson has pursued enactive and nondualist approaches to being and consciousness extensively.[3] Evan Thompson and Robert Hanna (2003) also reconfigured the mind-body dualism, recasting it as the mind-body-body problem (see chapter 16). Following Buijtendijk and Plessner (1925), Thompson and Hanna distinguish two ways in which we are bodies: as the phenomenal lived body (*leib*) and the body as the object of observation (*körper*), a distinction we are intuitively familiar with. For instance, when I touch my knee, the knee takes the role as *körper*, the finger as *leib*.

In her work on *prereflective self-consciousness*, Dorothée Legrand (2006) makes distinctions similar to those of Thompson and Hanna, arguing that a prereflective bodily self-consciousness is a necessary precursor for self-awareness. She argues that this neurological ground zero for selfhood is the experience of sensorimotor integration—that is, the feeling that the self is where action and perception converge. This prereflective awareness creates the ground upon which both proprioception and intentionality can exist.

Susan Hurley (1998), working from Wittgenstein and Kant, brings contemporary neuroscience to bear on questions of consciousness and, in the process, buries several Enlightenment ghosts. In her view, consistent with arguments by Lakoff, Gallese, and others, conscious agency arises out of nonconscious sensorimotor feedback—structurally coupled with the world, an enactivist would say. The self, for Hurley, is not hidden in the dark recesses of the mind, pulling levers like the Wizard of Oz behind the curtain, but is and always has been *embodied and embedded*, to use Haugeland's phrase.

The opposition of emotion and reason is one of the more stubborn skeletons in the Enlightenment closet. It has been famously challenged by

Damasio (1994) in his book *Descartes' Error*. More recently, Giovanna Colombetti (2013) has brought an enactivist perspective to her work on affective cognition, just as Rosalind Picard (1997) brought affect to the world of AI in her *Affective Computing*.

## Sensorimotor Experience and Art

Phenomenologist Alva Noë (2000) has emphasized the central importance of sensorimotor experience to experiencing art. In his paper "Experience and Experiment in Art," he identifies four artists—Serra, Smithson, Turrell, and Irwin—who exemplify his case for *experiential art*: art directed at the crafting not of objects but of experiences. This work, he says, "enables us to catch ourselves in the act of perceiving and can allow us thus to catch hold of the fact that experience is not a passive interior state, but a mode of active engagement with the world" (128).

The artists Noë identifies, it must be noted, occupy a special historical niche. Emerging in the late 1960s, their formative context included op art, a movement that specifically addressed the phenomena of visual perception, and work of the Art and Technology movement, much of which addresses questions of perception. This work was undergirded by the psychology of visual perception of R. L. Gregory, which was celebrated by the art critic Ernst Gombrich—who also followed the work of Karl Popper. The works of Gregory and Gombrich were required reading for art students through the latter 1960s and the 1970s, before this scientistic orientation (which also included a healthy helping of cybernetics, served up deliciously by Jack Burnham) was eclipsed by the rise of new theory inflected by poststructuralist thought.

Speaking about experiencing a work by Serra, Noë recalls the following: "To wander around a piece like this can cause a loss of balance. In this way the works make us reflect on how we feel, perceptually, in their presence. . . . The loss of balance, for example, introduces us to what are strictly non-visual (e.g., vestibular, kinesthetic) components of our 'visual' experience" (2000, 131). Citing Wittgenstein, Noë speaks about the attempt to gain a "perspicuous overview" when experiencing these works by assembling a global sense of the artist's work as a sum of specific views and approaches. Noë appears here to be balancing a deictic viewpoint with the development of a mental map—a representation that synthesizes these immediate experiences into an "authoritative" overall view. Yet some kinds of works—including immersive and virtual reality works— attempt precisely to destabilize this desire to resolve such a *God's-eye view*, continually reminding the spectactor of his subjective, deictic position.

These issues are particularly relevant to the design of game interfaces, which attempt to address precisely this problem on the small screen. In this case, the ability to jump between first- and third-person views (a technical kluge) encourages perhaps a less-than-principled compromise. A more rigorous attention to the underlying issues discussed here may lead to more aesthetically satisfactory solutions.

Reflecting on the kinds of knowledge that arise from proprioceptive or kinesthetic experience, Noë observes, "We can think of Serra's work, and that of other experiential artists, as providing opportunities for first-person phenomenological investigation" (2000, 133). He elaborates, "To investigate visual experience—that is, to do visual phenomenology—we must investigate the temporally extended pattern of exploratory activity in which seeing consists" (128). Noë's emphasis on vision is consistent with his field, yet the experience of these works is emphatically not simply visual. The temporally extended, embodied quality of the experience of these works, so *visual phenomenology* is too narrow. The experience of the work is fully kinesthetic and proprioceptive; the work itself is physically extended and requires walking around, moving back and forth, experiencing duration, and presenting one's embodied self to it in ways that go far beyond simply seeing. This is sculpture, large sculpture, and one engages it kinesthetically and spatiotemporally. It is thus inaccurate to call it *visual art*. This nomenclature covertly reinforces the erroneous notion that the role of the body in perception is simply to position the eye—as the only veracious extension of the mind—in the optimum position for data collection. This is not art for the "seeing couch potato" but art for the enactive, deictic subject. The nature of experience of these works is also the quality of experience in installation art.

Noë provides a succinct synopsis of the sensorimotor paradigm, which reminds us of Gibson's ambient optic array in the "skill-based confidence that you can acquire the information at will by probing the world" (128). I have emphasized the way that the experience of interactive art destabilizes the subject-object dualism. Noë similarly affirms this when he says, "The knowledge one thus attains is knowledge of the character of one's experience" (132).[4] Noë connects his art theory to autopoietic biology and ecological psychology by emphasizing that "perceptual experience, in whatever sensory modality, is a temporally extended process of exploration of the environment on the part of an embodied animal" (2000, 128). As we establish an outline for an aesthetics of behavior, Noë's observations remind us of the need for a phenomenology of engagement with ongoing multimodal cultural activity. This will have several aspects: that of the artist and the design/making process; that of the spectactor; that of the machine system, which behaves; and that of the heterogeneous assemblage that is the larger spectactor/work system.

Noë's remarks, we must remember, are about traditional forms of plastic arts that do not inhere capacities of movement or behavior. However, CACA is not always, or simply not, about depiction nor concerned with communicating a representation of an idea about the world. CACA builds a context in which a spectactor can have a special kind of experience and reflect on the nature of that experience. This is the radical proposition of interactive forms: the reader, the audience—the *spectactor*—is the protagonist. It is the job of the artist to create a catalytic context. This is, as Andy Pickering would say, art in the performative mode. The *subject matter* (if such a term is even applicable) is comprehended not through literary simile ("What would I do if I were in her position?") but directly ("What should I do now?"). The real *subject* matter is the spectactor's subjective experience. From this perspective, literature and traditional art are elaborations of voyeurism.

## Conclusion: Postcognitivism and Art Practice

The entire question of what constitutes cognition and how we characterize cognition is brought into question in this conversation. It is a question central to any discussion of the cognitive aspect of art practices. It seems that many of the terms of reference in the language of conventional cognition (knowledge, information, reasoning, symbols) are of scant value. The symbol-grounding problem shows us how profoundly different the ontology of the arts is from the ontology of computer science, and it goes some way to explaining the deep philosophical confusions encountered as computing moves into the arts. One might posit that art practice is not a symbol system at all, in the sense that arts practices are always already grounded and may be nonsymbolic. If symbols arise, they too are automatically grounded, so the symbol-grounding problem never comes up. While cognitivist theory fails to have explanatory power, phenomenology, enactive and distributed cognition, ANT, and a probing of the cognitive unconscious are valuable resources for the development of an aesthetics of behavior.

Hubert Dreyfus (1996) relates a study of flight instructors in which the flight instructors instructed their students to monitor cockpit instruments in a particular order, but they were unaware that they themselves did not follow their own prescribed procedures. In other words, experienced pilots develop a cognitive/perceptual procedure for observing their instruments, which they themselves are unconscious of. To elucidate such practices in (cognitivist) language is as challenging as attempting to dance the theory of relativity. Polanyi alerted us to the unknowability of tacit knowledge, and it was upon these rocks that AI foundered, in the form of Minsky's common sense problem and Harnad's closely related symbol-grounding problem. Tim Ingold and others have emphasized in various ways the unspeakability of embodied knowledge (see chapter 14). As language inhabits consciousness, so the nonconscious is beyond its reach. Yet much of what we understand as intelligence, in the sense of intelligent action in the world, is nonconscious. Cultural practices deal in intelligence in this larger sense, often beyond the reach of language. That is why such experiences seem inarticulable!

The distributed cognition research of Hutchins (2010) and Kirsh and Maglio (1994) offer ways of asking *how* the process of interaction *means*. The work is concerned with how bodily action plays a role in cognitive processes involving manipulation of artifacts and exploitation of images. Lakoff and Johnson have shown how we build abstract concepts out of sensorimotor behavior. Part of the aesthetics of behavior then constitutes the study of how bodily action in the world constructs meanings. This understanding can be applied to consider how actions elicited in artworks contribute to their meaning as experienced. It is crucial to allow that such knowing can be proprioceptive and dynamical, nonconscious, and nonrepresentational. We might ask what kinds of experiences can be developed through interaction dynamics alone while eschewing "content" entirely. Clearly, sensorimotor action is a kind of content, but it is content of a different kind from the representational, citational mode of pictures and comparably representational sound.

Art is the crafting of embodied, sensorial experience, expertise as old as human culture itself.[5] The movement toward embodiment in cognitive science meets media artists coming the other way, as it were, exploring the application of computational technologies to embodied, material, and situated cultural practices.[6] With hindsight, it has become clear that many of the R&D projects of *media artists* through the 1990s focused on the problematics of interfacing representational abstraction and embodied experience. As such, they explored questions that more recently have become associated with ubiquitous computing.

The realms of art and cultural practices have until recently been off-limits to cognitive scientists. A noncognitivist or more-than-cognitivist approach offers the tantalizing possibility of shedding new light on a range of human practices that are culturally regarded as epitomes of human intelligence and yet have been largely excluded from understanding as cognition precisely because they tend not to trade in the symbolic languages of those realms. The finely honed, living practice of the arts offers a veritable goldmine of sophisticated embodied, situated, and distributed practices waiting for examination by cognitive science.[7] However, any attempt to reduce the experience of art to information, in a purely mental or computational sense, is misguided.

## Coda: Art, Brain-centrism, and the Neuroaesthetic Fallacy

To look to evidence from contemporary neuroscience as a way of understanding art practice may at first glance seem counterintuitive (the current rise in fashionability of neuroaesthetics notwithstanding), but over the last fifty years a significant body of experimental work has arisen that I believe can be usefully marshaled. The scenario of scientists of one stripe or another "explaining" art is as familiar as it is annoying, so I hasten to note that it is not my goal to explain (away) art practice by (ostensibly) rendering mental operations transparent under the glare of scientific explanation. Nor do I want to naïvely deploy a superficial reading of scientific or theoretical research to support any argument in the arts.

As noted, it is ironic that although cultural practices are regarded as pinnacles of human achievement, conventional cognitive science has been hard-pressed to say anything useful about painting, dancing, or composing and playing music. Much of what *has* been said falls into the category of *neuroaesthetics* (for example, by Zeki [1999]). Regrettably, much of that work has been unreflexively internalist and so provides little insight into the "doing" of art, the enactive embodied practices by which art comes into being. Any attempt to pursue a neuroscientific analysis of creative practices must be vigilant not to reenact the neuroaesthetic fallacy, itself a case of *fundamental attribution error*. A certain kind of brain activity might be measured when a person is engaged in some task, but this does not confirm that "thinking" is contained within that measured phenomenon; it simply means that the phenomenon is concurrent with or temporally related to what we call thinking. It is a testament to the plasticity of the mind that we can mold our conception of ourselves around various theoretical armatures.

To hold onto internalist ideas about art is to impede a clearer understanding of what it is to be human in the world. Some contributions in the new wave of so-called neuroaesthetics exhibit this flat-footedness. The assumption that art is about beauty is of course laughably anachronistic, as is the idea that there might be some Platonically general, abstract, and timeless quality of beauty. The idea that this quality might be found in a *beauty neuron* or an *aesthetics gene* is naive determinism. Again, we see a tendency to focus on the (purportedly) immaterial while eliding the embodied and situated dimensions of the phenomenon.

An outrageous recent example of this is found in "Specificity of Esthetic Experience for Artworks: An fMRI Study" (Di Dio et al. 2011) in which photographs of two classical Greek sculptures are compared with photographs of two contemporary young men in underwear. The paper purports to derive some useful knowledge about the nature of aesthetic judgement. The study begs this question: "What is the difference between looking at a Greek sculpture and looking at a dude in the gym change room?" This question itself is rife with cultural theory booby traps that the researchers seem to step into obliviously. The first complexity is the question of who is looking? Gay, straight, male, female, young, old, "white," not "white" . . . ? I found myself wondering if one of the young men looked like a neo-Nazi skinhead. Not a question I would ask about a classical sculpture.

Semiotically speaking, these images are several orders removed from the thing itself. My viewing is of a reproduction of a black-and-white photo, so all kinds of questions of the aesthetics of the photography intervene. At root, this paper reveals major uninterrogated assumptions. Centrally, the authors seem confident that there is such a thing as "art," that we can distinguish between art and non-art, and that these Greek sculptures epitomize it. In this case,  a dose of interdisciplinarity and a shot of critical technical practice might have inoculated this team against foot-in-mouth disease.

# 22  Embodiment and Interaction

It serves one well not to dabble in abstractions too long.
—J. W. Goethe

It may have come as a surprise to many readers that interactive art predates
the era of the personal computer—and, in some cases, even predates digital
computing, as in the case of Nicolas Schöffer and Gordon Pask (see chapter
19). Commodity software packages—the mechanics of which are safely protected from meddling hands by a friendly GUI—have substantially closed
down the range of interactive art practices due to the proscription of menu
options, limitations of the keyboard/screen interface, and limitations of
standard input and output modalities (such as screen presentation of text
and image or two-channel audio). As discussed in chapter 18, we cannot
begin to address the aesthetics of embodied interaction without first recognizing the deep theoretical tensions and practical challenges implicit in
attempting to deploy computational systems for the creation of artworks.
The advent of *computer art* was something like the moment of atomic fis-
sion. The structure of mutually repelling magnetic fields of humanist modernism had kept reason and emotion apart, kept mind and body separate,
until this great conflagration.

After developing several generations of embodied interactive systems,
the lasting impression I have gained from the making, testing, and presenting of these projects is that a substantial part of the meaning of the work
resides in or emerges from the sensorimotor experience of doing it. Like riding
a bicycle, we cannot "understand" the work without bodily engagement—not
simply *immersion*, which implies the possibility of inaction, but fully dynamic
proprioceptive/kinesthetic engagement. This necessity to *take action* implies
engaging the plastic arts in a way unknown in conventional genres that are
embedded in concepts of perception and contemplation, which enforce and
reinforce a subject-object dualism.

In the pages that follow, I elaborate upon some of the fundamentals of interactive, embodied, enactive installation art as they have become apparent to me through thirty years of active practice involving the development of custom robotics, sensor and actuator technologies, and machine vision systems. Making interactive digital-cultural works involves designing an armature for an ongoing structural coupling between a system and its environment. Making such works involves *designing behavior*: imagining and specifying the shape of an ongoing chain of interactions between a system and its environment. It involves building a context in which a coherent and engaging chain of interactions occur between a person (or people) and the system, embracing the possibility of a wide range of admissible or appropriate human behaviors. Such systems are better understood by analogy to an organism or agent as opposed to an artifact.

Our most common *interactive modalities* enlist sensorimotor behaviors and (likely) draw upon DNA hardcodings. Aside from the trivially Pavlovian modality (press the button and get the reward/food pellet), what are the key interactive modalities in artworks? In installation and robotic work, many examples exploit what I call the *puppy paradigm*—a modality of interaction based on approach and withdrawal, trust and fear—that is beguiling, for a while, at least. Is the charm of this modality somehow natural to us as humans, perhaps hardcoded into our DNA as parenting animals? This question opens a field of inquiry at the intersection of neuroethology and interactive aesthetics. Whatever the case, the next question is how to move aesthetic development of the field beyond this biocultural ground zero.

## Interaction Dynamics: Fundamentals of Cultural Interaction

Interaction is something you do. It is embodied, dynamic, and performative. Interaction design encompasses not just doing and not just the awareness of doing, but the cognitive dimensions of doing. An array of utensils and ingredients on a kitchen bench might suggest action; the particular shape of a knife might suggest chopping or filleting. The arrangement and design of implements supports a kind of abstract thought, cued and prompted by memories and muscular gestalts arising from previous (bodily) experience of things like these. How is meaning developed dynamically, in the *doing*? Does the arrangement and design of implements support thinking? Does an arrangement arrange thought and a shape shape it? Once we embrace an enactivist or extended conception of cognition, the presumed separation between characteristics of the external world and thinking must be reconsidered.

The key difference between interactive systems and conventional artworks is that interactive systems change responsively through time. Interactive systems disrupt conventional aesthetics because the very mode of engagement is *processual, performative,* and *enactive,* and thus incompatible with conventional modes of engagement with conventional art forms. When a person engages a system designed as an interactive cultural system or artifact, the involvement is more complex than the relation with a conventional static work, such as a painting or sculpture, or with a temporally linear artwork, like a film or video, and certainly more complex than the instrumental interactivity of software tools. Modalities of interaction in cultural applications are often more than instrumental. They exploit the dynamics of interaction in a performative way, as a means of engaging the user and of developing meaning. The nature of interaction in cultural applications, at least in exemplary cases, has a poetic dimension that permits allusion, association, and metaphor as part of the mechanics of interaction and often involves surprise, humor, and intellectual engagement with process.

### Sensorimotor Integration: Taking Embodiment Seriously

As embodied beings, we conduct our path through the world in the form of sensorimotor circuits that have no beginning or end. Contrary to received wisdom, humans rarely perceive then act, but instead understand the world in a synesthetic and proprioceptive fusion of sensing and action, often acting to perceive. An aesthetic theory of interaction, then, must include a dynamic, enactive understanding of perception and action.

Making a user complicit in the construction of an unfolding experience is a powerful technique for establishing engagement and commitment. If seeing a video in which a person is pushed off a balcony is disturbing, then pushing someone yourself—or being put in the position of choosing to— magnifies the disturbance by a large order. (Unless of course such action is routinely trivialized, as in first-person shooter games.) Aside from ethical issues, basic sensorimotor realities anchor interaction in a way that emotionally distanced contemplative vision never can.

### Cognitive Mechanics of Interaction

To be successful, interactivity must be both coherent and engaging. Coherency means the experience *makes sense*; it demands that the data collected about the user adequately represents the behavior of the user and that the system presents back to the user behavior construed as being directly related to the user's behavior—usually his recent behavior. *Engaging* means more than entertaining. It is the successful manipulation of the interest of the user to be drawn in and drawn along. While content can offer this quality, the creative development of beguiling dynamics of interaction can also contribute substantially. Predictably instrumental interaction is boring but remains in the realm of coherency. Randomness is incoherent. Between these two lies a realm analogous to the onset of chaos—neither linear nor random, a zone of unpredictable variety that remains in the realm of coherence. Between didacticism and perceived disorder lies the territory of a poetics of interaction—the territory of a novel field of aesthetics.

We may say that an exemplary interactive artwork provides a context in which engagement with the work constructs a condition that requires further action to be resolved—that is, in which artifacts and effects are arrayed spatially and temporally to encourage the formulation of novel ideas. The temporality of the process is unavoidable, and its design constitutes a kind of synthetic enactionism, or a context in which cultural enaction can occur. The arrangement of such conditions in a way that optimally stimulates such processes (bearing in mind questions of demographics and cultural specifics) is a cognitive dimension of interaction design for aesthetic purposes. Interaction dynamics are not the only dimension of meaning construction in interactive art. Interactive art, like opera, is a *gesamtkunstwerk*; all the aesthetic modalities of the contributing media remain in play: spatial and graphic design, imagery, music and sound, and so on. The design task is to bring these modalities into synergistic relation.

## Ontology of Interaction

How does behavior *mean*? How does interaction impart meaning? How are such valences to be manipulated for enriched affective practice? These are fundamental questions in the aesthetics of interactive art. There are no answers to these questions in the traditional aesthetics of the plastic arts. Because this is a *new* problem, precious little in the traditions of the arts has much bearing on the task, so we scramble to find practices in other fields that have some relevance as models. (Chapter 23 explores this matter in greater detail.) To the extent that the mechanisms of interaction are naturalized, automatic, or intuitive, they do not play a significant part in the epistemological circuits of the work. It is only when such actions are present-at-hand that they take part in a circuit of meaning. When I have to bend *this way*, climb *that* ladder, or stand with my feet in cold water—then the *doing* of these actions, the embodied and performative dimensions, can be mobilized as major components in the overall meaning of the work.

In some interactive work, interactive modalities are taken as transparent and given: The dynamics of interaction were conceived as a means to an end, which was primarily found in the so-called content of the work (as if interaction dynamics were not always part of the *performative* content). In other cases, the dynamics of interaction play a key role in the overall construction of meaning. It is important to make a distinction between interface and interaction modalities deployed as mechanisms for exploring content (which are automatic, intuitive, ready-to-hand) and modalities that *themselves constitute content* or contribute to the accumulated meaning or experience of a work.[1]

## Embodiment and Interaction

HCI in general and embodied interaction in particular are in a state of tension with both general computational theory and art theory, for similar reasons. In embodied interaction, the centrality of spatial immersion and temporal extension casts or inscribes the human subject as deictic and engaged in a way that does not permit the kinds of authoritative, objective viewpoints of external control that characterize paradigms of computer science and also characterize paradigms of contemplative and passive consumption of art objects. This enactive processuality is consistent with postcognitivist conceptions of perception as dynamical, as discussed by Randall Beer (see chapter 15).

There is beginning to be a groundswell in the theorization of cultural practices that is sympathetic with phenomenological approaches and by extension with emerging postcognitivist cognitive science.[2] I see this trend as a critical paradigm shift with major implications for the theory and practice of interactive art and the study of computer interaction in general. Indeed, it is this conceptual and historical synchronicity that points to postcognitive theory as particularly relevant for thinking about CACA. Both arose as somewhat disruptive developments of conventional computing and computationalist theory.

Embodied interaction, as a cultural practice, occupies a radically interdisciplinary position between disciplines commonly regarded as being antithetical—namely, the arts and the computer sciences. The worldview of computing culture and that of the arts are fundamentally different and in tension. In general terms, the commitment of computer science to the idea of disembodied symbolic information and to abstraction as a goal and a virtue is orthogonal to art and cultural practices as they have a commitment to the immediately experiential, the concrete, and the specific. We engage artworks in a directly sensorial and bodily way. Modeling and manipulation of (sensory) experience is a primary skill of the artist. For the cognitivist and the computationalist, embodied experience is an almost irrelevant distraction.

Strangely, due to the historical formation of the field, it is necessary to emphasize the seemingly obvious fact that *interaction is done by physically embodied and culturally situated people*. That is to say, anthropological and sociological theorization of computer use, at least in the first decades of the discipline, was almost completely absent. To the extent that there was such theorization, there was usually an implicit commitment to an internalist cognitivism that elided the significance of embodied being, even in human interaction. While fields like industrial design attended closely to ergonomics, designers of interactive computer systems paid little attention to human dynamics, as if the movement of information from human mind to computer and back was as straightforward as Claude Shannon's communication theory would suggest.

Contrarily, whether we speak of the plastic or the performing arts, embodied practice has always been central to the doing of art (if not to its theorization or its consumption). In a way that speaks to Michael Polanyi's notion of tacit knowledge, those practices have been resistant to textual capture—a situation exacerbated by a traditional reticence among artists to attempt to bridge this gap. This has been seen as an expression of a characteristic anti-intellectualism in many aspects of the arts, but may be more charitably seen as a tacit acknowledgment of the reality of tacit knowledge. One thing is clear: The intellectual traditions of the arts and of computing constitute quite separate worlds, and their meeting in digital cultural practices has been as calamitous as any meeting of previously separate cultures. There are many ways to characterize the crisis of theory that has developed in digital cultural practices. I have advocated the usefulness of Andy Pickering's ontological binary between modes of knowledge that he characterized as, respectively, the *representational* and the *performative* idioms. This idea has the merit of digging deeply into the commitments and axiomatic assumptions of the two fields in question.

**Is Enactivism Heresy?**

The desire to surpass bodily labor in the form of hand-eye coordination via direct neural implants is symptomatic of an extropian drive among those who see embodiment as an encumbrance, an idea that runs deep in the Christian heritage of Western culture. How tiresome these body-denying sentiments are! Why can the perpetrators and their followers not see them for what they are: quasi-religious yearnings for freedom from materiality, from the body, from the source of sin! We are irreducibly embodied and should rejoice in the fact. There is no mind separate from body; we must allow that the body is suffused with mind and at least entertain the possibility that while mind might occur in concentrations in certain body areas such as inside the cranium, the self is the embodied self. The instinct to exclude embodiment from cognition, inspired by this neo-Platonic and Christian legacy, creates a skewed view of selfhood.

If we consider interaction from an embodied, enactive standpoint, we see embodied actions not as mechanical operations driven by control signals from the homunculus but as inherently intelligent in themselves. In so doing, we can liberate our thinking from the constraints of fallacious dualism and come to see interaction with digital media as embodied meaning-making, as a situated, distributed, performative, and enactive process, as a specific case of our general interaction in the world, the world we are given by virtue of our particular capabilities, our umwelts.

Some may want to qualify embodied interaction in terms of degree. They might say that jumping about with the Kinect is a qualitatively different thing from tapping on a QWERTY. However, as Kirsh and Maglio have shown us, the very act of externalizing cognitive operations produces qualitatively and quantitatively different cognitive phenomena, whether the external manipulation is performed with physical objects like rocks and sticks, with symbols drawn on paper, or with interactive animations on a computer. There are differences in these modalities, of course, and deeper research into these phenomena is required. Any such inquiry must begin with the following question: Is meaning extracted from representational tokens, or is it enactively constructed in doing?

## The Implicit, Enactive, Performative Body

Discussions of interactive art have a dialectical quality. On one hand, an arts/humanistic approach all but ignores the nature of the technological vehicle. On the other hand, technocentric approaches tend toward instrumentalization of the user and the trivialization of precisely the phenomenon in need of explication. There is some value in each of these approaches, diametrically opposed as they are. However, considering the behavior of the user-machine system as a whole will provide insights neither of the approaches can provide.

In his discussion of interactive art, Nathaniel Stern (2013) marshals insights from performance studies to formulate a conception of the "implicit body," a Deleuzian "body in motion." Central to his analysis is an awareness of the dynamical condition of interaction—a perspective that is, in cognitive terms, *enactive*. As interdisciplinary interventions, projects like Stern's have the salutary effect of balancing the weight of a technocentric and instrumental approach that often has the effect of rendering the user as robot-like or as a Pavlovian subject capable of a limited range of behaviors elicited by specific stimuli. Crucial to Stern's analysis is an understanding of temporally and spatially ongoing embodiment as the locus within which meaning is created. This is a theme we have seen emerge in the postcognitivism of Hutchins, Kirsh, Agre, Pickering, and others.[3] It points to a new ontological perspective from which interaction and the interactor can be usefully reformulated and from which advances in interaction design practice and its theorization might be made. A significant challenge in the formulation of an aesthetics of behavior is to understand how meaning emerges in the trajectory of a spectactor through a work, in an experiential and nondidactic mode that has been a hallmark of art in the modern period and is quite unlike the interactional modalities of commodity software products. We might think of the design of interaction in terms of what we could call *aesthetic affordances*—the way the artist or designer makes cultural references or facilitates associations.

# 23 Improvisation, Interaction, and Play

In foregoing chapters, I have suggested that the conventional aesthetics of the plastic arts has no capacity to engage the design of behavior and that therefore we must look elsewhere for practices that might offer models for the design of interaction between machines and humans. The advent of interactive cultural practices and the emergence of their design as a field of aesthetic decision-making presents practitioners with a theory vacuum, because most of the areas of precomputational cultural practices that inform such new forms are static or temporally locked. That is, none of those forms involve artifacts that possess behavior, that *make decisions* and *take actions* based on changes in their context in real time.

Here, I propose that improvisatory practices hold some promise in this regard, because such traditions embrace the possibility of real-time response. Examples that come to mind most readily include jazz improvisation, improv theater, and contact improv in dance. Yet in the wider cultural arena, all manner of practices are improvisatory: tango, aikido, bullfighting, football, and cooking, to name a few. Perhaps the kind of performativity that makes interactive art seem such a misfit in the arts is a reflection upon the strangeness of the plastic arts rather than the strangeness of interactivity.

The performance of a musical score or the script of a play always involves a certain amount of interpretation and a modicum of real-time adaptation. In football, in wrestling, and in certain musical forms, such as Carnatic music of South India, "play" occurs within the constraint of physical limits and rules. Some things are permissible, others are not, and occasionally some gifted player comes up with a new move. Improvisation tends to involve skilled physical activity; in this sense, it is nontrivially embodied. Rene Limacher (2011) said about watching the great jazz pianist Keith Jarrett perform, "He was crouched over the piano, he moaned and groaned, and his whole body got into it. Playing jazz is definitely not just a cognitive activity." We might quibble with "not just cognitive," but the meaning is clear.

Improvisatory actions, to the extent that they are not explicitly planned and scored, are immediate expressions of nonconscious intelligence. Such creative acts cannot be predicted, nor can a player plan out an improvisation in detail. Military action is improvisational, as General Dwight Eisenhower wisely observed: "Plans are useless, but planning is indispensable." Improvisational forms are done well only when the performer has pursued extensive training. Good improvisation requires discipline and internalized skill. A performer has to spend years engaged in the daily tedium of repeating scales and other patterns over and over and over again until, as a musician might say, the notes are "in your bones." As Pasteur (1854) remarked, "Chance favors the prepared mind."

## The Representational Idiom as Master Discourse

Improvisation and interactivity occupy marginal positions with respect to conventional arts practices. According to the logic of this chapter, these two practices are also linked in the sense that interactivity can be thought of as automated improvisation. Thus, it is in these evanescent areas of performative practice, in which invention takes place in the moment, that we might look for experience and strategies useful in the construction of interactive art.

Improvisatory cultural practices are often regarded as outsider or nonconformist practices. Improvisatory cultural practices exhibit a commitment to the emergent possibilities of an embodied present and a resulting unwillingness to commit to the ossification of the representational. As such, improvisational practices stand as exemplary of a performative ontology. Characteristic of the politics of such practices is a resistance to the process of validation of materially engaged and temporally embodied practice via translation into regimes of symbolic representation—that is, a resistance to the procedures of a representationalist epistemology.

This performative quality is also definitive of (much) interactive art. In interactive art, the user's active commitment to actions and the experience of effecting such actions and perceiving their results constitutes the work itself. By contrast, interactivity of an instrumental variety—say, working with a word processor or navigating the web—produces action that is designed to be as transparent and automatic as possible (as discussed in chapter 22). We must be cautious of falling into the comfortable and customary oversimplification of binaries by adopting a strict representational/performative dichotomy. There is much representationalism within performance and the performative. In particular, the coding that underlies interaction is a representational pursuit par excellence. Furthermore, one can deploy representations but not be representationalist.

## Interaction, Improvisation, and Freedom

Computer-based interactive cultural practices offer the user(s)/player(s) a *constrained freedom*: the opportunity of free action within a constrained gamut of possibilities defined by code, interface design, and input modalities. Improvisation in cultural practices likewise permits a freedom of action within a frame. In musical improvisation, for instance, behavior is constrained by key, rhythm, and mode; in Carnatic music, *sruti*, *ragam*, and *tālam*; and so forth. Karlheinz Stockhausen was clear on this matter: "One always connects improvisation with the presentation of underlying schemata, formulae and stylistic elements" (quoted in Lewis 2003, 195). Naïve views of improvisation and computer interaction have both been characterized in terms of a utopian rhetoric of *freedom*. Improvisation is in fact an intellectually rigorous exploration of possibilities within a domain the constraints of which are understood by the improviser.

Here, again, the trope of Gödelian incompleteness provides a useful metaphor, as does Cariani's concept of combinatoric emergence (see chapter 8), each in its own way informing a consideration of questions about the constraints on improvisatory practices and the nature of the defining frame. This idea of *constrained freedom* is central to the proposed isomorphism between improvisation and interaction. Reference to distributed and enactive cognition discourse and theory of self-organizing and emergent systems provides a ground for the following discussion, which will provide for a more developed theorization of the interactive cultural artifact. As such, this conversation is undergirded by theoretical questions regarding emergence, novelty, and the nature of creativity itself, in human, biological, evolutionary, and computational contexts, which have been touched upon in previous chapters.

There is a structural isomorphism between computer-based interaction and improvisatory practices in the fine and performing arts, as well as other points of relatedness. This isomorphism exists because a truly interactive cultural artifact reacts to changes in its environment in an aesthetically intelligent way, similar to the way a human improviser reacts. That isomorphism points to ways in which such practices might provide aesthetic models and theoretical insights that can inform the design of more aesthetically rich interactive cultural artifacts. Recognition of this isomorphism leads us into an interdisciplinary conversation concerning emergence and creativity in computational systems. These discussions triangulate the trajectories of several traditions—such as improvisation, interactive art, and artificial life discourses. In the pages that follow, I will discuss improvisation with respect to several areas of technological discourse, including artificial intelligence and artificial life, and will relate improvisation to generativity, emergence, and dynamical and self-organizing systems, as well as to concepts of responsiveness, creativity, invention, novelty, surprise, and play.

## Machines, Creativity, and Interaction

Machines, as normally construed, do not improvise. When they do something that is unexpected, they are broken and need repair. The screw-cutting lathe that creates a thread of varying pitch must be fixed. The blender that contributes shards of metal to the smoothie is bound for the recycle bin. The desktop computer is framed around such instrumental functionality. The last thing I want is topsdbns

   ;lr

    '

. . . exactly. In other words, we want our word processor to be predictable and ready-to-hand. This is not something we expect from an artwork (though, of course, we do expect this quality in the tools we use to make the work).

In discussing computer-based interaction and specifically interactive art and cultural practices vis-à-vis improvisation, we recognize that an interactive system designed for cultural purposes is expected to behave in an inventive or mildly surprising way with respect to user behavior. The interaction dynamics of the word processor are designed to be predictable. Being uninteresting is a virtue in this context. On the other hand, system responses that correspond to variables the user is not cognizant of create an experience that is indistinguishable from random behavior and therefore confusing or simply tedious. Between utter predictability and perceived chaos lies a zone of *interaction poetics*.

For those in the world of the fine and plastic arts, it is easy to forget that computer music, as a field, already had a long history before computer art emerged as a practice in the 1990s. As such, discussion about computational creativity and automated improvisation in that field is well established. Electronic music composer Christopher Dobrian elucidates a distinction between interactivity and reactivity in terms sympathetic to my approach:

Interactivity is a term too often employed to describe any use of a computer in live performance or installation. A computer might act independently, or might *react* to human actions (responding slavishly to triggers, or tracking continuous input), but this is not *interactivity*. The prefix *inter-* implies that both human and computer can act independently and react responsively to the actions of the other. Thus, true interactivity must involve mutual influence, and cannot be all deterministically programmed. (2001; emphasis in original)[1]

This, we must recall, was the interactional logic of the first interactive art work: Gordon Pask's *Musicolour* (1953), built over several years with Robin McKinnon Wood, using World War II surplus parts. Of this period, Pask memorably opined: "You need a mellow, elegant, South Kensington period in developing any cybernetic art form" (1971). We observe with some sadness that in over sixty years—the entire history of digital computing—the aesthetics of interaction has not developed much beyond this pioneering example. What then constitutes an interesting response by a machine to a human action? One might propose something like a Turing test: relevant yet provocative, able to propel the exchange forward. Such a response would resemble the kind one might get in a rewarding conversation with an intelligent, informed, and motivated partner—a response that surprises yet tacitly acknowledges the current frame (see Penny 2011b). Joseph Weizenbaum's Eliza, lauded as the first chatbot, passed the Turing test with only sixteen rules. At the time of its test in 1966, it easily duped MIT grad students into thinking it was human. But Eliza, in emulation of Rogerian therapy, specialized in saying as little as possible. She wasn't trying to be interesting.

Interactive responses are always constrained by the already given structure of the machine system, the output of which must be codified in terms of the available output modalities, usually limited to two-channel audio and the presentation of colored pixels on a flat rectangular surface. This narrow, codified, and commodified expressive range is a major limitation in the potential for interactivity using conventional systems. Such a system can never juggle or spray pheromones or raise its eyebrow, no matter what the context or internal computation. Output is always (already) constrained. To paraphrase Henry Ford, you can have any color, as long as it falls within the gamut. You can have any note as long as it falls within the designed range and modality of your audio system; microtonality usually is not an option, and sound can emanate from any of two places. In the same way that you can't (easily) get a quarter-tone out of a conventional piano, all computers perform predefined procedures (algorithms) upon a stream of already structured data within the constraints of their hardware. Their operations are rule based and, like any engineering pursuit, such rules allow no room for interpretation. An instruction like "make a jazz noise here"[2] does not compute.

### Improvisation in Living

In music, dance, theater, and any other temporal performance practice formalized by systems of textual codification, improvisation is unusual, and when it does happen it takes the form of highly constrained freedom of action within the defined practices of a canon or genre.[3] Further afield from such high cultural pursuits, in martial arts, football (of various sorts), and dancing, improvisation is the rule rather than the exception, despite defined structures. Improvisation is an integral part of these activities, but the range of invention remains within constraining conventions—or, in the case of football, rules. In mundane life, whether gardening or doing the dishes, it's improvisation "all the way down." The constraining structures are multifarious, flexible, and contingent. The law is present but inconsistently imposed. If I speed on the freeway, I *may* get a ticket.

Improvisation characterizes much of what people do most of the time in their lives, just as most of what people do most of the time also is largely routine. The complex webs of contingency we navigate in daily life were to downfall of the grand dreams of GOFAI (see chapter 6). The routineness of daily life challenged the conception of cognition as *problem solving*. These were issues Philip Agre (1988) identified and addressed in his PhD.

It may seem paradoxical to propose that life is characteristically both improvisational and routine. Yet this seems irrefutable, cybernetically and phenomenologically speaking. Living is adaptation, and adaptation is the application of known and relevant routines to novel contexts. If the idea seems strange, it may be due to the prevalence of a particular notion of intelligence. *Routines* are flexible rules, aspects of tacit knowledge. The general model is of learned routines, applied variably, with judgment, in varying contexts. Routines are themselves the subjects of higher-level improvisation. Etiquette is an extreme case, highly formalized in some cultures, not so much in the contemporary United States.

Agre observed, "Life is mostly routine" (1997a, 188). Contra the stance of Cold War cognitivism, the world is not full of novel contexts and dire consequences requiring explicit problem solving (see chapter 4). No, the world is mostly routine, and when novelty presents itself we tend to address it using approaches that are largely routine. As Hubert Dreyfus (1996) wittily observed, "The expert does what usually works, and 'of course it usually works.'"

## Improvisation and Temporality

Our perception of improvisation is constrained by our biologically determined perceptual capabilities and timescales (von Uexküll, Merleau-Ponty, Dreyfus). Dogs may have a highly developed olfactory art form. A tree might be said to be improvising when it sprouts leaves according to the seasons, responding heliotropically to the movement of the sun and adjacent areas of shadow cast by other (similarly improvising) trees at various times of day. Slime molds and communities of bacteria perform delicate improvisational dances in relation to changing biophysical contexts. The performances of the bacteria, slime molds, and trees are out of our perceptual range in terms of their temporal and physical scales. The growth patterns of cities and towns may be read in similar terms.

Although cultural pursuits such as Carnatic improvisation involve sophisticated mentation, we might drop our anthropocentrist guard for a moment to consider creative invention among other species as well: the complex architectures and group behaviors of ants and bees, for instance. Such connections usefully triangulate our discussions of the behavior of computational machines, which produce behaviors capable of emulating or resembling improvisatory behavior, with ethology (see chapter 2).

We are entranced by the aerial sculptures made by flocking birds: emergent improvisation on a social level. Crowd movement and traffic patterns have the quality of emergent adaptive pattern too. What about the activities of the painter? The action painting of Jackson Pollock was as close to musical improvisation as painting gets. Can we say that a painter is engaged in a slow solo improvisation as she paints?[4]

Notions of adaptation and emergence in biology and artificial life are relevant here too. The consideration of improvisation in non-anthropocentric terms engages the literature of emergence. This perspective begs the question: Does improvisation imply conscious action? The answer seems to be no, and as such, discussions of the cognitive unconscious acquire new significance (see chapter 16). This intersection of improvisation and emergence—bringing with it the legacy of artificial life and dynamical system theory (see chapters 7 and 8)—provides rich theoretical ground for elaboration of the aesthetics of behavior.

## Rules, Logical Frames, Surprise, and Play

Improvisation, in the sense we have been discussing it, is performance in which the performers have a freedom of action constrained by preset scores, scripts, rules, and cultural and artistic conventions. A person improvises within a defined domain. Infinite improvisation looks like chaos. A musician may play strange notes, but it is inadmissible to pour glacial nitric acid into the horn of your partner's saxophone. You may play soccer, but it is unacceptable to shoot the ball with a bullet from a gun. I may improvise with the materials with which I build my house, but only from within a range of viable materials—soap bubbles and birthday cake are out.

Improvisation is a structured opportunity for constrained surprise, a game of exploration and experimentation. Any realm of improvisation implies a frame, a domain. Canons and genres are quasi-logical domains—contexts with axioms, frames, and rules. Per Gödel, a domain has a language that is operational within that domain. A more encompassing language is required to move outside the domain in question, into a domain in which the domain in question is then a subset. These domains also vary in breadth. The range of improvisatory possibility in, say, a Bach toccata is narrower than that in free jazz.

## Frames

Conventional creative practices generally involve the manipulation of formal variables within a frame (not specifically a picture frame). Characteristically, avant-gardism, in various contexts, identifies and breaks frames, activity captured in the popular expression "thinking out of the box." All manner of watercolor paintings are possible, but an attempt to make a watercolor painting 3-D would go beyond the conventional frame. Following Cariani, we can identify the former as a combinatoric kind of invention, a kind of invention that operates within Gödelian limits. The latter—an intentional pushing through the genre envelope, makes explicit the frame itself and then moves beyond it. This has been the modus operandi of the avant-garde throughout the twentieth century. In some cases, this has been an almost algebraic process of inversion of a single term in an equation: contesting representationalism in painting or contesting the fourth wall in theater.

## It's All about Agency

My purpose here has been to help to enrich discourses around computer-based interaction by considering what designers of digital interactive systems can learn from improvisatory practices in human culture and beyond. There is an extensive history of improvisatory cultural machines, from Pask's *Musicolour* (1953), including milestones such as James Meehan's Tale-Spin (1976) (see chapter 6), George Lewis's Voyager (1986) (see

Lewis 2000), and continuing to the present with the contemporary work of David Cope (1991, 1996, 2000, 2005).

Documenting the history of this work is a book-length project in itself, not attempted here. Since the easy availability of personal computers in the late 1980s, the expansion of interface modalities in the 1990s, and the development of user-friendly programming environments and software tools, such practices have developed rampantly—much of it falling prey to the dangers outlined in chapter 18.

Improvisational practices open a space for skilled play and real-time response to changing scenarios; these cases have direct relevance to interaction design. In such contexts, enhancing the user's sense of agency is always a good thing. However, the user's sense of agency is not constituted by undirected liberty but rather by having a purpose and a sense of knowing the right thing to do, the right kind of thing to do, or the best choice of possible actions in a given situation. In the conclusion of his essay "The Secret Love between Interactivity and Improvisation; or, Missing in Interaction: A Prehistory of Computer Interactivity," George Lewis says, "If we allow interactivity and improvisation to finally consummate their relationship through an interdisciplinary study of how meaning is exchanged in real-time interaction, combining the insights of artists, cultural theorists, and technologists, we could witness the development of far more powerful new user interfaces engaging new forms of art and more sophisticated interactive computer applications" (2003, 203). Indeed, we can begin to build a formally elaborated theory of the aesthetics of behavior that bears general relevance to real-time computational cultural practices.

# 24 The Representational, the Performative, and the Processual

Performance is the ground from which knowledge emerges and to which it returns.
—Andrew Pickering, "Ontological Theatre: Gordon Pask, Cybernetics, and the Arts"
(2007, 44)

In many of the previous chapters we have reflected upon representationalism and related concepts of functionalism, computationalism, and cognitivism. According to these theories, knowledge resides in representation of the world—in maps, plans, algorithms, and symbols, the vernacular of artificial intelligence. Phenomenologists and postcognitivists have argued against this representationalist view, arguing that the world is not experienced via internal representations in some Cartesian theater (with one or more homunculi watching the screen and munching popcorn). According to externalists and antirepresentationalists, the world is not experienced secondhand through representations projected in a theater of the mind; it is experienced *out there*, where the body extends out into the world via sensorimotor loops.

Andrew Pickering developed the notion of the *performative idiom* to describe the way science is performed in the world, characterized by contingencies, accidents, improvisations, and even dreams. This idea is in opposition to the conventional notion of experiment guided in lockstep by hypothesis, which he calls the *representational idiom*, the way science as a practice is conventionally *represented*. He argued that the performative idiom is ontologically prior to the representational idiom (1995). According to Pickering, in this performative "dance of agency" a human actor proceeds through lively interactions with other agents, human and nonhuman. Such conduct has little in common with a scientific-humanist conception of objectivist mastery of the world. The actor-network theory of Latour, Callon, and Law has much in common with Pickering's decentered, agentic, and non-human-exceptionalist sensibility (see chapter 21). Pickering (2009) has argued that the mid-twentieth-century cybernetics of Pask, Walter, Ashby, and Beer remains impenetrable to most contemporary scientists because it stands on ontological premises fundamentally different from positivistic science. He argues that though "normal" science works in a representational mode, British cybernetics worked in a performative mode.[1] As mentioned in earlier chapters, Karen Barad's *agential realism* is a more radically relational ontology of *phenomena* (2003). It is rooted in the writings of Neils Bohr, which in a poetically pleasing way brings the performative cycle of thought back to the original moment of posthumanist destabilization: the uncertainty or indeterminacy of the quantum physics of Schrödinger, Heisenberg, and Bohr.

The idea of process figures strongly in the revolutionary art practices of the 1960s, as discussed in chapter 19. Procedural modeling (Reynolds 2007) became an important theme in the simulation of multiagent dynamics before and during the artificial life movement. Performativity, in both its feminist/humanist and its sociology of science contexts, affirms its ontological difference from the textual mode.

In the development of an aesthetics of behavior, process art, artificial life, process ontology, and performativity theory must be negotiated together. If we take this preoccupation with process in 1960s art along with traditions of improvisatory practice, combine them with sensibilities of procedurality in complexity theory and artificial life, and add to this mix the richness of discourses in performativity in the humanities and social sciences, I believe we have an excellent interdisciplinary recipe for advancing discourse and practices of interactive art.

## Disambiguating Performativity

In discourses of performativity and dynamical approaches to cognition, a remarkable sympathy in spirit has been occluded by disciplinary partitions and the suspicions of the science wars. It is clear, for instance, that though Butler's performativity and Beer's dynamical approaches do not map one to one and there will be much haggling over assumptions and commitments, there is much to be gained by theoretical miscegenation, queering, and hybridizing. As Pickering (1995) observes, "Humanist and antihumanist discourses run deeply through everyday thought. . . . They are also the very stuff from which the traditional academic disciplines are created and that holds them apart. . . . To be a traditional sociologist *is* to be a humanist; to be a physicist *is* to be an antihumanist (in technical practice, I mean). But the mangle, like the actor-network approach, corrodes the distinctions these discourses and disciplines enforce" (25; emphasis in original). In this context, it is interesting to note that Pickering—by his own report—deployed the term *performative* without knowledge of its use in literary performance studies (pers. comm). Barad has taken him to task on this matter.[2] While he does not refer to such traditions, his conception of the performative idiom also shares sensibilities with feminist performance theory.

Scholarly research involving the root word *perform* has a history in the humanities and particularly in feminist theory. It has been deployed in various ways to address the intersections between language and lived experience. In the humanities, performance studies, as a field that straddles theater studies and anthropology, has been driven by the work of Richard Schechner and Victor Turner, undergirded by the work of Geertz and Goffman. Language philosopher J. L. Austin introduced the notion of performative utterances in the early 1960s. The term *performative utterances* emphasizes the effects that such speech has in the world, as opposed to just "saying" or "describing" something. If I say, "I will buy the milk," I am doing something more than just saying something or describing what I will do, I am making a contract. Performative utterances are neither true nor false; that is, they are not truth evaluable.[3]

Feminist theorists reacted to what they rightly perceived as Victorian and patriarchal relegation of women to the (lowly) bodily and the retention of the Cartesian high ground for men. Rather than contesting the so-called high ground, they took up questions of embodiment, often in relation to questions of gender. It was in this context that feminist philosopher Judith Butler—informed by Derrida and Foucault—offered a reading of the notion of performativity as "that reiterative power of discourse to produce the phenomena that it regulates and constrains" (quoted in Hall 2000, 28). Elsewhere, she elaborates:

Performativity cannot be understood outside of a process of iterability, a regularized and constrained repetition of norms. And this repetition is not performed by a subject; this repetition is what enables a subject and constitutes the temporal condition for the subject. This iterability implies that "performance" is not a singular "act" or event, but a ritualized production, a ritual reiterated under and through constraint, under and through the force of prohibition and taboo, with the threat of ostracism and even death controlling and compelling the shape of the production, but not, I will insist, determining it fully in advance. (Butler 1993, 95; emphasis in original)

Note that this *iterability* resonates closely with the ongoing structural coupling of enactive cognition and recalls sensorimotor loops. One might go so far as to assert that this kind of performativity *is* enactive cognition. In the humanities, *performance* has differing inflections in theater studies, language philosophy, anthropology, and feminist, gender, and identity theory. All these have bearing on the development of an aesthetics of behavior.

## Art and the Performative Idiom

Pickering's distinction between representational and performative modes is just as relevant in discussions of the arts as the sciences. Originally applied to questions of scientific knowledge and practice, this binary is ripe for application to art practices. The plastic arts and the performing arts have been mostly representational, not simply in the naïve sense of "a picture of something," but rather in Pickering's more deeply ontological terms, yet practice is quintessentially performative.

Pickering's formulation that the representational and performative idioms are distinct and perhaps incommensurable is thus of particular relevance to our discussion of interactive art. Interactive cultural practices, though deploying representational components, prescribe a performative ontology—some more so than others. To argue that interactive art is *performative* is to expose the ontological core of its substantial shift away from conventional modes of practice. The recognition that interaction is both embodied and quintessentially performative provides a position from which to build an aesthetic theory.[4]

The practice of many cultural forms involves translation into and out of the representational, in the form of texts, scores, schedules, plans, designs and scripts, and computer code. In the arts, perhaps more so than in the sciences, the representational and the performative, like the pragmatic and epistemic, are deeply entangled. To draw simplistic dualisms would be naive. Elucidation of these ontological tangles in specific kinds of practices would advance theorization of practice.

Improvisational and interactive forms deploy representations in various ways, computer code being perhaps the most paradoxical—a representation that performs (as discussed below). In CACA, representational and performative modalities are combined on all levels, from the cognitive to the artifactual. Persisting around the edges of these representational idioms, performative practices by their nature resist—and often by their politics refuse—the codification upon which the representational aspects of disciplines have built their institutional edifices. These include, for example, documents, libraries, archives, databases, manuals, laws, rules, regulations, and constitutions.

## Process Ontology and (Artificial) Life

A concern with processes occurring in systems was a fundamental concept in systems theory, operations research, and cybernetics. Indeed, it was a biologist, von Bertalanffy, who originated general systems theory. The destabilization of the subject-object dualism was philosophically developed in second-order cybernetics (von Foerster) and finds echoes in autopoietic biology (Maturana). The process ontology inherent in autopoietic biology resurfaces in the enactive cognition theory of Varela, Thompson, and Rosch, which affirms the tight and iterative integration of an agent with its environment. The focus on systems and feedback loops in the cybernetic period can be seen as a precursor to an ontological shift, which, as mentioned, rendered some cybernetics research quite "strange" according to conventional scientific subject-object ontology. As argued in part I, this relativistic and performative spirit was held in check by a resurgence of neo-Cartesianism through the second half of the twentieth century, typified by, if not driven by, the rise of digital computing and symbolic AI.[5]

John Horton Conway's *Game of Life* (1970)—the mathematical game that became an icon of artificial life—generated surprisingly complex emergent behaviors from simple iterative mathematical rules. The dynamics of the game echo themes of the self-organizing systems theory of the cybernetic period. While conventional robotics in the 1980s hewed closely to the representationalist AI paradigm, Rodney Brooks developed an antirepresentationalist theory of embodied and situated robotics. Brooks's robots are performative in the sense that they "do in the world" and act without explicit internal representation. This notion of intelligence as "doing in the world" resonates with the theories of the performative that emerged within the humanities and the social sciences in the latter part of the twentieth century.

Dynamical, processual, and procedural ideas arising out of complexity theory and related research have been integral to the development of emergent and holistic techniques that refute or address the failings of top-down cognitivist models. They are thus directly relevant to the development of CACA.

## Process Ontology and the Arts

Buckminster Fuller's (1970) cybernetically inspired locution—"I seem to be a verb"—captures the spirit of much of the rhetoric of emerging art practices of the 1960s, which emphasized process—in performance, site-specific art of various kinds, and other art forms. Such a transitive or process oriented attitude was common in 1960s countercultural rhetoric and was informed by the ubiquity of cybernetic ideas, popularized in various contexts by Bateson, Burnham, and many others. This relational ontology is also the ontology of analog electronics, a modality of electronics roundly misunderstood or simply unknown to practitioners of today's digital electronics. The analog electronic signal is doubly continuous, being temporally continuous and amenable to infinite resolution. Both of these conditions are curtailed by the discrete nature of digital data—a fact that, via the rhetoric of object-oriented programming and the like, may have informed the object-centric nature of instrumental interaction. To posit such suggestions is to wade into the murk of computer etymology: what exactly is an *object* in object-oriented programming?[6] This erasure of temporal process is typical of the object-centric ways we tend to explain experience. Here, the analog, as transitive, corresponds to the performative, the digital to the representational.

Processual sensibilities underlay much 1960s art. We might again note the prescient but inchoate way such concepts arise first in the arts. Yet how can the tacit, performative, and embodied be anything but inchoate, without the development of a discursive skin? Many experiments in interactivity, like many experimental projects generally that occur in advance of a discursive context, remain unrecognized or uncomprehended. In their day, works like Pask's *Musicolour*, Ihnatowicz's *Senster*, and Kreuger's *Videoplace* fell into an explanatory abyss. In the years since, such a discursive skin has indeed begun to appear, in patches. My goal here is to stitch some of those patches together, although the image of a continuous fabric would be inappropriate. Perhaps a crocheted topological manifold?[7]

In contemporary discourse, the terms *dynamical, processual, procedural, performative, situated, enactive,* and *relational,* each in its own theoretical context, capture the evanescent process of contextualized doing. This demonstrates a groundswell in the theorization of cultural practices sympathetic with phenomenological approaches and by extension with emerging postcognitivist cognitive science. I see this trend as a critical paradigm shift with major implications for the theory and practice of interactive art.

The diversity of emerging forms in the arts through the 1960s can be baffling, but the performative/representational dualism provides an instructive armature for analysis. As discussed in chapter 21, happenings, performance, installations, site-specific art, and interventionist and socially situated arts practices affirmed materiality, embodiment, context, and temporal engagement. Other practices, grouped around rubrics of idea art and conceptual and post-object and information art, had a distinctly neo-Platonist taint; they clung to notions of symbols and abstraction and rejected, often vociferously, materiality, affirming a representationalist stance and operating within the representational idiom. As I have argued, there is a fascinating contemporaneity between the emergence of artificial intelligence and the emergence of conceptual art. Indeed, we may fairly refer to conceptual art as *cultural software.*

This bifurcation between the contextualized and the abstracted was profound. The drive toward disembodiment drew strength from the rhetoric of the information revolution and the linguistic turn in critical theory. On the other side, feminist theorists were developing discourses around the inescapable realities of embodied living, from the realities of reproductive biology to the ascription of gender roles. On the larger philosophical stage, Anglo-American analytic philosophy, true to its Enlightenment humanist roots, was enamored with immaterial abstraction, whereas so-called continental philosophy (existentialism and phenomenology) was fundamentally materialist and concerned with lived being.

In the arts, one way this bifurcation was elaborated was in a derisive distinction between merely artisanal crafts and high art. Of course, this hierarchy simply mirrored an existing hierarchy in the academy and the world at large, which denigrates "merely technical" work and elevates the types of work that tradesmen and machinists derisively referred to as done by "Professor Pinkhands." Yet a concern with process remained strongly felt in the arts because the material, temporal, and artisanal dimensions of practice can never be denied. Whether we talk of painting or dance, arts practices are quintessentially performative.

## Code: Performative Representation

The design of interaction is the specification, as text in a text-machine, of a process (or at least one side of a process). Code is a paradoxical object: It is a text and it is also a machine. Programming languages, as systems for specification for behavior, occupy a novel position in terms of cultural artifacts, being texts that are both representational and performative. It behaves, and it can be generative—but can the behavior of code be said to be improvisatory? Or should we say that it is the machine that performs the code? If so, code would retain its simple representational status. If we cast the hardware as a performer rather than simply an executor of instructions, then we disrupt the hierarchy of the software-hardware dualism.

If a machine simply number-crunches to execute code in order to perform some mathematical calculation (such as pi to a million places), then the code/machine complex is utterly deterministic, performing set instructions.

However, if the machine employs sensors that monitor some aspect of the world through time, then the code/machine/sensor system ceases to be so simplistically deterministic. Instead, it begins to take on the characteristics we ascribe to improvisatory practice, in the sense that though the system will act in accordance with the constraints and directives of the code, its behavior will nonetheless be influenced by environmental factors and will thus be unpredictable—to the extent that the data derived from the sensors with which the system interacts is unpredictable. This way of thinking preserves an subject-object dualism for the machine, which is precisely the dual that the experience of interactive art destabilizes—for the spectactor. Is it inconsistent to permit the machine an objectivist position while dismantling it for the spectactor? One way around this difficulty is to think *systematically*, to see the whole system—computer, user etc.—as a distributed cognitive network. In this case, the entire system of computers and people behaves in a way characteristic of that system. This would be consistent with distributed cognition and with ANT. It introduces a relational perspective and illustrates the potential value of process ontology to the development of an aesthetics of behavior.

## A Theoretical Mélange

Agre and Chapman proposed deictic programming, which contested the objectivist God's-eye view assumptions of conventional AI. The situated and reactive robotics of Brooks et al. were similarly inclined, as were Kelso's discourses of emergence and iterative processes in artificial life, self-organization, and dynamical systems theory. In cognitive science, enactivism and situated and distributed cognition challenge cognitivist attitudes.[8] In the humanities, the rise of performance theory (in some forms) contests the excesses of the linguistic turn. In science studies, ANT and Pickering's mangle destabilize conventional objectivist science discourses. In art theory, we see the rise of relational aesthetics. In philosophy, there is a resurgence of interest in Spinoza and Henri Bergson—brokered by Deleuze and later Brian Massumi—and a resurgence of pragmatism (e.g., William James, John Dewey, Alfred North Whitehead). Across diverse fields in the late twentieth century, such approaches have lurked on the margins of positivist disciplinary discourses. It is quite a patchwork; some of the moves might feel a little strained. The feeling of strain indicates the breadth of interdisciplinary reach and theoretical rigor demanded by a negotiation of the aesthetics of behavior. This is strenuous work.

## When All Is Said and Done, We Dwell in Representation

It is not my intention to make an argument that simply inverts the mind-body hierarchy, nor the performative/representational dualism. We should not hold out much hope for the resolution of the problem of cognition in either full-blown internalism or full-blown externalism. While I concur with Haugeland that "we abide in the meaningful" and "the meaningful is the world itself," human culture is representational, and human thinking seems to us to have (mental) representations—even if we have no clue what or where they are, neurologically.

As artificial life was the antithesis of AI, so reactive robotics countered the SMPA paradigm. However, it was not long before researchers were seeing the value and deficits in both approaches and attempting a synthesis. In a similar spirit, though Anthony Chemero (2009) has characterized radical embodied cognitive science in opposition to both overtly and covertly cognitivist approaches, the synthetic moment of the cognitivist/anticognitivist dialectic would seem to be upon us.

When we abandon the false distinction between intelligence and skill, we see that much intelligent action in the world is demonstrably not driven or coordinated by conscious abstract reasoning on symbols. But it is equally true that we, as humans, dwell in representation. Artistic practices—perhaps all human practices—involve aspects that are embodied and unconscious, as well as processes of conscious ratiocination and design. Our task is to grapple with how these two modes work together. Across a diverse range of disciplines, we are on the cusp of a veritable Kuhnian paradigm shift toward a performative ontology. In such a Kuhnian shift, the intractable is rendered trivial by an orthogonal shift of perspective. In my opinion, the practice and performance of interactive art itself is an integral part of that ontological shift, and that shift offers leverage on theoretical questions that have seemed vexing under previous theoretical approaches.

## Conclusion

We are processual beings immersed in temporal flow. This is the lesson of enactive cognition and of O'Regan's sensorimotor loops (see O'Regan and Noë 2001). The concept of enactive cognition of Varela, Thompson, and Rosch captures the ongoing structurally coupled nature of experience as "laying down a path in walking."[9] It is precisely this (erformative) aspect of the aesthetics of interaction that demands theoretical elaboration.[10]

Mark Johnson's explanation of the transition from bodily situation to abstract concept seems to be sometimes stuck in a temporal freeze—a "frame-wise" way of thinking, much as conventional frame-by-frame machine-vision analysis are incommensurable techniques of optic flow. Hutchins makes tentative steps toward a translation of Johnson's notion into the temporal dimension in his elaboration of thinking with the body. Our task is to think art in the present-continuous—as process-oriented rather than goal-oriented. Such a commitment to process has been a leitmotif of mid-twentieth century avant-gardism (specifically process art and performance art). This idea remained largely incomprehensible outside the community of arts practitioners, at least until the emergence of performance theory.

The ontological ramifications of process art are captured by Barad (2003), who argues that the very construction of subject and object are historically contingent and proposes a radically materialist and performative ontology that sees phenomena as primary and subjects and objects contingently forming or falling out of a process of *intra-action*. Such an approach would be consistent with the performative ontology of Pickering, *the-laying-down-a-path-in-walking* of enactivism, and the *ongoingness* of O'Regan and Noë. This ontological reformulation has direct relevance to the theorization of, and the creation of, interactive artifacts.

The lesson of performativity is that *the experience,* the doing of the action by the subject in the context of the work, *is what constitutes the work.* It is less the destination, or chain of destinations, and more the temporal process that constitutes the experience. (To call the experience *content* would be again to slip into objectivizing language.) Central to any useful analysis of the aesthetics of behavior is the recognition that recourse to a conception of the art phenomenon as being exclusively beyond the spectator is recourse to an imaginary condition. Interactive art destabilizes the subject-object dualism, because the experience of the work is in part the reflexive experience of the activity of the spectactor. An understanding of performativity in interactive art leads to the dissolution of one of the key humanistic dualisms upon which both science and art are premised: the separation of self and world or, in cybernetic terms, of observer and observed.

# 25  Theory and Practice

The difference between theory and practice is greater in practice than in theory.
—Author unknown

The motivation to write this book *arose out of practice*—my own creative practice utilizing electronics, robotics, and computing in pursuit of interactive art, which began in the mid-1980s. My prior experience in sculpture, installation, performance, and other spatially and materially engaged practices led me to pursue projects that engaged the public in a fully embodied way—in contrast to most "new media" work that perpetuated (and still perpetuates) an obsession with the screen and the image, inherited from video art, television, film, and ultimately, photography and painting. Such work demanded intensive technical research and development and prototyping novel sensor, effector, and control systems from low-level components. This practice granted me a hard-won familiarity with the nuts and volts of programming and computer engineering—with an outsider's perspective.

My prior experience in the arts equipped me with an understanding of the tasks of designing computational technologies for direct human sensorimotor engagement that was very different from that of my colleagues in computer science, HCI, and robotics; my approach took human experience seriously and as central to the exercise, rather than seeing it as the phenomenon on the other end of a peripheral, or as an inconvenience on the way to mental abstraction. Over the years, a general unease about the mismatch or misalignment between the goals of my art practice and the goals and values underlying computing technology led me into extended historical review and critical analysis of computing and especially artificial intelligence, as well as psychology, ethology, and other fields. This work was simultaneous with the creation of works that were increasingly conceived as critical interventions into discourses of computer science, AI, and HCI. My growing understanding of this misalignment between the value system underlying (digital) computing and the values inherent in embodied cultural practices made emerging discourses of cognition from embodied, situated, and enactive perspectives particularly relevant. Further research increasingly suggested that these new paradigms of cognition could be leveraged to address problems, not just in computer-based creative practices, and could provide ways of thinking about arts practices generally, which would provide release from the cognitivist straightjacket.

## Humanism

The overt goal of this book has been to explore the value of emerging post-cognitivist research for the development of new ways of understanding arts practices. The embodied, situated, and enactive cognition paradigms offer resources for a new way of thinking about cognition, which provides real explanatory power in understanding the cognitive dimensions of cultural practices, providing explication of kinds of cognition in which material and temporal integration is fundamental—what I've been calling *the intelligences of the arts*.

A particular focus has been the new aesthetic realm facilitated by computational technologies. The development of digital cultures has moved apace, and the miniaturized, networked, mobile digital appliances in our pockets bristling with apps bear scant resemblance to the giant brains of the military-industrial complex of sixty years ago. Online social spaces are populated with chatbots, and games are populated with nonplayer characters, or "AIs." Yet the values around which the computer was constructed inhere, skeuomorphically, even as they are obscured by ever more sumptuous surfaces. Nonetheless, the principles informing what we do with computers and how we do it has not changed much—nor have paradigmatic procedures, nested inside algorithms inside languages inside authoring environments inside operating systems, all smothered over with the mayonnaise of the GUI. Now more than ever, a critical technical practice (Agre 1997b) must be part of any education in digital technologies.

The use of these technologies for cultural practices has generated new modalities of practice, in particular the *designing of behavior*: behavior of machine systems and behavior of heterogeneous networks of people and machines, which characterizes the technosocial complexes we increasingly inhabit. This behavior and these networks are embodied and materially instantiated. As such, the old "brain is a computer" explanation of cognition—preserving as it does the humanist values of rationalism, internalism, individualism, and dualism—is found wanting. It is ironic that a conception of cognition based on computing is perceived as inadequate when systems that are elaborations of that technology are considered.

Such thinking draws us into longer historical consideration of computing as continuous with humanist themes in Western culture. The way computers are and the way we are with computers—both products of the values of humanist modernism—involve dualisms that structure our understanding of ourselves and of our relation with the world. These dualisms—prime among them the mind-body dualism and the closely associated subject-object and self-world dualisms—are axiomatic assumptions upon which both scientific ideas and philosophy are based. They are—and it must be shouted—BELIEFS! They have no grounding in scientifically derived fact.

These beliefs support certain kinds of ideas about mind, body, and cognition, and preclude other ways of thinking. Beyond consideration of the complexities of media arts practices, beyond a historical critique of the role of Enlightenment values in science and technology, beyond advocating for the usefulness of postcognitivist ideas for a theory of practice, my mission here is to consign the notion that thinking occurs exclusively in the brain to the philosophical dumpster. To locate thinking exclusively in the brain is a case of fundamental attribution error. Without doubt, thinking *involves* the brain, but to suggest, on the basis of detection of certain signals, that these signals fully comprise the phenomenon of thinking reinforces dubious internalism.

The idea that thinking occurs exclusively in the brain has precluded proper understanding of the intelligences of the arts. In order to come to grips with the nature of our existence in the world, it is time we abandoned these ideas. This prescription is intended to have practical and pragmatic value; it not only promises to generate a new discourse around (creative, cultural) practices but should also be applicable and useful to practitioners as a way of understanding their practices.

## Not Knowing and Not Caring

If 90 percent of all cognitive activity is unconscious, then artistic decision-making can be partly or wholly nonconscious, which explains the traditional reticence of artists to explain their work—they can't. There is no way we can understand the process or verbalize it, because introspection only has access to what becomes conscious. Moreover, the idea that introspection provides a clear and comprehensive view of even that tip of the iceberg with any accuracy is dubious. Psychological and neuroscience research has shown us that *what we think we think* often has little veracity. Our sense of what our minds are doing is chimerical, a mirage. As we have no access to 90 percent of what is going on in the brain; we also have no sense of what role noncranial and nonneural tissues play; our belief that we know anything with accuracy about the other 10 percent is, as noted, dubious. Based on our lived experience, what we can say with any confidence about who we are, what we know, or how we know it seems minimal.

Introspection and its object (conscious thought) are mutually co-constituting, so discerning *what it is that is aware* is a circular conundrum. Consciousness is a hallucination shown to a hallucination. The conclusion that we must resign ourselves to the fallibility of our conscious awareness as a way to understand ourselves is anathema to an Enlightenment rationalist, yet there seems no alternative.

## What I Said

The following ten points sum up the main arguments of this book:

1. The generally held beliefs regarding mind and selfhood and their relation to embodiment and the world are historically contingent products of a Western humanist, Judeo-Christian worldview.
2. The values of this worldview are embedded in our digital technologies.
3. Mind-body and self-world dualisms are characteristics of that dominant worldview, but we can trace a tradition of alternative views in philosophy, science, and the arts.
4. Art and cultural practices are intelligent. They deploy modalities of intelligence in which embodiment, artifacts, context, and temporality are actively involved. This notion of intelligence is incommensurable with the ideas of cognition we are naturalized to through cognitivism. These ideas have been reinforced by the paradigmatic presence of digital computing in many walks of life.
5. The computer has provided us with new material for cultural practices and a novel capability—that of real-time computing, which permits the design of behavior. This is a new aesthetic realm. The aesthetics of the design of behavior and the experience of behaving artifacts are not well developed.
6. The computer, as it morphed from being the giant brain of the military-industrial complex to a personal digital appliance, has promulgated a retrogressive intellectual imperialism, in the sense that it has reified rationalist Enlightenment ideas and imposed them on diverse contexts in which such ideas are of dubious relevance.

7. The collapse of cognitivism led to new approaches to cognition that attend to the shortcomings of cognitivism by addressing embodiment, context, and temporal engagement.

8. These new postcognitivist approaches provide us with a basis on which to build a new way of thinking about the intelligences of the arts and an aesthetics relevant to the design of behavior.

9. Contemporary neuroscience and philosophy of mind are rapidly destabilizing the dualist individualist and humanist notions of self and mind, and the autocracy of consciousness is giving way to a more distributed, contingent, and relational conception of cognition.

10. Acknowledgment of the performative, embodied, and situated dimensions of cognition can lead to a reassessment of the hierarchical Cartesianism that privileges immateriality and abstraction, qualities which our academies and education systems.

## Postcognitivism

The corpus of postcognitivist ideas, suitably elaborated, offers a range of exciting possibilities for ongoing research and study. It provides perspectives from which to critique modernist philosophical history and technological development. They offer purchase on the shortcomings of the cognitivist paradigm, as applied to human cognition and to technology. They provide a tool for analysis and critique of the ideas embedded in the technology, offering a way forward for HCI out of the cul-de-sac of reified cognitivism. They help us understand the qualities of embodied interaction—phenomena that cognitivist approaches have no purchase on.

Postcognitivist ideas provide new purchase on the cognitive dimensions of all arts and cultural practices. They provide a way of understanding the doing of embodied, sensorially mediated, temporally extended behaving artworks and will allow new perspectives on the design of computational artifacts, CACA or not. A new way of speaking of the intelligences of practice is facilitated by critical application of ideas of situated, distributed, embodied, enactive, and extended cognition. Understanding mind-body-world in nondualist ways will encourage more complete understandings of *cultural cognition.*

# Epilogue: Art, Cognition, Disciplinarity, and Institutions

In order to do interdisciplinary work, it is not enough to take a "subject" (a theme) and to arrange two or three sciences around it. Interdisciplinary study consists of creating a new object, which belongs to no one.
—Roland Barthes, *The Rustle of Language* (1989, 72)


"All knowledge presents itself within a conceptual framework adapted to account for previous experience and that any such frame may prove too narrow to comprehend new experiences."
—Niels Bohr, *Essays 1958–1962 on Atomic Physics and Human Knowledge* (1987, 67)


If we follow the disciplinary habits of tracing disciplinary-defined causes through to the corresponding disciplinary-defined effects, we will miss all the crucial intra-actions among these forces that fly in the face of any specific set of disciplinary concerns.
—Karen Barad, "Posthumanist Performativity: Toward an Understanding of How Matter Comes to Matter" (2003, 810)


"To a man with a hammer, everything looks like a nail."
—Variously attributed to Maslow, Twain, Baruch, and others[1]


In this book, I have sought to enunciate a problem regarding the explication of embodied intelligences. Having recognized that this problem exceeded any established disciplinary domain—or, to put it differently, having realized that various disciplines offer partial and sometimes conflicting answers—I sought to marshal ideas, perspectives, and experimental reports from diverse fields that seemed relevant. I have evaluated and compared positions with respect to each other, noting that ideas that are "commonsense" in some disciplines are regarded as absurd or incomprehensible in others. This process leads necessarily to reflection on the construction of disciplines and the way they function to regulate knowledge. The importance of cross-disciplinary inquiry becomes clear: It is a requirement for a useful discussion of cross-disciplinary phenomena, not simply in the sense of bringing different perspectives to the table but more profoundly, such inquiry can shed light on the uninterrogated axiomatic assumptions hidden in the cultures of existing subject disciplines. Contra disciplinary hubris, I maintain that *anyone who can coherently draw a rhetorical vector through knowledge space (arranged in any definable way) has a claim to expertise.*

## As Many Disjunctions as Convergences

Postcognitivist research is often commendably interdisciplinary—and necessarily so. However, there are many cases in which developments are not well communicated between disciplines and seemingly obvious exchanges have not occurred. As discussed in previous chapters, the notion of performativity and some of its intellectual roots (i.e., speech act theory) were part of Winograd and Flores's HCI and Pickering's sociology of science, yet neither Winograd and Flores nor Pickering seemed aware of the simultaneous blossoming of performance theory in the humanities. Similarly, though the feminist science studies of Donna Haraway, Evelyn Fox Keller, and others had a strong influence on the development of the social studies of science and technology (SSST, STS, etc.), feminist embodiment theory seems to have had little impact on the emerging postcognitive cognitive science. There has been surprisingly little exchange between the distributed cognition community and those connected with the contemporaneous actor-network theory in the social sciences, and the history of research into interaction in the media arts remains almost entirely unknown in HCI circles.

At root, this failure is a symptom of disciplinarity itself. A discipline defines itself in large part by what kinds of knowledge, methods, and subject matter are (understood as) outside its boundaries. As we saw in the review of AI, in technical fields, relevant knowledge is often assumed to be exclusively technical. Geoff Bowker and Leigh Star see it differently:

Why should computer scientists read African-American poets? What does information science have to do with race-critical or feminist methods and metaphysics? The collective wisdom in those domains is one of the richest places from which to understand these core problems in information systems design: how to preserve the integrity of information without a priori standardization and its often attendant violence. In turn, if those lessons can be taken seriously within the emerging cyberworld, there may yet be a chance to strengthen its democratic ethical aspects. (1999, 302)

By the same token, media artists should read phenomenology, artificial life, and dynamical systems theory. Philip Agre saw that artificial intelligence sealed itself off from highly relevant ideas from outside the discipline; making insights from outside perspectives incomprehensible. Disciplinary hubris is almost always folly.

New disciplines do arise and in their formative stages are always interdisciplinary. George Miller's recollections of his 1978 representations to the Sloan Foundation regarding the need to support the establishment of the *cognitive sciences* is instructive:

I argued that at least six disciplines were involved: psychology, linguistics, neuroscience, computer science, anthropology and philosophy. I saw psychology, linguistics and computer science as central, the other three as peripheral. These fields represented, and still represent, an institutionally convenient but intellectually awkward division. Each, by historical accident, had inherited a particular way of looking at cognition and each had progressed far enough to recognize that the solution to some of its problems depended crucially on the solution of problems traditionally allocated to other disciplines. The Sloan Foundation accepted my argument. (2003, 143)

## Disciplines and Institutions

Institutions resist change. The names of disciplines are carved in stone, both metaphorically and literally on the buildings of our campuses. This creates an illusion of permanence. Yet the university and all the disciplines in it are historically contingent human inventions. Contrary to the impression created by institutions, human knowledge and learning are in constant flux. Institutions accommodate such flux, but appropriately slowly. Like a filter capacitor, they dampen the more rapid oscillations. Fifty years ago, many of the disciplines upon which the conversations in this book are grounded were nascent or did not exist: computer science, cognitive science, HCI, robotics, dynamical system theory, artificial intelligence, artificial life, poststructuralist theory, feminist theory, postcolonial theory, science and technology studies, performance studies, media theory, and new media arts. More recently, we have seen the emergence of game studies, software studies, and other fields of digital cultural practices. We should expect and encourage such transformations.

Disciplines arise as a result of external contexts. Mechanical engineering arose in response to the increasing proliferation of mechanisms in the Industrial Revolution, professionalizing a field that had once been the territory of amateurs, experimenters, and inventors. Computer science, similarly, came into existence in parallel with the rise of the information economy. It follows then, that in periods of rapid technocultural change, disciplinary conservatism— hewing to the practices of established disciplines— is probably an impediment to real progress in discourse and in technological development.

The ossification of the disciplines has a major negative effect in encouraging the silo effect in academic structures, endorsing epistemological tunnel vision in faculty and providing students with a narrow view of the world and the role of their discipline. Given the self-justifying nature of disciplines, attempts to cross boundaries are usually met with dismissive accusations of dilettantism and shortage of specialized expertise.

Such conceptions of expertise are themselves a product of the historically contingent, and by no means entirely rational, divisions of knowledge into defined areas called disciplines. Not unlike the national boundaries of Africa, which are a legacy of the colonial period, the division of the academy into schools, disciplines, and departments is always inconsistent and anomalous. Subject areas are occupied by multiple disciplines with incompatible methodologies, logically unified fields are divided, and epistemologically separate fields are lumped together. What unifies such "disciplines" are often uninterrogated commitments to sets of axiomatic assumptions that are, in a Gödelian way, out of reach of critical analysis using the tools of the discipline itself. Some disciplines (as Agre shows about AI) are stubbornly resistant to reflexive inquiry. (Others perhaps overindulge in what can amount to navel-gazing.)

It is important to note that those who forge new areas of research— *amateurs* in the best sense—almost always do so without institutional support. Machiavelli knew this in 1513: "Innovation makes enemies of all those who prospered under the old regime, and only lukewarm support is forthcoming from those who would prosper under the new" (1992, 17). It is only when such ideas become institutionalized that institutions reward such researchers—by which time those ideas are, by definition, no longer cutting edge. This is a major paradox confronting institutions dedicated to inquiry and "new knowledge": While interdisciplinarity is rightly lauded by institutions as a significant source of innovation and new knowledge, to the extent that an idea is interdisciplinary and innovative it will usually be judged unscientific, unfeasible, outrageous, irrelevant, or otherwise unacceptable by disciplines in those same institutions.

A great power of interdisciplinary research is its ability to note not just disjunctions but commonalities between the concerns and methods of diverse pursuits. Such comparisons can be generative of new research agendas. As with biology and with human culture, hybridity in the academy is generative. By the same token, it is often unwelcome in established disciplines because it can be disruptive. "Disruptive thinking" is another catchphrase of innovation coaches—just don't be too disruptive. (Suggesting that the basic premise of a major corporation is fundamentally unethical is not the kind of disruption they want to hear about.) Interdisciplinarity of any meaningful kind entails a willingness to question assumptions and boundaries, and to generally go beyond the comfort of known territories and familiar discourses. Such challenges cause deep discomfort in many, which in their most blatant cases amounts to little more than unwillingness to interrogate habitual behaviors, or simple intellectual cowardice, sometimes veiled with bombastic rhetoric about specialization, tradition, and rigor. This is well documented in the history of media technologies by Brian Winston, who coined his *law of suppression of radical potential* to describe the pattern of suppression of new technologies by those with vested interests in the technologies of the previous generation (1998).

The following story I have come to call the parable of the locksmith. During the renovation of buildings on a university campus, a tradesman was sent to fix a problem with a door. When I encountered him, he was enlarging a hole in the doorframe with a grinder so the bolt would latch. I looked at the door and noticed that it was not latching because door was not aligned. Further inspection revealed that the screws holding the hinges to the doorframe had corroded and the door had dropped. I pointed this out to the tradesman and suggested that he replace the screws in the hinges. He looked at me with pathetic incomprehension, saying, "I'm a lock guy; I'm not a door guy." I was speechless. His response had an appalling profundity to it, and it captures a kind of blinkered thinking not unknown in centers of higher learning.

**Asking the Right Question: Beyond "Problem Solving"**

Contemporary pedagogy, belying its cognitivist influences, valorizes "problem solving." Such a preoccupation assumes that a problem is given or self-evident. While this might be the case for a set problem in a college engineering textbook, in the real world nothing could be farther from the truth. More importantly, the analytic, reductive skills of conventional problem solving have scant value in the task of asking the right question. In institutions of higher learning, emphasis is commonly placed on problem solving, as if problems were lying around like shells on the beach, just waiting to be picked up. In order to be solved, a problem must first be *enunciated* and *framed*—and problems can be constructed with more or less astuteness. Except in isolated and informal pockets, few attempt teaching the skill of asking the right question or knowing how to ask the right question or knowing how to know if it's right. Courses in critical and analytical thinking are rare.

## Wicked Problems

In his paper "Wicked Problems in Design Thinking" (1992), Richard Buchanan reviews the development of the idea by German design theorist Horst Ritell, who borrowed the term from Karl Popper. Buchanan cites Rittel's characterization of wicked problems as follows:

(1) Wicked problems have no definitive formulation, but every formulation of a wicked problem corresponds to the formulation of a solution. (2) Wicked problems have no stopping rules. (3) Solutions to wicked problems cannot be true or false, only good or bad. (4) In solving wicked problems there is no exhaustive list of admissible operations. (5) For every wicked problem there is always more than one possible explanation, with explanations depending on the Weltanschauung of the designer. (6) Every wicked problem is a symptom of another, "higher level," problem. (7) No formulation and solution of a wicked problem has a definitive test. (8) Solving a wicked problem is a "one shot" operation, with no room for trial and error. (9) Every wicked problem is unique. (10) The wicked problem solver has no right to be wrong—they are fully responsible for their actions. (1992, 16)

This quotation captures an approach to problem solving which has been a consistent characteristic in design disciplines since the 1960s, especially in Europe and the UK. It emphasizes the heterogenous nature of real world problems. Point 1 emphasises the reflexive isomorphism between a proposed solution and the particular formulation of the problem. This is a constant danger in discipline-based problem solving.

In the real world, problems seldom observe disciplinary borders. Problem formulation requires a kind of intellectual process that is diametrically opposed to problem solving. It requires the ability to grapple with incongruities and incompatibilities and discontinuities. We are good at teaching the deductive processes of problem solving, but this only permits students to solve already framed textbook-style problems. As previously noted (see chapter 15), Varela, Thompson, and Rosch say, "The usual tendency (of conventional cognitive science) is to treat cognition as problem solving in some pre-given task domain. The greatest ability of living cognition, however, consists in being able to pose, within broad constraints, the relevant issues that need to be addressed at each moment" (1991, 145).

Determining salience—asking the right question—is an act of intelligence as substantial as, but incommensurable with, the reductive analytics of problem solving. Asking the (right) question—a good (or appropriate) question—always precedes getting the right answer. Getting the right answer to a bad (inappropriate, impractical, unwise) question can be disastrous. Discerning what the right question is from the cacophony, heterogeneity, incongruities, and noise of the everyday lived world requires a kind of intelligence that is orthogonal to the analytic mode valorized as "reasoning" in cognitivism. To return to the Gödelian metaphor, analytic problem solving occurs within a predefined and closed logical framework; the construction of such frameworks and their contents are of quite a different order of mentation. This scenario is reminiscent of the "common sense problem," reminding us that deductive logical operations themselves might be inadequate or inappropriate.

As an undergraduate, one of my professors at art school gave me a piece of what I now see as sage advice: "Art is not about getting the right answer, it is about asking the right question."[2] I now recognize that this determination of salience is central to artistic judgment and moreover, that visual arts pedagogy is one of the few areas in the academy where the importance of asking the right question—and the skills required in order to ask the right question—is taught from the outset. Artworks often create, rather than solve, problems—and this is a good thing.

## The Two Cultures and the Tacit/Performative

In a world where education is predominantly verbal, highly educated people find it all but impossible to pay serious attention to anything but words and notions.

—Aldous Huxley, *The Doors of Perception* (1954, 62)

Long ago, C. P. Snow made famous his idea of the basic difference between humanistic and scientific knowledge. Whatever the differences in attitude between Snow's two cultures, they both partake in an Enlightenment drive toward abstraction. While much is made of the humanities/sciences rift on campuses, both engage in scholarly practices of symbolic discourse, the reaping of symbols from the world. They harvest knowledge from the world to produce abstract representations (texts, equations, databases), which, in our epistemology, constitute knowledge. This predilection for the (ultimately Platonic) qualities of generality and abstraction is a characteristic of the academy and the university as we know it. Snow's binary today seems less significant than the distinction between doing things in the world and extracting knowledge from the world—between representational and performative ontology.

Throughout our society, symbolic abstraction has privileged status. The academy, the university—the institutions that support and validate scientific knowledge—play a major role in this. The ivory tower is built around the valorization of abstraction and the power of generality, be it in philosophy or physics. Even our intelligence tests emphasize extractions from the world of abstract truths, which can then be manipulated in the immaterial realm of mental computation. Alfred Jarry offered an alternative science of pataphysics: "Pataphysics will be, above all, the science of the particular, despite the common opinion that the only science is that of the general" (1996, 21). Generality is not a universal good, and specificity is just as useful in its place. Art often dwells on the specificities of the particular, and thus acts counter to the scientistic drive to generality and abstraction.

Conventional academic or scholarly ontology involves extraction of knowledge from the world and encapsulation in forms of symbolic representation, whether we are speaking of equations, algorithms, postulates, or even sonnets. The ability to perform such dematerializing actions (conventionally) defines intelligence. Yet in the day-to-day world, we are confronted with endless examples of intelligent actions that do not culminate in dematerialized symbolic abstractions and, in many cases, arguably do not even detour through that territory: the work of the chicken sexer, the potato roguer, the juggler, the stonemason, the shipwright, and all the rest.

Agre makes a complementary point when he observes that computational fields "concentrate on the aspects of representation that writing normally captures. As a result, theories will naturally tend to lean on distinctions that writing captures and not on the many distinctions that it doesn't" (2003, 290). It is precisely this discontinuity that creates a deep tension in the modern academy, between the ontology of the textual-symbolic regime and the ontology of the arts and other embodied practices. With these different ontologies follow different pedagogies. The apprenticeship, so sneered upon by modern liberal arts pedagogues, is clearly well suited to training in tacit and embodied knowledges (and has been considered so for millennia), where the guidance of the movement of an arm or a leg efficiently conveys understandings extensive textual elaboration cannot.

The rubrics of the performative turn and material turn are new in the humanities and social sciences. It's all we've ever had in the arts. The humanities are now *posthumanist*, yet there is a long tradition of these now characteristically posthumanist ideas in American pragmatist and continental phenomenologist philosophy. One of the ramifications of this posthumanism is that the Cartesian dualism and other Enlightenment baggage are not above interrogation. Sadly, the conception that mind and matter are somehow inherently separate is reproduced daily in the commitments of cognitivists and computer scientists. A small but growing number are aware that practice—whether that practice is in the studio, the lab, or the operating room—implies modalities of cognition which are performative and materially engaged.

## Bypassing the False Precision of Formalism

Arts practices do not usually pursue a one-way serial conversion of world into symbols. *Artists turn the world into more world*, sometimes taking a detour into the world of symbolic representation, but usually manifesting material artifacts or temporal performances. The predicament of the arts on the modern campus is that this turning the world into more world is incompatible with a conception of intelligence rooted in symbolic abstraction.

To pretend that arts practices trade exclusively in the currency of symbol manipulation has the effect that Agre exquisitely referred to as being "hollowed through the false precision of formalism" (1997b, 148). As there is "more in heaven and earth than ever dreamed of in your philosophy," so there is also more in art practice. The little that passes through the dualist sieve is impoverished without the rest. To deploy a different analogy, illuminating arts practices with the flashlight of rationalism illuminates a narrow cone. What is outside this illuminated cone—the structures and networks that support the part illuminated—remains obscure, unseen, and unspeakable. As a practitioner, I know—as artists and artisans of all ages before me have known—the ineffability of practice: the way that active engagement with a heterogeneous constellation of tools and materials, smells and associations, arguments, images, ideas, and passions exceeds and evades rational encapsulation or description.

Cultural artifacts play a role in culture. Culture comprises the activities of groups of people in structured spaces or storied places populated with crafted artifacts and eloquent objects. In this light, all of culture is distributed cognition, broadly construed—whether it be a Niuginian singsing, an Appalachian quilting bee, or online coverage of computer game competitions in Korea. Today, social media has created a context in which cultural effects can be physically distributed, heterogeneous combinations of the virtual and physically real.

The monumentality of edifices such as museums and concert halls attests to the fact that cultural objects and events are regarded generally as important markers of human achievement. Yet paradoxically, as a result of the ontological commitments of the liberal arts model, the arts are rendered second-class disciplines on the campus. A closely related irony is that though we, as a culture, value cultural works and sing the praises of their makers, conventional measures of intelligence have little to say about those with such abilities. As Lambros Malafouris lamented, "I am afraid that, as long as cognition and material culture remain separated by this ontological gulf, our efforts to understand the nature of either is doomed to failure" (2004, 53–54). Cognition and material culture remain separated on the campus. Changing the way we think about cognition can have far-reaching effects for the arts, for the academy, and for the place of the arts in the academy.

## New Knowledge

As any scientific researcher knows, to be a good candidate for research, a project must conform to two main conditions: It must be novel and interesting, and it must be amenable to methodology; that is, it must have the potential to result in new knowledge within the context in which knowledge is (locally) defined. The problem, as Hamlet knew, is that there are many more interesting questions than are amenable to any particular methodology. More often than one would prefer, interesting topics are jettisoned because the likelihood of producing results according to what constitutes "good results" within a particular disciplinary method are low. The case of neuroaesthetics exemplifies the difficulties created in the attempt to fuse the profoundly different types of complexity confronted by neuroscientific modeling and the performance and scholarly traditions of the arts and humanities. This is emblematic of the challenges involved in the undertaking of such radical interdisciplinarity—an interdisciplinarity implicit in the task of finding modes of neurocognitive analysis with which to approach evidence of human construction of meaning provided by five thousand years of historical record and current practices in the arts.

## Disciplinary Auslanders

If we insist that a question is interesting, but contest the validity of a given methodology to produce results that capture the interestingness of the matter, we become a kind of disciplinary auslander, hawking interestingness outside the city walls. How do you validate knowledge outside disciplinary and methodological constructs? This is a key problem for inter/trans/anti/nondisciplinary practice. Such questions lead us into an epistemological dilemma at the heart of debates, from the two cultures to the science wars—the kind captured in aphorisms like: Science exists to establish objective truth about the world and the humanities exist because it (establising objective truth) is not possible. Einstein's witty observation that "not everything that can be counted counts, and not everything that counts can be counted" is another way of saying: that which quantitative measures can measure is limited to quantities, but each quantity is of a qualitatively defined category. In the same way, we can say that reductivism sometimes succeeds only in reducing things. The idea that valuable knowledge about poetry can be produced by statistical analysis of word occurrences in Shakespeare's sonnets is just silly. Data of some kind are produced, data of the kind that fill the vast server farms of Amazon and eBay, but these data hardly deserve the moniker *information*, let alone knowledge. As T. S. Eliot presciently asked in 1934, "Where is the knowledge we have lost in information?"

The corollary is also true. More than once I have been asked if I have performed "user testing" on my artworks. My response to this question is usually incredulity. The idea of running user studies or usability studies on an object the use of which is not defined—or is built intentionally to confound discourses of usability—is absurd. How can one measure the effectiveness of a work if the conditions of fulfillment are not only *not* stated but *never* stated and perhaps not even considered? What if "success" meant that user response was unpredictably surprising? In order to submit to the rigors of tractability, user studies of artworks, if they happen, confine themselves to the dimensions of artworks that conform to nonart structures. We might see studies of the ergonomics of keyboard operations for a desktop game, and those results might tell us something about the details of ergonomic design—but little about the game experience.

## Toy Problems

AI was criticized for working with "toy problems" like "block worlds," which constrained variables to permit tractability, but in the process tacitly abandoned hopes of scalability or broader applicability. It was in response to the failures of such approaches to building viable robots in the real world that Brooks insisted that every module of his subsumption robots be tested and proven in real-world conditions before it was integrated into larger systems. The AI aphorism "In AI we believe in the work ethic—it has to work" seems to speak of pragmatism and practicality, but such systems often "worked" in a controlled and constrained domain.

Many animal behavior and psychology of perception experiments in the same period (i.e., 1960s–1980s) were similarly conducted in highly constrained (laboratory) environments. (The example of Hubel and Wiesel's experiments [1959] on the visual neurology of cats was discussed in chapter 2.) The neuroethological approach was developed in recognition of the failure of that reductivist logic. Results in such studies have minimal relevance in real-world situations. Chemero and Heyser (2005) published a metastudy of the history of experiments concerning the exploratory behavior of rats under different circumstances in which new objects are introduced to the rats' environment. They explain that for male rats, climbability is a key affordance of objects, affording keeping lookout. For females, the quality of enclosure or protection was key, affording nesting. They note that of 116 experiments over two decades, they found all but thirty-two methodologically suspect because the experimental reports made no explicit record of the kinds of objects introduced for rat exploratory behavior! Clearly, a pencil, a brick, a box, and a banana are all objects, but what each affords any particular rat is different.

The choice of Tetris as an experimental environment by Kirsh and Maglio (1994) was canny, as what was of interest (epistemic action) was in this context controllable, quantifiable (in the simplest measures of units/ time), and repeatable. As such, part of the charm of the experiment was how it mapped so nicely onto experimental methodology. Operating a photocopier—as in Suchman's (1987) case study—is a task with a defined result that is achieved or not achieved. Likewise, in finding the museum (Clark and Chalmers's Extended Mind thought experiment), there is a clear measure of success and failure. Cases in which the end states and results are not so clear, are unspecified or unspecifiable, challenge these kinds of methods and measures. We confront this situation in the extreme when considering works of art and culture cognitively or quantitatively.

An approach that works in some cases is to treat an aspect of the mechanics of the cultural pratice as if it were an HCI user study. Evelyn Tribble (2005) has done this in her analysis of diagrammatic and notational systems employed in Shakespeare's Globe Theatre, which have been something of an academic conundrum. Tribble's analysis, modeled on Hutchins's distributed cognition, is an exemplary piece of interdisciplinary research.

## Catamarans and Locomotives

In his discussion of anthropological research regarding Micronesian navigation, Hutchins (1995) reports that when asked a question regarding navigation, framed in terms of Western traditions, the Micronesian navigator found the question almost incomprehensible. It wasn't that he wasn't clever or got the wrong answer, but that the question would not parse within the worldview. Yet, as we know, Micronesians used their system with substantial success for centuries. This example reminds us that systems of knowledge can be incomensurable; systems can be effective while being incompatible with each other. Importantly, any explanatory system—built necessarily on axioms, assumptions and analogies—makes certain things easy to think and, by the same token, makes other things difficult or impossible. Hutchins gave the useful example of geocentric and heliocentric views of the "heavens": Each facilitates different kinds of thinking (and computation). As previously mentioned, John Haugeland described Descartes's constitution of the mental as an independent ontological domain with a charmingly hokey image: "Behind that engine have trailed the sorry boxcars of hyperbolic doubt, the mind-body problem, the problem of the external world, the problem of other minds, and so on" (1998, 207). Descartes's formulation of mind and body as ontologically separate has facilitated all kinds of philosophical inquiry regarding the ego and its relation to the world. By the same token, it makes it impossible to think of self and being in nondualist terms. One must maintain constant vigilance lest one's metaphors drive one's ontology, putting the cart before the horse.

## Cognitive Studies of Art

An effective approach to the study of cognitive dimensions of arts practices must, in my opinion, take an approach akin to neuroethology or cognitive archeology—that is, neither internalist nor externalist but ecological and relational, acknowledging know-how, actor networks, and the mangle of practice, with full recognition of the cultural and dynamical dimensions of the context. This may well have the effect of precluding the kind of reductivism upon which conventional scientific research depends.

Artworks are neither scripts nor navigational aids, nor can we think of an artwork as an artifact or a tool. Especially in the modern period, the cognitive modality of artworks is transitive, and as William James said about consciousness, "It is nothing jointed, it flows." We can confidently ascribe a didactic and pedagogical role to the stained glass and relief sculpture of a gothic cathedral, and place them discursively into a sociopolitical context in which the church had control of literacy and information. However, we cannot speak of a Serra sculpture in the same terms that we speak of a Michelangelo, to say nothing of an activist media-cultural intervention such as the Barbie Liberation Organization (BLO)—a feminist/queer initiative in which talking Barbie and GI Joe dolls were purchased, their voice recordings switched (so that

GI Joe complained "math is hard!"), repackaged, and stealthily replaced on store shelves in acts of reverse shoplifting.

Without going more deeply into case studies across a variety of traditional and contemporary forms and media, we are reduced to generalizations. Among those generalizations, we can with some confidence say that didacticism plays a minimal role in the ways a contemporary artwork functions, and functioning as a catalyst for evoking associations in a provocative and open-ended way is primary. Indeed, leaving viewers with a sense of disquiet or irresolution would be regarded by many as a successful intervention: Not in the sense of being trivially disruptive, but in the sense of provoking ongoing active inquiry—disruptive thinking at its best.

Artworks (at least, good ones) are metacognitive. They provoke us to consider, for instance, not just what we are seeing but also the experience of seeing itself and our assumptions about it. James Turrell's work is paradigmatic: Take, for instance, *Pleiades* (1983), installed at the Mattress Factory in Pittsburgh. In this work, the perceptual experience is so subtle, at such low light levels, that one is left with more questions than answers regarding what it is one experienced. Of the work, Turrell said, "In this work, what is generated in you and what is actually out there become a little more equal" (1983). This example suffices to caution us that consideration of the cognitive roles and modalities of (at least contemporary) artworks in terms of *communication* or other didactical conceptions would be foolishly naïve. On the other hand, it would be similarly naïve to assume one could say much useful *in general* about contemporary art, because one could find exceptions for whatever one says—and if one couldn't find such an example, then this would be provocation enough for someone to make it. Such is the perversity of art.

To take another example, consider Bill Viola's early video installation *Sleep of Reason* (1988). You walk into a medium-sized white room, lit with a single table lamp. Facing you against the far wall is an ordinary-looking domestic dresser with a nine-inch black-and-white video monitor on it. On the monitor, a completely uneventful video plays, showing the head of a sleeping man on a pillow. Suddenly, the screen goes black, the entire room goes dark, and the three walls of the room light up in floor-to-ceiling slow motion, grainy, monochrome video—a house on fire at night, a close-up of an owl in flight, ocean waves crashing, or other scenes, accompanied with inchoate and troubling sounds. Just as suddenly, the images and sounds vanish, the room is quiet, the lamp and the monitor come on again. The sleeper perhaps stirs. We could say vague things about dreams, but any attempt to "explain" the work seems fatuous. As per the title, the work evades explication or seeks to capture the quality of an experience that evades explication. The installation is "about" the unspeakability of things that are as quotidian as they are unspeakable.

Perhaps this is why cognitive scientists have, so far and perhaps wisely, swerved to avoid contemporary art: It is just too difficult. Attempts that have been made often seem flat-footed, almost as flat-footed as the majority of early computer graphic "art" (which, in the catalog of all flat-footed things, is a pinnacle of achievement—a pinnacle rivaled, it must be said, by the silliness of Photoshop pointillist and charcoal-sketch filters, objects of much mirth in the art world). On the other hand, some contemporary art can seem aggressively obfuscating, such as Joseph Beuys's famous action performance *How to Explain Pictures to a Dead Hare* (1965), in which he sat, his face daubed with gold leaf and honey, mumbling indistinguishable things to a dead hare he cradled in his arms.

Recently, in an interview about his (collaborative) work *Coal Fired Computers*, British media artist Graham Harwood said, "We choose to use art as a method of inquiry . . . we're not trying to say 'here's a problem, lets solve it'; what we're trying to do is construct something like a physical diagram that allows people to reimagine . . . what kinds of ways can you construct something that will allow different kinds of public to negotiate the relationships" (2013). Remarks like this will seem quotidian to readers with a background in contemporary arts, but they may be surprising to readers from outside the art world. It is the nature of interdisciplinary conversations like this one that things sophomoric to one audience can be almost incomprehensible to another. Harwood's notion of an artwork as "a physical diagram that allows people to reimagine" describes a process of associative play with all the phenomena of the world, juxtaposed for their potential to elicit cognitive fireworks. We're not in Kansas anymore, and this is not square dancing. Marcel Duchamp, the godfather of contemporary art, gave up art for chess. He probably would have preferred the glass bead game.

## The Arts, Disciplines, and Society

Among the several perversities of art is its commitment to embrace and to grapple with the essential heterogeneity of things. Art, as understood since the mid twentieth century at least, is inherently non- or antidisciplinary. It is in the nature of a discipline that it can identify its domain, and that process immediately draws lines between inside and outside—like the autopoietic cell membrane—defining a logical environment beyond which the discipline cannot operate. The idea of a discipline as a logically coherent domain that cannot conceive of itself as part of something larger—cannot position itself in a larger context—is as depressing as it is poetic. Perhaps this is a wanton metaphorization of Gödel's incompleteness theorem, too loose to be rigorous, but we are searching here for structures to think with, not logical rules.

Art is just one of many nondisciplines that operates in human culture outside the dogmas of the academy, remixing aspects of culture (broadly construed) in ways that sometimes seem to make little sense. Sometimes, as noted, this is because such actions occur in advance of the development of an explanatory discourse. Within the academy, an important role for the arts is to reimagine what disciplines do and to review the appropriateness of such institutions and categories. Perhaps the arts do function as cultural early warning systems (McLuhan), and artists as "the antennae of the race" (Pound).

# Notes

## Preface

1. This was repeated in a number of pieces written about him after his death. See, for example, http://philosophy.uchicago.edu/faculty/haugeland.html.

2. Little of this exists in art education on liberal arts campuses today, where the culture of lectures and texts and exams reigns.

3. I am grateful for the vision and drive of my department head, the late Bryan Rogers.

## Introduction

1. See Penny 1997.

2. Initiatives in this area are emerging, such as the study of distributed cognition in choreographic development by David Kirsh (2011) with the Royal Ballet Company.

3. See Penny 2011a.

4. Ibid.

5. And who, in turn, were elaborating the aspirations in 1980s telematic art practices.

6. See Penny 2008a.

7. I have been preoccupied with this theme since the publication of my article "Simulation Digitization Interaction: The Impact of Computing in the Arts" (Penny 1987).

8. As Tom Standage amusingly showed in his book *The Victorian Internet: The Remarkable Story of the Telegraph and the Nineteenth Century's Online Pioneers* (1998).

9. See Penny 2008b.

10. A set of transitions beautifully described by Thomas L. Hankins and Robert J. Silverman in *Instruments and the Imagination* (1995).

11. *What Computers Can't Do: A Critique of Artificial Reason* (Dreyfus 1972), later updated as *What Computers Still Can't Do: A Critique of Artificial Reason* (Dreyfus 1992), a book that was roundly despised by most AI people. Stevan Harnad's paper titled "The Symbol Grounding Problem" (1990) addressed much the same territory. The matter is still being discussed in AI circles.

12. With apologies to Katherine Hayles.

**Intermezzo**

1. The Mercator projection was known in Britain for many years as the Wright projection, named for Edward Wright, the editor and publisher of an English exegesis of this projection (1599).

2. It is worth observing that in the construction of massively multiplayer games, the challenge of usable representations in virtual worlds has brought forth interfaces rooted in these conventions and that these would not be meaningful without prior acculturation.

**1   How Did We Get Here?**

1. Many have served this duty before me, far better than I am capable of—notably, Lewis Mumford and Otto Mayr.

2. See also Hanna and Thompson 2003.

3. It is worth noting that this binary is not explicit in Alan Turing's original work and that the idea of software as immaterial, formalized reasoning matured slowly. The notion was not so cut-and-dried even in the early 1970s, probably because programming was such a tangible process even then—pushing punch cards into readers in the right order.

4. The computer upon which Deep Blue's chess program ran in 1997 was ten million times faster than the Ferranti Mark 1 upon which Dietrich Prinz's chess program ran in 1951.

5. See, for instance, Moore 2015.

6. Elsewhere, I have reviewed the period of emergence of digital media arts in the 1990s in terms of the theoretical dilemmas generated by the grand collision of arts traditions and computing. See "Desire for Virtual Space: The Technological Imaginary in 90s Media Art" (Penny 2011a).

**2   The Biology of Cognition**

1. Over such time scales, there is no need to assume a generally steady rate of evolution. S. J. Gould's notion of punctuated equilibrium is entirely acceptable (Eldredge and Gould 1972).

2. Von Uexküll was also a friend of philosopher Walter Benjamin.

3. See Lettvin et al. 1959.

4. On the other hand, it's possible that the frog can distinguish flat pictures from spatial environments.

5. See Medina 2011.

6. Oliver Sacks beautifully relates one such story: "To See and Not See" in *An Anthropologist on Mars* (1995).

7. The term *radical constructivism* comes from Ernst von Glasersfeld (1980).

8. See Mayer 2011.

### 3  What Was Cybernetics?

1. The term *cyborg* (for *cybernetic organism*) was coined in 1960 by Manfred Clynes.

2. See, for instance, the work of Adrian Thompson (1997).

3. Or, as I more recently quipped, "Objectivity is in the eye of the beholder."

4. See also von Foerster 1995.

5. This notion was shared by the theory of autopoiesis, originated by Chilean biologist Humberto Maturana and developed with the assistance of Francisco Varela (his graduate student at the time; see chapter 2).

6. See, for instance, Cariani 2009.

### 4  Giant Brains of the Military-Industrial Complex

1. I am indebted to Paul Edwards's extraordinary work *The Closed World: Computers and the Politics of Discourse in Cold War America* (1997) for many of the historical details discussed in the chapter.

2. William (Bill) Phillips, a New Zealander, built a hydraulic economic simulator Monetary National Income Analogue Computer (MONIAC) in 1949 at the London School of Economics.

3. A *relay* is an electromagnetic switch that performs a function analogous to that of a simple transistor.

4. In yet another inaccurate and oversimplified story of individual genius, William Shockley of Bell Labs is usually credited with the invention of the transistor in 1947. It was clearly advantageous to Bell Labs to expend resources to write history in this way. There were in fact precedents in Canada (Lilienfeld in 1925) and Germany (Heil in 1934), and the Shockley point contact transistor was independently invented in France a few months later (Mataré and Welker in 1948).

5. This RAND is not to be confused with the Rand of Remington Rand. That Rand originates in James Rand Sr. and James Rand Jr., proprietors of the Rand Kardex Company, which merged with the Remington Typewriter company in 1927 (Campbell-Kelly and Aspray 1996, 34). Significantly, Sperry-Rand originated as the Sperry Gyroscope Company in 1910. In 1955, the Sperry Corporation acquired Remington Rand and the Eckert Mauchly computer corporation, changed its name to Sperry-Rand, and developed the UNIVAC computer.

6. It transpires that, at the time, the Soviet Union was doing the same.

7. Edwards continues, "Between SAGE and its work on the 'Bomb-Nav' analog guidance computer for the B52 strategic bomber, more than half of IBM's income in the 1950s came from military sources" (1997, 102).

8. Quickly renamed Terrorism Information Awareness—saving precious tax dollars by preserving the acronym.

9. The title of this chronology refers to *Giant Brains; or, Machines That Think* by Edmund C. Berkeley. Amusingly, chapter 3 details "the design of a very simple mechanical brain" called Simon (Berkeley 1949, 22–41).

10. ENIAC shared many features with a small-scale machine later known as the Atanasoff Berry Computer (ABC) that J. V. Atanasoff and Clifford Berry built at Iowa State University from 1937 to 1939. John Mauchly visited Atanasoff for several days in June 1940 and gained a detailed understanding of the ABC, yet later denied it had any influence on the design of ENIAC.

## 5   The Rise of Artificial Intelligence

1. The video *From Rosenblueth to Richmond* is a one-hour historical review of cybernetics that was delivered by Randall Whitaker on August 10, 2011, in the context of the American Society for Cybernetics' Conference on Listening. Randall Whitaker tells the story, in a staunchly partisan way, as one of betrayal and skullduggery:

By the mid-fifties, some of the things that have been associated with the people involved in Macy Conferences, like computers, like communication . . . and so forth, had gone in a different direction. The Dartmouth Conference in 1956 established what we would call *AI*: cognitivism—representationalism, not only in terms of computer models, but also in terms of an approach to studying cognition itself. . . . What they essentially threw out was everything about circularity. They managed . . . to wipe out interest in analog and neural models as far as engineering computing kinds of things, and they essentially wiped out interest in similarities that cut across both biological and technical systems. (2011)

2. Such as those arrayed in the wonderful display of mechanical musical instruments in Schloss Bruchsal in Baden Würtemburg, Germany.

3. Turing's choice of a game of deception and "passing" was presumably inflected by his experience of his own homosexuality in repressive social context.

4. The essay was republished one year later in a book of essays (with an additional article by Warren Weaver) entitled *The Mathematical Theory of Communication* (Shannon and Weaver 1949).

5. See, for instance, Kirsh 1991.

6. For instance, WordPerfect was first marketed in 1980, and its first PC version was available in 1982. The first PC version of WordStar was available the same year. Demo versions of Microsoft Word were distributed on disk (5¼-inch floppy) in issues of *PCWorld* in late 1983.

7. In 1981, Satya Pal Asija received the first US patent for a computer software program: "It was for a natural-language-interface program called Swift-Answer, an acronym for the contrived name Special Word-Indexed Full-Text Alpha-Numeric Storage with Easy Retrieval" (Ganapati 2009). This kind of labored acronym also was a characteristic of the field, humorously noted in the naming of TWAIN: "Technology Without An Interesting Name."

8. In the same year, McCarthy developed the idea of timesharing. His goal was to reduce the delays and bottlenecks of batch processing. Most of the time, the CPUs of big machines were idle, but researchers would regularly wait days for their jobs to be processed. Timesharing allowed multiple users to work interactively via data screens rather than via batch processing on paper. It interleaved the calculations of several users simultaneously connected to the machine via video display terminals (VDTs). This reduced input/output (i/o) bottlenecks and led to the real-time computation necessary for the military requirements of high-speed decision-making.

9. It is worth noting that this binary is not explicit in Turing's original work and that the idea of software as immaterial, formalized reasoning matured slowly. The notion was not so cut-and-dried even in the early 1970s, probably because programming, even then, was such a tangible process: pushing punch cards into readers in the right order.

## 6 "Gravity Drowned"

1. AI promoters had a distinct weakness for hyperbole. Along with artificial intelligence itself, which would have more appropriately been dubbed *automated reasoning*, the General Problem Solver might more modestly and accurately have been called *Local Feature-Guided Network Searcher*, according to Drew McDermott (Dreyfus 1992, 2). Dependency maintenance was once called *truth maintenance*. Similar things might be said of *knowledge engineering*.

2. Fernando Flores was the political director of Stafford Beer's Cybersyn project in Salvador Allende's Chile (see chapter 3). In this way, the socio-technological discourses of cybernetics reinserted themselves into computer science through the back door of HCI.

3. Famously, Marvin Minsky was, at one point, of the opinion that the common sense problem could be solved in a year or so, given some good grad students.

4. Philip Agre discusses this in his wonderful essay "Toward a Critical Technical Practice: Lessons Learned Trying to Reform AI" (1997b).

5. A later summary of the argument is found in Wilson and Keil 1999.

6. This scenario of infinite regress of mutually defining chains of reference is surprisingly similar to the postmodern critique of culture made by Jean Baudrillard in his influential essay "The Precession of the Simulacra," originally published in French in 1981 (Baudrillard 1983).

7. Notably, playing expert-level Go proved far more challenging. Recently, Google's AlphaGo has played well, but it is built around connectionist methods as opposed to symbolic AI.

8. Such language problems are now the territory of cognitive linguistics. Turner and Fauconnier refer to such constructions as "conceptual blends" (1995).

9. Thanks to Noah Wardrip-Fruin for reminding me of this Tale-Spin anecdote.

10. See Agre and Horswill 1997.

11. See also Agre 1988.

12. I first pursued such themes in Penny 1994.

## 7 Complexity, Nonlinear Dynamics, and Self-Organizing Systems

1. *Phlogiston* was a theory of combustion advanced by J. J. Becher in the seventeenth century. It held that in burning, an element called *phlogiston* was liberated. This theory was superseded by an understanding of the chemical process of oxidation.

2. "If the correction channel has a capacity equal to Hy(x) [the amount of additional information that must be supplied per second at the receiving point to correct the received message] it is possible to so encode the correction data as to send it over this channel and correct all but an arbitrarily small fraction of the errors. This is not possible if the channel capacity is less than Hy(x)" (Shannon and Weaver 1949, 68).

3. Pataphysics is a science or philosophy devised by absurdist French playwright Alfred Jarry in the early twentieth century. At least in one interpretation, pataphysics is antigeneralist.

4. The couplet is an erudite play on Jonathan Swift: "Naturalists observe, a flea / Has smaller fleas that on him prey; / And these have smaller still to bite 'em, / And so proceed ad infinitum"; Swift's lines were themselves a play on a nursery rhyme of the time, "The Siphonaptera."

**8 Artificial Life**

1. I refer to artificial life in the past tense as the field has dissipated and diversified.

2. Key figures in this work included Alex Fraser, Lawrence J. Fogel, Ingo Rechenberg, and Hans-Paul Schwefel.

3. See also Holland et al. 1986.

4. *Fast, Cheap & Out of Control* is the title of a 1997 documentary by Errol Morris, featuring Rodney Brooks.

5. See also Beer 1995 and Clark 1996.

6. See also the special issue of *Artificial Life* on stigmergy (Bedau 1999).

7. See, for instance, Cariani 2008 and Cariani 1998.

8. The very existence of the software-hardware dualism is, of course, an axiomatic construction quite as dubious as its Cartesian model.

9. Evolvable hardware was pursued with some limited success by Adrian Thompson (see Thompson 1997).

10. See, for instance, Cariani 1990 and Cariani 1993.

11. William Wundt (sometimes called the father of experimental psychology) developed the curve now named for him (the Wundt curve). It describes arousal and overstimulation. For instance, the taste of sugar is pleasurable to a certain intensity; above that intensity, enjoyment wanes and eventually becomes negative.

12. See, for instance, http://www.srl.org/ and http://www.lafura.com/.

13. Note that true random number generators depend on truly random events, such as the emission of radioactive particles from a radioactive isotope. The classic reference *A Million Random Digits with 100,000 Normal Deviates* (RAND Corporation 1955) was compiled this way. Tom Jennings quipped, "This is a fantastic book—guaranteed to contain no information."

14. Some years later, Ray made a proposal to promote *digital biodiversity:* a distributed digital wildlife preserve on the Internet in which digital organisms might evolve, circumnavigating diurnally to available CPUs. He noted, "Evolution just naturally comes up with useful things" (pers. comm.); he argued that these creatures would evolve unusual and unpredictable abilities (such as good Net navigation and CPU-sensing abilities) and that they could then be captured and domesticated.

15. See also Ventrella's works at http://www.ventrella.com/Darwin/darwin.html, http://www.ventrella.com/index.html, and http://www.Swimbots.com/; and Lintermann's works at http://www.bernd-lintermann.de/.

## 9  Rethinking Cognitivism

1. I became profoundly aware of this tension in the early 1990s when building an autonomous robot (Petit Mal). In the design of the device, I had explicitly assigned certain "problems" a mechanical solution, whereas others were addressed in analog electronics or in software. The question of the computational value of such solutions seemed unresolvable. Various computational solutions involved various analog-electronic (nondigital), electromechanical, and mechanical components that took part in the computational process but for which the computational value was itself unresolvable. Each process might be digitally emulated in more than one way, but any calculation of equivalence based on processor cycles of lines of code is necessarily fallacious. This unresolvability of the computational equivalence of analog procedures is everywhere, from automobile controls to the weighing of vegetables in the market to biology.

2. All these metaphors should remind us of Lakoff and Johnson's early work, *Metaphors We Live By* (1980).

3. Is there such a clear separation in other languages and other cultures? The little I know about non-Western cultures suggests that there is great diversity possible in conceptions of self, the individual, and group identity. Such cross-cultural research is not part of my project here, but my hunch is that different cultures construct mind-self-body-others-world relations differently. Does the construction of the English language erase such nonobjectification in translations from other languages? Do the preconceptions of Western-educated scholars render aspects of other cultures incomprehensible? Of course! Edwin Hutchins's second-order study of (Western anthropologists' reports of) Micronesian navigational practices is just one of many examples.

4. By Herbert Simon, Noam Chomsky, Jerry Fodor, Zenon Pylyshyn, Wilfrid Sellars, Hilary Putnam, Daniel Dennett, and others, going by such descriptors as cognitivism, internalism, representationalism, functionalism, and so on.

## 10  Mindful Bodies

1. Similarly, an oft-quoted definition of *cognition* is as follows: "Cognition is a term referring to the mental processes involved in gaining knowledge and comprehension. These processes include thinking, knowing, remembering, judging, and problem-solving. These are higher-level functions of the brain and encompass language, imagination, perception, and planning" (Cherry 2016). Not only are we on shifting sands with respect to definitions or conceptions of cognition, but the concepts in terms of which cognition is defined are as rubbery as the laundry list is long: problem solving, reasoning, information, thinking, knowledge, attention, memory, judgment, evaluation, representation, decision-making, comprehension, and, more abstractly, awareness, consciousness, intelligence, mind, the mental, and conceptions of self and being. These are all not only contested but also defined in terms of each other.

2. The only references to the word found by Google come from Hutchins or people quoting him.

3. Here, Sutton is summarizing Malafouris (2004, 59–60), and he goes on to argue that this rendering of artisanal practice cannot be the whole story (2008, 94).

4. The Western concept is not necessarily shared by other cultures and traditions. Pursuit of this matter goes beyond the already wide scope of this book.

5. A biological materialist would contend that I am nothing except my fleshy, wet, pulsing self. Per Ockham and his razor, I feel that resorting to explanations involving quantum physics, supernatural forces, or the immaterial *res cogitans* are unnecessary.

6. Indeed, a prime mystery of human cognition from this perspective is that there is intercourse between the spatially, socially, and materially engaged kinds of cognition and kinds of cognition that engage mental representation (whatever that is)—cultural practices being prime examples.

## 11   The New Cognitive Science

1. Certain sites where, by happy accident, radically interdisciplinary research was fostered became focal centers of such research. Key among these was the Centre for Cognitive Science (COGS) at the University of Sussex, which for two decades was an international interdisciplinary think tank at the crossroads of artificial life and embodied cognition, driven in large part by the vigor and vision of Margaret Boden, Inman Harvey, and Phil Husbands. The University of California, San Diego was also a center for such research, with pivotal players such as David Kirsh and Edwin Hutchins in cognitive science; Elizabeth Bates, Gilles Fauconnier, and Mark Turner in linguistics; and Gerald Edelmann and Vilayanur Ramachandran in neuroscience. The work of Gallese, Rizzolati, and the group centered at the University of Parma (where mirror neurons were studied) has also been highly influential.

2. See, for instance, the work of Randall Beer, Scott Kelso, and Alicia Juarrero.

3. A feminist-inclined student of a colleague once brilliantly (if rhetorically) asked, "Why are men so preoccupied with their extensions?"

4. Hutchins reflects,

Sometimes my colleagues ask me whether I feel safe metaphorically extending the language of what's happening inside people's heads to these worlds. My response is "It's not a metaphorical extension at all." The computer was made in the image of a sociocultural system, and the human was remade in the image of the computer, so the language we use for mental events is the language that we should have used for these kinds of sociocultural systems to begin with. These are not examples of metaphorical extension from the base domain of mental events to the target domain of cultural activity. Rather, the *original* source domain for the language of thought was a particular highly elaborate and culturally specific world of human activity: that of formal symbol systems. (1995, 363–364; emphasis in original)

5. He bases this retelling on an interpretation of Turing's work: "The heart of Turing's great discovery was that the embodied actions of the mathematician and the world in which the mathematician acted could be idealized and abstracted in such a way that the mathematician could be eliminated. What remained was . . . the application of rules to strings of symbols" (Hutchins 1995, 362). Following this logic, Hutchins argues that the processes Turing abstracted "involve the patterns of manipulations of the symbols, but they expressly do *not* involve the psychological processes which the mathematician uses in order to accomplish the manipulations. The essentials of the abstract manipulation of symbols are precisely not what the person does. What Turing modeled was the computational properties of a sociocultural system" (1995, 362; emphasis in original).

6. The enactive approach has continued to be elaborated by others, notably Alva Noë and Kevin O'Regan.

7. Examples of such an approach are found in the work of Evelyn Tribble, Carrie Noland, Deidre Sklar, and Sally Ann Ness.

8. It is also of note that interdisciplinary practice (often referred to as *intermedia*) was central to 1960s and 1970s art.

9. Not to mention the work of Luce Irigaray, Julia Kristeva, Judith Butler, Elizabeth Grosz, Sandra Harding, Donna Haraway, Emily Martin, Evelyn Fox Keller, and many others.

10. Gallop comments, "Although French departments in the early seventies were full of female students, the faculty was predominantly male, the powerful professors were nearly all male, and it was the male graduate students who were treated and took themselves to be 'professional,' who were being groomed to take the place of the faculty" (1988, 42).

11. This may have something to do with the fact that the United States, which ironically often takes the civil rights high road in international relations, has never managed to pass an equal rights amendment.

## 12  Mind, Body, World

1. The first major paradigm of psychology, the structuralism of Edward Titchener (1867–1927), was staunchly introspective.

2. For an overview, see MacIver 2009.

3. As noted, Rodney Brooks's *subsumption architecture*—a biologically grounded approach to robot behavior—is functionally identical to the kinds of simple and self-contained sensorimotor loops Uexküll proposes.

4. Anglo-American analytic philosophers generally derided the traditions of *continental* philosophy: the phenomenology of Husserl, Heidegger, and Merleau-Ponty.

5. See Culham and Kanwisher 2001.

6. Characterized by the embodied, environmentally situated, nonrepresentational system of robot behavior developed by Rodney Brooks in the late 1980s.

7. See, for instance, Deák 2014.

8. The dualist nature of the Western philosophical tradition (and its tendency toward body denial) is thrown into relief when we note that in Buddhist meditation exercise a practitioner is required to master awareness of body before he begins to work on (what we call) the mind. Such observations also help to explain why Varela, Thompson, and Rosch find Buddhist philosophy immediately relevant to embodied cognition.

9. This makes the equilateral triangular geometry of the grid cells quite surprising. Triangles are geometrically fundamental, but we are not triangular. Whether we are culturally naturalized to rectilinear grids or whether a conception of them is innate, we find it hard to think in a triangular grid.

10. Yes, you can scratch your butt and, with practice, assemble a rifle in the dark.

11. This was one of the fallacies of 1990s virtual reality research: the assumption that functional stereoscopy was crucial for immersion and for the simulation of spatiality.

12. The derivation of the term "dead" is unknown, and seems to have nothing to do with death. OED first records it in 1613, and it has affinity with usages such as "dead level" and "dead right," though these infer exactness, and dead reckoning is understood to be an approximation. Go figure.

13. This and other arguments are conventionally explained by the arithmetic fact that the duodecimal system has a large number of factors and thus makes computing fractions far easier than in a decimal system. The sexagesimal system (base sixty—retained in our system of 360 degrees) was deployed by the Babylonians for much the same reasons.

### 13  Mind beyond Brain

1. See, for instance, Marsh and Onof 2008.

2. See also Giere and Moffat 2003.

3. However, see other authors, such as Menary 2012.

### 14  Tools, Cognition, and Skill

1. See Anderson 2009.

2. From "The Windhover" by Gerard Manley Hopkins (1918).

3. A few years ago, I decided to wash a large carpet. It took some time to decide how to best exploit the site available—a slightly sloping concrete driveway—to best effect for flushing out the grit from deep in the pile. Gravity and water flow would be my friends. I hosed the carpet down and soaped it up and scrubbed it with a scrubbing brush, then turned it over, face down, and hosed it again to wash out the dirt from deep in the pile. I then turned it over again and squeegeed the water out of it with a length of two-by-four. It was hard work, moving barefoot crabwise, bent over, pressing heavily and evenly on the wooden squeegee in long strokes to squeeze the water out. The pressure and direction of each stroke was adjusted to force maximum water out of the carpet and down the incline.

4. Cf. A. C. Graham's translation: "If I chip at a wheel too slowly, the chisel slides and does not grip; if too fast, it jams and catches in the wood" (Chuang-Tzŭ 2001, 139–140).

5. This is a pithier paraphrase of the following: "In theory, there is no difference between theory and practice. But in practice there is" (attributed to Jan L. A. van de Snepscheut, among others).

6. The same can be observed in the various cultures of defecation. The first encounter by Westerners with a Chinese squat toilet usually produces consternation—although they are simpler, anatomically better, and more hygienic than the Western type. Chinese encountering Western toilets often have a similar experience, which explains finding muddy footprints on (Western) toilet seats in China.

7. See Penny 2007.

## 15  Representation

1. Or as the New Zealand dairy farmer and philosopher Fred Dagg noted,

Now of all the many turning points and crucial stages from primitive ape-like creatures through to the sophisticated and marginally less primitive and ape like creatures you see around you today at zoos and football matches, the most curious development of all is that of the human brain. The human brain has got man into a lot more trouble than has previously been supposed, and unless we come up with some way of putting the brain out of commission or obviating some of the more ludicrous effects of the brain, then I don't think life's going to get any better. Now the main shortcoming of the human brain is that it has led to all this discussion of the meaning of life, which is not really very healthy. It's quite a dangerous business really, because the more you think about life the less likely you are to reach a conclusion . . . that is if you don't count realizing that you aren't going to reach a conclusion as an actual conclusion. (2010)

2. Malafouris's provocative suggestion (in "Before and Beyond Representation" [2007]) is that Paleolithic cave marking bootstrapped the mind into representation. Our capacity to do mental arithmetic may be rooted in and derived from embodied action.

3. As my colleague Tom Jennings observed, the behavior of my own reactive robot Petit Mal (1989–1995), whose behavior is implemented in C code on an early

68hc11-based microcontroller, could be implemented in operational amplifiers, the quintessential analog electronic device.

4. This is evidenced by the following exchange on Yahoo! Answers: *MotoGirl* wrote: "Define Transduction and explain its significance to the sensory organs." The best answer as chosen by voters was from *flemon99*: "Transduction refers to the conversion of a signal from one form to another, in sensory terms, it is important for converting external stimuli in to [*sic*] a form that our brain can understand. For example, light hits photoreceptors in the retina of the eye, and causes a chemical change. This chemical change is then converted to a an [*sic*] electrical impulse which can be transmitted across neurons" (Yahoo! Answers 2012). In so saying, flemon99 reinforces a naïve Cartesianism and proscribes any possibility of a holistic consideration of embodied being. Such an explanation denies the realities of morphological computing and makes all cognition exclusive to cranial neural matter.

5. More recently, Hanna and Thompson (2003) made a similar argument when they asserted the falsity of the mind-body problem by proposing that both mind and subjective embodiment arise out of our *animality*.

6. We are unlikely to have considered the kind of setup necessary to take such photographs—wide angle and other special lenses and floodlighting, which tend to flatten the image. This is the importance of Werner Herzog's stereoscopic (3-D) documentary, *Cave of Forgotten Dreams* (2010).

## 16 Consciousness, Selfhood, and the Cognitive Unconscious

1. C. I. Lewis first used the term *qualia* in its modern sense in *Mind and the World Order* (1929).

2. See also Kornhüber and Deecke 1965 and Libet 1985.

3. This sketch about eating dog features Graham Chapman as a fatuous and pompous doctor:

*Doctor:* [Graham Chapman, eating] I am afraid he is suffering from what we doctors call whooping cough. That is the failure of the autonomic nervous section of the brain to deal with the nerve impulses that enable you or I to retain some facts and eliminate others. The human brain [we hear the sound of a dog barking in the background] is like an enormous fish; it is flat and slimy and has gills through which it can see. [We hear the sound of a gun firing and of what sounds like meat sizzling on a hot plate.] Should one of these gills fail to open, the messages transmitted by the lungs don't reach the brain. It is as simple as that. (Monty Python 1973)

4. According to Myers,

The muscles have spindles that measure length change (and over time, rate of length change) in the muscles. Even these spindles can be seen as fascial receptors, but let's be kind and give them to the muscles (Van der Wal 2009). For each spindle, there are about 10 receptors in the surrounding fascia—in the surface epimysium, the tendon and attachment fascia, the nearby ligaments and the superficial layers. These receptors include the Golgi tendon organs that measure load (by measuring the stretch in the fibers), paciniform endings to measure pressure, Ruffini endings to inform the central nervous system of shear forces in the soft tissues, and ubiquitous small interstitial nerve endings that can report on all these plus, apparently, pain (Stecco et al. 2009; Taguchi et al. 2009). (2011)

5. This work is exactly contemporaneous with the very similar crisis in AI, but Johnson does not partake in that conversation and evinces no knowledge of it.

6. See Rizzolatti 2005; Rizzolatti, Fogassi, and Gallese 2001; Baldissera et al. 2001; Buccino et al. 2001; and Craighero et al. 2002.

7. Historically, the distinction between what it is to be a body (in German, *leibsein*) and what it is to have a body (*körperhaben*) originated with the German philosophical anthropologist Helmuth Plessner. Merleau-Ponty explicitly nods to Buijtendijk, Plessner, and Max Scheler. See Buijtendijk and Plessner 1925 and Krüger 2010.

8. Elsewhere Malafouris writes,

If the notions of human agency and intentionality did not make any sense for the Homeric person who "does not yet regard himself as the source of his own decisions" (Snell 1960, p. 8), then why assume, as archaeology so often does, that they made sense for humans in the Palaeolithic? . . . As Bernard (1993, p. 23) correctly observes, criticizing Snell's thesis, "[t]here is certainly one thing that Homer's descriptions of people did without, and that was a dualistic distinction between soul and the body." (2008, 1994–1995)

## 17  Postcognitivism and the Aesthetics of Behavior

1. This hearkens back to the early socially oriented work in HCI by Terry Winograd and Fernando Flores (1986).

2. As an example, in recent years David Kirsh has been working with the Royal Ballet on distributed cognition in choreographic development.

3. For instance, the game *1979 Revolution Black Friday* (banned in Iran) develops a historically accurate and richly complex experience of the 1970s revolution in Iran.

4. See Donald 1991 and Malafouris 2004, 2007.

5. See Penny 2008b.

6. See short video interview with Barney: https://www.sfmoma.org/watch/matthew -barney-on-using-plastics-and-petroleum-jelly/.

## 18  The Trouble with Computers

1. Although conceptions of computing, in both technical and cultural aspects, have moved beyond this mindset in progressive areas of research and scholarship, few of these reconceptualizations have trickled down to express themselves in

the consumer commodity or popular imagination. The computer on your lap, in your hand, or mounted on your head, is always two decades behind cutting-edge research.

## 19  The Roots of New Media Art

1. See, for instance, the writings of Meyer (1972), Lippard (1973), Battcock (1973), and Alberro and Stimson (2000).

2. Lawrence Weiner's *Statement of Intent* (1969) reads as follows:

1. The artist may construct the piece.
2. The piece may be fabricated.

3. The piece need not be built. Each being equal and consistent with the intent of the artist, the decision as to condition rests with the receiver upon the occasion of receivership.

3. See Penny 2011a.

4. See also Steels 2008.

## 20  A Critical Aesthetics of Performative Technologies

1. In support of my argument, I intend to marshal evidence from, among other sources, contemporary neurophysiology, ethology, psychology of perception, cognitive science, neuroscience, and phenomenology, and situated and enactive cognition, and to support these with theory of mind and embodied being, especially the work of Evan Thompson, Eleanor Rosch, Francisco Varela, Hubert Dreyfus, Mark Johnson, George Lakoff, Alva Noë, Andy Clark, J. J. Gibson, Elizabeth Wilson, and others.

2. As I am a practitioner, these questions have arisen out of practice. I'm interested in providing a theory that is useful to practice—a body of theory that helps practitioners think about what they do in productive ways and helps them to do it better.

3. Happily, a new generation of interdisciplinary scholars has marked out fields such as software studies (Fuller 2008), platform studies (Montfort and Bogost 2009), game studies (Wardrip-Fruin 2009), and new perspectives on networks and interfaces (Galloway 2012).

4. My own work, such as *Fugitive* (1996–1997), follows such a mode.

5. For examples of such work, see Penny 2011b.

6. Artists often fail miserably at this task, but they cannot be blamed for the glazed-eyed processions of tourists through the halls of famous art museums. Still, the audience does bear some responsibility for preparation. Some familiarity with history does make old paintings more interesting.

## 21 Applying Postcognitivist Approaches to Arts and Cultural Practices

1. See Latour's (1995) review of Hutchins.

2. See Law and Lodge 1984, for an early statement, and Latour 1987.

3. See, for instance, Thompson and Stapleton 2009, and Thompson 2005.

4. Noë (2000) says that it was after developing these ideas that he became aware that several highly regarded art theorists (such as Rosalind Krauss, Hal Foster, and Yve-Alain Bois) "have anticipated me in this or that respect." Such are the perils of interdisciplinarity.

5. Donald (1991) argues that this mimetic intelligence is fundamental to human culture. It is a telling and persistent failure of interdisciplinarity that though media artists were at the forefront of such research, media art communities and media technology development communities had limited connection. Certain initiatives stand out as beacons through the 1990s, such as the artist-in-residence program at Xerox PARC, the Ars Electronica Futurelab, V2 in Rotterdam, ZKM, the Banff New Media Institute, the Australian Network for Art and Technology, and, more recently, Intel Labs.

6. See Penny 2011a.

7. As Kirsh and others have begun to explore. See, for instance, Welsh 2009.

## 22 Embodiment and Interaction

1. For examples of such work, see Penny 2011b.

2. See J. Hall 2015.

3. We might add Evan Thompson, Ezequiel Di Paolo, Bruno Latour, Karen Barad, Susan Hurley, and others.

## 23 Improvisation, Interaction, and Play

1. He goes on to say, "In a truly interactive instrument, the computer will have the capability to act independently and to react indeterminately to input. These characteristics are inherently contrary to an attempt to produce a fully controlled, determinate, predictable work of music. One can program an instrument that responds in a known manner to all likely input data, but that is just reactive, not interactive" (Dobrian 2001).

2. The title of a 1991 album by Frank Zappa.

3. This is not to say that there is not a fractality of microimprovisation on the level of nuance, gesture, emphasis, and tone.

4. As in the 1950 Alain Resnais film of Pablo Picasso painting.

**24  The Representational, the Performative, and the Processual**

1. See Pickering 2009.

2. Barad on Pickering's use of *performative*:

Andrew Pickering (1995) explicitly eschews the representationalist idiom in favor of a performative idiom. It is important to note, however, that Pickering's notion of performativity would not be recognizable as such to poststructuralists, despite their shared embrace of *performativity* as a remedy to representationalism, and despite their shared rejection of humanism. Pickering's appropriation of the term does not include any acknowledgement of its politically important—arguably inherently queer—genealogy (see Sedgwick 1993) or why it has been and continues to be important to contemporary critical theorists, especially feminist and queer studies scholars/activists. Indeed, he evacuates its important political historicity along with many of its crucial insights. In particular, Pickering ignores important discursive dimensions, including questions of meaning, intelligibility, significance, identity formation, and power, which are central to poststructuralist invocations of "performativity." And he takes for granted the humanist notion of agency as a *property* of individual entities (such as humans, but also weather systems, scallops, and stereos), which poststructuralists problematize. On the other hand, poststructuralist approaches fail to take account of "nonhuman agency," which is a central focus of Pickering's account. (2003, 807; emphasis in original)

3. Austin (1962) later referred to performative utterances as *illocutionary acts*.

4. In my opinion, a major aspect of the importance of the Exploratorium—the visionary science museum in San Francisco—is that it respects the performative idiom and engages a dialog between the representational and performative modes.

5. It is tempting to see parallels here with the political landscape, particularly in the United States, as the liberalism of the 1960s gave way to a conservative swing in the later 1970s. It was the Cold War, after all (sung to the tune of "It's a small world after all").

6. The oracle java tutorial (https://docs.oracle.com/javase/tutorial/java/concepts/object.html) says this about "objects": "Real-world objects share two characteristics: They all have state and behavior. Dogs have state (name, color, breed, hungry) and behavior (barking, fetching, wagging tail). Bicycles also have state (current gear, current pedal cadence, current speed) and behavior (changing gear, changing pedal cadence, applying brakes). Identifying the state and behavior for real-world objects is a great way to begin thinking in terms of object-oriented programming." This is both enlightening and confusing.

7. Which reminds me of Wertheim and Wertheim 2015.

8. Enactivism, situated cognition, and distributed cognition are three major variants of postcognitivist cognitive science.

9. This phrase is the title of chapter 11 of *The Embodied Mind: Cognitive Science and Human Experience* by Varela, Thompson, and Rosch (1991). The authors note, "Our guiding metaphor is that a path exists only in walking" (241). The term has been taken up in aspects of contemporary cognitive science and philosophy of mind—notably, the work of O'Regan and Noë (2001).

10. Much of the thinking behind academic and industrial machine-vision research still labors under the naïve conception that frames are a fundamental aspect of reality (rather than a skeuomorphic convention) and likewise that lines in images can be unproblematically associated with objects or edges in a physical space. Computer science libraries and journals are replete with papers on topics such as "edge detection." In some cases, the authors seem unaware that a video image depends on optics developed in film cameras, themselves designed to implement the graphical perspective, a conventionalized geometrical system for representing spatial depth on a plane, developed as a drawing technique in the Renaissance.

### Epilogue

1. In 1964, Abraham Kaplan published *The Conduct of Inquiry: Methodology for Behavioral Science*. In it, he included a passage about the *law of the instrument*: "It may be formulated as follows: *Give a small boy a hammer, and he will find that everything he encounters needs pounding*. It comes as no particular surprise to discover that a scientist formulates problems in a way which requires for their solution just those techniques in which he himself is especially skilled" (28; emphasis mine).

2. The speaker was Bert (Herbert) Flugelman, a sculptor and a professor at the South Australian School of Art, circa 1978.

# References


Adam, Alison. 1998. *Artificial Knowing: Gender and the Thinking Machine*. New York: Routledge.

Adams, Frederick, and Kenneth Aizawa. 2008. *The Bounds of Cognition*. Malden, MA: Wiley-Blackwell.

Agre, Philip E. 1988. "The Dynamic Structure of Everyday Life." PhD diss., Massachusetts Institute of Technology.

Agre, Philip E. 1997a. *Computation and Human Experience*. New York: Cambridge University Press.

Agre, Philip E. 1997b. "Toward a Critical Technical Practice: Lessons Learned Trying to Reform AI." In *Social Science, Technical Systems, and Cooperative Work: Beyond the Great Divide*, edited by Geoffrey Bowker, Susan Leigh Star, Les Gasser, and William Turner, 131–157. Mahwah, NJ: Erlbaum.

Agre, Philip E. 2003. "Writing and Representation." In *Narrative Intelligence*, edited by Michael Mateas and Phoebe Sengers, 281–303. Philadelphia: John Benjamins.

Agre, Philip E., and David Chapman. 1987. "Pengi: An Implementation of a Theory of Activity." *Proceedings of the American Association for Artificial Intelligence* (AAAI '87), 268–272. https://www.aaai.org/Papers/AAAI/1987/AAAI87-048.pdf.

Agre, Philip E., and David Chapman. 1990. "What Are Plans For?" *Robotics and Autonomous Systems* 6 (1–2): 17–34.

Agre, Philip E., and Ian Horswill. 1997. "Lifeworld Analysis." *Journal of Artificial Intelligence Research* 6 (1): 111–145.

Alberro, Alexander, and Blake Stimson, eds. 2000. *Conceptual Art: A Critical Anthology*. Cambridge, MA: MIT Press.

Anderson, Botan. 2009. "Scythe Workshop: How to Mow with a Scythe." YouTube video, October 15. https://www.youtube.com/watch?v=YzdjOkLQw1s.

Ascott, Roy, ed. 1999. *Reframing Consciousness: Art, Mind and Technology*. Portland, OR: Intellect Books.

Ashby, W. Ross. 1952. *Design for a Brain*. London: Chapman & Hall.

Ashby, W. Ross. 1962. "Principles of the Self-Organizing System." In *Principles of Self-Organization: Transactions of the University of Illinois Symposium on Self-Organization*, edited by Heinz Von Foerster and George W. Zopf, 255–278. London: Pergamon Press.

Austin, J. L. 1962. *How to Do Things with Words*. New York: Oxford University Press.

Bach-y-Rita, Paul. 1967. "Sensory Plasticity: Applications to a Vision Substitution System." *Acta Neurologica Scandinavica* 43 (4): 417–426.

Bach-y-Rita, Paul, Carter C. Collins, Frank A. Saunders, Benjamin White, and Lawrence Scadden. 1969. "Vision Substitution by Tactile Image Projection." *Nature* 221:963–964.

Bach-y-Rita, Paul, Kurt A. Kaczmarek, Mitchell E. Tyler, and Jorge Garcia-Lara. 1998. "Form Perception with a 49-Point Electrotactile Stimulus Array on the Tongue: A Technical Note." *Journal of Rehabilitation Research and Development* 35 (4): 427–430.

Baldissera, F., P. Cavallari, L. Craighero, and L. Fadiga. 2001. "Modulation of Spinal Excitability during Observation of Hand Actions in Humans." *European Journal of Neuroscience* 13 (1): 190–194.

Ballard, Dana H., Mary M. Hayhoe, Polly K. Pook, and Rajesh P. N. Rao. 1997. "Deictic Codes for the Embodiment of Cognition." *Behavioral and Brain Sciences* 20 (4): 723–742.

Barad, Karen. 2003. "Posthumanist Performativity: Toward an Understanding of How Matter Comes to Matter." *Signs* 28 (3): 801–831.

Barad, Karen. 2012. *Agentieller Realismus: Über die Bedeutung materiell-diskursiver Praktiken*. Berlin: Suhrkamp.

Barry, Robert. 1969. *Inert Gas Series/Helium, Neon, Argon, Krypton, Xenon/From a Measured Volume to Indefinite Expansion*. New York.

Barthes, Roland. 1989. *The Rustle of Language*. Translated by R. Howard. Berkeley: University of California Press.

Bates, Elizabeth, and Brian MacWhinney. 1988. "What Is Functionalism?" *Papers and Reports on Child Language Development* 27:137–152.

Bateson, Gregory. 1972. *Steps to an Ecology of Mind*. Chicago: University of Chicago Press.

Battcock, Gregory, ed. 1973. *Idea Art: A Critical Anthology*. New York: Plume.

Baudrillard, Jean. 1983. "The Precession of Simulacra." In *Simulations*, trans. Phil Beitchman, Paul Foss, and Paul Patton, 1–79. Cambridge, MA: MIT Press.

Beckers, R., O. E. Holland, and J. L. Deneubourg. 1994. "From Local Actions to Global Tasks: Stigmergy and Collective Robotics." In *Artificial Life IV*, edited by Rodney A. Brooks and Pattie Maes, 181–189. Cambridge, MA: MIT Press.

Bedau, Mark A., ed. 1999. "Stigmergy." Special issue, *Artificial Life* 5 (2).

Beer, Randall D. 2014. "Dynamical Systems and Embedded Cognition." In *The Cambridge Handbook of Artificial Intelligence*, edited by Keith Frankish and William M. Ramsey, 128–149. Cambridge: Cambridge University Press.

Beer, Randall D., Hillel J. Chiel, and Leon S. Sterling. 1990. "A Biological Perspective on Autonomous Agent Design." In *Designing Autonomous Agents: Theory and Practice from Biology to Engineering and Back*, edited by Pattie Maes, 169–186. Cambridge, MA: MIT Press.

Beer, Stafford. 1995. *Designing Freedom*. Hoboken, NJ: Wiley.

Berkeley, Edmund Callis. 1949. *Giant Brains; or, Machines That Think*. New York: John Wiley and Sons.

Bernard, Claude. 1974. *Lectures on the Phenomena of Life Common to Animals and Plants*. Translated by H. E. Hoff, R. Guillemin, and L. Guillemin. Springfield, IL: Charles C. Thomas.

Bernard, W. 1993. *Shame and Necessity*. Los Angeles: University of California Press.

Beuys, Joseph. 1965. *How to Explain Pictures to a Dead Hare*. Galerie Schmela, Düsseldorf, November 26.

Boal, Augusto. 1985. *Theatre of the Oppressed*. Translated by Charles A. McBride and Maria-Odilia Leal McBride. New York: Theatre Communications Group.

Bohr, Neils. 1987. *Essays 1958–1962 on Atomic Physics and Human Knowledge*. Vol. II, *The Philosophical Writings of Niels Bohr*. Woodbridge, CT: Ox Bow Press.

Bolter, J. David. 1984. *Turing's Man: Western Culture in the Computer Age*. Chapel Hill: University of North Carolina Press.

Boston Women's Health Book Collective. 1971. *Our Bodies, Ourselves*. Boston: New England Free Press.

Bourdieu, Pierre. 1972. *Esquisse d'une théorie de la pratique, précédé de trois études d'ethnologie Kabyle*. Paris: Droz.

Bourriaud, Nicolas. 1998. *Relational Aesthetics*. Paris: Les presses du réel.

Bowker, Geoffrey C., and Susan Leigh Star. 1999. *Sorting Things Out: Classification and Its Consequences*. Cambridge, MA: MIT Press.

Broad, William J. 2000. "U.S. Planned Nuclear Blast on the Moon, Physicist Says." *New York Times*, May 16. http://www.nytimes.com/.

Brooks, Rodney A. 1990. "Elephants Don't Play Chess." *Robotics and Autonomous Systems* 6 (1–2): 3–15.

Brooks, Rodney A. 1991a. "Intelligence without Reason." AI Memo no. 1293. Cambridge, MA.

Brooks, Rodney A. 1991b. "Intelligence without Representation." *Artificial Intelligence* 47:139–159.

Buccino, G., F. Binkofski, G. R. Fink, L. Fadiga, L. Fogassi, V. Gallese, R. J. Seitz, K. Zilles, G. Rizzolatti, and H. J. Freund. 2001. "Action Observation Activates Premotor and Parietal Areas in a Somatotopic Manner: An fMRI Study." *European Journal of Neuroscience* 13 (2): 400–404.

Buchanan, Richard. 1992. "Wicked Problems in Design Thinking." *Design Issues* 8 (2): 5–21.

Buijtendijk, Frederik J. J., and Helmuth Plessner. 1925. "Die Deutung Des Mimischen Ausdrucks: Ein Beitrag Zur Lehre Vom Bewusstsein Des Anderen Ichs." *Philosophischer Anzeiger* 1:72–126.

Burnham, Jack. 1968a. *Beyond Modern Sculpture: The Effects of Science and Technology on the Sculpture of This Century*. New York: George Braziller.

Burnham, Jack. 1968b. "Systems Esthetics." *Artforum* 7 (1): 30–35.

Butler, Judith. 1993. *Bodies That Matter: On the Discursive Limits of Sex*. New York: Routledge.

Cage, John. 1961. *Silence: Lectures and Writings*. Middletown, CT: Wesleyan University Press.

Campbell-Kelly, Martin, and William Aspray. 1996. *Computer: A History of the Information Machine*. New York: Basic Books.

Canguilhem, George. 1992. "Machine and Organism." Translated by M. Cohen and R. Cherry. In *Incorporations*, edited by Jonathan Crary and Sanford Kwinter, 45–69. New York: Zone Books.

Cannon, Walter B. 1926. "Physiological Regulation of Normal States: Some Tentative Postulates Concerning Biological Homeostasis." In *Charles Richet: Ses Amis, Ses Collègues, Ses Élèves*, edited by A. Pettit, 91–93. Paris: Editions Médicales.

Cannon, Walter B. 1929. "Organization for Physiological Homeostasis." *Physiological Reviews* 9 (3): 399–431.

Cannon, Walter B. 1932. *The Wisdom of the Body*. New York: W. W. Norton.

Cardew, Cornelius. 1971. *The Great Learning*, Paragraphs 2 and 7. Deutsche Grammophon/Universal Classics 471572.

Cariani, Peter. 1990. "Adaptive Connection to the World through Self-Organizing Sensors and Effectors." In *Proceedings of the Fifth IEEE International Symposium on Intelligent Control*, edited by A. Meystel, J. Herath, and S. Gray, 73–78. Philadelphia: IEEE.

Cariani, Peter. 1992. "Emergence and Artificial Life." In *Artificial Life II*, edited by Christopher G. Langton, Charles Taylor, J. Doyne Farmer, and Steen Rasmussen, 775–797. Boston: Addison-Wesley.

Cariani, Peter. 1993. "To Evolve an Ear: Epistemological Implications of Gordon Pask's Electrochemical Devices." *Systems Research 10* (3): 19–33.

Cariani, Peter. 1998. "Epistemic Autonomy through Adaptive Sensing." In *Proceedings of the 1998 IEEE ISIC/CIRA/ISAS Joint Conference*, 718–723. Gaithersburg, MD: IEEE.

Cariani, Peter. 2008. "Design Strategies for Open-Ended Evolution." In *Artificial Life XI: Proceedings of the Eleventh International Conference on the Simulation and Synthesis of Living Systems*, edited by Seth Bullock, Jason Noble, Richard A. Watson, and Mark A. Bedau, 94–101. Cambridge, MA: MIT Press.

Cariani, Peter A. 2009. "The Homeostat as Embodiment of Adaptive Control." *International Journal of General Systems* 38 (2): 139–154.

Cariani, Peter. 2012. "Creating New Informational Primitives in Minds and Machines." In *Computers and Creativity*, edited by Jon McCormack and Mark D'Inverno, 383–417. Berlin: Springer Verlag.

Chalmers, David J. 1995. "Facing Up to the Problem of Consciousness." *Journal of Consciousness Studies* 2 (3): 200–219.

Chemero, Anthony. 2009. *Radical Embodied Cognitive Science*. Cambridge, MA: MIT Press.

Chemero, Anthony, and Charles Heyser. 2005. "Object Exploration and a Problem with Reductionism." *Synthese* 147 (3): 403–423.

Cherry, Kendra. 2016. "What Is Cognition?" *Verywell*. Last modified May 6. https://www.verywell.com/what-is-cognition-2794982.

Cho, Sung-Bae, and Thomas S. Ray. 1995. "An Evolutionary Approach to Program Transformation and Synthesis." *International Journal of Software Engineering and Knowledge Engineering* 5 (2): 179–192.

Chuang-Tzŭ. 2001. *The Inner Chapters*. Translated by A. C. Graham. Indianapolis: Hackett.

Cisek, Paul. 1999. "Beyond the Computer Metaphor: Behavior as Interaction." *Journal of Consciousness Studies* 6 (11–12): 125–142.

Cisek, Paul. 2008. "The Affordance Competition Hypothesis: A Framework for Embodied Behavior." In *Embodiment, Ego-Space, and Action*, edited by Roberta L.

Klatzky, Brian MacWhinney, and Marlene Behrmann, 203–246. New York: Psychology Press.

Clark, Andy. 1996. *Being There: Putting Brain, Body, and World Together Again*. Cambridge, MA: MIT Press.

Clark, Andy. 1998. "Embodiment and the Philosophy of Mind." In *Contemporary Issues in the Philosophy of Mind*, edited by Anthony O'Hear, 35–52. Cambridge: Cambridge University Press.

Clark, Andy, and David Chalmers. 1998. "The Extended Mind." *Analysis* 58 (1): 7–19.

Colombetti, Giovanna. 2013. *The Feeling Body: Affective Science Meets the Enactive Mind*. Cambridge, MA: MIT Press.

Conway, John. 1970. "Life." YouTube video, January 3, 2009. https://www.youtube .com/watch?v=23MBR2pZoDQ.

Cope, David. 1991. *Computers and Musical Style*. Middleton, WI: A-R Editions.

Cope, David. 1996. *Experiments in Musical Intelligence*. Middleton, WI: A-R Editions.

Cope, David. 2000. *The Algorithmic Composer*. Middleton, WI: A-R Editions.

Cope, David. 2005. *Computer Models of Musical Creativity*. Cambridge, MA: MIT Press.

Cosmelli, Diego, and Evan Thompson. 2010. "Embodiment or Envatment? Reflections on the Bodily Basis of Consciousness." In *Enaction: Toward a New Paradigm for Cognitive Science*, edited by John Stewart, Olivier Gapenne, and Ezequiel A. Di Paolo, 361–386. Cambridge, MA: MIT Press.

Costall, Alan. 1991. "'Graceful Degradation': Cognitivism and the Metaphors of the Computer." In *Against Cognitivism: Alternative Foundations for Cognitive Psychology*, edited by Arthur Still and Alan Costall, 151–169. New York: Harvester Wheatsheaf.

Craighero, L., A. Bello, L. Fadiga, and G. Rizzolatti. 2002. "Hand Action Preparation Influences the Responses to Hand Pictures." *Neuropsychologia* 40 (5): 492–502.

Crutchfield, James P. 1994. "The Calculi of Emergence: Computation, Dynamics and Induction." *Physica D: Nonlinear Phenomena* 75 (1–3): 11–54.

Crutchfield, James P., J. Doyne Farmer, Norman H. Packard, and Robert S. Shaw. 1986. "Chaos." *Scientific American* 254 (12): 46–57.

Culham, Jody C., and Nancy G. Kanwisher. 2001. "Neuroimaging of Cognitive Functions in Human Parietal Cortex." *Current Opinion in Neurobiology* 11 (2): 157–163.

*Cybernetic Serendipity*. 1968. Curated by Jasia Reichardt. London: Institute of Contemporary Arts.

Dagg, Fred. 2010. "The Meaning of Life." YouTube video, July 4. https://www.you tube.com/watch?v=KaFFesrS8aE&feature=youtu.be.

Damasio, Antonio R. 1994. *Descartes' Error: Emotion, Reason, and the Human Brain.* New York: G. P. Putnam's Sons.

Deák, Gedeon O. 2014. "Development of Adaptive Tool-Use in Early Childhood: Sensorimotor, Social, and Conceptual Factors." In *Advances in Child Development and Behavior,* vol. 46, edited by Janette B. Benson, 149–181. Burlington, MA: Academic Press.

DeLanda, Manuel. 1992. "Nonorganic Life." In *Incorporations,* edited by Jonathan Crary and Sanford Kwinter, 129–167. New York: Zone Books.

Dennett, Daniel. 1996. *Kinds of Minds.* New York: Basic Books.

Descartes, René. 1991. *The Correspondence.* Vol. 3, *The Philosophical Writings of Descartes.* Translated by J. Cottingham, R. Stoothoff, D. Murdoch, and A. Kenny. New York: Cambridge University Press.

Dewey, John. 1928. "Body and Mind." *Bulletin of the New York Academy of Medicine* 4 (1): 3–19.

Dewey, John. 2008. *The Later Works of John Dewey, 1925–1953.* Vol. 1, *1925: Experience and Nature.* Edited by Jo Ann Boydston and with an introduction by Sidney Hook. Carbondale: Southern Illinois University Press.

Di Dio, Cinzia, Nicola Canessa, Stefano F. Cappa, and Giacomo Rizzolatti. 2011. "Specificity of Esthetic Experience for Artworks: An fMRI Study." *Frontiers in Human Neuroscience* 5, Article 139. https://doi.org/10.3389/fnhum.2011.00139.

Di Paolo, Ezequiel A. 2005. "Autopoiesis, Adaptivity, Teleology, Agency." *Phenomenology and the Cognitive Sciences* 4:429–452.

Di Paolo, Ezequiel. 2009. "Extended Life." *Topoi* 28 (1): 9–21.

Di Pellegrino, G., L. Fadiga, L. Fogassi, V. Gallese, and G. Rizzolatti. 1992. "Understanding Motor Events: A Neurophysiological Study." *Experimental Brain Research* 91 (1): 176–180.

Dijkstra, Edsger W. 1982. "How Do We Tell Truths That Might Hurt?" In *Selected Writings on Computing: A Personal Perspective,* 129–131. New York: Springer-Verlag.

Dobrian, Christopher. 2001. "Aesthetic Considerations in the Use of 'Virtual' Music Instruments." Paper presented at the Workshop on Current Research Directions in Computer Music, Barcelona, November 15–17, Institut Universitari de l'Audiovisual, Universitat Pompeu Fabra.

Donald, Merlin. 1991. *Origins of the Modern Mind: Three Stages in the Evolution of Culture and Cognition.* Cambridge, MA: Harvard University Press.

Doyle, Richard M. 1998. "Emergent Power: Vitality and Theology in Artificial Life." In *Inscribing Science: Scientific Texts and the Materiality of Communication*, edited by Timothy Lenoir, 304–327. Stanford, CA: Stanford University Press.

Dretske, Fred. 1996. "Phenomenal Externalism; or, If Meanings Ain't in the Head, Where Are Qualia?" *Philosophical Issues* 7:143–158.

Dreyfus, Hubert L. 1972. *What Computers Can't Do: A Critique of Artificial Reason.* New York: Harper & Row.

Dreyfus, Hubert L. 1979. *What Computers Can't Do: A Critique of Artificial Reason.* Rev. ed. New York: Harper & Row.

Dreyfus, Hubert L. 1992. *What Computers Still Can't Do: A Critique of Artificial Reason.* Cambridge, MA: MIT Press.

Dreyfus, Hubert L. 1996. "The Current Relevance of Merleau-Ponty's Phenomenology of Embodiment." *The Electronic Journal of Analytic Philosophy* 4. http://ejap .louisiana.edu/EJAP/1996.spring/dreyfus.1996.spring.html.

Dreyfus, Hubert L. 2005. "Overcoming the Myth of the Mental: How Philosophers Can Profit from the Phenomenology of Everyday Expertise." *Proceedings and Addresses of the American Philosophical Association* 79 (2): 47–65.

Dreyfus, Hubert L., and Stuart E. Dreyfus. 1986. *Mind over Machine: The Power of Human Intuition and Expertise in the Era of the Computer.* New York: Free Press.

Dreyfus, Stuart E., and Hubert L. Dreyfus. 1980. "A Five-Stage Model of the Mental Activities Involved in Directed Skill Acquisition." University of California, Berkeley. http://www.dtic.mil/dtic/tr/fulltext/u2/a084551.pdf.

Durham, Frank, and Richard D. Purrington. 1990. "Newton, Nonlinearity and Determinism." In *Some Truer Method: Reflections on the Heritage of Newton*, edited by Frank Durham and Richard D. Purrington, 175–226. New York: Columbia University Press.

Edelman, Gerald M. 1987. *Neural Darwinism: The Theory of Neuronal Group Selection.* New York: Basic Books.

Edwards, Paul N. 1990. "The Army and the Microworld: Computers and the Politics of Gender Identity." *Signs* 16 (1): 102–127.

Edwards, Paul N. 1997. *The Closed World: Computers and the Politics of Discourse in Cold War America.* Cambridge, MA: MIT Press.

Egelhaaf, M., R. Kern, H. G. Krapp, J. Kretzberg, R. Kurtz, and A. K. Warzecha. 2002. "Neural Encoding of Behaviorally Relevant Visual-Motion Information in the Fly." *Trends in Neurosciences* 25 (2): 96–102.

Eisenhower, Dwight D. 2005. "Farewell Radio and Television Address to the American People, January 17, 1961." In *Dwight D. Eisenhower: 1960–61: Containing the*

*Public Messages, Speeches, and Statements of the President, January 1, 1960, to January 20, 1961*, 1035–1040. Washington, DC: Office of the Federal Register, National Archives and Records Service, General Services Administration.

Eldredge, Niles, and Stephen Jay Gould. 1972. "Punctuated Equilibria: An Alternative to Phyletic Gradualism." In *Models in Paleobiology*, edited by Thomas J. M. Schopf, 82–115. San Francisco: Freeman Cooper.

Eliot, T. S. 1963. "Choruses from 'The Rock.'" In *T. S. Eliot: Collected Poems, 1909–1962*, 145–210. San Diego: Harcourt Brace.

Fitzpatrick, Anne, Tatiana Kazakova, and Simon Berkovich. 2006. "MESM and the Beginning of the Computer Era in the Soviet Union." *IEEE Annals of the History of Computing* 28 (3): 4–16.

Fodor, Jerry A. 1981. *RePresentations: Philosophical Essays on the Foundations of Cognitive Science*. Cambridge, MA: MIT Press.

Freeth, Tony, and Alexander Jones. 2012. "The Cosmos in the Antikythera Mechanism." *ISAW Papers 4*. http://dlib.nyu.edu/awdl/isaw/isaw-papers/4/.

Fuller, Matthew, ed. 2008. *Software Studies: A Lexicon*. Cambridge, MA: MIT Press.

Fuller, R. Buckminster. 1970. *I Seem to Be a Verb: Environment and Man's Future*. New York: Bantam Books.

Fyhn, Marianne, Sturla Molden, Menno P. Witter, Edvard I. Moser, and May-Britt Moser. 2004. "Spatial Representation in the Entorhinal Cortex." *Science* 305 (5688): 1258–1264.

Gallagher, Shaun. 2005. *How the Body Shapes the Mind*. New York: Oxford University Press.

Gallese, Vittorio, and George Lakoff. 2005. "The Brain's Concepts: The Role of the Sensory-Motor System in Conceptual Knowledge." *Cognitive Neuropsychology* 22 (3/4): 455–479.

Gallop, Jane. 1988. *Thinking through the Body*. New York: Columbia University Press.

Galloway, Alexander R. 2012. *The Interface Effect*. Malden, MA: Polity Press.

Galloway, Kit, and Sherrie Rabinowitz. 1980. "Hole in Space." YouTube video, December 6, 2013. https://www.youtube.com/watch?v=SyIJJr6Ldg8.

Ganapati, Priya. 2009. "May 26, 1981: Programmer-Attorney Wins First U.S. Software Patent." *Wired*, May 26.

Gibson, James J. 1966. *The Senses Considered as Perceptual Systems*. Oxford: Houghton Mifflin.

Gibson, James J. 1971. "The Information Available in Pictures." *Leonardo* 4 (1): 27–35.

Gibson, James J. 1973. "Further Note on Formless Invariants as Optical Information for Perception." Unpublished manuscript, Cornell University.

Gibson, James J. 1978. "The Ecological Approach to the Visual Perception of Pictures." *Leonardo 11* (3): 227–235.

Gibson, James J. 1979. *The Ecological Approach to Visual Perception.* Boston: Houghton Mifflin.

Gibson, James J. 1982a. "Gibson-Shaw Discussion." In *Cognition and the Symbolic Processes*, vol. 2, edited by Walter B. Weimer and David S. Palermo, 227–239. Hillsdale, NJ: Lawrence Erlbaum.

Gibson, James J. 1982b. "Notes on Action." In *Reasons for Realism: Selected Essays of James J. Gibson*, edited by Edward Reed and Rebecca Jones, 385–392. Hillsdale, NJ: Lawrence Erlbaum.

Gibson, James J. 1982c. "Notes on Affordances." In *Reasons for Realism: Selected Essays of James J. Gibson*, edited by Edward Reed and Rebecca Jones, 401–418. Hillsdale, NJ: Lawrence Erlbaum.

Giere, Ronald N., and Barton Moffatt. 2003. "Where the Cognitive and the Social Merge." *Social Studies of Science* 33 (2): 301–310.

Gigerenzer, Gerd. 2007. *Gut Feelings: The Intelligence of the Unconscious.* New York: Viking.

Glanville, Ranulph. 2003. "Second-Order Cybernetics." In *Systems Science and Cybernetics*, edited by Francisco Parra-Luna, 175–204. Oxford: Encyclopedia of Life Support Systems.

Google. 2016. "Cognition." Accessed July 21. https://www.google.com/?ion=1&espv =2#q=cognition.

Grassé, Pierre-Paul. 1959. "La Reconstruction du Nid et Les Coordinations Inter-individuelles chez Bellicosi-termes Natalensis et Cubitermes sp. La Theorie de La Stigmergie: Essai d'Interpretation des Termites Constructeurs." *Insectes Sociaux* 6:41–83.

Grillner, Sten. 1996. "Neural Networks for Vertebrate Locomotion." *Scientific American* 274 (1): 64–69.

Grosz, Elizabeth A. 1994. *Volatile Bodies: Toward a Corporeal Feminism.* Bloomington: Indiana University Press.

Haacke, Hans. 1965. *Condensation Cube.* http://www.macba.cat/en/condensation-cube -1523.

Haacke, Hans. 1971. *Shapolsky et al. Manhattan Real Estate Holdings, a Real-Time Social System, as of May 1, 1971.* http://collection.whitney.org/object/29487.

Hafting, Torkel, Marianne Fyhn, Sturla Molden, May-Britt Moser, and Edvard I. Moser. 2005. "Microstructure of a Spatial Map in the Entorhinal Cortex." *Nature* 436: 801–806.

Hall, Jennifer. 2015. "An Autopoietic Aesthetic in Interactive Art." In *Aesthetics and the Embodied Mind: Beyond Art Theory and the Cartesian Mind-Body Dichotomy*, edited by Alfonsina Scarinzi, 297–314. New York: Springer.

Hall, Stuart. 2000. "Who Needs 'Identity?'" In *Identity: A Reader*, edited by Paul du Gay, Jessica Evans, and Peter Redman, 15–30. Thousand Oaks, CA: Sage.

Hankins, Thomas L., and Robert J. Silverman. 1995. *Instruments and the Imagination.* Princeton, NJ: Princeton University Press.

Hanna, Robert, and Evan Thompson. 2003. "The Mind-Body-Body Problem." *Theoria et Historia Scientiarum: International Journal for Interdisciplinary Studies* 7 (1): 23–42.

Haraway, Donna. 1988. "Situated Knowledges: The Science Question in Feminism and the Privilege of Partial Perspective." *Feminist Studies* 14 (3): 575–599.

Harding, Sandra. 2004. "A Socially Relevant Philosophy of Science? Resources from Standpoint Theory's Controversiality." *Hypatia* 19 (1): 25–47.

Harnad, Stevan. 1990. "The Symbol Grounding Problem." *Physica D: Nonlinear Phenomena* 42:335–346.

Harvey, David. 1989. *The Condition of Postmodernity.* Oxford: Blackwell.

Harwood, Graham. 2013. "Coal-Fired Computers." YouTube video, June 30. https://www.youtube.com/watch?v=WfgkzplMxWA.

Hasler Vane Gear. n.d. "Small Pendulum—Servo Gear for Yachts up to 9m (30ft) Aprox. [*sic*]." Southampton, England. *M. S. GIBB Ltd.*

Haugeland, John. 1998. "Mind Embodied and Embedded." In *Having Thought: Essays in the Metaphysics of the Mind*, 207–237. Cambridge, MA: Harvard University Press.

Hayles, N. Katherine. 1999. *How We Became Posthuman: Virtual Bodies in Cybernetics, Literature, and Informatics.* Chicago: University of Chicago Press.

Hayles, N. Katherine. 2017. *Unthought: The Power of the Cognitive Nonconscious.* Chicago: University of Chicago Press.

Hayman, Robin, Madeleine A. Verriotis, Aleksandar Jovalekic, André A. Fenton, and Kathryn J. Jeffery. 2011. "Anisotropic Encoding of Three-Dimensional Space by Place Cells and Grid Cells." *Nature Neuroscience* 14 (9): 1182–1188.

Heims, Steve Joshua. 1993. *Constructing a Social Science for Postwar America: The Cybernetics Group, 1946–1953*. Cambridge, MA: MIT Press.

Hein, Hilde. 1972. "The Endurance of the Mechanism—Vitalism Controversy." *Journal of the History of Biology* 5 (1): 159–188.

Held, Richard, and Alan Hein. 1963. "Movement-Produced Stimulation in the Development of Visually Guided Behavior." *Journal of Comparative and Physiological Psychology* 56 (5): 872–876.

Higgins, Dick. [1981] 1995. "[Fluxus Chart], Intermedia Chart." *George Macunias Foundation, Inc.* Accessed August 13, 2016. http://georgemaciunas.com/exhibitions/.

Hobbes, Thomas. 2016. *Leviathan*. Adelaide: University of Adelaide.

Holland, John H. 1975. *Adaptation in Natural and Artificial Systems: An Introductory Analysis with Applications to Biology, Control, and Artificial Intelligence*. Ann Arbor: University of Michigan Press.

Holland, J. H., K. J. Holyoak, R. E. Nisbett, and P. Thagard. 1986. *Induction: Processes of Inference, Learning, and Discovery*. Cambridge, MA: MIT Press.

Holst, Per A. 1982. "George A. Philbrick and Polyphemus: The First Electronic Training Simulator." *Annals of the History of Computing* 4 (2): 143–156.

Honner, John. 1987. *The Description of Nature: Neils Bohr and the Philosophy of Quantum Physics*. New York: Oxford University Press.

Hopkins, Gerard Manley. [1918] 1985. "The Windhover." In *Gerard Manley Hopkins: Poems and Prose*, edited by W. H. Gardner, 30. New York: Penguin Classics.

Hubel, D. H., and T. N. Wiesel. 1959. "Receptive Fields of Single Neurones in the Cat's Striate Cortex." *Journal of Physiology* 148 (3): 574–591.

Huhtamo, Erkki. 2012. "From Dole to the Pole; or, Professor Huhtamo's Daring Adventures." Performance at The Velaslavasay Panorama, Los Angeles, California, August 2–3.

Huizinga, Johan. 1950. *Homo Ludens: A Study of the Play Element in Culture*. New York: Roy Publishers.

Hurley, Susan L. 1998. *Consciousness in Action*. Cambridge, MA: Harvard University Press.

Hutchins, Edwin. 1995. *Cognition in the Wild*. Cambridge, MA: MIT Press.

Hutchins, Edwin. 2000. "Distributed Cognition." *International Encyclopedia of the Social & Behavioral Sciences*. Last modified May 18. https://www.elsevier.com/books/international-encyclopedia-of-the-social-andampamp-behavioral-sciences/wright/978-0-08-097086-8.

Hutchins, Edwin. 2010a. "Enaction, Imagination, and Insight." In *Enaction: Toward a New Paradigm for Cognitive Science*, edited by John Robert Steward, Olivier Gapenne, and Ezequiel A. Di Paolo, 425–450. Cambridge, MA: MIT Press.

Hutchins, Edwin. 2010b. "Imagining the Cognitive Life of Things." In *The Cognitive Life of Things: Recasting the Boundaries of the Mind*, edited by Lambros Malafouris and Colin Renfrew, 91–101. Cambridge: McDonald Institute.

Huxley, Aldous. 1954. *The Doors of Perception*. New York: Harper & Row.

Ihnatowicz, Edward. 1970. "The Senster." YouTube video, January 12, 2008. https://www.youtube.com/watch?v=1jDt5unArNk.

Ijspeert, Auke Jan. 2008. "Central Pattern Generators for Locomotion Control in Animals and Robots: A Review." *Neural Networks* 21 (4): 642–653.

*Information*. 1970. Curated by Kynaston McShine. New York: Museum of Modern Art.

Ingold, Tim. 2001. "Beyond Art and Technology: The Anthropology of Skill." In *Anthropological Perspectives on Technology*, edited by Michael Brian Schiffer, 17–31. Albuquerque: University of New Mexico Press.

Ingold, Tim. 2006. "Walking the Plank: Meditations on a Process of Skill." In *Defining Technological Literacy: Towards an Epistemological Framework*, edited by John R. Dakers, 65–80. London: Palgrave Macmillan.

Ingold, Tim. 2011. *The Perception of the Environment: Essays on Livelihood, Dwelling and Skill*. New York: Routledge.

Jacobs, Joshua, Christoph T. Weidemann, Jonathan F. Miller, Alec Solway, John F. Burke, Xue-Xin Wei, Nanthia Suthana, Michael R. Sperling, Ashwini D. Sharan, Itzhak Fried, and Michael J. Kahana. 2013. "Direct Recordings of Grid-like Neuronal Activity in Human Spatial Navigation." *Nature Neuroscience* 16 (9): 1188–1190.

James, William. 1950. *The Principles of Psychology*. Vol. 1. Mineola, NY: Dover.

Jarry, Alfred. 1996. *Exploits and Opinions of Dr. Faustroll, Pataphysician*. Cambridge, MA: Exact Change.

Johnson, Mark. 1987. *The Body in the Mind: The Bodily Basis of Meaning, Imagination, and Reason*. Chicago: University of Chicago Press.

Juarrero, Alicia. 2002. *Dynamics in Action: Intentional Behavior as a Complex System*. Cambridge, MA: MIT Press.

Kaplan, Abraham. 1964. *The Conduct of Inquiry: Methodology for Behavioral Science*. San Francisco: Chandler.

Kauffman, Stuart A. 1993. *The Origins of Order: Self-Organization and Selection in Evolution*. New York: Oxford University Press.

Kawaguchi, Yoichiro. 1995. "Gigalopolis." YouTube video, December 15, 2012. https://www.youtube.com/watch?v=nlCbw4WVynw.

Kelso, J. A. Scott. 1995. *Dynamic Patterns: The Self-Organization of Brain and Behavior.* Cambridge, MA: MIT Press.

Kennedy, Noah. 1990. *Industrialization of Intelligence: Mind and Machine in the Modern Age.* London: Unwin Hyman.

Kirsh, David. 1991. "Foundations of AI: The Big Issues." *Artificial Intelligence* 47 (1–3): 3–30.

Kirsh, David. 2011. "How Marking in Dance Constitutes Thinking with the Body." *Versus: Quaderni Di Studi Semiotici* 113–115:179–210.

Kirsh, David, and Paul Maglio. 1994. "On Distinguishing Epistemic from Pragmatic Action." *Cognitive Science* 18 (4): 513–549.

Kittler, Friedrich. 1995. "There Is No Software." *ctheory*, Oct. 18. https://journals .uvic.ca/index.php/ctheory/article/view/14655/5522.

Kornhüber, H. H., and L. Deecke. 1965. "Changes in the Brain Potential in Voluntary Movements and Passive Movements in Man: Readiness Potential and Reafferent Potentials." *Pflügers Archiv für die Gesamte Physiologie des Menschen und der Tiere* 284:1–17.

Krüger, Hans-Peter. 2010. "Persons and Their Bodies: The *Körper/Leib* Distinction and Helmuth Plessner's Theories of Ex-Centric Positionality and *Homo absconditus.*" *Journal of Speculative Philosophy* 24 (3): 256–274.

Kwa, Chunglin. 1994. "Modelling Technologies of Control." *Science as Culture* 4 (3): 363–391.

Kubie, John. 2013. "Place Cells, Remapping and Memory." http://blog.brainfacts.org/ 2013/10/place-cells-remapping-and-memory/#.WMbFw4X7DKM.

Lakoff, George. 1987. *Women, Fire and Dangerous Things: What Categories Reveal about the Mind.* Chicago: University of Chicago Press.

Lakoff, George, and Mark Johnson. 1980. *Metaphors We Live By.* Chicago: University of Chicago Press.

Lakoff, George, and Mark Johnson. 1999. *Philosophy in the Flesh: The Embodied Mind and Its Challenge to Western Thought.* New York: Basic Books.

La Mettrie, Julien Offray de. 1996. "Machine Man." In *Machine Man and Other Writings*, edited by Ann Thomson, 1–40. New York: Cambridge University Press.

Langton, Christopher G. 1986. "Studying Artificial Life with Cellular Automata." *Physica D: Nonlinear Phenomena* 22 (1–3): 120–149.

Langton, Christopher G., ed. 1989. *Artificial Life: Proceedings of an Interdisciplinary Workshop on the Synthesis and Simulation of Living Systems*. Boston: Addison-Wesley Longman.

Latour, Bruno. 1987. *Science in Action: How to Follow Scientists and Engineers through Society*. Milton Keynes: Open University Press.

Latour, Bruno. 1995. "Cogito Ergo Sumus! Or, Psychology Swept Inside Out by the Fresh Air of the Upper Deck . . . ." *Mind, Culture, and Activity: An International Journal* 3 (1): 54–63.

Law, John, and Peter Lodge. 1984. *Science for Social Scientists*. London: Palgrave Macmillan.

Legrand, Dorothée. 2006. "The Bodily Self: The Sensori-Motor Roots of Pre-reflective Self-Consciousness." *Phenomenology and the Cognitive Sciences* 5 (1): 89–118.

Leitan, Nuwan D., and Greg Murray. 2014. "The Mind-Body Relationship in Psychotherapy: Grounded Cognition as an Explanatory Framework." *Frontiers in Psychology* 5:1–8.

Lettvin, Jerome Y., Humberto R. Maturana, Warren S. McCulloch, and Walter H. Pitts. 1959. "What the Frog's Eye Tells the Frog's Brain." *Proceedings of the Institute of Radio Engineers* 47: 1940–1951.

Lettvin, Jerome Y., Humberto R. Maturana, Warren S. McCulloch, and Walter H. Pitts. 1968. "What the Frog's Eye Tells the Frog's Brain." In *The Mind: Biological Approaches to its Functions*, edited by William C. Corning and Martin Balaban, 233–258. Hoboken, NJ: John Wiley & Sons.

Levidow, Les. 1994. "The Gulf Massacre as Paranoid Rationality." In *Culture on the Brink: Ideologies of Technology*, edited by Gretchen Bender and Timothy Druckrey, 317–327. Seattle: Bay Press.

Levy, Pierre. 1997. *Collective Intelligence: Mankind's Emerging World in Cyberspace*. Translated by R. Bononno. New York: Plenum Trade.

Lewis, C. I. 1929. *Mind and the World Order*. New York: Charles Scribner's Sons.

Lewis, George E. 2000. "Too Many Notes: Complexity and Culture in Voyager." *Leonardo Music Journal* 10:33–39.

Lewis, George E. 2003. "The Secret Love between Interactivity and Improvisation; or, Missing in Interaction: A Prehistory of Computer Interactivity." In *Improvisation V: 14 Beiträge*, edited by Walter Fähndrich, 193–203. Winterthur: Amadeus.

LeWitt, Sol. 1967. "Paragraphs on Conceptual Art." *Artforum* 5 (10): 79–83.

Libet, Benjamin. 1985. "Unconscious Cerebral Initiative and the Role of Conscious Will in Voluntary Action." *Behavioral and Brain Sciences* 8 (4): 529–566.

Libet, Benjamin. 1993. *Neurophysiology of Consciousness*. Boston: Birkhäuser.

Limacher, Rene. 2011. "Jazz, Embodied Cognition and Strategy." *StrategyHub*, March 11. http://www.strategyhub.net/2011/03/jazz-embodied-cognition-and-strategy.html.

Lippard, Lucy R. 1973. *Six Years: Dematerialization of the Art Object from 1966 to 1972*. London: Studio Vista.

Lorenz, Edward. 1972. "Predictability: Does the Flap of a Butterfly's Wings in Brazil Set Off a Tornado in Texas?" Paper presented at the AAAS Section on Environmental Sciences, New Approaches to Global Weather: GARP, Boston, December 29.

Machiavelli, Niccolò. 1992. *The Prince*. 2nd ed. Translated by R. M. Adams. New York: Norton.

MacIver, Malcolm A. 2009. "Neuroethology: From Morphological Computation to Planning." In *The Cambridge Handbook of Situated Cognition*, edited by M. Aydede and P. Robbins, 480–504. New York: Cambridge University Press.

MacWhinney, B. 1995. *The CHILDES Project: Tools for Analyzing Talk*. 2nd ed. Hillsdale, NJ: Lawrence Erlbaum.

Malafouris, Lambros. 2004. "The Cognitive Basis of Material Engagement: Where Brain, Body and Culture Conflate." In *Rethinking Materiality: The Engagement of Mind with the Material World*, edited by Elizabeth DeMarrais, Chris Gosden, and Colin Renfrew, 53–62. Cambridge: McDonald Institute.

Malafouris, Lambros. 2007. "Before and Beyond Representation: Towards an Enactive Conception of the Paleolithic Image." In *Image and Imagination: A Global Prehistory of Figurative Representation*, edited by Colin Renfrew and Iain Morley, 287–300. Cambridge: McDonald Institute.

Malafouris, Lambros. 2008. "Between Brains, Bodies and Things: *Tectonoetic* Awareness and the Extended Self." *Philosophical Transactions of the Royal Society of London. Series B, Biological Sciences* 363 (1499): 1993–2002.

Mandelbrot, Benoit B. 1967. "How Long Is the Coast of Britain?" *Science* 156:636–638.

Mandelbrot, Benoit B. 1982. *The Fractal Geometry of Nature*. New York: W. H. Freeman and Co.

Manovich, Lev. 2002. *The Language of New Media*. Cambridge, MA: MIT Press.

Marr, David. 1982. *Vision: A Computational Investigation into the Human Representation and Processing of Visual Information*. New York: W. H. Freeman.

Marsh, Leslie, and Christian Onof. 2008. "Stigmergic Epistemology, Stigmergic Cognition." *Cognitive Systems Research* 9 (1–2): 136–149.

Marvin, Carolyn. 1990. *When Old Technologies Were New: Thinking about Electric Communication in the Late Nineteenth Century*. Oxford: Oxford University Press.

Mattelart, Armand. 2000. *Networking the World, 1794–2000*. Translated by L. Carey-Libbrecht and J. A. Cohen. Minneapolis: University of Minnesota Press.

Maturana, Humberto R. 2002. "Autopoiesis, Structural Coupling and Cognition: A History of These and Other Notions in the Biology of Cognition." *Cybernetics and Human Knowing: A Journal of Second-Order Cybernetics, Autopoiesis and Cyber-Semiotics* 9 (3–4): 5–34.

Maturana, Humberto R., and Francisco J. Varela. 1980. *Autopoiesis and Cognition: The Realization of the Living*. Dordrecht, Netherlands: D. Reidel.

Maturana, Humberto R., and Francisco J. Varela. 1987. *The Tree of Knowledge: The Biological Roots of Human Understanding*. Boston: Shambhala.

Mauss, Marcel. 1934. "Les techniques du corps." *Journal de Psychologie* 32 (3–4).

Maxim, Hiram S. 1891. "Aerial Navigation: The Power Required." *Center Magazine* 42 (6): 829–836.

Maxim, Hiram S. 1895. "A New Flying-Machine: Maxim's Experiments in Aerial Navigation." *Center Magazine* 44 (3): 444–456.

Mayer, Emeran A. 2011. "Gut Feelings: The Emerging Biology of Gut-Brain Communication." *Nature Reviews. Neuroscience* 12:453–466.

McBeath, M. K., D. M. Shaffer, and M. K. Kaiser. 1995. "How Baseball Outfielders Determine where to Run to Catch Fly Balls." *Science* 268 (5210): 569–573.

McCarthy, John, Marvin L. Minsky, Nathaniel Rochester, and Claude E. Shannon. 2006. "A Proposal for the Dartmouth Summer Research Project on Artificial Intelligence, August 31, 1955." *AI Magazine* 27 (4): 12–14.

McCulloch, Warren S., and Walter H. Pitts. 1943. "A Logical Calculus of the Ideas Immanent in Nervous Activity." *Bulletin of Mathematical Biophysics* 5: 115–133.

McLuhan, Marshall. 1964. *Understanding Media: The Extensions of Man*. New York: McGraw-Hill.

Medina, Eden. 2011. *Cybernetic Revolutionaries: Technology and Politics in Allende's Chile*. Cambridge, MA: MIT Press.

Meehan, James R. 1976. "The Metanovel: Writing Stories by Computer." PhD diss., Yale University.

Menary, Richard, ed. 2012. *The Extended Mind*. Cambridge, MA: MIT Press.

Merleau-Ponty, Maurice. 2002. *Phenomenology of Perception*. 2nd ed. Translated by Routledge and Kegan Paul. New York: Routledge.

Meyer, Ursula. 1972. *Conceptual Art*. New York: E. P. Dutton.

Mill, John Stuart. 2009. *A System of Logic, Ratiocinative and Inductive*. Project Gutenberg. https://archive.org/details/asystemoflogicra35421gut.

Miller, George A. 1951. *Language and Communication*. New York: McGraw-Hill.

Miller, George A. 2003. "The Cognitive Revolution: A Historical Perspective." *Trends in Cognitive Sciences* 7 (3): 141–144.

Miller, George A., Eugene Galanter, and Karl H. Pribam. 1960. *Plans and the Structure of Behavior*. New York: Henry Holt.

Mindell, David A. 2002. *Between Human and Machine: Feedback, Control, and Computing before Cybernetics*. Baltimore, MD: The Johns Hopkins University Press.

Minsky, Marvin. 1986. *The Society of Mind*. New York: Simon & Schuster.

Minsky, Marvin, and Seymour A. Papert. 1969. *Perceptrons*. Cambridge, MA: MIT Press.

Mintz, Sidney. 1985. *Sweetness and Power: The Place of Sugar in Modern History*. New York: Viking-Penguin.

Montfort, Nick, and Ian Bogost. 2009. *Racing the Beam: The Atari Video Computer System*. Cambridge, MA: MIT Press.

Monty Python. 1973. "The Adventures of Ralph Mellish/Hot Dogs and Knickers." *The Monty Python Matching Tie and Handkerchief*. Charisma Records (UK), catalog no. CAS 1080, vinyl LP, side 1, track 6. Also released in 1975 on Arista Records (US), catalog no. AL 4039.

Moore, David S. 2015. *The Developing Genome: An Introduction to Behavioral Epigenetics*. New York: Oxford University Press.

Moravec, Hans. 1988. *Mind Children: The Future of Robot and Human Intelligence*. Cambridge, MA: Harvard University Press.

Moreno, Alvaro, Arantza Etxeberria, and Jon Umerez. 1994. "Universality without Matter?" In *Artificial Life IV: Proceedings of the Fourth International Workshop on the Synthesis and Simulation of Living Systems*, edited by Rodney A. Brooks and Pattie Maes, 406–410. Cambridge, MA: MIT Press.

Morris, Errol. 1997. *Fast, Cheap & Out of Control*. DVD, Sony Pictures Classics.

Morris, Robert. 1961. *Box with the Sounds of Its Own Making*. http://www.seattleartmuseum.org.

Myers, Thomas. 2011. "Fascial Fitness: Training in the Neuromyofascial Web." *IDEA Health & Fitness Association*. Accessed July 31, 2015. http://www.ideafit.com/fitness-library/fascial-fitness.

Nagel, Thomas. 1974. "What Is It Like to Be a Bat?" *Philosophical Review* 83 (4): 435–450.

Nauman, Bruce. 1969–1970. *Video Surveillance Piece: Public Room, Private Room.* http://www.medienkunstnetz.de/.

Neisser, Ulric. 1967. *Cognitive Psychology.* New York: Meredith.

Newell, Allen, Paul S. Rosenbloom, and John E. Laird. 1989. "Symbolic Architectures for Cognition." In *Foundations of Cognitive Science*, edited by Michael I. Posner, 93–131. Cambridge, MA: MIT Press.

Newell, Allen, J. C. Shaw, and Herbert A. Simon. 1958. "Elements of a Theory of Human Problem Solving." *Psychological Review* 65 (3): 151–166.

Newell, Allen, and Herbert A. Simon. 1976. "Computer Science as Empirical Inquiry: Symbols and Search." *Communications of the ACM* 19 (3): 113–126.

Noë, Alva. 2000. "Experience and Experiment in Art." *Journal of Consciousness Studies* 7 (8–9): 123–135.

O'Keefe, J., and J. Dostrovsky. 1971. "The Hippocampus as a Spatial Map: Preliminary Evidence from Unit Activity in the Freely-Moving Rat." *Brain Research* 34 (1): 171–175.

O'Regan, Kevin, and Alva Noë. 2001. "A Sensorimotor Account of Vision and Visual Consciousness." *Behavioral and Brain Sciences* 24:939–1031.

Paik, Nam June. 1966. "Cybernated Art." In *Manifestos*, 24. New York: Something Else Press.

Papert, Seymour. 1988. "One AI or Many?" *Daedalus* 117 (1): 1–14.

Pask, Gordon. 1968. *The Colloquy of Mobiles.* http://www.medienkunstnetz.de/works/colloquy-of-mobiles/.

Pask, Gordon. 1971. "A Comment, a Case History and a Plan." In *Cybernetics, Art and Ideas*, edited by Jasia Reichardt, 76–99. London: Studio Vista.

Pasteur, Louis. 1854. Lecture, University of Lille, December 7.

Penny, Simon. 1987. "Simulation Digitization Interaction: The Impact of Computing in the Arts." *Artlink* 7 (3): 4.

Penny, Simon. 1994. "VR as the End of the Enlightenment Project." In *Culture on the Brink: Ideologies of Technology*, edited by Gretchen Bender and Timothy Druckrey, 231–248. Seattle: Bay Press.

Penny, Simon. 1996–1997. "Fugitive." Interactive artwork. http://simonpenny.net/works/fugitive.html.

Penny, Simon. 1997. "The Virtualization of Art Practice: Body Knowledge and the Engineering Worldview." *Art Journal* 56 (3): 30–38.

Penny, Simon. 2007. "Enaction and the Ethics of Simulation." In *4th International Conference on Enactive Interfaces 2007*, 213–216. Grenoble, France: Association ACROE.

Penny, Simon. 2008a. "Bridging Two Cultures: Towards a History of the Artist-Inventor." In *Artists as Inventors—Inventors as Artists*, edited by Dieter Daniels and Barbara U. Schmidt, 142–157. Berlin: Hatje Cantz.

Penny, Simon. 2008b. "Experience and Abstraction: The Arts and the Logic of Machines." Fibreculture Online Journal.

Penny, Simon. 2011a. "Desire for Virtual Space: The Technological Imaginary in 90s Media Art." In *Space and Desire: Scenographic Strategies in Theatre, Art and Media*, edited by Thea Brejzek, Wolfgang Greisenegger, and Lawrence Wallen, 168–181. Zurich: Zurich University of the Arts.

Penny, Simon. 2011b. "Towards a Performative Aesthetics of Interactivity." *The Fibreculture Journal*, no. 19: 72–108.

Picard, Rosalind W. 1997. *Affective Computing*. Cambridge, MA: MIT Press.

Piccinini, Gualtiero. 2004. "Functionalism, Computationalism, and Mental States." *Studies in History and Philosophy of Science* 35 (4): 811–833.

Pickering, Andrew. 1995. *The Mangle of Practice: Time, Agency, and Science*. Chicago: University of Chicago Press.

Pickering, Andrew. 2007. "Ontological Theatre: Gordon Pask, Cybernetics, and the Arts." *Cybernetics and Human Knowing: A Journal of Second-Order Cybernetics, Autopoiesis and Cyber-Semiotics* 14 (4): 43–57.

Pickering, Andrew. 2009. *The Cybernetic Brain: Sketches of Another Future*. Chicago: University of Chicago Press.

Poerksen, Bernhard. 2004. *The Certainty of Uncertainty: Dialogues Introducing Constructivism*. Translated by A. R. Koeck and W. K. Koeck. Charlottesville, VA: Imprint Academic.

Polanyi, Michael. 1962. *Personal Knowledge: Towards a Post-Critical Philosophy*. Chicago: The University of Chicago Press.

Polanyi, Michael. 1966. *The Tacit Dimension*. Chicago: University of Chicago Press.

Pound, Ezra, and Ernest Francisco Fenollosa. 1967. *Instigations of Ezra Pound*. Freeport, NY: Books for Libraries Press.

Prigogine, Ilya. 1997. *The End of Certainty: Time, Chaos, and the New Laws of Nature*. New York: The Free Press.

Prigogine, Ilya, and Gregoire Nicolis. 1977. *Self-Organization in Non-equilibrium Systems*. New York: Wiley.

Prix Ars Electronica. 1992. "Golden Nica: RD Texture Buttons." *Ars Electronica Archive*. http://90.146.8.18/en/archives/prix_archive/prix_projekt.asp?iProjectID=2465.

Pylyshyn, Zenon W. 1979. "Metaphorical Imprecision and the 'Top-Down' Research Strategy." In *Metaphor and Thought*, edited by Andrew Ortony, 420–436. Cambridge: Cambridge University Press.

Pylyshyn, Zenon W. 1989. "Computing in Cognitive Science." In *Foundations of Cognitive Science*, edited by Michael I. Posner, 49–92. Cambridge, MA: MIT Press.

Raibert, Marc H. 1986. "Legged Robots." *Communications of the ACM* 29 (6): 499–514.

RAND Corporation. 1955. *A Million Random Digits with 100,000 Normal Deviates*. Santa Monica, CA: RAND.

Randerson, James. 2008. "You Really Can Smell Fear, Say Scientists." *The Guardian*, December 3.

Reynolds, Craig. 2007. "Boids: Background and Update." Last modified July 30. http://www.red3d.com/cwr/boids/.

Rich, Adrienne. 1976. *Of Woman Born: Motherhood as Experience and Institution*. New York: Norton.

Richardson, Lewis F. 1922. *Weather Prediction by Numerical Process*. Cambridge: Cambridge University Press.

Rieffel, John A., Francisco J. Valero-Cuevas, and Hod Lipson. 2010. "Morphological Communication: Exploiting Coupled Dynamics in a Complex Mechanical Structure to Achieve Locomotion." *Journal of the Royal Society Interface* 7:613–621.

Rizzolatti, Giacomo. 2005. "The Mirror Neuron System and Imitation." In *Mechanisms of Imitation and Imitation in Animals*. Vol. 1, *Perspectives on Imitation: From Neuroscience to Social Science*, edited by Susan Hurley and Nick Chater, 55–76. Cambridge, MA: MIT Press.

Rizzolatti, Giacomo, and Laila Craighero. 2004. "The Mirror-Neuron System." *Annual Review of Neuroscience* 27:169–192.

Rizzolatti, Giacomo, Leonardo Fogassi, and Vittorio Gallese. 2001. "Neurophysiological Mechanisms Underlying the Understanding and Imitation of Action." *Nature Reviews: Neuroscience* 2 (9): 661–670.

Rizzolatti, Giacomo, Leonardo Fogassi, and Vittorio Gallese. 2009. "The Mirror Neuron System: A Motor-Based Mechanism for Action and Intention Understanding." In *The Cognitive Neurosciences*, 4th ed., ed. Michael S. Gazzaniga, 625–640. Cambridge, MA: MIT Press.

Robins, Kevin, and Les Levidow. 1995. "Soldier, Cyborg, Citizen." In *Resisting the Virtual Life: The Culture and Politics of Information*, edited by James Brook and Iain A. Boal, 105–113. San Francisco: City Lights.

Rorty, Richard. 1989. *Contingency, Irony, and Solidarity.* New York: Cambridge University Press.

Rosen, Clifford J. 2009. "Serotonin Rising—The Bone, Brain, Bowel Connection." *New England Journal of Medicine* 360 (10): 957–959.

Rosenblueth, Arturo, and Norbert Wiener. 1945. "The Role of Models in Science." *Philosophy of Science* 12 (4): 316–321.

Rosenblueth, Arturo, Norbert Wiener, and Julian Bigelow. 1943. "Behavior, Purpose and Teleology." *Philosophy of Science* 10 (1): 18–24.

Roszak, Theodore. 1986. *The Cult of Information: The Folklore of Computers and the True Art of Thinking.* New York: Pantheon.

Rowlands, Mark. 1999. *The Body in Mind: Understanding Cognitive Processes.* Cambridge: Cambridge University Press.

Rumelhart, D. E., G. E. Hinton, and J. L. McClelland. 1986. "A General Framework for Parallel Distributed Processing." In *Parallel Distributed Processing: Explorations in the Microstructure of Cognition.* Vol. 1, *Foundations,* edited by David E. Rumelhart, James L. McClelland, and the PDP Research Group, 45–76. Cambridge, MA: MIT Press.

Rumelhart, David E., and James L. McClelland, and the PDP Research Group. 1986. *Parallel Distributed Processing: Explorations in the Microstructure of Cognition.* Vol. 1, *Foundations,* edited by David E. Rumelhart, James L. McClelland, and the PDP Research Group, Cambridge, MA: MIT Press.

Rumelhart, D. E., P. Smolensky, J. L. McClelland, and G. E. Hinton. 1986. "Schemata and Sequential Thought Processes in PDP Models." In *Psychological and Biological Models.* Vol. 2, *Parallel Distributed Processing: Explorations in the Microstructure of Cognition,* edited by James L. McClelland, David E. Rumelhart, and the PDP Research Group, 7–57. Cambridge, MA: MIT Press.

Russell, James. 1984. *Explaining Mental Life: Some Philosophical Issues in Psychology.* London: St. Martin's Press.

Ryle, Gilbert. 1946. "Knowing How and Knowing That: The Presidential Address." *Proceedings of the Aristotelian Society* 46:1–16.

Ryle, Gilbert. 1949. *The Concept of Mind.* Chicago: University of Chicago Press.

Sacks, Oliver. 1995. *An Anthropologist on Mars: Seven Paradoxical Tales.* New York: Knopf.

Sandlin, Destin. 2015. "The Backwards Brain Bicycle." YouTube video, April 24. https://www.youtube.com/watch?v=MFzDaBzBlL0.

Sargolini, Francesca, Marianne Fyhn, Torkel Hafting, Bruce L. McNaughton, Menno P. Witter, May-Britt Moser, and Edvard I. Moser. 2006. "Conjunctive Representation of Position, Direction, and Velocity in Entorhinal Cortex." *Science* 312 (5774): 758–762.

Schöffer, Nicolas. 1956. *CYSP 1*. https://monoskop.org/.

Searle, John R. 1980. "Minds, Brains, and Programs." *Behavioral and Brain Sciences* 3 (3): 417–424.

"The Secret to a Happy Life—Courtesy of Tolstoy." 2015. *BBC News Magazine*, January 1. http://www.bbc.com/news/magazine-30536963.

Sengers, Phoebe. 1998. "Anti-Boxology: Agent Design in Cultural Context." PhD diss., Carnegie Mellon University.

Shakespeare, William. n.d. *The Tragedy of Hamlet Prince of Denmark*. Edited by Barbara A. Mowat and Paul Werstine. Folger Shakespeare Library. Web edition.

Shannon, Claude E. 1948. "A Mathematical Theory of Communication." *Bell System Technical Journal* 27 (3–4): 379–423, 623–656.

Shannon, Claude E., and Warren Weaver. 1949. *The Mathematical Theory of Communication*. Champaign: The University of Illinois Press.

Shaw, Jeffrey. 1993. "Modalities of Interactivity and Virtuality." In *Artistic Exchange, Proceedings XXVIIIth International Congress of the History of Arts/Kunstler Austauch: Kongressakten XXVIIIth Internationaler Kongress für Kunstgeschichte Berlin, 15–20 Juli 1992*, edited by Thomas W. Gaehtgens, 295–300. Berlin: Academie Verlag.

Sheets-Johnstone, Maxine, ed. 1992. *Giving the Body Its Due*. Albany: State University of New York Press.

Sheets-Johnstone, Maxine. 2010. "Thinking in Movement: Further Analyses and Validations." In *Enaction: Toward a New Paradigm for Cognitive Science*, edited by John Stewart, Olivier Gapenne, and Ezequiel A. Di Paolo, 165–182. Cambridge, MA: MIT Press.

Silberstein, Michael, and Anthony Chemero. 2011. "Dynamics, Agency and Intentional Action." *Humana.Mente* 15:1–19.

Simon, Herbert A. 1996. *The Sciences of the Artificial*. 3rd ed. Cambridge, MA: MIT Press.

Sims, Karl. 1991. "Artificial Evolution for Computer Graphics." *Computer Graphics* 25 (4): 319–328.

Sims, Karl. 1994a. "Evolved Virtual Creatures." Internet Archive video. https://archive.org/details/sims_evolved_virtual_creatures_1994.

Sims, Karl. 1994b. "Evolving Virtual Creatures." In *SIGGRAPH 1994 Conference Proceedings: Computer Graphics Annual Conference Series*, 15–22. Boston: Addison-Wesley.

Small, J. S. 1993. "General-Purpose Electronic Analog Computing: 1945–1965." *IEEE Annals of the History of Computing* 15 (2): 8–18.

Snell, B. 1960. *The Discovery of the Mind*. New York: Harper & Row.

*Software*. 1970. Curated by Jack Burnham. Brooklyn, NY: Jewish Museum.

Standage, Tom. 1998. *The Victorian Internet: The Remarkable Story of the Telegraph and the Nineteenth Century's Online Pioneers*. Princeton, NJ: Princeton University Press.

Steels, Luc. 2008. "The Symbol Grounding Problem Has Been Solved, So What's Next?" In *Symbols and Embodiment: Debates on Meaning and Cognition*, edited by Manuel de Vega, Arthur Glenberg, and Arthur Graesser, 223–244. New York: Oxford University Press.

Stern, Nathaniel. 2013. *Interactive Art and Embodiment: The Implicit Body as Performance*. Canterbury, UK: Gylphi Limited.

Stilwell, Donald L. 1957. "Regional Variations in the Innervation of the Deep Fasciae and Aponeuroses." *Anatomical Record* 127 (4): 635–653.

Stratton, George M. 1896. "Some Preliminary Experiments on Vision Without Inversion of the Retinal Image." Paper presented at the Third International Congress for Psychology, Munich, August.

Suchman, Lucy A. 1987. *Plans and Situated Actions: The Problem of Human-Machine Communication*. New York: Cambridge University Press.

SunSpiral, Vytas. 2010. "The Brain Is for Motion!" *BeingHuman*, February 14. http://www.magicalrobot.org/BeingHuman/2010/02/the-brain-is-for-motion.

Sutton, John. 2007. "Batting, Habit and Memory: The Embodied Mind and the Nature of Skill." *Sport in Society: Cultures, Commerce, Media, Politics* 10 (5): 763–786.

Sutton, John. 2008. "Material Agency, Skills and History: Distributed Cognition and the Archaeology of Memory." In *Material Agency: Towards a Non-anthropocentric Approach*, edited by Carl Knappett and Lambros Malafouris, 37–55. New York: Springer.

Thompson, Adrian. 1997. "An Evolved Circuit, Intrinsic in Silicon, Entwined with Physics." In *Evolvable Systems: From Biology to Hardware*, edited by Tetsuya Higuchi, Masaya Iwata, and Weixin Liu, 390–405. Berlin: Springer.

Thompson, D'Arcy Wentworth. 1917. *On Growth and Form*. Cambridge: Cambridge University Press.

Thompson, Evan. 2005. "Sensorimotor Subjectivity and the Enactive Approach to Experience." *Phenomenology and the Cognitive Sciences* 4 (4): 407–427.

Thompson, Evan, and Mog Stapleton. 2009. "Making Sense of Sense-Making: Reflections on Enactive and Extended Mind Theories." *Topoi* 28 (1): 23–30.

Thoreau, Henry David. [1854] 1966. *Walden*. Location: Peter Pauper Press.

Tolman, Edward C. 1948. "Cognitive Maps in Rats and Men." *Psychological Review* 55 (4): 189–208.

Tomasello, Michael. 1999. *The Cultural Origins of Human Cognition*. Cambridge, MA: Harvard University Press.

Tribble, Evelyn B. 2005. "Distributing Cognition in the Globe." *Shakespeare Quarterly* 56 (2): 135–155.

Turing, Alan M. 1936. "On Computable Numbers, with an Application to the *Entscheidungsproblem*." *Proceedings of the London Mathematical Society 42*, ser. 2: 230–265, 544–546.

Turing, Alan M. 1950. "Computing Machinery and Intelligence." *Mind* 59 (236): 433–460.

Turner, Mark, and Gilles Fauconnier. 1995. "Conceptual Integration and Formal Expression." *Metaphor and Symbolic Activity* 10 (3): 183–204.

Turrell, James. 1983. "Pleiades." Mattress Factory: ActiveArchive. Accessed August 17, 2016. http://www.mattress.org/archive/.

Varela, Francisco J. 1980. "Describing the Logic of the Living: The Adequacy and Limitations of the Idea of Autopoiesis." In *Autopoiesis: A Theory of Living Organization*, edited by Milan Zeleny, 36–48. New York: North-Holland.

Varela, Francisco J., Evan Thompson, and Eleanor Rosch. 1991. *The Embodied Mind: Cognitive Science and Human Experience*. Cambridge, MA: MIT Press.

Viola, Bill. 1988. "Sleep of Reason." Carnegie Museum of Art, Pittsburgh. Accessed August 22, 2013. https://www.sfmoma.org/media/features/viola/BV03.html.

von Bertalanffy, Ludwig. 1968. *General System Theory: Foundations, Development, Applications*. New York: George Braziller.

von Foerster, Heinz. 1980. "On Constructing a Reality." In *The Invented Reality: How Do We Know What We Believe We Know?*, edited by Paul Watzlawick, 41–62. New York: W. W. Norton.

von Foerster, Heinz. 1995. *Cybernetics of Cybernetics*. 2nd ed. Minneapolis: Future Systems.

von Glasersfeld, Ernst. 1980. "An Introduction to Radical Constructivism." In *The Invented Reality: How Do We Know What We Believe We Know?*, edited by Paul Watzlawick, 17–40. New York: W. W. Norton.

von Uexküll, Jakob. 1909. *Umwelt Und Innenwelt Der Tiere*. Berlin: J. Springer.

von Uexküll, Jakob. 1957. "A Stroll through the Worlds of Animals and Men: A Picture Book of Invisible Worlds." In *Instinctive Behavior: The Development of a Modern Concept*, edited by Claire H. Schiller, 5–80. New York: International Universities Press.

von Uexküll, Jakob, and G. Kriszat. 1934. *Streifzüge Durch Die Umwelten von Tieren Und Menschen: Ein Bilderbuch Unsichtbarer Welten*. Sammlung: Verständliche Wissenschaft.

Wardrip-Fruin, Noah. 2009. *Expressive Processing: Digital Fictions, Computer Games, and Software Studies*. Cambridge, MA: MIT Press.

Weiner, Lawrence. 1969. *Statement of Intent*. New York: Seth Siegelaub. Exhibition catalog. http://www.lissongallery.com/artists/lawrence-weiner.

Weiser, Mark, and John Seely Brown. 1995. "Designing Calm Technology." Xerox PARC, December 21. http://www.ubiq.com/weiser/calmtech/calmtech.htm.

Weizenbaum, Joseph. 1976. *Computer Power and Human Reason: From Judgment to Calculation*. San Francisco: W. H. Freeman.

Welsh, Anne Marie. 2009. "Cognitive Scientists Seek to Quantify Body Movement." *LA Times*, March 8.

Wertheim, Margaret, and Christine Wertheim. 2015. *Crochet Coral Reef*. Los Angeles: Institute for Figuring.

Wertheimer, Max. 1924. "Gestalt Theory." Address to the Kant Society, Berlin, December 7. http://gestalttheory.net/archive/wert1.html#fn1.

Wheeler, Michael. 2008. "Autopoiesis, Enactivism, and the Extended Mind." In *Artificial Life XI: Proceedings of the Eleventh International Conference on the Simulation and Synthesis of Living Systems*, edited by Seth Bullock, Jason Noble, Richard Watson, and Mark A. Bedau, 819. Cambridge, MA: MIT Press.

Wheeler, Michael. 2010. "Minds, Things and Materiality." In *The Cognitive Life of Things: Recasting the Boundaries of the Mind*, edited by Lambros Malafouris and Colin Renfrew, 29–37. Cambridge: McDonald Institute.

Whitaker, Randall, 2011. "From Rosenblueth to Richmond—Part 4/6." YouTube video, August 20. https://www.youtube.com/watch?v=AUEkZU-1zck.

Whitehead, Alfred North, and Bertrand Russell. 1910. *Principia Mathematica*. Cambridge: Cambridge University Press.

Wiener, Norbert. 1948. *Cybernetics; or, Control and Communication in the Animal and the Machine*. New York: John Wiley & Sons.

Wiener, Norbert. 1961. *Cybernetics; or, Control and Communication in the Animal and the Machine*. Cambridge, MA: MIT Press.

Wilson, Robert A., and Frank C. Keil, eds. 1999. "Chinese Room Argument." In *The MIT Encyclopedia of the Cognitive Sciences*, 115. Cambridge, MA: MIT Press.

Wikipedia contributors. n.d. "Embodied Embedded Cognition." *Wikipedia*. Last modified February 19, 2016. https://en.wikipedia.org/wiki/Embodied_embedded_cognition.

Winograd, Terry, and Fernando Flores. 1986. *Understanding Computers and Cognition: A New Foundation for Design*. Norwood, NJ: Ablex.

Winston, Brian. 1998. *Media Technology and Society: A History from the Telegraph to the Internet*. New York: Routledge.

Wolfram, Stephen. 2002. *A New Kind of Science*. Champaign, IL: Wolfram Science.

Wooten, Janine M., Tim Haresign, and James A. Simmons. 1995. "Spatially Dependent Acoustic Cues Generated by the External Ear of the Big Brown Bat, *Eptesicus fuscus*." *Journal of the Acoustical Society of America* 98: 1423–1445.

Young, Iris M. 1980. "Throwing like a Girl: A Phenomenology of Feminine Body Comportment Motility and Spatiality." *Human Studies* 3 (2): 137–156.

Zeki, Semir. 1999. *Inner Vision: An Exploration of Art and the Brain*. New York: Oxford University Press.

# Index